HERMENEUTICS, AUTHORITY, and CANON

HERMENEUTICS, AUTHORITY, and CANON

edited by

D. A. Carson
and
John D. Woodbridge

Wipf & Stock
PUBLISHERS
Eugene, Oregon

Wipf and Stock Publishers
199 W 8th Ave, Suite 3
Eugene, OR 97401

Hermeneutics, Authority, and Canon
Edited by Carson, D. A. and Woodbridge, John D.
Copyright©1986 by Carson, D. A.
ISBN: 1-59752-118-3
Publication date 3/9/2005
Previously published by Zondervan, 1986

Contents

ix

Preface

xi

Abbreviations for the Books of the Bible

xii

Transliterations

1

CHAPTER ONE

RECENT DEVELOPMENTS IN THE DOCTRINE OF SCRIPTURE

D. A. Carson

This essay attempts to classify and evaluate some of the
more important issues raised in the past two or three
decades regarding the doctrine of Scripture, including
re-writing its history, the phenomena of the Bible,
debates over terminology and the concursive theory,
"proposition" and "literary genre," the new hermeneutic,
and the waning authority of Scripture in the churches.

49

CHAPTER TWO

THE SEMANTICS OF BIBLICAL LITERATURE: TRUTH AND
SCRIPTURE'S DIVERSE LITERARY FORMS

Kevin J. Vanhoozer

Examining how Scripture's literary forms affect biblical
authority, meaning, and truth, this chapter suggests that
Evangelicals, in their zeal to defend "propositional
revelation," have overlooked certain important features
of biblical literature. The author provides a model of
biblical revelation as "ordinary literature" in order to do
justice to the forms as well as the content of Scripture.

105

CHAPTER THREE

THE PLACE OF HISTORICAL RECONSTRUCTION IN NEW
TESTAMENT CRITICISM

Moisés Silva

Believers in the authority of the Bible are disturbed when
scholars disagree widely in the way they reconstruct
biblical events. By focusing on two specific problems—
the character of Pharisaism and the conflict between
Jewish and Gentile Christianity—this chapter seeks to
identify the reasons for such scholarly disagreement.

135

CHAPTER FOUR

THE LEGITIMACY AND LIMITS OF HARMONIZATION

Craig L. Blomberg

Harmonization offers neither a panacea nor a cul-de-sac
for historians faced with apparent contradictions between parallel accounts of ancient events. Rather, it
provides one method among many, including, most
notably, redaction criticism. Suggested resolutions of
seeming inconsistencies in the Synoptics, Kings--
Chronicles, the writings of Josephus, and the biographies of Alexander the Great illustrate these various
methods.

175

CHAPTER FIVE

THE PROBLEM OF *SENSUS PLENIOR*

Douglas J. Moo

The doctrine of inerrancy must come to grips with the
phenomenon of apparently "new" meanings that New
Testament authors discovered in Old Testament texts.
After defining the problem, a brief historical survey
highlights some of the issues, and contemporary explanations of the phenomenon are analyzed. A broad
"canonical" approach is proposed as the most promising
solution.

213

CHAPTER SIX

THE SPIRIT AND THE SCRIPTURES

John M. Frame

The Holy Spirit inspired the Bible in its "problematic" form so as to better *communicate* God's truth in all its variety and mystery. His internal testimony is to the whole text of Scripture, and it opens hearts and minds to accept the truth, reinforcing the words themselves and helping people recognize the cogency of Scripture itself.

237

CHAPTER SEVEN

SOME MISCONCEPTIONS OF THE IMPACT OF THE "ENLIGHTENMENT" ON THE DOCTRINE OF SCRIPTURE

John D. Woodbridge

In current debates regarding biblical authority, it has been proposed that the "Fundamentalist" doctrine of biblical inerrancy originated during the age of the "Enlightenment." This chapter argues that many Christians before the "Enlightenment" believed the Bible is infallible, not for salvation truths alone, but even when it treats matters of history and the natural world.

271

CHAPTER EIGHT

THE AUTHORITY OF SCRIPTURE IN KARL BARTH

Geoffrey W. Bromiley

This chapter focuses on biblical authority in the theology and practice of Karl Barth. Beginning with Barth's revolutionary return to the Bible during World War I, it documents his view of the Bible as norm in his early statements and the *Church Dogmatics* and then presents his use of Scripture in his preaching, theology, and counseling. It concludes by assessing the weaknesses and merits of his position.

295

CHAPTER NINE

THE BIBLICAL CANON

David G. Dunbar

The second half of the twentieth century has seen a renewal of interest in the formation of the Old and New Testament canons, both from historical and theological perspectives. This chapter contends that the idea of a canon is the outgrowth of salvation history and arises when God's people regard the process of revelation as complete or, at least, in abeyance.

361

Abbreviations for Works Cited

363

Notes

447

Index of Persons

459

Index of Subjects

463

Index of Scripture References

Preface

The present study—*Hermeneutics, Authority, and Canon*—has, in one sense, its own self-identity. As editors, we chose topics that we believe are among the most significant ones in the contemporary discussion of the doctrine of Scripture—e.g., the formation of the canon, Karl Barth's distinctive views regarding Holy Scripture, the relationship between truth and literary genre, and the work of the Holy Spirit in regard to Scripture. Christian theologians, pastors, and laypersons are once again reflecting upon these issues in the mid-1980s. This study should aid in that reflection.

This volume is a companion to an earlier book we edited, *Scripture and Truth* (Zondervan, 1983). If you will, this study treats important topics not broached in the earlier volume. Together, the two volumes constitute a whole. Whatever laudatory quality they possess we attribute to our esteemed colleagues who worked so graciously and so knowledgeably in this joint undertaking.

We see ourselves in line with the central tradition of the church's understanding of the Bible—but pressing beyond that tradition at points to address new questions and to articulate as carefully as possible a responsible doctrine of Scripture in the light of those new questions. Theological controversy can, of course, be destructive of the church; but in God's providence it sometimes serves to sharpen thinking and to promote greater care in exegesis and in the formulation of theological truth. As the upheaval over Arianism fostered profound christological reflection, and as the Reformation spawned equally profound soteriological reflection, so also the critical and epistemological crises characteristic of contemporary Western Christendom may serve under God to encourage thoughtful and reverent reflection on God's gracious self-disclosure in the pages of Scripture. That, at least, is our hope and prayer; and if the essays in this volume contribute even a small part to such progress, we shall be grateful.

Each contributor is responsible only for his own essay; and the editors bear sole responsibility for the topics selected for inclusion in this volume. In some ways, the first essay in this book might have served as an introduction to both volumes; but because it could not easily have been written until most of the other essays had come to hand, it makes its appearance in the second volume. Particular thanks go to Sherry Kull, who typed many of the corrections and revisions in several of the manuscripts, and to Joseph Anderson, who proofread the galleys and compiled two of the indexes.

Soli Deo gloria!

The Editors

Abbreviations for the Books of the Bible

Genesis	Ge	Nahum	Na
Exodus	Ex	Habakkuk	Hab
Leviticus	Lev	Zephaniah	Zep
Numbers	Nu	Haggai	Hag
Deuteronomy	Dt	Zechariah	Zec
Joshua	Jos	Malachi	Mal
Judges	Jdg	Matthew	Mt
Ruth	Ru	Mark	Mk
1 Samuel	1Sa	Luke	Lk
2 Samuel	2Sa	John	Jn
1 Kings	1Ki	Acts	Ac
2 Kings	2Ki	Romans	Ro
1 Chronicles	1Ch	1 Corinthians	1Co
2 Chronicles	2Ch	2 Corinthians	2Co
Ezra	Ezr	Galatians	Gal
Nehemiah	Ne	Ephesians	Eph
Esther	Est	Philippians	Php
Job	Job	Colossians	Col
Psalms	Ps	1 Thessalonians	1Th
Proverbs	Pr	2 Thessalonians	1Th
Ecclesiastes	Ecc	1 Timothy	1Ti
Song of Songs	SS	2 Timothy	2Ti
Isaiah	Isa	Titus	Tit
Jeremiah	Jer	Philemon	Phm
Lamentations	La	Hebrews	Heb
Ezekiel	Eze	James	Jas
Daniel	Da	1 Peter	1Pe
Hosea	Hos	2 Peter	2Pe
Joel	Joel	1 John	1Jn
Amos	Am	2 John	2Jn
Obadiah	Ob	3 John	3Jn
Jonah	Jnh	Jude	Jude
Micah	Mic	Revelation	Rev

Transliterations

Hebrew

א = '	ד = *d*	י = *y*	ס = *s*	ר = *r*
בּ = *b*	ה = *h*	כ = *k*	ע = '	שׂ = *ś*
ב = *b*	ו = *w*	ךּ כ = *k*	פ = *p*	שׁ = *š*
ג = *g*	ז = *z*	ל = *l*	ף פ = *p*	ת = *t*
ג = *g*	ח = *ḥ*	ם מ = *m*	ץ צ = *ṣ*	ת = *t*
ד = *d*	ט = *ṭ*	ן נ = *n*	ק = *q*	

(ה)ָ = *â (h)*	ָ = *ā*	ַ = *a*	ֲ = *a*
יֵ = *ê*	ֵ = *ē*	ֶ = *e*	ֱ = *e*
יִ = *î*	ֹ = *ō*	ִ = *i*	ְ = *e (if vocal)*
וֹ = *ô*		ָ = *o*	ֳ = *o*
וּ = *û*		ֻ = *u*	

Greek

α = *a*	η = *ē*	ν = *n*	τ = *t*
β = *b*	θ = *th*	ξ = *x*	υ = *y*
γ = *g*	ι = *i*	ο = *o*	φ = *ph*
δ = *d*	κ = *k*	π = *p*	χ = *ch*
ε = *e*	λ = *l*	ρ = *r*	ψ = *ps*
ζ = *z*	μ = *m*	σ,ς = *s*	ω = *ō*

αυ = *au*	γγ = *ng*	ᾳ = *ā*	' = *h*
ευ = *eu*	γκ = *nk*	ῃ = *ē*	ῥ = *rh*
ηυ = *ēu*	γξ = *nx*	ῳ = *ō*	
ου = *ou*	γχ = *nch*		
υι = *ui*			

CHAPTER ONE
RECENT DEVELOPMENTS IN THE DOCTRINE OF SCRIPTURE

D. A. Carson

D. A. Carson

D. A. Carson is Professor of New Testament at Trinity Evangelical Divinity School, Deerfield, Illinois. He is a graduate of McGill University (B.Sc.), Central Baptist Seminary in Toronto (M.Div.), and Cambridge University (Ph.D.), and he has studied at Regent College and in Germany. He has served both as a church planter and as a pastor, and he lectures frequently in Canada, the United States, and the United Kingdom. Before moving to Trinity, he taught at Northwest Baptist Theological College and Seminary in Vancouver. He is editor of the *Trinity Journal* and the author or editor of fifteen books, including *Divine Sovereignty and Human Responsibility*, *From Sabbath to Lord's Day*, the Matthew commentary in *EBC*, and *Greek Accents: A Student's Manual*—and of many articles. He holds membership in *Studiorum Novi Testamenti Societas*, the Society of Biblical Literature, the Canadian Society of Biblical Studies, the Tyndale Fellowship for Biblical Research, the Institute for Biblical Research, and the Evangelical Theological Society.

CHAPTER ONE

RECENT DEVELOPMENTS IN THE DOCTRINE OF SCRIPTURE

The pattern of Christian thought that emerged from the Reformation is often summed up under the three phrases: *sola gratia, sola fides,* and *sola Scriptura*. When I was a boy, I sometimes wondered how logic could be preserved if there were *three* statements each claiming that something or other was "sola"; but in due course I learned that grace is the sole ground of salvation, faith is the sole means of salvation, and the Scriptures are the sole ultimate authority for faith and life—all set in the context of the polemics of the Reformation period.

Precisely because the Reformers' theological formulations were shaped by the controversies of their age, it is clear that the "faith and life" formula was meant to be an all-embracing rubric, not a limiting one. They claimed that the deposit of truth lies in the Bible, not in the church or in the magisterium of the church. Their concern, in other words, was to spell out the locus of authority in order to rebut their Roman Catholic opponents, not to restrict the range of the Bible's authority to religious life and thought, away from history and the natural world.[1] The modern disjunction would have seemed strange to them.

This side of the Enlightenment, debate over the Scriptures soon moved on to broader matters. Although the history of these debates has been chronicled many times,[2] a great deal of detailed work still needs to be done. But perhaps the most difficult period to comprehend, in some ways, is the most recent. We do not yet have the advantage of distance; and the twists in the debate are many and intricate. Not a few of the issues raised are so fresh or are so much a part of modern scholarly thought that evenhanded and disinterested evaluation is extraordinarily difficult.

The essays printed in this volume and in the companion volume[3] have been written in order to address the most important of these issues. We have written as Evangelicals; and so far as the doctrine of Scripture is concerned, we believe we stand within the central tradition of the church and in line with the teaching of the Scriptures themselves. This ancient tradition is worth defending, examining, and rearticulating as theological fashions raise new questions. The present essay attempts to scan rather rapidly some of these recent

5

developments, in the hope that a bird's-eye view will provide these volumes with breadth and unity that might otherwise be lacking. The aim is not to deal with denominational bodies (e.g., the Missouri Synod or the Southern Baptist Convention) or particular publications that have agonized over the issue (e.g., *Churchman)* but to focus on theological, philosophical, and historical matters that in the modern debate impinge directly on how we view the Bible.

The resurgence of interest in the doctrine of Scripture can be traced to many factors; but four deserve brief mention. The *first* is the growing strength of Evangelicals. It is no longer possible to ignore them. Their churches are growing, their seminaries are bulging, their books keep pouring off the presses. In any large movement, of course, much of the momentum is kept up at the purely popular level; but Evangelicalism can no longer be responsibly dismissed as an academic wasteland. While nonconservative seminaries are lowering academic standards, multiplying D.Min. tracks, and reducing Greek and Hebrew requirements in order to avoid disastrous collapse of student enrollment, seminaries within Evangelicalism continue to blossom. At some Ivy League seminaries, only thirty percent of the students take any Greek; most evangelical institutions require at least one year of Greek as a prerequisite for entrance and insist on a minimum of one year of Greek beyond that. One of the results is that a disproportionate number of current doctoral candidates both in America and in Britain spring from conservative backgrounds; they are more likely to have the linguistic competence for advanced training. The rising tide of interest in the doctrine of Scripture in nonconservative circles[4] is not a reaction against conservatives who are becoming even more conservative than the heritage from which they have emerged (as some have suggested).[5] Rather, it is at least partly a reaction to the increasing visibility of conservatives.

The *second* factor is scarcely less important: Evangelicalism is becoming somewhat fragmented. Never a truly monolithic movement, Evangelicalism long enjoyed a fair measure of agreement over certain central teachings; but in its contemporary guise it is pulling itself apart on several different doctrinal fronts—and one of these is the doctrine of Scripture. Some of this fragmentation is the predictable but tragic fruit of remarkable numerical growth. Whatever the reason, some of the strongest attacks on the Evangelicals' traditional understanding of Scripture—even some of the least temperate criticisms— have been penned by those who today are viewed as Evangelicals[6]— though it is by no means certain that the Evangelicals of forty years ago, were they somehow to reappear on the scene, would recognize them as fellow travellers. Perhaps it should be mentioned that this fragmentation of Evangelicals' views on Scripture is not restricted to North America—as, for instance, a comparison of the papers of the Keele and Nottingham conferences quickly proves with reference to England (with similar evidence available for other places).

It is astonishing how much of the literature written by mainline Evangelicals on the doctrine of Scripture has been penned in response to one or both of these first two trends. Conservatives have often been accused of fixating on Scripture; but careful perusal of the treatments of the last fifteen years shows that, if anything, the reverse is true: nonconservatives have taken up the theme, and conservatives have responded. That may not say much for the creativity of conservatives; but it does exonerate them from the charge of endlessly banging the drum. The creation of the ICBI (International Council on Biblical Inerrancy) was prompted by apologetic concerns; and only a few of the authors who have published under its aegis have attempted new and more profound analysis of the nature of Scripture. The majority have simply aimed to restate the traditional positions and delineate the weaknesses of their opponents. Like the works of the nonconservatives, the essays of those who have contributed to ICBI have varied from the average and the shallow to the acute and the insightful.[7] As an instance of the latter, it would be a great help to clarity of thought if no one would comment on the appropriateness or otherwise of the term "inerrancy" without reading the essay of Paul Feinberg that deals with this subject.[8]

ICBI is perhaps simultaneously too encompassing and too unrepresentative in its membership. Because it is too encompassing, it has sometimes published essays of doubtful worth along with far better pieces; but this policy, though it has encouraged the involvement of many, has set the organization up for caricature that is not itself entirely fair. Owing to the prominence of the organization, some have failed to recognize that many Evangelicals in America and abroad have contributed to the debate without any organizational connection to ICBI; in that sense, ICBI is somewhat unrepresentative.[9]

In any case, it would be quite mistaken to suppose that conservatives on the doctrine of Scripture are an embattled few who can manage nothing more credible than throwing a few defensive javelins into the crowd, hurled from the safety of a stony rampart called "orthodoxy." In addition to the *magnum opus* of Henry,[10] there is a plethora of studies prepared by Evangelicals—philosophical, exegetical, hermeneutical, historical, critical—that do not address directly the question of the truthfulness of Scripture, but operate within the framework of that "functional nonnegotiable"[11] and, by demonstrating a certain coherence and maturity, contribute to the same end.

The fragmentation of Evangelicalism, therefore, has produced mixed fruit. On one end of the spectrum, it has weakened its distinctiveness; on the other end, it has flirted with obscurantism. Yet there still remains a considerable strength; and part of the resurgence of interest in the doctrine of Scripture reflects the self-examination of the movement as it struggles with its own identity. But of this I shall say more in a few moments.

The *third* factor that has helped to raise again the subject of Scripture is the crisis of authority that stamps so much of modern, Western Christianity—especially in academic circles. Children of the Enlightenment, like moths to a light we are drawn to the incandescence of the autonomy of reason. But having destroyed all the pretensions of external authority, we have discovered, somewhat aghast, that reason is corruptible, that one human mind does not often agree in great detail with another human mind, that reason by itself is a rather stumbling criterion of truth, beset as it is by a smorgasbord of values, theories, and predispositions shaped in remarkable independence of reason.

In the ensuing vacuum, there has arisen a muted hunger for authority. Finding all the gods dead, some people have manufactured their own: faddish gurus, unrestrained hedonism, and the pious pursuit of self-fulfillment are among the current contenders. But many wonder if the authority of Scripture should not be looked at again. Nor is this a concern of conservatives alone. The crisis of authority infects every stratum of our society; and, therefore, many people—unable to bear the sight of the epistemological abyss, yet unwilling to call in question the proposition that the human race is the final measure of all things—have come to affirm the authority of Scripture, though in some attenuated sense. The nature of such attenuation is a recurring theme in this essay; but for now it is enough to point out that the search for meaningful authority has contributed to the renascence of interest in the doctrine of Scripture.

The *fourth* factor contributing to this renascence is the theological revolution that has taken place and is taking place in the Roman Catholic Church. Pope John XXIII and Vatican II have had a profound influence on academic Roman Catholic theology, confirming and accelerating the more "liberal" wing of the church in its adoption of a position on Scripture that is almost indistinguishable from that of "liberal" Protestantism. By and large, this trend has not been as uncontrolled in Catholicism as in Protestantism, owing in part to the constraints of Catholicism's theology of tradition; but the changes are so far-reaching that to compare the academic publications of the Roman Catholic Church of forty or fifty years ago with those of the past two decades is to enter two entirely different worlds. The dramatic change is attested even by the successive drafts at Vatican II. The first draft schema, reflecting the longstanding tradition of the church, dealt with inerrancy as follows:

> Since divine inspiration extends to all things [in the Bible], it follows directly and necessarily that the entire Sacred Scripture is absolutely immune from error. By the ancient and constant faith of the Church we are taught that it is

absolutely wrong to concede that a sacred writer has erred, since divine inspiration by its very nature excludes and rejects every error in every field, religious or profane. This necessarily follows because God, the supreme truth, can be the author of no error whatever.

However, it was the fifth draft that was actually adopted:

Since everything which the inspired author or sacred writer asserted must be held to have been asserted by the Holy Spirit, it must equally be held that the books of Scripture teach firmly, faithfully, and without error that truth which God willed to be put down in the sacred writings for the sake of our salvation.[12]

The changes are dramatic. First, the Bible is now restricted to truth "for the sake of our salvation," and, second—and more importantly—the expression "that truth which God willed to be put down in the sacred writings" not only comes short of making God's truth at least as extensive as the writings but also thereby leaves it entirely open to each reader (or to the church) to decide which parts of the sacred writings embody God's truth. Everyone from a Fundamentalist to a "Christian atheist" could assent to this formulation—which is, another way of saying that this final draft masks massive disagreement in the Roman Catholic Church. Creedally speaking, its fine phrases are worth less than the ink that enables us to read them.

This revolution is evident not only in the content of much Roman Catholic scholarship[13] but now also in the self-conscious defense of these developments.[14] Roman Catholic scholars who adopt a conservative stance on the Scriptures continue to publish their findings;[15] but by and large they have neither advanced a well-thought-out defense of their position nor devised a mature critique of their more liberal colleagues. The few explicit attempts to accomplish the latter are too personal and insufficiently knowledgeable to carry much weight in the academic marketplace.[16]

Whatever the factors that have contributed to bringing about renewed discussion of the nature of Scripture, this essay attempts to chart some of the most important of the recent developments. The eight sections in the rest of this paper do not attempt to be comprehensive; rather, the focus is on those issues that seem to have the greatest bearing on the traditional view of the authority and truthfulness of Scripture held by the church across the centuries.[17] Among other things, this means that a disproportionate amount of space is devoted to positions that are *nearest to but somewhat divergent from* the traditional view. Moreover, issues discussed at length in one of the other articles in these two volumes are usually accorded only brief discussion in this essay, along with a note drawing attention to the more extensive treatment.

I. REVISIONIST HISTORIOGRAPHY

A. SUMMARY OF RECENT HISTORIOGRAPHY

As late as 1975, Martin E. Marty, in an essay largely devoted to tracing the *differences* between Fundamentalism and Evangelicalism,[18] could nevertheless insist that so far as the doctrine of the inerrancy of Scripture is concerned there was no difference between the two groups.[19] That may have been a slight exaggeration, for even in 1975 there were a few scholars who called themselves Evangelicals but who expressed their displeasure with any notion of "inerrancy" as traditionally understood. But Marty's assessment highlights a point of some importance: until fairly recently, the infallibility or inerrancy of Scripture was one of the self-identifying flags of Evangelicalism, recognized by friend and foe alike. In debates with nonconservatives, both sides agreed that the conservatives were in line with the historic tradition of the church. Nonconservatives simply argued that such a position was no longer tenable in any intellectually respectable climate; and conservatives sought to show that the position was not only defensible but one without which the heart of the gospel too easily slipped from one's grasp. Of course, there have been a few exceptions to this understanding. In his debates with Warfield, for instance, Charles Briggs[20] sought to show that the position he held was in line with Reformation teaching; but his argument was not taken up and developed by others. Karl Barth likewise insisted that his understanding of Scripture was but a modern restatement of historic and especially Reformation Christianity; but although in his strong defense of the Bible's authority there is considerable justification for his claim, nevertheless there are nuances in his position that remove him somewhat from the heritage to which he lays claim.[21] By and large, then, conservatives and nonconservatives alike have in the past agreed that the witness of history has favored the conservatives.

That consensus is rapidly dissipating. A new generation of historians is arguing that the modern conservative position on Scripture is something of an aberration that owes its impetus in part to scholastic theology of the post-Reformation period and in part to the Princetonians, especially Charles Hodge and Benjamin B. Warfield. Probably the best known work to espouse this view is that of Jack Rogers and Donald McKim.[22] They seek to establish this thesis by a comprehensive outline of the way the Bible was described and treated throughout (largely Western) church history. Their conclusion is that the historic position of the church defends the Bible's authority in the areas of faith and practice (understood in a restrictive sense), not its reliable truthfulness in every area on which it chooses to speak.

Initial response was largely affirming; but it was not long before major weaknesses came to light. Owing not least to the detailed rebuttal by John D. Woodbridge,[23] rising numbers of scholars have pointed out the fatal flaws. While Rogers and McKim accuse conservatives of reading Warfield into Calvin and the Fathers, it soon becomes apparent that they read Barth and Berkouwer into Calvin and the Fathers. Misunderstanding some of their sources and quoting others with prejudicial selectivity, they finally succumb to a certain "ahistoricism" that neglects the church's sustained attempt to guard the form of the message as well as the message itself.[24]

The work of Rogers and McKim is based in one small part on an influential book by Ernest Sandeen,[25] who argues that belief in "the inerrancy of the Scriptures in the original documents" was innovatively raised to the level of creedal standard by Benjamin Warfield and Archibald Alexander in an 1881 essay on "Inspiration." This part of Sandeen's examination of Fundamentalism's roots was woven into the larger pattern spun by Rogers and McKim. One of the benefits of their work has been a renewed interest in this and related historical questions. As a result, major essays have been written to show, *inter alia*, that primary sources (letters, magazine articles, books, and manuscripts) of the nineteenth century amply attest that the view articulated by Warfield and Hodge was popular long before 1881,[26] that the magisterial reformers were consistent in their defense of an inerrant Scripture,[27] that Abraham Kuyper and Herman Bavinck of the "Old Amsterdam" school cannot legitimately be taken as forerunners of Barth and Berkouwer,[28] and much more. We anticipate more of these careful historical treatments in the next few years.

B. RENNIE'S PROPOSAL

This much of recent revisionist historiography and the responses it has called forth is common knowledge. But subtler influences are at work. In a conference held in June 1981 at the Institute for Christian Studies in Toronto, Ian Rennie delivered a paper written as a response to Rogers and McKim but containing several important and innovative proposals.[29] Rennie argues that the view expounded by Rogers and McKim has conceptual links with "plenary inspiration" as understood in Britain in the nineteenth century. Plenary inspiration, according to Rennie, was distinguished from verbal inspiration and was characterized by (1) a willingness to recognize several different modes of inspiration, (2) insistence nonetheless that all the Bible is inspired, (3) confidence that because all the Bible is authoritative it will not lead anyone aside from the truth on any subject (though it is peculiarly authoritative when it deals with the central Christian truths), and (4) greater openness to interpretative innovation than its competitor. Plenary inspiration could describe the Bible as infallible and without error. It is the view closest to the relatively unformed doctrine of Scripture held by the church until the Reformation.

By contrast, the Germanic lands in the sixteenth century began to

advance the verbal inspiration view—a view that held sway in
countries heavily influenced by Germany but one that made almost
no impact on the Anglo-American world until the nineteenth century,
when it began to be defended by Alexander Carson, Robert Haldane,
J. C. Ryle, and many others. The plenary inspiration theory is
painfully literalistic in its approach, and it becomes characteristic of
Christianity in decline and defensiveness. The plenary view reflects a
Christianity that is both orthodox and robust, and it becomes one of
the vehicles of the First and Second Evangelical Awakenings. Historically, it even enabled those who opposed the slave trade to "break
through the literalism that sanctioned slavery, and affirm that in such
issues it was the spirit of love and redemptive freedom that validly
reinterpreted texts that otherwise possessed the death-disseminating
quality of the culture-bound."[30]

There are two rather substantial weaknesses with Rennie's
proposal. The first is the conceptual inappropriateness of the
disjunction he draws. As Rennie characterizes plenary and verbal
inspiration, it appears that the differences between the two viewpoints center around competing hermeneutical systems and have
almost nothing to do with either inspiration or the Bible's truthfulness. Thus, he affirms that the verbal inspiration view is quick to
say the Bible is without error and is fully authoritative; but, of course,
the plenary inspiration viewpoint would not want to disagree.
According to Rennie, the verbal inspiration view sees the locus of
inspiration in the words themselves and tends to develop formulations in deductivist or Aristotelian fashion. By contrast, the plenary
inspiration view sees the locus of inspiration in the human authors
and tends to develop its formulations from the actual phenomena of
Scripture. The irony in this disjunction is that the one passage where
inspiration is overtly brought up in the Bible (surely, therefore, one of
the "phenomena" to be embraced) tells the reader that it is the
Scripture itself that is "inspired" ("God-breathed," 2Ti 3:16)—not the
human authors. But apart from such distinctions, about which I'll say
more in a later section, the primary disjunctions Rennie draws
between the two viewpoints are hermeneutical and functional:
plenary inspiration is open-minded, aware of the Enlightenment and
able to come to terms with it, relevant, prophetic, against slavery,
while verbal inspiration is defensive, incapable of relevantly addressing the age, strong on literalism and the defense of slavery.

These observations drive us to the second substantial weakness
in Rennie's analysis.[31] His argument, of course, is essentially a
historical one, based on his reading of certain texts; but it is not at all
certain that he has understood those texts correctly. Certainly in the
nineteenth century there were some who preferred to adopt the
plenary inspiration viewpoint, and others were happier to label their
view verbal inspiration. On the other hand, there is little evidence that

the two labels were set over against each other. Those who upheld verbal inspiration were also happy to affirm plenary inspiration;[32] and *both* sides adopted the plenary inspiration label over against the Unitarians, who opted for a much "lower" view of the Bible.[33] In other words, all Evangelicals labeled their view "plenary inspiration" when they were distinguishing their position from the "limited inspiration" of the Unitarians. More telling yet, at least some of those who disparaged verbal inspiration while affirming plenary inspiration did so because they mistakenly equated the former with a theory of mechanical dictation—a theory the ablest defenders of verbal inspiration disavowed—and with such things as verbatim reportage, which rendered Gospel harmonization principally impossible.[34] Similarly, even into the first third of the twentieth century, a few British Evangelicals so associated the term "inerrancy" with crude literalism, or with a failure to recognize the progressive nature of revelation, that they therefore avoided associating themselves with the term—even though, by modern usage, that is what they believed.[35] As for those who in the early part of the twentieth century adopted the view that the Scriptures contained many errors on all sorts of incidental matters (e.g., James Orr, James Denney, and Marcus Dods), not only was their view outside the classic formulations of Scriptural infallibility and plenary inspiration, but it was supported by surprisingly little exegesis.

It appears, then, that Rennie's assessment needs some major qualifications. It is true that the verbal inspiration viewpoint was prominent in Germanic lands, owing in part to the struggles Protestants found themselves engaged in with Roman Catholics and Socinians; but contra Rennie, it is not true that this viewpoint was first introduced into Britain through the hyper-Calvinist John Gill in his *Body of Practical Divinity* (1770). For instance, forty years earlier Ridgley had argued at some length "that the inspired writers have given us a true narration of things, and consequently that the words, as well as the matter, are truly divine."[36] Indeed, his argument is shaped by the assumption that his view is shared by the vast majority of his readers. In any case, it is not at all clear that those who held to verbal inspiration in the nineteenth century were reflections of Christianity in decline. To support this rather startling thesis, Rennie merely offers the judgment that the opposing view opened up interpretative possibilities that made antislavery and other social reform movements possible. But a staunch supporter of verbal inspiration like Edward Kirk (1802–74), the translator of Louis Gaussen's influential *Theopneustia*, was a leader in the American Anti-Slavery Society[37] and a champion of relief for the poor.[38] Rennie's underlying thesis is, on any reading, too generalizing: Christianity given to thoughtful doctrinal precision may not be in decline but in faithful consolidation and advance. Very frequently in the history of

the church the attacks of new philosophical and theological positions
have proved to be the occasion for the orthodox to formulate their
own positions more carefully. These are the historical circumstances
that under God breed an Athanasius or a Calvin.

C. THE "FAITH AND PRACTICE" RESTRICTION

Another example of revisionist historiography merits mention.
For some time it has been popular in many circles to speak of the
Bible's authority, and even its inerrancy, in the realms of "faith and
practice"—but not in such realms as history and science. All sides
agree that the Bible is not a textbook on, say, high energy physics; but
those who hold a high view of Scripture argue that wherever Scripture
speaks, it speaks truthfully. As the essays in this pair of volumes show,
appropriate allowance is made for the genre of any biblical text,
generalizing language, phenomenological descriptions, the problem
of the hermeneutical circle, and so forth; but there is still in this camp
a reasoned defense of the view that *whatever* the Scripture says,
properly interpreted, is true. The restriction offered by the opposing
camp—namely, that the Bible is necessarily true *only* when it
addresses questions of faith and practice—is sometimes now read
back into the history of the church as if the restriction belonged to the
mainstream of the church's understanding of the Bible. One of the
more influential articulations of this perspective is the work of Bruce
Vawter.[39] His argument depends in part on a certain understanding of
"accommodation," about which I shall say more in a subsequent
section; but more central yet to his position is his repeated insistence
that the "inerrancy" or "infallibility" position he freely concedes to be
in the Fathers, in the Middle Ages, and in the Reformers is restricted
to matters of faith and practice.

This reconstruction of history does not appear to stand up very
well to close scrutiny. In the third of his recent W. H. Griffith Thomas
lectures, John Woodbridge[40] has carefully documented, in a preliminary way, some of the hurdles such a reconstruction must overcome.
Vawter insists that the modern inerrantist who sees in the Bible a
source of knowledge instead of a source of religious experience is
hopelessly ensnared by modern scientific paradigms of "knowledge"
illegitimately transferred to the Scripture. Too great a dependence on
a "paradigmatic" view of the development of science is one of the
weaknesses in Vawter's proposal;[41] but, more important, he fails to
recognize that in the Middle Ages, for instance, the Bible held the
supreme place of honor as the highest source of knowledge.

> Manuscript collections were organized under three rubrics: manuscripts of
> Scripture standing supremely by themselves, manuscripts which helped
> readers understand the Scriptures, and diverse manuscripts. Archivists know
> of few, if any, exceptions to this organizational division for medieval
> manuscript collections.[42]

Moreover, the heavy weather that the Copernican theory faced from Catholic, Lutheran, and Calvinist thinkers alike stemmed from the fact that they thought the Bible flatly contradicted a heliocentric view of the universe—which, of course, presupposes that they believed the Bible could address such scientific issues. When Johannes Kepler (1571–1630) sided with Copernicus, he tried to persuade his critics that the theory of Copernicus could be squared with the Bible, not that the Bible does not address such questions or that it may be in error over them.[43] In fact, Kepler went so far as to say that he would willingly abandon whatever parts of the Copernican hypotheses could be shown to be contrary to Scripture.[44] The conclusion Woodbridge documents is inescapable:

> Contrary to the interpretations found in the works of Vawter, Rogers and McKim, and Roland Mushat Frye, the choice that Christians faced until the middle of the seventeenth century was generally this: Should each passage of an infallible Bible which speaks of the natural world be interpreted literally or should some interpretive allowance be made for the fact that a number of passages are couched in the language of appearance? The choice was not between a belief in a completely infallible Bible and a Bible whose infallibility was limited to faith and practice. Parties from both sides of this debate included "science" and history within their definition of infallibility, but they interpreted passages which dealt with the natural world in differing ways. Those persons who did believe the Bible contained errors included, among others, Socinians, libertines, skeptics, deists, remonstrants like Grotius, and members of smaller radical rationalist sects.[45]

The Bible was well on its way to being uncoupled from science, at least in many intellectual circles, by the second half of the seventeenth century; but this uncoupling was normally accompanied by a shift to a theological position that no longer affirmed the infallibility of Scripture. Therefore, those who now wish to affirm the Bible's infallibility in the spheres of "faith and practice" but not in all areas on which it speaks are doubly removed from the mainstream of historical antecedents. Whatever the merits or demerits of their theological position, they cannot legitimately appeal to the sustained commitment of the church in order to bolster that position.

D. COMMON SENSE REALISM

Another sector of modern historiography has become extremely influential—namely, the reassessment of the role and influence of Scottish Common Sense Realism.[46] This offspring of Thomas Reid[47] is charged with so influencing American Evangelicalism that it introduced profound distortions. Common Sense traditions are said to have been influential in generating the Princetonians' doctrine of Scripture,[48] in pushing the "fundamentalist mentality" toward a commitment to "inductive rationalism,"[49] in focusing too much attention on biblical "facts" and "truths" at the expense of knowing

God, in developing certain approaches to systematic theology that resulted in dispensationalism, in engendering assorted Arminianisms, verbal inspiration, evidential apologetics, an overemphasis on individual conversion as over against group conversion, and much more.

The point of these essays, more frequently insinuated than enunciated, is that if Evangelicalism/Fundamentalism were to strip itself of the warping influence of Common Sense Realism, then these other unfortunate accretions, including the doctrine of inerrancy, would wither away, or at the very least lose a substantial part of their support. If we have taken deep draughts from the wells of Baconianism and Scottish Common Sense Realism, we are inescapably corrupted and, therefore, need to revise our views along several doctrinal fronts. In short, Common Sense is perilously close to becoming the whipping boy for certain features in the life of American Evangelicalism that some church historians do not like.

It is no doubt true that Common Sense traditions had a wide impact on nineteenth-century America; and some of this influence was doubtless pernicious. But it is not at all clear that an evenhanded analysis of the extent to which Common Sense actually shaped American Evangelicalism, and in particular its doctrine of Scripture, has yet been written. We have already surveyed some of the studies that show the doctrine of inerrancy not only antedates Thomas Reid but characterizes the church's view of Holy Scripture across the centuries until fairly recent times. Similar things could be said in some other doctrinal areas. For instance, it is not true to history to lay the blame for all evidentialism at the feet of Common Sense traditions (see further discussion in Section VI below).

More broadly, the popularity of certain doctrines is too commonly explained in monocausational terms, especially in Marsden's work; or, to put the matter in a broader framework, simple causal relationships are often affirmed without being demonstrated. Besides being *a priori* methodologically suspect,[50] the approach fails to weigh certain important evidence. If Hodge was so hopelessly ensnared by Common Sense traditions, how was he able to rigorously critique certain points in Reid's position, as well as the positions of such supporters of Common Sense as William Hamilton and Dugald Stewart?[51] If Scottish Common Sense was so determinative in the Princetonians and in subsequent Evangelicalism so far as their doctrine of Scripture was concerned, how was it that other groups equally under the spell of Common Sense did *not* generate such a doctrine of Scripture?[52] How many of these studies have adequately examined the book and journal trade both before and after the alleged impact of Common Sense Realism in order to determine what doctrines and concepts arose only after that impact, what ones were common both before and after that impact, and what ones were in some way modified or slightly reformulated as a result of that impact?[53] How many of the studies have adequately weighed competing explanations of the same historical phenomena?[54]

The Princetonians were extraordinarily widely read scholars. Warfield was as familiar with Augustine, Calvin, and the Westminster divines as he was with Thomas Reid. Such breadth of learning is likely to militate against a controlling dependence on any òne tradition. Hodge was accused of being a slavish follower of Turretin—who had *no* connection with Common Sense. More positively, certain doctrines, including the doctrine of the Scripture's infallibility, are so widely distributed throughout the history of the church that one must conclude they are not paradigmatically determined by any single undergirding philosophy. After all, no one can write without reflecting the philosophical systems that have contributed to his or her thinking; but it does not necessarily follow that a reasonable knowledge of those systems will enable the historian to predict each doctrine the writer will hold. To the extent that the Princetonians used Common Sense categories to express themselves (a point still not adequately examined, in my view), they were thinkers of their time; but it does not necessarily follow that the categories of their time made their doctrine of Scripture innovative. Perhaps that is why one recent writer is able to argue that the Princetonians—and later Machen—used the Scottish Common Sense traditions in a self-critical way to defend and articulate the *historic* doctrine of Scripture.[55]

Frequently quoted as proof of his irremediable dependence on Scottish Common Sense are the following words from Charles Hodge:

> The Bible is to the theologian what nature is to the man of science. It is his storehouse of facts; and his method of ascertaining what the Bible teaches is the same as that which the natural philosopher adopts to ascertain what nature teaches.[56]

These words are commonly taken to reflect at least two unfortunate shifts: first, an uncritical dependence on induction in theology, a method taken over directly from Baconianism mediated through Scottish Common Sense; and, second, a novel view of the Bible that deemphasizes its role as a guide for life, a source for truths necessary for salvation, and a means of grace, while seeing it as a "storehouse of facts," the quarry from which systematic theology is hewn.

Probably too much is being made of this sentence. It is essential to recognize that Hodge makes his remark *in the context of his treatment of the inductive method as applied to theology*—and to nothing else. Hodge develops the thought further to show such principles as the importance of collecting, if possible, *all* that the Bible has to say on a subject before proceeding to inductive statements on the subject, undertaking the collection (like the collection of facts in science) with care, and constantly revising the induction in the light of fresh information. He does not in this section of his work seek to establish the nature of the Bible's truthfulness; his subject is prolegomena, not bibliology. When Hodge does, in fact, turn to the doctrine of Scripture, he is immensely sophisticated and balanced; but here his focus is elsewhere. The most that could be deduced from this one passage about Hodge's doctrine of Scripture are his beliefs that all the Bible is true, that its content is the stuff of systematic theology, and that its material is sufficiently interrelated to belong to the same system. It is hard to see how anyone with a truly high view of Scripture could say much less, even though much more needs to be said (much of which Hodge himself says elsewhere). Like most analogies, this one between science and theology is not perfect; for instance, the nature of experimentation in science is rather different from the trial and error of formulating systematic theology. Certainly there is a place in theology for experience, a place rather different from anything in the empirical sciences;[57] and the role of the Holy Spirit must be incorporated into the discussion. These, however, are steps that Hodge himself undertakes in other sections of his *magnum opus*. But so far as the narrow subject of induction is concerned, the analogy is not all that bad.[58] I shall say more about induction in the next section; but granted what else Hodge writes on Scripture, truth, and method, there is little warrant for reading too much into this one sentence. For exactly the same reason, the admittedly positivistic nature of nineteenth-century science cannot legitimately be held to tarnish his sophisticated epistemology.

E. THE SIGNIFICANCE OF RECENT HISTORIOGRAPHY

This rather introductory survey of recent revisionist historiography is not an attempt to establish a certain doctrine of Scripture by simple appeal to the tradition of the church. The discipline of church history cannot by itself establish the rightness or wrongness of what ought to be believed. On the other hand, Evangelicals in particular, precisely because of their high view of Scripture, have often been content to know far too little about the history of the church; and efforts to overcome this common ignorance can only be commended. Thoughtful Christians who sincerely seek to base their beliefs on the Scriptures will be a little nervous if the beliefs they think are biblical form no part of the major streams of tradition throughout the history of the church; and, therefore, historical theology, though it cannot in itself justify a belief system, not only sharpens the categories and informs the debate but serves as a major checkpoint to help us prevent uncontrolled speculation, purely private theological articulation, and overly imaginative exegesis.

That is precisely why at least some of this recent historiography is rather important. If it is basically right, at the very least it shifts the burden of proof. In the past, inerrantists could comfort themselves that their position was in line with the historical position of most thoughtful Christians in most generations since the first century, even if in the modern environment their position needs fresh defense and articulation; but if now (as they are told) they must admit to being the innovators, they must contend not only with the larger part of modern biblical scholarship arrayed against them but also with the weighty witness of the history of the church. If, on the other hand, the recent historiography has embraced some fundamental misjudgments on these matters, the *perception* that the burden of proof has shifted remains. That is why so many essays in this pair of volumes have dealt with essentially historical matters.

To put the matter another way, this recent historiography has necessarily set a certain agenda. Those convinced it is right must conclude that a major redefinition of Evangelicalism is called for. In one sense, this can only be applauded. There are, after all, so many theological aberrations, cultural hangups, and differences of opinion within Evangelicalism that the movement *ought* to go back to basics again and again to examine how much of its intellectual structure is based on the Bible, its putative authority. But the redefinition envisaged by some of Evangelicalism's recent historians frequently ignores, sidesteps, or downplays—on alleged historical grounds— one of the central planks that binds the diverse strands of Evangelicalism together and to church history.[59] The redefinition, in other words, is in danger of destroying what it seeks to define.

What cannot escape notice is that the driving figures in this movement are historians, not exegetes or theologians. That, of course, is as it should be; they are engaged in historical theology. But quite apart from whether or not this or that historical conclusion is valid, a larger question looms: at what point do the historians who are setting a theological agenda need to interact more directly with scriptural and theological data themselves?[60] The question grows in importance if it is claimed that the observable cultural forces can be identified without making theological judgments in the process:

> While [the historian] must keep in mind certain theological criteria, he may refrain from explicit judgments on what is properly Christian while he concentrates on observable cultural forces. By identifying these forces, he provides material which individuals of various theological persuasions may use to help distinguish God's genuine work from practices that have no greater authority than the customs or ways of thinking of a particular time and place. How one judges any religious phenomenon will, however, depend more on one's theological stance than on one's identification of the historical conditions in which it arose.[61]

The last sentence is surely largely true; but the rest of the quotation, by distancing the historian from the theological matrix where judgments are made, almost sounds as if the historian is able to

provide value-free data, grist for the theological mill turned by
colleagues in another department.

In short, while some of the revisionist historians have been much
concerned, and rightly so, to explain more adequately the intellectual
roots of Fundamentalism and Evangelicalism, they have not always
displayed a critical awareness of the direction from which they
themselves are coming.

II. FOCUS ON THE PHENOMENA OF THE BIBLE

In the exchange of views on the doctrine of Scripture between
James D. G. Dunn and Roger Nicole, to which reference has already
been made, there was a final exchange of open letters that attempted
to delineate the substantive issues that lie between the two viewpoints.[62] Dunn argues that such qualifications to their position as the
inerrantists make (e.g., precision is not the issue, not all commandments in the Old Testament are equally binding today, and so forth)
are generated and demonstrated by studying Scripture itself. In his
words: "*It is the recognition of what Scripture actually consists of
which makes such qualifications of the inerrancy position necessary.*
But once you grant this methodological principle . . . you must surely
also recognize that my position emerges from an application of that
same principle."[63] The difficulties in, say, synoptic relationships are
such that Dunn asks the question, "Do inerrantists *take with sufficient
seriousness even the most basic exegetical findings*, particularly with
regard to the synoptic gospels?"[64] Exactly the same charge appears in
many recent discussions. Paul Achtemeier writes:

> Faced with the overwhelming evidence which critical scholarship has
> uncovered concerning the way in which Scriptures have been composed of
> traditions that are used and reused, reinterpreted and recombined, conserv-
> ative scholarship has sought to defend its precritical view of Scripture by
> imposing that view on Scripture as a prior principle. Unless evidence can be
> turned or bent to show the inerrancy of Scripture, the evidence is denied
> (e.g., it did not appear in the errorless autographs). . . . Critical scholarship is
> therefore an attempt to allow Scripture itself to tell us what it is rather than
> to impose upon Scripture, for whatever worthy motives, a concept of its
> nature which is not derived from the materials, the "phenomena," found in
> Scripture itself.[65]

James Barr puts the matter even more forcefully:

> My argument is simply and squarely that fundamentalist interpretation,
> because it insists that the Bible cannot err, not even in historical regards, has
> been forced to interpret the Bible wrongly; conversely, it is the critical
> analysis, and not the fundamentalist approach, that has taken the Bible for
> what it is and interpreted it accordingly. The problem of fundamentalism is
> that, far from being a biblical religion, an interpretation of scripture in its

own terms, it has evaded the natural and literal sense of the Bible in order to imprison it within a particular tradition of human interpretation. The fact that this tradition—one drawn from older Protestant orthodoxy—assigns an extremely high place to the nature and authority of the Bible in no way alters the situation described, namely that it functions as a human tradition which obscures and imprisons the meaning of Scripture.[66]

It is important to understand the nature of this charge. Inerrantists, we are told, do not shape their doctrine of Scripture by the Scripture itself; or, if they do, they—while constructing their doctrine of Scripture from a few passages that seem to justify the high view they espouse—ignore the actual *phenomena* of Scripture. Worse, once this doctrine is in place, it so distorts their approach to the text that they become the least "biblical" of all.

The issues involved turn out to be surprisingly complex: but at least the following observations are relevant:

A. EVANGELICALS' DISTORTION OF EXEGESIS

Certainly Evangelicals can be as guilty of distorting exegesis as non-Evangelicals. The real question is whether or not that distortion is primarily the result of a high view of Scripture. Clarity of thought is not gained when one particularly notorious example (e.g., the suggestion that the difficulties in reconciling the accounts of Peter's denials can be accomplished by an additive harmonization that postulates six cock crowings)[67] is paraded about as if it were typical of evangelical scholarship. It is most emphatically not, as a quick scan of recent commentaries on the Gospels testifies.[68] Such charges do not seem much fairer than those by conservatives who point out, with some glee, that nonconservatives have sometimes adopted preposterous positions as well (e.g., what really happened at the feeding of the five thousand was that the little boy's generosity shamed everybody else into sharing the lunches they had surreptitiously hidden).

In fact, it is somewhat frustrating to be told again and again that Evangelicals don't really understand the Bible, without being offered realistic test cases where responsible "scholarly consensus" is pitted against responsible consensus of Evangelicals. Without hard cases, the charge against conservatives is emotive (Who, after all, wants to be told he does not understand what he reads?) but not particularly compelling. The few cases that are brought up have usually been discussed at considerable length in the literature; and there we discover that the conservative position is often defended by many scholars who would not call themselves conservatives. One thinks of a John A. T. Robinson, for instance, certainly not an "Evangelical" but many of whose critical views are more conservative than those of the present writer. Even though not many scholars have agreed with him, few of his colleagues would charge him with fundamentally distorting the text. It appears, then, that it is not the individual exegetical position that critics find distasteful or obscurantist; rather, it is a configuration of positions in line with a high view of Scripture. In other words, it is not so much the exegesis that is offensive after all, as the high view of Scripture itself.

Be that as it may, Evangelicals as well as others have needed for some time to articulate the exegetical procedures they follow and the reasons for choosing this or that option—and to do so in such a way that numerous hard cases are used as tests. That is part of the reasoning behind the essays by Silva and Blomberg in these two volumes.

B. "QUALIFICATIONS" OF INERRANCY

Dunn's estimate of the way "qualifications" to the doctrine of inerrancy have come about deserves further reflection. At various points, he raises three such "qualifications"—the contention that precision is not a determining factor in any estimate of the Scripture's truth content, the recognition that not all commandments in the Old Testament are perceived to be equally binding today, and the insistence that the considerable diversity of interpretations is not injurious to the doctrine—and argues that these "qualifications" have been wrung out of the conservatives by the phenomena of the Scriptures themselves. But although there is some merit in his assessment, it is injudiciously cast. Statements about the truthfulness of Scripture are not dependent upon the accuracy or uniformity with which the Scripture may be interpreted. There is an immense conceptual difference between the effort to interpret a certainly truthful text and the effort to interpret a doubtfully truthful text— regardless of the validity of the interpretative effort. Moreover, the lack of precision in many biblical statements is not the primary source of a qualification begrudgingly conceded by entrenched conservatives forced to face up to unavoidable phenomena. Far more important is the fact that the Scriptures themselves, though they lead the reader to expect the Scriptures to be true, do not lead the reader to expect the Scriptures to be *uniformly* precise. Signals as to degree of precision to be expected, like signals as to genre, are often subtle things; but a difficulty would arise only where all the signals point unambiguously to one degree of precision when a considerably lower one is present. This question has been discussed in the companion to this volume.[69] Also, no thoughtful conservative from Irenaeus or Augustine to the present has found the intricate question of the relationships between the covenants to be a threat to his doctrine of Scripture, precisely because the Scripture itself teaches that it covers salvation-historical development: there is before and after, prophecy and fulfillment, type and antitype, as well as mere command. The truthfulness of Scripture does not necessitate viewing all commands in Scripture on the same covenantal footing. What is somewhat astonishing is that this should have been perceived as a weakness in the conservative position.

C. SCRIPTURE'S PHENOMENA AND TRUTH CLAIMS

The central question being raised, I think, may be put like this: Granted for the moment that the Scriptures *claim* to be entirely truthful (a point some critics would concede and others deny), do the hard phenomena of the Scriptures allow the claim to stand? Do the conservatives who accept the authority of the Scripture's truth claims equally accept the authority of the phenomena that must be set in juxtaposition with and perhaps in antithesis to those truth claims?

The question is extremely important. Unfortunately it is often cast in such a way as to suggest that the Bible's claims in support of its own truthfulness are slight and indirect, while the difficulties cast up by larger categories—e.g., the use of the Old Testament in the New, logical or chronological contradictions, historical impossibilities, and the like—are so pervasive that there is only one possible conclusion for a fair-minded scholar. Nothing could be farther from the truth. The Scripture's self-attesting truth-claims are extremely pervasive;[70] and the difficulties raised by the biblical phenomena are on the whole a good deal less intractable than is sometimes suggested.

Part of the problem is that many critics have come to accept as true a certain tradition of critical exegesis that not only highlights problems but sometimes discovers them where there are none. As a result, it is a certain interpretation of the phenomena of the text, not the phenomena themselves, that are being set over against the Scripture's truth claims. The careful reader does not need more than a couple of hours with, say, Bultmann's *magnum opus* on the Synoptics[71] before discovering dozens of alleged contradictions based on little more than assertion and disjunctive thinking.

Nevertheless, it must be admitted that a substantial proportion of evangelical writing has avoided the difficulties or provided facile answers. This sad state of affairs came about in part because of the decimation of Evangelicalism's intellectual leadership in the wake of the Fundamentalist/Modernist controversies. In part (if only in part), this loss has been retrieved: now there are not only older works dealing with some of the difficult phenomena of Scripture[72] but also major commentaries[73] and technical essays on particular passages (e.g., Mt 27:3–10[74] or Eph 4:7–9[75]).

Behind this debate lurks an important methodological question: Granted that there are many statements about Scripture in the Bible, and granted that there are many biblical phenomena to consider when it comes to constructing a doctrine of Scripture, what should be the relation between the two kinds of data? Critics of the traditional view increasingly stress the primacy of induction from the phenomena; but this approach must be challenged. Twenty years ago Nicole, in a review of the first edition of Beegle's book on Scripture,[76] wrote the following:

Dr. Beegle very vigorously contends that a proper approach to the doctrine of inspiration is to start with induction from what he calls "the phenomena of Scripture" rather than with deduction from certain Biblical statements about the Scripture. . . . This particular point needs to be controverted. If the Bible does make certain express statements about itself, these manifestly must have a priority in our attempts to formulate a doctrine of Scripture. Quite obviously, induction from Bible phenomena will also have its due place, for it may tend to correct certain inaccuracies which might take place in the deductive process. The statements of Scripture, however, are always primary. To apply the method advocated by Dr. Beegle in other areas would quite probably lead to seriously erroneous results. For instance, if we attempted to construct our view of the relation of Christ to sin merely in terms of the concrete data given us in the Gospels about His life, and without regard to certain express statements found in the New Testament about His sinlessness, we might mistakenly conclude that Christ was not sinless. . . . [This] is not meant to disallow induction as a legitimate factor, but it is meant to deny it the priority in religious matters. First must come the statements of revelation, and then induction may be introduced as a legitimate confirmation, and, in some cases, as a corrective in areas where our interpretation of these statements and their implications may be at fault.[77]

In other words, if particular texts, despite evenhanded exegetical coaxing, cannot fit into the theological theory (for that is what a doctrine is) that has emerged from explicit statements of Scripture on the subject, then the theory may have to be modified, recast, reformulated—or, alternatively, the exegesis may have to begin again. But because hard cases make not only bad law but bad theology, one should not give *priority* to them in the articulation of doctrine, even though each one must be thoughtfully considered.

D. THE RELATION OF DEDUCTION AND INDUCTION

Related to this debate is the broader question of the proper relation between deduction and induction in theological inquiry. This question has both historical and methodological foci. In the historical focus, Rogers and McKim, as we have seen, charge the scholastic Reformed theologians and the Princetonians after them with an innovative dependence on deduction; infected by Baconianism, it is alleged, they began with a central proposition (such as "God cannot lie") and deduced a sweeping doctrine of Scripture.[78] More recently, others (as we saw in the last section) have charged the Princetonians in particular with too heavy a reliance on induction. It is alleged that they treat the Bible as a mere sourcebook of facts from which, by the process of induction, they create their theological theories. It is doubtful if the charge of innovation is historically justifiable in either case; and, in any case, if the Princetonians are to be permitted neither induction nor deduction, it might be easier to dismiss them just because they think.

At the methodological level, the problem is much deeper. In the first place, Sproul has pointed out how distinct groups of inerrantists have defended the doctrine on quite different grounds—i.e., the doctrine is not entirely hostage to a particular form of reasoning.[79] More important, any complex theory in any field of human thought (some areas of mathematics possibly excluded) depends not only on intricate interplay between induction and deduction but on what is variously called adduction, abduction, or retroduction—which is not so much a category entirely distinct from induction and deduction as a label that incorporates these two processes while going beyond them to include the creative thought, sudden insight, and perception of links that are essential to all intellectual advance. These matters are commonplace among those who deal with theory formation and justification;[80] and it is, therefore, disconcerting to find them so consistently overlooked.

III. DEBATES OVER VARIOUS TERMS

Packer warns us of the dangers in oversimplifications:

> I am sure that my evangelical readers have all had abundant experience of this particular evil. I am sure we have all had cause in our time to complain of over-simplifications which others have forced on us in the debate about Scripture—the facile antithesis, for instance, between revelation as propositional or as personal, when it has to be the first in order to be the second; or the false question as to whether the Bible is or becomes the Word of God, when both alternatives, rightly understood, are true; or the choice between the theory of mechanical dictation and the presence of human error in the Bible, when in fact we are not shut up to either option. I am sure we have all found how hard it is to explain the evangelical view of Scripture to persons whose minds have once embraced these over-simplifications as controlling concepts.[81]

These oversimplifications are in no small measure the result of defective definitions. *Truth* is one such term frequently subjected to reductionism; but as it was discussed in the first of this pair of volumes,[82] I shall largely leave it aside and make brief mention of three other terms that have become important in recent discussion. But two remarks about *truth* seem in order. First, although it is sometimes suggested that conservatives reduce truth to words and propositions—and thereby ignore the centrality of Christ as truth incarnate—this failing is rare in conservatives of any stature. It is far more common for the reductionism to work the other way: the nonconservative of stature is more likely to affirm the centrality of Christ while ignoring the truth claims of the Scriptures themselves. Second, the diversity of meanings bound up in the word *true* and its cognates (and ably expounded by Nicole) does not itself jeopardize allegiance to a correspondence theory of truth, on which the doctrine of a truthful Scripture is partly based. For instance, I might say, "My wife is my true friend"—even though I do hold to a correspondence theory of truth. My sample sentence merely demonstrates that the semantic range of "true" and its cognates cannot be reduced to usages congenial to the correspondence theory of truth. Opponents would have to show either that the Hebrew and Greek words for truth never take on the correspondence meaning, or at least that they never have such force when they refer to Scripture.

A. ACCOMMODATION

The *first* additional term to consider is *accommodation*. If the transcendent, personal God is to communicate with us, His finite and sinful creatures, He must in some measure *accommodate* Himself to and *condescend* to our capacity to receive that revelation. The point has been recognized from the earliest centuries of the church, and it received considerable attention during the Reformation. In recent discussion, however, this notion of accommodation as applied to the Scriptures is frequently assumed to entail error. Thus, Barth writes:

> If God was not ashamed of the fallibility of all the human words of the Bible, of their historical and scientific inaccuracies, their theological contradictions, the uncertainty of their tradition, and, above all, their Judaism, but adopted and made use of these expressions in all their fallibility, we do not need to be ashamed when He wills to renew it to us in all its fallibility as witness, and it is mere self-will and disobedience to try to find some infallible elements in the Bible.[83]

Less ambiguously, Vawter writes:

> We should think of inspiration as always a positive divine and human interaction in which the principle of condescension has been taken at face value. To conceive of an absolute inerrancy as the effect of the inspiration was not really to believe that God had condescended to the human sphere but rather that He had transmuted it into something else. A human literature containing no error would indeed be a contradiction in terms, since nothing is more human than to err.[84]

Similarly, in his latest book, Clark Pinnock attempts to relate the possibility of error to the principle of accommodation:

> What we all have to deal with is a Bible with apparent errors in it whose exact status we cannot precisely know. Whether in his inspiration or in his providence, God has permitted them to exist. . . . What God aims to do through inspiration is to stir up faith in the gospel through the word of Scripture, which remains a human text beset by normal weaknesses.[85]

There are numerous other examples of the same approach, often accompanied by the assumption that this is the view of accommodation that has prevailed throughout much of church history.

The first thing that must be said by way of response is that some of these treatments are not very consistent. In the same context as the last quotation, for instance, Pinnock writes: "The Bible does not attempt to give the impression that it is flawless in historical or scientific ways. God uses writers with weaknesses and still teaches the truth of revelation through them."[86] But here there is a shift from error in certain spheres of thought (history and science) to error caused by the humanity of Scripture. One begins to suspect that the latter argument is being used to restrict the Bible's authority to purely religious matters, not to whatever subject it chooses to address. But the argument is more dangerous than Pinnock seems to think; for if the potential for error is grounded in Scripture's humanity, by what argument should that error be restricted to the fields of history and science? Why does not human fallibility also entail error in the religious and theological spheres? Or conversely, if someone wishes to argue that God has preserved the human authors from error in religion and theology, what prevents God from doing so in other areas of thought?

Second, this approach to accommodation is certainly far removed from the understanding of accommodation worked out both in the early church and in the Reformation. The most recent authority rightly insists:

> The Reformers and their scholastic followers all recognized that God in some way must condescend or accommodate himself to human ways of knowing in order to reveal himself: this *accommodatio* occurs specifically in the use of human words and concepts for the communication of the law and the gospel, but it in no way implies the loss of truth or the lessening of scriptural authority. The *accommodatio* or *condescensio* refers to the manner or mode of revelation, the gift of wisdom of infinite God in finite form, not to the quality of the revelation or to the matter revealed. A parallel idea occurs in the scholastic protestant distinction between *theologia archetype* and *theologia ectype*. Note that the sense of *accommodatio* which implies not only a divine condescension but also a use of time-bound and even erroneous statements as a medium for revelation arose in the eighteenth century in the thought of Semler and his contemporaries and has no relation either to the position of the Reformers or to that of the protestant scholastics, either Lutheran or Reformed.[87]

Third, the argument that error is essentially human ("nothing is more human than to err," writes Vawter) is extremely problematic and cries out for further analysis. Error, of course, is distinguishable from sin and can be the result of nothing more than finitude; but much human error results from the play of sin on human finitude. The question is whether it is error that is essential to humanness, or finitude. If the latter, it is difficult to see why Scripture would be any less "human" if God so superintended its writing that no error was committed. Human beings are always finite; but it does not follow

they are always in error. Error does not seem to be essential to
humanness. But if someone wishes to controvert the point, then to be
consistent that person must also insist that between the Fall and the
new heaven and the new earth, not only error but *sinfulness* is
essential to humanness. No writer of Scripture escaped the sinfulness
of his fallen nature while composing what came to be recognized as
Holy Writ: does this mean that the humanness of Scripture entails not
only error but sinfulness? And if not, why not? Who wishes to say
Scripture is sinful? This is not mere *reductio ad absurdem*: rather, it is
a way of showing that human beings who in the course of their lives
inevitably err and sin do not necessarily err and sin in any particular
circumstance. Their humanness is not compromised when they fail
to err or sin. By the same token, a God who safeguards them from
error in a particular circumstance—namely, the writing of Scripture—has not thereby vitiated their humanness.

Fourth, there is an unavoidable christological connection, raised
(perhaps unwittingly) by Vawter himself:

> The Fathers and the Church have always been fond of the analogy by which
> the Scripture as word of God in words of men may be compared with Christ
> the incarnate Word, the divine in human flesh. But if the incarnate Word
> disclaimed omniscience (Mk 13.32, etc.), it must seem singularly inappropri-
> ate to exploit the analogy as an argument for an utterly inerrant Scripture.[88]

The logic, of course, is faulty: to be a valid argument, Vawter would
have had to conclude with the words: " . . . it must seem singularly
inappropriate to exploit the analogy as an argument for an utterly
omniscient Scripture." I'm not sure what "omniscient Scripture"
would mean: presumably a Scripture that "knows" or "tells" or
"records" absolutely everything. But no one claims that. However, if
the Scripture/Christ analogy holds, Vawter's argument can be made to
stand on its head. If error is the *inevitable* result of lack of
omniscience, and if lack of omniscience is characteristic of all
humanness (including that of Jesus, according to the biblical passage
to which Vawter refers), then there are errors not only in Scripture but
in Jesus' teaching as well.

Calvin understood the problem and, therefore, appealed to
accommodation not only in his treatment of Scripture but as a
function of God's gracious self-disclosure to us in many forms: in the
use of language, in the use of anthropomorphism, in the doctrine of
Scripture—and in the Incarnation itself.[89] But it was precisely that
breadth of view that enabled him to see that whatever accommodation entails it *cannot* entail sin or error: the costs are too high right
across the spectrum of Christian theology.

B. INSPIRATION

A *second* term that is currently undergoing creative redefinition is *inspiration*. Most of the major proposals over the past fifty years or so for an appropriate meaning of the term are reasonably well known and need not be canvassed here. More recently, William J. Abraham has put forward another suggestion with some novel features.[90] He argues that during much of the church's history Christians believed the Bible was simply dictated by God. Advances in knowledge made so simple a view no longer tenable; and it was in that context that Warfield and others articulated their "concursive" theory of inspiration—i.e., that God in his sovereignty so supervised and controlled the human writers of Scripture that although what they wrote was genuinely their own, and in their own idiom, it was nevertheless the very word of God, right down to the individual words. The trouble with this view, Abraham argues, is that, for all intents and purposes, it remains indistinguishable from the older dictation theory. There are too many difficulties and contradictions in the Bible for the theory to be tenable (although he declines to enumerate any of these). What we must do is recognize that all talk about God is analogical talk; and, therefore, what we mean when we say "God inspires someone" must be determined by analogy to what we mean when we say something like "A teacher inspires his pupil." This does not mean that the pupil quotes the teacher verbatim, or even that the pupil remains entirely faithful to all that the teacher holds true. Some of what the pupil passes on will be accidental distortion of what the teacher taught; some may even be self-conscious revision of it; and some distortion may occur because of the pupil's limited capacity. But if the teacher is very "inspiring," the pupil will faithfully pass on the heart of what the teacher taught. So it is in the relationship between God and the writers of Scripture: He inspires them as a teacher does his pupils. But to claim "verbal inspiration" or inerrancy or infallibility in any strict sense would be a denial of the insights gained from an analogical approach to the way we talk about God.

Abraham's view has received adequate critique elsewhere,[91] but a few comments may be in order. First, one cannot help noting that while other historians accuse Warfield of tightening up the doctrine of Scripture (see the first section of this paper), Abraham charges him with loosening it—but not enough. The charge depends on the antecedent judgment that writers before Warfield, in particular Gaussen,[92] held to a dictation view of inspiration. Certainly such writers occasionally use the word "dictation," but it has been shown repeatedly that many older writers use "dictation" language to refer to the *results* of inspiration, not its *mode*—i.e., the *result* was nothing less than the very words of God. As for the mode, Gaussen himself forcefully insists that the human authors of Scripture are not merely

"the pens, hands, and secretaries of the Holy Ghost," for in much of
Scripture we can easily discern "the individual character of the
person who writes."[93] Warfield does not seem so innovative after all.

Second, Abraham attempts to formulate an entire doctrine of
Scripture on the basis of his treatment of inspiration. What he never
undertakes, however, is a close study of the wide-ranging ways in
which Scripture speaks of itself, claims to be truthful, identifies the
words of man with the words of God, and so forth—the kind of
material that Grudem has put together.[94] More important yet, in the
one passage in the New Testament that is closest to using our word
"inspiration" (2Ti 3:16), it is not the human author who is "inspired"
but the text: the Scripture itself is *theopneustos*. At a blow, the analogy
of a teacher inspiring his pupils falls to the ground—a point the
much-maligned Warfield treated with some rigor almost a century
ago.[95]

What strikes the evangelical reader who contemplates Abraham's
proposals is the degree of arbitrariness intrinsic to the selection of the
model. The same is true about other recent proposals. The "biblical
theology" movement, for instance, has often suggested that God has
revealed Himself through a sequence of revelatory events, to which
Scripture is added as the result of the Spirit's inspiring human minds
to bear witness to the revelation. The revelatory pattern as a whole is
the act of God; but because the human witness may be faulty,
individual steps along the line of that revelatory pattern may have to
be dismissed; and, in any case, there is certainly no identification of
God's words with man's words. These and many other proposals, as
insightful as they are at some points, are strikingly arbitrary in that
they select some model or other without dealing effectively with the
Bible's account of its own nature.

C. INERRANCY

A *third* term that has elicited some discussion is *inerrancy*.
Besides the fact that it is essentially a negative term, many have
charged that the use of the term in the modern debate is not only
innovative (Why move from, say, "infallibility"?) but also logically
inadequate. Marshall, for instance, comments that many propositions
about alleged historical phenomena can be meaningfully judged to be
inerrant (i.e., true); but many statements in Scripture cannot be so
treated. If Jesus says, "Take away the stone" (Jn 11:39), His command
is neither true nor false: the categories are inappropriate. What may
be true or false is the biblical proposition that Jesus actually uttered
this command, not the command itself. The same is true of much of
the advice of Job's comforters, of fictional narratives like Jotham's
fable or Jesus' parables, and of much more. As a result, Marshall
prefers to adopt the language of "infallibility," understood to mean
something like "entirely trustworthy for the purposes for which it is
given."[96]

In one sense there is wisdom here: if Evangelicals use words as frequently misunderstood and as easily mocked as this one, they may be erecting unnecessary barriers to others who are trying to understand their position. Certainly it is easy enough to articulate a comprehensive doctrine of Scripture without using that particular word,[97] even though "inerrant" and especially the longer "without error" have a notable pedigree.

On the other hand, it rather misses the point to say that "inerrant" is a term inappropriate to commands and parables. Inerrancy does not mean that every conceivable sequence of linguistic data in the Bible must be susceptible to the term "inerrant," only that no errant assertion occurs. In any case, even if "inerrancy" were inappropriate at the merely lexical level, any one-word summary of a complex doctrine must be understood as a construct. This is true even of a word like "God": what a writer who uses this term means cannot be established from a lexicon. Once again, Feinberg's essay on the meaning of inerrancy comes to mind.[98] More important, it is arguable that those who today defend the use of the term "inerrancy" mean no more and no less than did most of those who used the term "infallibility" forty years ago. One of the factors that has prompted the switch has been the progressive qualification of "infallibility": Marshall wants it to mean "entirely trustworthy for the purposes for which it is given." That qualification may be entirely laudable, if the "purposes" are discovered inductively and not arbitrarily narrowed to salvific matters, as if to imply that the Bible is not trustworthy when it treats of history or the external world. After all, one might suggest that the purpose of Scripture is to bring glory to God, or to explain truthfully God's nature and plan of redemption to a fallen race in order to bring many sons to glory: under such definitions of "purpose" the comprehensiveness of Scripture's truth claims cannot be so easily circumvented. In short, conservatives may in some measure be innovative in stressing one word above another as that which most accurately characterizes their views; but it is not at all clear that by so doing they have succumbed to doctrinal innovation insensitive to normal linguistic usage.

IV. UNCRITICAL ATTITUDES TOWARD LITERARY AND OTHER TOOLS

It must be frankly admitted that evangelicals have on the whole been somewhat slow to make use of genuine advances in literary criticism. On the other hand, it must also be admitted that some scholars have deposited a naive confidence in these same tools that would be touching if it were not so harmful to accurate biblical exegesis and to profound humility before the Word of God. We are already in some peril when we use our tools in Procrustean ways to make us masters of the Word, when it is far more important to be mastered by it.

In the first of these two volumes, one essay briefly discussed the limits and usefulness of redaction criticism and of its antecedents;[99] and for that reason this section may be kept short. Four observations, however, may be of value.

The first is that literary tools almost never bring with them the control of a mechanic's "tools." The label "literary tool" is, therefore, potentially deceptive. One need only read certain structuralist treatments of Jesus' parables,[100] for instance, to observe how often the interpretation turns out to be an invitation to authentic existence or an openness to world-view reversal or the like: Jesus would have been surprised. If, in days gone by, the "orthodox" Christians were the first to impose their theology on the text, they seem to have been displaced in recent scholarly discussion by a new generation so gifted in the use of their "tools" that they can find confirmation of their theology in every text they examine. This process has been speeded up by the impact of the new hermeneutic, about which I shall say more in the sixth section of this paper. For the moment it is enough to remark that although literary tools offer to interpreters of Scripture a variety of devices to bring out the meaning of the text, they have sometimes become ponderous ways of saying the obvious,[101] or (which is worse) refined ways of distorting the obvious.[102]

Second, new literary "tools" are being developed constantly; and frequently some time must elapse before profound understanding of the tool's nature and limits can be reached. This is true not only for something fairly simple, such as audience criticism, but also for the range of techniques and procedures covered by, say, "rhetorical criticism." There is no doubt, for instance, that Culpepper's recent book on John[103] breaks new ground; but, equally, there is no doubt that by appealing to the formal characteristics of a nineteenth- and twentieth-century novel as the grid by which the Fourth Gospel should be interpreted, there is a substantial loss both in accuracy of exegesis and in the book's real authority.[104] One common feature of rhetorical criticism is the removal of the external referent in the interpretative process *and* (in the hands of most interpreters) *in the final assessment of the text's relation to external reality*.[105] The result seems to be a two-tier approach to history and even to truth itself— one in the external world and one in the "story," with few obvious relations between the two. What that will do to the "scandal of particularity" inherent in the revelation of a self-incarnating God can only be imagined. It is probably still too early for deep assessments; but this "literary tool" clearly marks out an area where a great deal more work needs to be done.

The confusion extends well beyond conservative circles, of

course. At the 1983 meetings of *Studiorum Novi Testamenti Societas* held in Canterbury, the section on John spent many hours debating the proper relationships between rhetorical criticism and the older, more established "tools." In that sense, there is some gain; for if the evidence that serves to justify, say, source-critical division of a text can with equal or better reason serve to justify the unity of the text when read with rhetorical-critical questions in mind, one wonders what justification is left for the source criticism of the passage. It will not do to suggest that a source-critical reading of the text justifies the initial partition theory, and the rhetorical reading of the text justifies the unity imposed by the final redactor; for it is *the same evidence* to which appeal is being made. If that evidence is satisfactorily explained by rhetorical considerations, then it *cannot* serve to ground partition. It would not, of course, be fair to give the converse argument ("If that evidence is satisfactorily explained by source-critical considerations, then it *cannot* serve to ground unity.") equal weight, because we have the text as a unified whole before us. The *onus probandi* in this sort of debate always rests with the source critic. Thus, when Ackerman[106] contends that the doubling in the Joseph story has a literary purpose, he is inevitably calling in question the view that the doubling betrays a conflation of disparate sources. At some point the student must opt for one line of argument or the other, presumably on the basis of which method offers the best "fit." But we may at least be grateful that some of the new literary tools are again opening up questions that have too often been illegitimately closed.

Third, one of the more influential of the new approaches to Scripture is the application of the principles of sociological analysis to the exegesis of the text. There is much to be gained by such an approach. Just as the contemporary church can be studied using sociological categories, there is no intrinsic reason why the same categories cannot be used for groupings of people in the Scripture. Certainly social forces have real impact on individuals and groups; and sometimes those (like theologians) who prefer to focus on abstract ideas at the expense of thinking about social forces may overlook important factors that bear on the historical events described in the sacred texts. For this reason, many of these studies have considerable value.[107]

Nevertheless, we must differentiate between the numerous sociological appeals being made. Sometimes the Scripture is studied by a historian or exegete who is sensitive to sociological issues; sometimes explicitly sociological categories intrude: "class," "millenarian cult," "charismatic authority figure," and so forth. Already there are two crucial issues lurking behind the surface: (1) Are the sociological appeals presented in a reductionistic fashion that ultimately sidesteps or even deprecates questions of ultimate truth and authority? If sociology warns us against a too facile appeal to *deus ex machina*, does it also sometimes banish God altogether, or fail to see His sovereign hand over social forces? (2) Are the categories of modern sociology applied to ancient societies with requisite care? Are discontinuities as carefully observed as continuities?

But we may go further and note those studies that apply particular sociological theory to specific problems.[108] Here there are sometimes unrecognized difficulties, as Rodd[109] has pointed out. What begins as a heuristic device may end up as a reductionistic explanation. Moreover, sociology gains in accuracy when it can study at first hand large groups of people under carefully worked out controls; and, even then, different sociologists may interpret the data rather differently. How accurate then are sociological analyses and explanations of social forces to which we have only remote and indirect access through documents two thousand and more years old? In short, at what point does dependence upon the "tool" become not only exegetically distorting but thereby also destructive not only of biblical authority but even of elementary exegesis? Marshall's judgment is balanced:

> The scholar who studies religious history from a sociological point of view may well believe that sociological considerations are largely sufficient to explain it. He may be wrong in adopting such an absolute standpoint—a Christian believer would certainly want to claim this—but nevertheless the adoption of his standpoint will probably bring to light historical facts and explanations which would have eluded the historian who ignored the insights of sociology.[110]

Finally, although it is true that conservatives have often been the slowest to adopt what is useful and fair in the so-called "literary tools," in some cases the opposite is true: Evangelicals use certain "tools" with increasing skill, while their less conservative colleagues are engaged in depreciating the same tools. Precisely because they put such a high premium on the Word, conservatives have devoted large amounts of energy to the study of the biblical languages and to the principles of what is often called "grammatical-historical exegesis." To scan the abstracts of the 1984 meetings of the Society of Biblical Literature will convince most observers that such discipline is in decline in the larger community of biblical scholars, suspended by approaches and themes judged more current, not to say faddish. Or again, harmonization is so often presented as an unscholarly capitulation to conservatism that far too little thought has been given to its nature, proper use, and abuse. For that reason the essay by Blomberg[111] in this volume marks a step forward, even if—or indeed, precisely because—it cuts across the grain.

V. SENSITIVITY TO "PROPOSITIONS" AND "LITERARY GENRE"

By and large, conservatives during the past one hundred years have not been slow to focus on *words*. They have pointed out, rightly, that inspiration extends beyond revelation of mere concepts—concepts that the human authors are left to flesh out without any divine superintendence so far as the actual *words* are concerned—to the actual *words* of the sacred text. But they have been slower to deal at length with more substantial literary units. How are words related to propositions? How are propositions related to any particular literary genre? How are the truth questions related to words, propositions, and literary genres? What exactly does it mean to say that Acts 15, Matthew's genealogy of Jesus, and Jotham's fable are all *true?* What is to be made of the fact that the first four books of the New Testament are "Gospels"?

At a popular level, any reasonably conscientious and intelligent reader makes various literary distinctions as the various parts of the Bible are encountered. Parables may not be understood very well; but few readers take the narrative parables to be descriptive of historical events. All will make subtle, if inarticulate, adjustments as they pass from genealogy to discourse, from discourse to apocalyptic, from apocalyptic to psalm. Few will read Jeremiah's psalm of malediction as a literal curse on the man who brought his father the news of Jeremiah's birth or as a serious wish that his mother should have remained forever pregnant (Jer 20:14–18): thoughtful reading recognizes lament rather than vindictiveness. That intuitive "feel" for what a passage means, however, demands rigorous attention and analytical thought. For, otherwise, we may unhappily fall into one of two opposite errors: we may insist that Scripture is saying something it is not in fact saying; or, alternatively, we may appeal to literary genre in a vague and undisciplined way that enables us to escape what Scripture is saying.

The issue was thrust upon Evangelicals in North America in the painful debates occasioned by Gundry's commentary on Matthew.[112] This is not the place to offer a blow by blow account of the debate; but quite clearly a substantial part of the criticism leveled against him by conservatives was ill-conceived.[113] Gundry holds that whatever Matthew writes that is different from or in addition to Mark and Q (which he understands to be considerably longer than the 250 or so verses normally so labeled) has no historical referent: rather, it belongs to midrash, a genre of literature that happily expands on historical material in order to make theological (not historical) points. Moreover, Gundry holds this while also maintaining, with integrity, the full authority and inerrancy of Scripture. Entirely without merit is the charge that because Gundry denies that the referent in certain passages is historical, therefore he runs into flat contradiction with other passages that treat the same referent as historical; for in each such case, Gundry has a ready-made answer. In some instances, such as the accounts in Matthew and Luke of the virginal conception of Jesus, he denies the historicity of Matthew's account (on the grounds that Matthew is writing midrash) while upholding the historicity of Luke's account (on the grounds that Luke is writing history, or theologically tinged history). In other instances he might simply argue that his opponent has not found any passage where the referent can be judged historical, *once it is agreed that the relevant passages all belong to the category of midrash*. Several of Gundry's critics fail to see that the problem lies solely at the interpretative level. A Calvinist might as easily argue that the Arminian who denies that certain texts teach the unqualified sovereignty of God is in reality denying the authority and inerrancy of Scripture. The only legitimate way to offer telling critique of Gundry's interpretation of Matthew is to combine careful assessment of some of his methods with demonstration that his handling of the literary genre "midrash" is fundamentally mistaken.[114]

To take another example, the "Gospels" have often been compared with better known and more widely distributed literary genres from the ancient world, in an attempt to define the manner in which a "Gospel" may be expected to convey truth.[115] Most such efforts result in some depreciation of the importance of "history" in a Gospel. Individual efforts to treat individual Gospels in a more conservative vein have not been entirely lacking;[116] but one of the best treatments of the problem is an essay by Aune,[117] whose work is immaculately researched and whose conclusions are nuanced. One of the more important of these is that "genre" is a category frequently without fixed boundaries; and an individual genre is often some amalgamation or reshaping of antecedent genres. The result is a telling critique of reductionist approaches to the Gospels. Similar studies are required to tell us just what the "Epistles" are (here the essay by Longenecker in the first of these two volumes will be of use[118]) and just what sort of "history" is recorded in the Book of Acts.[119] No less pressing is the need for further studies of such hellenistic categories as the diatribe and of such Jewish categories as pesher.

Comparable ambiguities surround the nature of propositions. The central questions may be introduced by quoting from a review of the first of these two volumes:

> While some of the authors distinguish between the message or truth of Scripture and the words (e.g., Bromiley), others (e.g., Gruden [*sic*]) tend to equate the human witness and the divine revelation. The latter are prone to ignore those passages that imply the discontinuity between human speech and understanding on the one hand and the Word of God on the other (cf. Ps. 71:15; 119:18, 19; 139:6; Isa. 55:8, 9; Job 42:3; Dan. 12:8; I Cor. 2:8, 9; I Pet.

1:10, 11). Instead, they concentrate on the character of Scripture itself as revelation.[120]

The criticism is in certain respects telling, as we shall see; but it also muddies the central issues a little. In the first place, the biblical passages to which references are made are not all of a piece, and in any case they do not prove what the reviewer thinks they do. For instance, Isaiah 55:8–9 does not affirm that because God's thoughts are higher than our thoughts they cannot be "reduced" to human language. The context shows that God's thoughts are "higher" than ours in the moral realm, and therefore our response must be repentance, not some kind of awareness of the ineffable. Psalm 71:15 and similar passages make it clear that the psalmist recognizes the limitations on his knowledge; but equally they show that the psalmist can utter in human language what he *does* know of God's ways. Passages such as Psalm 119:18 and 1 Corinthians 2:8–9 presuppose that the epistemological cruxes to understanding the Word of God go beyond mere analysis of language (about which a little more will be said in the next section); but they do not suggest that there is a fundamental disjunction between Scripture and truth. Second, the reviewer does not attempt interaction with the voluminous biblical evidence Grudem adduces to show that the Scriptures themselves develop the view that what Scripture says, God says. And third, the review moves unexpectedly from a possible distinction between the message or the truth of Scripture and its words to a distinction between the human *witness* and the divine *revelation*—a change in categories that prematurely closes the discussion.

Nevertheless, the reviewer has raised some important points. Certainly there is a formal distinction between, say, Grudem and Bromiley. But the reviewer's own suggestion is a trifle disconcerting:

> We need to ask seriously whether words contain their meaning. Infallibility and inerrancy pertain to the revelatory meaning of the biblical words, but is this meaning endemic to the words themselves? Or is it given by the Holy Spirit to the eyes of faith when the words are seen in their integral relationship to God's self-revelation in Jesus Christ?[121]

The difficulty is that the infallible meaning is not only removed from the words but from the realm of the text: it is "given" by the Holy Spirit to the eyes of faith. Apart from the fact that the work of the Holy Spirit is crucial to all human knowing of things divine (see the essay by Frame in this volume),[122] the kind of transfer of the locus of authority envisaged by our reviewer cannot be made to square with the biblical evidence amassed in the Grudem essay. But may it not be that the apparent discrepancy between a Grudem and a Bromiley is merely formal? The one reflects the fact that the Bible itself treats its words as God's words; the other reflects the linguistic stance that treats words as concatenations of phonemes or orthographical conventions that are mere vehicles for meaning. The one treats words in a "popular" or "ordinary" way and is delighted to find that these very human words of Scripture are also God's words; the other treats words in the framework of modern theoretical linguistics and therefore sees a certain disjunction between naked words and meaning.[123] But our reviewer goes beyond both of these complementary positions to a new stance that locates meaning only in the Spirit-illumined knower.

The question, then, at least in part, is whether admittedly human words, when so superintended by God Himself, can convey divine truth—not exhaustively, of course, but truly. I think they can, and I find insuperable difficulties with any other position[124]—though this is not the place to defend that view. But there is a second question, namely, whether the "propositions" the words make up convey meaning or merely serve as meaning's vehicle. What quickly becomes obvious is that "proposition" is given various definitions that feed back and affect one's use of "propositional revelation" and even of "verbal inspiration."

It is here that Vanhoozer[125] is a reliable guide and makes significant advances in resolving these perplexing issues. He forces us to think through these slippery categories, and he points to ways in which we may preserve the substance of "propositional, verbal revelation" (i.e., the emphasis on verbal, cognitive communication with authority vested in the text itself) while simultaneously appreciating the ordinariness of the language of Scripture, the diversity of its literary forms, and therefore what it means to speak of Scripture's truthfulness.

VI. THE NEW HERMENEUTIC AND PROBLEMS OF EPISTEMOLOGY

Few questions are more persistent and more important in this decade than those dealing with hermeneutics. Among the most influential of the developments of this generation is that the older hermeneutical models that focused on the processes whereby the interpreter interpreted the objective text have been radically transformed into newer models that set up a "hermeneutical circle" between the text and its interpreter. Each time the interpreter asks questions of the text, the questions themselves emerge out of the limitations of the interpreter; and, therefore, the responses are skewed to fit that grid. But those responses shape the interpreter; they may radically alter one's world view if they provide sharp surprises. Therefore, when the interpreter returns to the text, the questions he or she now asks come out of a slightly different matrix—

and, therefore, the responses are correspondingly modified. Not only is the interpreter interpreting the text; the text in this model is "interpreting" the interpreter. Understanding does not depend in any important way on a grasp of the referents of words (i.e., that to which they refer) but emerges out of the heart of language itself. The text merely provides the room or the vehicle for the language-event, now understood to be the origin of all understanding.

Only recently have Evangelicals contributed tellingly to the contemporary discussion.[126] Generalizations about the outcome of the debate are still premature, owing not least to the fact that not all who appeal to the new hermeneutic adopt the full range of philosophical baggage that others want to associate with the movement. What is clear is that the authority and objective truthfulness of Scripture are bound up in the debate—and this at several levels.

A. DIFFERENT FRAMEWORKS

Achtemeier introduces one of these when he argues that conservatives have paid too little attention to the vastly different frameworks out of which interpreters in different generations approach the text:

> If Scripture is in fact free from error in the form in which it purveys divine truth, it must be free from such error not only for the time for which it was written but also for future times in which it will be read. Scripture therefore must be recognizably as free from error to the medieval scientist searching for the way to transmute base metal into gold as it must be free from error to the modern physicist seeking a field theory of physical forces, despite the widely differing presuppositions each brings to Scripture about the nature of the physical world. If truth is one, and the Bible as truth must exclude error, on whose presuppositions is that truth to be explained, the alchemist's or the modern physicist's? . . . The fact that this problem is seldom if ever addressed by conservatives points to a naive absolutizing of our current level of scientific theory and knowledge on the part of conservatives. . . . It is as though conservatives assumed that to our time and our time alone the final, unchanging truth of the universe had been revealed. . . . The need for apologetics for a particular world view and the idea of truth as unchangeable from age to age make the task of conservative apologetics for Scriptural inerrancy a uniquely unprofitable one.[127]

The telltale impact of the new hermeneutic is self-evident in this paragraph: a fundamental confusion of meaning and truth. It is possible to raise hermeneutical questions without raising truth questions—but not in the eyes of the strongest proponents of the new hermeneutic, who hold that where a different hermeneutic operates there must also be a different theory of truth. Achtemeier does not here discuss whether or not the biblical text is thoroughly truthful; rather, he discusses whether or not the biblical text can possibly be *perceived* to be perfectly truthful by people living under different intellectual paradigms.[128] If Achtemeier's argument were pushed hard, however, it would have a painful sting in its tail. Because each human being is different from every other human being, therefore, to some extent, each of us operates under antecedent knowledge and bias that are different from those of every other human being; and this suggests that the notion of objective truth disappears forever. If that is so, one cannot help but wonder why Achtemeier should bother to try to convince others of the soundness, the rightness, the truthfulness of his views. That the problem is endemic to the discussion may be exemplified by a recent review of a book by Rudolf Schnackenburg, in which the reviewer tells us that the commentary in question

> . . . remains a victim of . . . the penchant to oppose a univocal concept of history to the category of literature. And the very emphasis to seek the "original intention" of the writer or editors, frequently called the "intentional fallacy," artificially restricts literary criticism and implicitly denies the existence of a literary universe in which texts have meanings that authors may never have dreamed of. This is as assured an assertion as the law of acoustics affirming the existence of overtones independently of a composer's intentions.[129]

Joseph Cahill skirts rather quickly around the distinction many make between "meaning" and "significance." Moreover, he slightly distorts the "intentional fallacy," which historically has not sought to deny intent to the author of a text but, instead, warns against all interpretative procedures that seek to determine the author's intention independently of the text. In other words, one must adopt as a basic operating principle that the author's intention is expressed *in* the text. Some authors may produce texts *designed* to be evocative, to have a certain narrative world of their own; and others may produce texts *designed* to convey certain information or opinions—very much like Cahill's review. What is quite certain, however, is that Cahill reflects a sizable and growing body of opinion that understands the discipline of history itself to be less concerned with what actually took place at some point in time and space than with the creation of a theory about what took place, based on fragmentary evidence and controlled by the historian's biases. Exactly the same assessment is now commonly made of the discipline of exegesis.[130]

B. POSITIVISM OR SUBJECTIVITY

Some of these developments are nothing more than a healthy reaction to the positivism of von Ranke. But proponents of the new history and of the new hermeneutic sometimes offer us an unhelpful disjunction: either suffer the epistemological bankruptcy of wishful historical positivism or admit the unqualified subjectivity of the historical enterprise.

Passmore offers important insight on this matter.[131] He admits that history is not a science the way many branches of physics are a science—controllable under the rigorous terms of repeatable experiments and quantifiable to many decimal places of precision. But history is as objective a "science" as, say, geology and many other "natural" sciences. Passmore examines eight criteria for objectivity and argues compellingly that if they are applied rigorously they exclude geology as swiftly as history; and if the criteria are softened a little to allow geology into the academy of the sciences, history slips in as well. For instance, his "criterion six" reads as follows: "An inquiry is objective only if it does not select from within its material." "Criterion eight" reads: "In objective inquiries, conclusions are reached which are universally acceptable." A moment's reflection reveals how many of the natural sciences will suffer as much difficulty under a tight understanding of such criteria as will history.

Exactly the same point may be made with respect to exegesis, that is, with respect to the understanding of Scripture. The new hermeneutic has helpfully warned us of our finiteness, our ignorance, our biases, the influence of our individual world views. Its more sophisticated exponents have also insisted on the process of "distanciation" in the interpretative enterprise; *and distanciation presupposes an ultimate distinction between the knower (subject) and the text (object).* The interpreter must self-consciously distance self and its world view, its "horizon of understanding," from the world view or "horizon of understanding" of the text. Only then can progress be made toward bringing the interpreter's horizon of understanding in line with that of the text, toward fusing the two horizons. When such fusion takes place, even if it is not perfect (let alone exhaustive), it allows the objective meaning of the text to be understood by the knower. This interpreter's understanding may not capture the meaning of the text exhaustively; but there is no compelling reason why it cannot approach asymptotically toward the ideal of capturing it truly. This is assumed by most scholars when they try to convince their colleagues and others of the rightness of their exegetical conclusions; and ironically, it is also assumed by the proponents of uncontrolled polyvalence in meaning when they write articles of considerable learning in order to persuade their readers. If it is true that there is no direct access to pristine, empirical reality, it is equally true that the person who argues there is therefore no real world out there, but that every "world" depends on value-laden constructions of reality, has opted for a self-defeating position; for we cannot espouse both value-ladenness and ontological relativity, because in that case it becomes impossible to talk meaningfully about conceptual relativity.

The issue has come to practical expression in the contemporary debate over "contextualization."[132] When books and articles offer "a feminist reading" or "a Black reading" or "an African reading" or "a liberation theology reading" of this or that text, there can be no initial, principial objection; for, after all, some of us are busy giving *unwitting* White, Black, Protestant, Reformed or Arminian, conservative or nonconservative readings. If the readings from a different perspective challenge us to come to grips with our own biases, if they call in question the depth of our commitment to distanciation and thereby teach us humility, they perform an invaluable service. But it cannot follow that every reading is equally valuable or valid, for some of the interpretations are mutually exclusive. The tragedy is that many modern "readings" of Scripture go beyond inadvertent bias to a self-conscious adoption of a grid fundamentally at odds with the text—all in the name of the polyvalence of the text and under the authority of the new hermeneutic. The relationship between the meaning that pops into my head under the stimulus of the text and the meaning held by the writer becomes a matter of complete indifference. Utterly ignored is the crucial role that distanciation must play. By such hermeneutical irresponsibility the text can be made to authorize literally anything. As I have discussed contextualization theory at some length elsewhere,[133] however, I do not propose to pursue it again here.

C. SCRIPTURE'S USE OF SCRIPTURE

At quite another level, the hermeneutical debate has been pushed back *into* the canon. How does Scripture treat Scripture? How can we meaningfully talk about Scripture's authority if, as is alleged, later writers of Scripture not only self-consciously violate earlier Scripture but unconsciously impose on it an interpretative grid that makes a mockery of any natural reading of the text? What is left, if even the New Testament corpora reflect divergent views of the content of the Christian faith? Perhaps it is not too surprising to read in a recent work that the authority of the Bible for the modern believer does not extend beyond a minimalist affirmation: "Properly speaking, a believing reader shares with his biblical predecessors the God of Abraham, the God of Paul, and only coincidentally does he hold other beliefs which make his outlook similar to theirs."[134] One wonders how the author can be so certain that it is the same God, if what we think of Him has only coincidental overlap with the faith of Abraham or of Paul. Or again, one wonders how much genuine authority can be salvaged when the Bible is understood to be a casebook that leaves the interpreter free to seek the cases judged most relevant to the interpreter's situation. Thus, Kraft argues that each culture has the right, even the responsibility, to choose those parts of the Bible it finds most congenial and to downplay the rest—a stance that leads Kraft to suggest:

We need to ask which of these varieties of theology branded "heretical" were genuinely out of bounds (measured by scriptural standards), and which were valid contextualizations of scriptural truth within varieties of culture or subculture that the party in power refused to take seriously. *It is likely that most of the "heresies" can validly be classed as cultural adaptations rather than as theological aberrations.* They, therefore, *show what ought to be done today* rather than what ought to be feared. The "history of traditions" becomes intensely relevant when studied from this perspective.[135]

The "scriptural standards" to which Kraft refers are not what the Bible as a whole says but a range of disparate theologies each based on separate parts of the Bible, a range that sets the limits and nature of the allowable diversity. Kraft here heavily depends on the work of von Allmen, extensively discussed elsewhere.[136] Appeals to a "supra-cultural core" in order to preserve at least some unity in Christianity are far more problematic than is commonly recognized.[137] It is not clear how or why God's macrosalvific purposes should escape the vicissitudes of paradigm shifts or cultural expression: even as simple a statement as "Jesus is Lord" means something quite different when transposed to a Buddhist context.[138] Finite human beings have no culture-free access to truth, nor can they express it in culture-free ways. Our only hope—and it is adequate—is in every instance so to work through problems of distanciation and the fusion of horizons of understanding that the meaning of the text is truly grasped. But if that is so for what I have called the macrosalvific truths, it is difficult to see why it should not be so for incidental details.[139]

Brown is only slightly oversimplifying the issue when he writes:

Prior to Bauer, the prevailing view was that Christianity, whether it was true or false, was at least a relatively well-defined and fixed body of doctrine; after Bauer, it was more often assumed that doctrine was constantly in the process of development and that "historic Christian orthodoxy," far from having been a constant for close to two thousand years, was only the theological fashion of a particular age.[140]

The related issues are so complex that four essays in this pair of volumes have been devoted to them: Moisés Silva has written two of them, one dealing with the text form of the Old Testament as it is quoted by the New[141] and the other with the place of historical reconstruction in biblical exegesis;[142] Douglas Moo has discussed the way the New Testament actually cites the Old, and he ties his discussion to modern debates over *sensus plenior;*[143] and a fourth essay has attempted to point a way toward a recognition of the genuine unity in the New Testament when it is interpreted within a certain salvation-historical framework.[144]

Such innercanonical questions inevitably raise again the question of the nature of the canon: what justification is there for treating these books and not others as the authoritative Word of God? None, some would reply.[145] Others, impressed by the canon criticism of Sanders[146] or of Childs[147] or convinced by traditional Roman Catholic arguments, adopt the general framework of the canon largely on the basis of the established tradition of the church. These issues, too, are extremely complex, and only infrequently discussed with knowledge and care by conservatives; and, therefore, David Dunbar's well-researched essay will prove particularly welcome to many.[148]

D. EPISTEMOLOGICAL QUESTIONS

At the deepest level, however, the questions raised by the new hermeneutic are epistemological. Some recent Reformed thought has unwittingly played into the hands of the more radical exponents of the new hermeneutic by dismissing both evidentialism and classical foundationalism and seeking to build a system on the view that belief in God is itself foundational, properly basic. If so, it is argued, Reformed epistemology and our belief in God enable us to escape the weaknesses of foundationalism and to stand above the mere amassing of bits of evidence. This line of approach is then sometimes projected back onto Calvin himself.

Quite apart from whether or not Calvin can be claimed in support for this view,[149] it seems open to the criticisms of van Hook,[150] who, arguing primarily against Nicholas Wolterstorff and Alvin Plantinga,[151] convincingly demonstrates that this new "Reformed epistemology" may justify the *rationality* of belief in God, but it is wholly inadequate to justify any God-talk as *knowledge*.[152] Van Hook, therefore, suggests we should follow the proposals of Rorty: redefine knowledge, defining it not epistemologically but sociologically—knowledge is "what our peers let us get away with saying." That means that whether any particular datum is to be considered knowledge very largely depends on the locus of the "peers": a different set of peers may generate a different assessment as to whether or not the datum is to be classified as knowledge.[153] The parallels to the subjective and relative interpretations generated by a skeptical handling of the new hermeneutic are obvious.

Perhaps part of the problem is that we have been so frightened by the extreme claims of philosophically naive evidentialists that some of us have been catapulted into a reactionary insistence that evidences are useless.[154] One inevitable result is the depreciation of such evidence as exists, the establishment of an unbridgeable gulf between hard data and theological truth-claims. Another part of the problem may be that much conservative writing has a wholly inadequate treatment of the work of the Holy Spirit.

Be that as it may, two essays in this pair of volumes have attempted to take steps to alleviate the need. Paul Helm[155] argues for a modified fideism to justify belief in the Bible as the authoritative Word of God, and John Frame[156] discusses the role of the Holy Spirit both in the creation of the written Word and in bringing people to place their confidence in it. These are seminal essays in an area where a great deal more work needs to be done.

VII. DISCOUNTING OF THE CONCURSIVE THEORY

It is safe to say that the central line of evangelical thought on the truthfulness of the Scriptures has entailed the adoption of the concursive theory: God in His sovereignty so superintended the freely composed human writings we call the Scriptures that the result was nothing less than God's words and, therefore, entirely truthful. Recently, however, the Basinger brothers,[157] in an apparent attempt to discount the concursive theory, have argued that it is illogical to defend simultaneously the concursive theory in bibliology and the free will defense (FWD) in theodicy. The former means one has accepted as true some such proposition as the following: "Human activities (such as penning a book) can be totally controlled by God without violating human freedom."[158] And that, of course, stands in contradiction to most formulations of the FWD. One must, therefore, choose between inerrancy (and the concursive theory on which it depends) and the FWD.

As the argument stands, it is valid; but perhaps it is revealing that the Basingers do not extend their argument to the major redemptive events. For instance, the death of Jesus Christ is presented as a conspiracy of leaders of Jews and Gentiles (Ac 4:27); yet those leaders "did what [God's] power and will had decided beforehand should happen" (Ac 4:28). God is not presented as a great chess player who brilliantly outfoxes His opponents by anticipating and allowing for their every move: the conspirators did what God Himself decided beforehand should happen. Yet the conspirators are not thereby excused: they are still regarded as guilty. Any other view will either depreciate the heinousness of the sin or render the Cross a last minute arrangement by which God cleverly snatched victory out of the jaws of defeat, rather than the heart of His redemptive purposes. If some sort of concursive theory is not maintained in this instance, one wonders what is left of an orthodox doctrine of God. And if the concursive theory is required here, why may it not be permitted elsewhere? Is it possible for any true theist with any degree of consistency to believe Romans 8:28 while arguing against a concursive theory of inspiration?

The philosophical issues cannot be probed here; but it is worth mentioning that human responsibility can be grounded in something other than "free will," where free will is understood to entail absolute power to the contrary.[159] And theodicy has other options than the FWD.[160]

VIII. THE DIMINISHING AUTHORITY OF THE SCRIPTURES IN THE CHURCHES

A high view of Scripture is of little value to us if we do not enthusiastically embrace the Scripture's authority. But today we multiply the means for circumventing or dissipating that authority. I am not here speaking of those who formally deny the Scripture's authority: it is only to be expected that they should avoid the hard sayings and uncomfortable truths. But those of us who uphold the thorough truthfulness of God's Word have no excuse.

The reasons for such failure are many. In part, we reflect the antiauthoritarian stance that is currently endemic to the Western world, and we forget that the Bible portrays true freedom not as absolute but as freedom from sin. This libertarianism has engendered two surprising children. The first is a new love of authoritarianism amongst some believers: they do not feel safe and orthodox unless some leader is telling them exactly what to say, do, and think. Inevitably this brings some power lovers to positions of religious leadership, supported sometimes by a theology that ascribes "apostleship" or some other special, charismatic enduement to them, sometimes by a theology of churchmanship that makes each pastor a pope. The authority of the Scriptures is in such instances almost always formally affirmed; but an observer may be forgiven if he or she senses that these self-promoted leaders characteristically so elevate their opinions over the Scripture, often in the name of the Scripture, that the Word of God becomes muted. The church cries out for those who proclaim the Scriptures with unction and authority while simultaneously demonstrating that they stand under that authority themselves.

The second is a fairly conservative mood, a reaction to the times, that some interpret as a great blessing. But this conservative swing does not appear to be characterized by brokenness and contrition. Far from it: it is imbued with a "can do" mentality not far removed from arrogance. Many of the most respected religious leaders amongst us are those who project an image of total command, endless competence, glorious success, formulaic cleverness. We are experts, and we live in a generation of experts. But the cost is high: we gradually lose our sense of indebtedness to grace, we no longer cherish our complete dependence on the God of all grace, and we begin to reject themes like self-sacrifice and discipleship in favor of courses on successful living and leadership in the church. We forget that the God of the Bible declares: "This is the one I esteem: he who is humble and contrite in spirit, and trembles at my word" (Isa 66:2). Mere conservatism must not be confused with godliness, mere discipline with discipleship, mere assent to orthodox doctrine with wholehearted delight in the truth. If Tozer were still alive, he would pronounce no improvement in the years that have elapsed since the publication of his moving lament on "The Waning Authority of Christ in the Churches."[161]

Along with the arrogance has come the exegetical and philosophical sophistication that enables us to make Scripture support almost anything we want. Henry incisively comments:

> . . . in recent years a . . . type of theft has emerged as some fellow evangelicals, along with non-evangelicals, wrest from the Bible segments that they derogate as no longer Word of God. Some now even introduce authorial intention or the cultural context of language as specious rationalizations for this crime against the Bible, much as some rapist might assure me that he is assaulting my wife for my own or for her good. They misuse Scripture in order to champion as biblically true what in fact does violence to Scripture.[162]

Worse, even some of us who would never dream of formally disentangling some parts of the Bible from the rest and declaring them less authoritative than other parts can by exegetical ingenuity get the Scriptures to say just about whatever we want—and this we thunder to the age as if it were a prophetic word, when it is little more than the message of the age bounced off Holy Scripture. To our shame, we have hungered to be masters of the Word much more than we have hungered to be mastered by it.

The pervasiveness of the problem erupts in the "Christian" merchant whose faith has no bearing on the integrity of his or her dealings, or in the way material possessions are assessed. It is reflected in an accelerating divorce rate in Christian homes and among the clergy themselves—with little sense of shame and no entailment in their "ministries." It is seen in its most pathetic garb when considerable exegetical skill goes into proving, say, that the Bible condemns promiscuous homosexuality but not homosexuality itself (though careful handling of the evidence overturns the thesis),[163] or that the Bible's use of "head" in passages dealing with male/female relationships follows allegedly characteristic Greek usage and, therefore, means "source" (when close scrutiny of the primary evidence fails to turn up more than a handful of disputable instances of the meaning "source" in over two thousand occurrences).[164] It finds new lease when popular Evangelicals publicly abandon any mention of "sin"—allegedly on the ground that the term no longer "communicates"—without recognizing that adjacent truths (e.g., those dealing with the Fall, the law of God, the nature of transgression, the wrath of God, and even the gracious atonement itself) undergo telling transformation.

While I fear that Evangelicalism is heading for another severe conflict on the doctrine of Scripture, and while it is necessary to face these impending debates with humility and courage, what is far more alarming is the diminishing authority of the Scriptures in the churches. This is taking place not only among those who depreciate the consistent truthfulness of Scripture but also (if for different reasons) among those who most vociferously defend it. To some extent we are all part of the problem; and perhaps we can do most to salvage something of value from the growing fragmentation by pledging ourselves in repentance and faith to learning and obeying God's most holy Word. Then we shall also be reminded that the challenge to preserve and articulate a fully self-consistent and orthodox doctrine of Scripture cannot be met by intellectual powers alone, but only on our knees and by the power of God.

CHAPTER TWO

THE SEMANTICS OF BIBLICAL LITERATURE: TRUTH AND SCRIPTURE'S DIVERSE LITERARY FORMS

Kevin J. Vanhoozer

Kevin J. Vanhoozer

Kevin J. Vanhoozer is the 1985–86 Burney Student in Philosophy of Religion at Cambridge University and Junior Research Fellow at Wolfson College, Cambridge, England. He is a graduate of Westmont College (B.A.), Westminster Theological Seminary (M.Div.), and Cambridge University (Ph.D.). He is currently working on a book dealing with contemporary hermeneutics and the use of the Gospel narratives in recent theology. He has contributed articles to *Theology* and the *Trinity Journal*. He is a member of the American Academy of Religion.

THE SEMANTICS OF BIBLICAL LITERATURE: TRUTH AND SCRIPTURE'S DIVERSE LITERARY FORMS

... many traditional philosophical perplexities have arisen through a mistake—the mistake of taking as straightforward statements of fact utterances which are ... intended as something quite different.

—J. L. Austin, *How to Do Things with Words*

"A proposition is a queer thing!" Here we have in germ the subliming of our whole account of logic. The tendency to assume a pure intermediary between the propositional *signs* and the facts. Or even to try to purify, to sublime, the signs themselves.—For our forms of expression prevent us in all sorts of ways from seeing that nothing out of the ordinary is involved, by sending us in pursuit of chimeras.

—Ludwig Wittgenstein, *Philosophical Investigations*

Reading maketh a full man ...

—Francis Bacon, *Essays*

I. THE SEMANTICS OF BIBLICAL LITERATURE

Polonius: What do you read, my Lord?
Hamlet: Words, words, words.

What in Scripture is susceptible to being characterized as true? Is it the biblical words, concepts, sentences, propositions, beliefs, or images? The so-called Biblical Theology movement's reading, like Hamlet's, focused on words, words, words—until *The Semantics of Biblical Language*[1] by James Barr provided a needed corrective to the movement's penchant for playing fast and loose with the linguistic phenomena of Scripture. Barr's book constituted a "trumpet blast against the monstrous regiment of shoddy linguistics."[2] Barr submitted various illegitimate uses of linguistic evidence in theological discussion to a searching critique. In particular, Barr rejected the fashionable notion that postulated a distinction between Hebrew (concrete) and Greek (abstract) thought—a contrast supposedly mirrored in the etymology and syntax of these languages. While Barr's linguistic rebuke has been for the most part heeded, a similar trumpet blast—this time against the tendency to mishandle the *literary* phenomena of Scripture—needs to be sounded. The new battleground is no longer biblical words, but larger units of discourse: sentences, paragraphs, entire books. The crucial questions of meaning and truth are now located on the textual level—thus the need for a semantics of biblical *literature* rather than biblical *language*.[3]

Barr pointed out the way beyond the lexical trees to the literary forest by observing that the new content of the Judaeo-Christian tradition was expressed linguistically in sentence form. The distinctive content with which any biblical theology is concerned is found not in the terminology so much as the various sentences and forms of discourse in Scripture.[4] Ironically, the "New Biblical Theology" (for lack of a better epithet) is in danger of repeating the linguistic sins of its forefathers, only this time on the literary rather than the lexical level.[5]

The earlier Biblical Theology movement adduced linguistic arguments to support the theologically significant distinction between Greek and Hebrew thought. According to Barr, the main points of Greek-Hebrew contrast involved (a) a static versus a dynamic conception of reality, (b) an abstract versus a concrete mode of thought, and (c) a literature with analytic distinctions versus a literature of imaginative totality.[6] Interestingly enough, these same contrasts (though temporarily banished by Barr's linguistic rebuke) have slipped back into contemporary theological discussion of biblical literature. What the older Biblical Theology movement could not accomplish with its Greek-Hebrew contrast, the New Biblical Theology has effected with its distinction between *descriptive* (informative) and *poetic* (religious) *texts*. Barr states that there are two kinds of writing; one is valued mainly for the information it gives, the other for its structure, shape, images.[7] Whereas the Biblical Theology movement claimed that Greek thought imposed an unbiblical philosophy onto scriptural language, the New Biblical Theology claims that descriptive, informative discourse is uncharacteristic of the biblical literature. Not lexical, but rather literary arguments are put forward to support this conclusion. Whereas the earlier Biblical Theology read theology off of Hebrew etymology and syntax, the New Biblical Theology reads theology off of literary shape or form (e.g., "narrative theology").

The older and newer forms of Biblical Theology share two important similarities. First, both movements rely on the dichotomy that exists between the descriptive-abstract-scientific and the poetic-concrete-imaginative types of thought—a dichotomy reflected both in language and literature. Second, theologians who use lexical and literary arguments to support this distinction manifest a common aversion to biblical statements, as well as to the "proof-texting" method. Barr correctly observes:

> Modern biblical theology in its fear and dislike of the "proposition" as the basis of religious truth has often simply adopted in its place the smaller linguistic unit of the word, and has then been forced to overload the word with meaning in order to relate it to the "inner world of thought."[8]

Similarly, the New Biblical Theology rejects the proposition as the basic vehicle of religious truth. Biblical statements are too large for those who insist that words are the building blocks of meaning, and they are too small for those who insist that the key to meaning is a text's literary form. In the one case, the proposition is the sum of its lexical components; in the other, the meaning of a given proposition is a function of its *literary* context. In support of the latter contention, John Lyons writes that "the context of a sentence in a written work must be understood to include the conventions governing the literary genre of which the work in question is an example."[9] Rightly or wrongly, biblical propositions are often caught between the Scylla and Charybdis of lexical and literary semantics.

As a case in point, Barr cites the example of theologians who try to derive a theory about the nature of time from biblical terminology: "It is the lack of actual statements about what time is like, more than anything else, that has forced exegetes into trying to get a view of time out of the *words* themselves."[10] Again, the New Biblical Theology supplies a literary counterpart to this very same theological argument about time. Rather than appealing to biblical words, some theologians have appealed to the nature of narrative as indicative of the nature of time and human temporal experience.[11] If read as history, the biblical narrative suggests that time is linear and history teleological. If read as myth, the biblical narrative displays a cyclic view of time, with history subject to infinite repetition. Whole philosophies of history are thus derived from and attached to literary forms.[12]

To this point we have drawn parallels between the Biblical Theology movement and the New Biblical Theology. Two significant differences, however, must not be overlooked. Firstly, the New Biblical Theology does not claim that there are unique, inspired literary forms peculiar to Scripture as did those earlier scholars who held that the Holy Spirit had transformed certain Greek linguistic elements so that they could convey new Christian content.[13] For the New Biblical Theology, the biblical literary forms function as do their secular counterparts. Secondly, unlike the earlier practitioners of "shoddy linguistics," the New Biblical Theology is able to draw upon the work of professional literary critics, some of whom will be considered below.[14] For this reason, the theological struggle over the nature of Scripture will be all the fiercer, because both sides can appeal to their respective literary champions in order to determine how the Bible should be read.

As opposed to the Biblical Theology movement and the New

Biblical Theology, Evangelicals neither fear nor despise the proposition. Indeed, Evangelicals go so far as to speak of "propositional"
revelation.[15] In a later book, *The Bible in the Modern World*, Barr
challenges the Evangelicals' view of revelation by noting that the
logical status of biblical sentences and God's communication to
human beings are two separate questions. Of course the Bible
contains propositions, says Barr, but whether or not they are to be
construed as revelation is another matter. Moreover, Barr argues that
the real issue is not about propositional revelation or whether a given
sentence is propositional but about the *right function* of propositions
and what literary category they belong to.

   Evangelicals claim that the biblical propositions convey information, but Barr sees this as a "literary category-mistake": "Failures to
comprehend the literary genre lead to a use of the biblical assertions
with a wrong function."[16] According to Barr, Evangelicals are not so
much believers in propositional revelation as representatives of a
particular way of viewing the genre or function of propositions (i.e., as
descriptive, informative). Barr concludes: "Genre mistakes cause the
wrong kind of truth values to be attached to biblical sentences. Literary
embellishments then come to be regarded as scientifically true
assertions, kerygmatic words of grace and promise come to be taken
as text-book doctrine."[17] This is a typical affirmation of the New
Biblical Theology, and Barr is one of its leading proponents.

   Barr's *"J'accuse"* is a serious challenge to Evangelicals. In plain
English, Barr accuses Evangelicals of doing interpretive violence to
Scripture, holding a doctrine of inerrancy that insists on reading the
biblical narrative as history in order to preserve the truth of every
proposition. Barr identifies the desire for an inerrant Bible to be the
"real guiding principle of fundamentalist interpretation."[18] In short,
Barr argues that Evangelicals are so preoccupied with truth that they
do not allow Scripture to be what it in fact is.

   How then can Evangelicals best refute this accusation and best
do justice to the biblical statements, to "propositional" revelation? We
have seen that the literary context partly determines the *kind* of
proposition with which we are dealing. There is a world of difference,
for instance, between a historical and a poetic statement—and
between the *kinds* of truth claims involved in each. This brings us to
the major concern of our essay: how does the diversity of Scripture's
literary forms affect the way we take biblical propositions and
understand scriptural truth?

II. PROPOSITIONAL PARADISE LOST?
SOME PROBLEMS WITH THE CONCEPT OF REVELATION

   Just what do Evangelicals mean by speaking of Scripture as
"propositional" revelation? Both defenders and attackers alike betray

no little confusion about the nature of propositions.[19] This confusion is not restricted to theologians; it extends to philosophers as well. Indeed, we shall see fit to take a detour over the somewhat rocky terrain of philosophical debate about propositions. This daunting detour is necessary because of the pride of place that propositions enjoy in traditional Evangelical statements concerning revelation and inerrancy.

Besides becoming clear as to the nature of propositions, we will be primarily interested in how propositions relate to Scripture's diverse literary forms. Are all of the Scripture's literary genres equally "propositional" or susceptible to propositional paraphrase? Are some not so susceptible? And what is the relationship between the literary forms and the propositions they convey? How are they conveyed? Is the task of theology to "translate" texts in various literary garb into "naked" propositions? But before addressing these questions, we turn first to an examination of Evangelicals' attempts to explain the nature of propositional revelation.

Ronald Nash says that propositions are the minimal vehicles of truth and that propositional revelation is the divine communication of knowledge or truth.[20] This accords with the view of John Hick: "In the propositional view, that which is revealed is a body of religious truths capable of being expressed in propositions."[21] Concerning the actual phrase "propositional revelation," however, Nash notes that it "has been in use for only forty years or so, and that it probably was not coined by Evangelicals."[22] The historical context for the use of the phrase was the neoorthodox attack on the idea that the divine revelation is rationally communicated to human beings. Barth and Brunner stressed the notion of revelation as personal encounter with God: God discloses Himself by divine acts in history, not by dispensing information about Himself. H. D. McDonald can thus write: "The watchword of the modern era might then be put like this: revelation is personal encounter, not propositional disclosure."[23]

But while the term may be of recent vintage, the issue is not. McDonald's two-volume study of theories of revelation from 1700 to 1960 clearly shows that the debate about the existence and nature of revealed truth has a long heritage. Indeed, J. I. Packer writes: "From the earliest days of Christianity, the whole Church regarded the Bible as a web of revealed truths, the recorded utterances of God bearing witness to himself."[24] By qualifying revelation as "propositional," says Nash, we underline the cognitive, informative function of revelation against modern attempts to deny it.

Interestingly, Nash refuses to equate propositional revelation with verbal inspiration: "Theoretically, a person could accept propositional revelation but reject verbal inspiration."[25] Verbal inspiration pertains to "the extent to which God's revelation is conveyed in *words*, notably the written words of the Bible."[26] There would thus seem to be a logical hiatus between propositional revelation and the actual words in Scripture. Nash goes on to say that the advocate of propositional revelation does not believe that written revelation must always take the form of assertions. Those who discuss propositional revelation "should not equate revealed propositions with sentences" and should remember "that this revealed truth is deposited in the various literary forms found in the Bible."[27] Behind the actual sentences, then, there lies the revealed deposit from which the theologian withdraws his propositions.

This logical gap between revealed propositions and biblical sentences has been further examined by Stanley Obitts, who offers a philosophical analysis of the doctrinal statement of the Evangelical Theological Society, which reads as follows: "The Bible alone, and the Bible in its entirety, is the Word of God written and is therefore inerrant in the autographs." Obitts contends that the statement suffers from a confusion in referring to "inerrant" autographs, a confusion stemming from a mistaken identification of linguistic phenomena (black marks on papyri) with the locus of revelation. Obitts writes: "As has been said many times, propositions—not sentences—are in the primary sense what can be true or false. Sentences can be effective or ineffective in expressing a statement or proposition."[28]

Obitts proceeds to endorse a suggestion made by Gordon R. Lewis to the effect that the term "infallible" be reserved for the capacity of sentences unfailingly to convey certain propositions or revealed truths, while "inerrant" be restricted to the propositions conveyed by the sentences. This is an important distinction for Lewis because "Logically, errorlessness or truth is a quality not of words, but of meanings."[29] The doctrinal statement thus labors under a category mistake: inerrancy is not a property of written sentences or autographs. Obitt's analysis trades on the distinction between the inerrant Word of God (revealed propositions) and infallible Scripture (inspired sentences).[30] The perhaps inevitable result is a certain measure of carelessness regarding the actual words of Scripture, as can be seen in this quotation from Lewis: "One benefit of regarding truth as a quality of propositions rather than sentences is a diminishing of the problem of some of the variations in the Gospel accounts, in other historical passages relating to the same event (Kings and Chronicles) and in the NT wordings of OT references."[31]

In so distinguishing revealed propositions from biblical sentences, Nash, Lewis, and Obitts may have inadvertently become strange bedfellows with a quasi-Barthian view of Scripture. While these Evangelicals repudiate Barth's noncognitive view of revelation, they seem to share Barth's idea that Scripture is a *witness* (albeit inspired) *to* revelation. For by insisting that sentences *convey* propositions, they locate revelation outside the actual biblical texts, creating a logical gap between revelation and the Bible. The biblical sentences, though pointing to revealed propositions, are not themselves to be regarded as revealed or inerrant. Nash, Lewis, and Obitts thus represent one Evangelical perspective on propositions.

Carl F. H. Henry and Clark Pinnock have presented a second approach, maintaining that the divine revelation is a rational communication conveyed by intelligible ideas and meaningful words, that is, in conceptual-verbal form.[32] But, in contrast to Nash and Obitts, Henry gives the following definition of a proposition: "As generally understood, a proposition is a verbal statement that is either true or false."[33] The crucial sentence-proposition distinction is absent in Henry's view of revelation. Consequently, Henry's understanding of inerrancy is at odds with the view propounded by Lewis and Obitts. Henry writes: "Verbal inerrancy implies that God's truth inheres *in the very words* of Scripture, that is, in the propositions or sentences of the Bible, and not merely in the concepts and thoughts of the writers."[34]

Whereas Lewis and Obitts restrict inerrancy to the propositions conveyed by the biblical sentences, Henry here claims that words can be true and sentences inerrant. This leads Henry to postulate infallibility to be the capacity of the *copies* of the autographs to reliably communicate God's revealed truth.[35] Similarly, Pinnock also understands revelation to be meaningful verbal communication:

> Historic Christian theology has employed the term *propositional revelation* to describe the cognitive truth-content of Scripture. The expression is not intended to deny that Scripture contains a rich multiplicity of literary forms in conveying its message. It merely points to the valid conceptual side of divine revelation.[36]

Yet a third approach to propositional revelation is that of Gordon Clark, who writes that "aside from imperative sentences and a few exclamations in the Psalms, the Bible is composed of propositions."[37] This view of propositions differs from that of Henry and Pinnock by identifying propositions with *certain kinds of sentences*, presumably declarative statements in the indicative.

Here then are three disparate views regarding "biblical propositions": (a) conceptual-verbal communication in general (Henry, Pinnock), (b) declarative sentences or statements (Clark), and (c) meaning-content—conveyed by sentences—that is true or false (Nash, Lewis, Obitts). While all three positions are agreed as to the general thrust of "propositional revelation" (viz., that revelation discloses truth in a cognitive manner), significant discrepancies remain as to the *nature* of the biblical propositions, discrepancies that affect one's reading of Scripture and subsequent theological method. The reason for this confusion among Evangelicals about propositions is simply stated: both ordinary usage and philosophical debate have given "propositions" an ambiguous status. The term has a long history and a wide semantic range.[38]

Propositions first came to be explicitly studied in Aristotle's *On Interpretation*, where they are distinguished from sentences. After defining a sentence as "significant speech," Aristotle goes on to say that "while every sentence has meaning . . . not all can be called propositions. We call propositions those only that have truth or falsity in them. A prayer is, for instance, a sentence but neither has truth nor has falsity."[39]

After more than two thousand years of discussion, philosophers remain divided over this sentence-proposition distinction. According to Richard M. Gale, "One of the most heatedly disputed questions in modern philosophy concerns whether there are propositions."[40] One wonders about the prudence of building a doctrine of revelation on such a problematic foundation! Indeed, Bernard Ramm calls "propositional revelation" an "inept" phrase and an "unhappy" expression.[41]

In what follows we will distinguish the "ordinary" sense of propositions (i.e., verbal statements) from the "philosophical" sense of propositions (which remains to be seen). Of the Evangelicals considered, Clark appears to understand propositions in their ordinary sense, while Nash, Lewis, and Obitts use the philosophical sense. Henry and Pinnock borrow from each sense for their understanding of propositions. Three initial questions about propositions must first be discussed before we go on to consider "propositional" possibilities for hermeneutics and theological method: (1) *Are* there propositions in the *philosophical* sense? (2) If so, *what* are they and how do they differ from sentences and statements? (3) How are propositions related to facts, to truth?

1.   Two related arguments constitute the basic case for the reality of propositions. First of all, communication would not be possible except for the ability to share our judgments. Several persons can have the same belief, for instance, not because their mental acts are identical, but because *what is thought* is in each case the same.[42] The second argument notes that *what is meant* by different sentences can be the same. "It's raining," "Il pleut," and "Es regnet" all express the same proposition or meaning.[43] This meaning is "abstract" because it can be rendered by many particular sentences. The apparent sameness of meaning that sentences may share is the strongest argument for the existence of propositions.

W. V. Quine, on the other hand, questions the need for propositions, which he terms "intangible intervening elements" and "shadows of sentences."[44] For Quine, propositions are a misleading philosophical fiction: "Once a philosopher, whether through inattention to ambiguity or simply through an excess of hospitality, has admitted propositions to his ontology, he invariably proceeds to view propositions rather than sentences as the things that are true or false."[45] Quine contends that there is no way to tell whether two sentences express the same proposition or meaning—we simply do not have the appropriate criteria. For the *kind* of sameness of meaning here relevant is, according to Quine, the "sameness of objective information, without regard to attitude or to poetic qualities."[46] But for "real life" sentences there is no evident rule for extracting the "objective meaning" from stylistic or other immaterial features of the sentences. Quine's work testifies that today the existence of propositions is no longer a foregone conclusion.

2. Assuming for the moment, however, that there are propositions, what are they and how do they differ from sentences and statements? While sentences may be so many inches long, in bold type, in a particular language, none of these things is true of propositions, at least in the philosophical sense. Are propositions, then, semi-Platonic entities, continuously hovering in an autonomous realm until they are expressed by sentences? Gottlob Frege seemed to think so: he spoke of propositions as belonging to a "third realm," a timeless order of nonphysical, nonmental objects. More recently Karl Popper has espoused a similar trichotomy. Popper speaks of three "worlds": the world of physical objects, the world of states of consciousness, and the "third world" (objective contents of thought). Human language, says Popper, belongs to all three worlds: it consists of physical sounds or symbols, it expresses a subjective state, and it conveys meaning and information. *"Theories, or propositions, or statements are the most important third-world linguistic entities."*[47] In another vein, E. J. Lemmon attempts to articulate the nature of propositions, distinguishing them from linguistic entities and spatio-temporal particulars and likening them to symphonies (as opposed to their performances)![48] Alan R. White, however, objects to the idea that a proposition has some sort of existence separate from sentences, for "no hint is provided of how to locate its abode."[49]

To complicate matters further, we must now consider how "statements" differ from both sentences and propositions. Lemmon notes that sentences vary in truth content from context to context, whereas statements are "timelessly" true or false. When *I* say "I am twenty-seven years old" I make a true statement, but someone else saying the same thing might make a false statement. The meaning of the sentence does not change, but the statement made does change depending on the occasion and context of the sentence. Lemmon concludes that "statements that sentences may be used to make are quite distinct from the propositions that they may express."[50] In other words, to determine what the sentence means (i.e., the proposition) is not necessarily to determine what statement is being made on any particular occasion.

We now have sentences conveying propositions and making statements. Must we admit the presence of these "intangible intervening elements" in our everyday speech and writing? White is unhappy with the equation of propositions and meanings of sentences: "But

what a sentence conveys—or, more correctly, what someone uses the
sentence to convey—is not its meaning or its use."[51] The proposition
conveyed by "It is raining," for instance, cannot be the *meaning* of the
sentence; the assertion is about the weather, not about the meaning
of "It is raining." But to continue distinguishing propositions from
other things is not to say what propositions *are*.[52] At this point, talk of
propositions becomes rather strained. If propositions are identical
neither with the words uttered, nor the meaning of the sentence, nor
the statement made, then just what *is* conveyed by sentences? And if
propositions are so elusive, how can we be sure *which* propositions
are being conveyed by various sentences?

For these and other reasons, many philosophers would just as
soon abandon the whole notion of propositions. They prefer to speak
of "what is said, asserted, stated." White comments: "The introduction of a special name for what is said in an utterance, e.g.,
'proposition,' 'statement,' or 'judgment,' leads us to overlook these
indissoluble connections between what is said and the medium in
which it is said."[53] This is a telling criticism, which, with one blow,
reinstates the primacy of the actual sentences.

3. We are interested in Scripture and truth. It has been said that
only propositions can be true or false. But if, with White and Quine,
one discards the notion of propositions, then to what do truth and
falsity apply? Quine believes that truth may be construed as
"semantic assent." To call a sentence "true" is to say something about
the world rather than language. "Snow is white" is true only if snow is
white.[54] Quine writes that the truth predicate serves "to point
through the sentence to the reality; it serves as a reminder that
though sentences are mentioned, reality is still the whole point."[55]
Quine concludes that "eternal" sentences stay true or false regardless
of context. For example, the sentence "God led Israelites out of Egypt
in 1280 B.C."—if true—is true timelessly.

In White's account, truth and falsity apply to "what is said," but
only when what is said states "that this is how things are." This is an
important proviso. In the same way that referring is not the only way
that sentences can "mean," so "making a statement" is only one of the
possible functions of sentences. In effect, White limits truth and falsity
to *what is asserted*. But much of what is said is not asserted. "Saying"
something is a broader notion than "stating" something. Given that
only sayings of the type "This is how things are, were, or will be" are
candidates for truth or falsity, can we still agree with Clark's
contention that *most* of the Bible is propositional (in the ordinary
sense)? If not, does that mean that some portions of Scripture are
neither true nor false?

Our philosophical detour completed, what remains of "propositional" revelation? Are only the assertions or statements made by the
Bible to be regarded as revealed and true? Perhaps the very first attack

on the notion of propositional revelation is recorded in Genesis 3:1. Here the serpent asks, *"Did God say?"* This is perhaps the critical question for all those who wish to defend the concept of biblical revelation. But what was the serpent attacking? If he wanted to claim that a "proposition" had not been conveyed by the divine utterance, he could have merely pointed out that what God said was a command or warning—not an assertion—and thus neither true nor false. But what disturbed the serpent was that God had said something at all. The serpent questioned whether sincere, intelligible communication had in fact taken place.

Only a portion of the Bible seems to qualify as "propositional," understood in its philosophical sense. However, Henry's loose use of "propositional" to refer to rational-verbal communication in general is one way of refuting the serpent's spurious insinuation that God did *not* say. Our task in the remainder of this chapter is to understand revelation in a way that does justice to *all* that God says, not only to the propositions (in the philosophical sense) conveyed by God's saying.

Two diverse attitudes can be taken regarding "biblical propositions." On the one hand, one may accept the view that the Bible is composed of "ordinary" propositions, that is, verbal statements. According to this view, the actual sentences assume primacy; textual criticism and translation are assigned paramount importance. The extreme of this position would be a "biblical theology" that merely repeated the Hebrew, Aramaic, and Greek sentences in the Bible (and their translated equivalents). Though this is one way of preserving the biblical propositions, it is hardly a practical option in contemporary theology. However, it remains a limiting case of what it means "to do justice to" biblical propositions.

On the other hand, one may claim that the Bible conveys propositions of the "philosophical" breed; accordingly, the actual sentences are translated into a clearer, more explicitly propositional form. The extreme of this view would entail deriving a set of propositions in a precise discursive language and calling *these* the "biblical propositions." Opponents of Evangelicals warn that this is the constant danger. As long ago as 1883, Henry Drummond proclaimed: "There is no worse enemy to a living Church than a propositional theology."[56] If skepticism is a problem for those who believe we cannot know the truth, dogmatism is the constant temptation for those who believe that the truth is available and within their grasp.

It should be obvious by now that one's stance toward biblical propositions has consequences for one's theological method. Is the role of theology to extract propositions from the Bible in their pristine form—to make withdrawals from a divine deposit, as it were? Can Scripture be translated into a theological Euclid? As we have seen, many modern theologians fear that this eventuality is the goal of Evangelicals' theology. They worry that propositional theology depersonalizes revelation by rendering it abstract and lifeless, dulling the call of the gospel for decision and obedience. Another concern is that revelation will be packaged into a neat propositional system that can then be manipulated by humans as they manipulate other objects. Instead of intellectual "control" over an abstract system of doctrine, the neoliberal theologians wish to have an existential encounter with an all-powerful Subject. This, at least, is the critique of Evangelicals' theology. Does the shoe fit?

We must recall the original purpose for which the phrase "propositional revelation" was brought into service. In debate with neoorthodoxy, the term stressed the cognitive aspect of the divine revelation. However, we have seen how Evangelicals have become entangled in philosophical controversies over the nature of propositions and over what is susceptible to truth and falsity. Consequently, we have wondered whether the concept of propositional revelation has outlived its usefulness. Consider two Articles from the 1982 "Chicago Statement on Biblical Hermeneutics,"[57] put forward as a major statement of Evangelicals on an important issue:

> Article VI: WE AFFIRM that the Bible expresses God's truth in propositional statements, and we declare that Biblical truth is both objective and absolute. We further affirm that a statement is true if it represents matters as they actually are but is an error if it misrepresents the facts.

> Article XIV: WE AFFIRM that the Biblical record of events, discourses and sayings, though presented in a variety of appropriate literary forms, corresponds to historical fact.

Despite the key ambiguity in the term "propositional statements" (does it intend "propositional" in its ordinary or philosophical sense?), the framers of these Articles suggest that biblical statements are true when they state facts, facts that seem to be exclusively historical in nature. But does all of Scripture "state facts"? We have shown that "what is said" includes more than "what is asserted." For the biblical record to "correspond" to historical fact, it must be read as containing assertions about the past. Is there a possibility that "what is said" has been collapsed into "what is asserted," so that every sentence of Scripture is read as fact-stating and proposition-conveying? That is the charge leveled at Evangelicals by Barr and David Kelsey.

As we mentioned above, Barr charged Evangelicals with making a literary category mistake in insisting that the function of biblical sentences is to convey propositions or information. When biblical narratives are read as history, Barr says that a theory of meaning as reference is presupposed, along with the concomitant theological method of proof-texting. This has led, according to Barr, to a sort of "biblical atomism." Similarly, Kelsey's analysis of the various ways in which the Bible is authoritative for theology concludes that Evangelicals (represented in his study by Warfield) consider "doctrinal content" the authoritative aspect of Scripture.[58] Warfield foregoes the proof-texting method, however, preferring rather to consider the doctrine of an entire book or writer and then collect it into a consistent system or "biblical theology." Kelsey calls this a "biblical positivism." In Barr and Kelsey, then, we see two criticisms of the Evangelical approach to biblical propositions: Barr objects to the use of biblical sentences ("ordinary" propositions) as proof texts; Kelsey criticizes the concern for doctrines ("philosophical" propositions) that are extracted from the text.

In the opinion of Barr and Kelsey, the issue at stake is the nature of language, meaning, and truth. Both Barr and Kelsey associate Evangelicals with the theory that the meaning of a sentence is its referents. The Chicago Statement on Biblical Hermeneutics seems to justify this interpretation: the biblical record was there said to refer to "historical fact." Evangelicals, thus, regard the Bible as a kind of *Tractatus Theologico-Philosophicus!*[59] This allusion to Ludwig Wittgenstein's earlier work is not coincidental. What the neoliberal critics of Evangelicals object to is a view of language and meaning that was best expressed (and later repudiated) by Wittgenstein. It is, therefore, of some interest to compare Wittgenstein's early work with how Evangelicals view biblical propositions. In a later section, we shall see fit to contrast Wittgenstein's earlier view of propositions with his later theory of language—one that displayed greater sensitivity to various literary forms.

Wittgenstein's major philosophical concern in his first published work—a concern that stayed with him throughout his life—was with the nature of language and its relation to the world.[60] Wittgenstein once wrote: "My *whole* task consists in explaining the nature of sentences."[61] How do marks on paper come to signify the world? Like Evangelicals, Wittgenstein answered this question by appealing to propositions and facts. A brief look at Wittgenstein's *Tractatus Logico-Philosophicus* will perhaps clarify the theory of meaning referred to by Barr and Kelsey when they speak of "biblical atomism" and "biblical positivism."[62]

For Wittgenstein, the world is the totality of facts (1.1). A fact is the existence of a state of affairs (2), and a state of affairs is a combination of objects (2.01). The world is thus comprised of the sum total of objects, things, or "atoms." So much for the world. What about language and propositions? Wittgenstein says that we "picture" facts to ourselves (2.1). These pictures are "laid against" reality like a measure (2.1512), and if the picture agrees with reality it is true (2.21). Now a thought is a logical picture of facts (3), and a "proposition" is

an expression of a thought (3.1). Language is thus made of propositions that "picture" the world. And, just as facts are made up of
combinations of objects, so propositions are made up of combinations of names. Wittgenstein's central assumption, an assumption
that he later retracted, was that "A name means an object. The object
is its meaning" (3.203). So Wittgenstein's "logical atomism" might be
roughly pictured as follows:

LANGUAGE	– – – – – – –	WORLD
comprised of		comprised of
PROPOSITIONS	– – – – – – – –	FACTS
comprised of		comprised of
NAMES	– – – – – – – –	*OBJECTS*

This way of correlating language and the world has been termed
the "picture theory" of the proposition.[63] "A proposition is a picture
of reality" (4.01). What is common to both reality and the propositional picture is the "logical form," the arrangement or ordering of the
elements (objects and names). Thus, for every simple object or "atom"
in the world, there is an elementary proposition that pictures (names)
it (4.22). If we could only state every proposition, the world would be
completely described.

Does the concept of propositional revelation commit Evangelicals
to a picture theory of the proposition? Does, say, Article VI of the
Chicago Statement do so? But forgetting momentarily the possible
parallels between Wittgenstein's and Evangelicals' understanding of
the language–world relation, what is wrong with Wittgenstein's
account of the proposition?

For our purposes, the theory of meaning and language put
forward in the *Tractatus* has two major faults. First of all, the account
wholly ignores the importance of circumstances in determining
meaning—the setting-in-life or extralinguistic context of sentences.
Before we say that a proposition pictures reality, we must observe
how the sentence is being used. Is it being used as a picture? If so, is
it being used as a scientifically accurate picture, a beautiful picture, a
morally edifying picture? Norman Malcolm, one of Wittgenstein's
commentators, observes: "How a picture is used will determine what
it is a picture of."[64] For this reason, we cannot assume that the
meaning of a proposition is the state of affairs with which it
corresponds. Indeed, Wittgenstein's later work was in large part an
attempt to correct his earlier mistakes in this regard and to do justice
to the actual uses of language in life.

Secondly, and perhaps more importantly, Wittgenstein regarded
ordinary language as inadequate: "Language disguises thought. So
much so, that from the outward form of the clothing it is impossible
to infer the form of the thought beneath it . . . " (4.002).

Ordinary language is, in Wittgenstein's opinion, unclear and obscures the logical form of the proposition. The solution: analyze the sentence into its atomic picture; this is the task of philosophy as Wittgenstein conceived it. When clarified, propositions will mirror the logical form of the world (4.112). Now part of the "outward clothing" of sentences is their literary form. Wittgenstein's theory of meaning seems to entail regarding the literary form not only as dispensable packaging but as an actual hindrance to the perception of meaning. The proper form of a proposition—and this is one of Wittgenstein's major theses in the *Tractatus* —is $[\bar{p},\bar{\xi},N(\bar{\xi})]$ (6). The significance of the symbolism is that it shows Wittgenstein's concern to construct a formal language, a language of "proper" propositions, untainted by the awkwardness and lack of clarity of ordinary language.[65] The search for transparent propositions thus seems to involve a disparaging of and cavalier attitude toward the everyday forms of language.

This "picture" view of language and meaning would seem to necessitate an unpalatable corollary for Evangelicals, namely, that there is some imperfection in Scripture, that God could have revealed His propositions with greater perspicuity—an idea that would have surprised the Reformers. Should theologians *analyze* what is said in Scripture and seek the exactness of the proposition, or should they *describe* what is said and respect the ordinary language? This alternative reflects the major shift in Wittgenstein's own thinking. In his later work, Wittgenstein was interested above all in describing the everyday forms and uses of language and in watching how they were employed in various contexts, rather than tinkering with sentences and translating them into a standard form.

It is not for us to judge whether or not some Evangelicals, in their zeal for propositional revelation, have avoided the pitfalls of the picture theory of the proposition. What is our concern is to provide a model of biblical revelation that will preserve the substance of "propositional" revelation (i.e., the emphasis on verbal, cognitive communication) while at the same time allowing for greater appreciation of the "ordinary" language of Scripture and its diverse literary forms.

III. THE "HERESY" OF PROPOSITIONAL PARAPHRASE

Some proponents of propositional revelation are quick to acknowledge the presence of literary forms in Scripture. Nash says that critics who assume that propositional revelation means that revelation must always have an assertorical form are mistaken.[66] This is well and good, but it fails to explain *how* one does justice to the rich multiplicity of literary forms. Wittgenstein, as we have seen, distrusted ordinary sentences because they *disguised* the proposition. Do literary forms convey propositions or provide smokescreens for them? Just what is the relation of Scripture's diverse literary forms and its truth content?

The "Chicago Statement on Biblical Hermeneutics" explicitly addressed this issue:[67]

> ARTICLE X: WE AFFIRM that Scripture communicates God's truth to us verbally through a wide variety of literary forms.

Here, then, is a declaration that diverse literary forms and truth are by no means incompatible. However, this apparently peaceful coexistence is threatened when read in light of the subsequent article:

> ARTICLE XIII: WE AFFIRM that awareness of the literary categories, formal and stylistic, of the various parts of Scripture is essential for proper exegesis, and hence we value genre criticism as one of the many disciplines of Biblical study.
>
> WE DENY that generic categories which negate historicity may rightly be imposed on Biblical narratives which present themselves as factual.

The affirmation states that biblical sentences must be read in light of their literary context, or genre. The denial, however, immediately rescinds the decisive importance of genre whenever historicity is at stake. But to suggest that all narratives that *appear* to be factual must *be* historical is to ride roughshod over the issue of literary genres. John Searle remarks that there are no formal features, no textual properties that identify a given text as a work of fiction.[68] Hence the "we value genre criticism" seems to pay mere lip-service to the actual role of literary forms in deciding what kind of truth claims are involved in a given narrative. The confusion in the Chicago Statement is exacerbated by the following article:

> Article XIV: WE AFFIRM that the Biblical record of events, discourses and sayings, though presented in a variety of appropriate literary forms, corresponds to historical fact.

The variety of literary forms is herein smoothed over to ensure the unity of historicity. Clearly, some other principle seems to be guiding the statement's attitude toward biblical propositions than that of recognizing literary genre. It is, we suggest, an apologetic rather than hermeneutical interest that dictates that historicity take precedence in spite of the variety of literary forms. Ironically, the "Chicago Statement on Biblical Inerrancy" handles Scripture's diverse literary forms more successfully:

> So history must be treated as history, poetry as poetry, hyperbole and metaphor as hyperbole and metaphor, generalization and approximation as what they are, and so forth.[69]

By contrast, the "Chicago Statement on Biblical Hermeneutics" comes perilously close to imposing an interpretive grid on Scripture rather than letting Scripture's literary forms be literary forms.

In the work of Henry we again find the claim that truth and diverse literary genres are not mutually exclusive: "Propositional disclosure is not limited to nor does it require only one particular literary genre. And of course the expression of truth in other forms than the customary prose does not preclude expressing the truth in declarative propositions."[70] In spite of this admission, Henry still seems to be partial to the simple declarative statement: "Regardless of the parables, allegories, emotive phrases and rhetorical questions used by these writers, their literary devices have a logical point which can be propositionally formulated and is objectively true or false."[71]

Henry elsewhere argues that the claim that the Bible is literally true in no way requires that only prose serve as the vehicle of this truth: "Some literary techniques more than others sharpen the communication of truth by rousing the imagination, stirring the emotions, and stimulating the will."[72] Henry thus acknowledges that literary forms are not merely ornamental trappings of truth content, but that they have a positive contribution to make in God's revelatory communication. At the same time, however, Henry is clear that the basic value of biblical symbols (and presumably other literary devices) "lies not simply in their capacity to move us but more fundamentally in what they presumably tell us about God."[73]

In short, the informative function of language continues to enjoy preeminence in Henry's understanding of revelation. Consider his attitude regarding poetry: "Poetry can usually be restated in prose form; prose is a kind of linguistic shorthand for poetic expression."[74] But to substitute prose "shorthand" for poetry is to be guilty of what Cleanth Brooks has termed the "heresy of paraphrase."[75] It is also to overlook Sir Philip Sidney's dictum: "The poet nothing affirmeth and therefore never lieth."[76] To believe, as Henry does, that what is said in poetry may be paraphrased so that its content is clearly stated is to invoke the wrath of literary critics who view poetry and other literary forms as other than informative.[77]

Barr presents the alternatives: should we read the Bible as descriptive information or as poetic literature? Perhaps, says Barr, the primary way the Bible influences the church is by the stories it tells that pattern our lives—and this regardless of whether or not the stories are historically true: "in the Bible as a whole . . . the parabolic, mythical, or literary mode of impact is experienced as the primary one, and this mode of impact becomes antecedent to the question of what actually happened or what external realities are referred to."[78]

This is, roughly, the position of what we have termed the New Biblical Theology; and, as we mentioned at the outset, the New Biblical Theologians can invoke the work of legion professional literary critics in support of their nonpropositional reading of Scripture. Thus, as we had recourse to detour into philosophy when investigating propositions, so we must now detour into literary criticism in order to explore the proposition-conveying potential of various literary forms.

"It is axiomatic for a large number of contemporary poetic theorists that a poem, as a poem, does not assert anything about the world."[79] So states Gerald Graff, a member of the minority opposition party, about mainstream twentieth-century literary critics. It may be recalled that the New Biblical Theology, in its opposition to cognitive revelation, took refuge in the distinction between descriptive and poetic language. Similarly, a fundamental, essentially Romanticist, dualism runs throughout modern literary criticism: "From Coleridge to Mallarmé, and from Yeats to Cleanth Brooks, Philip Wheelwright, and Northrop Frye, a dualism very like that between symbol and allegory is carried through as a distinction between the poetic or literary and the scientific or ordinary kinds of discourse."[80]

Throughout the English-speaking world, this dichotomy has been more or less *de rigueur* for modern literary critics. Literature is considered an autonomous realm, hermetically sealed off from "external" questions of history or science. Frank Lentricchia describes the situation: "The unique discourse of literature is closed off (it is centripetally directed) from all that externality which is attended to by the 'centrifugal,' 'descriptive,' and 'assertive' qualities of ordinary writing."[81]

For the English critic I. A. Richards, poetry is an emotive use of language. Scientific statements describe the external world; poetic statements express the inner world of values.[82] The poem is not so much an assertion of thought as it is the dramatic enactment of the process of thought, of the poet's coming to grips with an idea, event, or person. For the American critic Brooks and the New Critics in general, "a poem is a special mode of discourse whose statement-denying dynamic tends to keep the reader's consciousness trapped within an enclosed aesthetic space."[83] It was Brooks who explained how the New Critics avoided the "heresy of paraphrase" when discussing poetry: "Any proposition asserted in a poem is not to be taken in abstraction but is justified, in terms of the poem, if it is justified at all, not by virtue of its scientific or historical or philosophical truth, but is justified in terms of a principle analogous to that of dramatic propriety."[84]

In his reading of Keats' "Ode on a Grecian Urn," for example, Brooks does not take the line "Beauty is truth, truth beauty" as asserting a proposition. Rather, the lines are "justified" by their "fit" with the rest of the poem—the principle of dramatic propriety. By appealing to this principle, Brooks hoped to free literary texts from the burden of declarative statement and himself from the heresy of paraphrase. However, on reading T. S. Eliot's "The Waste Land," Brooks finds the proposition "that men have lost knowledge of good and evil," even though it is not explicitly stated in the poem. Brooks argues that the proposition is an abstraction of the complex dramatic action expressed in the poem. The poem does not assert "that men have lost knowledge of good and evil," but rather shows an attitude that is trying to come to terms with this idea.

The extent to which this kind of literary criticism has infiltrated and influenced both biblical studies and theology may be seen by examining the work of Northrop Frye. This Canadian critic has written that "questions of fact or truth are subordinated to the primary literary aim of producing a structure of words for its own sake."[85] Here, then, is a call for what Lentricchia calls a "clean severance of the literary mode from the centrifugal responsibilities to describe and to assert."[86] Frye differs from the New Critics in seeing the individual text not as an autonomous entity but as a member of a larger literary universe. Lentricchia calls this a poetics of "aesthetic humanism,"[87] wherein aesthetics "releases mankind from all the shackles of circumstance and frees him from everything that may be called constraint, whether physical or moral."[88]

Frye is of special interest as a literary critic because of the privileged place allocated the Bible in his literary universe. According to Frye, the biblical images and narratives constitute the imaginative, mythological universe within which all subsequent Western literature has lived, moved, and had its being.[89] For Frye, like Barr, the Bible's significance resides in its shaping of the Western imagination. In marked contrast to Clark's belief that most of the Bible is composed of propositions, Frye claims that Scripture's "use of objective and descriptive language is incidental throughout."[90] The Bible for Frye is a special kind of rhetoric—a *kerygma*—that is a mixture of the metaphorical and existential. Frye can still call the Bible "revelation," but this is not to be understood as the "conveying of information from an objective divine source to a subjective human receptor,"[91] for this would make Scripture a "descriptive" text.

What does the Bible literally mean? Frye replies that it means what it says. However, Frye notes that whereas some verbal structures are set up as counterparts to external events (histories), other verbal structures exist for their own sake and have no such counterpart (literature). Frye thus sanctions the now-familiar distinction that is at the heart of the New Biblical Theology, namely, the distinction between "descriptive" and "poetic" texts. Moreover, Frye retains the New Critical point that the primary aspect of a verbal structure is its self-referring, "centripetal" aspect. The Bible means literally what it says, but it can only so mean by *not* referring to some extratextual matter. Frye cites an example: "When Jesus says (Jn 10:9), 'I am the door,' the statement means literally just what it says, but there are no doors outside the verse in John to be pointed to."[92] The same is true, says Frye, of the great fish in the Book of Jonah. What makes a descriptive text true is its correspondence to an external reference; but a work of literature has another criterion for truth: inner verbal consistency.[93]

An outstanding example of a work emanating from the New Biblical Theology that relies on literary critical theories such as the ones we have been discussing is Hans Frei's *The Eclipse of the Biblical Narrative*.[94] As Frye held that the literal meaning of the Bible *is* the poetic meaning, so Frei says that the literal meaning of the Gospel narratives *is* its narrative shape. Frei laments that the meaning of the Gospel narratives has come to be associated with something other than the narratives themselves, namely, an external history. John Barton correctly observes: "In Frei's book we have a non-referential theory of biblical narrative texts, which is closely akin to the New Critical theory of literature in general as non-referential."[95] Because the meaning of the narrative is the narrative form itself, it cannot be paraphrased in nonnarrative form.

The challenge to propositional or cognitive revelation, therefore, comes not only from theologians but also from professional literary critics who question whether literature functions to inform. These literary critics particularly frown on two "heresies": the heresy that literary forms are merely ornamental gilding (e.g., Frei's insisting that narrative shape is essential to its meaning), and the heresy of paraphrase. These two heresies are perhaps, at root, one—the "propositional heresy"—the belief that the content of literature can be restated in nonliterary form.

Not all literary critics and philosophers agree that to paraphrase is simultaneously to commit heresy. One philosopher, D. H. Mellor, writes: "If a novel can properly be said to be true or false it makes statements."[96] More precisely, a novel makes a set of statements (S) other than the set of statements it ostensibly makes in its narrative (S'). The novel's truth will be determined by the truth or falsity of the statements in S—usually generalizations of a moral, psychological, or sociological kind about real people: "The truth conveyed in the novel is that of the generalization of S, which is independent of the truth or falsity of the illustrative statement S' by which it is conveyed."[97] Contrary to the mainstream of literary critics, Mellor claims that literature does affirm stateable truths.

In a similar fashion, Graff's *Poetic Statement and Critical Dogma*[98] is a bold manifesto that meets head-on the nonpropositional view of literature. Graff admits that form and content are often inseparable; any change in the wording of a poem risks changing its meaning or content. However, Graff argues that the form "follows from" its conceptual content: "Our very ability to recognize such common literary sins as . . . sentimentality . . . presupposes that an ideal of proportion between ground and consequent governs the relation between content and form."[99] Graff is saying that we can only judge the appropriateness of the form on the basis of the content. In the same way, the "poetic attitudes" championed by Brooks and the New Critics are intelligible only in light of the conceptual statements of the poem, which serve as their *raison d'être*.

Paraphrase does, according to Graff, constitute a *part* of a poem's meaning: "But if the aim of paraphrase is more modestly conceived as giving an equivalent not of the total meaning of the utterance paraphrased but only of the *conceptual* portion of that meaning, then we can speak of most utterances as accessible to paraphrase."[100] Graff suggests that nuances that resist paraphrase may nevertheless be described. Once the conceptual grounds of the attitudes expressed in literature are made clear, we can then assess the adequacy of the dramatized response that the poem is said to embody. Poetry is distinguished from paraphrase by virtue of the former's "highly developed and systematic employment of rhythm."[101]

Is biblical revelation, like poetry or literature, susceptible to conceptual paraphrase? This is undoubtedly the thesis of those who speak of "propositional" revelation. But even Graff, a staunch defender of the cognitive nature of poetry, admits that paraphrase captures only *part* of the total meaning. What, then, *escapes* propositional paraphrase? Perhaps some examples from other "languages" might prove helpful in considering this question. I, for one, have not come across a good paraphrase of Brahms' "Fourth Symphony" recently. Though the proposition "that life is grand but ultimately tragic" makes a game stab at stating the conceptual content of Brahms' music, something inevitably gets lost in translation. In the realm of art, someone has said that the whole Protestant doctrine of the human race is contained in Rembrandt's paintings. But here too a systematic theologian would be hard pressed to put this theology in propositional form.

Of course, it may be objected, music and art are nonverbal; surely words and texts may be paraphrased more easily? Take, for instance, the familiar story of "Little Red Riding Hood." What statements (S) does the story (S') make? A recent article in *Time* magazine reports that one hundred scholars could not agree about the meaning of this fairy tale: "Nearly everyone agrees that the story *Little Red Riding Hood* is an evocative tale of sex and violence, but exactly what it evokes is a matter of dispute among folklorists, anthropologists, Freudians, feminists and literary critics."[102] And one muses whether there would have been a greater consensus if theologians had figured among the participants.

Certainly one of the purposes of "Little Red Riding Hood" was to warn someone (girls, children?) about something (men, strangers, wolves?). But many of the Old Testament narratives have a similar purpose. The apostle Paul writes about the accounts of Israel's history: "These things happened to them as examples and were written down as warnings for us" (1Co 10:11). That is, the Old Testament record was written not only to convey information, but to *affect* its readers in certain ways. And as we have shown, paraphrase is weakest in its attempts to preserve the noncognitive aspects of a text's meaning. We might perhaps generalize and say that what is lost in conceptual paraphrase is the *power* and *beauty* of the *in*-formed content. Ironically, in its very concern to preserve the cognitive content of literature, conceptual paraphrase strips the content of precisely those aspects that are most likely to preserve it and its effect! Wordsworth's lines describe the lifeless residue of propositional analysis:

> Our meddling intellect
> Misshapes the beauteous forms of things:—
>   We murder to dissect.[103]

Some no doubt will object that this detour into literary criticism is irrelevant because the Bible is manifestly *not* literature like "Little Red Riding Hood." Norman Geisler, for example, argues from the nature of truth to conclusions about which literary genres can or cannot be in Scripture, along lines something like this:

1. Statements are true when they correspond to actual fact.
2. Midrash rejects the correspondence theory of truth.
3. The Bible is true in all that it states.
4. Therefore, midrash cannot be one of Scripture's literary forms.[104]

Whether or not his conclusion is correct, Geisler's argumentation is surely faulty, dictating as it does a *priori* the literary form the divine revelation must take. His is a case of putting the interpretive cart before the horse, of pronouncing exegetical conclusions that do not logically depend on a reading of the text. In similar fashion, Robert Preus states:

> Certain alleged forms are not compatible either with the purpose of Scripture or with its inerrancy. . . . Specifically, any literary genre that would in itself be immoral or involve deceit or error is not compatible with Biblical inerrancy and is not to be found in Scripture.[105]

It is difficult, however, to see how a literary form can inherently be immoral; only personal agents can be morally responsible. Furthermore, the writer, in using a genre, is invoking known conventions. So long as it is known *what* is being read, the reader is not deceived. Ramm goes so far as to say that if pseudonymity "were a recognized form in the culture of the scriptural writer . . . then we must be prepared to accept this as a proper form of special revelation."[106]

In contrast to Geisler and Preus, Ramm writes: "There is no *inherent* harm in a literary genre; there is only harm or danger in how a scholar may use such a genre against a document. If such a genre plays a *positive* role in the communication of revelation . . . we should not shy away from it."[107] Ramm notes also that we are tempted to fix the literary forms of our day as the "standard" forms, forgetting that literary forms have undergone historical development. Because God's communication came at particular times and places, it comes in particular literary forms. Ramm concludes that "much harm has been done to Scripture by those within and without the Church by assuming that all statements in the Bible are on the same logical level, on which level they are either true or false."[108]

The genres that prove most worrisome to Evangelicals include legend, myth, midrash, and saga—genres that appear *prima facie* to vitiate Scripture's truthfulness. But even to read the Bible as history (as many biblical critics do) does not guarantee its truthfulness, for many liberal critics conclude that the Bible presents *false* history. One's reading of Scripture, then, ought not to harbor prejudices against some literary genres out of a concern for what the truth "must" be. This is the only way to avoid criticisms such as John Barton's that claim that Fundamentalists are seldom students of the humanities and mainly read nonfiction and that *consequently they do not know how to read the Bible.*[109] It would perhaps be beneficial to look at a counter-example to this serious charge.

IV. C. S. LEWIS: CHRISTIAN READER

The mention of C. S. Lewis immediately adds another dimension into our discussion of Scripture and truth: the role of the imagination. Lewis approaches Scripture not as a theologian but as a literary critic—a Christian reader—because the Bible as such is not a systematic theology but divinely inspired literature.[110] Lewis evidences an appreciation of the nonpropositional aspect of biblical literature—an appreciation that has hitherto been lacking in our study. It would be a gross injustice, however, to attribute to Lewis a purely "literary" reading of Scripture. Indeed, he has some harsh things to say about those who read the Bible as "mere" literature: "Those who talk of reading the Bible 'as literature' sometimes mean, I think, reading it without attending to the main thing it is about; like reading Burke with no interest in politics, or reading the *Aeneid* with no interest in Rome."[111] This thought accords well with Lewis's general emphasis on the "real things" seen in literary texts, as opposed to a focus on the style, personality, or poetic attitude of the author.[112]

But at the same time there is a sense in which the Bible clearly *is* literature for Lewis, so that each part must be read as the kind of literature it is. The importance of determining literary genre—or simply *genus*—is one of Lewis's most stringent principles for correct interpretation: "The first qualification for judging any piece of workmanship from a corkscrew to a cathedral is to know *what* it is— what it was intended to do and how it is meant to be used."[113] What is true for interpretation in general holds also for literary interpretation: "Every poem can be considered in two ways—as what the poet has to say, and as a *thing* which he *makes*."[114] A poem or work of literature has, says Lewis, two "parents": the "mother," or content (thought, experience), and the "father," or preexisting form (genre). Good reading will not put asunder what the author has joined together.

I would like to suggest that Lewis's model of reading—honoring both "father" and "mother"—allows the truth of literature to shine through while at the same time avoiding the excesses of propositional paraphrase. The intellect for Lewis is incurably abstract, "yet the only realities we can experience are concrete—this pain, this pleasure, this dog, this man."[115] Lewis thus distinguishes two modes of knowledge: *savoir*, or propositional truth (descriptive knowledge about reality), and *connaître*, or participatory truth (knowledge by personal acquaintance). When we are loving the person or bearing the pain, we cannot also be intellectually apprehending personality or pain:

> This is our dilemma—either to taste and not to know or to know and not to taste—or, more strictly, to lack one kind of knowledge because we are in an experience or to lack another kind because we are outside it. As thinkers we are cut off from what we think about; as tasting, touching, willing, loving, hating, we do not clearly understand.[116]

Myth or story is the "partial solution" to this dilemma. In the imaginative enjoyment of a great myth "we come nearest to experiencing as a concrete what can otherwise be understood only as an abstraction."[117] Paul Holmer believes that reality for Lewis cannot be summarized in a theory: "Literature is not a disguised theory, nor an implied didacticism. Instead, it communicates in such a way that, when successful, it creates new capabilities and capacities."[118] Myth is not abstract, as is truth; nor is it bound to particulars, as is direct experience. As a "middle way," myth is admirably suited to offer a concrete taste of a universal reality.[119] The main problem with propositional paraphrase is that it yields a "tasteless" knowing, a knowing bereft of the power and beauty perceived and apprehended by the imagination.

It is important to note that Lewis understood "myth" to include accounts of historical fact. He speaks of the gospel story as "myth become fact." This mythic appreciation of Christianity did not come easily for Lewis. Though he could rationally accept theism, for a long while he could not accept Christ nor understand the significance of such crucial aspects of the gospel as "sacrifice" and "propitiation." A late night conversation with J. R. R. Tolkien and "Hugo" Dyson showed him that it was possible imaginatively and emotionally to "feel the myth as profound and suggestive of meanings beyond my grasp even tho' I could not say in cold prose 'what it meant.'"[120] Lewis held that the doctrines derived from myths are *less* true; they are but conceptual translations of what God has already, and more adequately, expressed—namely, the actual Incarnation, Cross, and Resurrection.

For Lewis, therefore, we might say that the gospel "myth" gave him a profound *taste of history*—of history's relevance, power, and beauty. Peter Schakel argues that "tasting" reality imaginatively became more and more important for Lewis as he grew older, even influencing the particular genres with which he chose to write his own work. *Letters to Malcolm*[121] uses the literary device of an imaginary correspondence to achieve its purpose—"to fuse the 'knowing' of ideas crucial to Christian growth with the 'taste' of experienced reality necessary to give that knowledge vitality."[122] Literature for Lewis serves to give power, life, and "taste" to the information it conveys.

Poetic language and imaginative literature serve other purposes in Lewis's opinion as well. Poetic language gives *qualitative* information, whereas scientific language yields quantitative information and precision.[123] Poetic language expresses emotion not for emotion's sake but in order to inform us about the *object* that evoked the emotion. And, as with myth, Lewis declares that poetic language may be used of fact as well as fiction. Moreover, Lewis disparages the reader who is on the lookout for information alone: "As the unmusical listener wants only the Tune, so the unliterary reader wants only the Event."[124] But Lewis contends that some events cannot be conveyed as they are *without* engaging the heart—thus the necessity of poetic language. Perhaps the most impressive example of this principle at work would be the Psalms. Though we can pull any standard systematic theology off the shelf and read about God's eternal nature, the Psalms offer their own, more eloquent, "description" of God. So Lewis: "The most valuable thing the Psalms do for me is to express the same delight in God which made David dance."[125]

The indispensability of literary form is a theme that Lewis repeats in his treatment of the epistemological value of the "pupil's metaphor."[126] Some metaphors, says Lewis, are "our only method of reaching a given idea at all."[127] In some cases, we just cannot know the object without the metaphor; in these cases, a nonmetaphorical, or propositional, paraphrase is out of the question. While perhaps more technical (though Lewis remarks that it is still metaphorical), calling God the "transcendent Ground of Being" is simply not as inviting, nor as rich in meaning, as "Our Father who art in heaven."

Why did God "take up" certain human literary forms and press them into His service? "We might have expected, we may think we should have preferred, an unrefracted light giving us ultimate truth in systematic form—something we could have tabulated and memorised and relied on like the multiplication table."[128] Even Jesus' teaching lacks systematicity: "He preaches but He does not lecture."[129] To pin down Jesus' teaching in neat propositions is "like trying to bottle a sunbeam."[130] Lewis suggests that the reason why Jesus' teaching eludes our systematizing intellect is that, in so doing, it demands a response from the *whole* person: "No net less wide than a man's whole heart . . . will hold the sacred Fish."[131] Compare the similar thought on the part of the theologian Abraham Kuyper:

> The rationale for the diverse literary forms in Scripture is that revelation strikes all the chords of the soul, and not just one, e.g., the rational one. This makes it clear that the historical doctrine of revelation is not the barren propositional one it is often charged with being.[132]

This demand for a total response is central to one of Lewis's later works, *An Experiment in Criticism*. Lewis here makes the novel suggestion that books should be judged on the basis of how they are *read:* "Now the true reader reads every work seriously in the sense that he reads it wholeheartedly, makes himself as receptive as he can."[133] Good readers *receive* the literary text; bad readers *use* it.[134] Whereas the receiver "rests" in the vision of the work, the user wants to make the vision into, say, a life philosophy. As Schakel summarizes: "Reading involves an imaginative, emotional, and intellectual interaction between the words an author writes and a reader's understanding of and response to them."[135] By Lewis's criterion, the Bible is the paradigmatic good book. One cannot "use" it, for example, to pass away the time. Rather, it demands a response, an "uptake." In sum, good reading calls for the response of the rationalist (who approaches the Bible as truth to be believed), as well as the "romantic" (who approaches the Bible as a reality to be received).[136] Lewis the Christian reader has an appreciation for both the propositional, or rational, truth-bearing function and the nonpropositional, or imaginative, reality-bearing function of good literature.

V. SCRIPTURE'S DIVERSE FORMS: LANGUAGE GAMES AND LITERARY GENRES

Which literary forms has God "taken up" into the service of His Word? Lewis finds chronicle, poetry, political diatribe, moral romance; Ramm adds dramatic epic, apocalypse, wise sayings, and witnessing materials.[137] Ramm notes the significance for hermeneutics of Scripture's diverse literary forms: "Our stance about the literary genre of the book determines our entire interpretation of the book."[138] Reformation scholarship, standing in the philological tradition, recognized the role of genre in its exegesis and interpretation. Indeed, recognition of Scripture's literary forms—"literary competence" is the phrase used by Barton—is of paramount importance for the solid grammatical-historical exegesis that has traditionally been the staple of Evangelicals' commentaries.[139]

Corkscrew or cathedral? Romance or history? Epic or chronicle? The decisions we make as to what we read the Bible *as* (or what kind of thing it is) condition our expectations regarding the kinds of truth claims we find therein. If, asks Lewis, "sound critical reading revealed different *kinds* of narrative in the Bible, surely it would be illogical to suppose that these different kinds should all be read in the same way?"[140] He suggests that two biblical passages may not be inerrant in exactly the same way; that is, not every biblical statement must state historical truth.[141] Inerrancy must be construed broadly enough to encompass the truth expressed in Scripture's poetry, romances, proverbs, parables—as well as histories.

In spite of the affirmation in Hebrews 1:1 that God spoke "through the prophets at many times and in various ways," real appreciation of Scripture's literary pluralism has been somewhat overshadowed by the paradigm of God as author. A thoroughgoing acknowledgment of Scripture's diverse forms better helps us to understand the *humanity* of Scripture, without surrendering the notion of divine authorship. God used linguistic and literary convention in order to communicate with human beings. The diverse literary forms, far from being a weakness of Scripture, ensure a rich communication and are actually one of Scripture's perfections.

One of the first modern advocates of "genre-criticism" was the French exegete Marie-Joseph Lagrange. At the turn of the century he wrote several key works on the subject of inspiration and Scripture's literary forms.[142] Lagrange was a staunch defender of verbal inspiration and rejected "content inspiration," a rival theory that held that God *supplied* the "formal" component of Scripture (viz., its truth content) but only *assisted* with the "material" elements (the actual sentences and literary forms).[143] Lagrange maintained that the chief mistake of content inspiration lay "not in removing the wording of the Bible from God's control, but in removing the thoughts and ideas from that of man."[144] The very notion of authorial intent—the key to correct interpretation for Lagrange—would be rendered superfluous if the human authors were mere passive recipients of divine ideas. "But if it be granted that the full and troublesome task of assembling the very fabric and stuff of the Bible's thought falls to human writers, then the burden of his message will emerge from his distinctive manner of presenting it."[145]

God works with the human author's ordinary faculties and so ensures that what is written is fully human and fully divine. "Whatever the human writers affirm, God affirms, and Lagrange will defend it as absolutely inerrant."[146] To ascertain the human author's intentions and thus determine *when* he is affirming, it is necessary to examine the kind of literature he wrote. Lagrange is adamant that "the customs and usages of the East in bygone days ought, therefore, to be the standard by which we test our ideas of fitness and unfitness."[147]

We have seen that genre-recognition is part and parcel of the grammatical-historical method of exegesis. Grant R. Osborne acknowledges this connection when he calls genre an "epistemological tool" for discovering the *sensus literalis*—the literal sense, or intended meaning—of Scripture.[148] Problems, however, remain: to *which* genre should we assign this biblical text, this passage? How may genres be discerned? This is a disputed area in literary criticism; some critics say that textual form determines genre, others that internal factors (content) are more important. The truth is probably somewhere in between; for, as Graff has shown, the content demands a certain form, and the form is adequate to the matter. We should also not forget that the form-content distinction is a· precarious one: it is only in analysis—and not in reading—that they may be separated.

Recent literary studies show that literary forms serve more than classificatory purposes. The genre provides the *literary context* for a given sentence and, therefore, partly determines what the sentence means and how it should be taken. Mere classification ("Oh, that's an epic") satisfies our curiosity. But genre as constitutive of meaning conditions our expectations as readers and permits understanding to take place. E. D. Hirsch suggests that verbal meaning is always genre-bound. Hirsch defines genre as the "controlling idea of the whole," which governs and constitutes *what* a text *is*.[149] Genre thus enables the reader to interpret meaning and to recognize what kinds of truth claims are being made in and by a text.

With the burgeoning interest in genre among literary critics has come a commensurate interest in biblical genres among biblical scholars and theologians. Gordon Fee and Douglas Stuart have written a how-to-understand-the-Bible book that concentrates on Scripture's diverse literary forms and contains a wealth of practical guidelines for a competent reading of the Bible in all its variety. The authors note that the very diversity of literary forms permits Scripture to speak to the whole spectrum of human conditions. To the various forms we have already mentioned they add riddles, genealogies, biographical sketches, and sermons. They point out that narrative is the most abundant literary type in Scripture, and they suggest that narrative well serves God's revelatory design by "allowing us vicariously to live through events and experiences rather than simply learning *about* the issues involved in those events and experiences."[150] Fee and Stuart wish to make it quite clear that "the Bible, however, is *not* a series of propositions and imperatives; it is not simply a collection of 'Sayings from Chairman God' . . . ."[151] While Old Testament narratives "illustrate doctrine taught propositionally elsewhere,"[152] Acts serves to "entertain" and "encourage" as well as inform.[153]

Besides the role of literary forms in correct interpretation (Fee and Stuart) and determining truth claims (Lagrange), we will now see that literary forms have a properly *theological* significance—and this in three ways. First, Paul Ricoeur states the impact of Scripture's literary diversity on the doctrine of revelation: "So instead of having to confront a monolithic concept of revelation, which is only obtained by transforming these different forms of discourse into propositions, we encounter a concept of revelation that is pluralistic, polysemic, and at most analogical in form."[154] With Barr, Ricoeur argues that the traditional concept of revelation is based on the prophetic paradigm ("Thus saith the Lord"): "Revelation is the speech of another behind the speech of the prophet."[155] Yet not all portions of Scripture are prefaced by a "Thus saith the Lord" (e.g., Judges, Song of Solomon, Philemon). Luke, for instance, claims to have compiled his narrative not by divine revelation but through his own research, using his own eyes and ears.[156] Does his Gospel fit the prophetic paradigm?

Ricoeur concludes that doing justice to revelation means giving priority to the original forms of biblical discourse. To reduce the ordinary language of faith to second-order theological propositions is to mistake the literary forms as mere rhetorical facades that conceal a bare thought-content behind them. For Ricoeur, however, the literary forms themselves are theologically significant: "Not just any theology may be attached to the story form."[157] Furthermore, that prescriptive discourse (e.g., the Ten Commandments) can be embedded in narrative discourse (e.g., the Exodus account) suggests to Ricoeur that "the memory of deliverance qualifies the instruction in an intimate way."[158]

The second theologically significant area of Scripture's literary pluralism pertains to biblical authority. David L. Bartlett, with a nod of indebtedness to Ricoeur, agrees that the mode of authority proper to the prophetic and preaching genre "is its claim to speak a word given by God."[159] Bartlett's *The Shape of Scriptural Authority* proposes that each literary form in Scripture has its own proper authority. Narrative authority, for example, "is the authority which shifts our sight"[160] by displaying a new normative perspective with which to view the world.

On another level, one's decision about the "genre" (loosely conceived) of Scripture determines the way in which it functions authoritatively for theology. This is Kelsey's thesis, at least, and he argues that our imaginative construals of Scripture (as doctrine, or myth, or record of God's acts in history, etc.) dictate how Scripture will function in theological argumentation. This brings us to the third area in which genre has theological significance: questions about canon. While "canon" is not a literary form in the strict sense, Brevard Childs seems to use it as such when he postulates canon as the ultimate literary context of a biblical passage or even a biblical book.[161] Whether or not canon functions as does a normal literary genre in governing the nature of the whole is a subject beyond the scope of this chapter, but Childs' canon criticism is at least another instance of genre's theological relevance.

Our consideration of genre leads naturally into a discussion about another theory of language and meaning. Our brief study of genre has shown us that literary competence involves recognizing the rules that a text follows. Hirsch compares genres with games: "Coming to understand the meaning of an utterance is like learning the rules of a game."[162] Following rules is thus the point of "family resemblance" shared by the notions of literary genres and language games, the latter being the key image of Wittgenstein's later philosophy and theory of meaning, to which we now turn.

In his *Philosophical Investigations*, Wittgenstein rejected many of the earlier themes he had assumed in the *Tractatus*. Simply put, he abandoned the uniform *logic* of the *Tractatus* and stressed in his *Philosophical Investigations* the multifarious forms of *life*. We shall look first at Wittgenstein's new thoughts about language and meaning, then at the attempt of Anthony Thiselton to apply these insights to semantics, New Testament interpretation, and biblical authority. By thus comparing the earlier and later Wittgenstein, two important ways of understanding language and meaning may be contrasted.

Wittgenstein begins his *Philosophical Investigations* with a celebrated citation from Augustine's *Confessions*[163] in which Augustine explains how he learned as a child to grasp the names of objects. Wittgenstein reads Augustine as giving an account of the *essence* of language, namely, that words name objects and that meaning is the object to which a word refers.[164] Augustine erred in applying and extending this correct description of naming to *all* of language. In Wittgenstein's opinion, Augustine describes one "language game" and only one. In dismissing Augustine's account, Wittgenstein rejects ostensive reference as the "essence" of language.[165] The view that meaning is reference leads to a number of misunderstandings and philosophical difficulties. Wittgenstein's therapy consists in making a "radical break with the idea that language always functions in one way, always serves the same purpose: to convey thoughts."[166] Stanley Cavell expresses the same idea: "The philosopher who asks about everything we do, 'Voluntary or not?' has a poor view of action (as the philosopher who asks of everything we say, 'True or false?' . . . has a poor view of communication)."[167]

Why is Augustine's account of language so plausible, so difficult to shake? Thiselton cites two reasons: first, we tend to confuse grammatical and logical structures. Wittgenstein himself is the outstanding example of this confusion: in the *Tractatus*, he said that the "general form" of a proposition was "this is how things are." A large part of Wittgenstein's later effort was aimed at discriminating the "surface" from the "depth" grammar.[168] Second, we tend to assume that there is a basic kind of language use—usually the declarative statement. Again referring to his own misjudgment, Wittgenstein writes: "A *picture* held us captive."[169]

In fact, Wittgenstein later came to believe that there are myriad uses of sentences. Declaring that "this is how things are" is but one of these uses—and not even a specially privileged one at that. In a famous analogy, he compares words to tools: "Think of the tools in a tool-box: there is a hammer, pliers, a saw, a screw-driver, a rule, a glue-pot, glue, nails and screws. The functions of words are as diverse as the function of these objects."[170]

There seems to be little difference in principle between language-games and literary forms. Consider these language-games listed by Wittgenstein and their possible literary counterparts: "reporting an event" (history); "making up a story" (fiction, parable); "singing catches" (song, Psalm); "giving orders" (law). Each of these language-games would appear to correspond to a biblical literary form.

Besides having a number of different uses, language is grounded in many forms of life. This is another substantial contrast with the *Tractatus*, where language was divorced from its setting in life in the quest for a sentence's logical form. While the language-world relation still occupies the later Wittgenstein's thought, it is no longer in terms of name labels for world objects. Rather, language and world are learned together in various life contexts. Thiselton correlates this emphasis on the particular historical-cultural setting with the concerns of hermeneutics.[171] And again, understanding a sentence in its "form of life" parallels comprehending a sentence in its "form of literature": both language-games and literary forms are context-bound and rule-governed.

What is true for sentences applies to concepts as well. Many concepts have a given meaning only in particular language-games. Knowing which game is being played is essential if one wants to play along; and not only philosophical but also theological concepts are affected in their meaning by the language-game being played.[172] Take, for instance, the concept of inerrancy. Wittgenstein considers the sentence "Stand roughly here" and asks whether is it an exact or inexact answer to the query "Where should I stand?" But what does "inexact" mean? It does not mean "unusable," for someone could follow the advice in some situations (e.g., lining up for a photograph). And what, asks Wittgenstein, is "ideal" exactness? His point is that "exact" varies in meaning from one language-game to another: "Am I inexact when I do not give our distance from the sun to the nearest foot . . . ?"[173] One man's exactness is another's trivia.

Though Wittgenstein does not explicitly mention them, we might extend these comments about exactness to diverse literary forms— forms for which "exactness" does not mean the same thing. It is here that we see the implications for a doctrine of inerrancy. The art of poetic diction is, perhaps, just as "exacting" as scientific statements, though it is not the same *kind* of exactness. With C. S. Lewis, we might say that poetry strains for "qualitative" exactness, whereas descriptive language aims at quantitative exactness. Which kind of exactness is required by the doctrine of inerrancy? Surely the kind and degree of exactness required must vary with the particular literary form and a consideration of its communicative context.

The stakes are raised when the notion of language-games infiltrates discussions about truth. If each language-game or literary form has its own kind of truth, does not "truth" flounder in a sea of relativity? Thiselton asks: "Is it possible to say what the 'essence' of truth is in the biblical writings, apart from its meanings in given language-games?"[174] The truth of a poem is different from the truth of a historical report. Thiselton contends that Wittgenstein's "picture theory" of the proposition erred in claiming that the relationship between truth and *all* forms of language could be explained in the same way, viz., the correspondence of fact and proposition.[175] After examining the various uses of "true" and "truth" in the Bible, Thiselton concludes: "We cannot ask questions about 'the New Testament concept of truth,' or even 'John's concept of truth,' *outside* a given context of language-game."[176] In other words, Thiselton is encouraging readers to be more sensitive to the relativity of the concept "truth"—relative, that is, to particular language-games in Scripture.[177]

Some followers of the later Wittgenstein (including D. Z. Phillipps, Norman Malcolm, and Paul Holmer) have applied the notion of language-game to *religion as a whole*. Like other language-games, religion is simply taken as a given and therefore needs no "justification" before it can be played. Recently, however, there has been some debate about whether something as large as religion can be a "form of life" with its own "language-game."[178] If the Christian religion is a form of life, is the Christian canon its language-game? Some theologians seem to say as much when they affirm the Scripture has its own kind of truth—*saving truth*. In this scenario, "inerrancy" would refer only to "religious" or "saving" truths in Scripture. But as we have shown at some length, Scripture is composed of many genres, including "reporting an event." To regard the canon as a language-game in itself with its own kind of truth is to ignore Scripture's literary pluralism, the actual textual phenomena.[179]

What is the relation, then, between Scripture and truth? Because

God is all-knowing and omnipresent, we feel that Truth must be comprehensive and unified (at least for God, if not always for us). Truth, like Reality, is in one sense One. However, Reality is so rich and multifaceted that it, like white light, can only be conveyed (verbally) by an equally rich "spectrum"—diverse literary forms. While Truth may be "about" Reality (what *is*), we only receive the full picture *of* Reality (*what* is) by contemplating "true" history, "true" parable, "true" song, "true" poetry.[180] That Scripture has many literary forms is no impediment to the Truth; instead, it is the very possibility of Truth's expression. The diversity of literary forms does not imply that Scripture contains competing kinds of Truth; it shows rather that Scripture is about various kinds of *fact* (i.e., historical, metaphysical, moral, etc.). A sentence or text is true if things are as it says they are, but as Aristotle observed, "Being may be said in many ways."[181]

VI. "ORDINARY LITERATURE"—A PROPOSAL

Scripture is composed of "ordinary" language and "ordinary" literature. To say this in no way disparages Scripture, nor does it dispute its status as "God's Word." "Mere" language is itself miraculous; it is the currency of our everyday transactions, of our personal, business, and even spiritual relationships. Jesus prayed and taught in "ordinary" language. There is no such thing as "religious language" as such; poetry and science are two artificial perfections of ordinary language.[182] That God's Word has been communicated in everyday language is not a fault so much as a perfection of divine revelation, for only as "ordinary" language could Scripture communicate to "ordinary" people in "ordinary" situations. We should no more consider it a "weakness" that the Bible is a human book than we should deem Jesus' humanity an "imperfection." Indeed, these ordinary human forms were essential both for revelation and redemption.

Considering the Bible as ordinary language and literature has implications for theology. It would appear to rule out the basic premise of the Biblical Theology movement, viz., that there are biblical or "religious" words that have a special theological significance. Similarly, the presupposition of the New Biblical Theology also becomes doubtful. The "shape" of the biblical genres does not have an additional theological significance that is appended to the normal functioning of its literary forms.[183] The attempt to read theological significance into literary forms is ill-advised—particularly when "literary" is taken to mean "poetic," hence nonreferential. But lastly, the attempt to derive a series of propositions from the biblical texts must be, if considered in isolation, ruled a partially correct but ultimately inadequate reading. Conceptual paraphrase varies with regard to its practicality and legitimacy from genre to genre: often the

power (and sometimes meaning) of the message is lost in propositional translation.

What seems to be needed is a "philosophy" of language and
literature that does justice to the "ordinariness" of the biblical texts.
Why a "philosophy"? Can we not simply read the Bible, unhampered
by scholarly debates? Of course one *can* so read, but every reading
necessarily presupposes implicit judgments as to *what* literary
meaning is and *how* texts signify the world.

However, the model we would like to propose has the distinct
advantage of being palatable to common sense. This model tries to
explain how ordinary literature *works* rather than seeking to "perfect"
it by putting it into some other form. What we have in mind is a
variation of the "speech act" theory of language—which was fathered
by J. L. Austin and brought to conceptual maturity by John Searle.[184]
Speech act theory has been on the market for nearly three decades;
and at the outset, the sentence was the focus of the speech act
theorists' attention. Only recently have its proponents begun to
consider possible implications for literary meaning.

Austin's *How to Do Things with Words* questions the "age-old
assumption of philosophy" that to say something significant is always
and simply to *state* something.[185] Austin agrees with Wittgenstein
that surface grammar can be deceptive. When the bride utters the
words "I do" in the course of her wedding ceremony, she not only
states that she is marrying; she actually *does* something (viz., marry).
Austin calls this type of saying a "performative" utterance and says
that it is neither true nor false. As with other doings, however, the
performance may "misfire." Austin calls things that can go wrong on
the occasion of performative utterances "infelicities." If the minister
were an imposter, for example, his "I now pronounce you husband
and wife" (another performative) would be null and void.

How many things do we do with words? Austin distinguished
three components of the total speech act: (a) the *locutionary act* "is
roughly equivalent to 'meaning' in the traditional sense,"[186] (b) the
illocutionary act is what we do *in* saying something, and (c) the
perlocutionary act is "what we bring about or achieve *by* saying
something, such as convincing, persuading."[187] For our purposes,
Austin's significance lies in his discovering a whole new realm of
acts—illocutions—what we do *in* saying something.[188] With the
notion of the illocutionary act, Austin was able to distinguish between
the *meaning* of what we say and the *force* of what we say. When
Jeremiah writes that "A lion has gone up from his thicket, a destroyer
of nations has set out" (Jer 4:7 RSV), he not only writes a meaningful
sentence but also *warns* Judah. If the people had responded to
Jeremiah by simply nodding their heads or saying "Yes. That's
interesting, Jeremiah," they would have failed to appreciate Jeremiah's illocution, his warning. A complete understanding of a speech

act involves, therefore, an apprehension not only of the *meaning* but also of the *force*. For the warning to be successful, Austin says that "illocutionary uptake" must be secured.[189] William P. Alston writes: "If this is the line along which meaning should be analyzed, then the concept of an illocutionary act is the most fundamental concept in semantics and, hence, in the philosophy of language."[190]

Austin later found his early distinction between "performatives" and statements or "constatives" unsatisfactory: "Can we be sure that stating truly is a different *class* of assessment from arguing soundly, advising well, judging fairly, and blaming justifiably? Do these not have something to do in complicated ways with facts?"[191] "Stating" does not have a privileged relationship to facts; stating is just one of many illocutionary acts and is not unique in saying truth. Moreover, Austin agrees with Wittgenstein that the intentions and context of the utterance affect the statement made: "There are various *degrees and dimensions* of success in making statements: the statements fit the facts always more or less loosely, in different ways on different occasions, for different intents and purposes."[192] As we suggested above, truth may be said in many ways: truth and falsity need not be restricted to statements, for other speech acts also stand "in correspondence with" the facts.[193] Thus, God's promise (a performative) may be said to be "true" (Ps 18:30).

Austin concluded that the real distinction was not between performatives and statements or constatives but between various illocutionary forces.[194] In the statement, the illocutionary aspect is abstracted from the speech act, and truth is understood to be "what would be right to say in all circumstances, for any purpose, to any audience, &c."[195] Austin doubts that there are many statements that actually achieve such a universal intelligibility; most utterances are context-bound. In the performative utterance, we attend more to the illocutionary force and less to the propositional content and its correspondence with the facts. Both dimensions, however, are important; and Austin concludes his study of ordinary language by saying that every genuine speech act has both the locutionary and illocutionary dimension.

In Searle's work, Austin's seminal suggestions are modified and systematized in thorough analytic fashion. Searle defines language as a "rule-governed form of behavior."[196] Although Searle's *Speech Acts* is primarily concerned with sentences, literary forms and writing may also be viewed as "rule-governed" forms of behavior. Certain rules, for instance, govern "tragedy" (Aristotle's *Poetics* elaborates them) just as the convention of having the hero wear a white hat "governs" the genre of cowboy films.

According to Searle, the basic unit of linguistic communication is not the word nor the sentence but the speech act. A study of speech acts involves both *intention* (speaker's meaning) and *convention* (sentence meaning).[197] This incorporation of speaker's meaning and sentence meaning into speech act theory paves the way for a reconciliation between those biblical exegetes who investigate the formal features of the text in its final form and those who reconstruct the historical circumstances of the text in order to recover authorial intent. Or, in other words, the speech act approach combines the insights of Wittgenstein's early focus on sentence meaning with his later emphasis on sentence use.[198]

As did Austin before him, Searle works with the logical distinction between the meaning and force of the speech act. Consider four sentences:

1. David smote Goliath.
2. David smote Goliath?
3. David, smite Goliath!
4. May David smite Goliath.

Here we have four different speech acts. But note that what Austin termed the sense and reference (meaning) and what Searle calls the predication and reference (propositional content) is the same in each of the four sentences.[199] The referring expression ("David") serves to identify an individual person or object to whom the predication ("smiting Goliath") applies. The reference and predication together comprise the "proposition." In Searle's analysis, the *same proposition* (David smiting Goliath) is expressed in each of the four sentences: "Whenever two illocutionary acts contain the same reference and predication, provided that the meaning of the referring expression is the same, I shall say the same proposition is expressed."[200]

In treating the Bible as "ordinary literature," propositions are regained, although in revised form. With Searle and also P. T. Geach, we may define "proposition" as "a form of words in which something is propounded, put forward for consideration."[201] It is important to note that on Geach's account, there is a difference between "putting forward for consideration" and "putting forward for consideration *as true*" (assertion). We thus agree with Helm's description of Geach and Searle: "Both claim that the question 'Is it true or false' cannot be asked of propositions *simpliciter*, only of particular kinds of utterances."[202]

Searle identifies three things we do in speaking: utterance acts, propositional acts, and illocutionary acts. Significantly enough, Searle claims that the propositional act cannot stand on its own: "Propositional acts cannot occur alone; that is, one cannot *just* refer and predicate without making an assertion or asking a question or performing some other illocutionary act."[203]

Searle's understanding of propositional acts and propositions seems to conflict with the traditional concept of propositional revelation. For one thing, propositional acts cannot occur alone; there is always an illocutionary act that is simultaneously performed. More importantly, Searle holds that "*a proposition is to be sharply distinguished from an assertion or statement of it.*"[204] Though the propositional content (reference and predication) of sentences (1)–(4) above is identical, the illocutionary acts (force) is not. Searle offers "*F(p)*" as the symbolism of a speech act, where "*F*" stands for the kind of illocutionary force and "*p*" for the proposition. To put it simply, "*F*" indicates *how* a proposition is to be taken; "*F*" makes a proposition *count as* a warning, statement, etc.

How a proposition is to be taken is a matter of rules or convention. Some rules define, create, or "constitute" a form of activity. A promise *counts as* an obligation to do something in the future, just as a touchdown *counts as* six points in the language-game of football. In English, "I promise" conventionally counts as the making of a promise. Thus, what one *intends* to do (promise) is not just randomly related to what the sentence *means* ("I promise"). What, then, is the connection between the intentional act and the conventional meaning? Searle answers that the speaker intends his hearer to recognize his intention *by virtue of* his sentence meaning. By uttering "I promise," the speaker invokes the rules that govern the use of this expression and so attempts to get his audience to recognize his intention. If I say "My house is on fire," a correct understanding would involve recognizing that my intent is not to state an interesting fact about my domicile but to *warn* its inhabitants to flee and to *request* help.[205] Illocutionary uptake involves understanding not merely the meaning of a sentence but the force with which that meaning is to be taken. Unless the hearer recognizes my intent to warn, he has not truly understood my sentence, even if he knows what it "means" (its propositional content). Understanding, therefore, is knowing what the sentence *means* and what it *counts as*.

Instead of speech acts suffering from "infelicities," Searle prefers to speak of "defects." An illocutionary act is defective if the four conditions for its successful performance are not all satisfied. We illustrate these conditions with Searle's analysis of promising:

(1) Preparatory condition: the speaker believes his audience would like him to perform an act (if they did not, he would be making a threat rather than a promise).

(2) Propositional content condition: to make a promise, the proposition must predicate an act of the speaker, and it cannot be a past act.

(3) Sincerity condition: the speaker must truly intend to perform the future act predicated of him.

(4) Essential condition: the speaker intends for his utterance to count as an obligation to do a future action.

This last condition, as the name implies, is the most important, for it determines what an utterance counts as (e.g., promise, warning, request). Similarly, to make an assertion, the speaker must have evidence or reasons for supposing his proposition true (preparatory condition), he must believe his assertion to be true (sincerity condition), and he must intend his utterance to count as a representation of an actual state of affairs (essential condition).[206]

How many types of illocutionary acts are there, how many "*Fs*" of *F(p)*? Wittgenstein in his later phase believed that there were countless ways of using language, countless language-games. Searle, however, disagrees: "the illusion of limitless uses of language is engendered by an enormous unclarity about what constitutes the criteria for delimiting one language game or use of language from another."[207] In Searle's opinion, the essential condition forms the best basis for a "taxonomy" of illocutionary acts. The essential condition helps define the illocutionary point, not to be confused with illocutionary force. While the illocutionary *point* of both demanding and asking is to "get someone to do something," the illocutionary *force* of each varies in degree.

Searle also demarcates illocutionary acts according to the "direction of fit" between words and world. Assertions match propositional content with the world, but requests attempt to match the world with the words. Correctly perceiving the illocutionary point of an utterance is thus vital for determining how the propositional content is to be taken with regard to the world. Finally, Searle appeals to the different attitudes that the speaker expresses toward his propositional content (the sincerity condition)—"belief" for assertions and "desire" for requests.

On the basis of these three criteria—illocutionary point, direction of fit between words and world, speaker's attitude—Searle declares that there are only five basic things we do with language: "we tell people how things are, we try to get them to do things, we commit ourselves to doing things, we express our feelings and attitudes and we bring about changes through our utterances. Often, we do more than one of these at once in the same utterance."[208]

To this point we have limited our discussion to sentence-sized speech acts. Can we transpose the theory and consider literature rather than a speaker's utterance? To the extent that illocutionary force depends on facial expressions or vocal intonations, it is less inscribable than is propositional content. Yet Ricoeur admits that the "intentional exteriorization" of discourse in writing does succeed in inscribing the whole speech act.[209] Searle himself has made one foray into literary criticism by claiming that the only way to identify a work of literature as fictional is to determine the illocutionary intentions of the author.[210] In a work of fiction, writes Searle, the illocutionary acts are feigned: "What distinguishes fiction from lies is the existence of a separate set of conventions which enables the author to go through the motions of making statements which he knows to be not true even though he has no intention to deceive."[211] At the same time, Searle acknowledges the "serious" illocutionary acts performed by fictions: "Almost any important work of fiction conveys a 'message' or 'messages' which are conveyed *by* the text but are not *in* the text."[212] One example of a piece of fiction that carries a serious message would be Jesus' parables.[213]

Searle's programmatic suggestions for applying speech act theory to a theory of literature remain to be developed. Some preliminary work has been done. Mary Louise Pratt argues that literature too is a speech-context.[214] Like other speech acts, literary works depend upon culturally shared rules and conventions: "One of the most obvious kinds of contextual information we bring to bear in confronting a literary work is our knowledge of its genre."[215] Genre defines the *nature* of the communication situation. Susan S. Lanser has extended speech act theory to a study of narratives in particular: "In speech act theory I found a philosophical basis for understanding literature as communicative act and text as message-in-context."[216] As Barr has dismantled the linguistic theory behind the Biblical Theology movement, so Lanser is concerned to rebuke modern literary critics who deny the referential nature of literature: "Literature *is* communicative both in usage and intent, and the distinction between "literary" and "ordinary" language which poeticians have tended to assume is not supported by linguistic research."[217]

In light of these first steps in applying speech act theory to literature, we would like to propose (moving beyond Searle) that *there is a correlation between a text's genre, or literary form, and a text's illocutionary point and force.* If this principle is correct, then insensitivity to literary form entails a diminished appreciation of a text's peculiar force. While proponents of propositional revelation have cherished the (*p*) of the speech act *F(p)*, we have been arguing that the *F*'s have largely been overlooked, at least in formulations of a doctrine about Scripture. All five illocutionary points enumerated by Searle can be found in Scripture, and many biblical texts perform more than one act at once (e.g., report and warn or encourage).

A thorough analysis of the semantics of biblical literature needs to take account of four factors:

1. Proposition	— Fact	— Issue
2. Purpose	— Function	— Intention
3. Presence	— Form	— Incarnation
4. Power	— Force	— Illocution

1. Every text is "about" something, whether it is "David's smiting Goliath" or, in the case of Jesus' parable of the prodigal son, God's

forgiveness of repentant sinners.[218] Something in every text—the proposition—is propounded for some type of consideration. The issue of a text is "neutral" (in that we are not told how to take the particular fact propounded for consideration).

2. There is usually a reason for discourse. We speak or write in order to communicate something about something to someone. The propositional content is intended to function or count *as* something in the communicative act. The propositional content serves a specific purpose.

3. Once an author purposes to say something about something, he then seeks to express it in a particular form, a form that is appropriate for the purpose of his proposition.[219] The author's communicative intent is thus "incarnate" in a literary form that suits the message. The author is perhaps most "present" in the literary form of the letter, but his "voice" is present in other genres as well.[220] In the Gospel of John, for example, the authorial voice is that of the narrator, who is present to the reader as eyewitness to the things recounted.

4. The power, force, or illocution of a text depends on the combination of the proposition, the purpose of the author, and the particular form in which the author "incarnates" his authoritative voice and presence.

Throughout this study we have tried to supplement a concern for the truth of propositions with an appreciation of the power and purposes of Scripture's diverse literary forms. We have revised the notion of a proposition, following Searle and Geach, so that it means "something propounded for consideration." In its revised sense, "propositional revelation" has reference to the things that God has propounded for our consideration in Scripture. As Christian readers, we ought to be interested not only in the propositions themselves but in the manifold ways these propositions are presented for our consideration. In the context of Scripture's various genres, these propositions count as warnings, commands, prayers, questions, etc. as well as assertions.

We have seen that the Bible is eminently human—not in the sense that it errs, but in the sense of communicating to ordinary people in ordinary language and ordinary literature. In this way, the whole person, not only the intellect, is addressed by Scripture. As the apparent weakness of the incarnate Son of God was actually an essential factor in His accomplishing of God's redemptive purpose, so the apparent weakness of the incarnate biblical texts—their "humanity"—is an essential ingredient in their fulfilling of God's revelatory purpose.

VII. IMPLICATIONS FOR EXEGESIS AND THEOLOGY

A. GOD REVEALS HIMSELF IN THE BIBLE THROUGH INSCRIBED DISCOURSE ACTS

God makes Himself known through what He does and through what He says. And one of the things God *does* is speak. The "personal versus propositional" nature of God's revelation is a false dichotomy; God personally confronts us by means of the scriptural propositions that He propounds in various ways for our consideration. God spoke to Israel in Scripture, and Scripture itself is a collection of divine speech acts, which have been inscribed by human authors.

By speaking of revelation as divine discourse acts rather than as propositions, we intend to stress both the *meaning* and *force* of the divine revelation. John Frame observes that whereas liberalism emptied the Bible of power, neoorthodoxy emptied it of meaning.[221] Evangelicals, on the other hand, seek to acknowledge both meaning and power, and the model of the Bible as "ordinary literature" does this by holding the propositional and illocutionary acts together.

What Scripture says, God says. In Hebrews 1-2 alone, citations from canonical books as diverse as 2 Samuel, Deuteronomy, Isaiah, and the Psalms are attributed to God's saying.[222] Because God has performed these speech acts, we may say that revelation is verbal, rational, and informative. But revelation is also powerful, beautiful, memorable, encouraging, awesome, and demanding. These latter qualities are often lost under the heading of "propositional revelation" as traditionally conceived, which attends to Scripture's meaning at the expense of its power. The Bible is divine discourse act. The "divine" qualifies the literary forms of Scripture (the "microgenres," as it were) and so renders them "revelatory" (the "macrogenre"). Revealed truth may be said in many ways.

B. EXEGETES SHOULD NOT MAKE A PRIORI DECISIONS ABOUT BIBLICAL GENRES

The nature of a biblical text (the kind of discourse it is) should be determined only after a close reading and, if possible, a critical comparison with other ancient literary forms of the same type. Arguments from the supposed nature of truth to conclusions about what a genre "must" be are unsound. The purpose of exegesis is not to protect a correspondence theory of truth so much as to make clear what has been said in Scripture. Thus, the goal of exegesis will be a competent reading of the text, heeding both illocutionary intent (historical context) and literary convention (grammatical context). In this way, speech act theory continues the Reformation tradition of grammatical-historical exegesis and the priority of the literal sense.

C. SCRIPTURE DOES MANY THINGS WITH WORDS AND HENCE ITS AUTHORITY IS MULTIFACETED

The appropriate response to authoritative doctrine is intellectual belief or *assent*. But as we have seen, Scripture contains several other illocutionary points besides the Assertive. The Directives of Scripture are also authoritative, and obedience rather than intellectual assent is the appropriate response. Consider two types of Directives with varying degrees of force or intensity. The Proverbs have the authority of "wise sayings" and, as such, require thoughtful consideration and gradual integration into the very fabric of one's life. The Ten Commandments, on the other hand, are a more intense form of Directive and solicit absolute *obedience*.

Much of the Old Testament literature contains Commissive speech acts associated with the Covenant, whereby God commits Himself to a future course of action. God's promises of covenant blessings and deliverance have the authority of divine Commissives, the proper response to which is wholehearted *trust*. Assent, obedience, trust: these are all aspects of faith, but this should not be surprising. The richness of the faith-response simply matches the richness of the divine communication.

What of the authority of biblical texts with an Expressive illocutionary point? What kind of authority is shared by the Psalms, the Song of Moses (Ex 15), and Mary's Magnificat (Lk 1:46-55)? We may say that God is here using human Expressives to communicate something of the nature of human response when confronted with the majesty and character of God. As C. S. Lewis rightly observed, the response speaks eloquently (in a qualitatively precise manner) about the person who evoked it. These Expressives thus constitute normative responses in which the reader is invited to share and participate. We too must respond to injustice with laments and prayers for justice. We too must respond to God's mercy and love with sincere praise. We too must have imaginations captive to the vision of the kingdom of God. Not only our minds, but also our emotional responses are brought under scriptural authority.

D. INFALLIBILITY MEANS THAT SCRIPTURE'S DIVERSE ILLOCUTIONARY FORCES WILL INVARIABLY ACHIEVE THEIR RESPECTIVE PURPOSES

Perhaps the most surprising consequence of considering Scripture as a collection of divinely inspired discourse acts is the rehabilitation of the concept of infallibility. We have seen that both Austin and Searle allowed for the failure of some speech act performances; speech acts could be "infelicitous" or "defective." Like all other human acts, speech acts are fallible—liable to fail. God's speech, however, is not so susceptible. In any divine communication, the four conditions necessary for felicitous or nondefective speech acts are always fulfilled. God's locutions are always meaningful; the performance of the discourse act is always appropriate; the author is always sincere; the propositional content (predication and reference) is true (fitting) for its illocutionary mode. Isaiah said it better: "So shall my word be that goes forth from my mouth; it shall not return to me empty, but it shall accomplish that which I purpose, and prosper in the thing for which I sent it" (Isa 55:11 RSV).

Scripture is, therefore, indefatigable in its illocutionary intent. It encourages, warns, asserts, reproves, instructs, commands—all infallibly. Note that this makes inerrancy a *subset* of infallibility. On those occasions when Scripture does affirm something, the affirmation is true. Thus, we may continue to hold to inerrancy while at the same time acknowledging that Scripture does many other things besides assert. Logically, however, infallibility is prior to inerrancy. God's Word invariably accomplishes its purpose (infallibility); and when this purpose is assertion, the proposition of the speech act is true (inerrancy). Note too that inerrancy is subject to the intention and context of the assertive speech act. The parable of the prodigal son asserts that God forgives repentant sinners; it is not concerned to affirm that, in actual fact, a certain man had two sons who had a certain experience. However, the fact that Jesus uses the literary form of a parable results in the lesson being more memorable, vital, and powerful. When exegetes examine the total speech act situation, it will be seen that biblical texts are often more concerned with effective communication rather than scientific precision or exactness.

The Gospels, according to Ramm, "are *witnessing* or *kerygmatic* or *preaching* or *teaching* materials."[223] We might say that the illocutionary force of the Gospels is "proclaiming good news" (*euangelizo*). But, as Austin says, for any "performative utterance to be happy, certain statements have *to be true.*"[224] Not only must it be true that I *am* proclaiming good news, but it must also be true that there *is* good news to proclaim. The Gospels are not intelligible apart from their presupposition that there is in fact good news to proclaim. The Gospels, however, are not works of modern historians who are concerned with accurate documentation and "objective" description. Rather, the main purpose of the Gospels is to proclaim the good news of what has been done in Jesus Christ. Moreover, their canonical home makes the Gospels "authorized" announcements. Their illocutionary authority not only commands assent but also calls for repentance.

Is every sentence of the Gospels "true"? This question errs in ignoring the total discourse act context and literary form. Is it "true" that "A certain man had two sons"? The point is that we must determine the particular illocutionary force of the biblical texts before we ask whether they are true or false. For this reason, the predominant category in considering biblical authority should be that of infallibility rather than inerrancy. Infallibility is broader in scope, logically prior, and covers all of Scripture's authoritative functions.

At this point, because of the intrinsic importance and contemporary relevance of this our fourth implication, three possible objections to our proposal will now be considered. These three criticisms pertain to the (often subtle) distinctions between the *success, efficacy,* and *truth* of the divine speech acts. The first criticisms focus on the conditions for a successful and effective speech act; the third situates our proposed understanding of infallibility vis-à-vis other modern definitions.

The first objection runs as follows: could not a speech act conceivably contain an "error" and yet successfully achieve its purpose? Might not a warning that there is a bull loose in the china shop cause me to precipitate my departure from the premises, even if it should prove later to have only been a domesticated cow? Are we not, with our understanding of infallibility as "not liable to fail," defining the *success* of a speech act in terms of its *efficacy* rather than its *truth?* If so, then could not the Bible achieve its overall saving purpose and yet contain scientific, historical, and even doctrinal errors?

To meet this objection, we must review the necessary conditions for a successful performance of a speech act. We must also seek to specify exactly what it means for a speech act to "achieve its purpose." How do speech acts in general satisfy the three requisite conditions—sincere, propositional, preparatory—for a successful performance, and how are these three conditions "infallibly" satisfied by divine speech acts?

The sincerity condition simply stipulates that the speaker must be sincere. In the case of warning, for example, the speaker must really believe that a certain event is not in the best interest of the hearer. For an assertion, the speaker must really believe what is being said. Of course, the speaker who issued the warning about the bull may well have been sincere, even though he was mistaken. Significantly enough, we call his mistake a "false" alarm, whereas an insincere warning does not even qualify as a genuine warning. Sincerity, then, is a necessary condition for a successful speech act, but it is not a sufficient condition for the truth of warnings, promises, assertions, and so on. God's speech acts infallibly fulfill the sincerity condition because God never lies.

The propositional condition specifies the kinds of content that are appropriate for various illocutionary forces. Warnings, for example, must have as their propositional content some future event or state of affairs. A speech act that has some past event for its content ("Yesterday there *was* a bull in the china shop") cannot be a warning. *Successful* speech acts, then, have content that is suited to the illocution. Speech acts that say *truly*, on the other hand, are related to propositions in a more complicated way. A "true" warning, for instance, presupposes the truth of certain states of affairs and thus contains some tacit assertions to which the speaker is committed. A warning might be analyzed accordingly:

(1) There is now a bull in the china shop.
(2) This bull is dangerous.
(3) Take evasive action.

(Signed) A Friend

The speaker implicitly sanctions the truth of the tacit assertions (1) and (2) by crying out, "There's a bull in the china shop!" If either of the two assertions is false, then the warning is in some sense vitiated or falsified—even though it may prove *effective* in, say, vacating the shop floor in less than sixty seconds.

The preparatory condition tells us what the speaker *implies* in the performance of the speech act. By asserting, a speaker implies that there is evidence for the proposition; by warning, the speaker implies that there is reason to believe that something will occur that is not in the hearer's best interest. In the performance of any illocutionary act, the speaker implies that the preparatory conditions are satisfied (that the speaker is justified in the illocutionary intent). God's speech acts infallibly fulfill the propositional and preparatory conditions, for God is all-knowing.

A review of these three conditions has served to remind us that a speech act can be sincere, formally in order, justified, and yet false. To this extent the first objection makes a legitimate point: a speech act can achieve its illocutionary intent—that is, be successful—and yet be untrue. The real question raised by the first objection, therefore, pertains to the nature of the relation between the *success* of a speech act and the *truth* of a speech act; and the real concern behind the first objection is with the nature of Scripture's truth. By saying that speech acts infallibly achieve their purpose, it is objected that we are defining the truth of speech acts in terms of what is successful or effective—in terms of what *works*. This "pragmatic" theory of truth must be viewed as inadequate for defining Scripture's truth, for could not Scripture "work" in spite of its "errors"? Barr, indeed, seems to suggest as much when he claims that the power (i.e., "effect") of the biblical story comes from its literary features and does not depend on the events in the story having actually happened.

For Barr, perhaps, the truth of Scripture can be defined by its efficacy, but this is clearly insufficient for a doctrine of Scripture informed by speech act theory. The "pragmatic" theory of truth is confused in two important respects: it confuses (a) the *truth* of speech acts with their *success* and (b) the *success* of speech acts with their *efficacy*. Our review of the necessary conditions for speech acts was intended to show that for speech acts to be *successful*, certain formal conditions must obtain (sincere, propositional, preparatory). But for speech acts to be *true*, certain presupposed states of affairs must obtain.

Consequently, the pragmatic theory of the truth of speech acts is neither adequate to nor called for by speech act theory. Successful performance of speech acts alone does not guarantee truth. Indeed, the most telling point against the pragmatic construal of truth is that often something works for the wrong reason. Perhaps the clearest example of this is the epistemological situation where S may make a true assertion about X—but based on wrong or partial evidence. This situation is quite common. For example, I may conclude that someone is out of money *because* he is unemployed; but unbeknown to me he has inherited a good deal of money that he (still unbeknown to me) promptly donated to charity. My judgment about his fiscal state will be correct, but can it be said to be knowledge? I think not, for the correctness of my judgment was accidental. I believed the right thing for the wrong reason, and I was not entirely justified in deducing so much from so little.

Justification plays an important role in other speech acts as well. Consider once more the warning about the bull: the preparatory condition of this warning is that the speaker has *reason to believe* that an event (the bull's injuring me) will occur and not be in my best interest. Now imagine that I, in response to the speaker's warning, flee the building, which then immediately collapses, not as a result of the bull's charging, but because of an earthquake. I will have escaped unharmed, but can the speaker be said to have warned me? No, for he was not at all justified in warning me about an earthquake. Moreover, since the raging bull turned out to be a harmless cow, the speaker may have had reason to believe that danger was imminent, but he would have been wrong. If the speaker had been justified in believing me in danger from a bull, his speech act would have been at best successful but still false. However, divine warnings, since they infallibly fulfill the preparatory condition, will always be true, for God is all-knowing and will not only be justified in thinking that something is not in my best interest; He will be certain of it. When God asserts, His speech act implies that He has *certain* evidence for the truth of His assertion; when God warns, He has infallible reason to believe that something is not in the hearer's best interest.

To sum up our response to the first objection: an utterance may be a successful speech act, yet still be false. This is similar to being right for the wrong reason or accidentally. However, the divine speech acts will not only be successful; in infallibly satisfying the conditions that constitute a successful speech act, God's utterances will also be true. For not only is He sincere, but He also has an infallible justification for what He says. *God is never right for the wrong reason!*

While a "successful" speech act is based on certain formal conditions (sincere, preparatory, propositional), a "true" speech act is based on certain presuppositions that themselves must be true. These presuppositions pertain to the propositional content of the speech act, namely, the predication and reference. The predicate and reference indicate which state of affairs the speaker is committing himself to, and the illocutionary force determines the particular mode in which the question of the truth of the predicate expression is raised vis-à-vis the referent. If a divine warning depends upon latent assertions ("There is a bull in the china shop") for its truth, they must be true assertions, for God cannot fail to have *certain* knowledge of the states of affairs and preparatory conditions presupposed by His speech. In short, the success of a speech act must not be confused with its truth; but in the case of divine speech acts, infallible success implies infallible truth.

A second objection to our notion of infallibility is conversely related to the first: whereas the first maintained that success did not guarantee the truth of speech acts, the second criticism asks how a speech act can be considered true if it does *not* produce an effect on the hearer. Can a speech act be deemed true and successful if its effect is unfelt by the hearer? Can the Gospels infallibly succeed in their proclamatory purpose if readers refuse to believe?

This objection is related to the first, for both assume that to successfully achieve the purpose of a speech act is to be efficacious (to "work"). We have shown that such a pragmatic theory of truth is inappropriate for speech acts. But the error of the second objection is essentially its confusion of success and efficacy, or of the illocutionary and perlocutionary effects of speech acts. In the strict parameters of speech act theory, the illocutionary purpose does not involve producing an effect in the hearers. Searle explains the nature of the illocutionary effect: "But the 'effect' on the hearer is not a belief or response, it consists simply in the hearer understanding the utterance of the speaker. It is this effect that I have been calling the illocutionary effect."[225]

In other words, the intention or purpose of an illocutionary act is simply to be felt or understood for what it is. It is a matter of the hearer recognizing the nature of the speaker's meaning (i.e., as assertion, as warning, as question). What the hearer does after recognizing the kind of illocution of the utterance is irrelevant from the standpoint of the success of the speech act itself. We shall conclude, then, that the success of an illocutionary act is constituted not by its having an effect on a hearer (apart, that is, from the limited effect of producing recognition of the illocution) but rather by its satisfaction of the three conditions without which any speech act is defective.

This distinction between the success and efficacy of speech acts has some interesting implications for our doctrine of Scripture. Consider the following verses: "The heavens declare the glory of God; the skies proclaim the work of his hands. . . . There is no speech or language where their voice is not heard. Their voice goes out into all the earth, their words to the ends of the world" (Ps 19:1,3–4). Here the creation is said to "declare" or "proclaim" the glory of God—no mean illocutionary act! Of course, the heavens do not speak verbally, but their communication is nevertheless so clear that the psalmist speaks of their "voice." But now compare this with Paul's statement that God is angry with man for rejecting this cosmic communication "since what may be known about God is plain to them, because God has made it plain to them. For since the creation of the world God's invisible qualities—his eternal power and divine nature—have been clearly seen" (Ro 1:19–20a).

The point of this example is that the clarity—yes, success—of God's communication about Himself through nature does not depend on its producing a particular effect (belief, worship) on human beings. God's revelation is successful even if no one explicitly acknowledges it; the fault or lack of effect is not a weakness in God's speech act but rather a weakness in humans. The efficacy of speech acts (their successful realization of their illocutionary purpose) is to be understood simply as their satisfaction of the conditions necessary for bona fide speech acts. The "purpose" of speech acts is to mean—and to mean clearly. In this, Scripture succeeds admirably.

The third and last possible objection is the most serious. Does not our concept of infallibility lead to a theory of "partial" or "limited" inerrancy? If infallibility means that speech acts are performed successfully, could not some "successful" assertions turn out to be false? We have already admitted in discussing the first objection that success does not guarantee truthfulness. If it did, there could never be anything such as a false assertion, a false promise, a false alarm. I may successfully assert (i.e., satisfy all necessary conditions—including having a good reason for my assertion) that my tie is blue, but it may in fact be red. Success alone in illocution does not guarantee truth. Successfully performed assertions may be real assertions and still be false.

We need, therefore, to refine the meaning of "success," for speech acts are "liable to fail" in two quite different respects. In the strict sense, speech acts fail when something goes wrong with the speech act itself—a flaw, misfire, or abuse. In these cases the speech act never gets off the ground, as it were, and fails to perform its intended illocution. But in another sense of "liable to fail," speech acts fail when they are false. A false assertion or false alarm is in some sense a failure. Only divine speech acts are infallible; only divine speech acts are not "liable to fail" in either sense of the term.

But do we not fall into the class of those who limit the inerrancy of Scripture by relegating truth to only one category of speech acts, i.e., assertions? Are those passages or texts in Scripture whose illocutionary point is other than assertive not susceptible to truth or falsity? This way of construing the matter is clearly not adequate, for we have seen that the Bible itself (as well as ordinary language) refers to, say, "true" promises (Commissives). We have also seen that speech acts with nonassertive illocutionary points nevertheless presuppose certain states of affairs and believe they are "justified" in doing so. Nonassertive speech acts (warnings, promises) may thus be "true" in a secondary sense. These speech acts are true in a secondary sense because they do not "thematize" the question of truth. That is, while the principal issue of assertives is the truth or falsity of a certain state of affairs, the principal purposes of other types of illocutionary acts is something other than representing an actual state of affairs. However, we have discussed several examples where the truth of nonassertive illocutionary acts depends on the truth of certain presupposed states of affairs ("There really *is* a dangerous bull in the china shop").

What we need is an expanded notion of truth as correspondence, a notion that is broad enough to include this secondary sense in which nonassertive illocutions may be said to be true. I suggest that the *nature of the correspondence to reality* (and thus the nature of the truth) of an utterance is determined by its illocutionary aspect and literary form. Scientific statements involve one type of correspondence to reality, poetic statements another. But in this broader sense of the term, even speech acts that are not Assertives may properly be said to "correspond to" reality. The warning about the bull does not correspond to—does not "fit"—the situation, unless there *is* a dangerous bull on the shop floor. Conversely, should there be a dangerous bull in the china shop, the warning may be said to "fit" the situation and correspond to a concrete reality—or, in other words, to be "true."

To say, then, that speech acts are infallible is to say (1) that the speech acts satisfy the necessary formal conditions for the *successful* performance of a particular illocutionary act (i.e., the speaker sincerely believes that he is justified in what he is saying) and (2) that the speech acts *correspond to* reality in a manner appropriate for their particular illocutionary mode. Again, the nature of the correspondence (or the "kind" of truth) that is invoked by a speech act can only be determined by a close analysis of its illocutionary force or intent.

Perhaps a brief survey of the history of the term "infallible" will make even clearer the rather novel and yet traditional sense in which I am using it. "Infallible" has a long history and until recently was the church's near unanimous choice for expressing its high view of Scripture as "exempt from the liability to err" or "not liable to fail." This traditional sense of infallibility is virtually identical with the meaning of the more recent term "inerrancy"—freedom from error. "Inerrancy" was introduced into the discussion of Scripture only when "infallibility" was perceived no longer to function with the same meaning. Under duress from two centuries of biblical criticism, some modern theologians have declared that the Bible was no longer "wholly trustworthy" in matters of science and history. "Infallibility" has, in the twentieth century, come to be restricted to "matters of faith and practice." This second or revised sense of infallibility limits inerrancy to Scripture's speech on religious matters.

This revised sense of infallibility has surfaced in various quarters. Post-Vatican II Roman Catholic theology considers the Bible inerrant only when it touches on matters concerning the divine salvific intent. This viewpoint has its adherents among Protestants as well. Daniel P. Fuller, for example, in the judgment of Pinnock, "wants to define the macro-purpose of the Bible in soteric terms, and proportion inerrancy to it."[226] This revised notion of infallibility has even found its way into I. Howard Marshall's recent work: "The purpose of God in the composition of Scripture was to guide people to salvation. . . . We may therefore suggest that 'infallible' means that the Bible is entirely trustworthy for the purposes for which God inspired it."[227] In a review of the book, D. A. Carson observes: "Marshall argues that this analysis has the effect of shifting the focus away from the truth of the Bible to its adequacy for what God intends it to do."[228]

It should be obvious by now that this revised sense of infallibility is diametrically opposed to our proposed rehabilitation of the concept of infallibility as sketched out in this chapter. The revised, or limited, notion of infallibility errs in viewing the Bible as a single type of literature unified by its overarching salvific purpose. Despite the element of truth in this construal, the distinctive intents of the various literary genres are by and large smoothed over to make a seamless canon that is efficacious to God's salvific purpose and that thus enjoys "saving" truth. But to fit the diverse literary forms of Scripture into one mold—be it religious, salvific, or canonical literature—is to violate the semantics of biblical literature. Even an "infallible" Procrustean bed is too short! As we have seen in discussing the first objection, success in achieving a purpose—even a salvific purpose— cannot alone constitute the truth of a text or speech act.

Furthermore, by insisting that Scripture is trustworthy only in matters of faith and practice, a theological a priori is once again at work to frustrate the diverse illocutionary intents of Scripture as revealed by a careful examination of the literary phenomena them- selves. By noting the various illocutionary intents of the sundry literary genres, our proposed notion of infallibility affirms that Scripture is trustworthy in all matters on which it intends to speak. Against those who hold too narrow a view of inerrancy, we have pointed out that Scripture's truthfulness involves more than mere adherence to a principle of strict historical correspondence. The manifold ways in which texts say truly, we have argued, include more than wooden historical correspondence. On the other hand, our proposed view of infallibility must acknowledge those biblical texts that do indeed have as one of their primary purposes the communication of historical information (an acknowledgment that New Biblical theologians are reticent to give). In these cases too, as in any others, Scripture speaks infallibly.

Inerrancy and infallibility are mere terms, theological constructs that serve as convenient shorthand in expressing one's view regarding Scripture's truth and trustworthiness. Paul Feinberg states the real issue succinctly: "It is the concept of a *wholly true* Bible for which I contend. If some better word can be found, then let us use it."[229] Carson observes that the newer term "inerrancy" is merely intended to do the same work once accomplished by the older "infallibility."[230] Feinberg offers the following definition of inerrancy: "Inerrancy means that when all the facts are known, the Scriptures in their original autographs and properly interpreted will be shown to be wholly true in everything they affirm, whether that has to do with doctrine or morality or with the social, physical, or life sciences."[231]

Our proposed rejuvenation of the concept of infallibility set forth here preserves the substance of the above-mentioned definition of "inerrancy" and at the same time puts the semantics of biblical literature on the surer ground of a speech act philosophy of language and literature that does fullest justice to the notion of "not liable to fail." Our understanding of infallibility is thus in profound agreement with earlier statements of inerrancy (i.e., the Ligonier statement and the Chicago statement) even while moving beyond them. Our proposed view of infallibility assumes the concept of inerrancy and expands it to cover (in a secondary sense) all God's speech acts and all Scripture's literary forms, rather than having application only to direct affirmations or the "philosophical propositions" extracted from Scripture. Inerrancy is "expanded" because we have seen that Scripture "corresponds" in many ways to a variety of "facts" according to the illocutionary intent.

Scriptural truth is neither enslaved to the idea of correspondence to historical fact alone nor relegated to the realm of faith and practice. Rather, as infallible, Scripture successfully and truly speaks about many things in many ways, all of which "correspond" to reality. Far from limiting inerrancy, our proposed sense of infallibility actually enlarges it and makes clear the ways in which Scripture may be said to be both successful in its meaning-intents and wholly true. Scripture speaks truth in many ways.

E. THEOLOGY IS "ORDINARY LITERATURE" ANALYSIS OF AN EXTRAORDINARY BOOK

Though theology is undoubtedly *more* than critical reflection on Scripture, it is certainly not less. Barr and Kelsey maintain that some relation with Scripture is inherent in the very notion of Christian theology. Furthermore, even theologians who reject inerrancy often wish to remain "biblical." According to practitioners of analytic philosophy, a careful study of ordinary language is the "begin-all" if not the "end-all" of philosophical investigation. Austin believed that the subtle differences in ordinary language provide insights into philosophical concepts and tell us something about the world. Similarly, we suggest that theology may be viewed as an analysis of the "ordinary literature" of Scripture. As such, theology pursues an intelligent reading of Scripture, noting both propositions and illocutionary intents and rendering them coherent. In his "Ordinary Language Analysis and Theological Method," Arthur Holmes speaks of "ordinary" Scripture:

> Its literary diversity is more than a historic accident or a decorative device; it is a vehicle for imaginative thought and creative expression about things difficult to grasp. Analogy, metaphor, symbol, poetry—these and other forms cannot be translated without risking cognitive loss into univocal and pseudo-scientific form.[232]

Systematic theology attempts to give a coherent articulation of the Christian vision or world view, as presented through Scripture's literary forms. At the same time, theology is conscious of its second-order status as a discourse. Because it stresses logical consistency, theology is prone to lose noncognitive aspects of Scripture's communication (such as its force).

Does this mean that the actual literary form is indispensable, that we can only have, say, "narrative theology"? No, for theology can attempt to describe what it cannot conceptually paraphrase. But theologians are bound to their texts unlike secular literary critics, for theology's text is extraordinary: it is the word of God. Theologies, then, are never substitutes for Scripture (for what God has said in ordinary literature to ordinary people). Rather, theology is the humble attempt to receive God's extraordinary communication in all the fullness of its meaning, power, and truth.[233]

CHAPTER THREE

THE PLACE OF HISTORICAL RECONSTRUCTION IN NEW TESTAMENT CRITICISM

Moisés Silva

Moisés Silva

Moisés Silva is Professor of New Testament at Westminster
Theological Seminary, Philadelphia, Pennsylvania. He is a graduate of
Bob Jones University (B.A.), Westminster Theological Seminary (B.D.,
Th.M.), and the University of Manchester (Ph.D.). He also did graduate
work in Semitics at Dropsie University. Prior to his present position he
taught for nine years at Westmont College, where he also served as
chairman of the Department of Religious Studies. He has written two
books—*New Testament Survey* and *Biblical Words and Their Meaning*—and some periodical articles. He is the editor of the *Westminster
Theological Journal* and a member of the Society of Biblical Literature
and the International Organization for Septuagint and Cognate
Studies.

THE PLACE OF HISTORICAL RECONSTRUCTION IN NEW TESTAMENT CRITICISM

Not long ago, a biblical scholar polemicized against the doctrine of inerrancy by stating that the Bible is not a history textbook. I have heard that argument before, but all the same it reflects considerable naïveté with regard to how the doctrine of inerrancy is understood by those who hold to it. This particular scholar gave the distinct impression that, in his opinion, people holding to that doctrine have not given much thought to the character and purpose of the Bible. Surely—he appeared to reason—if we could briefly educate them on this issue, they will abandon their view of an inerrant Bible. How might he react if he knew that students in Fundamentalist schools are routinely warned not to misuse the Bible by treating it as a textbook for history, science, etc.?[1]

But then a related question comes to mind: To what extent have misunderstandings created unnecessary conflicts between a conservative and a nonconservative approach to critical questions? If the scholar mentioned above had understood that all responsible formulations of biblical inerrancy have emphasized that the Bible is *not* to be read as a scientific treatise, he might have discovered that at least some of his concerns were unnecessary. Conversely, those Evangelicals who take seriously their position that the Bible is not an academic textbook will discover that their suspicions of higher-critical methods and conclusions are not always well-founded.

It may be worth our while, therefore, to inquire more particularly whether the debates that arise from attempts to *reconstruct* biblical history are vitiated by misunderstandings on the part of both conservatives and nonconservatives. It would be a monumental error, of course, to suggest that the differences between these two groups can be reduced to a question of semantics. One cannot wish away the fundamental antithesis between a scholar who affirms that indeed *all* of Scripture is God's very breath (2Ti 3:16) and one who does not. Accordingly, this essay is not an attempt to minimize the differences, but to clarify them—not an effort to eliminate polemics, but to make sure that the debate focuses on the real issues.

I. THE TASK OF HISTORICAL RECONSTRUCTION

At the outset, some comments are necessary about the very concept of historical reconstruction. The term *reconstruction* suggests to many Evangelicals that the biblical data are being regarded as deficient and are therefore in need of revision. But this word need not be taken in a pejorative sense. Indeed, historical reconstruction is one of the favorite pastimes among Evangelicals, for that is precisely what goes on when a student seeks to harmonize two narratives.

For example, even an unsophisticated Bible student will notice, sooner or later, that the order of Christ's temptations in Matthew 4:1–11 differs from that given in Luke 4:1–12. Both Evangelists agree on the *first* temptation (stones to bread), but what Matthew gives as the second (the pinnacle of the temple) appears as the third in Luke. Here our student is faced with a *formal* contradiction (that is, an "apparent discrepancy," to use a common label); he or she wants to know whether it is also a *material* (or "real") contradiction. The moment we ask "What was the actual order of events?" we are involved in historical reconstruction. Of course, several approaches are possible:

(1) There were really four temptations, with the second repeated after the third. (I have never seen this solution proposed, but it is not qualitatively different from certain other extreme attempts at harmonization.)

(2) Matthew gives the actual order, as suggested by *tote* "then" and *palin* "again" (4:5,8; contrast *kai* and *de* in Lk 4:5,9). Luke was not interested in the chronological question but wanted to emphasize the dramatic character of the second temptation and so put it at the end. (This is the most common conservative solution.)[2]

(3) The question cannot really be answered from the texts and is somewhat irrelevant anyway, for *neither* Evangelist appears to be concerned with chronological issues.[3]

(4) The narrative may be "the distillation of a conflict Jesus experienced again and again throughout his ministry."[4] Perhaps they were visionary experiences that cannot be adequately handled under the rubric of historicity.

(5) The story is laden with supernatural elements beyond the reach of the historian; the account is, therefore, legendary, with little or no basis in fact.

Most readers of this study will find reconstructions (1) and (5) unacceptable. Option (4), though adopted by some Evangelicals, is generally avoided in the conservative camp. Either (2) or (3) would be viewed as clearly compatible with biblical inerrancy, but option (3) in particular helps us to identify the nature of our difficulty, namely, *uncertainty due to incomplete information.* For some conservative Christians, certainty about historical details appears to be inseparable from a high view of Scripture. Such a connection is valid, however, only where Scripture speaks directly and unambiguously on the historical question involved.

Hardly anything is more crucial to the Christian faith than the historicity of Jesus' life, death, and resurrection, yet no one knows for sure the date of Jesus' birth nor the year of His death and resurrection. Because biblical information regarding the time of Jesus' birth is *incomplete*, Evangelicals accept the reality of *uncertainty* on that issue. Any attempts to fill the gaps in our knowledge, to collect other kinds of evidence, to draw inferences, and to synthesize the results of this research by theorizing when Jesus may have been born—this is historical reconstruction.

Most Evangelicals, then, would agree that historical statements asserted in the Bible may be incomplete but not false. A more delicate question arises when it is suggested that incomplete information, in the very nature of the case, is defective and inevitably distorts the picture. This inference, however, is legitimate only when the given information is put to a use different from that intended by the writer. An architect might regard Jesus' parable of the wise and foolish builders (Mt 7:24–27) as "defective" if one treats the passage as a manual for the construction of skyscrapers. Some nonconservatives are too quick to use terms like "inadequate" and "faulty" when describing biblical information that was written down with a purpose quite different from that for which they are using it.

Sometimes, however, conservatives are equally at fault in neglecting the purpose of specific portions of Scripture. If a narrative in the Bible has a clear polemic intent, we can hardly treat it as we might treat an encyclopedia article. Take, for example, the figure of Herod Agrippa I. He appears in Scripture only in Acts 12, where we read that he (1) executed James, (2) imprisoned Peter, (3) executed the soldiers assigned to guard Peter, (4) accepted the blasphemous compliments of the Phoenician representatives, and (5) was struck down by an angel of the Lord. If this is all we know about Herod Agrippa I, and if we assume that the narrative is intended to give a balanced assessment of the king's total administration, we will conclude that the man was a monster.

In fact, however, Agrippa's three-year reign over Judea was regarded by the people as incomparably better than the rule they had experienced under Herod the Great, Archelaus, and the Roman governors. Josephus tells us that Agrippa "had a gentle disposition and he was a benefactor to all [Jews and Gentiles] alike. He was benevolent to those of other nations and exhibited his generosity to them also." In dealing with an opponent "he considered mildness a more royal trait than passion, and was convinced that considerate behavior is more becoming in the great than wrath."[5] No doubt for reasons of political expediency, Agrippa favored the Pharisees, conformed to the Jewish customs, and treated the people well. The spread of Christianity threatened his plans, however, and so he attempted to crush the church; in his pride he took upon himself the glory that belongs to God, and the divine judgment upon him was swift. The facts affirmed in Acts 12 are correct and also adequate to the writer's purpose, but they are "inadequate" for a modern historian who seeks to provide a total picture of Agrippa's reign. It would be wrong to deny the accuracy of Josephus' account (which does not really contradict Acts) or to reject a historical reconstruction that seems to put Agrippa in a better light than Acts does. But it is not less objectionable to describe the account in Acts as erroneous or untrustworthy simply because the information is incomplete and slanted toward the particular purpose of that book.

These introductory comments have focused on three examples that present relatively minor problems: the order of Jesus' temptation, the precise dates of Jesus' birth and death, and the evaluation of Agrippa's reign. They are "minor" problems because they have little effect on fundamental questions. Thus, whether we date Jesus' crucifixion in A.D. 30 or 33 does not significantly alter any basic element of biblical history (that Jesus did die under Pontius Pilate during Passover week), nor does it alter the theological implications of that history. If I may assume agreement with the salient points of the discussion so far, we may move on to historical issues of greater moment.

II. RECONSTRUCTING FIRST-CENTURY PHARISAISM

A. THE PROBLEM

Our first major problem area not only affects a significant historical question regarding the social and religious setting of the New Testament; it also raises doubts concerning the trustworthiness of Jesus' teaching as recorded in the Gospels. I refer to the New Testament depiction of the Pharisees. On the basis of the Gospel narratives, many conservative Christians have formed a wholly negative impression of first-century Judaism, especially as represented by the Pharisees. If John the Baptist called them vipers (Mt 3:7) and Jesus referred to them as hypocrites (Mt 23:13,15, etc.); if they performed religious duties for show (Mt 23:5–7), were full of greed (v 25), and placed obstacles on those who sought to enter the kingdom (v 13); if they plotted Jesus' death and were thus instrumental in having Him crucified (Mk 3:6; Jn 11:47–53; 18:3)—if all this and more is true, then apparently these Jewish leaders had no redeeming qualities. Accordingly, the usual modern conception or *reconstruction* of the Pharisees is that of a self-righteous group, full of pride and wickedness, parading an external show of religion, misinterpreters of the law who oppressed the common folk with their unreasonable legalism.

To be sure, a careful reader of the Gospel material will notice some items that conflict with such a reconstruction. In Matthew 23:3, for example, Jesus appears to commend the teaching of the Pharisees (though the meaning of this verse is debated). Again, the parable of the Pharisee and the publican (Lk 18:9–14), while it condemns the Pharisee, makes sense only if we appreciate the role reversal it implies: the wicked publican, not the one *generally regarded as righteous*, goes home justified. But these and other elements have traditionally been ignored in conservative reconstructions of Pharisaic Judaism. For example, a Bible dictionary widely used in the nineteenth and early twentieth centuries says of the Pharisees that "they had in Christ's day degenerated largely into a self-conscious and formal religiosity" that made piety dependent on "ritual rather than moral" acts. We are further told that "pride and hypocrisy were their prominent characteristics," and they were "the slaves of lust, and avarice, and pride."[6] A recent and very popular reference work characterizes Pharisaism (in contrast to Christianity) with five points: (1) the Pharisees taught "a servile adherence to the letter of the law," so that its moral precepts were undermined; (2) "the Pharisees multiplied minute precepts," so that "the law was almost, if not wholly, lost sight of"; (3) they "undervalued and neglected the "inward spirit" and "great rules of life," so that "the idea of religion as that which should have its seat in the heart disappeared"; (4) they "sought mainly to attract attention and excite the admiration of men"; and (5) they "made a prey of the friendless" and "were in reality avaricious, sensual, and dissolute."[7]

Contrast these descriptions to that found in a highly regarded non-Evangelical Bible dictionary, which argues that the negative view of the Pharisees "is being corrected by scientific research, both Christian and Jewish." "A wide historical study discovers moral dignity and greatness in Pharisaism." In contrast to the exclusiveness of the priesthood, "the Pharisees and the Scribes opened a great career to all the talents." When a reader "notes the striking freedom of the New Testament from ritualistic and sacerdotal ideas, he should give credit to Pharisaism as one of the historical forces which made these supreme qualities possible."[8] This positive reinterpretation of the Pharisees has received considerable impetus from current Jewish-Christian dialogue (indeed, one wonders at times whether the ecumenical spirit has not tended to distort history in its own way). At any rate, nonconservative scholars frequently suggest—and at times explicitly state—that the Gospel material is untrustworthy. One interesting approach is simply to ignore that material. A recent and very significant work, for example, introduces the subject of the Pharisees by pointing out that our main sources (the Gospels, Josephus, the Mishnah) are biased; the author then manages to reconstruct first-century Pharisaism without one reference to the negative portrait in the Gospels.[9]

In support of a positive view of the Pharisees, one can appeal to Josephus, who makes several references to them in his writings. In one passage he states that the Pharisees are

> extremely influential among the townsfolk; and all prayers and sacred rites of divine worship are performed according to their exposition. This is the great tribute that the inhabitants of the cities, by practising the highest ideal both in their way of living and in their discourse, have paid to the excellence of the Pharisees.[10]

Even after we make allowance for Josephus' prejudices, his testimony appears to conflict with that of the Gospels. Is it really likely that large groups of religious people would have admired the Pharisees if they had been avaricious and dissolute? Even more significant than Josephus are the documents of rabbinic Judaism, such as the Mishnah, the Talmud, and Midrashim—writings that are generally thought to reflect the views of Pharisaic Judaism (but see below). While these works contain features that suggest the need for some of Jesus' criticisms, one is hard pressed to find evidence of greed, hypocrisy, lack of concern for the "spirit" of the law, or an emphasis on ritual acts at the expense of moral acts.

B. THE SOLUTION

In the light of this apparently conflicting evidence, how does one proceed to reconstruct first-century Pharisaism? The conservative Christian is jealous to guard the infallibility of our Lord's teaching, much of which He expressed by contrasting it to the views of the Pharisees. If His assessment of the rabbis was off the mark, the validity of His message becomes suspect at a fundamental level.[11] On the other hand, for those who do not accept the infallibility of Jesus' teaching as recorded in the Gospels, an interest in historical objectivity—defined in such a way as to preclude divine revelation—takes priority. Given these opposing starting points, it is almost inevitable that divergent reconstructions of Pharisaism will result; yet one can argue that a considerable measure of agreement on this question is possible if the following points are taken into account.

1. The Gospels confirm Josephus' testimony that the common people generally held the Pharisees in high regard as religious and moral leaders. As pointed out earlier, the parable of the Pharisee and the publican has a shock value—it *assumes* that Pharisees are viewed

as paragons of virtue. In fact, the very nature of Jesus' controversy with them makes sense only if Josephus' description is basically correct. This point is granted by conservatives and nonconservatives alike. What some conservatives have failed to appreciate, however, is that the people's high regard for the Pharisees *as moral examples* is inexplicable if the Pharisees as a group were "the slaves of lust, and avarice, and pride," if they "made a prey of the friendless" and could be characterized as "dissolute." In other words, it is clear that one important element in some conservative reconstructions clashes with the very testimony of the Gospels and, therefore, must be jettisoned.

2. Not all Pharisees were alike. The Mishnah itself speaks of the "wounds" (or "plagues") of the Pharisees (*Sota*, 3.4). The commentary on this passage in the Babylonian Talmud contains the famous description of seven types of Pharisees, including those who were actuated by impure motives, those who practiced their religion ostentatiously, etc.[12] The biblical material itself suggests that Jesus' more severe criticisms, particularly those that addressed *moral* weaknesses (e.g., Mk 12:40; Lk 16:14), applied restrictively to some, not all, Pharisees; consider, for example, Jesus' commendation of a wise scribe (Mk 12:34), John's portrayal of Nicodemus (Jn 7:50–51), and the presence of Christian Pharisees in the church (Ac 15:5).

The methodological significance of this point is that *informal generalizations* in the Bible (or elsewhere) *should not be confused with a historian's endeavor to generalize in a more or less scientific fashion.* In daily conversations and informal speeches, we accept without offense broad generalizations that we know cannot be substantiated. ("Car mechanics are thieves" in this type of context means, "The last two times I had my car worked on I paid more money than seems fair.") Thus, when Jesus says that the Pharisees "love the place of honor at banquets," we may understand that criticism as an informal generalization: those who are listening and who know that Jesus cannot be describing all (perhaps not even most) Pharisees understand the contextual restrictiveness of the statement and appreciate its force—self-importance was a temptation to which Pharisees, because of their position, were particularly susceptible.

3. Closely related to the previous point is the legitimate role that hyperbole can play in Scripture. According to Matthew 23:5, Jesus said: "Everything they do is done for men to see." This is more than generalization—it is an "absolutization," but clearly it is not meant in an absolute sense. In verse 3 Jesus had told the crowds to "do everything they tell you," but I know of no one who would take that statement literally.

4. Another consideration of a semantic nature is the use of the word "hypocrite," which in English has an unusually strong pejorative sense. The Greek *hypokritēs*, like its English cognate, indicates inconsistency between what one says and what one does, but it

would be difficult to prove that the Greek word carries the offensive overtones (such as dishonorable motives) that we normally associate with the English word. Paul describes the behavior of Peter and other Jews in Antioch as *hypokrisis*, but it is unlikely that he was thereby impugning their motives.

5. As noted earlier in connection with Acts 12, a statement made with a polemical purpose cannot be treated as one would treat an "objective" encyclopedia article. Jesus' woes in Matthew 23 were not intended to address the questions that twentieth-century historians might ask concerning Pharisaism. The Pharisaic features Jesus chose to point out and the tone of the descriptions were intended to serve a particular purpose; therefore, when this material, infallible as it is, is used for quite a different purpose, one must guard against possible distortion.

6. What is true of Jesus' statements in their historical setting is also true of the Gospel narrative in its literary setting. We must not ignore the fact that the extensive discourse of Matthew 23 is distinctive to Matthew and that it fits the polemic so characteristic of this Gospel. Without suggesting that the Evangelist has misrepresented Jesus' teaching, we may readily agree that Matthew's particular slant has affected his presentation: perhaps this chapter reflects some of the author's own struggles with Judaism at the time of composition.

7. We move to a different set of questions when we consider the proper use of the rabbinic literature. The earliest of these writings (the Mishnah) was not published until well over a century after the Gospels were composed. To be sure, the document embodies a corpus of oral traditions that had been passed on for generations, but the dating of these traditions is fraught with difficulties, and some scholars, notably Jacob Neusner, are very skeptical about how much we can know about pre-A.D. 70 Pharisaism.[13] Against any extreme skepticism, one can argue plausibly that the *main features* of Jewish religious attitudes and the *basic outlines* of rabbinic thought as represented in the Mishnah accurately reflect Palestinian Judaism at the time of Jesus (even if we are uncertain about the dating of specific customs and laws). Nonetheless, it cannot be doubted that the destruction of the temple played a fundamental role in the development of Jewish tradition; the resulting discontinuity between pre-70 and post-70 Judaism may account for some of the discrepancies between the Gospels and rabbinic literature.

8. But even if we grant a significant measure of continuity between first-century Judaism and the Mishnah, we still face a problem of interpretation. Most scholars operate within a framework that identifies the Pharisees depicted in the Gospels as the precursors of rabbinic Judaism. This seems to me a defensible interpretation of the evidence, but not all specialists agree. In particular, one should

acknowledge the work of Phillip Sigal, who views the Pharisees as "a complex of pietists and separatists who made up a segment of Judaism and included such known entities as Essenes and Qumranites as well as other unknown groups that proliferated at the time."[14] According to Sigal, the Pharisees constituted only one element in the formation of rabbinic Judaism, whereas the true "proto-rabbis"—a somewhat insignificant force in the first part of the first century— were not among Jesus' antagonists. If one accepts this reconstruction, then our problems are solved with one stroke. I do not believe that Sigal's views will be generally accepted (the similarities between the Pharisees of the Gospels and the later rabbis are too significant, as we shall see below), but he has brought together considerable evidence to prove that a simple identification of the Pharisees with the rabbis is quite unacceptable. In other words, we have good reason to believe that *some* of the objectionable features of the Pharisees were never characteristic of Jewish religious leadership in general and that therefore these features are not prominent in the rabbinic literature.

9. The evidence from Josephus too has come under scrutiny. Some scholars have noted that his presentation (particularly in *Antiquities*) differs in some important respects from what both the Gospels and the rabbinic literature preserve. While the differences do not affect directly our primary concerns, it is important to point out that even Josephus, though he writes at much greater length than the Evangelists, cannot avoid a very selective, and therefore incomplete, depiction of the Pharisees.[15]

We have thus far noted that our three primary sources—the Gospels (1–6), the rabbinic literature (7–8), and Josephus (9)—give us very limited information and are therefore somewhat inadequate *for the purpose of historical reconstruction*. But now we must address a more significant set of questions, namely, the precise nature of the conflict between Jesus and the Pharisees.

10. Is it accurate to say that Jesus condemned the Pharisees for their *legalism?* The answer to this question would be easy if all parties involved were to agree on the meaning of *legalism* and its derivatives.

a. Most commonly, the term is used as a "slur word" to describe and condemn anyone who happens to take a stricter view of conduct than that taken by the speaker. We may ignore this particular use, but as we shall presently see, we make a serious error when we consider the Pharisees as "too strict."

b. Closely related is the use of *legalist* to refer to people who appear to us to be "picky," overly concerned with relatively trivial matters, particularly when such an attitude is accompanied by lack of concern for significant issues. One can argue, on the basis of Matthew 23:23–24, that at least some of the Pharisees could be characterized this way, but this type of criticism is not prominent in Jesus' teaching and does not by itself disclose the heart of the issue.

c. A third meaning is that which focuses more formally on questions of *law*. That the Jews were preoccupied with legal issues goes without saying: the massive amount of material brought together in the Talmud consists primarily of attempts to interpret, apply, and expand those Old Testament laws intended to regulate the life of God's people. Some Christians who seem too ready to scoff at the many involved legal discussions of the Talmud forget that our modern legal system is incomparably more detailed. (Tax regulations alone could easily challenge the whole of Jewish *halakah* for complexity!) To be sure, one may point out that our legal system is not intended to legislate our religious behavior; no doubt the rabbis were often in danger of equating the divine will with their precise definitions and distinctions. All the same, it would be a grievous mistake not to appreciate the positive qualities that motivated rabbinic debates. The rabbis

> believed that their task was to realize in everyday life the precepts of the revealed Torah. "To do justice, love mercy, and walk humbly with God"—to the rabbis these were not abstractions. They had to be effected in the world, and nothing is so difficult in secular affairs as to find exactly what is justice or mercy here and now—and what is to be done that is just and merciful. Since the Torah contained rules on many subjects, and since these rules had to be interpreted to apply to wholly new matters and to issues important only long after Sinai, we should not be surprised to find the sages concentrating on the minutiae of daily life.[16]

It is not farfetched to suggest an analogy between the rabbinic debates and the current controversy among Evangelicals about the ordination of women. We fool ourselves if we think that this sensitive issue is not a *legal* question. Who may or may not rule (*proistēmi*, 1Ti 5:17) is a matter of church order, regulation, law. Dozens of books (to say nothing of specialized articles) have appeared, many of them dealing with textual "minutiae" (the precise nuance of words, the force of Greek tenses, etc.). In short, the mere presence of extensive legal discussion among the rabbis does not help us to identify the nature of Jesus' criticism.

d. An explicitly theological sense for the term *legalism* brings us closer to the real issue. Serious writers who accuse the Pharisees of being legalistic have in mind a Jewish system of salvation that depends on human merit rather than divine grace. Unfortunately, several weaknesses can be detected in most characterizations. The first problem is a tendency to depict Jewish thought as monolithic. The rabbis themselves never attempted to formulate a coherent soteriology; and those who seek to infer a soteriology from the scattered comments in rabbinic writings face some serious pitfalls.[17] The second problem arises from the first: having assumed a monolithic Jewish theology, scholars find it easy to play down or altogether ignore rabbinic emphases on such topics as repentance and the need to depend on God's mercy.[18] Finally, rabbinic soteriology tends to be caricatured as teaching a crass "medieval" doctrine that sees God balancing our good and bad deeds, our only hope being that the good outweighs the bad. Of course, such a description is not even fair to medieval theologians, and one can produce evidence that it distorts Jewish teaching on salvation.[19]

When all of this is admitted, however, one must still acknowledge that human merit plays a very prominent role in broad segments of the rabbinic literature.[20] Of special significance is the opinion (to my knowledge not explicitly contradicted in the rabbinic writings) that certain human acts can expiate sin. Even in such a pre-rabbinic document as Ecclesiasticus (3:3,14,30), sins are said to be atoned by honoring one's parents and by practicing almsgiving. The rabbis viewed acts of loving-kindness, the penalty of lashes, and, in some cases, death as having the power to atone for sins.[21] It seems impossible to deny that, according to Jewish thought, good deeds should be viewed in some important sense as meritorious; *to the extent* that human beings may be regarded as contributing to their salvation, the biblical doctrine of grace is compromised in Jewish theology. But even these considerations do not pinpoint clearly enough the source of the conflict between Jesus and the Pharisees, and so we move on to our final concern.

e. Legalism, theologically understood, can manifest itself in a variety of ways. Whether or not the Pharisees explicitly taught a merit system such as was described in the previous paragraph, we must recognize that Jesus is never represented in the Gospels as criticizing them for believing that they could atone for their own sins. He does indeed condemn them for their legalism—but a legalism that finds expression in a somewhat different form, namely, *through the relaxation of God's standards.*

This point can be illustrated most clearly by referring to a well-known legal ruling, the *prozbul*, attributed to Hillel the Elder, who apparently lived during the reign of Herod the Great. This ruling in effect did away with the command that debts were to be cancelled every seven years (Dt 15:1–3). That command was accompanied by a solemn warning: "Be careful not to harbor this wicked thought: 'The seventh year, the year for canceling debts, is near,' so that you do not show ill will toward your needy brother and give him nothing. He may then appeal to the LORD against you, and you will be found guilty of sin" (v 9). During Hillel's time, however, the wealthy were in fact refusing to lend money, fearing they would lose it in the sabbatical year. Since the poor were the ones suffering, Hillel (if we may trust the rabbinic attribution) used the legal fiction that debts cease to be private when transferred to a court, and he ordained that in such cases the debts may be collected.[22] For humanitarian reasons, therefore, Hillel devised a way of "breaking" the Torah; the explanation, of course, would have been that such "innovations and amendments . . . fulfilled the basic reason of the commandment, whereas its literal observance nullified its original intent."[23]

This enactment—and other examples could be used—show that we miss the point when we view the Pharisees as being concerned with the letter rather than the spirit of the law. While that may well have been the case in some instances, it does not address the basic motivation for the rabbinic interpretation of the Torah. If we wish to identify an overly strict Jewish group, we should turn to the Qumran community; for example, while Jesus assumes that His hearers would certainly rescue an animal if it should fall into a pit on the Sabbath, the Qumranites explicitly prohibited such an act.[24] In a very important sense, the Pharisees made the Torah easier to obey. As a result of the *prozbul*, wealthy Jews no longer needed to be concerned about the solemn warning of Deuteronomy 15:9. The divine standard had been relaxed. The Torah had been accommodated to meet the weaknesses of the people. Alexander Guttmann sees this feature as the genius of the Pharisees' approach.

> Emerging from the ranks of the people, the rabbis spoke in terms intelligible to the populace and were therefore able to lead the people in accordance with their teachings, a feat the Prophets had been unable to accomplish. Uncompromising idealists, the Prophets demanded perfection and the establishment of God's kingdom on earth in their own time; therefore, they were doomed to failure. Prophetic Judaism never became a reality but remained only an ideal, a goal, like Plato's *Republic*. The rabbis were idealists, too, but they were at the same time pedagogues. In guiding their people, they took the realities of life (among them the weakness of human beings) into consideration. They upheld the Torah as the divine code, but at the same time they recognized the need for harmonizing the Torah with the ever-changing realities of life.[25]

It turns out, then, that Jesus, who like the Old Testament prophets demanded perfection (Mt 5:48), would have been critical of the Pharisees, not because they obeyed the Torah too strictly, but because they interpreted it too loosely.[26] This is clearly and precisely the point of Mark 7:1–13, generally recognized as a key passage for understanding the conflict between Jesus and the Pharisees. The controversy described in this passage centers on the law that ceremonial washing was required before eating. In fact, this is not an Old Testament law; it is not part of the *Written* Torah. But it was part of the *Oral* Torah, that is, the traditions of the elders. Scholars are generally agreed that the concept of the Twofold Law was the most distinctive feature of Pharisaic and later rabbinic Judaism. The Oral Law was viewed as on a par with the Written Law—indeed, in some respects, as more important, for a ruling that is part of the Oral Law may in effect set aside the Written Law, as in the case of the *prozbul*.

Jesus' response to the Pharisees in Mark 7 is that they "have let go of the commands of God and are holding on to the traditions of men" (v 8). And, after describing a particularly insidious example, He concludes: "Thus you nullify the word of God by your tradition that you have handed down" (v 13). This undermining of God's Word, moreover, resulted in a muted consciousness of sin, for normally there were ways of interpreting the divine commands that mitigated their force. This frame of mind is almost surely the background for Matthew 5, where Jesus is said to demand of His disciples a righteousness greater than that of the Pharisees (v 20). Then, to preclude any interpretive moves that might render the law innocuous, He goes on to *intensify* specific scriptural commands. Just in case anyone might have missed the point, He concludes, "Be perfect, therefore, as your heavenly Father is perfect" (v 48), the equivalent of Leviticus 11:45, " . . . therefore be holy, because I am holy."

The Pharisees were often in danger of thinking that they had adequately fulfilled their duty before God (cf. Lk 18:9–12,21), and therefore no great sense of dependence on God's grace was likely to arise. In contrast, Jesus emphasized that the true servants of God are those who are ever conscious of their unworthiness (Lk 17:7–10) and who have learned to pray, "God, have mercy on me, a sinner" (Lk 18:13).

The reader may wonder whether we have not moved too far from the subject of historical reconstruction in pursuing these questions. The excursion was essential, however, if we were to appreciate the complexities that a modern historian must face when reconstructing the past. Conservative Christians who forget that the Bible is not a history textbook will jump too quickly from the biblical data to create a picture of Pharisaic Judaism that is consistent with their presuppositions. Nonconservatives too, however, sometimes appear to ignore the character of New Testament narrative and tend to assume that the material is unreliable simply because it is incomplete and theologically slanted. The result is two opposing historical reconstructions. In the one, the positive qualities of the Pharisees are virtually ignored; in the other, Jesus' condemnation is not taken seriously. In both of them, the precise point of Jesus' criticism may be missed altogether.

III. RECONSTRUCTING FIRST-CENTURY CHRISTIANITY

To bring up, as I have just done, the role of presuppositions in historical work raises some other questions. In attempting to deal with these, it will be useful to address another controversial topic, namely, the New Testament picture of the conflict between Jewish and Gentile Christianity. In this case, it will not be necessary to explore the various facets of the debate in great detail. My interest is not to provide a new reconstruction but only to identify as clearly as possible what leads scholars to interpret the evidence in different and even contradictory ways.

A. F. C. BAUR

In 1831, the controversial scholar Ferdinand Christian Baur published a lengthy article that was to revolutionize the study of New Testament history.[27] Prior to the appearance of that essay, it had been generally assumed that the apostles and other leaders of the early church worked together in full harmony. True, the Book of Acts preserves evidence of occasional friction (e.g., 11:1–18; 15:1–21,36–40; 21:20–26), and Paul recounts a sharp dispute he had with Peter (Gal 2:11–21), but these were viewed as minor exceptions that proved the rule. The data in the Corinthian letters, however, persuaded Baur that a fundamental conflict existed between Paul and the other apostles, especially Peter, who represented Jewish Christianity. Further re-search led him to more radical ideas, such as his conclusion that most of the letters ascribed to Paul were inauthentic. Finally, he published in 1845 a magisterial synthesis of Paul's life and ministry that presented in coherent form the "Tübingen School" interpretation of early Christianity.[28]

In the introduction to this work, Baur emphasizes that, while we have two accounts of early Christianity (Paul and the Book of Acts), these two sources differ so much from each other that

> historical truth must be entirely on one side or entirely on the other. To which it does belong can only be decided by applying the undisputed historical canon that the statement which has the greatest claim to historical truth is that which appears most unprejudiced and nowhere betrays a desire to subordinate its historical material to any special subjective aim.[29]

Now one could readily argue that the Pauline letters, especially Galatians, being intensely polemical, are not to be trusted—that Paul, concerned to prove his authority, inevitably distorts the material. In fact, this approach does not at all occur to Baur, who instead focuses on the apologetic aim of Acts: "its chief tendency is to represent the difference between Peter and Paul as unessential and trifling." The resulting picture of Paul is that of someone sympathetic to the Judaizing party, but this is so clearly contrary to the thrust of Paul's writing that the historical character of Acts "can only be maintained at the cost of the moral character of the Apostle." Without denying the importance of Acts as a source of apostolic history, Baur claims that the author is a second-century writer willing "to sacrifice historical truth" as a means of harmonizing genuine Paulinism with its Judeo-Christian opposition.[30]

B. PRESUPPOSITIONS

We need not pursue the details of Baur's reconstruction, which in several respects set the agenda for subsequent New Testament scholarship.[31] What concerns us here is identifying the principles and processes that led Baur, a brilliant scholar, to interpret the data as he did. Why does a J. B. Lightfoot, after analyzing the same biblical data, come up with a reconstruction that is often taken as the definitive refutation of the Tübingen School? And why does a Johannes Munck go even further than Lightfoot in minimizing the significance of the Judaizing opposition to Paul? Why do a large number of scholars reject Baur's thesis of a monolithic party opposed to Paul, whereas Walther Schmithals sees in the New Testament text new evidence for such a uniform opposition—only not Jewish but Gnostic?[32]

The simple answer is: presuppositions. Unfortunately, this is too simple an answer, for not everyone means the same by that word. When applied to Baur, the term *presuppositions* usually refers to his adoption of a Hegelian schema whereby Jewish Christianity was viewed as the thesis, Pauline Christianity as the antithesis, and second-century catholicism as the synthesis.[33] It is doubtful, however, whether Baur's reconstruction would have been fundamentally different if Hegel had never existed. The evidence indicates that prior to his acquaintance with Hegel's dialectic, Baur had already identified the Pauline/Petrine conflict as the key issue of apostolic history.[34] While we need not play down the significance of Hegel's influence on Baur's philosophy of history, this particular "presupposition" does not account satisfactorily for Baur's handling of the biblical data.

Another approach is that of Horton Harris, who argues that Baur's radical interpretation of church history resulted from *broad* dogmatic presuppositions that precluded a transcendent personal God and miracles.[35] But there are several difficulties with this analysis. Other scholars starting out with that same set of presuppositions have developed widely divergent reconstructions of the apostolic age; conversely, as we shall soon see, biblical students who allow for the truth of supernatural events may also differ significantly among themselves in the interpretation of the data.

A second difficulty is that broad criticisms of this kind can easily encourage inexact descriptions of a scholar's view. It is quite unfair to Baur, for example, to say that he was "prejudiced in advance . . . against the historicity of Acts,"[36] for as late as 1829, when he had already given up supernaturalism, his handling of Stephen's speech betrays "not a trace of doubt about the historicity of the speeches of Acts or of the book as a whole."[37] Again, it is an exaggeration to say that "the fundamental axiom of Baur's whole historical investigation was that the New Testament writings are not trustworthy historical documents,"[38] for the phrase "fundamental axiom" suggests that

Baur did not attempt to set forth any reasons for his skeptical approach.[39] Moreover, even with respect to Acts he stated that it "remains a highly-important source of the history of the Apostolic Age."[40]

To complicate matters even more, Harris concludes his book in a way that suggests that Baur was unconscious of his presuppositions:

> The problem which still confronts the investigation of the historical sources of Christianity is to set forth a total-view which takes full account of its dogmatic premises. For if we learn anything from the procedure of the Tübingen School it is this: that *Biblical exegesis and interpretation without conscious or unconscious dogmatic presuppositions is impossible.* The interpretation of the Bible and Biblical history demands an open, unconcealed, and honest statement of the fundamental historical principles by which it is to be interpreted. The validity of all Biblical exegesis and interpretation rests upon its readiness to set forth clearly and unflinchingly the dogmatic presuppositions on which it is based.[41]

But did Baur, as this statement seems to imply, fail to be open and honest about his "fundamental historical principles"? Harris himself had earlier made clear that "Baur leaves us in no doubt" with regard to his "central presupposition." His basic principle was that of a purely historical approach such as excludes the appeal to miracles as an explanation for what happened in the past.[42] Now it is true that Baur seems to have persuaded himself that his approach, if successfully carried through, would insure complete objectivity, but he was quite ready "to set forth clearly and unflinchingly" his antisupernaturalistic standpoint.[43] The irony, in fact, is that Harris himself falls, as all of us do, into the very pitfall that he warns us against. "And yet one has to read through the Clementine writings *with an open mind* to see that Baur's hypothesis is utterly untenable. . . . Whether anyone who was *not prejudiced in advance* would recognize Paul in this description is indeed doubtful."[44]

These strictures are not meant to undermine Harris's main concern, which is not precisely the same as ours. One can hardly deny that a scholar's fundamental assumptions about God will radically affect one's handling of the biblical material. Unfortunately, there is seldom (never?) a one-to-one correspondence between those assumptions and the scholar's historical reconstruction; therefore, to dismiss the reconstruction on the grounds that the basic world view is faulty does not solve our problem (particularly since faulty presuppositions sometimes open up legitimate options that another scholar may resist due to "correct" presuppositions; more on that matter below).

One other, more fruitful, approach to the role of presuppositions is to focus on the narrower network of mental associations that provides a meaningful interpretive framework for the scholar. In this sense of the term, presuppositions need to be viewed not merely as valid but also as essential for understanding information. Learning does not take place by appropriating individual facts in isolation but by integrating them (consciously or not) into a prior coherent framework. Or to put it somewhat tritely: it is by a knowledge of the whole that we understand the parts. Baur was keenly aware of this fact and deliberately exploited it. For example, he knew well that many features of the Acts narrative did not clearly conform to the apologetic aim; but since such an aim (the whole) is so clear, "we need not give it up even though there should be some passages" (the parts) whose purpose seems to be historical. More specifically, with reference to the second part of Acts: " . . . although the narrative of the Apostle's travels might seem to contain more personal and special details than the apologetic aim required, still it is clear that this very narrative is coloured throughout in accordance with that aim."[45] It is plain that, for Baur, once the general thesis has been ascertained, any details that appear to contradict it are simply to be adjusted to it.[46]

Particularly interesting is the preface to *Paul*, where Baur challenges his opponents to prove him wrong: " . . . let [my results] be denied and destroyed by the power of facts and arguments, if any one feels that he can do so!" Of course, he knows full well that at numerous points his interpretation of the data is subject to debate, and thus he must qualify himself:

> There is no limit to controversy on points of detail. The abstract possibility of this and that detail can never be disproved: but this is not the way to dispose of a comprehensive historical theory. Such a theory appeals to its broad general truth, to which details are subordinate, and on which they depend: to the logical coherence of the whole, the preponderating inner probability and necessity of the case, as it impresses itself quietly upon the thoughtful mind; and against this the party interests of the day will sooner or later cease to assert themselves.[47]

Baur is not thereby seeking to dodge the issue. The validity of a scientific theory is not necessarily disproven by the existence of contradictory data—what is needed is an alternate theory that has greater power to account for the facts.[48] Yet one can also argue—with a justifiable measure of frustration—that, according to Baur's thoroughgoing application of this method, the facts seem to count for very little.

C.   J. B. LIGHTFOOT

An interesting illustration of how facts—even a large number of them—may be easily ignored in the interests of a broad thesis is furnished by diverging reactions to Bishop Lightfoot's response to the book *Supernatural Religion*. In his essays, Lightfoot sought to refute the claim that the Gospels are historically worthless. Stephen Neill views Lightfoot's refutation as "tearing to shreds" the author of *Supernatural Religion* and unequivocally disproving its thesis.[49] But another scholar, Otto Pfleiderer, thinks that Lightfoot's answer was "extraordinarily weak." Pfleiderer regrets that "the short-sighted scholar found nothing better to do than to submit the author's examination of references in the Fathers to the Gospels to petty criticism; while, even if all the Bishop's deductions were correct, the general result of the author's inquiries would not be in any way altered."[50] It is clear that agreement on a vast array of details does not insure a common interpretation of the larger picture.

The reference to J. B. Lightfoot is useful in another way, however, since he is usually regarded as having put to rest Baur's reconstruction of early Christianity. Of singular importance for our purposes is Lightfoot's essay, "St Paul and the Three," an eighty-two-page monograph that ranks among the very finest works of modern biblical scholarship.[51] In erudition, logical power, and lucidity, it remains a model of scholarly writing. Significantly, Lightfoot's answer to the Tübingen theories does not take the form of listing objections to them or answering Baur's arguments one by one. Rather, Lightfoot proceeds by presenting a positive reconstruction of his own. Indeed, anyone reading this essay who happened to miss a couple of footnotes would not be aware at all that it was written as a polemic against Baur and his colleagues. This matter needs emphasis because here Lightfoot certainly did not fall into the trap of debating the many points that Baur himself acknowledged were debatable (in other words, Pfleiderer's criticisms of Lightfoot's *Essays on 'Supernatural Religion'* do not apply in this case). On the contrary, Lightfoot set forth an alternate and coherent theory that, to apply Baur's words, "appeals to its broad general truth, to which details are subordinate, and on which they depend."[52]

What is seldom pointed out, however, is how many important features Lightfoot's reconstruction shares with Baur's. In the preface to his commentary on Galatians, Lightfoot refers to the "extravagant" views of the Tübingen School, then adds: "But even in extreme cases mere denunciation may be unjust and is certainly unavailing. Moreover, for our own sakes we should try and discover the element of truth which underlies even the greatest exaggerations of able men, and correct our impressions thereby."[53] That Lightfoot is not merely paying lip service to the value of radical scholarship becomes clear from the commentary itself, where he shows remarkable sensitivity to the tensions between Paul and the Jerusalem apostles. His comments on 2:4 bear quoting:

> What part was taken in the dispute by the Apostles of the Circumcision? This question, which forces itself upon us at this stage of St Paul's narrative, is not easily answered. On the whole it seems probable that they recommended St

Paul to yield the point, as a charitable concession to the prejudices of the Jewish converts: but convinced at length by his representations, that such a concession at such a time would be fatal, they withdrew their counsel and gave him their support. . . . [This interpretation] best explains St Paul's language here. The sensible undercurrent of feeling, the broken grammar of the sentence, the obvious tenour of particular phrases, all convey the impression, that though the final victory was complete, it was not attained without a struggle, in which St Paul maintained at one time single-handed the cause of Gentile freedom.[54]

And in the next paragraph he penned that memorable sentence (in a way the key to his interpretation of Galatians): "The counsels of the Apostles of the Circumcision are the hidden rock on which the grammar of the sentence is wrecked."

But this is not all. What characterized the apostle's ministry after the Jerusalem Council? Lightfoot's answer is in "St Paul and the Three":

Henceforth St Paul's career was one of life-long conflict with Judaizing antagonists. Setting aside the Epistles to the Thessalonians, which were written too early to be affected by this struggle, all his letters addressed to churches, with but one exception [Ephesians], refer more or less directly to such opposition. . . . The systematic hatred of St Paul is an important fact, which we are too apt to overlook, but without which the whole history of the Apostolic ages will be misread and misunderstood.[55]

Significantly, he ends the essay by disabusing us of the notion that the New Testament period was characterized by "an ideal excellence." On the contrary, "the theological differences and religious animosities of our own time . . . are far surpassed in magnitude by the distractions of" that age.[56]

It is ironic that nonconservative, even radical, scholars in our day would probably view Lightfoot's reconstruction as simplistic—as a casualty from the days when the Tübingen theories affected every scholar's thinking. It is, of course, impossible to determine whether the basic outlines of Lightfoot's position would have developed even if he had never heard of Baur. In any case, he openly acknowledges, as we have seen, a measure of indebtedness to the Tübingen School, and one could plausibly argue that the extreme conclusions of a scholar with wrong presuppositions was what made possible significant progress in uncovering the history of the apostolic period.

Lightfoot, of course, opposed a fundamental feature of Baur's thesis: for Lightfoot, all the apostles were in substantial agreement regarding the message of the gospel. Closely related to this point, moreover, is his high regard for the reliability of Acts. Paradoxically, Lightfoot criticizes Baur for valuing Paul's letters too highly as a source for historical reconstruction! While it is doubtful whether Lightfoot himself would have put it in such terms, note how he approaches the problem:

> *St Paul* himself is so clearly reflected in his own writings, that a distorted
> image of his life and doctrine would seem to be due only to defective vision.
> Yet our first impressions require to be corrected or rather supplemented by
> an after consideration. Seeing him chiefly as the champion of Gentile liberty,
> the constant antagonist of Jew and Judaizer, we are apt to forget that his
> character has another side also. By birth and education he was a Hebrew of
> the Hebrews: and the traditions and feelings of his race hold him in
> honourable captivity to the very last.[57]

Lightfoot openly admits that the tone of the Acts narrative "differs
somewhat from the tone of the epistles," but the reason is that the
latter were "written in the heat of the conflict, written to confute
unscrupulous antagonists and to guard against dangerous errors." In
short, "St Paul's language could not give a complete picture of his
relations with the Apostles and the Church of the Circumcision."[58]

There is intense irony in the possibility that Baur was led astray
because he treated the Pauline letters as a history textbook![59] Though
he was perfectly aware that they were written for quite a different
purpose—to meet specific problems—Baur's broader concern to
preserve Paul's personal integrity[60] kept him from perceiving the
fragmented and slanted character of the historical picture provided
by those letters. Here, then, is another crucial factor in Baur's
"preunderstanding" that materially affected his reconstruction. Indeed, we might be able to identify numerous other factors that
provided Baur with a mental grid through which alone individual
facts could be filtered and appropriated.

But if that is the way a historian works, we can begin to
appreciate how difficult—nay, how hopeless and irrelevant—are the
attempts to dismiss a theory on the grounds that its author had come
up with it before examining the facts. As Barth once remarked, "Only
God knows whether Baur found this historical line *a priori* or *a
posteriori*."[61] Baur himself could not have told us. We are not very
accurate judges of our own mental and psychological processes, and
we do well to take with a grain of salt the frequent and no doubt
sincere claims of authors who tell us they have approached their
material with no preliminary hypothesis or even with a hypothesis
quite different from the actual conclusions.

D. HISTORICAL OBJECTIVITY

What does all of this do to the goal of historical objectivity? Is it a
complete illusion? Some writers have argued, sincerely, that knowledge of the past is quite beyond our reach.[62] Practicing historians are
seldom bothered by this philosophical problem; and specifically with
regard to objectivity—an issue that cannot be ignored so easily—
they tend to be fairly optimistic. Consider, for example, the high
regard with which Herbert Butterfield is held as an objective
historian. In the introduction to that author's posthumous work, *The
Origins of History*, Adam Watson commented:

> Butterfield approached this vast and largely uncharted subject in a characteristic way, with no preconceptions, not knowing in what direction his researches would lead him. . . . The trouble [with broad interpretations such as Spengler's or Toynbee's] was that in all of them the theory of interpretation or diagram came first. They were *a priori* intuitions. Sometimes, as he once said to me, it was a grandiose and imaginative one, but derived only very partially from the facts and owing more to other beliefs and other purposes in this world. . . . Butterfield was concerned to start with the facts [followed by more detailed research and reflection]. He developed an extraordinary flair for this kind of open-minded deduction. . . . [The] refusal to force the facts, [the willingness] to suspend judgment until they offered you their own answer, the ability not to prejudge anything, Butterfield called elasticity of mind.[63]

One cannot avoid detecting a measure of naïveté in Butterfield's judgment. Note, for instance, how he judges the credibility of the Gospels when they describe the disciples' reaction to Jesus' death:

> The description of their shortcomings must have come from the confessions of the disciples themselves, for the authors of the Gospels *could hardly have had any motive for inventing such things* if they had not been known to be true, even though these pictures of human frailty do add realism to the narrative, and it might be argued that they served a purpose, bringing into greater relief the transformation that took place in the disciples immediately afterwards.[64]

In this one sentence, Butterfield himself gives us two perfectly plausible *motives* for fabricating the accounts: to heighten the realism of the narratives and to exploit the apologetic value of the disciples' later change. Yet these two reasons are relegated to a long clause that is grammatically subordinate to the main point, namely, that the accounts are authentic, since the Evangelists had no motive for inventing them!

Lapses and inconsistencies of this sort, however, do not give us sufficient reason to doubt all of Butterfield's conclusions, or to reject his method, or to abandon his goal. The fact that controversial interpretations of history occupy most of our attention tends to obscure another, more significant fact, namely, the enormous amount of accessible historical data about which no one expresses any doubt. Moreover, there are vast areas of research in which scholars have provided reconstructions that remain unchallenged (save for details that do not substantially affect the larger picture). We may wish to question Butterfield's criticism of historians that begin with a general theory; we dare not question his call to exercise restraint in making the facts fit the theory. We can argue that presuppositions play a much more positive role than Butterfield allows for; we cannot give up the struggle for objectivity in historical interpretation.[65]

But is it really meaningful to use the term *objectivity* once we have conceded so much that seems incompatible with it? The standard answer is that scholars should seek to attain as much objectivity "as is possible," but this tells us nothing. The only kind of objectivity that we can sink our teeth into is that which is recognized as such by the community of scholars who evaluate historical interpretations. Asking a scholar to be objective is not a demand that he or she adopt a particular psychological attitude or an acceptable step-by-step mental process. It does mean that the scholar should seek to persuade other scholars who scrutinize any new interpretation according to agreed-upon canons of historical persuasiveness. Such a community process does not guarantee that any one historian will be objective, but it is a compelling force in determining whether a particular reconstruction approaches objectivity.

The much used—and abused—analogy with the judicial process in criminal cases helps us here. Although prospective jurors are rejected if they appear prejudiced, no juror can be expected to be free of the subjective element. Yet, we are all satisfied that, in the vast majority of cases, agreement among the jurors insures an acceptable measure of objectivity—enough, at least, that we are unwilling to replace this process with an "arbitrary" system. The rapid disintegration of the Tübingen School is, therefore, the clearest evidence that Baur's handling of the facts can hardly be regarded as objective—quite irrespective of whether or not Baur had an *a priori* theory and whether or not he was aware of his fitting (forcing?) pieces into the large picture.

IV. CONCLUSIONS

It is now time to return to our initial question: Have misunderstandings created unnecessary conflicts between conservative and nonconservative historical reconstructions? The answer is certainly yes. But this issue must be distinguished from a very different question: Can we avoid widely divergent historical reconstructions? This second question requires a negative answer. Even authors who share a large number of significant premises will often interpret the data quite differently.[66] Besides, highly idiosyncratic theories—obnoxious and harmful as they sometimes may be—force us to face new questions that can open productive new avenues of research. At any rate, it would be an illusion to think that individual scholars could submit themselves to carefully defined reasoning steps or to arbitrary limits on their imagination.

On the other hand, it *is* possible to acknowledge the existence of misunderstandings and thus to avoid unnecessary polarization of viewpoints. To begin with, we all need to watch our language. As we have seen, nonconservatives tend all too easily to use terms such as "unreliable" when all they have shown is that the material so described will not serve them to solve a problem that actually lies outside the scope of the biblical writer.

For their part, conservatives tend to read too much into some terms that are perceived, perhaps rightly, as objectionable. For example, Evangelicals understandably cringe when they hear a certain saying of Jesus described as "inauthentic." Often such a description does indeed contradict biblical infallibility, but in some cases all that is meant is that the saying was not recorded in the Gospels in its original form. Evangelical scholars have always insisted that infallibility does not demand verbatim quotations: when a saying of Jesus occurs with different wording in two Gospels, it is quite possible that one of the Gospel writers may be giving an abbreviated or paraphrased form of the saying. In such a case, a scholar may ask which of the two is "authentic"—perhaps an unfortunate choice of terms but one that does not necessarily impugn the authority of Scripture if the scholar is merely concerned with establishing which Gospel has preserved the "primitive" form of the saying.

Similarly, unnecessary polarization has often resulted through the insensitive use of language in describing the diversity of theological expression that is found in the New Testament. The presence of such diversity does not at all undermine the divine unity of scriptural revelation. Conservatives, however, sometimes appear to impose an artificial uniformity on the New Testament (though Lightfoot taught us otherwise!), while nonconservatives very quickly identify diversity as contradiction. There will always be points of material disagreement in these areas as long as Evangelicals hold to an infallible Bible and non-Evangelicals do not; but some present conflicts do not belong in this class, and a genuine effort must be made to identify them.

In addition to the need for more careful use of language, another item that requires further reflection is the by now commonplace plea for scholars to show a sharper awareness of their presuppositions. The truth is (strange as it may appear to some) that most biblical scholars are not fools; they know full well there are limits to their objectivity, and their writings generally indicate some degree of self-consciousness as to what those limits are. We cannot give in to the temptation of simply dismissing what we don't like on the grounds that "those liberals" (or "those conservatives"!) are slaves to their presuppositions. Still, there is something to be said for the view that scholars should make a greater effort to identify those premises that provide their framework for selecting, interpreting, and synthesizing the data.

Finally, an effort must be made to refine and make explicit those "agreed-upon canons of historical persuasiveness" that make it possible for the community of biblical scholars to weed out unacceptable theories. Considerable frustration will persist as long as the scholarly orthodoxy appears to use a measure of arbitrariness in determining what is allowed as proper evidence.

The perennial focus of controversy, of course, is the Book of Acts. Lightfoot once stated that this book "in the multiplicity and variety of its details probably affords greater means of testing its general character for truth than any other ancient narrative in existence; and in my opinion it satisfies the tests fully."[67] At the turn of the century, the extensive research of William Ramsay provided further means of checking the book's veracity at numerous points.[68] Virtually everything that the book asserts, where it *can* be verified, checks out; yet most contemporary scholars maintain that the book is not to be trusted at those points where it *cannot* be falsified![69] This would not be so bad if a serious attempt were made to refute the significant body of evidence that has been brought to bear. Routinely, however, the evidence is simply ignored. The standard critical commentary on Acts knows not Ramsay,[70] and the innocent reader of a recent and important synthesis can only deduce that all thinking persons regard Acts as a basically legendary work that happens to incorporate a handful of historical passages.[71]

Conservative scholarship can hardly be expected to take these judgments seriously—let alone agree with them—as long as they are evidently not based on a sober analysis of all the relevant data. To be sure, we can argue just as easily that conservative scholars have a good deal of homework to do in refining *their* criteria for what constitutes acceptable and persuasive evidence. The frequency with which Evangelicals use isolated bits of data *ad hoc* to support their positions has understandably alienated the scholarly establishment and provided an excuse for ignoring responsible work.

In either case, it should be marked, the impasse arises because of *the scholar's perception as to where the burden of proof lies.* An F. C. Baur is impressed with the differences between Acts and the Epistles; that leads him to place the *onus probandi* on the scholar who would argue for the reliability of Luke's description of Paul. A William Ramsay is stunned by the accuracy that characterizes Luke's habit of mind; therefore, he will not be budged unless someone shows him overwhelming evidence to the contrary. Perhaps it is possible for the scholarly community to define with some clarity the place and limits of the *onus probandi* in historical argumentation.

One must not think, however, that progress in these areas will resolve the basic conflict. By and large, modern critical scholars have persuaded themselves that the biblical view of the relation between faith and history must be totally reversed—the risk of faith, we are told, must not be avoided by appealing to objective historical reality.[72] So long as historical veracity is viewed by one party as more or less irrelevant or secondary, genuine rapprochement is impossible. The Evangelical, convinced that any faith not based on historical truth is illusory (e.g., 1Co 15:17; 2Pe 3:16), will continue to be scoffed at for failing to adopt a post-Kantian dichotomy between the religious and the scientific. This very commitment by Evangelicals, however, argues for a fearless approach to historical questions. An intelligent reliance on the authority of Scripture, coupled with sensitivity to its true character and purpose, yields the best prescription for responsible historical reconstruction.

CHAPTER FOUR
THE LEGITIMACY AND LIMITS OF HARMONIZATION

Craig L. Blomberg

Craig L. Blomberg

Craig L. Blomberg is Assistant Professor of Religion at Palm Beach Atlantic College, West Palm Beach, Florida. He is a graduate of Augustana College (B.A.), Trinity Evangelical Divinity School (M.A.), and the University of Aberdeen (Ph.D.). He has contributed a number of articles to journals and has written "Midrash, Chiasmus, and the Outline of Luke's Central Section" and "Tradition and Redaction in the Parables of the Gospel of Thomas" for the six-volume work *Gospel Perspectives*.

CHAPTER FOUR

THE LEGITIMACY AND LIMITS OF HARMONIZATION

I. INTRODUCTION

The consensus of modern biblical scholarship disparages virtually all attempts to "harmonize" the scriptural data. The implausibility
of the proposed harmonizations of certain conservative scholars only
reinforces the criticism of the majority. Nevertheless, all historians,
whether they employ the term or not, practice some kind of
harmonization as they seek to reconstruct the truth of past events.
The purpose of this chapter is to explore both the legitimacy and
limitations of this method.

A major part of the debate stems from varying definitions of the
word *harmonization*. Paul Achtemeier's otherwise lucidly written
work on the inspiration of Scripture nicely illustrates this problem.
Achtemeier quotes James Packer as representative of the inerrantist
position, a position that commits one "in advance to harmonize and
integrate all that we find Scripture teaching, without remainder."[1]
Then, after discussing examples of what he believes are errors in
Scripture, Achtemeier returns to the problem of harmonization,
which he rejects because of its artificial or contrived nature. But here
it becomes clear that he has equivocated on the meaning of the term,
since the method he rejects is that of trying "to show that seemingly
discrepant accounts can be reconciled by showing that they are only
partial accounts of an actual event."[2] As will become clear, however,
this is but one of many methods by which apparent discrepancies
between parallel historical narratives can be reconciled. To reject
harmonization in this narrower sense in no way calls into question
the viability or even the necessity of attempting, via *whatever* method,
a harmonization in Packer's broader sense of the term—that is,
showing that no real discrepancy exists.[3]

The investigation of the legitimacy of harmonization in this
broader sense lies outside of the scope of this study and is virtually
identical with inquiry into the legitimacy of systematic theology *per
se*[4] or into unity and diversity of biblical theology.[5] At this point it
need only be noted that it is not merely evangelical scholars who have
defended the propriety of this type of harmonization; even the most
"radical" of biblical commentators recognize that certain apparently

conflicting data can be brought into agreement with each other. For example, among recent Synoptic studies, F. W. Beare's work on Matthew is one of the most skeptical of that Gospel's historical accuracy; yet Beare resorts to very traditional, harmonizing exegesis (in the broad sense of the term) when he explains that Matthew 7:1 does not preclude the judgments Scripture elsewhere enjoins upon Christians but merely stresses that such judgment "must not be harsh."[6] Simple common sense dictates such exegesis; one cannot escape harmonizations of some kind. And, as will be discussed further below, this is a technique all historians utilize—even with somewhat errant documents.

On the other hand, if the interpretation is to be fair, certain tensions within documents representing similar religious or philosophical systems must be allowed to stand. One thinks of the way Scripture holds together seemingly disparate themes (e.g., predestination and free will, security and apostasy, the preservation and yet supersession of Old Testament law). The compatibility of the two members of each pair is not easily proved, but neither is their incompatibility; and the biblical writers' regular juxtaposing of contrasting themes suggests that *they* did not find the tension that severe.[7]

The key question for this study, therefore, remains that of the use and abuse of harmonization, narrowly defined.[8] Yet even here, critique is not leveled only by those who would disassociate themselves from an Evangelical view of Scripture. Robert Gundry, writing as an avowed inerrantist, laments the fact that "conservative Protestants bend over backward for harmonizations," appealing to linguistic or literary solutions as well as the straightforward "additive" reconstructions noted by Achtemeier. Yet such harmonizations "often become so complicated that they are not only unbelievable, but also damaging to the clarity of Scripture."[9] Gundry believes that redaction criticism is the preferable method, its application revealing that the Gospel of Matthew is a midrashic mixture of fact and fiction. Unfortunately, Gundry has employed the term "redaction criticism" in a much broader sense than is customary,[10] with the result that several even more conservative scholars have overreacted (though not for this reason alone) by calling for Evangelicals to abandon redaction criticism altogether.[11]

With all of this terminological confusion, a study of the proper and improper types of solutions to the apparent discrepancies of Scripture is absolutely crucial. Moisés Silva has graphically illustrated the problem, showing the varying amounts of liberties the Gospel writers seem to have taken with their sources,[12] and D. A. Carson has called for a balance between adopting "glib harmonizations" and refusing "easy" (i.e., obvious, common-sensical) ones.[13] But no one has attempted to draw up a road map to point the way out of this methodological maze. Hopefully, this essay can begin to chart a few directions toward that end. In short, its thesis is that "additive" harmonization (what will be called the "narrower" sense) and redaction criticism are but two of several methods that can be legitimately employed to explain apparent discrepancies among documents of various historical genres. These methods will be discussed with somewhat detailed illustrations from the Synoptics and then applied more briefly to selected problems between parallel passages in Kings-Chronicles, Josephus, and ancient historians of Alexander the Great.

II. DEFINITIONS

At least eight main categories of types of resolutions of apparently conflicting historical data warrant attention here. Redaction criticism and harmonization, narrowly defined, are perhaps the two most controversial, so they will be treated last and in slightly more detail. Six other methods and the assumptions on which they are predicated, however, deserve brief treatment first.

A. TEXTUAL CRITICISM

In most study of ancient historical writing, the autographs of the relevant texts no longer exist. Conflicting testimony may, therefore, result from copyists' errors where the original manuscripts would not have disagreed with each other. The situation with Scripture is no different; most scholarly inerrantists (at least in Protestant circles) would emphasize that their doctrine of inerrancy applies only to the autographs.[14]

B. LINGUISTICS

Apparent contradictions may arise due to inadequate understanding of the meaning of words, phrases, clauses, sentences, and even larger units of writing. When works of antiquity are under consideration, the "culture gap" makes this problem prevalent. Where the translation of foreign languages is involved, the potential for misunderstanding becomes even greater. The trend in recent biblical scholarship has been to emphasize the difference in meaning between words that could be synonyms, and this often makes parallel accounts of the same event seem more divergent than they really are.[15]

C. HISTORICAL CONTEXT

Due to the limited information available, modern historians have problems using apparently contradictory testimony to reconstruct the facts of an event. In some cases, a formal contradiction exists between statements that were both true in some limited context but that could not both be true if universalized, either temporally or geographically. In other instances, a writer may assume knowledge on the part of his audience—knowledge that would resolve an apparent contradiction but that he has not preserved for later readers' access.

D. FORM CRITICISM

Much more often than is true of modern writings, documents of antiquity were based on long periods of oral tradition before any written text appeared. If there is reason to assume such an oral stage behind a given text, the ways in which that tradition might have altered the text need to be taken into consideration when trying to explain conflicting accounts. On the other hand, it could be that originally parallel testimony agreed with itself, and later errors—and therefore contradictions—crept in during oral transmission. Evangelical scholars have rightly recognized that this type of assumption could not coexist with a belief in biblical inerrancy, but their rejection of these form-critical presuppositions is for the most part based not on this recognition but on valid observations about the differences between the formation of the historical writings of Scripture and that of other orally transmitted traditions of old.[16] On the other hand, many stylistic variations between biblical parallels, especially in the Synoptics, most likely do arise due to form-critical processes, and the awareness of valid tendencies of transmission can help to explain otherwise perplexing differences among the Evangelists.

E. AUDIENCE CRITICISM

Based on J. A. Baird's pioneering work, this approach assumes, *contra* the prevailing fashions of biblical criticism, that the narrative settings and, more particularly, the audiences ascribed to the various Gospel pericopae are reliable.[17] The paucity of such specific settings throughout the Gospels makes Baird's position highly probable; had the Evangelists felt free to invent settings at will, many more ought to appear than actually do. Some problems between apparent parallels may, therefore, best be resolved by acknowledging that the different settings given them show that they are probably not genuine parallels after all.[18]

F. SOURCE CRITICISM

Many ancient writings have a complex literary as well as preliterary history. In the case of the Synoptics, the two-document hypothesis remains the most probable, as the comprehensive studies of C. M. Tuckett and K. Uchida have demonstrated.[19] A recent trend among certain conservatives to herald some form of Matthean priority as more amenable to a high view of Scripture seems misguided;[20] commentators may just as consistently hold to Markan priority and the Q hypothesis along with a high view of the editorial accuracy of Matthew and Luke.[21] In general, however, the significance of source criticism is that it enables one to locate at what stratum of a book's composition potential problem passages appear, information which may turn what appears to be deliberate contradiction into an unwitting coincidence of noncomplementary but noncontradictory terminology. The epistolary example of James versus Paul on faith and works springs naturally to mind.[22]

G. REDACTION CRITICISM

As noted, the biggest problem here is certainly one of definition. This chapter will use *redaction criticism* to refer merely to what many Christians have been doing ever since the Gospels were written—and to what all modern historians do to all sorts of ancient texts—namely, reflecting upon the distinctive themes, purposes, motives, and emphases of a given writer, especially in comparison with others who have written on the same topic(s). This method takes seriously the vast amount of material that any historian of any age could have chosen to include in his work and yet omitted; as a result, it asks why the author included what he did. Selectivity, however, scarcely implies errancy. The words of Lord Macaulay merit frequent repetition in the modern *Weltgeist*: "What is told in the fullest and most accurate annals bears an infinitely small proportion to what is suppressed," and "he who is deficient in the art of selection may, by sharing nothing but the truth, produce all the effect of the grossest falsehood."[23] Generalizations, summaries, and excisions must punctuate any chronicle in order for it to become intelligible history.

Evangelicals do well to reject the type of redaction criticism practiced by some extremely "radical" scholars, in which negative presuppositions about historicity are, by definition, part of the method.[24] But this is not always the case, even in so-called liberal circles. For example, W. G. Kümmel's standard textbook refers to redaction criticism merely as attending to "the literary, sociological, and theological presuppositions, methods, and tendencies of the individual evangelists."[25] Of course, Kümmel sees some of those tendencies involve distortion of part of the tradition beyond the bounds of historical accuracy, but nothing in his definition itself requires this.

Rather, redaction criticism can be neutral, in which various questions are raised to account for the editorial activity of the author. Where particular themes, distinctive vocabulary, and stylistic characteristics appear far more often in one writer than in another, especially when comparing closely paralleled material, it is reasonable to attribute the distinctives to conscious editorial preference. Such analysis is necessarily subjective, but proper statistical methods can identify with virtual certainty a limited number of features whose frequency of occurrence precludes coincidence.[26] But the attribution of a word, sentence, or theme to a redactional origin in this sense proves nothing about its historical accuracy, which may only be determined by an application of valid criteria for authenticity and inauthenticity.[27] In fact, redaction criticism, as will be argued below, can become a powerful tool for defending the accuracy of Scripture rather than impugning it; for, without resorting to artificial and discrediting harmonizations, it can give reasonable explanations for why one writer altered a canonical source.

H. HARMONIZATION

In this narrower sense of one among many methods, harmonization refers to the explanation of apparent discrepancies between parallel accounts where it is assumed that both accounts are correct because similar events happened more than once or because each author has chosen to recount different parts of a fuller, original narrative. Not nearly as many of the classic problems in reconciling Scripture warrant a harmonizing explanation, in this limited sense, as those that have received one, and it is for this reason that the method is often rejected wholesale. Such, however, is standard practice among secular historians of both written and oral traditions,[28] and Gilbert Garraghan emphasizes that "almost any critical history that discusses the evidence for important statements will furnish examples of discrepant or contradictory accounts and the attempts which are made to reconcile them."[29] Garraghan's examples show as many instances of "additive" harmonization as of the other methods noted. Implausibility usually arises only when harmonistic hypotheses have to be multiplied, as for example in the coincidence of not only two but perhaps three or more people with the same name involved in similar circumstances.[30]

Before turning to specific examples of each of these eight methods for resolving apparent contradictions, some objections to this entire enterprise need to be addressed. Although harmonization, both broadly and narrowly defined, is a standard practice among virtually all historians, many students of the Gospels would want to argue that the genre of the Synoptics is not a sufficiently historical one for the principles of modern historiography to be applied to them. Stewart Goetz and I have addressed that problem in our article on the burden of proof.[31] Suffice it here to say that the two major works on this topic published since then, both dealing with Matthew, have not overturned the evidence cited therein. On the one hand, Gundry's analysis of Matthew as midrash has generally failed to convince both "conservative" and "liberal" reviewers, while on the other, Philip Shuler's identification of Matthew as encomium biography compares that Evangelist favorably with Polybius, Cicero, Plutarch, and Lucian, all of whom rank among the more respected historians of the ancient Greco-Roman world.[32]

Of course, part of the problem in discussing "historical" genres is again the question of definition,[33] but if all one requires is that the document be a narrative of purportedly factual events where a strong likelihood is present of recovering a fair amount of accurate information about the past, then the Synoptics fit the bill handily.[34] The seemingly indestructible tendency to pit history against theology must just as consistently be exposed for the false dichotomy that it is, but the editorial concerns of each Evangelist do suggest that a redaction-critical explanation may account for the differences between the Gospels more often than a traditional harmonization. Moreover, as Werner Kelber stresses, when one uses harmonization not for historical reconstruction but to interpret one Gospel in the light of information in its parallels, the exegesis runs the inevitable risk of doing "violence to the integrity of both."[35]

III. SYNOPTIC EXAMPLES

It is probably impossible to specify in advance any detailed criteria for establishing when each of the eight methods enumerated above should come into play. For all but the simplest of examples, a combination of two or more methods may well work the best. Nevertheless, a few introductory suggestions for the use of each method appear below, with at least two examples from the Synoptics to illustrate each method. The literature on each of the passages selected for examples has been scrutinized in some detail, although this minimizes the number of passages that can be examined. But because so many superficial discussions of the phenomena of Scripture seldom seriously interact with the exegetical studies of competing perspectives, this seems to be a preferable method.

A. TEXTUAL-CRITICAL SOLUTIONS

The establishment of the original text of the New Testament remains far more certain in all but a handful of instances than for any other important text of antiquity; conjectural emendation is, therefore, virtually never appropriate. Caution must be exercised, however, against making the latest Nestle/UBS a new Textus Receptus;[36] and a specially relevant problem is that, due to the principle of *lectio difficilior*, harmonizing variants are almost never accepted as original.[37] The harder reading, though, can be too hard,[38] and in two instances it seems at least plausible to suggest that adopting a different reading than that chosen by Aland's committee provides a good solution to apparent discrepancies.

1. Did Jesus promise that His heavenly Father would give good gifts or the Holy Spirit to His children (Mt 7:11/Lk 11:13)? The high degree of verbal parallelism between the rest of the two versions of

this pericope (cf. esp. Mt 7:7–8 and Lk 11:9–10) seems to preclude the recourse to assuming two different sayings from two different occasions in the life of Jesus, although this is not impossible.[39] The frequent conclusion that Luke prefers to add references to the Holy Spirit to his source material seems less certain since the study of C. S. Rodd.[40] Grundmann therefore suggests that the Lukan variant (πνεῦμα ἀγαθόν)—attested by p[45] L *pc* aur vg—is perhaps original.[41] It is a *lectio dificilior* of sorts, since "good Spirit" is not a common biblical term, and it adequately accounts both for Matthew's abbreviating ἀγαθά and for the later scribal change of Luke's text to the more standard πνεῦμα ἅγιον.

2. To which side of the Sea of Galilee did the disciples head after the feeding of the five thousand (Mt 14:22/Mk 6:45)? Although at first glance the problem seems to be between Mark's reference to Bethsaida (east bank) and Matthew's reference to the "other side" (west bank; cf. Jn 6:17, which explicitly mentions Capernaum), the mention in Mark 6:53 of Gennesaret makes it clear that there is an internal tension in Mark's own account as well. The critical consensus is that Mark is simply careless in his geographical references or uses them in service of theology rather than topography.[42] But such specific place names are so rare in Mark that this seems improbable. The traditional conservative responses usually employ additive harmonization, either arguing for two Bethsaidas—one on each shore of the lake—or for two meanings of "the other side" so that Mark refers only to the other side of the small bay just outside of Bethsaida.[43] But there is no archaeological evidence for any Bethsaida west of the Galilean sea—John 12:21 must not be pressed[44]—nor would Mark's readers have any way of distinguishing this Bethsaida from the one referred to in Mark 8:22. The latter harmonization runs aground on the fact that εἰς τὸ πέραν is a stock phrase in the Gospels, referring to a trip across the entire sea (cf. Mk 4:35; 5:1,21; 8:13; 10:1).

Carson prefers a linguistic solution, noting that Matthew's ἕως οὗ plus the subjunctive strictly implies "until," whereas Mark's ἕως plus the indicative means "while." Thus, Jesus sent the disciples ahead to Bethsaida while He dismissed the crowds, and then they headed on across to the western shore.[45] The syntax, however, only sustains this interpretation with difficulty, since πρὸς Βηθσαϊδάν reads more naturally as a definition of εἰς τὸ πέραν. The best solution, therefore, appears to be a textual-critical one, à la Lane, Cranfield, and Taylor.[46] "To the other side" is omitted by p[45] W λ q sy[s], and if this were a later, harmonizing variant, it would have made even more sense to omit "to Bethsaida." Rather, it seems that the disciples did start out by boat for Bethsaida Julias but were blown off course and landed on the west bank instead. The very severity of a storm capable of carrying them this far from their destination makes the need for the subsequent miracle more intelligible. It also provides incidental corroboration that the reference to the storm is an integral part of the setting of the story, not an interpolation into an original narrative that told only of Jesus walking on the water.

B. LINGUISTIC SOLUTIONS

The plausibility of an alternate translation to remove an apparent contradiction between texts increases in direct proportion to the unusual nature of the construction in the original language or to the coherence of the proposed, new translation. Some examples may be helpful at this point.

(1) Did Jesus preach his great sermon on the mount or on the plain (Mt 5:1/Lk 6:17)? The answer seems to hinge on Luke's word πεδινός in both its diachronic and synchronic contexts. In Luke 6:12, Jesus is already in the mountains; and Matthew can scarcely have envisioned the large throng of people gathered on a steep incline. Some type of level place, or plateau, of which there were many in the Galilean hills, naturally suggests itself.[47] Isaiah 13:2 (LXX) clearly reflects this usage of πεδινός; and the other Septuagintal references, while often contrasting πεδινός with ὄρος, also regularly employ it as one of several geographical categories and as one of apparently higher elevation than the coast (Jos 9:1), the Negev (Jos 10:40), the low country (Shephelah; 2Ch 26:10), and the valley (Jer 31:8).[48] Gundry's objection that all the diseased people (Mt 4:24/Lk 6:17–18) would scarcely have climbed into the hills to reach Jesus not only underestimates the length to which sick people will go to find cures but also renders major portions of the Gospels unintelligible, since those who are ill confront Jesus at nearly every turn of the hilly, Galilean terrain that He traverses. However, to resort to believing that Jesus preached two different, programmatic sermons with remarkably similar introductions, conclusions, structure, details, *and* setting (apart from the mount/plain problem) leaves one unnecessarily vulnerable to hasty rejection by those who are already skeptical of harmonizing methods.[49]

(2) Who was high priest when David ate the sacred showbread, Abiathar or Ahimelech (Mk 2:26/1Sa 21:1–6)? A textual-critical solution falters on the lack of any early manuscript supporting the omission of ἐπὶ Ἀβιαθάρ.[50] Most scholars simply acknowledge that Mark contains a historical error but give no plausible explanation of how this entered into what shows all signs of being at the very least an early Palestinian tradition from a Jewish-Christian community that knew well its Old Testament.[51] William Hendriksen squeezes the texts entirely out of shape to suggest that both father and son gave the bread to David![52] The best solution again appears to be a linguistic one. John Wenham has called attention to the parallel construction in Mark 12:26 (ἐπὶ τοῦ βάτου), in which ἐπί means "in the passage about."[53] Ahimelech is certainly the more dominant of the two high

priests in the larger context of the latter portion of 1 Samuel, making Wenham's application to Mark 2:26 extremely plausible. Moreover, in eighteen of the twenty-one Markan uses of the preposition, $\epsilon\pi\iota$ has a local or spatial rather than a temporal sense, rendering the traditional translation ("when Abiathar was high priest") less likely.

There are certainly other problem passages in the Synoptics where a linguistic solution seems best. Included among these would be (3) Mark 14:66–72 and its parallels. Any scenario that envisions Peter denying Jesus more than three times entirely trivializes the force of Jesus' original prediction;[54] similarly, "the" maid of Mark 14:69 need not be resumptive, and the "man" of Luke 22:58 could be generic.[55] Also included are (4) the Old Testament fulfillment quotations, especially in Matthew 1–2; the semantic range of $\pi\lambda\eta\rho\delta\omega$ in these formulae certainly exceeds the mere occurrence of what was straightforwardly predicted. Likewise, (5) "three days and three nights" (Mt 12:40) almost certainly does not equal seventy-two hours. Similarly, (6) the Gerasene/Gergesene/Gadarene demoniac(s) of Mark 5:1 and its parallels probably hailed from Khersa,[56] (7) the linguistic convention of citing only one source for a composite quotation explains the reference to Jeremiah in Matthew 27:9,[57] and (8) the problem of determining the day of the week on which Jesus was crucified is removed by recognizing that the "Passover" could refer both to the initial day of the feast as well as to its week-long celebration.[58]

A specially significant type of linguistic analysis may account for several additional examples of the apparent license taken by the Synoptists in rewriting their sources. This subcategory perhaps ought to appear under redaction criticism or—if the changes be attributed to a traditional stage—as an example of form criticism. But the parallels with issues raised by the science of modern Bible translation justify its inclusion here. The procedure has been called dynamic equivalence,[59] contextualization,[60] or contemporization, but Joachim Jeremias's term *representational change*[61] is the most descriptive.

In brief, the concept behind these terms is that the imagery and idioms that prove meaningful to one community or culture may need to be re-presented in quite different terms for a different audience in order to preserve their original meaning. Bible translations sometimes employ this procedure (most notably, with units of measure), and more paraphrastic compositions do so regularly (cf. the striking "flashlight" of Ps 119:105 or the "shake hands warmly" of Ro 16:16 in the *Living Bible*). Probable Synoptic examples of representational change include Luke's versions of the parables of the two builders and of the mustard seed (Lk 6:47–49/Mt 7:24–27; Lk 13:18–19/Mt 13:31–32). Thus, Luke turns Matthew's distinctively Palestinian wadi (a waterless ravine with steep sides that occasionally turned into a raging river after severe rains) into a broad river like the Orontes at

Syrian Antioch, where temporary summer shelters had to be abandoned before the winter rains set in.[62] Similarly, Luke's mustard seed grows in a domestic garden rather than a rural field, again reflecting a concern for intelligibility in a more urban, Hellenistic context.

Even most conservative commentators seem relatively comfortable with applications of representational change like those discussed above. But is it not possible that such contemporization is in fact more widespread in the Gospels than they have generally recognized? For example, Grant Osborne suggested that the Trinitarian formula of the Great Commission (Mt 28:19) was a redactional expansion of an original monadic expression.[63] Yet the criticism he received for this view later led him to back away from his suggestion.[64] Of course, the standard critical assumption—that Jesus could not have spoken of Father, Son, and Holy Spirit, because Trinitarian theology developed only in a later stage of the history of Christianity—cannot be the motive for adopting a position like Osborne's initial one.[65]

But what if the disciples had begun to realize that when Jesus spoke of His Father, He referred to a God with whom He and the Spirit were also uniquely one? Suppose also that Jesus only commissioned them to baptize in the name of the Father. Matthew could scarcely have recorded such words verbatim and expected an audience (whether Jew or Gentile) familiar with traditional Jewish monotheism to understand the new meaning that Jesus had invested in the word "Father." Some kind of clarifying expansion would be essential for the very purpose of *preserving* the meaning of Jesus' original utterance intact. Now this may well not be the best explanation of Matthew 28:19—and, in fact, I suspect rather strongly that it is not—but *in principle* the Evangelical should not dismiss it on the grounds that it contradicts a belief in inerrancy; quite the opposite, it suggests at least one way in which Matthew *could* have chosen accurately to communicate the original meaning of Jesus' terminology and to avoid the misconceptions that a new audience might derive from it. Blanket criticism of a view of *ipsissima vox* that allows for this type of representational freedom is entirely unwarranted.[66]

C. HISTORICAL-CONTEXTUAL SOLUTIONS

The types of limitations imposed by historical context emerge most clearly in a discussion of "progressive revelation." Logical contradictions between Old and New Testament teaching do occur (consider all the so-called ceremonial laws that the New Testament no longer enjoins upon God's people) until one recognizes the New Testament belief that the Old Testament no longer applies as it did before the coming of Jesus. This altered historical perspective also accounts for seeming discrepancies *within* the Gospels (and Acts), since these books describe the events (from the Crucifixion through Pentecost) that brought about this change.

1. Thus, in Matthew 10:5–6 Jesus commands the disciples to go nowhere among the Gentiles but only to the lost sheep of the house of Israel, while in the Great Commission (Matt. 28:18–20) He sends them to all the ἔθνη of the earth. Despite elaborate attempts to explain this change of heart in terms of some division within the Matthean community,[67] the best explanation remains the traditional one— Jesus (like Paul) came first for the Jews, and after He and His disciples had preached almost exclusively to them, they turned their attention to the larger Gentile world surrounding them.

2. Similarly, the perplexing inconsistencies of Luke-Acts, with its portrait of the first Christians' somewhat schizophrenic attitudes toward the law, most likely reflect accurate historical reminiscence of a fledgling religion frequently uncertain as to how to identify itself over and against Judaism. As I have argued in detail elsewhere, Luke must not be pitted against other New Testament writers as a more conservative defender of the Law. Rather, a careful study of his redactional tendencies reveals that he strongly emphasizes the freedom and newness of the inaugurated kingdom.[68]

A more subtle problem in historical-contextual analysis surfaces when authors assume knowledge on the part of their audiences that may no longer be recoverable. The historian (secular or religious) often has to postulate a resolution of conflicting data that may be far from demonstrable. At other times, supplementary historical information may grant a particular reconstruction greater probability.

3. For example, did Jesus allow for an exception to His mandate against divorce (Mt 19:9/Mk 10:11)? Carson's thorough resumé of the complex literature on this issue permits omission of detail here.[69] The traditional explanation of this formal contradiction remains the best. Mark's version assumes the reader's familiarity with the contemporary debate on divorce, in which all parties agreed that adultery offered legitimate grounds. Matthew merely makes this assumption explicit. The recent reply from Charles Ryrie and his students that this interpretation leaves Jesus' position no different from that of Shammai[70] misses the full force of the overall pericope (Mt 19:3–12/Mk 10:2–12), in which Jesus challenges even the strictest Pharisaic position ("for your hardness of heart he wrote you this commandment"—i.e., Dt 24:1–4). Moreover, neither Evangelist gives any grounds for supporting Ryrie's alternate interpretation, in which Jesus, in the middle of the dialogue, changes the meaning of ἀπολύω from "divorce" to "annul."

4. The likelihood that gaps in historical knowledge provide the key to an alleged error in Scripture greatly increases when that "error" involves a conflict with extrabiblical data. The classic Synoptic example is the problem of dating the census under Quirinius.[71] The linguistic explanation that says αὕτη ἀπογραφὴ πρώτη ἐγένετο should be translated "this was before the census" rather than "this

was the first census" substitutes a rather rare usage of πρῶτος for a moderately awkward one. The developments since Ramsay's proposal of an earlier administration of some kind by Quirinius, though, have only questioned certain details of his argument and have raised many new possibilities for a historical-contextual solution. John Thorley has surely not overstated his recent conclusion from a classicist's standpoint: "Until we can prove conclusively that Luke was wrong, perhaps we should at least allow that he may yet prove not to have misled Theophilus."[72] More positively, E. Jerry Vardaman has discovered micrographic lettering on coins and inscriptions of the time of Christ that appear to substantiate a proconsulate for Quirinius in Syria and Cilicia from 11 B.C. until after Herod's death.[73]

5. A similarly classic example, from the Book of Acts, is the alleged contradiction between Luke and Josephus on the chronology of Theudas and Judas (Ac 5:36; *Ant.* 20:97–98). I. H. Marshall cites this as the clearest example of the scriptural phenomena that make him uneasy with the term "inerrancy," especially since the rarity of the name "Theudas" weighs against arguing for two different men of the same name leading similar rebellions.[74] Yet the similarities between the accounts end there, as E. Yamauchi has emphasized,[75] and Theudas can be a contraction of Theodotus, Theodorus, or Theodosius.[76] That Luke and Josephus had two separate people in view remains the most probable explanation, even from the standpoint of a secular historian.[77] Who is to say that archaeologists will not yet unearth some documentation or inscription to corroborate Luke here as they have done for him consistently elsewhere?

D. FORM-CRITICAL SOLUTIONS

1. The Role of Oral Transmission

The exhaustive study by E. P. Sanders of the tendencies of oral transmission in early Christian tradition dealt a fatal blow to Bultmann's "law of increasing distinctness," and Leslie Keylock's subsequent work should have buried it.[78] Instead, a tendency towards abbreviation frequently appears, as I have discussed in some detail in connection with the *Gospel of Thomas*.[79] But many stylistic tendencies peculiar to the oral retelling of the various forms that Bultmann enumerated remain valid.[80] For example, the Lukan account of the parable of the wicked husbandmen streamlines and restructures the arrival of the various servants into a climactic threefold sequence (Lk 20:9–16a/Mk 12:1–9). So too the famous inversion of the killing and casting out of the son in the same parable (common to Luke and Matthew) probably reflects no theological allegorization of the crucifixion of Jesus outside the walls of Jerusalem but only a stylistic improvement to create climactic order. The most likely locus for both (1) and (2) is in oral tradition.[81]

Matthew's omission of the Capernaum centurion's Jewish embassy to mediate between him and Jesus to request healing for his slave probably also reflects form-critical processes at work. Ancient convention permitted referring to someone speaking or acting when it was a subordinate who actually carried out the command (cf. Mt 27:26 on Pilate scourging Jesus, 2Ki 21:10 with 2Ch 33:10 on God speaking to Manasseh by His prophets, and Plutarch's *Life of Alexander* 73:1 with Arrian's *Anabasis* 7:16.5 on Alexander "meeting" the Chaldean seers through Nearchus), and modern convention is not that different (e.g., saying that "the president announced . . . " when in fact it was his press secretary who spoke with reporters). But form criticism supplies the motive for this type of shorthand. H. J. Held labels it the "law of scenic twofoldness." In other words, the oral transmission of a detailed narrative tends to simplify the story so that no more than two characters engage in conversation at any one time.[82] No theological distinctive or correction of earlier tradition is intended.[83]

2. The Stereotype Form of a Pericope

A second way that form criticism can help to explain differences between parallels (without implying a distortion of meaning) involves the stereotype form of a pericope. The parable of the rich man and Lazarus (Lk 16:19–31) provides a fairly noncontroversial example (at least for biblical, though not always for systematic, theologians!). Since a parable makes an extremely limited number of main points,[84] one need not worry if this picture of the afterlife differs from every other Scripture on the topic. Local color from Jewish and Egyptian folklore has dramatized the depiction of Hades and Abraham's bosom, but the exegete is not committed to view Jesus' appropriation of this imagery as doctrinal endorsement. Rather, Jesus' emphasis lies in verses 27–31, for which no parallel emerges in the extrabiblical literature. The rich man's sin lay not in his wealth *per se* but in his lack of repentance—to which the law directed him and for which even a resurrection would provide no compelling stimulus.

A more controversial example might be the saying about the coin in the fish's mouth (Mt 17:27). At first glance, most assume Matthew is here relating what he believed was a genuine miracle of Jesus. Yet even a superficial rereading reveals that no event is ever narrated; Jesus merely gives a cryptic command. This passage cannot be categorized along with the other miracle stories, because it is not a *story*. Matthew never tells us that Peter obeyed the command; and given his propensity for disbelief and misunderstanding, that obedience can scarcely be taken for granted. Even if Peter did go to the sea, we have no record of how he interpreted his Lord's words. Marcus Ward suggests that perhaps Jesus meant for Peter "to catch fish which can be sold to pay the tax for them both."[85] Alternately, G. M. Lee likens the saying to a picturesque and slightly humorous injunction to "Go and catch a fish, and it will be useful for our purpose as one of those fabled fishes with a coin in their mouth."[86]

Conservative commentators who do not believe that Jesus meant this command to be taken literally are troubled—not because they have an antisupernatural bias but because this is a rather uncharacteristic, seemingly trivial, and unnecessarily spectacular action simply to pay a tax. Richard Bauckham diminishes this distinctiveness somewhat by suggesting that this is a gift-miracle like the feedings of the multitudes and an occasion when Jesus and the Twelve were quite destitute.[87] Unfortunately, nothing in the context corroborates this otherwise attractive suggestion, whereas the immediately preceding verses do disclose that Jesus has just been speaking in a parabolic mode. Tellingly, Bauckham admits that the primary unsolved question for his thesis is the form of verse 27. Recognizing this entirely distinct form and the juxtaposition of a short metaphor in verses 25–26 makes opting for an ironic or metaphorical rather than a literal interpretation of Jesus' words very attractive, even if we may not know for sure the precise import of that metaphor. To cite Lee again: "I yield to no one in the belief that miracles happen, but when a miracle seems more characteristic of D. D. Home than of Christ, I think we should . . . ask whether a non-miraculous explanation is possible."[88] A rather elementary form-critical observation in this instance suggests that one is.

E. AUDIENCE-CRITICAL SOLUTIONS

If the Evangelists supply obviously distinct settings for what synopses nevertheless present as parallel passages, those pericopae deserve *a priori* consideration as different sayings or events from different times in Jesus' ministry. Two examples that I have discussed elsewhere are the Matthean and Lukan "versions" of the parables of the talents (pounds) (Mt 25:14–30/Lk 19:11–27) and of the lost sheep (Mt 18:12–14/Lk 15:3–7).[89]

An apparent doublet within one Gospel offers another type of illustration. Many critics, for example, assume that Mark (or his tradition) invented the feeding of the 4,000 (Mk 8:1–10) on the basis of the feeding of the 5,000 (6:33–44).[90] Yet Mark implicitly contrasts a largely Jewish (the 5,000) audience with a largely Gentile (the 4,000) one, with the latter narrative grouped together with other stories of Jesus' travel outside of the land of Galilee (7:24–37; cf. also the distinctive words for "basket" in 6:43 and 8:8[91]). Moreover, Mark subsequently depicts Jesus referring back to both events as separate incidents (Mk 8:19–20). The only real stumbling block to agreeing with Mark's presentation is the apparent absurdity of the disciples not recalling the first feeding as they question Jesus before the second (8:4). Yet Knackstedt points out that the Matthean parallel (Mt 15:33) strongly emphasizes that the disciples' question could refer only to their inability to deal with the problem *alone*.[92] Carson concurs, considering that the new Gentile audience, Jesus' rebuke in John 6:26, and the "vast capacity for unbelief" inherent in humanity all ensure that the disciples' response is "not sufficient to prove this pericope a doublet."[93]

In fact, audience criticism regularly provides the antidote to hypotheses of apparent doublets. An important line must be drawn between the modification and the invention of Gospel material, whether at the traditional or at the redactional stage. As Goldingay emphasizes, even precritical historiography rarely employs wholesale creation *de novo*.[94]

F. SOURCE-CRITICAL SOLUTIONS

The ascription of specific settings or audiences in the Gospels is rare enough that even when audience criticism cannot demonstrate that two apparently parallel pericopae in fact represent different events, this possibility must be entertained. In some instances, it may be source criticism that points in this direction.

1. Major portions of Luke's central section, for example, probably stem from sources peculiar to that Evangelist, and a selection of the parables scattered throughout these chapters, including all of those obviously unparalleled, form a chiastic sequence suggesting some kind of pre-Lukan unity.[95] Included in this chiasmus, however, are the parables of the watchful servants (Lk 12:35–38) and of the great supper (Lk 14:16–24)—for which many have found parallels in Mark 13:34–37 and Matthew 22:1–10, respectively. Source criticism (including an analysis of vocabulary as well as structure[96]) points in the opposite direction, and the problems inherent in assuming that such drastically different "parallels" developed from a common original disappear.

2. Did Jesus command His disciples to take a staff and sandals on their "missionary" journey or not (Mt 10:10/Mk 6:8–9/Lk 9:3)? The absolute antithesis here between Mark and Matthew/Luke has convinced even very conservative scholars of Scripture's errancy.[97] Inerrantists' replies vary. (a) Two different types of staffs and sandals are envisioned[98]—but there is no difference in the Greek diction to support this. (b) Matthew's κτίζω means "acquire" (i.e., extra items), while Mark's αἴρω refers to what they are already carrying/wearing[99]—but Luke also uses αἴρω, and in any event this solution permits too much; Matthew would then be permitting the disciples to carry the money that Mark denies them. (c) All three Gospels agree on the basic concept of traveling light; only the details differ[100]—but this solution must still admit the presence of a contradiction, even if it seems incidental.

The critical consensus, therefore, opts for a source-critical explanation for the differences, the commonest of which is that

Matthew conflated two different accounts of the commission—Mark's and Q's (reflected in Luke). This, however, only pushes the problem back a stage and does not remove the discrepancy. A historical-contextual solution, in which Mark is making an implicit assumption explicit, works for Luke's omission of any reference to sandals[101] but not for Matthew's version nor for either Evangelist's prohibition of a staff. A source-critical solution does seem preferable—but with the somewhat distinct nuances offered by Osborne. Luke 10:1–12 describes Jesus' subsequent sending of the seventy (-two), which contains some closer parallels to Matthew 9:37–10:16 than does Luke 9:1–6. Matthew has consequently conflated Mark's account of the sending of the twelve with Luke's account of the seventy (whether from Q or from some other source), while Luke has assimilated some of his material from chapter 10 into his account in chapter 9.[102] In other words, the prohibitions against staff and sandals originally stemmed only from the latter mission; in the former Jesus did permit these two items.

Is this reconstruction compatible with a doctrine of inerrancy? Indiscriminate conflation and assimilation certainly is not, but in this case Osborne's solution works, precisely because the twelve were most likely part of the seventy.[103] Luke's use of ἑτέρους in 10:1 at first seems to contradict this claim; but on closer examination it contrasts with the three who reject discipleship in 9:57–62 and not with the twelve, who do not reappear until 10:17, 23, where they seem to overlap with the seventy. Neither Matthew nor Luke expected readers to compare his Gospel with Mark's; taken on its own, Matthew and Luke each presents entirely factual reports of what Jesus told His disciples before sending them out to minister in His name, even if they do not spell out the number and nature of these missions as clearly as modern readers might have wished.

G. REDACTION-CRITICAL SOLUTIONS

The abuse of redaction criticism by its more radical practitioners should not blind the more cautious critic to its immense value.[104] In many cases, it provides a more convincing explanation for the differences between the Gospels than does traditional harmonization, without jeopardizing the reliability of any of the canonical versions. The Evangelists' editorial activity includes both stylistic and theological re-presentation of tradition, and one of the reasons redaction criticism sometimes seems so suspect is that certain critics have too often appealed to the latter rather than to the former.

1. Stylistic Redaction

The following two examples present parallel passages where stylistic motivations probably best account for the seeming contradictions, despite the fashion of scholarship to favor more radical evaluations.

a. Did Jesus rebuke the disciples for their lack of faith before or after stilling the storm, and how harsh was He (Mt 8:26/Mk 4:39–40)? Ever since Bornkamm's pioneering redactional study, many have argued that Matthew here contradicts Mark by reversing the order of miracle and rebuke and by substituting "little faith" for "no faith" in order to stress the positive side of the disciples' belief in Jesus.[105] Yet it is hard to see how ὀλιγόπιστοι is any less harsh than οὔπω ἔχετε πίστιν; One could even argue the reverse, that Matthew's declarative label leaves no room for the possibility which Mark preserves for answering his interrogative with a partially positive reply! Matthew does emphasize discipleship (note his addition in 8:23b) but not so as to contradict Mark. As for the change in order, if either evangelist is intending a chronological sequence at this point, it would more likely be Matthew (τότε [Mt 8:26] vs δέ [Mk 4:39]). Mark is content to preserve his typically paratactic narrative without implying that Jesus did not speak to the disciples until after the miracle. Stylistic improvement and characteristic diction best account for Matthew's language, and no contradiction with the Markan narrative need be inferred.[106]

b. Did Jesus cure blind Bartimaeus before or after entering Jericho (Mk 10:46/Lk 18:35)? Here a redactional analysis of Luke's style suggests a better approach than traditional harmonization. Many have argued that Jesus was leaving "old Jericho" and heading toward "new Jericho," since the rebuilt city had left the old ruins intact at a separate nearby site.[107] But what reader would ever suspect that Mark had this former, virtually uninhabited location in mind, especially when he describes Jesus as leaving with "a great multitude"? Hiebert adopts a linguistic solution in which Luke's ἐγγίζειν refers merely to being in the vicinity without the specific connotation of "drawing near."[108] This view would resolve the apparent contradiction, but it supplies no motive for Luke's alteration. A study of Luke's redactional tendencies, however, offers the missing motive. Luke (or the tradition he inherited) consistently abbreviated Mark, as word counts from parallel passages readily show.[109] For Luke's purposes, Mark is unnecessarily detailed (lit., "and they come to Jericho, and as he was leaving Jericho . . . "); so Luke streamlines the narrative while substituting a sufficiently ambiguous verb so as not to contradict Mark (ἐγγίζω for ἔρχομαι). But why not avoid the potential confusion altogether by omitting mention of Jericho as well?[110]

The answer emerges from a study of Luke's geographical references. Despite the impression that Luke 9:51–18:34 is a travel narrative, fewer specific place names occur in these chapters than in any other section of similar length in the Gospels. A topical rather than a chronological outline best accounts for this material.[111] With the reference to Jericho in 18:35, the situation reverses itself dramatically. Luke locates each succeeding pericope in or near a specific city until Jesus and His entourage finally enter Jerusalem (18:35;

19:1,11,28–29). The proximity of all cities to Jerusalem (Jericho, Bethphage, and Bethany) reinforces the previously dormant emphasis of 9:51 and prepares the reader for the climactic arrival in the holy capital and the events that await Jesus there.

Assuming Mark 10:46 is accurate, the conversion of Zacchaeus (Lk 19:1–10) must have occurred before the healing of the beggar, but Luke inverts their order to create a climax within three closely linked pericopae (18:35–43; 19:1–10; 19:11–27; and note the closure in 19:28a). All portray Jesus upending traditional Jewish expectation, but each successive scene causes severer shock waves—healing a blind and so presumably sinful man, fellowshipping with a tax collector, and destroying servants and enemies in a parable in which they clearly stand for the Jewish leaders. Nevertheless, Luke's inversion creates no chronological error, since 19:1 supplies no temporal link with the preceding paragraph.[112]

The examples of the differences between the parallel versions of the storm-stilling and Bartimaeus miracles have raised the question of topical versus chronological narrative in the Gospels. One of the most significant contributions of redaction criticism (some would distinguish this by calling it "composition criticism") is its emphasis on the structure of the Gospels and the original outline and literary design of each Evangelist. The dictum of modern biblical criticism that not one of the Gospels gives enough data for a detailed reconstruction of the chronology of Jesus' ministry merits acceptance—for no other reason than that the data themselves bear this out. A careful analysis shows that no two Gospels contradict each other's chronology—but only if no chronology is read into the juxtaposition of pericopae *except where undeniably temporal connectives appear.*[113]

Granted this principle, it is, therefore, methodologically inconsistent to infer chronology from mere narrative sequence, even where no potential conflicts with parallels arise. Moreover, all three Synoptists regularly group pericopae by form or topic with few temporal connectives (e.g., the miracles of Mt 8–9, the controversy stories of Mk 2:1–3:6, and Luke's central section), so that it is a priori likely that other sections of the Gospels less clearly demarcated in structure also follow a logical rather than chronological outline. Mark's Gospel, often felt to be the most chronological of the three, may in fact be the most topical.[114] Luke's claim to have written in order (Lk 1:3) does not make his Gospel any different; καθεξῆς may refer just as easily to topical as to temporal sequence.[115] An important implication of these findings is that a detailed harmony of the life of Christ is no longer recoverable, not because the Gospels contradict each other in chronology but because they provide too little chronological data. At best, any harmony must be judged merely "possible" and not "demonstrable," and exegesis should base few conclusions upon the hypothetical order of events proposed.[116]

2. Theological Redaction

The second main category of editorial activity is theologically motivated redaction. Certain cases are clear-cut and widely recognized even among conservatives.

a. For example, Luke reverses the order of the second and third temptations of Jesus and replaces the potentially temporal connective τότε with a simple δέ (Lk 4:9/Mt 4:5) in order for the ordeal to climax at the Jerusalem temple. Luke consistently emphasizes Jesus' relationship with that site; his entire two-volume work is probably best outlined geographically, with chiastic parallelism centering attention on the resurrection appearances in and around Jerusalem.[117] Other examples prove more controversial, as with the two that follow.

b. Did Jesus curse the fig tree before or after He cleansed the temple (Mt 21:18–22/Mk 11:12–14,20–25)? Close attention to transitional vocabulary again demonstrates that no necessary contradiction exists. Mark has apparently preserved the more complex historical sequence, which Matthew telescopes and presents as an uninterrupted event. Translations of πρωΐ that include a definite article (e.g., "in the morning") may mislead the reader of Matthew 21:18; Matthew himself gives no indication of the day to which he is referring. Similarly, there is no problem presupposing a gap between Matthew 21:19 and 20, since Matthew never reveals when the disciples saw the withered tree ("at once" only governs the withering, and Mark 11:14 suggests that the disciples only *heard* Jesus' original curse from a distance). The Synoptists omit much information that one could wish they had preserved, so that postulating gaps of this nature is scarcely special pleading. Rather, it fits exactly with the type of redaction that lies behind virtually every page of the Gospels.

Theologically, both Matthew's and Mark's presentations sandwich the cursing miracle and the temple ministry (Mt 21:12–17,18–19,20ff./Mk 11:12–14,15–19,20–25), thus interpreting the former in light of latter. Jesus' *Strafwunder* acts out the parable of the fig tree (Lk 13:6–9), pointing to God's coming judgment upon the faithless, Jewish leaders. Only this type of symbolic or metaphorical explanation of Jesus' actions can save them from seeming extremely capricious, and Matthew's and Mark's redactional linkage in fact clarifies Jesus' historical intentions. The juxtaposition of Jesus' sayings on faith (Mt 21:21–22/Mk 11:22–25) does not refute this interpretation, since the mountain to be cast into the sea probably stands for the temple on Mount Zion and its impending obsolescence.[118] Redaction criticism and a presumption of historical authenticity actually complement one another in service of a coherent exegesis.

c. Did the rich young ruler ask Jesus about the good or did he call Him good (Mt 19:17/Mk 10:18)? An additive harmonization simply affirms both, but the grammatical thread on which this hangs (the continuous force of ἐπηρώτα in Mk 10:17) is extremely slender.[119] A typical redaction-critical explanation alleges that Matthew wanted to avoid the potential mistake that Mark's readers might have made if they inferred that Jesus denied either His divinity or His essential goodness.[120] If such an explanation derives from an invalid reconstruction of the development of primitive Christology, then it of course must be rejected. But it need prove no more problematic than, say, Luke's insertion into the parable of the wicked husbandmen of "perhaps" (ἴσως) before the vineyard owner's declaration that "they will respect" his son (Lk 20:13; cf. Mk 12:6), lest it appear that Jesus thought that God really believed the Jews would accept Him as their Messiah. Furthermore, the result of Matthew's modification of the rich young ruler's dialogue with Jesus in fact shifts the focus of attention from Christology to the Law, thereby making any emphasis on a heightened view of Jesus unlikely.[121]

Redaction criticism, then, supplies a motive for Matthew's change, but does his resultant narrative remain within the bounds of the *ipsissima vox Jesu*? Here a more traditional (but not "additive") harmonization provides a method for replying affirmatively. If the man, as in Mark, originally asked "Good teacher, what must I do to inherit eternal life?" Matthew would be entirely justified in interpreting the question as one about a good work (ἀγαθόν). Jesus could then very easily have replied in a way deliberately susceptible of a double meaning. Even in Greek, τί με λέγεις ἀγαθόν can just conceivably be translated, "Why do you say to me 'good'?"—which could then hark back to either Mark's or Matthew's use of the adjective.[122] A harmonization that might seem at first like a desperate expedient and a redactional analysis reminiscent of an unwarranted skepticism in fact combine to lend credence to each other. Neither Evangelist has distorted Jesus' original meaning, and the motives of both become intelligible.

Similar marriages of these odd bedfellows undoubtedly occur much more often than commentators of any ideological commitment have suspected. At least two other probable examples include the chronology of the Transfiguration (six days or eight after the first passion prediction?—cf. Mk 9:2 and Lk 9:28) and the centurion's cry at the Crucifixion (Son of God or innocent man?—cf. Mk 15:39 and Lk 23:47). In the former instance, Luke's "about" (ὡσεί) avoids a formal contradiction with Mark, but only a realization of the theological parallels between the Transfiguration and the ministry of Moses (which included a six-day preparation for revelation—Ex 24:16) makes any sense of the difference. In the latter instance, a nonadditive harmonization can supply an original saying of the centurion from which both Mark's and Luke's versions can be derived as faithful interpretations (e.g., "Certainly this man was justified in calling God his Father.").[123] Yet only the recognition of Mark's emphasis on "Son of God" and Luke's apologetic for the legality of Christianity account for such drastic editing.

H. HARMONIZATION

The last examples above form a natural bridge to this final category of solutions to discrepancies between Synoptic parallels. In certain limited instances—especially where the Gospel writers greatly abbreviate accounts of complex events that occur in several stages or over long periods of time—applications of harmonization in its narrower, additive sense do seem justified.

1. George E. Ladd's reconstruction of the sequence of events surrounding Jesus' resurrection offers a good example. The four Evangelists chose to record primarily divergent features of a complex Easter-event, yet without entangling themselves in any necessary historical contradictions.[124] For shorter narratives, however, usually some type of external evidence that key details are missing is needed before one can feel very comfortable with harmonization.

2. For example, Luke's love of logical inversion leads one to suspect that, for some topical purpose, he has simply switched the order of the bread and the cup in his account of the Last Supper (Lk 22:15–19a/cf. Mk 14:22–25). No such purpose, however, readily presents itself, and familiarity with the *four* cups drunk during the Passover haggadah makes probable the explanation that Luke and Mark are referring to different portions of the ceremony. The resurgent favor with which text critics look upon Luke 22:19b–20 greatly enhances this hypothesis.[125]

3. Or consider the "trials" of Jesus before the Sanhedrin (Mk 14:55–65, 15:1/Lk 22:66–71). The discrepancy between Mark's night-time and Luke's daytime hearings seems inescapable until one realizes that the Sanhedrin probably could not reach a legal verdict at night and that Mark 15:1a refers to some type of brief postdawn proceedings.[126] Yet, in their ecstasy of finally having captured Jesus, it is historically incredible that the Jewish authorities should not have begun the unofficial nighttime interrogation that Mark depicts.[127] The only obstacle to this reconstruction lies in the close similarity between the Markan and Lukan dialogues. Would Jesus so graciously have indicted Himself a second time (Lk 22:69), even despite His more muted response (vv 67–68,70)? Yet, even a veiled affirmative (v 70) to the question of His identity with the Son of God would have satisfied the Sanhedrin, and Luke may have simply assimilated additions from Mark's narrative into his own version, knowing that the council had, in some sense, to repeat its agenda. As Carson cautions,

> the sad fact is that there are few methodologically reliable tools for distinguishing between, say, two forms of one aphoristic saying, two reports

of the same saying uttered on two occasions, or one report of one such saying often repeated in various forms but preserved in the tradition in one form (surely not problematic if only the *ipsissima vox* is usually what is at stake).[128]

Although the trial narratives are not aphorisms, the proposed assimilations involve only brief, memorable utterances, so an application of Carson's principle to this new situation seems safe.

4. Additional applications of straightforward harmonizing seem plausible for the famous examples of character doubling (two blind men—Mt 20:30/cf. Mk 10:46; two demoniacs—Mt 8:28/cf. Mk 5:2; two men by the empty tomb—Lk 24:4/cf. Mk 16:5). If there were two, then obviously there was one. Examples of such doubling are too rare to attribute them to either form or redaction-critical processes, and the Evangelists make nothing of the additions.[129] Harmonization seems sanest; one member of a pair (or group) often stands out from the other(s) and thereby receives exclusive attention. In the Gospels, this focus usually falls on the person who acts as a spokesman.[130]

I. CONCLUSIONS

This survey of problem passages has admittedly proved sketchy. Some will prefer solutions for certain passages different than those suggested here. Appreciation of the categories of types of solutions and of the principles involved in applying them is more important than complete agreement with the category chosen under which to subsume each individual illustration. As Carl Henry stresses, "evangelical scholars do not insist that historical realities conform to all their proposals for harmonization; their intent, rather, is to show that their premises do not cancel the logical possibility of reconciling apparently divergent reports."[131]

Two fundamental conclusions, however, do merit more widespread acceptance than they have received. First, "additive" harmonization is entirely legitimate as one among many tools for alleviating tension between Gospel parallels, but a survey of the classic "contradictions" suggests that in most cases it is not the best tool. Second, the newer branches of Gospel study (source, form, and redaction criticism), far from necessarily proving Scripture's errancy, regularly enable the exegete to reconcile apparent contradictions in a much less contrived and artificial manner than traditional harmonization. Of course, complex problems regularly require a combination of methods, and the innovative conjunction of redaction criticism with harmonization emerges as a powerful but little-used tool for breaking down some of the most resistant barriers to belief in the accuracy of the Evangelists' narratives.

IV. OTHER BIBLICAL AND EXTRABIBLICAL PARALLELS

The methods for solving conflicts among the Synoptics have not developed in a vacuum but out of the study of the other historical writings in Scripture along with noncanonical literature, both religious and secular. If the principles outlined here have any validity, then they should also suggest solutions to seeming discrepancies between other pairs of paralleled narratives. In fact, that is precisely what happens. The conclusions of this final major section of our study show divergences among "synoptic" corpora elsewhere in ancient historiography yielding to the same spectrum of solutions as employed with Matthew, Mark, and Luke. The other main "synoptic" problem in the New Testament contrasts Acts with autobiographical portions of the Pauline epistles. Conservatives have regularly emphasized that much of the tension between Acts and Paul dissipates when the distinctive genres and purposes of the different books receive due emphasis, while the critical consensus clings to skepticism concerning the historical accuracy of Acts. Ironically, the more liberal approach thus downplays the redaction-critical type of argument that the conservatives utilize, although neither "camp" seems aware that it is taking a different position from the one it generally adopts when studying the Gospels. But more closely analogous to the problems of harmonizing the Synoptics are some examples further removed from the New Testament, to which we now turn.

A. CHRONICLES-KINGS

The classic problem of the Old Testament contrasts the works of the Chronicler and the so-called Deuteronomic historian. Chronicles has generally received short shrift in scholarly circles, but recent studies have rehabilitated the reputation of its author as a theologian[132] and even to a limited extent as a historian.[133] In fact, all eight categories applied to Synoptic divergences come into play in a study of Chronicles.

1. The Old Testament autographs prove vastly more difficult to reconstruct than their New Testament counterparts. The undeniable contradictions that punctuate the extant texts of Samuel through Chronicles most likely reflect copyists' errors. Numbers and names have become distorted most easily; on the former, John Wenham cogently stresses that "the more absurd the figures the less likely it is that they were invented," and the "absurdity suggests the likelihood that someone has been trying to transmit records faithfully, in spite of the fact that they do not seem to make sense."[134] Wenham itemizes eight types of textual corruption and then discusses at length twelve possible meanings of אֶלֶף besides "thousand."[135] J. Barton Payne supplements Wenham with an exhaustive listing of the 213 numerals

that Chronicles contains for which parallels occur elsewhere in Scripture, and he notes that only nineteen create contradictions. The maxim that Chronicles consistently embellished its sources fails utterly—and all the more so since it contains the higher of the divergent figures in only eleven of the nineteen cases.[136]

A more famous contradiction pits Elhanan against David as the slayer of Goliath (cf. 1Ch 20:5 with 1Sa 17:4,7,50 and 2Sa 21:19). The Chronicler has preserved what was most likely the original text of 2 Samuel, with Elhanan slaying Lahmi the brother of Goliath and not Goliath himself. It is easy to see how אֶת־לַחְמִי אֲחִי גָּלְיָת could give rise to בֵּית־הַלַּחְמִי אֵת גָּלְיָת.[137] Interestingly, traditional Jewish exegesis opts for a less likely, additive harmonization in which there were two different giants with the same name or title![138]

2. Contextual analysis suggests that the "help" Tiglath-pileser gave Ahaz (2Ki 16:7–9) proved short-lived and misguided, so that the Chronicles can deliver the verdict of a later generation that Ahaz received *no* help (2Ch 28:16,21). Chronicles also uses the word "war" in a sense that excludes minor border skirmishes, so that it can claim that Asa and Baasha lived in peace with each other for twenty years (2Ch 15:10,19) despite the apparent disagreement of 1 Kings 15:16.[139] An appreciation of the Chronicler's redactional motives makes both of these linguistic explanations intelligible, since he sought to summarize each king's reign with sweeping, moralistic generalizations.

More controversial are some apparent representational changes. Did Solomon's "molten sea" hold two thousand (1Ki 7:23–26) or three thousand baths (2Ch 4:2–5)? Wenham and Payne favor textual corruption; Curtis and Madsen, a historical error; and the Targums harmonize by assuming that one bath is a dry and the other a liquid measure.[140] Evidence shows, though, that the capacity of a bath had changed over time, so that Chronicles alters the number precisely to preserve the original measure, just as English translations often provide British or American equivalents.[141]

The Chronicler similarly turns the temple guard, including foreign mercenaries (Carites), into Levites (2Ch 23:1–11/2Ki 11:4–12, 2Ch 24:4–14a/2Ki 12:4–16). The typical conservative harmonization that centurions, Carites, and Levites all worked together[142] does not seem to do justice either to the Chronicler's overwhelming preoccupation with the Levites or to their almost total absence from all of Samuel-Kings (Chronicles—99 times, Samuel-Kings—3 times). The critical consensus still concludes that no Levites functioned during the early monarchy, because it is thought that that part of the "mosaic" code did not develop until later; but this requires the references that do occur in the Deuteronomist's work (note also the 14 in Joshua and 10 in Judges) all to be later interpolations. May not a mediating view that sees a contemporization occurring prove best? As R. J. Coggins says, "we should not dismiss this as falsification;

the Chronicler is concerned to tell the story in terms that would be appropriate for his own day, when there was no closer equivalent to a royal bodyguard than the religious leaders of Jerusalem."[143] Goldingay concurs: "Thus he describes as Levites those who would have been Levites in his day."[144]

3. The most famous illustration of extrabiblical history helping to solve discrepancies within Kings-Chronicles involves the Assyrian king lists aiding in synchronizing the chronology of the Israelite and Judean kings' reigns. The scholar who almost single-handedly discovered a reconciliation for all the apparently conflicting data is Edwin R. Thiele.[145] The type of critique that his work deserves far outstrips the bounds of this study, and several of the problems that he solves by historical criticism may instead reflect textual corruption.[146] Siegfried Horn, nevertheless, concludes that "Thiele's chronological scheme with its logic and historical integrity has gradually become accepted by an everwidening circle of biblical scholars of all persuasions."[147]

4. Almost no form-critical study of Chronicles exists, primarily because its author claims to have worked almost exclusively from written sources (1Ch 29:29; 2Ch 9:29; 12:15; etc.). Nevertheless, he occasionally presents a narrative more abbreviated and freely rewritten than typically; perhaps the tendencies of oral tradition account for a few of these (esp. 1Ki 3:6–14 and 2Ch 1:9–12).

5. Audience criticism also rarely enters into the study of Kings-Chronicles, but 1 Chronicles 23:1 and 29:22 present one apparent doublet. Was Solomon really proclaimed king of Israel twice? The contexts suggest that the first ceremony involved only Israel's leaders, while the second enacted David's decree in front of all the people of Jerusalem.

6. On the other hand, source criticism looms even larger in the study of Kings and Chronicles than it did for the Synoptics. The detailed lists of sources scattered throughout these works makes their unparalleled material readily attributable to these long-lost documents. One "microlevel" and one "macrolevel" example illustrate further. First, the Chronicler lists additional "mighty men" of David not found in his primary source (1Ch 11:41b–47/2Sa 23:24–39). Stylistic variations and authentic trans-Jordanian locations suggest that this material stems from a different source—one that supplements the earlier list rather than contradicting it.[148] Second, the most striking omission of 1 and 2 Chronicles is the large amount of information about the court history of David and about Elijah and Elisha. Since some of this material could have enhanced the Chronicler's narrative and coheres with his purposes, the omission proves puzzling. Yet recent studies favor viewing the "succession narrative" and the Elijah-Elisha cycles as independent sources supplementing the Deuteronomist's work; thus, A. G. Auld speculates that the Chronicler simply may not have had access to them.[149]

7. Redaction criticism again combines with harmonization to solve two of the strangest differences between the Chronicles and the Deuteronomist—one very famous and one rather obscure. The classic "contradiction" comes with David's infamous census. Did God or Satan move David to number Israel (2Sa 24:1/1Ch 21:1)? Almost all agree that the Chronicler wanted to avoid the mistaken inference that God directly causes evil, and more conservative commentators stress that Scripture always portrays Satan as subordinate to God.[150] Chronicles, therefore, does not contradict Samuel. The Targum to 1 Chronicles 21:1, in fact, conflates the two, having Yahweh incite Satan to move David to number Israel! As with the pericopae of the rich young ruler and Jesus, a canonical writer markedly alters his source—but for the very purpose of preventing a tragic misinterpretation of it. Redaction criticism supplies the motive for the change and rescues an accompanying harmonization from the charge of being arbitrary.

A second illustration comes from a comparison of 2 Chronicles 2:13–14 with 1 Kings 7:13–14. Was Huram-abi's mother from Dan or Naphtali? The contiguity of these two territories makes a mistake unlikely and points toward Dillard's harmonization as the most probable of several proposed; one is her geographical residence and the other her genealogical relationship. But why would Chronicles bother to notice this? Dillard continues: "rather than be distracted by a harmonistic problem, it is more important in this case to see that the Chronicler has assigned Huram-abi a Danite ancestry to perfect further the parallel with Oholiab."[151] Oholiab, from the tribe of Dan, was one of the two master craftsmen who constructed much of the tabernacle in the wilderness (Ex 38:22–23), and many commentators have noted that the Chronicler viewed Solomon and Huram (the suffix *-abi* actually means "my master") and their work in God's temple in a similar light. Redaction criticism explains even an obscure change from Kings to Chronicles and prevents the inference that either author erred.

8. "Additive" harmonization has already come into play in the previous two examples; two others afford instances of its use apart from other critical tools. The last pair of parallels notes also that Huram comes from Tyre, but so does the king of that city who has the identical name (2Ch 2:11). Surprisingly, I have not discovered anyone claiming that these texts should not be harmonized and taken to refer to two different people, presumably because Solomon could scarcely have conscripted a foreign king into manual labor (1Ki 7:13). But then similar harmonizations elsewhere should not receive the undue scorn sometimes unleashed. A second example involves the sources for Asa's reign. Were the rest of his actions recorded in the Book of the Chronicles of the Kings of Judah (1Ki 15:23) or in the Book of the Kings of Judah and Israel (2Ch 16:11)? The proliferation of sources cited in

Kings and Chronicles makes "both" the most likely answer; it is even possible that the two names refer to the same work.[152]

The conclusions arising at the end of this survey strikingly resemble those from the study of the Synoptics. None of the "contradictions" cited proves irreconcilable with its parallel, but harmonization, narrowly defined, is only a relatively unimportant tool among many for solving the various problems. In some instances, however, its legitimacy increases as it joins hands with redaction criticism to provide probable solutions, when either method alone would fall far short of convincing.

B. THE WRITINGS OF JOSEPHUS

Turning to extracanonical Jewish literature, one might study the synoptic problems that surface from a comparison of the midrashim with the Old Testament[153] or of the different Targums with each other.[154] But critical texts, translations, concordances, and redactional analyses of these works are frequently lacking; more groundwork is needed than can be laid in a survey of this nature. Robert Johnston's comprehensive catalogue of the Tannaitic parables provides such a foundation for a comparison of parallels within that corpus;[155] I have elsewhere begun such a comparison and there noted that the types of changes between parallels often closely mirror the development of the Synoptic tradition, while rarely precluding the preservation of the *ipsissima vox* of the original rabbinic speakers.[156]

Among Hellenistic Jewish sources, the critical tools are more developed, and perhaps the most significant parallels for comparison come from the works of Josephus. Historical overlap occurs between the *Antiquities* and the Old Testament (including the Apocrypha),[157] and between the *War* and the *Life*,[158] but the closest parallels to the problems already encountered in Scripture seem to emerge from a comparison of the later *Antiquities* and the earlier *War*.[159] Because the same author penned both works, attempts to reconcile conflicts between the narratives are all the more appropriate, unless one assumes that he either corrected or forgot his earlier writing.

1. Students of Josephus have regularly attributed his inflated figures for populations, armies, and casualties to a tendency to embellish, but textual corruption is increasingly becoming a more satisfactory solution. The parallels with Kings-Chronicles are obvious. Cohen's caution, that "prudence dictates that we refrain from any conclusions [of historical inaccuracy] based on these variations,"[160] needs regular repetition in biblical circles. A. Byatt, in fact, argues that the figures Josephus gives are actually more often consistent with other historical data than is usually recognized.[161]

2. Did Herod see his enemies run past him when he was outside or inside of his bathhouse (*War* 1:340/*Ant.* 14:462)? Grammatical analysis removes the apparent discrepancy. The use of the participle

in the former instead of the preposition plus infinitive in the latter (εἰσελθών/πρὶν . . . εἰσελθεῖν) creates some ambiguity and is probably circumstantial rather than temporal. Since Josephus seldom quotes himself verbatim, the change is probably entirely stylistic. Did Herod order the immediate (παραχρῆμα) execution of both Mariamme and Joseph (*War* 1:444), or did he pardon Mariamme until the later death of Soemius (*Ant.* 15:80–87, 218–31)? The *War* probably just omitted the latter detail for brevity's sake; "immediately" is merely a literary device to dramatize the story (cf. Mark's consistent use of εὐθύς).

3. Could there really have been two different Sanballat's who opposed Israel in similar fashion (*Ant.* 11:7–8/Ne 2–6)? The discovery of additional historical data in the Samaria papyri corroborates Josephus' record and validates a harmonization that many previously rejected outright.[162]

4. Form criticism scarcely enters into a comparison of Josephus' works, since it is implausible to imagine either his writing circulating in oral tradition or his dependence on such a tradition in subsequent historical composition. This is regularly the case with extrabiblical literature, as Bruce Waltke has emphasized, although his wholesale rejection of *Traditionsgeschichte* remains rather extreme.[163]

5. Did Agrippa pray for Tiberius' death and Gaius' accession at a feast or during a chariot ride (*War* 2:178–80/*Ant.* 18:168)? The narratives otherwise differ markedly; the audience-critical presumption in favor of two different events gains credence when one realizes that Agrippa courted Gaius over a considerable period of time. The wording of the prayers, moreover, reveals no verbal parallelism apart from the names of the two men, although Josephus' redactional style precludes any wide-ranging deductions from this fact.

6. Source criticism has dominated Josephan study even more than it did with Kings-Chronicles. Where Josephus cites no source, he is generally very brief, suggesting that he does not fill the gaps in his sources with creative invention.[164] Even those briefer sections probably rely on unidentified writings, as recent comparisons with the Babylonian chronicles demonstrate.[165]

7. Redaction criticism of Josephus remains in its infancy, but great strides have been taken.[166] Both the *Antiquities* and the *War* disclose dominant themes and interpretations with which Josephus' contemporaries would not always have agreed, but neither is demonstrably more or less historical than the other, at least with respect to first-century events.[167] Josephus' paraphrastic style reminds us, as F. G. Downing puts it, that "it is not the divergencies among the synoptists (or even between them and John), in parallel contexts, that are remarkable; it is the extraordinary extent of verbal similarities." Again, "the relationship may betoken a much greater respect, one for the other, even than Josephus' for Scripture."[168]

An excellent example of more "theological" editing emerges in *Antiquities* 14:177–84 and *War* 1:212–13. In the former, Hyrcanus advises Herod to flee Jerusalem due to the Sanhedrin's murderous plots; in the latter, Herod imagines (ὑπολαμβάνω) that his escape was contrary to the king's wishes. But Herod could have easily imagined that Hyrcanus' advice was a trap due to the ongoing enmity between the two men (cf. *War* 1:214, *Ant.* 14:180). More importantly, the motives for the shift in perspective seem clear. In the *War*, Josephus tries to discredit his countrymen who defied what he viewed as the providentially-ordained Roman empire, and this highlighting of internal Jewish conflict colors his narrative of earlier history as well. In the *Antiquities*, though, he deals more dispassionately with this material in order to portray Jewish history as positively as possible, as he defends the merits of his heritage before a pagan audience.

8. An obvious candidate for simple harmonization comes with *Antiquities* 19:188 ("four cohorts who regarded freedom from imperial rule as more honorable than tyranny") and *War* 2:205 ("three that remained loyal"). Neither passage claims that its number is a total, despite the impressions of some English translations.[169] Perhaps Josephus learned of an extra character involved in those not too distant events (ca. A.D. 41) and so augmented the number in his later work.

The above illustrations do not prove that all of the discrepancies among Josephus' writings can be eliminated. Perhaps even some of the examples cited here are simple errors on his part. But as with our previous surveys, the point is to note the wide spectrum of methods—harmonization included but not dominant—that seem in many instances to vindicate the general reliability of the author. No theological commitments lead any Josephan scholar always to seek for an alleviation of tension between parallels in the way that they do for conservative students of Scripture. But a catena of quotations from Rajak's masterful study makes one pause to consider their *a fortiori* application to the biblical literature: "as long as what Josephus tells us is *possible*, we have no right to correct it," "if we find no internal grounds for impugning the historian's story, then, in the absence of evidence from outside, it must have *prima facie* claim on our belief," and "Josephus' story, the best we have for the Jewish revolt, is the one that should stand."[170] Rajak herself regularly offers examples of harmonization in both its broad and narrow sense to vindicate Josephus' accuracy;[171] how much more ought biblical scholars abandon once and for all the notion that attempts to reconcile apparent tensions in Scripture as somehow unscientific or only confessionally motivated!

C. ARRIAN'S AND PLUTARCH'S LIVES OF ALEXANDER

Examples from historians in every historical period could be endlessly multiplied to prove this last point. This survey will conclude, however, with only one more, this time from secular Greek historiography. C. B. Welles summarizes the reasons for choosing the biographies of Alexander the Great as an apt parallel to the Synoptic problems for harmonization:

> Usually in Ancient History we are confronted with fragmentary and inadequate sources, from which the most probable story must be reconstructed, or, more rarely, with a single overpowering source from which we vainly struggle to escape: a Thucydides or a Tacitus. The problem of Alexander is comparable, actually, only to the problem of Jesus. In both cases there exists ample evidence, each appropriate to the career and importance of the individual. In both cases the evidence is a generation or two later than the events in question . . . and in both cases the evidence is contradictory and tendentious.[172]

In the case of the canonical evidence for Jesus, "apparently contradictory" is a more accurate assessment, but otherwise Welles' analysis stands. The discussion here will limit itself to Alexander's Greek biographers (Arrian and Plutarch); if the later Latin writers were added (Quintus Curtius, Diodorus, and Justin), a short treatment would become impossible. Generally, though, this so-called "Vulgate" tradition is not held to contain nearly as much reliable history,[173] so its omission from this survey seems justified. Parallels with the Gospels also extend to the emergence of apocryphal, legendary traditions, but these later "Alexander-romances" are sufficiently separated in time from his historians that they too may be passed over.[174]

An important difference between Arrian and Plutarch on the one hand and Matthew, Mark, and Luke on the other is that the former often admit that their sources contradict each other and that they have had to choose among them or attempt a harmonization (see, e.g., *Anab.* 2:12.8 or 3:30.5).[175] They agree that Aristobulus and Ptolemy provide the most reliable eyewitness testimony, though even here they make no pretense for the inerrancy of their most trusted authorities (see esp. *Anab.* 4:14.3–4). Alan Wardman elaborates:

> It was an accepted practice for ancient historians to decide between different or conflicting versions of the same event by appealing to the criterion of probability. . . . As source criticism in the modern sense was virtually unknown, writers could do little else than keep in mind the more obvious bias or prejudice of their sources and follow what seemed to be the more likely account.[176]

Yet even this "crude" method resembles modern redaction criticism more than traditional harmonization, reinforcing the claim of the former to an ancient pedigree. Oral tradition also comes into play, as many ancient historians wrote from a combination of notes and highly trained (though fallible) memories.[177] Occasionally form-critical processes will therefore reveal themselves, too. In fact, once again all eight of the categories utilized throughout this article take turns in accounting for discrepancies between Arrian and Plutarch.

1. Textual corruption again plagues the transmission of numbers. Arrian, for example, allows Alexander not much more (οὐ πολλῷ πλείους) than 30,000 infantry and 5,000 cavalry for his march to the Hellespont (*Anab.* 1:11.2). Plutarch frankly admits that his sources vary, with figures from 30,000 to 43,000 footmen and from 4,000 to 5,000 horses (*Alex.* 15:1). A. B. Bosworth, nevertheless, offers an additive harmonization by claiming it "extremely likely" that the higher figures "include the forces already across" the river,[178] while P. A. Brunt believes they include additional mercenaries.[179] Here are two expert, contemporary classicists putting forward the very type of harmonizations that most biblical critics would reject out of hand if they came from Evangelicals.

2. When they heard of Alexander's conquest of Thebes, did the Athenians abandon their mystery festivals because of consternation (ἐκπλαγέντες—*Anab.* 1:10.2) or due to mourning (ὑπὸ πένθους—*Alex.* 13:1)? The semantic overlap between these expressions suggests that one need reject neither, although Hamilton correctly points out that Arrian is more precise.[180] A linguistic solution similarly accounts for a more trivial discrepancy involving names, yet one that is regularly paralleled in biblical orthographic variation (recall the example of the "Gadarene" demoniac). In *Alexander* 66:1, Plutarch notes that Alexander calls a certain island Σκιλλοῦστιν whereas others call it Ψιλτοῦκιν. Arrian accounts for the disagreement; neither is completely precise, for the natives name their homeland Κιλλουτά (*Anab.* 6:19.3).

3. New historical data have made plausible one of the most incredible episodes in Alexander's adventures, the crossing of the ravine to the Rock of Chorienes by the impromptu erection of a massive causeway of tree trunks. Arrian describes the bridge-work done from above and below, requiring the narrowest part of the valley to be somewhere between the top and the bottom (*Anab.* 4:21). Sir Aurel Stein discovered a ravine of approximately the right shape and size at Aornos,[181] so that J. G. Lloyd can claim: "At first reading Arrian's account of its capture seems impossible. No man and no army could achieve such things. But archaeology has proved it. The site is as Arrian describes, and Alexander virtually redesigned the landscape to make the hill accessible."[182]

4. As with Chronicles and Josephus, Plutarch and Arrian depend primarily upon written sources for their information, so form-critical tendencies appear only occasionally. The virtually complete lack of

verbal parallelism between these historians of Alexander—even where they are following the same source and including the same sequence of details—highlights the occasional exception all the more. A few memorable sayings appear in almost identical form in both; these suggest careful transmission in oral tradition. Three good examples involve (a) the oracle of Orpheus, when Aristandrus commanded Alexander to cheer up (*Anab.* 1:11.2/*Alex.* 14:5), (b) the description of Alexander breaking the Gordian knot (*Anab.* 2:3.7/*Alex.* 18:2), and (c) Alexander's rejection of Callisthenes' kiss (*Anab.* 4:12.5/*Alex.* 54:4). In other instances, closely paralleled *content* (i.e., conceptual rather than verbal parallelism) will suddenly intrude into otherwise highly divergent (noncomplementary, though usually noncontradictory) narratives, thus lending credence to the singly attested material as well. Two illustrations here arise out of the stories of Alexander and Parmenio crossing the Granicus (*Anab.* 1:13.6–7/*Alex.* 16:2–3) and Cleitus taunting Alexander (*Anab.* 4:8/*Alex.* 50–54).

5. The similar missions of Phratapliernes and Stasanor during subsequent winters (329–28, 328–27 B.C.) lead Bosworth to label them doublets (*Anab.* 4:7.1, 18.1),[183] but audience criticism corroborates Arrian. In the first passage, the two men have returned from arresting Arsames, Barzanes, and the rebel compatriots of Bessus; in the latter, Alexander dispatches Phratapliernes to bring back Autophradates and Stasanor to become satrap of Media. The similarities between passages are clearly quite meager. An example of apparently conflicting audiences between Plutarch and Arrian also proves harmonizable. Who advised Alexander to attack Darius by night at Gaugamela—Parmenio only (*Anab.* 3:10.1) or a group of lower-ranking advisors (*Alex.* 31:6)? Plutarch's earlier mention of Parmenio (*Alex.* 31:6) actually suggests he was part of the group, while Arrian's later reference to others who were listening (*Anab.* 3:10.2) also shows that Parmenio was not alone.

6. Regular reference to explicit sources throughout the lives of Alexander makes a written origin for undocumented material again very probable. An interesting phenomenon noted also in Josephus strengthens traditional views of Synoptic literary dependence. Even where Arrian and Plutarch narrate the same event from the same source, verbal parallelism is virtually absent. As noted above, the rare exceptions are often attributable to oral tradition, suggesting that ancient historians felt a need to rephrase their sources, even when they had nothing new to add.[184]

This should warn the Synoptic scholar against too quickly reading major implications into minor differences between parallels, and it should also strengthen the Q-hypothesis. Gospel commentators are used to observing the greater variation between Matthew's and Luke's shared material than between either of those Evangelists and Mark. Reading other parallel histories of antiquity, however, underlines the marked parallelism between Matthew and Luke that does exist. The linguistic evidence for some type of Q considerably outweighs that for written sources behind Josephus or the Alexander-historians, where such sources are undeniable!

7. More so than for Chronicles or Josephus, a redactional study of Alexander's biographers reveals periodic interruptions of a basically chronological narrative with topical digressions. Plutarch is especially this way (e.g., *Alex.* 21:5–23; 28; and 39:1–42:4, which illuminate Alexander's self-control, attitude toward divinity, and generosity or loyalty, respectively),[185] but Arrian also evidences "dischronologization." For example, he explicitly acknowledges that "all this which took place not long afterwards, I have related as part of the story of Cleitus, regarding it as really akin to Cleitus' story for the purpose of narration" (*Anab.* 4:14.3–4). Such topical narration may well account for the baffling differences between Plutarch and Arrian on the dating of Darius' embassy to Alexander proposing an early truce (*Anab.* 2:25.1—during the siege of Tyre; *Alex.* 29:4—after returning from the Egyptian oracle to Phoenicia). Bosworth assumes that Arrian has erred, while Hamilton distrusts Plutarch;[186] the tendency to prefer the testimony of any source other than that on which one is commenting seems to extend outside of biblical circles! Yet it seems plausible that Plutarch is simply writing topically at this point. He links his new material to the previous paragraph only loosely (δέ), 28:1 suggests the theme that connects the passages ("In general, he bore himself haughtily toward the barbarians"), and 31:1 clearly resumes a chronological outline.

Redaction criticism can also identify clear emphases and "biases" distinguishing Arrian from Plutarch. Arrian's work is an "encomium," noticeably paralleling Chronicles' preference for praiseworthy material dealing with public—and especially military—accomplishments. Plutarch, on the other hand, "psychologizes" by probing into Alexander's inner motives and recounting more private events, not unlike the presentation of John *vis-à-vis* the Synoptics.

These distinctives may explain the contrasting depictions of Alexander's response to Parmenio's urgent cry for help in the battle of Gaugamela. According to Arrian, he rushes to help him at once (*Anab.* 3:15.1), while Plutarch portrays him rebuking Parmenio's embassy (*Alex.* 32:4). Yet Plutarch narrates a second summons for which Arrian has no parallel; and Alexander eventually does leave his phalanx (*Alex.* 33:7). Arrian seems similarly incomplete, and *Anabasis* 3:15.5 offers incidental corroboration of Plutarch's version; Alexander rests his cavalry ἐπὶ μέσα νύκτας, implying that the battle took longer than a superficial reading might suggest. A complete harmonization may no longer be possible, but Hamilton agrees that Plutarch's sources "evidently spoke of two requests" (and the "Vulgate" tradition corroborates this hypothesis).[187] Alexander probably scorned the first plea for help but responded to the second. More importantly, redaction criticism justifies our historians' selectivity. Philip Stadter's assessment of Arrian's silence merits acceptance:

> The omissions for which Arrian has been faulted, such as his silence on the efforts for the Persian right wing under Mazaeus to outflank Parmenio, seem for the most part the result not of ignorance, or confusion, or of the limited scope of Ptolemy's narrative, but of deliberate decision. Throughout Arrian concentrates on the essentials, making clear the sequence of the events and the tactical genius of Alexander. He avoids completely the romantic, the spectacular, the melodramatic which so dominate our other sources.[188]

8. A straightforward harmonization suggests itself for the problem of how many soldiers had statues erected in their honor after the battle of the river Granicus. Plutarch cites Aristobulus, who records that nine footmen out of thirty-four on Alexander's side were memorialized in this manner (*Alex.* 16:7–8). Arrian, however, awards the honor to twenty-five territorial troops (ἑταίρων—*Anab.* 1:16.4). Is it pure coincidence that $25 + 9 = 34$, or might it not make sense to assume that both authors are correct?

There are probable errors in Arrian and Plutarch; and, again, a few of the passages surveyed may just contain simple mistakes. As with Josephus, though, such errors are not the focus of attention. Rather, the findings of this section again reinforce the general historical trustworthiness of the authors studied; parallel problems in Scripture should seem rather less insoluble as a result.

V. CONCLUSION

The results of these studies of the Synoptics, Chronicles, Josephus, and Alexander dovetail remarkably. The more one studies extrabiblical historiography, the more inescapable the legitimacy of harmonization becomes, even in its narrower, additive sense. At the same time, even the least tendential of annals reveals principles of selectivity that justify a thoroughgoing application of redaction criticism and, although usually less significant, of all of the other branches of literary and historical criticism as well.

Yet what applies to noncanonical literature applies, *mutatis mutandi*, to the biblical writings. As A. Momigliano emphasizes, the problems of understanding the text, discovering sources, and determining the truth are basically the same for both biblical and Greco-Roman history.[189] But, as he continues, the really serious problem of the day is the "widespread tendency . . . to treat historiography as another genre of fiction."[190] A reassessment of the historical accuracy of more than one ancient document is in order. For the results to be unprejudiced, apparent discrepancies between paralleled texts should be subjected to all eight of the methods enumerated above (and these may, in turn, be subdivided or combined in many ways) to see if any yield plausible explanations. Until this has been done, any verdict that equates a given discrepancy with a genuine error will have to remain suspect. In addition, utilizing one category to suggest an implausible solution does not mean that another category may not supply a perfectly valid one.

As for the biblical texts in particular, the sample of some of the most obvious candidates for errors in the Gospels and Chronicles shows that this presumption is rash; all can be explained, even if competing explanations are not equally probable. The tools of higher criticism not only do not have to be viewed as inherently destructive but can, in fact, join hands with traditional harmonization in the service of a high view of Scripture.

CHAPTER FIVE
THE PROBLEM OF *SENSUS PLENIOR*

Douglas J. Moo

Douglas J. Moo

Douglas J. Moo is Associate Professor of New Testament at Trinity Evangelical Divinity School, Deerfield, Illinois. He is a graduate of DePauw University (B.A.), Trinity Evangelical Divinity School (M.Div.), and the University of St. Andrews (Ph.D.). He has authored *The Old Testament in the Gospel Passion Narratives* and *The Epistle of James: An Introduction and Commentary* (TNTC) and co-authored *The Rapture: Pre-, Mid-, or Post-Tribulational?*

CHAPTER FIVE

THE PROBLEM OF SENSUS PLENIOR

I. INTRODUCTION

No factor is cited as an argument against the inerrancy of Scripture more often than the Bible itself. Whatever conclusions about the nature of Scripture that can be demonstrated by theological deduction or on the basis of the claims of the Bible for itself must be tested against the data of the text. And, many conclude, when these phenomena are considered, the idea that the Bible is true in all that it affirms becomes clearly impossible. Careful, objective study of the text reveals numerous errors of one kind or another—historical inaccuracies, discrepancies between the scriptural record and the findings of modern science, and, above all, contradictions between and within biblical books.

Inerrantists, it is often alleged, are guilty either of sweeping these phenomena under the rug of pure deduction or of doing a disservice to the biblical text by foisting on it unlikely and sometimes fantastic harmonistic explanations in order to save their theory. This criticism comes from some within the inerrancy camp as well as from those without. Robert Gundry, for instance, finds numerous clear, theologically motivated contradictions between Matthew on the one hand and Mark and Luke on the other. He criticizes fellow Evangelicals for failing to take seriously the force of this evidence and concludes that inerrancy can be upheld only by adopting the extreme (and most unlikely) hypothesis that Matthew has written in a "midrashic" style and is therefore often uninterested in reporting historical fact.[1] More typically, the weight of the phenomena is held to invalidate the notion of inerrancy altogether. As William Abraham put it, "[The doctrine of inerrancy] involves enormous strain when it comes into contact with inductive study of the text. Indeed the strain is too great for any reasonable person to want to bear."[2]

What may be said in reply to such a claim? "Induction"—the process by which theological conclusions are drawn only as they emerge from the data—certainly has a legitimate place in formulating a doctrine of Scripture. But two things need to be said. First, as Warfield pointed out long ago, the claims made by the biblical authors for their writings is also evidence from the texts, capable of being molded into an inductively based argument for the nature of Scripture. *Some parts* of the phenomena of the text may present a problem; but it is wrong to cast the issue as one of induction versus deduction.³ Second, it should be recognized that induction and deduction need to be used together in formulating a doctrine of Scripture; not even "pure" scientists use induction *to the exclusion of* deduction in the construction of theoretical models.⁴

Nevertheless, it is true that *all* the phenomena of the biblical text must ultimately be considered in the formulation of a satisfactory doctrine of Scripture. Too many discrepancies between these phenomena and the doctrine of inerrancy would cast serious doubt on the validity of the doctrine. But, though often claimed, it is by no means clear that the phenomena of Scripture present so great a problem for the view that the Bible is completely truthful. Specific issues relative to this problem are dealt with in several essays in these two volumes: here, however, I will examine the problem created by the use of the Old Testament in the New. Long a matter of fascination, perplexity, and fruitful study to Christian preachers, theologians, and laypeople, the general issue of the Old Testament in the New has received much scholarly attention in the last forty years.⁵ Numerous offshoots of the problem have taken root in the course of the discussion, involving textual criticism, hermeneutics, and Jewish exegetical history, to name only three of the more important.

The implications of the subject for the nature of Scripture have also received considerable attention. Of specific interest to us is the allegation that the way in which the New Testament uses the Old Testament is incompatible with the notion that the Bible is completely true in all that it teaches. Paul Achtemeier's statement of the case is typical. To attribute inerrancy to the books of the Bible, he claims, is to ignore the New Testament authors' attitude to the Old Testament, as demonstrated in their actual use of the Old Testament. Their frequent modifications of the Old Testament text and their habit of reading into that text meanings obviously not intended in the original demonstrate clearly that they did not regard the Old Testament as an eternal, unchanging, inerrant document. Rather, Achtemeier argues, their use of the Old Testament shows that the New Testament authors regarded the canonical books as part of a living tradition that could be freely modified in order to fit new situations. If we would be true to the New Testament itself, then, we will not impose on the Bible a static, oracular status such as the doctrine of inerrancy implies; we will view it and use it as the living, changing, tradition that it is.⁶

In formulating his argument, Achtemeier has two specific phenomena in mind: (1) places where the New Testament uses a text form of an Old Testament passage that differs from the accepted Masoretic tradition and (2) places where the New Testament gives a meaning to an Old Testament passage that does not appear to agree with the intention of the original. That the issues are intertwined is obvious: new meanings are often given to an Old Testament passage by means of a change in text. However, since Moisés Silva has dealt competently with the textual side of the problem in his essay "The New Testament Use of the Old Testament" in *Scripture and Truth*, we will focus in this essay on the second issue. To put the problem simply: how can we accord complete truthfulness to writings that appear to misunderstand and misapply those texts from which they claim to derive the authority and rationale for their most basic claims and teaching? Although not always framed in just this way, this question has been one that has challenged Christian theologians from the earliest days of the church. We would do well to glance at some of the more important responses to this issue in the history of theology.

II. SOME HISTORICAL PERSPECTIVE

A. REJECTION OF THE OLD TESTAMENT

The appropriation of the Old Testament by the New Testament is one aspect, or manifestation, of a larger theological issue: the relation between the Testaments, in particular the degree to which, and manner in which, the Old Testament can be considered a "Christian" book. Of course, some—Marcion in the ancient church, Harnack more recently—have rid themselves of the problem by essentially dismissing the Old Testament from the Christian canon. But this radical alternative has wisely been rejected by the vast majority of Christian theologians. For, in a very important sense, the identity and viability of Christianity itself hinges on its relationship to the Old Testament. Jesus was none other than the Messiah of the Old Testament, and this meant that the church was forced to find a "Christian" meaning of the Old Testament.

B. ALLEGORIZATION

The method that quickly became the most important way of finding this "Christian" meaning was allegorization. Allegory finds meanings hidden behind the words of the text; the text is treated as a series of symbols that provides the discerning reader with a "higher" or "deeper" meaning. Origen's role in making the allegorical approach *the* Christian approach to the Old Testament was central. Without denying the "literal" sense, he held up the "spiritual" sense as ultimately the most important. This sense, however, could be perceived only by the spiritually "enlightened."[7] Since this method takes the New Testament as the "code" that provides the insight into the "spiritual" meaning of the Old Testament, there was naturally no "problem" in the way the New Testament used the Old.

While the allegorical method, then, quickly came to dominate patristic interpretation of the Old Testament—as Henri de Lubac says, "The so-called mystical or allegorical meaning was always considered as the doctrinal meaning par excellence"[8]—other options were explored. The "Antiochene" school is well-known for its opposition to the excesses of Alexandrian allegory. In place of allegory, they advocated a more historically based *theoria* concept, according to which the Old Testament author's own vision was seen as embracing both the ultimate Christian fulfillment and his immediate perspective.[9] Still, the Antiochenes saw this Christian meaning as a "higher sense" beyond the literal meaning, and their differences from the dominant Alexandrian approach must not be overemphasized.[10]

The ultimate codification of the allegorical approach came with the formulation (by about the fifth century) of the famous *quadriga* ("four horse chariot"), which outlined the four meanings to be found in every Old Testament text: (1) the literal meaning, (2) the "allegorical" meaning (the most important basis for doctrine), (3) the "tropological" meaning (specifying the moral implications of the text), and (4) the "anagogical" meaning (which provided the eschatological focus of the text).[11] In practice, the basic distinction was between the "literal" and the "spiritual" sense—or, to use the terms that often were associated with the two meanings, the "letter" and the "spirit." A central motivating factor in the insistence on the spiritual sense was the need for the church to show that its interpretation was the "correct" meaning of the Old Testament, over against both the merely literal, "Judaizing" interpretation of the Jews and the literal but disparaging interpretations of the Gnostics.[12]

As some Christians became reacquainted with Jewish interpretations—and some, including Andrew of St. Victor (twelfth century), adopted many of them—the relationship of the literal and spiritual sense was explored anew.[13] Thomas Aquinas' solution was widely received. The literal sense is based on the *words* of Scripture and should include all that those words may signify by means of metaphor, symbolism, and the like. The spiritual sense, on the other hand, is found in the *things* to which the words refer. Since the Bible is the only book with both a human and a divine author, only it can possess this twofold sense.[14]

Others, however, insisted that the "spiritual," Christian sense was the *only* true, literal sense, while some, more interested in finding better historical justification for the Christian interpretation, proposed a "double literal sense." James Perez of Valencia (d. 1490) distinguished between the grammatical sense and the hidden sense spoken by the Spirit—an idea resembling the currently popular *sensus plenior* approach that will be examined below.[15] These different proposals seem to be trying to take the "spiritualizing" approach to the Old Testament that had become standard and to put it on solid footings by providing some systematic hermeneutical foundations for the process.

C. THE REFORMATION

As is well-known, a key ingredient in the Reformers' interpretation of Scripture was their general rejection of the traditional "spiritual" meaning. Luther, after "driving" the "four horse chariot" in his early biblical expositions, violently rejected the system. Indeed, James Samuel Preus has argued that Luther's recovery of a genuine historical appreciation for the Old Testament was a prime factor in his theology and deeply significant for the course of the Reformation.[16] Luther gave to Old Testament Israel a religious experience in its own right; and the Old Testament was viewed not simply as a quarry for Christian symbolism but as a book with its own significance. This meant, in practice, that Luther was freed from the necessity of using an allegorical method to find Christian meaning in the Old Testament; he recaptured a genuine sense of salvation history. Thus, Luther's interpretations, as Heinrich Bornkamm says, are characterized above all by a "comprehensive prophetic application of the Old Testament to Christ."[17] If anything, Calvin was even more insistent on the importance of the literal sense, as his many fine biblical commentaries demonstrate.

Still, the Reformers and their followers certainly did not abandon allegory entirely. Luther approves of an allegorical interpretation where theological sense can be derived from a text in no other way; and the "hermeneutical textbook" written by the Lutheran Flacius (d. 1575) contains limited approval for allegorical methods. In addition, Protestant interpreters retained a *sensus mysticus* or *spiritualis* alongside the *sensus literalis*, although there was concern to distinguish this secondary sense from Roman Catholic notions of the mystical sense by insisting that it was part of the one sense intended by the true author of Scripture, the Holy Spirit.[18] The centuries of "Protestant orthodoxy" (not to be as sharply distinguished from the sixteenth-century Reformers as is all too common) saw a continuation of these methods, with a greater emphasis in some circles on "typology" as a hermeneutical key. The "Cocceian" school is especially famous for an overuse of typology, in which petty details of the Old Testament text were accorded symbolic significance.[19]

D. "SCIENTIFIC" HISTORICAL EXEGESIS

Throughout the period we have surveyed, most theologians, however they explained the relationship, assumed that the New Testament use of the Old Testament was valid and authoritative. This assumption began to be seriously challenged in the seventeenth and eighteenth centuries.[20] With the onset of higher criticism, the New

Testament use of the Old came in for even more criticism. Insistence on the "grammatical-historical" meaning as the *only* legitimate meaning of the text sounded the death knell for an approach that gave theological meaning to the Old Testament mainly by means of spiritualizing exegesis or by reading back into it the meaning found there by the New Testament.[21] No longer, naturally, was the New Testament interpretation of Old Testament texts considered, *ipso facto*, to be the correct interpretation. Where the New Testament interpretation of the Old differed from the findings of modern, "scientific" historical exegesis, so much the worse for the New Testament. New Testament exegesis of the Old Testament was no longer considered to provide the normative key by which the unity of the Testaments could be asserted; and the New Testament authors were accused of arbitrary and illegitimate exegetical procedures.

E. REACTIONS TO THIS "RATIONALISM"

Responses to this new attitude were numerous and varied. From the Protestant side, J. C. K. von Hofmann sought to reassert the unity of the Testaments by demonstrating that the Scripture presents as its basic structure a *Heilsgeschichte* (a "history of salvation") and that this historical process is what binds the Testaments together as anticipation and realization.[22] The title of Ernst W. Hengstenberg's magisterial survey, *The Christology of the Old Testament*, reveals that he, too, is convinced of the essential unity of the Testaments: they both, in different ways, speak of Jesus the Messiah.[23] Patrick Fairbairn advocated a properly defined, sober use of typology as an explanation for the correspondence between Old Testament and New.[24] From the Roman Catholic side, John H. Newman strongly criticized "rationalists" for denuding the text of its spiritual import by refusing to go beyond the literal sense. He argued that it was necessary to recapture the early church emphasis on the "mystical" sense as the clue to the divine intention in Scripture.[25] Similar proposals have been made by Henri de Lubac and Jean Daniélou.[26] Other responses to the difficulty will be canvassed below.

III. INITIAL CONSIDERATIONS

The problem, then, with which we are dealing is very much a modern one—the product *not*, it should be emphasized, of a new, innovative way to view Scripture but of the modern insistence on the "historical" sense as the only legitimate meaning of a text.

A. A FIDEISTIC APPROACH

One way, then, of dealing with the problem, advocated both by some Protestants and some Roman Catholics, is to argue that it is the modern view of exegetical procedure, not the New Testament, that is at fault. The revelatory stance of the New Testament is the validation for their interpretations; and when we cannot discover this meaning in the Old Testament through our exegetical techniques, then we should either abandon that method or else admit the inadequacy of it.[27]

There is no doubt some point to this proposal. The danger of "modern snobbishness"—the conviction that only we moderns have somehow transcended cultural bias and are uniquely able to understand things correctly—is real. As Moisés Silva reminds us, we must be careful not to think that "the authority and validity of apostolic interpretation . . . depend on its conformity to modern exegetical method."[28] In this, as in all other matters, Scripture itself must judge our understanding, not we it; and ultimately, we will conclude, it is impossible to "validate" the New Testament use of the Old, in general or in detail, without a prior decision to accept what they say as true and authoritative.

But while this kind of response is, at a certain level, adequate for the problem, it is ultimately less than satisfactory. First, constant dismissal of these kinds of problems by appeal to the uncertainties and fallibility of all knowledge—the record of ancient history is far from complete, modern science could very well be wrong, etc.—while appropriate to a degree, would in the last resort place Scripture in a realm above any real historical investigation or criticism. At some point, the weight of unexplained discrepancies would be too much for the doctrine to bear. Moreover, if apparent discrepancies between our reading of the Old Testament and the apostles' reading are dismissed out of hand because of the fallibility of our interpretation, we are in a rather vicious circle; for we can know what the apostles' interpretation of the Old Testament is only by using those same methods that we have rejected.

A second reason for wanting to go beyond the fideistic course outlined above is that the New Testament appeal to the Old Testament is too basic to the church's very identity to leave it in the realm of unexplained assertion. For all our legitimate emphasis on Christ as the center and fulfillment of revelation and as the "hermeneutical key" to the Old Testament, we sacrifice too much by refusing to allow the Old Testament to stand, to some extent at least, as an independent witness to the New. J. A. Sanders puts it well: "All the while that we insist that nothing is exempt from the judgment of Christ—even our faith-understanding of the Old Testament—we must remember that the Old Testament was and, in some sense, is the criterion whereby Christ is Christ."[29] How can the church's claim that it, not Judaism, is the true "completion" of the Old Testament be validated if its (rather than Judaism's) use of the Old Testament cannot be shown to best accord with the meaning of the Old Testament?

B. THE SUBJECTIVITY APPROACH

Another possible response to the problem is to eliminate it by recourse to the inevitable subjectivity of all meaning and interpretation. A. T. Hanson, in dealing with this issue, for instance, criticizes the notion that there is any "correct" meaning of a text, arguing that one's presuppositions (one's *Vorverständnis*) decisively determine the meaning one arrives at.[30] It is true, as we will argue below, that presuppositions play a critical role in the way the Old Testament is read and applied. And it is also true that one's presuppositions about what the Old Testament is saying are due in part to faith rather than to unaided reason. But without gainsaying any of this, we must insist that presuppositions themselves can and must be adjusted to "fit" the material under investigation: the "horizon" of the text and that of the interpreter *can* be "fused." Thus, without denying the problem of subjectivity in interpretation, the notion that a "correct" interpretation of a text exists and can be found is both reasonable and necessary.[31]

What we can say, however, is that our ultimate decision about the validity of the New Testament use of the Old will depend considerably on our decision to reject or accept the presuppositions on which the detailed applications of specific texts are based. These presuppositions must themselves, of course, be evaluated; and one of the ways to test them is to consider whether their acceptance leads to a more natural understanding of the Old Testament than, say, the presuppositions at work in the Qumran community or among the rabbis. The process is inevitably circular, but the circle is not a closed one. We want to "break into" it at the level of the actual use of the Old Testament in the New, consider this use in light of certain fundamental theological and hermeneutical presuppositions, and show that, granted these presuppositions, the interpretations given these texts need not be considered erroneous.

We conclude, then, that the apparently novel meaning attributed to Old Testament texts by Jesus and the writers of the New Testament *do* constitute a potentially legitimate objection to the inerrancy of Scripture. Theirs was no casual appeal or an argument by analogy: they repeatedly assert that we are to believe or do certain things *because* of the witness of specific Old Testament texts. It is the frequently *causal* relationship between New Testament claim or teaching and Old Testament text that makes the problem a different one than that which Silva illustrates by appeal to news reports juxtaposing the Miami riots and the eruption of Mount Saint Helens in 1980.[32] Those reports did not claim either that the volcanic eruption in Washington state caused the riots in Florida or that we must understand the riots in a certain specific way because of the mountain's eruption. If the New Testament errs in drawing these relationships, then it has erred in a fundamental way—affecting, by the way, not just incidentals but very basic matters "of faith and practice." S. Lewis Johnson is right: the doctrine of inerrancy "requires that the meaning the New Testament author finds in the Old Testament and uses in the New is really in the Old Testament."[33]

It will be the purpose of this study to investigate this idea of New-Testament-specified meaning being "really in" the Old Testament. On what basis does the New Testament so confidently apply text after text from the Old Testament? Before analyzing some of the most important explanations of the situation, it will be helpful to clear the way by removing what might be called some "phantom" difficulties.

IV. CORRECTLY DEFINING THE PROBLEM

Statements of the problem posed by the use of the Old Testament in the New for the doctrine of Scripture frequently magnify the difficulties by failing to take into account certain important factors. We will examine some of the most important of these.

A. THE NATURE OF INSPIRATION

Implicit in some discussions of the issue is the assumption that inerrancy necessarily involves a "dictation" theory of inspiration. Bruce Vawter, arguing that the New Testament exhibits great freedom in interpreting the Old Testament as a witness to Christ, goes on to say: "Clearly this was not done out of any belief that the prophetic word that it adapted so plastically was in any sense the oracular utterance of a delphic spirit, a word voiced from heaven fixed and immutable, once for all."[34] Now, as is well known, the vast majority of inerrantists do not assume a mechanical, dictation-type of inspiration theory such as Vawter's quotation implies. The words of Scripture are viewed as the product of a "concursive" operation whereby the human author freely wrote what he wanted while the divine author at the same time superintended and guided that writing. Once it is recognized, then, that the view of inspiration held by inerrantists does not entail the notion of an ahistorical, "oracular" process, scope for flexibility in quotation and attention to historical context can be allowed without invalidating inerrancy.[35] This, of course, does not solve all the problems that Vawter finds, but it does remove at least one of his objections.

B. THE NATURE AND PURPOSE OF REFERENCES
TO THE OLD TESTAMENT

Another way in which the scope of the problem is illegitimately expanded is by a failure to recognize the many different purposes for which New Testament writers cite the Old Testament. Authors and speakers "quote" for many reasons, not all of which depend for their legitimacy on the quotation being given an interpretation or application completely in accord with the original context. For instance, if I warn my children about the consequences of an action by reminding them that "what they sow they shall also reap," my applying Paul's words to a situation that he clearly never envisaged does not hurt the effectiveness of the warning. My intention was not to quote Paul as an authority, providing legitimate substantiation of my warning, but to borrow his language in order to express vividly my caution.

What is crucial is to determine whether the author intends to assert the "correct" meaning of the text and whether the "correct" interpretation of the text is necessary for the point that the author is making. Only in such cases does an apparent misinterpretation of a text create difficulty. Granted the prominence played by the Old Testament in the lives and cultural milieu of New Testament authors, it is more than probable that they frequently used scriptural language other than as authoritative proof. When in such cases they appear to deduce a new meaning from the text or apply it to a new situation, it is unjustifiable to accuse them of misusing the text or to infer from their usage that they did not think the text was inerrant. We will examine some specific categories of usage that should not, for this reason, be included in our consideration of the problem.[36]

1. Use of Scriptural Language as a Vehicle of Expression

Much like the speech of a person raised on the classics will be sprinkled with terminology and idioms drawn from those texts, New Testament writers often—without intending to provide a "correct" interpretation of the Old Testament text—use Old Testament language as a vehicle of expression. Such usage will often suggest a certain atmosphere or underlying concept that is important for what the speaker or writer is trying to communicate.

We may take Jesus' words of lament in Gethsemane as an example: *perilypos estin hē psychē mou heōs thanatou* ("My soul is sorrowful, even unto death," Mk 14:34/Mt 26:38). The rarity of *perilypos* (only eight times in the LXX, never in Philo or Josephus, only twice in the NT), especially in combination with *psychē*, renders an allusion to the "refrain" of Psalms 42 and 43 (perhaps originally a single psalm) virtually certain.[37] But there is little evidence that we should find in Jesus' allusion an attempt to cite the psalm(s) as authoritative prefigurement of His sufferings in the Garden. Jesus appears simply to be using familiar biblical language to express His emotions. To be sure, Jesus' use of this language may suggest a general identification of His plight with the psalmist's—oppressed by enemies, seeking God's vindication and rescue—but we would be wrong to accuse him of misusing the text or reading into it new meaning if we were to find no evidence that Psalms 42–43 were predictive of Jesus' agony in Gethsemane. Moisés Silva cites Paul's use of Deuteronomy 19:15 in 2 Corinthians 13:1 as a similar case.[38] Realizing the familiarity of all the New Testament authors with the Old Testament, we can expect many such instances; and none is germane to the issue discussed here.

2. The Application or Accommodation of Old Testament Principles

In his important study of hermeneutics, E. D. Hirsch describes the idea of what he calls a "willed type." This involves the extension or application of an author's language, particularly in legal texts, such that the application is not part of the author's specific, conscious intention but at the same time can legitimately be seen as included within the author's general meaning.[39] This phenomenon can be observed in places where the New Testament applies an Old Testament principle or law to a new situation.

As an example of one such instance, we can take Paul's oft-criticized quotation of Deuteronomy 25:4 ("Do not muzzle an ox while it is treading out the grain") in support of giving money to Christian ministers (1Co 9:9). First, it is considered fanciful in the extreme that a law providing for the welfare of animals should be applied by Paul to the Christian ministry; and, second, he appears categorically to deny in his next words that the law had anything to do with animals: "Is it for oxen that God is concerned? Does he not speak entirely for our sake? It was written for our sake" (RSV). Here Paul appears to equate the "literal" sense with the "spiritual," Christian sense.

Numerous explanations of Paul's procedure have been offered. Longenecker sees this as one of the few examples of allegory in Paul.[40] Others think that Paul has adopted a Hellenistic Jewish exegetical principle by which interpreters such as Philo were able to avoid the crassly literal sense of such laws by appealing to the "higher sense" really intended by God.[41] Walter Kaiser, however, expanding on the approach taken by Calvin and Godet, argues that Paul's use of the text depends strictly on the original meaning of the text, which in its context is intended to inculcate in masters and owners a concern for their laborers (whether animal or human). What Paul does is to draw out in a legitimate way the *significance* of the law for the situation of churches and their "workers." Paul is also right, then, in claiming that the law *is* given for "us" (e.g., human beings), not (primarily) the oxen.[42] Moreover, Paul is probably not saying that this is the *only* meaning of the law; the crucial word *pantōs* is best translated not "entirely" (as in the RSV) but "certainly" or "undoubtedly."[43]

Another possibility is that the phrase had become a popular proverb to express the idea that a worker deserves to be paid. In this case, Paul's application would not have to cohere in any sense with the original, since his purpose in quoting it had nothing to do with the authority of the text as God's law. While there is some evidence for the proverbial use of the phrase, Paul's use of it appears to go further than this. In either case, however, Paul cannot be accused of misusing the text. To claim that the application of a law beyond anything the original author specifically intended is a misinterpretation of that law is to apply an unfairly rigid concept of meaning. A better test is to seek to determine whether the application can legitimately be included in the scope of the law—whether the original author, if asked, would have acknowledged the validity of the further application.

3. Old Testament Texts That Are Cited to Represent Alternative Points of View

That some statements in 1 Corinthians are not so much Paul's own teaching as slogans of the Corinthians is generally recognized (e.g., "all things are lawful" [6:12; 10:23 rsv]; "it is well for a man not to touch a woman" [7:1 rsv]; "all of us possess knowledge" [8:1 rsv]). In a similar manner, it may be that some Old Testament quotations are used not to express the teaching of the author but to represent the opinion or teaching of someone else.

At least some of the quotations set in antithesis to Jesus' teaching in Matthew 5 are to be so explained. The clearest instance of this is the final quotation (Mt 5:43), in which the addition of "hate your enemies" to the love commandment of Leviticus 19:15 expresses the teaching current among some Jews (perhaps Essenes).[44] Here, of course, clear contextual indicators are present: the addition of language not found in the Old Testament (nor fairly representative of Old Testament teaching) and the introductory formula, "you have heard that it was said," which suggests something of a distance from the Old Testament per se.

In situations where contextual indicators of this sort are not present, the hypothesis that an author quotes the Old Testament to represent the opinion of his listeners or opponents must be advanced with great caution. Nevertheless, the possibility cannot be excluded when this option offers the best explanation of the flow of an author's thought. Thus, as Silva points out in his essay, the difficulty of Paul's quotation of Leviticus 18:5 (Gal 3:12; Ro 10:5), where the original sense of the passage appears to be disregarded and where a straightforward reading creates an apparent conflict with what Paul says elsewhere about the law (cf. Gal 3:21), has led a number of expositors to view the quotation as a slogan drawn from the apostle's Judaizing opponents.[45]

Interestingly, both Achtemeier and Vawter cite this quotation as a clear instance of misuse of the Old Testament in the New.[46] Now it is entirely possible that the explanation of this quotation given above is incorrect. And, as a general principle, the adoption of an interpretation that attributes the words of a book to the author's opponents should be supported by compelling evidence—clear contextual indicators or the conclusion that the only way to make any sense of a passage is to read it in this way. The alternative we are considering here, then, will not help us with our problem very often. Nevertheless, the category should be considered as a possibility when faced with a difficult quotation; and it is instructive that neither Vawter nor Achtemeier even mentions this alternative in criticizing Paul's use of Leviticus 18:5.

C. THE MEANING OF FULFILLMENT LANGUAGE

As one instance of the misuse of the Old Testament in the New, Dewey Beegle cites Matthew's use of Hosea 11:1 to furnish "authoritative proof from the Old Testament for an event in the life of Jesus."[47] The quotation in question is one of Matthew's well-known "formula citations," a body of quotations that offers more textual and hermeneutical difficulty than any others in the New Testament.[48] The stay of Jesus and His family in Egypt, and their subsequent return to Palestine, "fulfills," according to Matthew, Hosea's statement, "Out of Egypt have I called my son" (Mt 2:15 RSV).

Many things could be said about this frequently discussed quotation, but what I want to focus on here is the use of *plēroō* to introduce it. Although Beegle does not explain why he thinks that Matthew regards the citation as an "authoritative proof," it is probable that it is the use of *plēroō* that is decisive. Indeed, it is common to think that the "fulfillment" of the Old Testament in Jesus' advent refers basically to His doing and saying what specific Old Testament prophecies said the Messiah would do or say. And if this is so, Matthew 2:15 presents a problem, since Hosea 11:1 appears to be a simple statement of fact and gives no indication of being a "prophecy" of the Messiah's departure from Egypt.

But, in fact, *plēroō* cannot be confined to so narrow a compass. The word is used in the New Testament to indicate the broad redemptive-historical relationship of the new, climactic revelation of God in Christ to the preparatory, incomplete revelation to and through Israel.[49] Thus, Mark can summarize Jesus' preaching as an announcement that time itself had been "filled up" and the kingdom of God was at hand (1:15); Jesus claims that His teaching is the ultimate, climactic expression of the will of God to which the Old Testament law pointed (Mt 5:17; cf. Mt 11:13).[50] What needs to be emphasized, then, is that the use of *plēroō* in an introductory formula need not mean that the author regards the Old Testament text he quotes as a direct prophecy; and accusations that a New Testament author misuses the Old Testament by using *plēroō* to introduce nonprophetic texts are unfounded. In the case of Matthew 2:15, then, the Evangelist may be suggesting that Jesus, God's "greater son," brings to a climax—"fills up"—the "Exodus motif," that had become, even in the Old Testament, an eschatologically oriented theme.[51]

The factors we have enumerated in the preceding paragraphs serve to reduce the scope of the problem we are considering. While some "conservatives" can justly be accused of forcing exegetically unlikely harmonizations on texts to preserve doctrinal purity, many of a more critical bent err in the opposite direction by failing to make sufficient allowance for these and other factors of similar sort. Nevertheless, the considerations we have cited mitigate but by no means eliminate the problem. There remain numerous passages in which the force of the author's argument depends on an Old Testament text being given its proper, authoritative meaning—when cited in support of theological conclusions, or where the author says specifically that the text prophesied the event he narrates, for instance—and yet where the author appears to give that text a meaning that cannot be demonstrated exegetically. What are we to do with these texts? We will survey and analyze the most popular answers to this question in the next section.

V. PROPOSED SOLUTIONS TO THE PROBLEM

A. THE USE OF JEWISH EXEGETICAL METHODS

The most popular explanation for the way in which the New Testament interprets the Old Testament likens the New Testament approach to that of first-century Judaism. Striking similarities, it is argued, are found between the New Testament use of the Old and the way the rabbis—especially the Qumran community—applied Scripture to their own situations. Some of the peculiar and, to modern eyes, unconvincing interpretations of Old Testament texts in the New Testament are to be seen, then, as examples of a "midrashic" or "pesher" approach such as was popular in the first-century Jewish environment. How should we view this explanation for the problem we are probing?

First, there can be no doubt that the New Testament often utilizes citation techniques that are quite similar to practices amply illustrated in first-century Jewish sources—combining verses on the basis of verbal resemblance (what the rabbis called *gezerah shawah;* cf. Ps 110:1 and 16:8–11 in Ac 2:25–34), argument from the less to the more significant (*qal wahomer;* cf. Jn 7:23), the use of subtle allusions to texts and themes to convey a message (cf. the use of the "lament psalms" in the Crucifixion narratives in the Synoptics especially), the choosing of textual forms that are most conducive to the point being made (e.g., Ac 15:16–18), and many others. Moreover, the New Testament shares with Qumran the conviction that the prophets spoke of their own times and experience. These similarities, and many others that have been amply documented, are undeniable. But what is considerably in doubt is the degree to which such methods are found and the implications of their use for inspiration and inerrancy. Many think that the New Testament authors have uncritically adopted improper and even fantastic Jewish exegetical methods and that the use of these methods discredits their exegetical conclusions. Beegle, for instance, attributes Matthew's "misuse" of Hosea 11:1, noted above, to his use of Jewish methods.[52] In response to this kind of criticism and in order to evaluate more accurately the significance of these methods for New Testament interpretation, the following points should be noted.

First, it is vitally important that certain key terms, such as "midrash" and "pesher," be carefully defined, if not in a definitive way, at least for the purposes of the discussion at hand. Thus, for instance, Richard Longenecker finds a considerable amount of "pesher" exegesis in the New Testament; but he appears to understand it broadly to refer to any "direct" application of the Old Testament to the New that proceeds from a revelatory basis.[53] Granted that definition, the use of pesher per se in the New Testament need not invalidate the exegetical conclusions thereby reached. Others, however, at least judging by their strictures against it, apparently understand pesher necessarily to involve a "reading into" an Old Testament text of what is not there. Similar problems crop up with regard to the term "midrash."[54] Without attempting definitions here, we simply point out that not all Jewish exegetical methods, whether they be called "pesher," "midrash," or "midrash pesher," necessarily result in a perversion of the meaning of the text.

A second consideration relates to the problem of cultural subjectivity. Without by any means endorsing the extreme position of those who open the door to complete exegetical relativity by claiming that our cultural context forbids us from finding the "correct" meaning of an ancient text, it is nevertheless important that we exercise humility with respect to our own exegetical method. At the least, we need to recognize that when we criticize rabbinic and Jewish interpretation procedures, we do so from the standpoint of our present understanding of good exegetical method. And it also means that we must consider the soundness of the argument that New Testament authors would not have used some Jewish techniques because they would have been logically unconvincing. They may be logically unconvincing to *us*, but it is not clear that they would have been to their immediate audience.

More importantly, we should recognize that the degree of influence of Jewish exegetical methods on New Testament procedure has often been considerably exaggerated. A vast gulf separates the often fantastic, purely verbal exegeses of the rabbis from the generally sober and clearly contextually oriented interpretations found in the New Testament.[55] Indeed, it is where Jewish exegesis strays furthest from what we would consider sound principles that the New Testament differs most from it.

A further helpful distinction is that between "appropriation techniques" and "hermeneutical axioms." By the former, I mean those specific, "on the surface" methods by which a text is "appropriated" for a new situation—straightforward identification of one situation or person with another, modification of the text to suit the application, association of several passages, etc. In this the New Testament shows undeniable similarities to the Qumran literature, rabbinic literature, and other early Jewish materials. But lying behind these techniques (and ultimately crucial for how and where they are employed) are the basic convictions of a community about Scripture, its own identity, and the movement of God in history.

For instance, the Qumran community—convinced that it was the people of God, that the last days had arrived, and that the prophets spoke in "riddles" about the last days—directly applied the details of Habakkuk's prophecy to themselves and their enemies. From our standpoint, not convinced of the truth of these, their "hermeneutical axioms," we find their exegesis strained and unconvincing. But from their standpoint, it obviously made perfect sense.

Similarly, New Testament exegesis proceeds on the assumption that Jesus Christ is the culmination of God's plan and that "all the law and the prophets" ultimately point to Him. Behind what may sometimes appear to be a mere verbal resemblance between an Old Testament text and its New Testament "fulfillment" may lie a deepened identification of Jesus with an Old Testament figure. This is not to say that valid exegesis is entirely a product of arbitrary, undemonstrable hermeneutical axioms; some axioms and exegeses provide a much better "fit" with the material itself than others. Rather, the point is that the New Testament can, at the level of appropriation technique, resemble closely contemporary Jewish methods, while below the surface, as it were, basic theological connections between the Testaments are at work, providing the "validating" matrix for what may seem to be an arbitrary exegesis.[56]

Thus far, we have argued that the New Testament use of Jewish exegetical methods does not lead necessarily to the misinterpretation of the Old Testament; nor does it, in itself, constitute a problem for the inspiration and inerrancy of the Scripture. On the other hand, it should be clear that neither does it provide a solution to the problem we are considering. Study of Jewish exegetical procedures may help to explain *what* the New Testament authors sometimes do with Scripture and *why* they do it; and it shows that Jesus and the writers of the New Testament often use methods that would have been familiar and acceptable to many of their contemporaries.

But the presence of first-century exegetical techniques provides no help in answering the question before us: is the meaning discovered by means of these techniques "really in" the Old Testament? Thus, conservatives who stress the presence of Jewish exegetical techniques in the New Testament often appeal for the validity of the exegesis to the "charismatic" stance of the interpreter. As E. Earle Ellis explains Paul's procedure: "His idea of a quotation was not a worshipping of the letter or 'parroting' of the text; neither was it an eisegesis which arbitrarily imposed a foreign meaning upon the text. It was rather, in his eyes, a quotation-exposition, a *midrash pesher*, which drew from the text the meaning originally implanted there by the Holy Spirit and expressed that meaning in the most appropriate words and phrases known to him."[57]

That the exegesis of the New Testament writers did, in fact, find in the Old Testament the meaning intended by the Spirit can no doubt be asserted on dogmatic grounds; and it may be that we will be left with no alternative but to accept their procedure because of the authority of the New Testament or to reject that authority because of its obvious misinterpretations of the Old Testament. But before casting the issue in terms of such stark alternatives, we should thoroughly explore the theoretical and hermeneutical foundations of the New Testament use of the Old, seeing if we can provide a clearer rationale for the validity and coherence of the biblical authors' practice.

B. TYPOLOGY

In the last thirty years, typology has reemerged, after a period of relative neglect, as one of the most popular ways of explaining the relationship between the Testaments. Typology is set forth by many scholars as the key to understanding the New Testament use of the Old.[58] Unfortunately, there is widespread disagreement about the definition and extent of typology.

Most would agree with David Baker's simple definition: "a *type* is a biblical event, person or institution which serves as an example or pattern for other events, persons or institutions."[59] Basic to typology, it is generally agreed, is the belief that God acts in similar ways in both Testaments; hence, there can be a real correspondence between the Old Testament and the New. That typology works from the narratives of God's activity in history is also a matter of general consensus— although whether the type must always be a *historical* figure, event, or institution is debated.[60] Most scholars also carefully distinguish typology from allegory—on the basis of the strongly historical character of typology and the "real" correspondence that must exist between type and antitype; where allegory looks for meaning *behind* the text, typology bases meaning on the events narrated *in* the text.[61] An eschatological "fullness" or advance (*Steigerung*) in the New Testament antitype over against the Old Testament type is also usually considered essential to true typology.[62]

Once we move beyond these general characteristics, however, considerable disagreement sets in. Particularly significant for our purposes is the debate about whether typology is prospective or retrospective. Does the Old Testament type have a genuinely predictive function, or is typology simply a way of looking back at the Old Testament and drawing out resemblances?[63] Related to this question is the matter of classifying typology. Is it a general way of viewing the relationship between Old Testament and New (a *"pneumatische Betrachtungsweise,"* as Leonhard Goppelt calls it[64]), a system of exegesis, a form of prophecy, or what? A certain circularity of procedure is often evident at this point, as scholars—according to the definition they have established—select what they think are genuine instances of New Testament typology.

Without attempting anything approaching a definitive definition, we suggest that typology is best viewed as a specific form of the larger "promise-fulfillment" scheme that provides the essential framework within which the relationship of the Testaments must be understood. This "salvation-historical" movement from Old to New Testament permeates the thinking of Jesus and the early church and is the ultimate validation for their extensive use of the Old Testament to depict and characterize their own situation.[65] The two Testaments are bound together by their common witness to the unfolding revelation of God's character, purpose, and plan. But the salvation wrought by God through Christ is the "fulfillment" of Old Testament history, law, and prophecy. This being the case, New Testament persons, events, and institutions will sometimes "fill up" Old Testament persons, events, and institutions by repeating at a deeper or more climactic level that which was true in the original situation.

If we ask whether the typological correspondence was intended in the Old Testament, we would answer differently according to what is meant. If by "intended" is meant that the participants in the Old Testament situation, or the author of the text that records it, were always cognizant of the typological significance, we would respond negatively. But 1 Corinthians 10 suggests that there is some kind of "prospective" element in typological events. In this passage, Paul warns the Corinthians about presuming that the sacraments will shield them from the judgment of God by pointing out that the Israelites also possessed a "baptism" and "spiritual food" but nevertheless suffered the judgment of God. What is significant is that Paul says that these events *"happened"* to the Israelites "as types" *(typikōs)*, by which he implies that there was typological significance to the events as they took place.[66] The "anticipatory" element in these typological experiences may sometimes have been more or less dimly perceived by the participants and human authors; but it is to be ascribed finally to God, who ordered these events in such a way that they would possess a "prophetic" function.

The use of Psalm 22 in the New Testament affords a good example of typological relationship. This psalm, usually categorized as an "individual lament," figures prominently in the narration of the crucifixion of Jesus. Jesus Himself uses its opening words to convey His sense of abandonment (Mk 15:34/Mt 27:46); John states that the dividing of Jesus' clothes "fulfilled" Psalm 22:18, and all four Evangelists allude to Psalm 22 in their depiction of the Crucifixion.

What is the basis for this significant application of language that appears to have no prospective force to Jesus' passion? Albert Vis finds no basis of any kind: he argues that the early church has arbitrarily and illegitimately applied the psalm to Christ for apologetic reasons.[67] But, taking David to be the author of the psalm, we must remember that he is much more than an "individual" righteous sufferer. The promises given to him and to his progeny and his status as Israel's king give to many of his psalms a corporate and even eschatological significance.[68]

Some, then, have viewed the psalm as a direct messianic prophecy, but the historical circumstances are too clear to accept this proposal. It has been popular more recently to see the psalm as part of a widespread "righteous sufferer" motif that the Evangelists used to show the innocence of Jesus.[69] Others see this as an instance of *sensus plenior* (for which, see below).[70]

But it is best to think that the use of the psalm is based on an underlying typological relationship: Jesus is the ultimate "fulfillment" of the experience and feelings that David undergoes in this passage. It is not clear that David would always have been aware of the ultimate significance of his language; but God could have so ordered his experiences and his recordings of them in Scripture that they become anticipatory of the sufferings of "David's greater son." It is this fundamental identification of Christ with David in a typological relationship, not chance verbal similarities, that undergird the extensive use of this psalm.[71]

It appears, then, that typology does have a "prospective" element, but the "prospective" nature of specific Old Testament incidents could often be recognized only retrospectively. In some cases, certainly, the Israelites themselves will have recognized the symbolic value of some of their history (e.g., the Exodus) and institutions (the cultus, to some extent). But not all typological correspondence involves recognizable symbols; and the prospective element in many Old Testament types, though intended by God in a general sense, would not have been recognized at the time by the Old Testament authors or the original audience. Without confining valid types to those specifically mentioned in the New Testament, then,[72] it is nevertheless true that we would not know of some types had the New Testament not revealed them to us and that any types we may suggest lack the authoritative status enjoyed by those singled out by the inspired authors.

That typology offers some help for the problem we are considering is obvious. What might at first sight appear to be arbitrary applications of Old Testament texts, based on mere verbal analogies or the like, can often be seen to be founded on a deeper, typological structure. On the other hand, it must be admitted that typology will itself be accorded legitimacy only if the basic assumptions on which it is founded are granted—that God had so ordered Old Testament history that it prefigures and anticipates His climactic redemptive acts and that the New Testament is the inspired record of those redemptive acts. An appropriate recognition of the place of typology in New Testament interpretation of the Old is important as providing a structure that gives coherence and legitimacy to many specific applications. On the other hand, however, it leaves unexplained many interpretations that involve an apparently strained interpretation of specific words or where the element of correspondence is not clear. While according to typology the significance it deserves, then, we must look for other explanations of some of the problem texts.

C. ELIMINATION OF THE PROBLEM THROUGH THEOLOGICAL EXEGESIS

Over the last two decades, no one has given more attention to the implications of the use of the Old Testament in the New for inspiration and inerrancy than Walter C. Kaiser, Jr.[73] Because of this, and because his approach raises in a particularly insistent form some of the most important questions involved in the problem we are considering, we will devote some space to an analysis of his solution.

From a doctrinal standpoint, he is convinced, it is illegitimate for a New Testament author to find more, or different, *meaning* in an Old Testament text than the original human author himself intended. As he puts it at one point, " . . . the whole revelation of God as revelation hangs in jeopardy if we, an apostle, or an angel from heaven try to add to, delete, rearrange, or reassign the sense or meaning that a prophet himself received."[74] Kaiser does allow that a New Testament author may draw out some of the implications or applications of an Old Testament text, but this involves *significance*, not meaning. Hermeneutically, Kaiser endorses an "intentionality" theory of meaning, according to which the meaning of any text is tied to what the author of that text intended to say.[75] This meaning, although potentially embracing more than one concept or application, is nevertheless one: it is wrong, as well as hermeneutically disastrous, to think that a text can have more than one meaning.

Kaiser does not rest with simple dogmatic assertion; he has sought to demonstrate the validity of his approach inductively by tackling over the years some of the knottiest problem quotations in the New Testament. We have noted above his treatment of one such text (1Co 9:9). His approach to the text is typical of his method: careful consideration is given to the context of the Old Testament text cited, particularly the larger theological context that too many exegetes ignore or fail to see. An illegitimately atomistic exegesis or a narrow, one-sided concern with form-critical questions frequently prevents the exegete from recognizing the "informing theology," the rich tapestry of unfolding theological themes and concepts within the Old Testament that provide the crucial context for many prophecies.[76] Once sufficient account is taken of this theological context, and the New Testament context is similarly understood in all its theological richness, apparent discrepancies between the meaning of an Old Testament text and the meaning given that text in the New Testament disappear.

Kaiser is to be commended for bringing to our attention the seriousness of the issue. And there is much in his approach that is right on target. Far too many approaches to Old Testament exegesis focus so exclusively on putative stages of tradition and interpret texts so rigidly in terms of hypothetical *Sitze im Leben* that the theological significance of the final product is entirely ignored or obscured. When this happens, it can legitimately be objected that the texts are no longer being given their natural, contextual, *theological* sense, and alleged discrepancies between findings reached by such methods and interpretations found in the New Testament should be accorded little significance. It is no wonder that when such an exegetical procedure is employed, New Testament authors—who read the Old Testament as a single, thoroughly theological book—are found to misinterpret the Old Testament.

Kaiser is also justified in his strictures against the "hermeneutical nihilism" that plagues much modern literary criticism; it is vital that we not surrender the insistence that a text has a single, determinative meaning. And finally, in what is the acid test for any theory, he succeeds in demonstrating that it is capable of explaining several otherwise problematic applications of Old Testament texts.

Several questions, however, have been raised with respect to this proposal. Some have criticized Kaiser for committing the "intentional fallacy," but this criticism is wide of the mark.[77] More serious is the criticism that he does not allow sufficiently for the intention of the divine author of Scripture or for the "added" meaning that a text takes on as a result of the ongoing canonical process. We will deal with both these issues below; here we will simply note that it is not so certain that meaning should be confined to the intention of the human author of Scripture.

What is ultimately crucial is the question whether the approach advocated by Kaiser can solve every "problem text" with which we are confronted in the New Testament use of the Old. The success of Kaiser's approach depends on the extent and nature of the "informing theology" that he claims as the undergirding context of many texts. While many Old Testament exegetes undoubtedly accept far too little by way of overarching theological constructs, it may be that Kaiser on occasion finds more than is clearly supported by the text. For example, in dealing with the quotation of Hosea 11:1 in Matthew 2:15, Kaiser argues that the key to the legitimacy of Matthew's interpretation is the fact that Hosea "no doubt understood the technical nature of 'my son' along with its implications for corporate solidarity."[78] But what is the evidence that Hosea intended this in his use of "son" here? He never elsewhere uses the word in a theological sense; nor is there a great deal of evidence that *ben* is a corporate concept in the Old Testament.

Another crucial issue is whether we can speak of "meaning" or "significance" in Old Testament texts as they are cited in the New Testament. If the latter, the New Testament application need not, according to Kaiser, be clearly present in the original author's intention; if the former, then it must be. In the case of the use of Deuteronomy 25:4 in 1 Corinthians 9:9, for instance, the *meaning* of the Old Testament text is the principle that workers (whether animal or human) deserve to be rewarded. Paul's application of the principle, then, to Christian ministers validly draws out the *significance* of that text.

But there are other texts where the distinction is not so neat and where the New Testament author appears to assign more, or different, "meaning" to an Old Testament text than can legitimately be inferred as being part of the human author's intention. A series of texts in which this seems to be the case are those in which Old Testament passages describing God or Yahweh are applied to Jesus in the New Testament. Romans 10:13, for instance, applies to faith in Jesus the words of Joel 2:32 (MT; LXX 3:5): "Everyone who calls on the name of the Lord will be saved." There is no evidence, either from Joel or from an "antecedent theology," that the prophet would have intended his words to refer to Christ. From the standpoint of the revelation of the nature of Jesus in the New Testament, of course, we can understand the legitimacy of applying Old Testament passages about God to Christ. Now perhaps Kaiser would regard this as an instance in which a New Testament author perceives further significance in the Joel text. But it seems to me that this kind of procedure goes beyond the drawing out of the significance of the text; the meaning of the word Yahweh (= LXX *kyrios*) is being expanded and, implicitly, more precisely defined by Paul.

A similar situation seems to exist in the application to Jesus of texts such as Psalm 2:7 ("You are my son, today I have begotten you" RSV) or 2 Samuel 7:14 ("I will be his father, and he will be my son"). Granted that there is behind both texts the concept of the Davidic King and his descendants as the heirs to the promise, it is nevertheless the case that the meaning of the word "son" is distinctly different when applied to David or Solomon than when applied to Jesus.

Therefore, while remaining extremely sympathetic to Kaiser's general approach, and, in fact, strongly supporting much of what he says, I am not convinced that his approach offers an ultimately satisfactory answer to all the problems raised by the use of the Old Testament in the New. There are places where the New Testament attributes to Old Testament texts more meaning than it can be legitimately inferred the human author was aware of. Nor do I think it is fatal to the doctrines of inspiration or inerrancy to suggest this. Only if the meaning of Old Testament texts *must* be confined to what we can prove their human authors intended does such a problem arise. Therefore, we will now look at some proposals that look beyond the original human author for a solution to these problem quotations.

D. SENSUS PLENIOR

Sensus Plenior, "fuller sense," is a phrase that was first coined by Catholic scholars, who have subjected the concept to thorough analysis and debate. But the concept denoted by the phrase—and often the phrase itself—is also popular among Protestants. Although precise definitions of the idea may differ, we will use it to designate the idea that there is in many scriptural texts a "fuller sense" than that consciously intended by the human author—a sense intended by God, the ultimate author of Scripture. It is this meaning, an integral part of the text, that is discerned and used by later interpreters who appear to find "new" meaning in Old Testament texts. This "new" meaning is, then, part of the author's intention—the divine author and not necessarily the human author.

Raymond Brown, whose monograph is the most important statement and defense of the approach, describes *sensus plenior* as *"that additional deeper meaning, intended by God but not clearly intended by the human author, which is seen to exist in the words of a biblical text (or group of texts, or even a whole book) when they are studied in the light of further revelation or development in the understanding of revelation."*[79] Several elements of this definition must be further explained if we are to understand the nature of this proposal.

First, Brown insists that the *sensus plenior*—though by definition involving a meaning not fully understood by the human author—could, nevertheless, have been dimly perceived by him at times. As he puts it, the human author's awareness of the *sensus plenior* could range "from absolute ignorance to near clarity."[80] Generally, however, *sensus plenior* is used to refer to a meaning that cannot be demonstrated by means of traditional grammatical-historical exegesis. Second, there must be a relation between the literal sense intended by the human author and the "fuller" sense intended by God.[81] Advocates of the approach insist on this control lest the concept be used as an excuse for uncontrolled allegorizing.

Third, the *sensus plenior* is to be distinguished from typology; the former has to do with the deeper meaning of *words*, the latter with the extended meaning of *things*.[82] The bronze serpent in the wilderness may be considered a "type" of Christ on the cross, but the application to Christ of Psalm 2:7 ("you are my son") involves a "deeper sense" of the words themselves. Fourth, the *sensus plenior* is also to be distinguished from what Roman Catholic scholars have called "accommodation," the application of a biblical text to a situation not envisaged in the text itself. ("Accommodation" in this sense is to be distinguished from "accommodation" as used with respect to God's adapting Himself to human words in the process of revelation.) Brown argues for the need of the *sensus plenior* approach by pointing to the inadequacy of "accommodation" to handle the data: "[The New Testament writers] certainly give no evidence that they are using the Scriptures in a sense not intended by God (accommodation); on the contrary, they make it clear that their spiritual meaning is precisely that meaning intended by God, but not realized by the Jews."[83]

Fifth, as the quotation above specifies, a valid *sensus plenior* can be adduced only on the basis of "revelation" or "further development in revelation." For Brown and other Roman Catholics, this authority includes the church (the "magisterium") and the New Testament.[84] The *sensus plenior* becomes very important, then, for Roman Catholics, in that it provides a way to justify through Scripture the development of Mariology and other such otherwise poorly supported theological concepts. But, as we suggested earlier, the *sensus plenior* approach is also very popular among Protestants—who, naturally, confine the "further revelation" on which a fuller sense can authoritatively be based to the New Testament.[85]

What are we to make of this proposal? Many object to the notion because the lack of objective controls renders it liable to abuse. On what basis does one decide what the Spirit might be saying through the words of a text?[86] Some respond that only those "deeper meanings" specifically enumerated in the New Testament should be accepted. But whether this restriction be accepted or not, it is a well-known logical principle that difficulties created by a theory are never sufficient to falsify that theory, if it is well-enough established on other grounds. If *sensus plenior* be demonstrated to be a viable concept, we will simply have to live with the difficulties, much as we live with the difficulties inherent in a teleological view of world history.

A second objection to the idea of a *sensus plenior* holds that the New Testament authors would not have appealed to a "hidden" meaning in the text, because this would have evaporated any apologetic value from the appeal. Would sceptical Jews be likely to accept the claims of the early church if they were based on unprovable assertions about what the Old Testament "really" meant? This objection has some point, but its force is mitigated by two considerations. First, we must be careful not to think that methods of proof not convincing to us would necessarily have been equally unconvincing to first-century Jews. The use of Scripture both at Qumran and by the rabbis gives little evidence that modern notions of biblical argument were considered important among ancient Jews. Second, we must ask to what extent the New Testament appeal to Scripture is intended for "general" consumption or with apologetic purpose. Much, if not most, of the use of the Old Testament in the New is designed to assure or convince Christians, for whom the general relevance of the Old Testament for the church was already assumed.[87]

Since no biblical text clearly teaches the concept and no biblical text clearly refutes it,[88] our final acceptance or rejection of the idea will depend on whether it is necessary and adequate to explain the phenomena and whether it coheres with an acceptable theory of inspiration. It is with respect to this second point that the most serious objection to the theory is raised. Inspiration, as we noted earlier, is generally conceived to be a "concursive" phenomenon whereby God so uses the human author that the final product, Scripture, is definitely and uniquely *God's* Word and, at the same time, the culturally, historically, linguistically conditioned words of human beings. If this is so, it is argued, the notion that God has placed in Scripture a meaning unknown to the human author (the "instrument" by which God produced Scripture) is inconsistent with inspiration. Whatever it is, then, this "fuller meaning" cannot be part of the *text*, since the meaning of that text is limited to what the divine/*human* author intended.[89] There is validity to this objection. A notion of inspiration that "divides" the divine and human authors of Scripture may be theologically as suspect as a Christology that too rigidly separates the divine and human natures of Christ.

However, this objection is not decisive. Brown, replying to such criticism, argues that the "instrumentality" of the human author of Scripture cannot be taken in the rigid, technical sense implied by some statements of the problem. As long as God uses that "instrument" (the human author) according to its "proper sphere" (viz., cognition and intention) and the human author always is really an instrument (in the sense that the "literal" sense is always present and not excluded by the "fuller" sense), then it is neither impossible nor objectionable to think that God could " . . . elevate that instrument to produce an additional effect outside the sphere of its proper activity." Brown goes on to quote Manuel de Tuya: "'From the fact that God is using an instrument which is *capable of knowledge*, it does not follow that God can use this intelligent instrument only in as much as he actually knows all that God wanted to express.'"[90] While not strictly parallel, since the production of inspired Scripture is not involved, the example of the "prophecy" of Caiaphas (Jn 11:49–52) is suggestive: as "high priest that year," he communicated a message from God that goes beyond anything he consciously intended.

Walter Kaiser objects, "Could God see or intend a sense in a particular text *separate* and *different* from that conceived and intended by his human instrument?"[91] But this is to erect a wider chasm between the "literal" and the "fuller" sense than advocates of a *sensus plenior* conceive. Brown insists that the *sensus plenior* be "homogeneous" with the literal sense,[92] and J. I. Packer, defending a limited "fuller sense," insists that this further meaning " . . . is simple extension, development, and application of what the writer was consciously expressing."[93] The question should rather be: Could God have intended a sense *related to* but *more than* that which the human author intended? I cannot see that the doctrine of inspiration demands that the answer to that question be negative.

It is not clear, then, that the usual objections brought against the idea of a *sensus plenior* are cogent. There does not appear to be any compelling reason for rejecting the hypothesis. On the other hand, there are reasons to hesitate before embracing it as a comprehensive explanation of the "problem" uses of the Old Testament in the New. For one thing, the New Testament sometimes appeals to the *human* author of the Old Testament text for what appears to be a questionable application. For instance, Peter specifically states that *David* spoke about the resurrection of the Messiah in Psalm 16 (Ac 2:25–28). Yet few scholars find any evidence in the text of that psalm that David had anyone but himself in mind as he wrote it.[94] Moreover, the New Testament generally gives the impression that the meaning they find in the Old Testament can be seen by others, too, once certain basic presuppositions are granted (see Jn 3:10; Mk 12:26). Yet if Jesus and the New Testament authors are appealing to a "hidden" sense of the text, revealed only by the Spirit to them, such an argument is nonsensical. Therefore, without at this point excluding the possibility that a *sensus plenior* may be the best explanation for some of the problematic quotations, we are encouraged by these remaining difficulties to investigate other possible approaches first.

E. A CANONICAL APPROACH

A renewed interest in the final, canonical form of the Old Testament and its significance for exegesis and interpretation has been a hallmark of recent Old Testament studies. Many scholars, who for various reasons find themselves unable to accept the *sensus plenior* approach in its usual form, have focused on the ultimate canonical context of any single scriptural text as the basis on which to find a "fuller" sense in that text than its human author may have been cognizant of. Norbert Lohfink, for instance, suggests that the need to posit a *sensus plenior* is largely due to the unnecessarily stringent restriction of the "literal sense" to what can be discovered through historical-grammatical exegesis. Instead, he argues, one should posit a "'theological' literal sense," which "means nothing other than the meaning of the scripture read as a whole and in the *analogia fidei.*"[95]

Without calling this further meaning the "'theological' literal sense"—a designation of questionable appropriateness, since it is liable to confusion with the human author's conscious intention, often "theological" in nature—a number of other scholars have advocated a similar proposal.[96] Common to them is the argument that any specific biblical text can legitimately be interpreted in light of its ultimate literary context—the whole canon, which receives its unity from the single divine author of the whole. The original human author may often have had an inkling that his words were pregnant with meaning he himself did not yet understand, but he would not have been in a position to see the entire context of his words; some biblical books written before him may not have been available to him, and, of course, he was unaware of the revelation that would be given after his time.

This way of looking at the phenomenon of the use of the Old Testament in the New has much to commend it. First, it builds on the scripturally sound basis of a redemptive-historical framework, in which the Old Testament as a whole points forward to, anticipates, and prefigures Christ and the church: "all the law and the prophets prophesied until John" (Mt 11:13 rsv); "Christ is the *telos* [goal and end] of the law" (Ro 10:4). These texts and others show that the New Testament views the Old Testament as a collection of books that, in each of its parts and in its whole, was somehow "incomplete" until "filled up" through the advent of Christ and the inauguration of the era of salvation. Jesus "fills up" Israel's law (Mt 5:17), her history (Mt 2:15), and her prophecy (Ac 3:18). That He might also "fill up" the meaning of many specific Old Testament texts would not be at all incommensurate with this characteristic pattern.

Second, this scheme can be shown to have its antecedents in what the Old Testament itself does with earlier revelation. Outstanding events like the Exodus take on more and more significance as they are used to model the future dealings of God with His people.[97] The significance of Israel's Davidic king as an anticipation of the messianic king becomes clearer and more specific as the Old Testament unfolds. The "meaning" of the choice of David to be king of Israel becomes deeper in the light of further Old Testament revelation, going beyond what would have been recognized by David's contemporaries, by Samuel, or even by David himself. And not until the greater son of David himself appears on the scene does this meaning reach its deepest level.

Third, the questionable division between the intention of the

human author and that of the divine author in a given text is
decreased, if not avoided altogether, in this approach. Appeal is made
not to a meaning of the divine author that somehow is deliberately
concealed from the human author in the process of inspiration—a
"*sensus occultus*"—but to the meaning of the text itself that takes on
deeper significance as God's plan unfolds—a "*sensus praegnans*." To
be sure, God knows, as He inspires the human authors to write, what
the ultimate meaning of their words will be; but it is not as if He has
deliberately created a *double entendre* or hidden a meaning in the
words that can only be uncovered through a special revelation. The
"added meaning" that the text takes on is the product of the ultimate
canonical shape—though, to be sure, often clearly perceived only on
a revelatory basis.

And this means, fourthly, that the "fuller sense" discovered by
Jesus and the apostles in Old Testament texts is, at least to some
extent, open to verification. One can, by reading the Old Testament in
the light of its completion and as a whole, as they did, often
demonstrate the validity of the added meaning they find in texts. But
this must also be qualified. It is no doubt true, though the point is
often exaggerated, that Jesus and the apostles did not always work by
conscious hermeneutical principles in their application of Old
Testament texts. The revelatory stance of the New Testament
interpreters of the Old must not be ignored; and some of the
applications they make would never have been discovered if they had
not told us of them. Who would have guessed, for instance, that
Rachel's weeping for her children (Jer 31:15) would have been "filled
up" in the weeping of the people of Bethlehem over their slaughtered
infants (Mt 2:17–18)? The specificity of the application could not have
been made without the benefit of revelation. On the other hand, it
needs to be stressed again that the "fulfillment" of this Old Testament
text does not imply that Matthew views it as a *prophecy;* and the
context of Jeremiah shows how appropriate and theologically profound Matthew's application of this text is.[98]

In the debate over whether we can "reproduce the exegesis of the
New Testament," then, our answer must be carefully nuanced. On the
one hand, we do not have the same revelatory authority to make the
specific identifications made in the New Testament. But, on the other
hand, we can usually see the theological structure and hermeneutical
principles on which the New Testament interpretation of the Old
rests; and we can follow the New Testament in applying similar
criteria in our own interpretation.[99]

The nature and usefulness of this approach can be better
appreciated if we apply it to some specific examples. We will look at
two Old Testament texts, one from the Psalms and the other from the
Prophets, whose extension of meaning in the New Testament is best
explained as due to deepening of meaning through further revelation.

In 1 Corinthians 15:27, Paul quotes Psalm 8:6 ("God has put all things in subjection under his feet" RSV) as proof that Christ's reign must culminate in His sovereignty over everything, even death itself (v 26). Unlike both the MT and the LXX, Paul's citation uses the third person singular verb rather than the second person, but this modification—being necessary to fit the verse into Paul's context—does not really affect the meaning. Psalm 8 praises God's majesty and expresses awe at the dignity and supremacy to which God had raised insignificant mankind. The "man" of the psalm is clearly the generic or representative man, particularly in his original created state.

What right, then, does Paul have to take language from the psalm and apply it to Christ? One possible response is that Paul does not really "quote" from the psalm but simply uses the language of the psalm to make his point (cf. our discussion about Old Testament language as a "vehicle of expression" above).[100] But although Paul does not use a formula to introduce the quotation, the significance of the appeal in its context suggests that he is adducing proof from an outside source. Others, then, consider this a case of *sensus plenior:* Paul, from his inspired standpoint, discerns in the verse the meaning that God had ultimately intended in it.[101] In the nature of the case, this possibility cannot be excluded, but other options should be explored first.

Since Psalm 8:4 uses the phrase "son of man," it has been suggested that an implicit Son of Man christology lies behind the use of Psalm 8 both here and in Hebrews 2.[102] Paul's application would then be validated by virtue of a typological or even prophetic understanding of Psalm 8. But Paul's failure to use an explicit "Son of Man" christology makes this suggestion questionable. A better approach is to recognize the significance of the Adam-Christ comparison in Paul's theology—specifically in 1 Corinthians 15. Paul sees Christ as the "second Adam," the "spiritual," "heavenly," eschatological Adam (1Co 15:45–47).[103] Christ, then, is both "like" Adam in his significance as "representative head" and different from Adam in origin, nature, and impact on humanity (cf. also Ro 5:12–21). In some sense, then, Paul views Christ as "perfect" man—the ideal not realized by Adam but now embodied in the "last Adam." Granted this perception of Christ, we can see how Paul would naturally attribute language about the "ideal man" to Christ. The psalm itself gives no indication that anything other than man in his ideal, created state is in view; but, in the light of New Testament revelation, it can now be seen that none other than Christ fulfills this role of the ideal man. Paul's use of this psalm, therefore, receives its validation from the legitimacy of regarding Christ as ideal man.[104] His is not an appeal to a meaning deliberately hidden in the text by God but to the meaning that that text can now be seen to have in the light of the significance of Christ.

No Old Testament text is more significant for Paul than Habakkuk 2:4b: "the righteous will live by his faith." It is cited in both Romans (1:17) and Galatians (3:11) as substantiation for Paul's crucial doctrine of justification by faith. The textual situation is complicated and debated. The MT adds after "faith" ('*ĕmūnâ*), the third person singular pronominal suffix ("his")—almost certainly referring to the "righteous one" (*ṣadîq*).[105] In the LXX, however, the first person singular possessive occurs (*pisteōs mou*, "my faith"), a reference, it seems, to the faith, or "faithfulness," of God.[106]

Paul's omission of any possessive is probably deliberate and has been variously explained. Some have suggested that Paul in Galatians 3:11 intends a reference to God's faithfulness rather than to man's faith, but this is unlikely.[107] It is more likely that Paul omits the qualifier to highlight his notion of faith as something *"extra nos"*—the gift of God, not a possession or quality of man.[108] Here, then, is a case in which a modification in the text effects a certain nuance of meaning. A further preliminary issue is the strongly contested issue of what Paul intends the prepositional phrase *ek pisteōs* to modify. Is he stressing that "the one who is righteous will *live* by faith" (taking *ek pisteōs* with *zēsetai*)[109] or that "the one who is *righteous* by faith will live" (taking *ek pisteos* with *dikaios*)?[110] Certainty is impossible, but the emphasis on righteousness in both Romans and Galatians favors the second translation.

What can be said, then, about Paul's hermeneutical procedure in using this text to support his teaching of justification by faith? It is true that each of the three key terms in the quotation has a specific theological nuance derived from Paul's distinctive theology.[111] For Paul, the one who is "righteous" is the one who has experienced the eschatological gift of Christ (not one who is "right" according to the standard of the law), "faith" takes on all the richness of Paul's characteristic, dynamic understanding, and "life" denotes eternal life.

However, the difference between Paul's use of these terms and their meaning in Habakkuk should not be exaggerated. In Habakkuk, the verse comes as God's answer to the prophet's complaint about the judgment to be visited upon Israel through the wicked "Chaldeans." The term *ṣadîq* means not simply those who are "morally upright" but, as often in the Old Testament, those who belong to God's covenant.[112] "Live" (*yiḥᵉyê*), to be sure, does not mean "eternal life," but neither does it mean no more than "exist"; the word connotes "life before God," the enjoyment of His covenant grace and blessings.[113] And '*ĕmūnâ* means a firm, settled trust in God that rises above the circumstances.[114] Thus, while there is no doubt that Paul gives to each of the terms a specific nuance that the original did not have, his interpretation preserves the essential thrust of Habakkuk's meaning—far different from the way the verse was used at Qumran and in some rabbinic texts, where keeping the law was brought into the situation.[115]

Once again, then, we find an Old Testament verse that is given an added depth, a new richness, a more precise significance in the light of the "revelation of the righteousness of God" (Ro 3:21).[116] That God foresaw this added dimension to His words through the prophet is obvious. But there is no evidence that Paul has cited the verse on the basis of a hidden meaning in the text. It is the further revelation of God that brings out from Habakkuk's great principle its ultimate meaning.

The use of the Old Testament in the New cannot be understood without setting it in the framework of the canon as witness to salvation history. This "canonical approach"—to be distinguished from the more specific and far-reaching concept advocated by Brevard S. Childs and others—is an essential and basic element in the answer to the problem we are considering.

But is it able to explain all the problems? R. E. Brown compares this kind of approach unfavorably to the *sensus plenior* explanation because, he claims, the New Testament authors are clear in ascribing the "added meaning" they find to the actual *text* they cite, not to a new appreciation for the place of that text in the history of redemption.[117] It was *David*, as we noted earlier, who "foresaw and spoke of the resurrection of the Christ" in Psalm 16 (Ac 2:31 RSV).

In this case, however, Brown's *sensus plenior* solution fares no better, since the meaning is directly ascribed to the human, not the divine, author. What is apparently happening here is not that Psalm 16 takes on added meaning in the light of further revelation but that further revelation enables us to understand for the first time the ultimate significance of David's words. And, in the case of Caiaphas, a still different situation seems to obtain: while John's recognition of the ironically prophetic significance of the high priest's words came long after the fact, on the basis of further revelation, he nevertheless implies that the words, at the time of their utterance, possessed a meaning unknown to Caiaphas. Here, perhaps, we come closest to a genuine *sensus plenior*, although we must keep in mind that Caiaphas is not an author of Scripture.

VI. CONCLUSION

These examples, and others like them, suggest that our explanation of instances where the New Testament finds meaning in Old Testament texts that cannot be demonstrated through normal exegetical procedure cannot be reduced to a single formula. The ultimate canonical context of all of Scripture is the basic starting point and is the ultimate validation of the New Testament approach. From this basic conviction, however, Jesus and the apostles appear to proceed in several different ways. Perhaps most frequent are occasions when later revelation provides the basis to draw out further meaning from the text—meaning not clearly envisaged by the human author but compatible with his intent. Typology is best viewed as a special form of this relationship. In other instances, the brute facts of who Jesus is and what He did, combined with the inspired authors' unique revelatory stance, serve to give them a knowledge of the meaning of the text that would otherwise not have been possible (e.g., Ps 16 in Ac 2). And, finally, it may be that some citations are best explained according to the traditional *sensus plenior* model: by direct, inspired apprehension, the New Testament authors perceive the meaning in a text put there by God but unknown to the human author. Even in this case, however, it is important to insist that this "deeper meaning" is based on and compatible with the meaning intended by the human author. And, while there is some truth to the assertion that the New Testament practice of interpreting the Old Testament should inform our own interpretation, we should be very cautious about suggesting "deeper meanings" in the text that are not clearly enunciated within Scripture.

We have now reached the end of our analysis of popular approaches to the problem of the Old Testament in the New. We have seen that many apparently "new" meanings discovered in Old Testament texts by New Testament authors are no more than the literal sense of those passages when read against the "informing" theology that precedes them.

Not all New Testament citations can be satisfactorily explained by this method, however. There remain some that actually do give to Old Testament texts meanings that do not correspond to the "grammatical-historical" meaning of the text, even when the "informing theology" is fully taken into account. When this happens, it is best to think that the New Testament authors have read the text against the background of the whole scope of revelation, preserved in the developing canon. The meaning intended by the human author of a particular text can take on a "fuller" meaning, legitimately developed from his meaning, in the light of the text's ultimate canonical context. Without necessarily appealing to the divine author as intending a meaning separate from, and hidden from, the human author at the point of inspiration, we would appeal to the divine author as providing the larger context of the developing canon as the framework within which the New Testament writers read the Old Testament. What is involved is not just the ultimate significance of a text, or its valid manifold applications, but the meaning of the text, not fully understood by the human author.

While advancing this viewpoint as the most important for understanding the New Testament use of the Old, we have admitted that not all of the "problem texts" can be satisfactorily fit into this approach. Acts 2 makes clear that the prophecy of the resurrection that Peter finds in Psalm 16 was David's intended meaning—a specificity of meaning that cannot be demonstrated from exegesis of the psalm. Here Peter is operating on a revelatory basis that is not open to proof or disproof. All that we can show is that the meaning Peter finds is not incommensurate with the original purpose and language of the psalm; but whether we think his interpretation is correct will depend on whether we consider him to be an inspired, accurate interpreter of the Old Testament.

In other words, when dealing with the problem before us, we must forthrightly admit that we cannot *prove* that the New Testament interpretation of the Old Testament is correct at every point. We can show that many are straightforward, legitimate interpretations and that many others can be considered valid if we admit the principle of the canon as the ultimate context of meaning. In other cases, while arguing that the meaning found by the New Testament author does not *violate* the meaning of the original, we will be unable to show how or why they arrived at the meaning they did—we will have to take them by faith, in the best sense of the word.

Does this admission mean that the phenomenon we have considered stands as an argument against inerrancy? We would answer no. For it to be considered as evidence against inerrancy, we would have to be able to show that Jesus or a New Testament author attributes meaning to an Old Testament text that appears to be entirely unrelated to the evident meaning of that text. Does this ever occur? To answer that question, we would have to conduct a thorough inductive study of every use of the Old Testament in the New. But what can be said is that the principles enumerated in this essay—allowing for the hermeneutical axioms of the interpreter, considering the larger theological framework of specific texts, recognizing the validity of the developing canonical context—suffice to explain any "problem text" of which I am aware.[118] The "ultimate," christological meaning discerned by New Testament authors in passage after passage of the Old Testament often extends beyond, but is always based on the meaning intended by the human author.

CHAPTER SIX
THE SPIRIT AND THE SCRIPTURES

John M. Frame

John M. Frame

John M. Frame is Associate Professor of Apologetics and Systematic Theology at Westminster Theological Seminary, Escondido, California. He is a graduate of Princeton University (A.B.), Westminster Theological Seminary (B.D.), and Yale University (M.A., M.Phil.). He has authored many articles, and his *Doctrine of the Knowledge of God* has been accepted for publication.

CHAPTER SIX

THE SPIRIT AND THE SCRIPTURES

The Holy Spirit is involved with the Bible in a wide variety of ways.[1] As the Third Person of the Trinity, He participated in formulating the eternal plan of creation and redemption, of which Scripture is a part (Eph 1:3, "spiritual" referring to the Holy Spirit). Further, He was involved in the creation of the heavens and the earth, without which Scripture, God's Word to his creatures, would have had no role (Ge 1:2; Ps 33:6 ["breath" suggests "spirit" in Hebrew]; Ps 104:30). Then, He was the author of revelation, the one who revealed God's truth to the prophets (Isa 61:1–4; Ac 2). Next, He was the one in charge of inspiration, the one who supervised the placing of God's Word in writing (1Co 2:9–10; 2Ti 3:16 ["spirit" being implicit in the Greek word for "inspired"]; 2Pe 1:21). Finally, by the internal testimony of the Spirit, He enables the "hearers" of the Word of God to savingly appropriate it (Ro 8:14–17; 1Co 2:10–16; 1Th 1:5; 2:13; 1Jn 2:27; 5:9). In all of these ways, the Spirit validates God's Word—planning it, creating the media for its communication, authoring it, recording it, driving it home to human hearts.

The present study will be concerned primarily with the Spirit's work in revelation, inspiration, and internal testimony.

I. THE SPIRIT'S WORK IN REVELATION AND INSPIRATION

In the areas of revelation and inspiration, a vast amount of literature has been published.[2] It is not necessary, therefore, to elaborate or justify these doctrines in detail. This study, rather, will assume the main outlines of the current common orthodox position and will address some questions that focus specifically on the *Spirit's* activity. Scripture, it will be assumed, is the Word of God, recorded inerrantly by the Spirit in the original manuscripts of the biblical books. Thus, the Spirit is the author of Scripture. Scripture, however, also has a number of *human* authors; and the questions before us focus on the relationship of the divine author to the human authors.

In many ways, Scripture does not *appear* to be written by one divine author. It contains a wide diversity of literary styles, reflecting the divergent personalities, gifts, educations, and environments of its human authors. The authors borrow from one another and seek

historical information in ways common to human writers of the
biblical period. Sometimes, between one author and another, there
appear to be contradictions, even misunderstandings, when, for
example, writers of the New Testament appeal to those of the Old.
Many Evangelicals have sought to explain or reconcile these apparent
contradictions; I will not add to that literature. My question, however,
is: how does the Holy Spirit figure in all of this? What role does He
play? How is the Bible different from what it would be if only human
writers were involved? Should we not expect, in a book inspired by
God, a greater uniformity, something more tidy, more easily distinguishable from merely human literature?

When questions of this sort arise, it is always well to ask, "What
would be the alternative?" We can imagine a more "uniform" book—
something like the Koran is thought by Muslims to be. Would that be
an improvement on the Bible? Scripture is written so that we might
believe in Christ and be complete in him (Jn 20:31; 2Ti 3:17). Would a
more uniform text help us in those ways?

Put in this way, the question appears less simple. Perhaps it
really requires more insight into God's mind than He has chosen to
give us. Do we know more than He does as to what it takes to save and
sanctify? Perhaps it is best just to leave these matters in His hands.
Yet, from what He has revealed about His purposes in revelation,
some further clarifications can be suggested.

A. COMMUNICATION

In giving us the Bible, God's purpose is communication. Clearly,
the art of communication is to speak the language of one's hearers.
When God communicates, therefore, He speaks as humanly as anyone
could possibly speak—the language humans are used to, in ways
humans are used to hearing. In the Incarnation, God became truly
human, enduring all the sufferings and temptations of human life.
Jesus did not live on earth with a halo or perpetually surrounded by
hosts of visible angels. Many would not have known by looking at Him
that He was the true God made flesh. God did this so that Jesus might
be sympathetic as High Priest, a true representative of humanity
before God (Heb 2:10–18; 4:14–16). Similarly, God's written Word is a
truly human word, one that captures all the nuances of human life
and human communication.

Some types of "uniformity" actually *hinder* communication. Utter
constancy of style can be monotonous. Recounting every detail of a
historical event with "pedantic precision" can detract from the point
of the story. (If someone asks my age, and I give it down to the hour,
minute, and second, surely I have, in most situations, placed a
roadblock in the process of communication.) If God had spoken to the
Hebrews using the precise language of twentieth-century science, He
would have been thoroughly incomprehensible. If every apparent

contradiction were explained in context, what would happen to the religious and emotional impact of the words?

Considerations like these help to reassure us that God's ways, after all, are best. The humanity of Scripture ought not to be an embarrassment to us, a weakness in an otherwise powerful document. Rather, the humanity of Scripture is its *strength*. It is an index of the *success* of God in speaking our language, in communicating His Word clearly to us.

B. VARIETY

The truth of God is *many-faceted*. It includes teaching about eternity past, time, and eternity future. It tells of the various parts of God's creation—heaven, earth, stars, and seas. It speaks to men, women, and children of all ages. It speaks of salvation as a comprehensive change in our hearts, affecting every aspect of life.

Describing all of these matters requires, sometimes artistry, sometimes conceptual sharpness, sometimes analytical clarity. It requires the poetic gifts of David, the wisdom of Solomon, the passion of Amos for social justice, the brilliant arguments of Paul, the intuitive clarity of John, the historical scholarship of Luke. A "more uniform" text would be poorer than the Bible we have; for it would not display as clearly the incredible richness of our salvation in Jesus Christ.

C. MYSTERY

How, then, did the Spirit work as He inspired Scripture? The answer is, mysteriously. That is what we expect from Him (Jn 3:8). He works, paradoxically, most divinely when He is speaking most humanly, for then He shows the perfection of His communication. Most writers on the subject of inspiration admit that Scripture tells us very little about the way in which God inspires. Sometimes, what He does seems to be "dictation," however much we may wish to deny a "dictation theory" (see Isa 6:9ff.; Rev 2; 3). Other times He works through methods of human reasoning (including an author's historical research—Lk 1:1–4). Sometimes He may give to a writer extraordinary knowledge of some historical information that is otherwise unknowable, but that is not usual. In every case the Spirit creates, by the human writer, a text that is God's Word, in the best form for communication.

II. THE SPIRIT'S INTERNAL TESTIMONY

More time will be spent on this aspect of the Spirit's work, since it is not as widely understood and expounded as are the doctrines of revelation and inspiration. Also, several problems that have emerged in recent theology deserve thorough analysis.

The Protestant Reformation contended for the gospel of justification by faith alone. But this doctrine contradicted the church
tradition, or so it was said. So the Reformers argued intensively, not
only about justification, but also about biblical authority and its
relation to tradition. A crucial weapon in the discussion was the
Reformers' doctrine of the "internal testimony of the Holy Spirit."
Rome was willing to grant the authority of Scripture; but, she insisted,
we cannot even know that Scripture is authoritative except by the
testimony of the church. Thus, church tradition became, at that point
at least, a more basic authority than Scripture. No, said Luther and
Calvin. Our final assurance of biblical authority is, not human
tradition, but the witness of God's own Spirit within us.

Calvin developed this doctrine in more detail than did Luther,
turning it into the centerpiece of his Christian epistemology.[3] In his
Institutes,[4] he sharply denies that "the eternal and inviolable truth of
God depended upon the decision of men." On the contrary, the
church itself is founded upon the "writings of the prophets and the
preaching of the apostles."[5] Although "sufficiently firm proofs are at
hand to establish the credibility of scripture,"[6] "we ought to seek our
conviction in a higher place than human reasons, judgments, or
conjectures, that is, in the secret testimony of the Spirit."[7] Calvin
denies that this doctrine leads to what we would today call
subjectivism. He opposes those "fanatics" who forsake Scripture for
alleged new revelations of the Spirit.[8] Word and Spirit go together, so
that the Spirit is recognized in His agreement with Scripture.[9]

Later in the *Institutes*, Calvin again discusses the Spirit's testimony, this time in its relation to individual faith and assurance. Using
many Scripture passages, Calvin indicates that faith is the work of the
Spirit.[10] Without the Spirit, we are incapable of faith.[11] Only the Spirit
can lead us to Christ.[12]

Since the Reformation, this doctrine has continued to play an
important role in Protestant theology—but with a wide range of
interpretations, applications, and emphases, provoking numerous
partisan debates. In our day, many have argued that the "orthodox"
tradition that followed the Reformation (Turretin, Voetius, et al.) either
ignored or seriously misunderstood this teaching, leading to similar
deficiencies in the "Old Princeton" theology (Hodge, Warfield), which
so strongly influenced modern Evangelicalism.

The present study will deal with three areas in which the
orthodox approach has been questioned: (A) the sovereignty, (B) the
objects, and (C) the rationality of the Spirit's testimony. But first we
must set the stage for this discussion.

As far as sovereignty is concerned, Karl Barth, especially, has
charged that the orthodox thinkers inadequately appreciated the
lordship of the Spirit in His testimony. They thought of Scripture as a
finished, permanent deposit of divine truth, while, in Barth's view,

they ought to have seen it as a human document that from time to time *becomes* God's Word to us as the Spirit sovereignly moves. On the orthodox view, Barth thinks, we may become complacent, believing that we "have" God's Word under our control.[13]

Moreover, in considering the objects of the Spirit's testimony, Gerrit C. Berkouwer[14] and others have argued that the orthodox tradition held too "formal" a view—a view of the Spirit witnessing to Scripture as a collection of inerrant truths on a wide variety of subjects. Berkouwer prefers to say that the Spirit witnesses to Christ, to the gospel of salvation, to our adoption as sons and daughters of God. The Spirit witnesses to Scripture also—but only as Scripture witnesses to these realities. Thus, the Spirit's concern is not to establish a "formal" principle of authority but to establish the "material" content of the gospel. He guarantees the truth of the gospel but not necessarily the accuracy of Scripture on such matters as history, geography, and science.

In regard to rationality, both Berkouwer[15] and others—such as Jack B. Rogers and Donald K. McKim[16]—think that the orthodox tradition misconstrued the place of reason in relation to Scripture, constructing a system of rational arguments to buttress biblical authority rather than relying entirely on the testimony of the Spirit.

In what follows, these questions will be considered in more detail—without entering into the historical questions of whether the modern critics have rightly interpreted the orthodox tradition.[17] We shall analyze the modern views, seeking to determine their meaning and their theological validity and to address the theological questions they raise. Although these views are complicated, I believe that this discussion will make the orthodox views look more compelling than their modern would-be replacements. In general, I will maintain that the modern formulations, while commendably reminding us of some biblical emphases, are too confused to stand serious theological scrutiny. These confusions can be overcome by formulations that, while recognizably orthodox, are stated to meet the contemporary questions.

A. THE SOVEREIGNTY OF THE WITNESS

One of the most exciting things about the Spirit's testimony is that it is an intimate, even "direct," relation between ourselves and God. Listening to Scripture is not merely a transaction between ourselves and a book, even a very extraordinary book; rather, in Scripture we meet God *Himself.* For Protestants (at least those outside "charismatic" circles), no experience offers a more profound closeness with God. It is this sense of the divine presence that pervades the Barthian analysis of the Spirit's witness. The same emphasis can be found in Calvin: "Thus, the highest proof of scripture derives in general from the fact that God in person speaks in it. . . . God alone is a fit witness of himself in his Word."[18]

Some modern writers, indeed, are even more bold in speaking of the closeness of our relation with God in the Spirit's testimony. Helmut Thielicke speaks of our having "a share in (God's) self-knowledge (I Cor. 2:10f; 13:12b)."[19] There is some danger of pantheism in this formulation, which Thielicke seeks to counter in various ways. Yet, the Scripture passages present the Spirit's witness as something uniquely wonderful, which we cannot adequately describe without taking some theological risks.

But if the internal testimony brings us face to face with God, at the same time it brings us face to face with His sovereignty and freedom. The doctrine must be formulated so as to do justice to God's lordship in His revelation.

1. The Position of Modern Theology

Both "orthodox" and "modern" thinkers find value in these sorts of considerations. But the modern thinkers also find in them some weapons against orthodoxy. For one thing, consider the traditional orthodox distinction between inspiration and the internal testimony of the Spirit. Orthodox thinkers have traditionally insisted that "inspiration" and "internal testimony" are quite distinct, though both are works of the Spirit.[20]

In modern theologians like Barth, however, this distinction loses its sharpness. For them, first, inspiration in the orthodox sense does not exist; God does not place His words on paper. For God to inspire words in this way would compromise His freedom and sovereignty; God Himself could not abrogate such words once He has spoken them. Thus, what the biblical writers experienced was, not inspiration in the orthodox sense, but a kind of illumination similar to what we experience today in the Spirit's witness. Furthermore, the distinction between inspiration and illumination becomes difficult to draw for theologians who are impressed with the immediacy of the divine presence in the Spirit's witness. What can "inspiration" be, if it is not the internal testimony? What more can we ask than an intimate participation in God's own self-knowledge?

But there is further implication. If inspiration in the traditional sense is rejected, then there is also a change in the basis of biblical authority. In orthodox Protestant theology, the inspiration of Scripture renders it authoritative, though the witness of the Spirit is essential if we are to perceive and accept that authority. In much modern theology, however, particularly in the Barthian tradition, not only is the witness of the Spirit essential to our acceptance of biblical authority; it is the one factor that *makes* Scripture authoritative. Without His witness (and therefore without our faithful response), Scripture has no more authority than the best books of human wisdom.[21] On this view, Scripture lacks authority until we believe it. But why should we believe a book that, before we believe it, has no authority over us?

Thus, in much modern theology the internal testimony *replaces* the traditional concept of inspiration. It was the internal testimony, not inspiration, in this view, that motivated the original writing of Scripture, and it is the internal testimony (presently occurring, as we read and hear), not inspiration, that grounds our faith in Scripture. The Bible is not inspired, if by "inspiration" we mean a unique divine action in the past that guarantees the truth of the text at all times and for all readers. If the word "inspiration" is to be of use, it must be used as a synonym for the internal testimony, so that we today are "inspired" as were the biblical writers, though our inspiration may in some respects depend upon theirs.[22]

This construction coheres well with three familiar concepts of neoorthodoxy. First, Scripture "becomes" the Word of God when the Spirit uses it to reach our hearts. Second, our response to the Word of God is a part of the revelation, so that there is no revelation without our (positive) response.[23] Third, the truth or error of the biblical text itself is irrelevant to faith, for the Spirit can reach the heart even by means of erroneous content.

These notions are thought to be essential to the freedom or sovereignty of God in the Spirit's witness. God is free to use, or not to use, any text as His Word, whether it be true or false. In the orthodox view, the Barthian argues, God is forced to honor a word spoken in the past; He is not free to contradict the canonical texts. Thus, we who "have" the canonical texts have God under our control.

But surely there is something odd about saying that an inerrant canonical text places God under our control. For one thing, Scripture never draws any such inference. In Scripture, God makes covenant promises, by which He *binds Himself*. In Christ, all these promises are Yes and Amen (2Co 1:20). God cannot lie or deny Himself (2Ti 2:13; Tit 1:2; Heb 6:18). Therefore, His Word abides forever (Isa 40:8). These divine words constitute a body of truth, a "tradition" (2Th 2:15; 3:6), a faith that was "once for all entrusted to the saints" and for which we are to contend earnestly (Jude 3). God commands His people to obey all His written words, statutes, and ordinances and to pass them on to their children (Dt 6:4–9; 8:3; Ps 1; 19:7–14; 119; Mt 5:17–20; 1Co 14:37; 2Th 2:15; 2Ti 3:15–17; 2Pe 1:19–21; 3:15–16).

Moreover, the biblical writers do not reason that these divine promises compromise God's sovereignty! On the contrary, God's sovereignty is expressed through the irresistible power of His Word. "So is my word that goes out from my mouth: It will not return to me empty, but will accomplish what I desire and achieve the purpose for which I sent it" (Isa 55:11). God's Word is an instrument of His sovereign rule. It is precisely the case that His sovereignty would be compromised if He did *not* speak such words.

Evidently we must use greater care in formulating our concept of divine sovereignty than has sometimes been shown among theologians. When we reason without such carefulness (relying on intuition, as it were), ambiguities emerge. To one theologian, God's sovereignty would be compromised if He were to utter an inspired, inerrant sentence. To another (and I believe this is the uniform position of Scripture) God's sovereignty *requires* the existence of such sentences.

The moral seems to be that "sovereignty" is a more complex concept than we often imagine. Use of it requires some careful thinking rather than jumping to conclusions that seem intuitive. What seems intuitive for one theologian will be counterintuitive for another. Intuition misleads us, because generally intuition does not make fine distinctions. Intuitively, we tend to formulate divine sovereignty by excluding anything that looks like it might be a "limitation" on God. However, when we reflect upon the matter, we can see easily that sovereignty cannot be taken to mean an absence of all such supposed limitations. Only the most extreme nominalists would conceive of sovereignty in that way. Some "fine distinctions" are needed to tell us what *kinds* of "limitations" are inappropriate to divine sovereignty—i.e., what sorts of "limitations" would *really* be limitations. Most theology books, even by Calvinists, recognize that God is "bound," at least by His own character—by, e.g., His goodness, rationality, and transcendent greatness; God *cannot* be evil, stupid, or weak. God is also bound by His covenant promises, as we have seen from Scripture.

There is, therefore, no *carte blanche* sovereignty, sovereignty without any "limitation" at all. Thus, a theologian must take pains to justify the types of qualifications he allows. The orthodox thinker must justify his assertion that God limits Himself to working within the framework of His covenant promises. (We have given an outline above of such a justification.) Barth, too, must justify the sort of limitation that he alleges, that God *cannot* guarantee the continuing truthfulness of written sentences. Barth, however, rarely if ever argues his distinctive view at this point; he seems to think that his particular view of God's sovereignty/limitation is intuitively obvious.

When such an argument is brought forward, we shall again consider the Barthian position. Until that time, we ought to remain content with the position of the Reformers, which (as we have seen in summary) is the position of Scripture itself:

2. The Orthodox Position

a. Contrary to neoorthodoxy, there *is* such a thing as an inspired text. God calls His people, not to listen to subjective inner promptings, but to listen to His "commands, decrees and laws" (Dt 6:1).[24] God holds His people responsible to obey His written Word.

b. The Spirit and the Word go together. This is the major emphasis of both Calvin and Luther over against the Roman church on the one side and the "enthusiasts" on the other. The Spirit witnesses to the Word—not against it or in addition to it, as the neoorthodox construction suggests. Scripture always represents the witness of the Spirit in this fashion: the Spirit calls us to hear what God says (see Jn 14:26; 15:26; 16:13; 1Th 1:5; 2:13). As Helmut Thielicke points out, the Spirit is poured out in fullness only after the Crucifixion and Resurrection (Jn 16:7), for He bears witness to the finished work of Christ (Jn 16:14). Thus, He "protects the givenness of the event." But, to complete Thielicke's point, the Spirit can witness to those objective events for us today only by witnessing to the apostolic *word* concerning those events, the word we have in Scripture.[25]

c. The word is self-authenticating. It is the ultimate authority for the believer, and therefore it is the ultimate ground even for its own authority. We cannot test Scripture by anything more authoritative than Scripture. God's written Word, in fact, is the means of testing spirits (1Co 14:37; 1Jn 4:1–3). No one, therefore, may dare to place any teaching of the Spirit over against the Word of God.[26]

d. What, then, is the ground of biblical authority? Is it to be found in inspiration or in the Spirit's testimony? There is some ambiguity here in the term "authority." The term can be used in an objective or subjective sense. Objectively, a civil law, for example, has authority over me whether I even know about it or not. Subjectively, however, that law will not rule me (in the sense of influencing my conduct toward obedience) unless I know about it and receive it favorably. Similarly, Scripture has objective authority over us by virtue of its inspiration. We are responsible to obey it whether or not the Spirit has witnessed to us. If we disobey, we are subject to divine judgment unless God forgives us through Christ. The subjective authority of Scripture, however, comes through the Spirit's witness; we cannot obey from the heart until/unless the Spirit testifies *in* our heart.[27]

e. Thus, the sovereignty and freedom of God in the Spirit's testimony are seen, not in God's ability to contradict or modify or add to His Word, but in His ability to drive it home to otherwise unwilling hearts and, indeed, to do everything He says He will do.

B. THE OBJECTS OF THE WITNESS

The chief burden of Gerrit C. Berkouwer's important work *Holy Scripture* is his critique of what he calls "abstract" and "formal" views of Scripture. "Whenever the words 'abstract' and 'formal' appear frequently in the discussion," he says, "what is meant is that scripture is received as writing, as a book of divine quality, while its content and message as such are thereby not taken into account from the out-set."[28] In discussing the Spirit's witness, then, Berkouwer wants to insist that the Spirit does not witness to scriptural authority in an "abstract" or "formal" way; rather, the Spirit testifies to the "content and message" of Scripture, and His testimony to the authority of Scripture occurs only in that context.

Berkouwer further insists that this witness to the biblical

"content and message" does not occur "apart from its connection with the condition of the religious subject."[29] It "first of all has a bearing on a person's sonship."[30] That is to say, the Spirit's witness to the Scripture is not a different witness from His witness to our adoption (described in Ro 8:14–17).[31] Thus, the Spirit validates the context of Scripture in its application to a faithful son or daughter of God.

Negatively, Berkouwer says (interpreting Bavinck) that the Spirit's testimony

> does not supply direct certainty regarding the authenticity, canonicity, or even the inspiration of Holy Scripture; nor regarding the historical, chronological, and geographical data "as such"; nor regarding the facts of salvation as *nuda facta*, nor, finally, regarding the closedness of the canon, as if it were possible to solve the problems regarding canonicity with an appeal to the witness of the Spirit.[32]

Berkouwer is a subtle thinker, and often it is not easy to describe precisely what he has in mind. There are always qualifiers that take the sharp edges off his more controversial statements. Note above, for example, that he does not deny that the Spirit witnesses to the biblical text, only that He so witnesses "in abstraction" from Scripture's "message."[33] Later on, in fact, he does clarify this point: "Reformed theology was not confronted with the dilemma of a dualism between authoritative scripture and the message it brings, because Reformed theology hears the message of salvation precisely in the witness of scripture."[34]

Nor does he quite deny that the Spirit witnesses concerning biblical authenticity, canonicity, inspiration, historical, chronological, and geographical data. If he did, then, of course, we would have to raise questions; for Scripture contains a great deal of material about such matters, and it is unclear why the Spirit would leave such data out of His purview. Rather, what Berkouwer denies is that the Spirit testifies to these "directly" or "as such" or "as *nuda facta*." What, we want to know, is the "cash value" of all this? What is Berkouwer, concretely, trying to rule in and to rule out?

Sometimes it seems as if what Berkouwer wants is a certain order of topics: "On the basis of the New Testament, the confession of the Spirit is first of all related to salvation in Christ; and *then* the Word of God is discussed."[35]

But it is hard to believe that Berkouwer's concern is as trivial (and formal!) as a mere order of discussion. Is he concerned, rather, about an *emphasis?* Sometimes we get that impression. But "emphasis" in theology is itself a rather subtle matter. Berkouwer does not mean, evidently, that the author of a paper on the Spirit's witness, for example, must spend, say, eighty percent of the text discussing salvation and only twenty percent discussing biblical authority. And surely an intelligent theologian like Berkouwer would not want to limit theological reflection to those topics "emphasized" in the New Testament, as if it were somehow impious to write about the veiling of women in 1 Corinthians 11. In what sense, then, are we required to "emphasize" matters of salvation when discussing the Spirit's witness? Perhaps Berkouwer's point, after all, is not well-described as a "matter of emphasis." But in that case, what is he saying? What does it mean to deny that the Spirit witnesses to historical data "as such"?

Berkouwer's chapter on the Spirit's witness leaves these matters rather unclear, but other parts of the book illumine his concern somewhat. In the chapter on "reliability," for instance, Berkouwer mentions differences in the Synoptic accounts, and concludes that the biblical concepts of witness, truth, and reliability are

> not in opposition to a freedom in composing and expressing the mystery of Christ; their purpose is rather to point in their testimony to that great light. . . . The aim of the portrayal was not to mislead and to deceive; it was not even a "pious fraud," for it was wholly focussed on the great mystery. This explains why the church through the ages was scarcely troubled by the difference pointed out long before, and by the inexact, non-notarial portrayal. A problem was created only as a result of attempts at harmonization and the criticism that followed. . . . But through a recognition of the true nature of the Gospels, the way is opened to hear and understand the one testimony.[36]

Here Berkouwer argues that since the purpose of Scripture is to proclaim the "great mystery," we should not expect a "notarial" precision in the biblical narratives. Scripture can witness adequately to its content and message without such exactness. Therefore, in making judgments about the "reliability" of Scripture, we must take into account its content, message, and purpose. Relating this discussion to the Spirit's work, then, we may say that, for Berkouwer, the Spirit does not testify to a "notarially precise" Scripture; He validates the *truth* of Scripture but only that kind of truth appropriate to the message.

All of this is true enough as far as it goes, but it is scarcely new. Orthodox Protestants have long denied that biblical inerrancy entails "pedantic precision."[37] How, then, does Berkouwer differ from those orthodox thinkers whom he seems to be criticizing? Chiefly, I think, in the vagueness of his formulation and also in his special agenda: Berkouwer throughout the book seems to be urging upon theological conservatives a greater openness toward current forms of biblical criticism,[38] often charging them with "fear"[39] or with avoiding questions[40] when they are not as open as he would like. But he rarely indicates that there are any limits at all to this openness. (He does, to be sure, indicate that Bultmann's demythologization is unacceptable).[41] The reader is left with a vague feeling, then, that he ought not to fuss too much over biblical criticism, that he should be open to almost any critical proposal. That vague feeling seems to be the "bottom line" of Berkouwer's analysis.

I suppose, then, that in evaluating Berkouwer's view we should ask whether he has succeeded in justifying this vague openness to biblical criticism. And, of course, the answer is no. Certainly, Scripture's purpose is to proclaim Christ, and it is worth pointing out as Berkouwer does (and most all the orthodox do) that this purpose does not necessitate "pedantic precision." But there is nothing about this purpose to warrant a vague openness concerning the theories of modern biblical scholarship.

On the contrary, there is much in Scripture to warn us *against* such openness. Scripture teaches us that we live in a fallen world, in which the fashionable currents of human learning are opposed to God and to His gospel (Ro 1; 1Co 1; 2). It warns us over and over again about the danger of false teaching from within the church (Mt 7:15–20; Gal 1; 2Th 2; 1Ti 1:3ff.; 4:1ff.; 2Ti 3:1ff.; 2Pe 2). Thus, if we are really to read Scripture in terms of its central message, we will be *suspicious* of modern biblical scholarship, particularly when it comes from those who have renounced the Bible's own supernatural world view. This does not mean that there is no truth in the writings of modern scholars; the question before us is one of our attitude or disposition toward them. Berkouwer has not succeeded in justifying his recommendation of sunny optimism.

Otherwise, much of Berkouwer's concern is legitimate. He is right in saying that we should not fear to investigate the difficult questions.[42] Berkouwer is also right to insist that the Spirit does not merely witness to the authority of a book. He witnesses to the gospel message, to what the book says. Believing Scripture is believing that message.[43] At the same time, believing the message entails believing the book,[44] for the message is the book's content. And, although the book is centrally focussed in certain great events—Jesus' life, death, and resurrection—it speaks out about everything in creation, including history, geography, and science. It speaks of a God who made the heavens, earth, and sea and who acted in earthly history and geography to save us from our sins. It urges us to do *all* things to His glory, whether we are preachers or carpenters or historians or scientists (1Co 10:31). As long as we read Scripture responsibly (yes, "in relation to its message"), we need not fear (as I believe Berkouwer does)[45] studying its implications for these and all areas of human life. Berkouwer's view is not only wrong but greatly harmful, insofar as he discourages such study, which study is in essence the attempt to "take captive every thought to make it obedient to Christ" (2Co 10:5).

Does the Spirit tell us what books belong in the canon? Does He help us decide between rival interpretations? Does He help us with scholarly questions about literary genre, variant readings, and the like? Not in the sense of whispering in our ears the solutions to these problems! On that question, the Reformers, the orthodox, and Berkouwer are agreed: Scripture never represents the Spirit's work as the giving of new information *about* the Bible. No one, for example, ought to claim that the Spirit has given him a list of canonical books; the actual list comes through historical and theological investigation of the contents of these books. Yet the Spirit has certainly played an important role in the history of the canon. By illumining and persuading the church concerning the true canonical books, He has helped the church to distinguish between false and true. He has motivated the church to seek out reasons for what He was teaching them in their hearts.[46]

Thus, the Spirit gets involved in everything we think and do as Christians. There is no area from which He, or His Scriptures, may be excluded. In that Berkouwer calls us to read those Scriptures responsibly, he should be applauded. But insofar as he discourages (as he does, at least by the ambiguity of his proposals) the comprehensive application of Scripture to all of life in opposition to unbelieving thought, he is not a reliable guide.[47]

C. THE RATIONALITY OF THE WITNESS

Now let us consider the question concerning the relation of the Spirit's testimony to evidences and rational arguments. Here it will be necessary to discuss some more general aspects of Christian episte-mology.[48]

Knowing always involves a knower, a knowable content, and some "laws of thought" or criteria for determining what is true about the knowable content. To put it more succinctly, knowing involves subject, object, and norm. These three factors are distinguishable in theory but very difficult to separate when we look at the actual experience of knowing. Where does the "subject" end and the "object" begin? Philosophical battles (between idealists like Berkeley or Hegel and realists like Moore and Russell) have been fought over this issue. Sometimes it seems that all our knowledge is really self-knowledge: after all, everything in my mind is *my* experience, is it not? But then, where is the "object" that stands over against the self? Other times it seems that I have no self-knowledge at all. Hume diligently searched his experience and couldn't find anything called "the self." So the debate continues: either the self is swallowed up in the object, or *vice versa*.

Similar problems arise in connection with the "norm." To the existentialist, the norm is indistinguishable from the self. (I am my own, and my only, law.) To the pure empiricist like John Stuart Mill, laws are generalizations from sense experiences, merely shorthand ways of speaking about objects. Thus does the norm get lost in the subject or the object. But the reverse problem also occurs. In Plato—

and perhaps in Kant and others—subject and object both get lost in the norm. Knowledge for them is faithfulness to a preexisting ideal (for Plato) or categorical structure in the mind (for Kant); anything short of such norms is inadequate and, in an important sense, unreal.

Christianity, too, recognizes this triad. God reveals Himself in the world (object), in His image (subject), and in His Word (law). As sinners, we hear but repress God's revelation in all three forms (Ro 1). In saving us, however, God overcomes this resistance. He performs wondrous, mighty deeds in the world to save us (object) and sets forth their meaning and application to us in His Word (norm).[49] Also, He transforms our own hearts and minds so that we will be able to believe His deeds as they are proclaimed in His Word. This transformation is the work of the Holy Spirit. His witness to the Word illumines and persuades us so that we have a saving knowledge of God's revelation.

In Christianity, the three factors—subject, object, and norm—are closely related but distinguishable. Knowledge of any one brings with it knowledge of the others. We cannot know the world without taking God's law into account; when God reveals Himself in the world, He also reveals His *ordinances* (Ro 1:32). We cannot know ourselves except in the light of God's Word. But, likewise, we cannot know the Word unless it comes to us through the world and through ourselves. We read the Bible as an object in the world among others, and we come to understand it through our own mental—and spiritual— gifts. Hence, it is not surprising that many have reduced some of our three elements to others. Besides, non-Christian thinkers have a special problem here. For the Christian, there is a God who has created the world and self and has spoken His norm-word. Thus, the Christian has confidence that object, subject, and norm will cohere; all three lead to the same place. But those who reject the theistic premise have no such basis for confidence. Therefore, they are tempted to choose one of the three, the one in which they have most confidence, as the *only* element of knowledge.

The Christian, though, knows that however inseparable these elements are in our knowledge, they are not identical. I am not the world, nor *vice versa*. God gave humans dominion over the world (Ge 1:28). Nor is God's word identical with the world or with myself. God's word is creator (Ge 1; Ps 33:6; Jn 1); the world and self are creatures.

Now the testimony of the Spirit to the written Word has a specific function in this triadic structure. The Spirit Himself, as we saw earlier, is active in all aspects of revelation—creation, incarnation (Lk 1:35), prophecy, inspiration.[50] But the internal testimony, as distinct from these other aspects of revelation, is focussed on the *subject* of knowledge. The internal testimony is not new revealed words (norms; see section I, above), nor is it a new saving act in history (object). Rather, in the internal testimony, the Spirit operates in our hearts and minds, in ourselves as subjects, to illumine and persuade us of the divine words and deeds.[51] This fact has important practical consequences for us when we seek God's guidance. When we lack knowledge of God's will, our need is not necessarily a need for new factual information (object), and it is never a need for new revelation in addition to Scripture (norms). Rather, most often (I think) it is a need for inward change, a need to reconcile ourselves to what God has already revealed. Guidance need not be either mystical (revelation apart from the Word), nor intellectualistic (arising from a merely academic study of Scripture). Our pride and doctrinal misunderstandings often lead us to think that if we have problems, either we can solve them through our own resources (intellectualism) or they are God's fault (because of inadequate revelation). But Scripture continually directs our attention to our own sinfulness as the source of such problems—to our need of the Spirit.[52]

Now since our theological question deals with the relation between the Spirit's witness and "rational argument," we must give some attention to human rationality.[53] Reason may be defined as a person's capacity for forming judgments, conclusions, inferences. So understood, reasoning is something we do all the time, not merely in academic or theoretical work. When a football quarterback sees a telltale motion in his opponents' backfield and moves to avoid the defensive players, he is reasoning; he has drawn an inference as to what the opposing players will do, and he has acted upon that inference. Logic is the science of inference, but people regularly draw inferences without having studied that science. Inference may fruitfully be seen as an *ethical* matter—and, therefore, as much a matter of conscience as of logical skill. A valid inference is an inference that we *ought* to acknowledge; and that "ought" is a *moral* "ought."[54]

So understood, reasoning takes place every time we make some use of God's revelation (in nature or Scripture). When a Christian is tempted to cheat on his taxes and resists that temptation, reasoning has taken place. He has drawn the conclusion—from Scripture, preaching, or conscience—that stealing is wrong, and he has drawn the further inference that cheating is stealing and therefore also wrong. Thus, every act of obedience to the Lord involves reasoning, whether or not some explicit argument is formulated.

Therefore, when we acknowledge Scripture as God's Word (also an act of obedience!), that acknowledgment is also a rational inference. We have looked at the data of Scripture and have come to this particular conclusion. Even if we "leap" to this conclusion by "blind faith," we have somehow come to the conclusion that our blind faith *ought* to leap to this conclusion rather than some other— meaning, of course, that our "blind faith" has not really been blind at all. Even a blind-faith conclusion is a conclusion, an inference.

Such reasoning can, of course, be bad reasoning. Sometimes people offer inadequate reasons for believing in Scripture. But we cannot conclude that *all* such reasoning is bad. To say that would be to say that there are no good reasons for believing the Bible. But that would mean that faith in Scripture is unwarranted; and that in turn would mean (recalling our ethical interpretation of logical inference) that we have no obligation to believe in Scripture. Scripture, then, would not have any authority at all.

Every warranted confession of Scripture, therefore, is a rational confession, a sound inference from experience. But then, what role remains for the testimony of the Spirit? Just what we said before. The Spirit's work is in the subject. Scripture tells us that sin blinds us to the truth (Ro 1; 1Co 1–2). This means that sin keeps us from acknowledging those things that we *ought* to acknowledge; it keeps us from acknowledging warranted conclusions, rational conclusions. The work of the Spirit is to remove those effects of sin, to overcome that resistance. The Spirit does not whisper to us special reasons that are not otherwise available; rather, He opens our eyes to acknowledge those that *are* available (and that, at one level of consciousness, we know already, Ro 1:21). Nor does the Spirit give us power to transcend reason altogether. That would mean either that no reasoning is involved at all (contrary to what we have established) or that the reasoning accompanying our conviction is invalid (but then our conclusion would be unwarranted, illegitimate).

According to our threefold scheme, therefore, in rational argument, norms (logical and others) are applied to an object (the data of experience). This process warrants a rational conclusion. But the sinner will resist this conclusion unless the Spirit opens his eyes. To come to rational conclusions, we need objects and norms, but we must also be the kind of people who can and will come to the right conclusions. The Spirit supplies that crucial third factor. He changes us so that we acknowledge what is rationally warranted.

Now just as secular philosophers have tended to confuse norm, object, and subject, so Christian thinkers have often confused the Spirit's witness with the other elements of the Christian's knowledge. This sort of confusion often occurs, in my opinion, when theologians consider the relation between the Spirit's work and human rationality. Calvin himself is not immune from criticism on this score. It is possible that Calvin's teaching can be reconciled to the sort of model I have presented,[55] but some of his expressions are problematic. Note:

> . . . we ought to seek our conviction in a higher place than human reasons, judgments, or conjectures, that is, in the secret testimony of the Spirit. . . . The testimony of the Spirit is more excellent than all reason. . . . Therefore, illumined by his power, we believe neither by our own nor by anyone else's judgment that scripture is from God; but above human judgment we affirm with utter certainty . . . that it has flowed to us from the very mouth of God

by the ministry of men. We seek no proofs, no marks of genuineness upon which our judgment may lean.[56]

Here Calvin talks as if the Spirit's testimony and rational arguments were competing factors, as it were, contributing to our assurance of Scripture. It sounds as if arguments are an inadequate means of assurance, the Spirit's testimony an adequate means. Now it is surely true that many arguments are unsound and do not truly warrant faith in Scripture and that, therefore, the testimony of the Spirit goes beyond those arguments. It is also true that even *sound* arguments without the Spirit's testimony will not lead anyone to saving knowledge of Christ and Scripture. Doubtless points of this sort were in Calvin's mind.

But Calvin's expressions might also be taken to mean that the case for the truth of Scripture is inadequate, and that we may come to belief in it only by irrational means. Such a view would certainly be illegitimate (and I think contrary to Calvin's own intent). Or, these statements might be understood as meaning that the Spirit *supplements* the evidence, giving us a legitimate warrant in place of inadequate ones. But what could this mean but that (1) Scripture lacks objective authority apart from the Spirit's witness (a notion we have refuted in section I), and (2) the Spirit gives us a new revelation to provide the adequate warrant, a notion that Calvin always rejects?

Such data have led to problems in the interpretation and theological use of Calvin's doctrine. We do not have the space for a historical excursus, but I do believe that the Dutch Calvinist theologians Kuyper and Bavinck, along with the philosopher Herman Dooyeweerd (not to mention Barth and Berkouwer, whom we discussed earlier) have pressed Calvin's teaching in a somewhat irrationalist direction. Similarly, the contemporary philosopher Alvin Plantinga has spoken of a "reformed epistemology" in which belief in God is accepted as "properly basic" (that is, not based on any reasoning or evidence). Jay M. Van Hook argues that although Plantinga can successfully defend the rationality of theistic belief on this basis (all systems of thought have to begin somewhere, therefore Christianity has a right to begin with God), he cannot show the *irrationality* of someone who *denies* Christianity (holding that something other than the biblical God, the Great Pumpkin for instance, is "properly basic").[57]

I think there is much value in Plantinga's concept of "proper basicality." God is the Christian's presupposition, the norm of all his thinking about everything else. More needs to be said, however, about how one distinguishes rational from irrational "presupposings" and about how the Christian presupposition has a rational basis in God's self-revelation.[58] And there is some danger now that reformed people will avoid wrestling with such questions, thinking that the doctrine of the Spirit's testimony answers them sufficiently.

That doctrine, however, is not suited to that particular purpose. Scripture does not present it for the purpose of overcoming inadequacies in the rational basis of Christianity. The point we need to remember is that there is no competition between the rationality of the Scriptures and the witness of the Spirit. We do not need to make the case for Scripture somehow irrational or inadequate in order to do justice to the Spirit's testimony. If knowledge of God is to be possible, both rationality and the Spirit are needed—rationality so that faith will be warranted, indeed obligatory, and the Spirit so that our sinful unbelief, our refusal to accept our obligation, will be overcome.

The above discussion will seem rationalistic to some. For the record, let me indicate my belief that human reason has a great many limitations,[59] especially in matters of faith. I freely grant that the "knowledge of God" in Scripture is far more than a theoretical contemplation, that it involves obedience, love, and trust. Further, coming to know God is far from a merely intellectual or academic experience. It involves all our faculties (as well as those of the Spirit!); it is more like coming to know a friend than coming to know, say, wave mechanics. For that matter, even learning wave mechanics is not a "purely intellectual" process, whatever that may mean. Intellectual operations are always dependent upon our experience, our emotional make-up, our religious and ideological commitments, etc.[60]

It should be said, too, that the testimony of the Spirit works in the Spirit's typically mysterious way (Jn 3:8). As we have said, He does not whisper in our ears; but neither does He work predictably through the normal channels of education so that those with advanced degrees automatically have the greatest spiritual perception. He gives us, rather, a sort of "intuition" for things divine, as many writers have put it. We recognize Scripture as the Word in the same way we recognize white to be white or sweet to be sweet. Suddenly, that Word, which we had, as unbelievers, despised, becomes fresh and exciting and precious to us. Arguments and reasons that, perhaps, we have heard many times and rejected display their cogency suddenly before our eyes. We recognize the *loveliness* of the gospel and respond with joy.[61]

Nor do I wish to say that we must be able to supply proofs and arguments in order to justify faith. As I have said, much of our reasoning is very informal, like that of the football quarterback. Generally it is not formulated into syllogisms, and usually it would be difficult, I think, even for a professional logician to identify the premises and the logical steps. God has simply given us a *sense* of what is reasonable, and usually that is sufficient. (Note how all reasoning, not just that which deals with matters of faith, may involve something like the Spirit's testimony.)[62] On the other hand, if someone has the God-given skill to develop some kind of formal proof,

I know of nothing in the doctrine of the Spirit's testimony that would prevent him from doing so.[63]

III. SUMMARY AND CONCLUSION

In this study I have sought to clarify some matters pertaining to the Spirit's work in revelation, inspiration, and internal witness. I have argued that although revelation and inspiration do not produce a "uniform" text, that fact need not be an embarrassment to us, unless it be an embarrassment of riches; for the Spirit gives us *more* than a "uniform" text, a text that conveys the truth with a fullness and clarity as appropriate to its depth and riches as is possible in human language.

Then I argued that debates over the sovereignty, objects, and rationality of the Spirit's internal witness ought themselves to be more carefully related to the riches of that inspired text. The weakness of theological discussions in these areas has been that they have seized upon certain biblical concepts (like "the sovereignty of God in revelation"), largely ignoring the qualifications, interpretations, and uses given to these concepts in the actual context of Scripture. Paradoxically, these modern theologians (most of whom would be quite opposed to the notion of "uniform" inspiration) have taken Scripture to be much more uniform that it really is! The biblical concept of sovereignty, for instance, is, as we have seen, much more nuanced than are the concepts of sovereignty in most modern theologies of revelation. The modern views owe more to philosophical discussions than to biblical data.

These are methodological problems in modern theology that are found in many areas beyond those discussed here. That fact will provide much for future study. For the time being, I advance this moral: if theologians would try to be more biblical in their doctrine of Scripture, they would be forming some habits that will be useful across the board, avoiding pitfalls in other areas of theology. It is important, then, even in the relatively "abstract" area of theological methodology, to hear the Spirit speaking in the Word. "He who has an ear, let him hear what the Spirit says to the churches" (Rev 2:7).

CHAPTER SEVEN

SOME MISCONCEPTIONS OF THE IMPACT OF THE "ENLIGHTENMENT" ON THE DOCTRINE OF SCRIPTURE

John D. Woodbridge

John D. Woodbridge

John D. Woodbridge is Professor and Chairman of the Department of Church History at Trinity Evangelical Divinity School, Deerfield, Illinois. He is a graduate of Wheaton College (B.A.), Michigan State University (M.A.), Trinity Evangelical Divinity School (M.Div.), and the University of Toulouse (Doctorat de troisième cycle). He has written *Biblical Authority: A Critique of the Rogers/McKim Proposal,* co-authored *The Gospel in America: Themes in the Story of America's Evangelicals* (with Nathan Hatch and Mark Noll), edited *Renewing Your Mind in a Secular World,* co-edited four other books, and contributed chapters and articles to numerous other publications.

SOME MISCONCEPTIONS OF THE IMPACT OF THE "ENLIGHTENMENT" ON THE DOCTRINE OF SCRIPTURE

I. THE CURRENT DEBATE

Orthodoxies of historical interpretation are often imposing edifices. Even when compelling evidence demonstrates that they are built on shifting foundations, they do not usually collapse in a heap. Those interpretations that commend a theological system are especially resistant to criticism.

Recently, I spoke with a distinguished German scholar about Luther's views of biblical authority. The professor's comments confirm how difficult it is to challenge "accepted" historical interpretations. One segment of the conversation went something like this:

"Did Martin Luther believe that the Bible was without error?"

"Yes."

"Did Martin Luther include within the purview of biblical authority the natural world?"

"Yes. Neoorthodox writers of this century created the idea that Lutherans of the sixteenth century did not think that the Bible spoke about the natural world. I published a volume by a Lutheran theologian of the sixteenth century who used the Bible as his sourcebook for a discussion of birds, fish, and animals. My study was not welcomed by some scholars in Germany, given its implications. It was published in Austria."

Here was a renowned specialist, with apparently no theological brief to deliver, who acknowledged without hesitation that Martin Luther upheld complete biblical infallibility and that it was a neoorthodox historiography that had contributed to a widespread misunderstanding of Luther and early Lutherans on that point.

This exchange with the professor underscores an age-old problem: the theological presuppositions of historians (including the present writer) sometimes get in the way of their honest effort to write scrupulously fair history. The spate of recent interpretations regarding the history of biblical authority may mirror the theological presuppositions of their authors more than unwary readers might suppose.

What has prompted the renewed interest in the history of biblical authority within recent decades?[1] Several eminent historians have turned to the topic because they are students of "secularism" and of "culture." They want to determine how the Bible lost its status as an authoritative, divinely inspired book in the minds of many Europeans or how its teachings helped shape a particular culture at a particular time. Other historians have written on the subject, motivated by a quest to legitimize their own beliefs. This seems especially true of several Roman Catholic theologians. At Vatican II, their church delimited the scope of biblical inerrancy to "that truth which God wanted put into the sacred writings for the sake of our salvation," thereby generally excluding the domains of history and science from the purview of inerrancy.[2] This was a new stance, perhaps dictated by the church's desire to seek an accommodation with higher criticism and macroevolution. For centuries, Roman Catholics had taken it for granted that the church upheld the Bible's complete infallibility (including the domains of history and science). Professor James T. Burtchaell of Notre Dame writes aptly:

> Christians early inherited from the Jews the belief that the biblical writers were somehow possessed by God, who was thus to be reckoned the Bible's proper author. Since God could not conceivably be the agent of falsehood, the Bible must be guaranteed free from any error. For centuries this doctrine lay dormant, as doctrines will: accepted by all, pondered by few. Not until the 16th century did inspiration and its corollary, inerrancy, come up for sustained review. The Reformers and Counter-Reformers were disputing whether all revealed truth was in Scripture alone, and whether it could be interpreted by private or by official scrutiny. Despite a radical disagreement on these issues both groups persevered in receiving the Bible as a compendium of inerrant oracles dictated by the Spirit.[3]

Post-Vatican II scholars sensed that the council's delimitation of inerrancy to "salvation truths" had to be explained. Several like Oswald Loretz wrote essays and books attempting to demonstrate that the new delimitation corresponded to what Christians of earlier generations had believed.[4] This concordance alone, it was felt, might help justify their claim that their church's new statement continued to reflect "orthodoxy" in the best sense of that expression.[5]

In their revisionist efforts, these Roman Catholic interpreters encountered a stubborn historiography that is very old. It has survived sharp criticisms from Johann Salomo Semler in the eighteenth century, Samuel Coleridge and Charles Briggs in the nineteenth, and Protestant liberal and neoorthodox historians in the twentieth. This historiography, summarized above by Professor Burtchaell, propounds the thesis that the so-called "central tradition" of the church retained the doctrine of biblical inerrancy until at least the eighteenth century.

For many contemporary critics this historiography has uncomfortable implications. It suggests quite strongly that their own beliefs about biblical authority are innovative and have probably departed from the basic teachings of the Christian churches. These scholars prefer to view biblical inerrancy as a novel doctrine created during one era or another of church history; they want to represent their own beliefs as reflecting what the Bible teaches and what wise Christians of earlier generations believed.

But when, according to these scholars, was biblical inerrancy created, and who were its originators? Here differences of opinion begin to multiply. The candidates for originators of biblical inerrancy have been numerous. During the heyday of neoorthodoxy, prominent scholars propounded the thesis that biblical inerrancy was created by Protestant Scholastics who sought certitude in the truthfulness of written text rather than being content with the authority of Christ, whom one encounters in the text. The creation of the doctrine of inerrancy allegedly took place in the late sixteenth century and is particularly associated with the names of Lambert Daneau, Flacius Illyricus, and other second- and third-generation Protestants.[6] With the recent work of Jill Raitt, Olivier Fatio, and Richard Muller, the historical synthesis sustaining a neoorthodox interpretation of theology is under considerable strain. Its very survival is in doubt.[7]

Persuasive monographs continue to appear that argue for greater continuity between the Reformers' theological teachings and those of their descendants. Professor Geoffrey Bromiley has well described the views of Scripture advocated by continental Protestant theologians of the late sixteenth and early seventeenth centuries as compared to the perspectives of Luther and Calvin:

> In these writers the doctrine of scripture is no doubt entering on a new phase. Tendencies may be discerned in the presentation which give evidence of some movement away from the Reformation emphases. The movement, however, has not yet proceeded very far. The tendencies are only tendencies. What change there has been is more in style, or materially, in elaboration. The substance of the Reformation doctrine of scripture has not yet been altered, let alone abandoned.[8]

The neoorthodox historiography regarding the Bible is less persuasive today than it was in the 1940s and 1950s.[9]

In 1979 Professors Jack Rogers and Donald McKim published *The Authority and Interpretation of the Bible: An Historical Approach*.[10] They moved the creation of the doctrine of biblical inerrancy back to the last decades of the seventeenth century, linking it to the work of Francis Turretin and the influence of Newton and Locke on theological reflection. In this fashion, Rogers and McKim, Presbyterians both, could deny that the Westminster divines' commitment to biblical infallibility was equivalent to a commitment to biblical inerrancy. Obviously, if the Westminster divines drew up their Confession in the 1640s, they did so before the doctrine of biblical inerrancy was fully fashioned.[11] For Professors Rogers and McKim, the Bible's infallibility excludes purposeful deceits but not "technical errors." It is infallible in accomplishing its saving purpose, but not infallible for matters such as history, science, and geography.

In 1980 the study by Professors Rogers and McKim was voted "Book of the Year" by reviewers of *Eternity* magazine. But eventually criticism of the volume began to build.[12] A good number of historians and theologians were unprepared to accept its linchpin thesis that when Augustine, Luther, and Calvin indicated that the Bible was without error, they simply meant that it contained no "purposeful deceits." This criticism stemmed from writers whose own theological outlooks differed considerably. The Rogers and McKim proposal did not ultimately weather its reviews very well.

Perhaps the most subtle of the newer interpretations to challenge the older "stubborn historiography" regarding biblical inerrancy is one that emphasizes a distinction between formulations of biblical inerrancy before the mid-seventeenth century and modern formulations of the doctrine. This interpretation acknowledges that biblical inerrancy was indeed espoused by earlier Christians but that the formulation of the doctrine advocated by today's proponents differs substantially from the one entertained by these earlier Christians. According to this interpretation, the modern formulation of biblical inerrancy is a product of "the scientific age and age of rationalism" (generally associated with the Enlightenment).[13]

This proposal has been championed by Professor Bruce Vawter (a Roman Catholic scholar) and, to a certain extent, by Professor George Marsden (a Protestant specialist in the history of American Fundamentalism). Professor Vawter concedes that the church fathers advocated a belief in biblical inerrancy. However, he quickly adds the caveat that they, unlike many modern defenders of biblical inerrancy, coupled it to a doctrine of "condescension." The doctrine of "condescension," then, is a major variable that sets off the early church's perception of biblical inerrancy from "Fundamentalist" conceptions of the same doctrine. Vawter explains:

> The fathers did of course believe that the Bible was an inerrant and, if you will, an infallible repository of revealed religion; but from right to left, from John Chrysostom, let us say, to Theodore of Mopsuestia, by theological recourses like *synkatabasis*, "condescension," to be discerned in the inspired word, they recognized its limitations and time-conditionedness in respect to a continually developing human awareness and factual knowledge which is also the gift of God.[14]

When did the later "Fundamentalist" doctrine of biblical inerrancy allegedly emerge? Professor Vawter perceives its origins in an age that is apparently associated with the "Enlightenment":

"Biblical inerrancy" or "infallibility" in the fundamentalist sense, as has often been observed, is the product of the scientific age and the age of rationalism, a simplistic response to both. It is definitely not one of the authentic heritages of mainline Christianity.[15]

Professor Vawter's influential interpretation is showcased in an essay that generally defends the Christian's acceptance of macro-evolution.[16]

Professor George Marsden has drafted a proposal that shares several of the same features as the one proferred by Professor Vawter. Like Vawter, he allows that the premise that the Bible does not err is an old one. But then he associates the "Fundamentalist" doctrine of inerrancy with the Bible perceived as a scientific textbook. According to Professor Marsden, this latter doctrine differs from the way the biblical authors perceived the truthfulness of their accounts and from the way earlier Christians spoke about the "errorless" character of the Scriptures. He summarizes his argument in this striking way:

It is incorrect then to think of fundamentalist thought as premodern. Its views of God's revelation, for example, although drawn from the Bible, are a long way from the modes of thought of the ancient Hebrews. For instance, fundamentalists' intense insistence on the "inerrancy" of the Bible in scientific and historical detail is related to this modern style of thinking. Although the idea that Scripture does not err is an old one, fundamentalists accentuate it partly because they often view the Bible virtually as though it were a scientific treatise.[17]

For Marsden, the "Fundamentalist" doctrine of biblical inerrancy is based on the scientific model associated with Newtonism and Baconian inductivism.[18] The impact of Common Sense philosophy also helped fashion its configuration.[19] Dispensational writers of the nineteenth century who allegedly submitted to these influences were pivotal in shaping the doctrine. Marsden observes:

It was vital to the dispensationalists that their information be not only absolutely reliable but also precise. They considered the term "inerrancy" to carry this implication. Statements found in Scripture would not deviate from the exact truth. The importance of this assumption for prophetic interpretation is obvious. Precise numbers of years had to be calculated and correlated with actual historical events.[20]

In sum, Marsden views the "Fundamentalist" definition of inerrancy as emphasizing the precision of biblical statements regarding history and science. And, like Vawter, he notes elements of "Enlightenment" thought that allegedly helped create the doctrine of inerrancy in its modern format—a format that is not completely commensurate with the earlier statements of the Christian churches that the Bible has no errors.

In contradistinction to the influential Augustinian tradition on the subject, Marsden does not apparently believe that the doctrine of inerrancy has much to do with the issue of the Bible's authority. He downplays the doctrine on a consistent basis, often identifying it solely as a Fundamentalist belief.[21] In defining who an Evangelical is, he declines to mention the doctrine; rather, he argues that the Evangelical is one who believes in "the Reformation doctrine of the final authority of the Bible."[22] In reality, the Reformers were Augustinian and would have had little truck for Marsden's ambivalence towards an affirmation of inerrancy. Augustine wrote: "For it seems to me that the most disastrous consequences must follow upon our believing that anything false is found in the sacred books."[23]

Whereas for both Vawter and Marsden, the "Enlightenment" created the intellectual context for the shaping of the "Fundamentalist" doctrine of biblical inerrancy, Bernard Ramm notes the fact that biblical scholars in the Enlightenment recognized the humanity of the biblical texts and in their biblical criticism challenged an unhealthy emphasis of "orthodox" Christians upon its divinity.[24] Ramm invites Evangelicals to come to grips with certain elements of the Enlightenment's view of the Bible in forming their own perceptions of biblical authority. For him, Karl Barth serves as a remarkable resource person in this regard. According to Ramm, Barth made his peace with the Enlightenment without succumbing to its more negative criticisms of the Christian faith.[25] If Evangelicals will do the same, they will avoid "obscurantism."[26]

The "Enlightenment," then, has emerged as a historical period of great significance for several recent interpreters of the history of biblical authority. For Professors Vawter and Marsden, it was during the Enlightenment that the modern "Fundamentalist" doctrine of biblical inerrancy began to be formulated; for Professor Ramm, it was during this period that scholars began to give due attention to the humanity of the Scriptures and to recognize its fallibility.

How valid are the claims of these distinguished scholars? Before we assess their claims, we should comment briefly about the difficulties associated with our authors' use of global expressions such as "scientific age and the age of rationalism" (Vawter), "modern style of thinking" (Marsden), and "Enlightenment" (Marsden, Ramm). These "paradigmatic" expressions are losing much force today as scholars grapple with the difficulties of defining what the "Enlightenment" may have represented.

II. THE ELUSIVE QUEST TO DEFINE THE ENLIGHTENMENT

Within the last several decades numerous scholars have become convinced that the eighteenth-century "Enlightenment" is a more elusive quarry to trap with a net of general characterizations than they had previously believed. A careful analysis shows that there are various connotations associated with the traditional words that designate the Enlightenment in several languages. Quite simply, the expressions *Enlightenment, Siècle des lumières, Aufklärung, Illuminismo, and Illustracion* are not exact synonyms.[27]

This point is made more understandable when we recall that Frenchmen, Germans, Englishmen, and Swiss, for example, did not experience the so-called "Enlightenment" in quite the same ways, if they encountered any "Enlightenment" at all. Large numbers of Europeans, especially illiterate peasants and workers, remained quite untouched by the movement. They continued to live in an oral culture.[28] Moreover, the "time-frame" for these national "Enlightenments" did not always overlap. Despite the wide-ranging influence of Christian Wolff in the first half of the eighteenth century, the *Aufklärung* did not become especially prevalent in the Lutheran towns and cities of northern Germany until the second half of the eighteenth century.[29] Lutheran orthodoxy and conservative Pietism reigned supreme in the hearts of many German Protestants until mid-century.[30] On the contrary, the deistic controversy that stirred the caldron of public debate during the Enlightenment in Anglican England became especially acrid much earlier (in the wake of the publication of John Locke's *The Reasonableness of Christianity* in 1695).[31] The more public phase of *Siècle des lumières* developed in Roman Catholic France in the decades following the publication of Montesquieu's *Spirit of the Laws* in 1748.[32] Before that date, "Enlightenment" literature often had passed from hand to hand in a more clandestine fashion. Fearing censorship and reprisal, "Enlightenment" authors like Voltaire and Montesquieu generally delivered glancing blows rather than direct verbal hits upon the "Old Order" before mid-century.[33]

With their growing realization that the "Enlightenments" took on various shadings in different religious, social, and political environments, scholars have tried to sort out the commonalities and distinctives of national experiences during the Enlightenment. The 1978 edition of the review *Dix-huitième Siècle* contains articles in which capable scholars attempt to discern the essential traits of the "Enlightenment" in specific countries (e.g., the United Provinces, the Pays-Bas [French], Poland, Portugal).[34] Professors Hans Bots and Jan de Vet, for example, write about the uniqueness of reactions to the Enlightenment in the United Provinces:

> The same *Lumières* which shone elsewhere during this period refracted in the United Provinces and divided into a spectrum of colors and of nuances which is not interchangeable with any of those which characterized the flourishing of the *Lumières* in the other countries. Much research will be yet

needed in order to appreciate the exact coloration of the *Lumières* in the
United Provinces.[35]

The authors were impressed by the staying power of the Christian
faith during the eighteenth century.

Specialists in the history of the book trade also want to track how
the books, broadsheets, journals and other printed materials purvey-
ing "Enlightenment ideas" moved through the cosmopolitan Republic
of Letters from one nation to another.[36] Are there chronological
sequences to be charted? Is the year 1680, associated with Paul
Hazard's dating of the "Crisis of the European Mind" (1680-1715), the
baseline from which any such tracking should begin? Or should
another year be selected? Complicating these issues even further is
another issue that Professor Aram Vartanian has brilliantly brought
into focus. In reviewing benchmark studies by Professors Michel
Vovelle, Daniel Roche, and Robert Darnton, Vartanian points out that
Michel Vovelle discovered signs of "dechristianization" in the province of Provence decades before the writings of the *philosophes*
Voltaire, Diderot, D'Alembert, La Mettrie, and others were widely
disseminated:

> What the graphs show, therefore, is that Lumières as a literary and
> philosophical enterprise, and dechristianization as a social process, were
> independent phenomena, though destined to converge in the Late Enlight-
> enment. Put another way, when the spirit of the Enlightenment eventually
> reached the general public, the latter had already prepared itself, by a
> different route, to receive, and practice it.[37]

Vartanian proposes that the crucial question on the agenda of present
research for French historians is to explain what forces were bringing
about the "dechristianization" processes that occurred in general
isolation from the "literary-philosophic" movement associated with
the French *philosophes*.[38]

Here the research of Professor Dale Van Kley may be of signal
importance.[39] He does not disparage the importance of interpretations that stress the influence of the *philosophes'* writings or the role
of economic factors in giving shape to the *Siècle des lumières* in
France. But he does suggest with sophisticated arguments and rich
documentation that the "unraveling of the Old Order" has much to do
with religious controversies between Jesuits and Jansenists that
spilled over into the political domain especially during the refusal of
sacraments dispute of the 1750s and the broils associated with the
expulsion of the Jesuits in the 1760s.[40] These controversies contributed to the breaking down of the loyalties of many Frenchmen to the
institutions of the *Ancien Régime*.

Van Kley's studies once again bring to the fore the seriousness
with which many eighteenth-century Europeans treated questions of
religion. It will not do to speak of the Enlightenment as a period of

unmitigated "secularism" or indifferentism. Even Christianity's most virulent foes (e.g., Voltaire) viewed the times as a mixed age of "lights" (the progress of *la philosophie*) and "darkness" (the superstition and fanaticism that he associated with the practitioners of the Christian religion).[41]

These brief comments should give us pause. Historians today are not at all certain that Immanuel Kant was speaking for a majority of Europeans when he penned his controversial definition of the age in the essay "Was ist Aufklärung?": "Enlightenment is man's leaving his self-caused immaturity. Immaturity is the incapacity to use one's intelligence without the guidance of another."[42] Professor Vartanian reminds us that the number of Frenchmen whose religious beliefs were molded by the writings of the *philosophes* was quite small: "Clearly, those whose religious attitudes were formed through exposure to the philosophes should be counted as an integral part of the Enlightenment proper. They must have been no more than 50,000 individuals, and their class-reference was no doubt quite diversified. . . ."[43]

Recent studies are taking far more note of the persistence of the Christian faith in the eighteenth century. Even Baron d'Holbach's famous coterie at Paris was not the hotbed of atheism that a longstanding historiography had announced with assurance.[44] Contemporaries often viewed the Seven Years War (1756-1763) as a war of religion pitting Roman Catholic against Protestant powers.

No longer is it possible to identify the age solely with Voltaire or Jean-Jacques Rousseau, both of whom died in 1778. Nor can we rely upon paradigmatic expressions such as the "scientific age and age of reason" (Vawter) without specifying exactly what we mean. The diversity of intellectual opinion and religious convictions in the period does not lend itself to overly bold categorizations of this type. In bolstering an argument, contemporaries frequently appealed to "everyday experience" as much as they did to reason.[45] John Wesley and George Whitefield lived their lives in the eighteenth century as vigorously as did Voltaire and Jean-Jacques Rousseau. In 1984, Professor Vartanian suggested that new research is forcing us to reconsider dramatically what the nature of the "Enlightenment" may have been.[46]

III. CHRISTIANS AND THE BIBLE IN THE "ENLIGHTENMENT"

Despite the surprising vitality of the Christian faith in the eighteenth century, there is little doubt that various forms of the Christian religion and the Bible's authority were severely buffeted during the "Enlightenment" (using the conventional term and dating its onset with a conventional date, 1680). Studies by Professors Michel Vovelle, Margaret Jacob, C. J. Betts, John Redwood, and Marie-Hélène Cotoni make this clear.[47] Critics did force Christians to ponder the best strategies with which to defend their faith; and many Christians did make one adaptation or another to teachings associated with the "Enlightenment." In fact, several leading pastors of the outlawed Church of the Desert in southern France became partisans of "philosophic ideas"—particularly after Voltaire's intervention in the Calas Affair between 1762 and 1765.[48]

But did Christians in general develop a "Fundamentalist" doctrine of biblical inerrancy in their interaction with the "Enlightenment"? Did they emphasize the precision and the truthfulness of Scripture and extend its infallibility to areas of history and science and thereby depart from a more "accommodating" view of earlier Christians? Have Professors Vawter and Marsden, esteemed and insightful thinkers both, deciphered a subtle but important doctrinal innovation? And is Professor Ramm correct to surmise that Neologian theologians in the "Enlightenment" made advances on the "Orthodox" in their understanding of the "humanity" of the Scriptures? These more restricted questions will direct the remainder of the present study.

IV. THE BIBLE'S TRUTHFULNESS AND "HISTORY"

To answer these questions, we must bear in mind what earlier Christians had believed about the Bible's infallibility in preceding centuries. Their beliefs will afford us with a foil against which suspected innovations by "Enlightenment" Christians might be measured. Moreover, we need to reconsider the interplay between post-Tridentine Roman Catholic and Protestant polemics regarding the Bible. In a remarkable way these polemics often set the stage for discussions about the Bible's authority in the "Enlightenment."

Following the Council of Trent (1545-63), Roman Catholic apologists often exploited arguments of the "new pyrrhonism" (a resurgence of skeptical argumentation in the second half of the sixteenth century) by indicating that even though Protestants and Roman Catholics concurred that the Bible was infallible, Protestants were doomed to fall into skepticism.[49] Protestants did not have an infallible interpreter to tell them what the Bible meant: thus, they would splinter into many sectarian groups, each following the personal fancies of ambitious headstrong leaders. For their part, Roman Catholics believed that they alone benefitted from possessing the "authentic" text of the Bible, the Vulgate; they alone enjoyed the direction of an infallible magisterium and infallible traditions that could instruct them regarding the meaning of their Bible. In fact, the Bible belonged to the church, the guardian of God's truth.

Protestants responded that the Roman Catholic analysis of the Protestants' inevitable slide into skepticism was patently wrong-headed. They said that the Holy Spirit, the ultimate author of Scripture, helps the reader of Scripture to understand its meaning; what better interpreter could a Christian have, far better than men (i.e., fallible priests, bishops, or a Pope)?[50] In response to Roman Catholic goading about the Holy Spirit's guidance in interpretation, Protestants also emphasized the role of regenerated reason in assisting the believer to understand Scripture. Moreover, they averred that Scripture interpreted Scripture, clearer passages enlightening darker ones. The Scriptures are sufficient and perspicuous concerning matters of essential faith and practice. There is no need to turn to fallible Roman Catholic traditions for additional information regarding those subjects.[51]

Skillful Roman Catholic apologists like Bellarmine, François Veron, François de Sales, and Jean Morin at the end of the sixteenth century and during the first decades of the seventeenth century did not acquiesce before the logic of the Protestants' apologetic. The Oratorian Jean Morin highlighted textual difficulties of the Scriptures in an attempt to demonstrate that the Bible was not as perspicuous as Protestants claimed.[52] François de Sales pointed out with biting irony that Protestants had divided into many groups despite the guidance of the Holy Spirit (de Sales arguing that the Holy Spirit works in conjunction with the Roman Catholic Church).[53] François Veron, the celebrated debater, tied up a number of Reformed disputants in knots by pointing out that although Protestants said they believed in *sola Scriptura*, they actually relied upon another authority (their own reason) in interpreting Scripture.[54] The Jesuits Genebrard and Guillaume Baile scored those Protestants who tried to uphold the certitude of the Old Testament by affirming the inspiration of the Masoretic pointing.[55]

Protestants were not reluctant to turn around the canons of pyrrhonical argumentation and to fire back with similar fusillades of "skeptical" flack. If the magisterium of the Roman Catholic Church is infallible in its interpretive role, why are there various groups within Catholicism itself? Does not the Jesuit and Jansenist controversy over the merits of Augustinianism demonstrate the weakness of the Roman Catholic argument?[56] Do not Roman Catholic traditions conflict with each other on many points?[57] Do Roman Catholics really believe that their beliefs about the Eucharist are "perpetual" as the Jansenists Arnauld and Nicole insisted in their debate with the Reformed pastor Jean Claude in the 1660s and 1670s?[58] And where in Scripture can one find passages to sustain the authority of the bishop of Rome as the head of Christ's church, let alone as the infallible interpreter of Christian doctrine? Does not the Bible teach that it is authoritative because God is its ultimate author, not because the church has deemed it to be so? Could not the uncertainty of Roman Catholic teachings lead to, of all things, skepticism?

In the second half of the seventeenth century the Roman Catholic and Protestant debate over these matters, conjoined with the impact of Cartesian thought and developments in science, elevated the issue of certitude to a very prominent place in the thinking of many philosophers and theologians. If pitched apologetic battles (as well as the tragic Wars of Religion) between the opposing churches had not revealed that God favored one party or another, then several contemporaries wondered if Christians could muster any rational argument to persuade their foes to change confessions.

For several thinkers, apologetical arguments between Christians (including Easterners), whether biblical or historical, had run their course. Pierre Bayle, for one, proposed that they had. He proposed that the truthfulness of religious beliefs cannot be determined by rational arguments—witness the longstanding confessional conflicts. Religious beliefs are essentially determined by faith commitments.

For many Christian apologists, however, the need to demonstrate the "rational" character of the Christian faith itself was becoming all the more imperative.[59] In hard-hitting invective and clever sideswiping rhetoric, deists were claiming that "natural religion" constituted a more rational belief than the Christian faith and that "Reason's" rights to judge revelation had been well established. In fact, "Revelation" was not necessary. In the *Moral Philosopher*, the deist Thomas Morgan responded to John Leland's defense of biblical infallibility in this way:

> And does he not see what an Advantage he has hereby given the Atheists and real Infidels? For in this Case, if they can give any plain Instances, or Proofs, of Errors, Mistakes, or Inconsistencies, in the sacred Writers, it will be enough to set aside their Inspiration and immediate divine Authority; for if they were not infallible in one Case, they might not in another; and if they were not immediately inspired in historical matters, who can prove that they were in Doctrinals? And such are the wretched Shifts to which all these must be driven, who place Infallibility and Certainty in any thing else but the necessary immutable Truth, Reason, and Fitness of Things. I think nothing can be plainer than this, that there is no such thing as *historical Infallibility*, but that all Men are liable to Error, not only in remote Facts and supernatural Events, but even with regard to the most common Affairs, and things near at hand.[60]

From Morgan's point of view, a belief in biblical infallibility abets the cause of "atheists" because they can exploit its actual errancy. Individuals should turn towards Reason as a final authority. Challenges of this kind often prompted "Enlightenment" Christians to construct their apologies in the various ways that they did. Professor Hugh D. McDonald's thoughtful assessment of the value of their apologetic choices stands as a heuristic counterevaluation to Professor Vawter's harsh judgments.[61]

In the last decades of the seventeenth century, daunting quests to determine criteria upon which religious belief could be established and to draw up a list of essential doctrines upon which Christians of all communions could agree captured the attention of such disparate thinkers as John Locke and William Stillingfleet in England and Gottfried Leibniz in Germany.[62] But the issues had become far more complex because critics were now questioning the infallibility of the Bible, thereby challenging it as a source of utterly truthful information and right doctrine.

In earlier centuries, Christians had simply assumed that the Bible was infallible, as Professor Burtchaell noted. This explains why several Roman Catholic scholars were dismayed when Erasmus not only seemed to dispute the infallibility of the Vulgate through his lower criticism but went a step further by suggesting that the original authors of the Scriptures could have made errors. John Eck counseled Erasmus about his disquieting comments on Matthew 2:6:

> Listen, dear Erasmus: do you suppose any Christian will patiently endure to be told that the evangelists in their Gospels made mistakes? If the authority of Holy Scripture at this point is shaky, can any other passage be free from the suspicion of error?[63]

Eck did not believe that "any Christian" would listen to the claim of the sage of Rotterdam with equanimity. Moreover, he cited Saint Augustine to the effect that if a genuine error existed in Holy Scripture, that fact alone would throw the authority of Scripture into jeopardy.[64] Perhaps due to negative reactions, Erasmus did ultimately revise his interpretation of Matthew 2:6. In the early sixteenth century, when the Reformers put quill to paper, few dared challenge the infallibility of Holy Writ.

However, by the second half of the seventeenth century, not only had a number of Socinians, Libertines, Remonstrants, La Peyrère, Hobbes, and members of several radical groups insisted that the Bible contained a few errors in minor matters, but Roman Catholic writers like Henry Holden (1596-1662) and the biblical critic Richard Simon (1638-1712) began to question the Bible's sufficiency to communicate revealed truth perfectly.[65] In his *Divinae fidei analysis* (first edition, 1652; 1655; 1685; 1767), Holden, using a "rational" method (whose inspiration was probably Cartesian), attempted to separate out what was "certain" from what was "doubtful" in Christianity.[66] Holden was perhaps the first major Roman Catholic thinker to limit inerrancy to matters of faith and practice.[67] In his *Histoire critique du Vieux Testament* (1678), the Oratorian Richard Simon apparently denied that Moses wrote all the Pentateuch.[68] Although Simon claimed that his controversial "public scribes" hypothesis actually responded to Baruch Spinoza's earlier criticisms against biblical infallibility and the Mosaic authorship of the Pentateuch in the latter's *Tractatus*

Theologico-Politicus (1670), a good number of contemporaries like Bossuet wondered if Simon could be a Spinozist in priest's garb.[69]

Modern scholars are so accustomed to theological pluralism that they often have difficulty grasping the fact that before 1680 most Christians believed that to challenge the Mosaic authorship of the Bible or the doctrine of biblical infallibility was tantamount to challenging the truth claims of the Christian religion. Little wonder, then, that Spinoza's *Tractatus*—which also contested the value of miracles and prophecy as validating pillars of Christian truth claims—transformed its author into a theological pariah in the eyes of the orthodox. Even Pierre Bayle described the book as "pernicious and detestable."[70] Little wonder that Simon was excluded from the Oratorian order in 1678 and that the first edition of the *Histoire critique du Vieux Testament* was confiscated and burned. Only a few volumes of this edition escaped the flames.[71]

But we should recall, as Professor Jacques Le Brun astutely observes, Holden and Simon belonged to a long line of Roman Catholic controversialists (Erasmus, François de Sales, Charron, Camus, Valeriano Magni, and others) who, in their attempts to exalt the authority of the church, emphasized the insufficiency of Scripture.[72] The alleged insufficiencies and weakness of Scripture "were apologetical arguments before they became the conclusions of criticism."[73] Simon, then, who has been hailed as the "Father of Biblical Criticism" (as has Spinoza), still worked ostensibly with the agenda of a traditional Roman Catholic disputant, but his hypotheses and conclusions ranged far beyond those of earlier more conservative apologists.[74]

The irony of the Roman Catholic "pyrrhonical," or skeptical, argumentation is that deists frequently exploited its arsenal not only in their attacks against the Protestants' perspectives on Scripture but against the Christian faith in general. For example, the free-thinkers John Toland and Anthony Collins cited the arguments of Simon to demonstrate that the Bible contained "errors."[75] The deist Matthew Tindal, in a tour de force, proceeded to argue that if the Scriptures are errant, God cannot hold us accountable to them. To what standard can God in justice hold us accountable if the teachings of the Bible and the churches are uncertain? Tindal's answer was plain: Reason. If we follow the light of our reason as best we can, God cannot help but judge us positively. We did the best we could with the light we had.[76]

Astute contemporaries perceived that deists were borrowing Roman Catholic pyrrhonical arguments. William Bentley, a shrewd critic of Anthony Collins, pinpointed this borrowing clearly. Collins had portrayed several Roman Catholic scholars (including Simon) as intent upon demonstrating the corruption of the texts of Scripture in order to force Protestants to accept the authority of the church.[77] To this Bentley responded:

> One confesses that the painstaking research of Father Simon had no other goal than to sap the foundations of the Reformed Religion and that this savant Roman Catholic thought nothing better for his own goals than to render Holy Scripture precarious. This ruse is thus a knavish ecclesiastical trick à la Roman; and how can it be, if you please, that a man [Collins] who professes to declare war on all Priests, and all knavish ecclesiastical tricks, feels so at home with a Roman Catholic priest, and supports him with so much warmth in the pious intention of maintaining the cause of Popes?[78]

Bentley also fended off Collins' claim that the Christian faith is uncertain because we no longer have the original documents of the Scriptures. Roman Catholics like Simon had earlier argued in a similar fashion, except the Oratorian had riposted that recourse to Roman Catholic traditions reestablished the certainty. Bentley was particularly galled because Collins had cited his own philological work to bolster the hypothesis. Collins had reasoned this way: if as the Cambridge scholar Bentley had argued, some thirty thousand variants exist in the New Testament alone, how can one know with assurance anything about what the Bible teaches?[79]

Bentley responded to Collins with a gloves-off counterstroke. He wisely remarked that the discovery of many manuscripts since the fifteenth century had provided biblical scholars with greater means for emending obvious faulty readings in the Greek texts than when they had fewer manuscripts.[80] In turning the tables on the freethinker Collins, Bentley was not striking a new pose among Christians. Richard Baxter had argued much the same way earlier in the seventeenth century.[81] Bentley's contemporary, Jacques Basnage, a French Protestant, argued at length against the Roman Catholic apologetic that tried to exploit the "lost originals" idea.[82] Basnage believed that the originals had been lost by Tertullian's day but that accurate copies nonetheless had been preserved. Protestants did not need to resort to Roman Catholic tradition to counterbalance the nefarious effects of the loss of the "originals."[83] For that matter, Augustine had recommended that students correct the mistakes in their copies of Holy Scripture.[84]

The emphasis by many Protestants in the eighteenth century upon the accuracy of the Bible's historical accounts and teachings regarding the natural world becomes more understandable when we perceive how deists—and to certain extent Roman Catholics—had exploited the issue. Moreover, at the beginning of the eighteenth century, various illuminist groups such as the French *Inspirés* seemed to deemphasize Scripture by their appeal to personal prophetic utterances.[85] But eighteenth-century Protestants who believed that the Bible was without error in historical detail were not innovators; they were defending a position long honored in the Christian churches.

Even a cursory reading of commentaries from earlier centuries reveals that Christians, whether Roman Catholic or Protestant, believed that the Bible gave truthful information in its historical allusions and comments about the natural world. Professor John Redwood describes the commitments of seventeenth-century Christians: "To the seventeenth-century biblical chronology, the account of Moses, and the science of geology were all part of the same world of learning. No one seeking to enquire into rocks or minerals, into earth history or the formation of the earth's configuration could afford to ignore or deny the value of his primary source, the Bible."[86] James Ussher in the early seventeenth century had based his dating of creation at 4004 B.C. on a detailed and literal reading of the historical accounts (whether we judge his interpretation right or wrong). Many seventeenth-century histories of the world began with recitations about Adam and Eve and assigned a specific date for creation and other events spoken of in the Scriptures. Johann Heinrich Alsted, Joseph Mede, James Ussher, and others propounded prophetical schemes that assumed that the historical accounts in Scripture were very accurate indeed.[87] In the early seventeenth century, exegetes went to great length to defend the accuracy of the Bible's description of the flood.[88] Moreover, in the sixteenth century, a Reformer like Martin Bucer assumed that the historical accounts of the Scriptures were utterly reliable.[89] It will not do to suggest that a concern for the historical infallibility of the "facts" of the biblical text first emerged in the "Enlightenment" due to the impact of "Baconianism," Common Sense Realism, Newtonian science, or some other factor. The freethinker Morgan perceived the "historical infallibility" of the Bible as a common belief to overthrow, not one that was just coming into existence.

In the last two decades of the seventeenth century, the task of "orthodox" Protestants was further complicated by the emergence of an openness to errancy among fellow Protestants, especially in Remonstrant circles in the United Provinces and in Latitudinarian circles in England. For example, Hugo Grotius (1583-1645)—the jurist, political theoretician, and biblical scholar—had, early in the seventeenth century, advocated a doctrine of accommodation, which was in turn taught at the Remonstrant Seminary at Amsterdam by Jean Le Clerc (1657-1736).[90] According to this Socinian teaching, God accommodated portions of the Bible to the understanding of the contemporaries of the biblical authors. Small errors occur in those passages where the Bible's human authors incorporate contemporary opinions about history and the natural world, even if these opinions were not "truthful."[91] This doctrine of accommodation regarding the Bible differed substantially from the doctrine of accommodation proposed by Saint Augustine and John Calvin.[92] According to their perspective, God did accommodate the Scriptures to the understanding of us humans, but He did so without allowing the text of Scripture to be alloyed with errors.

When the Roman Catholic Richard Simon and the Protestant Jean Le Clerc did battle royal in a four-volume match between 1685 and 1687, careful scorekeepers—and they were many in the Republic of Letters—noticed a peculiar twist.[93] Theoretically, each combatant represented a different confession. But Le Clerc's emphasis upon reason, an errant text, and criticism for traditional views of the Mosaic authorship of the Pentateuch did not seem too far removed from Simon's praise for a "criticism" of the text unhampered by a concern for theological presuppositions (despite his claim to defend Roman Catholic tradition) and Simon's own peculiar views of Mosaic authorship. In an earlier unpublished manuscript, Simon had defined a critic as a person who is "judicious," free from prejudice, impartial, and "a good man who loves truth."[94] Le Clerc probably would have concurred with this definition.

In sum, when orthodox defenders of the Bible's truthfulness wrote in the eighteenth century, they faced challenges from various quarters. Deists and Socinians highlighted the rights of reason to judge revelation; rationalistic Remonstrants like Le Clerc argued that an errant text had no negative entailments for the truthfulness of the gospel; even conservative Roman Catholics highlighted textual difficulties in the Scriptures as they continued to wage pyrrhonical warfare against Protestants; Protestant and Roman Catholic illuminist writers often separated Word from Spirit; and Spinoza criticized the Bible's authority from the vantage points of "morality" and a Cartesian emphasis upon reason.[95] The ranks of those who opposed biblical infallibility were swelling in number. The need to emphasize the truthfulness of the historical accounts in the Bible had become all the more urgent. Hostile critics like Spinoza, Toland, Collins, and others were, from their claim that the Bible was errant, drawing devastating conclusions about the Christian religion. Those Christians who accented the veracity of the historical accounts did not help create the doctrine of biblical inerrancy, but they may have emphasized this veracity more than earlier Christians, given the worrisome apologetical exigencies of the day.

V. THE BIBLE AND "NATURAL PHILOSOPHY"

If many Christian apologists were not innovative in affirming that the Bible was accurate in its historical detail, did they become so when they were writing about the relationship between Scripture and natural philosophy? Or, to put the matter another way, did certain eighteenth-century defenders of the Bible's authority extend the purview of the infallibility of Scripture to the natural world and treat Holy Writ as if it were a "scientific textbook" (as Marsden maintains)?

Undoubtedly, those writers who penned physico-theological tractates did, for apologetic purposes, emphasize passages in Scripture that speak of the natural world.[96] Countering those who seemed to remove God from an active role in nature by emphasizing secondary causes, they wanted to demonstrate that God was the "First Cause." These apologists attempted to demonstrate how the design of animals and insects reflected the handiwork of the great Designer, God Himself.

But to see the Bible as an accurate source of information about the natural world was certainly no novel gambit of Christians living during the "Enlightenment." A reading of Lambert Daneau's *The Wonderfull Workmanship of the World: wherein ,is conteined an excellent discourse of Christian naturall Philosophie, concerning the fourme, knowledge, and use of all thinges created* . . . (published in London, in 1578 [English edition of that text]) quickly dispels that hypothesis.[97] Citing Augustine, Chrysostom, and other church fathers, Daneau argued that general natural philosophy "is chiefly to bee learned out of holy Scripture."[98] Daneau did not deliver this argument in a rationalistic framework, as several neoorthodox writers like Ernst Bizer would have us believe.[99] Daneau argued that various church fathers maintained that general natural philosophy should be based on Scripture, and that Scripture itself commended the idea. Moreover, he specifically downplayed reason and the senses as adequate grounding for the natural sciences: "But whatsoever other things are recited touching Naturall Philosophie, they are not so sure and firme, because they bee only established by man's sense, and reason: which two things are no undoubted, and assured groundes. For man's reason is many times: and his senses are most times deceived."[100] According to Daneau, natural philosophy should be founded on the sure Word of God, and there were historical precedents, biblical admonitions, and reasons of faith for asserting this.

Many of Daneau's contemporaries also read their Bible for information about the natural world—as if it were a "scientific textbook." In his *Therobiblia Biblisch Thier-Vogel-und Fischbuch* (Leipzig, 1595), Hermann Heinrich Frey based his understanding of birds, fish, and animals upon his reading of Scripture.[101] Then again, as the astronomer Johannes Kepler (1571-1630) complained, "The whole world is full of men who are ready to throw all of astronomy, if it sides with Copernicus, off the earth."[102] Kepler understood only too well that large numbers of his contemporaries believed that the Bible's teachings militated against the acceptance of a heliocentric theory of the universe. Even if heterodox, Jean Bodin, the sixteenth-century man of letters, cited Melanchthon's reference to a verse of Scripture as the basis of his own rejection of the Copernican perspective.[103] For many sixteenth-century Christians, their interpretations of biblical passages had far more persuasive force than the mathematical calculations mustered by partisans of Copernicus.

Kepler, a Lutheran and mystic of sorts, also wanted to uphold the complete infallibility of the Bible. But he believed that he understood the accommodated language of the Bible better than did his detractors, who were frequently anti-Copernicans due to their reading of the Bible. In fact, Professor Edward Rosen remarks that "Lutheran theologians in Kepler's time looked upon the Bible as a textbook of astronomy."[104] Kepler's own description of the problem is telling: "Piety prevents many people from agreeing with Copernicus out of fear that the Holy Ghost speaking in Scripture will be branded as a liar if we say that the earth moves and the sun stands still."[105]

For his part Kepler argued somewhat like Calvin and Augustine that certain passages of Scripture were written from a "phenomeno-logical" point of view (based on the vantage point of what a common person would see). But he did not read all of the Scripture's statements about the natural world as those of a language of appearance. Nor did Calvin or Augustine. Moreover, the Bible is not errant in those portions that encompass this type of language. These sections are "truthful" as are other portions of Scripture. We do not find in Kepler's thought the premise of Professor Vawter (that accommodated language has the necessary corollary of an errant text). On the contrary, in chapter one of his *Mysterium Cosmographi-cum*, Kepler declared: "In general I promise to say nothing harmful to Holy Writ, and if Copernicus is convicted of anything with me, I shall consider him finished."[106] Unless he was writing in bad faith, Kepler formally announced that he would forsake Copernicus if any of the latter's hypotheses about the natural world were demonstrated to be contrary to the truthful Holy Scripture.

In Kepler's writings, natural philosophy had not yet been uncoupled from biblical authority as it would later become in the seventeenth century for some scholars. Debates regarding the pre-Adamite hypotheses of Isaac La Peyrère, for example, lay in the future.[107] Kepler still was concerned that his theories meshed with what, in passing, the Bible taught about the natural world. And obviously, his more literalistically inclined Lutheran opponents believed that the Bible's infallibility encompassed both history and teachings about that world.

Earlier on, Luther apparently rejected the Copernican perspective because it contradicted his interpretation of biblical passages and contemporary Aristotelian science. He commissioned the artist Lucas Cranach to do woodcuts that would illustrate the text of what became known as the Luther-Bibel of 1534.[108] The drawing illustrating the first chapters of Genesis reveals a geocentric cosmology. The dominant figure of God overlooks creation. A small sun along with other planets circles the much larger earth. Adam and Eve speak to each other while the animals stand in the foreground.[109] Lucas Cranach and undoubtedly Luther himself practiced a literalistic reading of the text in Genesis. There is little doubt that they believed the Bible provided authoritative and accurate teaching about the configuration of the natural world and its creation.

"New" data are now available to stir the simmering pot of controversy regarding Calvin's attitude towards Copernicus. For years, scholars had repeated the refrain that Calvin did not take a stand on the debate over the heliocentric hypothesis. Now we know that such is simply not the case. Citing Professor Richard Stauffer's research on Calvin's sermons, Professor Michel Heyd observes: "In a sermon on *I Corinthians X, 22*, Calvin dismissed people who held heliocentric ideas as being completely frenzied, comparing them to the Nicodemites who confounded good and evil and perverted the order of nature."[110] The exact reasons why he made this judgment will certainly be debated. The thesis that his reading of Scripture partially contributed to this stance should not be dismissed in a cavalier fashion, however.

The recent interpretation of Professor Roland M. Frye to the effect that Calvin viewed the Bible as a religious book with little or no prescriptive teaching about the natural world is highly problematical.[111] Frye does not cite Calvin's judgment about heliocentric ideas. Nor does he present Calvin's doctrine of accommodation in an especially accurate way. Calvin did not believe that the Bible is a "textbook" in astronomy, but this does not mean that Calvin completely excluded the natural world from the scope of the Bible's authority.

This latter extrapolation made by Professor Frye probably reflects his own desire to enlist Calvin as a thinker who would have been open to "evolution" if Darwin's hypotheses had been available to him.[112] According to this construction, Calvin would have had no biblical grounds to reject macroevolution; the Bible simply does not address issues related to the natural world in an authoritative way. In reality, Calvin was not any kind of evolutionist, theistic or otherwise. As Professor Henri Blocher observes, several studies have convincingly countermanded this characterization, one that B. B. Warfield apparently entertained: "B. B. Warfield had a very open attitude and thought that Calvin 'teaches a doctrine of evolution' because the creatures proceed from the confused mass of Genesis 1:2; that in fact was not what Calvin meant, as John Murray has shown and as R. Stauffer confirmed."[113] Those scholars who have argued this way have misunderstood Calvin's doctrine of creation based upon a careful exegesis of the biblical text.[114]

Copernicus suspected that one source of potential opposition to his *On the Revolutions of the Heavenly Orbs* (published posthumously in 1543) might come from Christians who perceived it as a challenge to the authority of Holy Writ. They would identify their interpretation of Scripture with what the Bible taught.[115] Thus, to challenge their interpretations was the same as challenging the Bible's authority. The astronomer's premonitions were prescient. Many Protestants and Roman Catholics believed that the Bible gave infallible and, if you will, "precise" information about the natural world.[116]

To argue that it was not until the Enlightenment that such a way of thinking emerged regarding Holy Scripture does not appear warranted. Contrary to the interpretations found in the studies by Professor Vawter, Professors Rogers and McKim, and Professor Roland Frye, the choice that Christians faced until the middle of the seventeenth century was generally this: should each passage of an infallible Bible that speaks of the natural world be interpreted literally, or should some interpretative allowance be made for the fact that a number of passages are couched in the language of appearance (the vantage point of the observer)?[117] The choice was generally not between belief in a completely infallible Bible and a "religious salvation book" whose infallibility was limited exclusively to matters of faith and practice. While differing in their interpretations of passages that dealt with the natural world, parties from both sides of this debate included "science" and history within their definition of infallibility. Those individuals who followed the Augustinian premise that certain portions of Scripture were written in phenomenological language, or proposed that the Bible treats the natural world only in passing, often found themselves criticized by other Christians who were more "literalistic" in their interpretations.[118]

In the second half of the seventeenth century, however, the writings by La Peyrère, Hobbes, and others led a few Christian scholars to claim that Scripture might contain "errors" regarding the natural world.[119] It followed that scientists who accepted this premise no longer strongly felt an imperative to align their findings with biblical teachings.[120] Moreover, several scientists, drawing upon the thought of Galileo and Bacon and others, argued that their investigations about the "real world" should be given more authority than the "phenomenological" statements of the Bible about the natural world.[121] After all, the Scriptures only deal with the natural world in passing. In a word, the Scriptures should conform with what science teaches and not vice versa.

This recommendation called for an innovative reversal of roles in the framework of a new kind of concordism. Many earlier Christians had attempted to align their "science" with Holy Writ, Scripture possessing the primary authority. For example, in 1634, the Englishman John Weemses offered a common understanding of the relationship that existed between "Sciences" and theology: "The conclusion of this is: All Sciences are found out for the benefit of man, but all of them can doe him but little good, untill Divinity come in and rectifie him. All Sciences are subordinate to Divinity in respect to the end; therefore every man should study to be holy, what science soever he professe."[122] A brief vignette rehearsing the establishment of the prestigious University of Leiden testifies to the high status that the Bible had as a source of knowledge for many sixteenth-century Christians:

> On the morning of the 8th of February 1574 a solemn procession wound through the streets of Leiden, to mark the dedication of the newly established University. Part of the tableau consisted of symbolic female figures, representing the four faculties; *Sancta Scriptura, Justitia, Medicina,* and *Minerva.* The last three figures were on horseback, but *Scriptura,* who led the way, was seated in the splendid triumphal chariot drawn by four horses. In her hand she held an open Bible. Next to her car of victory walked the four Evangelists.[123]

This recitation by H. J. De Jonge, a modern scholar, captures well the preeminent authority of Holy Scripture for the Protestants celebrating the founding of the University of Leiden, an institution that was to exert wide influence in Protestant Europe. According to these Protestants, the Bible was not to be subservient to any discipline. It judged them all, as it did for the Lutheran theologians who rejected the heliocentric theory due to their reading of Holy Scripture.[124]

That the Bible should enjoy such a privileged position in late sixteenth-century thought was no novelty. Many Roman Catholics had esteemed it in a similar fashion centuries before the birth of Martin Luther. During the Middle Ages, the Bible enjoyed a place of honor as a divinely authoritative source of knowledge. Manuscript collections were often organized under three rubrics: (1) manuscripts of the Holy Scripture standing supremely by themselves, (2) manuscripts that helped readers understand Holy Scripture, and (3) diverse manuscripts.[125]

A number of medieval scholars like John Wycliffe apparently believed that the Bible was a divine encyclopedia of all knowledge.[126] Other scholars did not support this idea but incorporated the Bible's teaching into their cosmologies and world views. Professor N. Max Wildiers, who introduced the writings of Teilhard de Chardin to a large public, describes their perspective in this fashion:

> The main question with which they were preoccupied and to which they devoted numerous writings, was precisely how a harmonious fusion of biblical data and Greek science could lead to a completely satisfactory and irrefutable picture of the universe. Countless texts were devoted to this venture.[127]

Many medieval scholars used three basic sources in constructing their views of the cosmos, as Wildiers observes: "1. the scientific conceptions of the ancient Greeks, supplemented by the works of Jewish and Arabian scholars; 2. the data of sacred Scriptures; 3. the teaching of the Church Fathers."[128] They assumed that the Scriptures were an "infallible" authority with truthful and binding teachings about the natural world.[129]

These illustrations should be sufficient to demonstrate that "Enlightenment" Christians engaged in no new exegetical move when they viewed those details of the Bible that speak of the natural world as authoritative and corresponding with what is the case. Undoubtedly, a number of writers did not take notice of the Augustinian insight regarding the accommodated character of some of the biblical passages regarding the external world. But even these commentators had precursors in the history of the Christian churches, who treated the Bible as if it were a "scientific textbook."

Nor will it do to suppose that "Enlightenment" Christians adopted from Newton a "precisionistic Newtonian" view of the Bible and thereafter developed a doctrine of inerrancy. For one thing, Newton apparently advocated an Augustinian version of accommodation and had the "give" of that approach in his exegesis.[130] He argued that Moses adapted his comments about creation to what common people would have seen if they had been there.[131] But in speaking in this accommodated fashion, Moses always told the truth:

> As to Moses, I do not think his description of ye creation either Philosophical or feigned, but that he described realities in a language artificially adapted to ye sense of ye vulgar. Thus when he speaks of two great lights I suppose he means their apparent, not real greatness.[132]

In Newton's discourse we hear echoes of Augustine's and Calvin's commentary on Genesis 1:16. With these two theologians, Newton asserted that Moses could have spoken with greater detail but chose not to do so because he knew the needs of his audience.[133] Newton's perspectives do not represent a doctrine of accommodation that entails errors in the biblical text; nor do they entail high levels of precision. The thesis that biblical inerrancy emerged when Enlightenment Christians forced Scripture's language to "conform to Newtonian notions of perfection" and Scripture's message to "accord with Lockean reason" (Rogers and McKim) stands in need of serious revision.[134] Newton did not establish a "precisionistic" standard by which to measure the Bible's truthfulness.

Newton's admirers may have done that, however. But even here the burden of proof remains on modern scholars like Professors Vawter and Marsden to clarify with care how their alleged "precisionistic" exegesis, for example, differed from the "literalistic" exegesis of many sixteenth-century Christians who opposed the Copernican hypothesis. To what extent did it differ from the harmonization efforts of Saint Augustine, who on occasion was concerned to explain how

one word of Scripture should be understood, so intent was he to
guard the infallibility of Holy Writ?[135] And why did eighteenth-
century and nineteenth-century Christians wrestle with some of the
same "Bible difficulties" as Calvin and Augustine did, if they were
locked in an intellectual paradigm that was incommensurable with
the "paradigms" of Calvin and Augustine?[136]

Nor should we accept Professor Vawter's interpretation that a
doctrine of condescension satisfactorily explains the difference
between these "precisionistic" moderns and the Reformers and
Augustine. For Professor Vawter incorrectly assumes that the doctrine
of accommodation accepted by Augustine and the Reformers dictated
that errors be found in the text of Scripture. He bases this judgment
on a misconstrued syllogism he applies in his discussion of accommodation: The Bible has human authors; to err is human; the Bible
possesses errors.[137] Regrettably, this is a misrepresentation of the
frame of reference out of which Augustine and the Reformers formed
their doctrines of accommodation.

Ironically, the "Fundamentalists" whom Professor Vawter carica-
tures undoubtedly represented views closer to the thinking of the
Reformers and Augustine than those of Professor Vawter himself.[138]
As noted earlier, Vawter's hypothesis that the accommodated language of Scripture must contain errors is an interpretation totally
alien to the thinking of the Reformers or Augustine.

More obviously in the "central tradition" of Christian thought
about Scripture's authority are the Evangelicals (e.g., British scholar
James I. Packer) who defend not only the complete infallibility of
Scripture but acknowledge an Augustinian definition of accommodation.[139] To dismiss their position as merely a parochial extension of
the nineteenth-century Princetonians or of American Fundamentalism betrays a genuine unfamiliarity with the history of biblical
authority.

VI. THE "ENLIGHTENMENT" AND THE HUMANITY OF THE BIBLICAL TEXT

Professor Ramm's positive evaluation about the contributions of
Enlightenment scholars to our understanding of the nature of
Scripture deserves further commentary. Only a few comments can be
made here. We hope to treat this topic more fully elsewhere.

Professor Ramm is particularly impressed by the writings of
German Neologians who emphasized the humanity of Scripture—
that is, the impress of the Bible's human writers upon its contents. He
suggests that the writings of the Neologians were virtually ignored
(except for specialists) in the Anglo-Saxon theological community in
which he received his education.[140] Unquestionably, literature regard-

ing the Neologians is not plentiful in English, but scholarly volumes in German by Karl Aner and others have been available for decades.[141] Presently, the refined analyses of Professors Peter Reill and Hans Frei do afford an interested English reader with the basic tenets of these eighteenth-century writers.[142]

Did the "orthodox" Christians stress the divinity of the Scriptures to such an extent that the Neologians were obliged to make a corrective and emphasize their humanity? This question should not be considered in the rather narrow optic that Professor Ramm presents to his readers. It is true that deep into the eighteenth century, many German Lutheran and Pietist writers upheld the complete infallibility of the Bible. But some went further and argued for the inspiration of the Masoretic pointing of the Hebrew text as well. Commenting upon the career of the Neologian biblical critic John David Michaelis, Eichorn in his *Allgemeine Bibliothek* noted this widespread commitment to these positions earlier in that century:

> A Bible with various readings had been printed at Halle, in the year 1720, and notwithstanding the use of the whole noble apparatus, they adhered still pertinaciously to the infallibility of the vulgar text. . . . They had discovered, upon investigation, and exposed to view in this edition of the Bible, the contradictions of the Masora—the most satisfactory evidence of their fallibility; and yet they had sworn, in as solemn a manner, to the absolute infallibility of the same, as they had sworn to their symbolical articles. . . .
>
> Michaelis, on his first appearance as a public teacher, was full, to overflowing, of this faith of his fathers. In the year 1739, he decked out, after his fashion, in a dissertation "de punctorum hebraicorum antiquitate." . . . In the year 1740, he came forward in the disputation *de Psalmo* xxii as an advocate of the infallibility of the entire text.[143]

Johann Jakob Rambach's *Instituiones Hermeneuticae Sacrae* (1723), the principal book on hermeneutics used by Pietist theologians, affirmed not only the inerrancy of Scripture but also the inspiration of the Masoretic pointing of the Hebrew text. Due to its popularity, the volume passed through eight editions by 1764.[144] Thus, some orthodox and Pietist authors in Germany did probably overemphasize the divinity of Scripture and did not sufficiently take into account developments in textual criticism and the human authorship of Scripture.[145]

In challenging the accent of the "orthodox" upon the Bible's divinity, however, the Neologians bypassed the positions of Luther and Calvin to espouse theories that made the humanity of the biblical writers the basis for the errancy of Scripture. John Calvin understood perfectly well that the Scriptures bore the marks of their human authors.[146] His commentaries give abundant evidence of this awareness. But the Reformer did not infer from the "humanity" of the Scriptures that they must be errant. Martin Bucer and Martin Luther did not make this connection either.[147]

But did not the Neologians see themselves as recovering the exegetical and theological insights of their Lutheran "predecessor" Martin Luther after the alleged dismal and dark days of Protestant Scholasticism? Have not recognized scholars like Professor Gottfried Hornig argued that Johann Salomo Semler did have a rightful claim upon Luther as one who shared similar convictions about the text of Scripture?[148]

Although Semler did evoke the name of Luther to give credence to his own ground-breaking studies, he also adduced the name of the Roman Catholic Richard Simon as the scholar (besides Erasmus) whose program of criticism he most appreciated.[149] In fact, Semler, like the learned John David Michaelis, claimed that Simon was the "founder" of historical criticism.[150] Moreover, Sémler's important doctrine of accommodation (which Hornig cites as a key for understanding his doctrine of Scripture) resembles more closely the "Socinian" version of that doctrine than the one that Reformers espoused.[151] The theologian from Halle upheld the time-bound character of some of the biblical writings and the fallibility of these same texts. This "Socinian" doctrine of accommodation that Semler probably borrowed from Jean Le Clerc became a vehicle by which higher criticism could enter more easily into theological debate during the last decade of the eighteenth century.[152] Professor Hornig tells us that between 1763 and 1817 there appeared no fewer than thirty-one titles that focused on the question of accommodation.[153]

Little wonder that Charles Hodge could criticize Semler and Van Hemert in 1825 and complain about this faulty version of the doctrine of accommodation: "Perhaps few causes have operated more extensively and effectually in promoting erroneous opinions than the problems of this doctrine [a false concept of accommodation]."[154] Hodge noted that those scholars who argued that the Bible's accommodated language encompassed errors were then obliged to pick and choose which sections of Holy Writ were truthful and which were not. That is, their reason judged Scripture: "It is evident that this doctrine is only a modification of the theory, which determines the sense of SS., by deciding what is, or is not reasonable; and which has as effectually excluded the doctrines of the Deity of Christ, and his atonement from the SS., because they are deemed inconsistent with reason."[155]

The neoorthodox claim that an errant text and principles of higher-criticism find rootage in the thought of Martin Luther is not warranted.[156] The assertions of the Neologians that they were the direct theological descendants of Luther are also unfounded. A growing number of scholars are beginning to realize this.

When Professor Ramm urges Evangelicals to come to grips with the "Enlightenment" (which he amorphously defines) and with the biblical studies of the Neologians, he is making a call that has serious implications. He is actually advising them to consider departing from the central tradition of the Christian churches regarding the authority of Scripture.

Professor Ramm should consider well what he is advocating to the Evangelical community. His cure for "obscurantism" is undoubtedly more costly than the supposed inconveniences of upholding the doctrine of biblical infallibility. For many Evangelicals, that latter stance represents what the Bible teaches about itself and reflects the central tradition of the Christian churches.[157] It is neither "scholastic" (Rogers and McKim), nor "orthodoxist," nor "obscurantist" (Ramm). Rather, it is sound doctrine.

If some "orthodox" Christians spoke without proper qualifications about the Bible's divinity, the Neologians fell into a more grievous error by subjecting God's Word to their personal judgments regarding what was authentic Scripture and what was not. In practice, they sometimes argued that the humanity of the Bible (including its alleged contradictions) confirmed the validity of the Scriptures as an authentic collection of religious books bearing God's moral message.[158] Many of their disciples drew out unhappy implications about the truthfulness of the Christian faith from the premises that the Neologian theologians and Gotthold Lessing had proferred.[159]

We would be well advised to follow the lead of Luther and Calvin, who believed that the Bible was both a fully divine and fully human book that does not err. Moreover the Reformers upheld the verbal inspiration of Holy Scripture without relying on a mechanical dictation theory.[160]

VII. CONCLUDING REMARKS

The present essay does not constitute a survey of the history of biblical authority in the "Enlightenment." That daunting topic is far more complex than many suppose; several scholars in Germany, for example, are presently engaged in a thorough reconsideration of developments in biblical criticism during the eighteenth century.[161] Rather, this essay's purpose has been more modest: to provide a preliminary assessment of the interpretations of several well-known authors who have claimed that modern beliefs in biblical inerrancy are essentially paradigmatically dependent upon "Enlightenment motifs."

In 1981, Professor Jack Rogers wrote: "In the late seventeenth century, the concept of the Bible's infallibility in religious matters was transmuted into a notion of Scripture's inerrancy in matters of science and history."[162] That is, during the beginning decades of the "Enlightenment," the doctrine of biblical inerrancy allegedly emerged.

Professors Bruce Vawter and George Marsden have attempted to portray biblical "inerrancy" as an innovative "Fundamentalist" doctrine forged in the eighteenth and nineteenth centuries. According to these authors, this modern version of inerrancy is not equivalent to what earlier Christians believed when they said that the Bible is without error. Professor Bernard Ramm, on the other hand, believes that Neologian scholars in the Enlightenment made a breakthrough in theology by coming to grips with the humanity of the Scriptures. From his perspective, Evangelicals must accept several of the conclusions about the Bible that eighteenth-century scholars proposed. If Evangelicals do not make their peace with these findings, they they will continue to be "obscurantist." For all of these writers, the "Enlightenment" represents a major watershed in the history of biblical authority.

We have argued that, on the contrary, the doctrine of biblical inerrancy—that the Bible speaks truthfully about all matters upon which it touches, including history and science—was not a creation of the "Enlightenment." Contemporaries of the late seventeenth century viewed this belief as one that the Christian churches had always held. If they were critics of the belief, they tried to point out specific errors (especially in the Pentateuch [1670s] and then in the Gospels [1680s]) with which to overthrow the position.[163] Deists acknowledged that they were attacking a position long esteemed by Christians, not one just coming into existence. Jean Le Clerc indicated self-consciously that his own beliefs clashed with what Protestants generally believed about the Bible's infallibility.[164] If contemporaries were defenders of the doctrine, they thought they were upholding a belief cherished since the early years of the Christian church.

It is misleading to argue that some Protestants and Roman Catholics in the "age of science and age of reason" were innovative because they made the Bible conform to higher standards of precision than had earlier Christians. Many Christians before the Enlightenment believed that the Bible afforded them with detailed histories and that the Bible was a "scientific textbook"; they could match nearly any eighteenth-century exegete's interest in small details in the Scripture. Moreover, it is misleading to claim (as does Professor Vawter) that all modern defenders of biblical inerrancy know nothing about a doctrine of accommodation. Admittedly, some do not. But many heartily endorse an Augustinian doctrine of accommodation and at the same time affirm the truthfulness of Scripture in the domains of both history and science. The interpretations of Professor Vawter and Professor Marsden cannot account for these Christians. This attractive centrist position is largely ignored in their studies.

Perhaps the nub of the matter is this. Professor Vawter and

Professor Marsden work with inappropriate visions of what constitutes the "central tradition" of the Christian church's thinking about biblical authority. Professor Vawter regrettably defines accommodation in such a way that Scripture must have errors; in addition, he assumes that Augustine and his disciples viewed accommodation in this fashion. On another tack, Professor Marsden does not perceive that the Augustinian tradition—which he, as a loyal Calvinist, attempts to uphold—viewed the infallibility of the Bible as an important component of its doctrine of biblical authority.[165]

It appears that a number of commentators today among post-Vatican II Roman Catholics and Protestant defenders of a "Reformed Epistemology" believe that a concern for the "christocentric focus" of Scripture and a concern for the Bible's infallibility are incompatible elements of a doctrine of biblical authority.[166] To our mind, they are fostering a false dichotomy, one quite foreign to the Augustinian tradition. For Luther and Calvin, a concern to portray Christ as the focal point of Scripture did not entail a loss of concern for the truthfulness of the biblical accounts. Like Augustine, the Reformers believed that to attack biblical infallibility was to question biblical authority.

Why are many historians and theologians today proposing that "the central tradition" of the Christian churches did not encompass the doctrine of biblical inerrancy? One possible explanation is this. They surmise that if the Bible is only infallible for faith and practice, then it cannot be negatively affected by developments in "higher criticism" and evolutionary hypotheses. But as we have seen, their historical interpretations are not always persuasive. Moreover, it seems that their attempts to make some kind of allowance for macroevolution, for example, may become unnecessary even from their point of view. The changing theories of evolutionists are presently up for rigorous scrutiny. In a remarkable essay, "Agnostic Evolutionists, The taxonomic case against Darwin," Tom Bethell writes:

> The theory of evolution has never been falsified. On the other hand, it is also surely true that the positive evidence for evolution is very much weaker than most laymen imagine, and than many scientists want us to imagine. Perhaps, as Patterson says, that positive evidence is missing entirely[167]

Is it possible that future generations will view "macroevolution" as one of those hoary but quaint theories of days past?[168]

Doubtless, Scripture itself should determine what our views of biblical authority are. On the other hand, it is instructive to learn that many Christians in centuries far removed from us affirmed a belief in the utter truthfulness of God's Word. Even if some of them employed the rather formidable theological word *accommodation*, they probably found it awe-inspiring to realize that the all-powerful Lord God, who was one and the same with their loving heavenly Father, had stooped to speak to humankind in mercy and in grace, using words that they basically understood. And for us today, if we sense even in a halting fashion the love that prompted this revelation, our hearts should be filled with gratitude for the Written Word, Holy Scripture, which speaks of the Living Word, our matchless Savior, Jesus Christ.

CHAPTER EIGHT
THE AUTHORITY OF SCRIPTURE IN KARL BARTH

Geoffrey W. Bromiley

Geoffrey W. Bromiley

Geoffrey W. Bromiley is Senior Professor of Church History and Historical Theology at Fuller Theological Seminary, Pasadena, California. He is a graduate of Emmanuel College, Cambridge (B.A. and M.A.), and New College, Edinburgh (Ph.D., D.Litt.). An ordained deacon and priest in the Church of England, he has served four parishes and been vice-principal of Trinity Theological College, Bristol. He has written a number of books, including *Historical Theology: An Introduction* and *An Introduction to the Theology of Karl Barth*. Also, he has edited such books as *Zwingli and Bullinger*, the *Theological Dictionary of the New Testament*, and the revision of *The International Standard Bible Encyclopedia*, edited and translated Barth's *Church Dogmatics*, and translated Ellul's *The Politics of God and the Politics of Man*, Kasemann's *Commentary on Romans*, and Thielicke's *Evangelical Faith*.

THE AUTHORITY OF SCRIPTURE IN KARL BARTH

I. INTRODUCTION

"In my work as a pastor I gradually turned back to the Bible and began my commentary on Romans."[1] In this statement in a radio interview, the older Barth drew attention to the decisive change at Safenwil that brought him not only to new biblical study but to a strong consistent reaffirmation of biblical authority.

As he pointed out, this was a turning back. Under his father's direction, which he recalled with gratitude, he had been nurtured in a conservative tradition. His roots were in the Swiss Reformed Church, with its historic attachment to the primacy of Scripture. In this church he had been confirmed and had received from Aeschbacher, his pastor, the impetus to pursue theological study. In this church he had prepared for ordination, taking courses and serving assistant-ships in the Bernese Oberland and the Jura. In this church he had been ordained and commenced his ministry at Geneva before moving on to the pastoral charge at Safenwil.

Yet Barth had succumbed to the allurements of more liberal teaching. Against his father's better judgment, he had done work at Berlin and Marburg, where he came under the powerful influence of Harnack and especially Herrmann, whom, during a whole year at Marburg, he had absorbed "through every pore." Schleiermacher and Kant were at this time his heroes, and by helping Martin Rade to edit the *Christliche Welt* he came into touch with many of those who were shaping contemporary religious and theological thought. The brief stay in Geneva renewed his interest in Calvin, in whose church he preached, but only to inspire him with the idea of a great synthesis of romantic and Reformation theology.

The situation at Safenwil shifted Barth's attention away from theological matters to social issues, in which he followed the lead of Ragaz and Kutter. Besides work done on sermons and confirmation classes, he spent much time in study of factory acts and in struggles on behalf of workers. So forcefully did he identify himself with the Social Democratic Party that he gained notoriety as "the red parson of Safenwil" and considered running for political office.

"A change came only with the outbreak of World War I," as he put it later.[2] This change took a threefold form. First, the support that his theological mentors gave to the German war effort compromised their theology beyond redemption. Second, the failure of the German Social Democrats to resist militarism brought him serious disillusionment regarding the possibilities of political and social progress. Third, as he found help in the message of the Blumhardts and perceived the eschatological dimension of the kingdom of God, he became concerned about his pulpit ministry, or, more specifically, "the textual basis" of his sermons.[3] Was he really proclaiming God's Word as his office demanded? What was this Word, and how could he proclaim it?

In some sense, of course, Barth had never really abandoned the authority of Scripture. He had thought he was preaching its message with his presentation of the liberal and social version of Christianity. The crisis of the war years involved biblical authority, not in the sense of a return to acceptance from total rejection but in the sense of a return to biblical teaching from an understanding that had obscured it and in that way eroded its authority. The task for Barth and his friend Thurneysen, according to a momentous decision in 1916, was to resume theological study so as to find out what the Bible itself says and by that means to restore to it an authentically normative and dynamic role. Surrounding himself with a stack of commentaries, Barth began at once the examination of Romans that would lead to his epoch-making book and initiate the revolution that changed the course of twentieth-century theology.

II. EARLY STATEMENTS

The renewed focus on the Bible quickly found expression in the addresses that Barth later collected as *The Word of God and the Word of Man*. In 1916, in a talk significantly entitled "The Strange New World Within the Bible," he stated some of his main themes. Having intrinsic force, the Scriptures "will interpret themselves in spite of all our human limitations."[4] Since their concern is "not to impact historical knowledge," they meet historians "with silence quite unparalleled."[5] Their true theme is divinity, "the religion of God." What they call for is acceptance or rejection of divine sovereignty.[6]

In an address on "Biblical Insights, Doctrines, and Vistas" (1920), Barth accepted the human side of Scripture as "the literary monument of an ancient racial religion" but argued that one must get beyond this ("this battle has had its time") to "the biblical object," compared to which the debate "whether figures like Abraham and Moses are products of later myth-making (believe it who can!)" is of little relevance.[7] Disenchantment with the extremes of the critical approach is apparent in this as in many other talks of the period.

In "The Need and Promise of Christian Preaching" (1922), Barth considered the implications of the Reformation principle that "the Word of God expressed in the Holy Scriptures is the foundation and final aim of the church."[8] "The Reformers, he said, "sternly took from us everything but the Bible."[9] Preachers must translate the questions of human life into "the inescapable question about God" that "one cannot ask or hear without hearing the answer." The minister speaks God's word when, submitting to this question, he answers "the people's question as one questioned by God."[10]

Discussing criticism in "The Doctrinal Task of the Reformed Churches" (1923), Barth argued that authority is beyond history; it is in Scripture and the Spirit, which must be free to "work their way to authority through criticism."[11] God alone is truth as He "speaks his own word" in them.[12] All doctrine must be "measured against an impassable and unchangeable standard discoverable in the Scriptures."[13] The whole Bible functions as a norm, not just a part "chosen to suit a preconceived theory."[14] Conformity to the Bible is not merely a formal principle; the Bible is "the first, the causal word."[15] As God's word, it expresses God's revelation given to the biblical witness and to those who accept it.[16] If in itself the Bible is "accidental, contingent, and human," God makes it, as serious witness to divine revelation, "*Holy* Scripture."[17] Faced with the questioning of its historical reliability, we do best to end "the guerilla warfare of apologetics, the blind fighting the blind," to focus on Christian reality, and to think through the category of revelation.[18]

In the parallel sermons of the period (published as *Come Holy Spirit*), Barth and Thurneysen were already espousing the important hermeneutical principle that "the heart of the Bible" is Jesus Christ.[19] They were also confident that the Bible can do its own work. One should not "handle it as a merchant handles his wares and his customers." Although it does not contradict "a sure knowledge of nature and life," "it disdains to speak where it is made a cheap ephemeral trifle."[20] Making room for itself, it is "at work in freedom." This freedom goes hand in hand with human freedom, but not all people "become free for the freedom of the Word." Nevertheless, the free word always has some effect, and this effect is to God's glory.[21]

The commentary on Romans, especially in its second and later editions, enabled Barth to reach a wider public. In the commentary itself he aimed to get through to Paul's own message, struggling, if not with entire success, to break free from external influences and to state what Paul himself was saying. In the preface to different editions he reasserted his convictions regarding biblical authority. Thus, in the first he candidly announced that if he had to choose between the critical method and "the venerable doctrine of Inspiration," he would "without hesitation adopt the latter."[22] In the second he pointed out that, although he had nothing against critics as such, recent commentators were offering an exposition that was "no commentary at all" but only "a point of departure for genuine exegesis." As he saw it, "the answers in the text must be related with the question," not with other questions. He accepted the charge of being a biblicist—so long as his critics would let him say what he meant by biblicism.[23] In the third preface he explained that, for him, biblicism meant "utter loyalty to the author." Anything less might produce a commentary *on* Paul but not *with* Paul. He admitted an affinity here "with the old doctrine of verbal inspiration," inasmuch as the spirit of a document can speak only "through the actual written words." He rejected the idea that Christ's spirit is a vantage-point "from which a ceaseless correction of Paul may be exercised schoolmaster-wise." Through the words we must seek "that which is struggling for expression in them."[24]

The third preface replied to criticisms by Bultmann, and the two friends pursued the matter in urgent discussions dating from Barth's move to Göttingen in 1921. Apart from the issue of a correction of Paul in the light of the sources—which Bultmann regarded as permissible exposition *with* Paul—the debate focused on the proper use of philosophical concepts. Bultmann's critical methods enabled him to find traces of romanticism and idealism in Barth's work on Romans that clearly did not evince utter loyalty to Paul's teaching. He tried to convince Barth of the need to find a suitable modern idiom in which to state the biblical message. He himself thought that he had found the right solution in Heidegger's existentialism.

Barth, in reply, claimed that he simply "reached out . . . for terms or concepts" that he found to be the "most appropriate, no matter where they came from." He could not accept the understanding of God's revelation as the Christian determination of human existence,[25] he had no enthusiasm for the subjection of the Bible to any philosophy, and he also resisted Bultmann's view that we should use the sources "to draw students into debate" and force them "to ask decisive questions."[26] Years later, when complaints about Bultmann's negative influence reached him, he expressed his conviction that if the church in Marburg would truly practice its belief in the risen Lord, it might prevent Bultmann from "tying the gospel to a pagan ontology, and make him a free expositor of the New Testament freely speaking for itself"—as he himself sought to be.[27]

Working his way back to a material as well as a formal acceptance of biblical authority, Barth necessarily had to reassess his own former hero, Schleiermacher, now seen as a prime example of aberration. In the Schleiermacher Lectures of 1923–24 he pointed out that even a genius like Schleiermacher "could not find his Christ, the Christ of synthesis, in the Bible." Indeed, Schleiermacher always had trouble with the Bible. "The whole of the Old Testament lay before him like a rock." The New Testament, in which he really found John's Gospel alone congenial, did not "fit smoothly into the schematism of his teaching."[28]

In general, he had what Barth called a "rather murky relation to the Bible."[29] He exalted spirit above word[30] and even argued that the Christmas feast was a better way to keep the beginning of Christianity "alive in human memory than the Bible or religious instruction."[31] His thought, Barth stated, "moves over the toughest biblical sayings like a roller, levelling and harmonizing everything."[32] He reduces the distinction between the New Testament and the early church to the chronological one of an "antithesis between beginning and continuation."[33] Only as that which comes first is the New Testament distinctive and normative.[34] His hermeneutic allowed no place for the concept of inspiration. Even the Holy Spirit could speak through the witnesses only "as if they spoke without him." The reality of the Spirit in them apparently amounted to little more than human impulse.[35] Schleiermacher consistently traced back to the subjective sphere that which the Bible and the church say objectively.[36] At the human level, Barth admired Schleiermacher's theology as a magnificent achievement, all his life asking whether he was interpreting it correctly. He wondered whether it might not be in its own way a theology of the Holy Spirit. Yet, its inadequacy both in the doctrine of biblical authority and under the measurement of the biblical norm seemed to Barth to disqualify it as real theology in any meaningful sense.

The addresses gathered in *Theology and Church* contain some of Barth's most forceful earlier statements on the authority and role of Scripture. In "A Universal Reformed Creed" (1925) he noted that the Roman Catholic Church, in distinction from the Reformed, "sets beside the Holy Scriptures as second and third authorities the apostolic tradition and the tradition of the church embodied in the doctrinal office of the pope." Liberal Protestantism also diverges from Reformed by giving history "the character of revelation which is not fundamentally but only quantitatively different from the revelation of the Bible." For Barth, the church has received from Scripture and the Spirit "the truth which is God's truth, whole and unchangeable."[37] Scripture, being "unique and incomparable," should be read as *Holy* Scripture, "not merely investigated for its religious interest but seen in its true character."[38]

Even so, in "The Word in Theology" (1927), Barth could take issue with biblicism on three counts. First, it wants the biblical content under the category of history. Second, it is anticonfessional and therefore subjective, giving no indication that "the human subject is really willing to let everything be said to him instead of saying everything himself." Third, it brings the truth of God into a system of knowledge, although such a system cannot be "created out of the word of God, even if it is introduced by thousands of biblical quotations." The scriptural proof, instead of taking precedence, "serves only as a supplementary corroboration," demonstrating what the Christian "already knows without it."[39]

In "The Principles of Dogmatics" (1925) Barth continued his criticism of the understanding of Scripture and dogma as "expressions of human faith" that are authoritative only as a spur to "the experience of which they speak." As the religious thoughts of others, the Bible and dogma neither have nor can they gain any true authority. The summons that Barth wants to hear is "to the matter itself, to the true theme, to him about whom everything centres in the Bible." God's word is spoken and heard only when teaching and acceptance "are perseveringly preserved" on their proper plane, which will be one of positive doctrine.[40]

In "Church and Theology" (1925) Barth referred to the "spoken and written word into which the Logos-revelation has entered in order to go out into all the world." This word is "the principle of all concrete representation of the revelation." Barth contended, too, for the parallel principle that since the word is God's, it is normative only as God the Holy Spirit "acknowledges this word of witness as his own Word," making it "ever and again incomparably true and powerful." The Spirit, then, is "the principle of all representation and revelation."[41] Yet this does not invalidate the role of Scripture, for pure doctrine is that which conforms to Scripture and the Spirit and sets the word "above the claims of all human speaking of and about God." As exegesis, theology must constantly raise "the fundamental question of the genuine witness to the revelation given in the canonical sources."[42]

Barth tried to show in his lectures on *Ethics* at Münster and Bonn how the Scripture principle works in practice. He related all theology to Scripture—exegesis as investigation of the word, dogmatics as the relating of the content of proclamation to the word, and homiletics as the relating of the form of proclamation to the word.[43] He suggested that a concern for the proper understanding of biblical authority should keep us from "overhasty biblicism" in applying the biblical commands, which he viewed as general summaries witnessing to "the absolutely concrete command received by Israel, the disciples, and the primitive church." Since biblicism leaves the application to us, Barth found in it "a secret lawlessness rather than legalism." As he saw it, "in and with the wording of the biblical witness to God's command the command itself is given."[44] At the opposite extreme to biblicism is trying to know God's law by referring to a philosophy or experience alongside the Bible. "We can point," said Barth, "only to the Bible, to Holy Scripture, as witness to the Word of God which he himself spoke once and for all and uniquely."[45] "We hear his (Christ's) Word in and through that of the prophets and apostles." By the Holy Spirit this word "acquires the power of truth of his own Word."[46] The one theme of the Bible is "the event of the incarnate Word and the quickening Spirit."[47]

On the specific basis of Reformation teaching, Barth strongly asserted the primacy of biblical authority in his famous Gifford Lectures of 1938, in which he expounded the Scots Confession under the title *The Knowledge of God and the Service of God*. He alluded here to the desire of Luther and Calvin "to see both the church and salvation founded on the Word of God alone, as God's revelation in Jesus Christ, as it is attested in the Scriptures." Reformation teaching acknowledges only "the spiritual law of Scripture." Hence the confession is a "signpost" to the Bible, which "authenticates but also criticises it."[48]

As human documents, the Scriptures are to be understood "in a human way . . . , by the scientific study of the Bible." Yet, although such study clarifies the human form, "it will not set before us the object of this testimony, which is God's revelation." Unless revelation awakens faith, "the scientific study of the Bible will certainly miss the divine content," and, if so, Barth wondered if "it can rightly clarify the human form."[49] The Bible exercises authority in the church as "the concrete form of Jesus Christ . . . the place where he can be sought and found, the Voice of the Holy Spirit which can be heard." This authority is God's, for "God Himself has here spoken of Himself."

Of real concern to the church is not the religious value of the Bible but the fact that it is "the human testimony in which the voice of God is to be heard," so that the church calls it alone "the Word of God."[50] The church realizes that its human authors were "fallible men like all of us." By the Word it means "Him to Whom this book and this book alone bears testimony." It can and should expound Scripture, but its exposition is always subject to Scripture as a judge to whom there must be constant appeal. Proper exposition is "faithful and attentive following after the exposition which Scripture desires to give to itself." Scripture interprets Scripture; human exposition must follow its self-exposition, in which the Holy Spirit is active, for "who can expound Scripture but God Himself?"[51] Good theology is critical, but it is truly critical when "it gives expression to the criticism passed by the Lord of the church and hence by Scripture,"[52] which, as a given factor within the church, "refuses to be silent."[53]

Barth made similar points in discussions of the Heidelberg Catechism in 1938 and 1947. In his *Introduction* he stressed that the catechism recognizes "only the one authority of Holy Scripture" and gives itself a secondary place—simply as a legitimate witness to Scripture.[54] In a later and fuller work, *Christian Doctrine according to the Heidelberg Catechism*, he argued that Christian doctrine has "a source and goal," for "above all Christian doctrine towers a form of Christian doctrine which is distinct from all other forms as the original form: the authentic, original, and therefore normative witness of the gospel of Jesus Christ as it is given in the Scriptures of the Old and New Testaments." He thus issued a warning against "every pursuit of theology which rejects the original task of theology, exegesis, that serious and difficult task to which the knowledge of Greek and Hebrew belongs."[55]

Finally, in his polemical *No* to Emil Brunner (1934), Barth defended his sharp attack precisely because he believed Brunner to be "in possession of more truth" than many others, i.e., "closer to the Scriptures."[56] Brunner alleged "an unconditional acceptance of the Reformers' principle of *sola scriptura–sola gratia*." But he abandons this principle when it "inopportunely blocks an important source of knowledge."[57] He also contradicts Calvin (notwithstanding his appeal to him), for Calvin's theology is "as a matter of principle only interpretation of Scripture and not also anthropology and philosophy of history and nature." Barth saw no need to look for other supports, as Brunner was doing. Instead, he commended "the confidence of which the Word of God and also the Holy Scriptures and therefore the sacraments and therefore also our weak and miserable preaching are worthy . . . because they are God or institutions of God."[58]

III. DOGMATIC PRESENTATION

In his early statements Barth expressed already all his main thoughts concerning biblical authority. He had quickly seen, however, that he needed to give orderly and constructive form to what he uttered first more as protest or correction. Already at Göttingen, then, he took advantage of his broad knowledge of Reformed theology to set a dogmatic course alongside his expository and historical series. Developing the beginnings of this course at Münster, he produced the abortive *Christian Dogmatics*. At Bonn he then undertook the revision that launched the bulky volumes of the *Church Dogmatics* that would dominate the rest of his teaching career. In this dogmatic venture Barth's task was to work out first a comprehensive doctrine of the Word of God and then within this doctrine a full and careful statement on Scripture and its normativeness for the church. "The Doctrine of the Word of God" is thus the title of volume 1 (Prolegomena) of the *Church Dogmatics*, and a chapter on Scripture forms part of the presentation.

In the introductory discussion, Barth advanced the thesis that the Word of God is the criterion of dogmatics and, therefore, of the church's proclamation. This Word, however, has a threefold form. It comprises the word preached and written as well as the word revealed.[59] Proclamation is God's word as the word is its commission, theme, judgment, and event.[60] But if this is to be so, proclamation must conform to the constitutive proclamation of Scripture—which, as the prophetic and apostolic witness, demands free exegesis and dynamically imposes itself as the canon.[61]

As witness, Scripture in turn points to the revealed word, which is itself not just record but revelation, which is thus God's word in a direct sense, which engenders Scripture and therefore has priority, which is indeed God's Word in the absolute sense of taking form as the incarnation of the eternal Word.[62] In analogy to the Trinity, to which revelation bears testimony in its form and structure, Barth perceived a perichoresis of the three forms of the word in which all are essential, since no one is present without the other two, and each, then, may with equal strictness, if not in the same sense, be described as the word.[63]

Developing the doctrine of Scripture more precisely in chapter 3 (vol. I, 2, §§ 19–21), Barth devoted to it three sections that should be studied as a totality, just as Scripture itself should be viewed as an integral part of the larger whole that comprises the word revealed and the word proclaimed. He turned first to Scripture as God's word for the church (§ 19). He began by stressing the importance of Scripture and the Scripture principle.[64] He then discussed the category of biblical witness. Taking the category from the Bible itself, he pointed out that it implies differentiation, for the Bible is not itself revelation, but it also means identification; for revelation reaches us through the spoken and written words of the immediate recipients whom God raised up within the event of revelation to be its authorized and authentic witnesses.[65] In this context Barth accepted the summons to study the Bible historically, but he insisted that true historical study means letting the Bible itself tell us what it has to say.[66] Above all, good hermeneutics must recognize that the Bible seeks to be heard as God's word. As is true of exposition in which the commentator does all the talking instead of genuinely listening, so, too, reading the Bible merely as the human words of human authors implies no real historical understanding.[67]

When he asked what it means for a human word to speak and be heard as God's word, Barth offered some important definitions. First, the Scripture at issue is canonical (that to which revelation bears witness and which the church confirms).[68] Second, the canon consists of the two Testaments in irreversible distinction and indissoluble unity.[69] Third, its theme is the unique contingent revelation of the incarnate Son, to which the primary witness corresponds as that of human authors discharging the unique and contingent function of giving the first and normative witness in both the passive and active senses.[70] Fourth, the revelational content and scriptural form are so united that we are "tied to these texts."[71] We may not seek some historical truth that lies behind or above them, for Christianity is valid only when "it is not ashamed to be actually and seriously a book-religion."[72] Fifth, Scripture is unique, not in intrinsic qualities but in the unique function whereby there arises, in analogy to the Incarnation, "an indirect identity of human existence with God Himself."[73] Sixth, Scripture "has priority over all other writings" as "itself the Word of God," not as a compendium of human knowledge, but in an act of the Holy Spirit. This act does not confer inerrancy on the Bible (although Barth knew no vantage-point from which to judge it to be in error) but causes the human words in their contextual meaning to be for us God's words.[74] In Barth's view, the fact that Scripture is God's Word implies no presence of God as an inherent attribute, but it entails, along with the human word, the control, act, miracle, and decision of God whereby "God says what the text says" and we discern God's word in it simply "by the fact that it is God's Word."[75]

Having tried to show how one should know and understand Scripture as God's Word, Barth (§ 20)—under the two heads of authority of and under the Word—took up the crucial theme of biblical authority. He stated at the outset that, since the witness of Scripture is that of the Holy Spirit, Scripture has a direct, absolute, material authority that alone can establish all indirect, relative, formal authorities in the church. Biblical authority consists not merely of chronological precedence, though that is a fact;[76] it derives from the unique relationship of the prophets and apostles to the revealed word, making these authors the specially commissioned witnesses of the revelation, so that to hear them is to hear God's word.[77]

This is the Scripture principle that the Reformed confessions state clearly and forcefully, that the Fathers hold (if rather equivocally), but that Roman Catholics weaken by advancing tradition as a second source of revelation and imposing the hermeneutical authority of the church as the living voice of the Spirit that finally comes to expression in infallible papal definitions.[78] As Barth saw it, Scripture replaces the spurious authority of the church's interpretation by an authentic authority that summons the church to obedience. It can do this precisely because it exists as an ongoing entity of its own with "the form of book and letter" that the church cannot subsume and in which, through the authors, there is heard "the voice of Him who called them to speak." The vitality of the church, in Barth's view, depends on its living by Scripture, whose presence grants the constant assurance of God's own presence and hence of a different and transcendent authority.[79]

Once he had established the unique and unchallengeable authority of Scripture, Barth could discuss the various forms of real but subsidiary authority that exist under it and are established by it. When the church hears and receives God's word, its responsive confession, both corporate and individual, constitutes the basic form of indirect, relative, formal authority.[80] From this basic form develop the three main historical manifestations—the canon, the Fathers, and the creedal formulations.[81] Unlike Scripture, all these are in principle reformable, although Scripture, along with all past and present voices, must be publicly heard before changes are made. The failure of liberal

Protestantism to make serious attempts at change on this level indicated, for Barth, its wise (if largely unconscious) realization that it had no real authority for its noisy, revolutionary criticisms and theorizings.[82]

Not unrelated to the matter of authority, in Barth's thinking, was that of freedom. He thus added to his treatment of Scripture a final section (§ 21)—under the parallel headings of freedom of and under the word—on the freedom of the word. Like true authority, true freedom is the freedom of the word itself on which the church's freedom must rest if it is to be authentic.[83] The word is free inasmuch as it is a living, acting, and speaking subject, constituted as such by its unique and divinely given theme.[84]

This freedom manifests itself as its power to maintain itself, to assimilate alien elements, to make an impact on the world, and to found, preserve, and rule the church.[85] Coming in human form, it involves a claim, command, and law that free us to hear and apply it.[86] Hence, freedom arises under it as active and responsible participation in "the great event by which Holy Scripture lives and rules in the church and world." This participation consists primarily of the threefold interpretation of Scripture in exposition, reflection, and application. In this process we unavoidably bring our own ideas, concepts, and convictions, but we must subordinate these consistently to the biblical witness and revelation if we are to achieve real freedom. Real freedom is freedom under the text, not from it.

In this regard Barth often pointed out that we must not identify God's word merely with passages that we find attractive. If God does not speak His word to us in one place today, He may well do so tomorrow. In any case, even in "its most debatable and least assimilable parts" the biblical message is always "truer and more important than the best and most necessary things that we ourselves have said or can say."[87]

As regards application, Barth issued a warning against confusing it with adaptation to ourselves and our own concerns.[88] What must take place is transposition away from the self to the word and the questions, concerns, and object of the word. Faith is a prerequisite for this transposition, for faith directs us to the focal point and enables us to receive what Scripture itself is saying. Obedient faith constitutes the exercise of the genuine freedom that arises under the free word.[89]

Finally, then, authority and freedom amount to much the same thing. The authoritative word has freedom, and the free word authority. The church that has authority under the word knows real freedom, and the church that has its freedom under the word has real authority. As Barth acutely observed, authoritarian churches need the authentic authority that also confers freedom, and churches that stress freedom need the authentic freedom that also brings authority.

IV. PRACTICAL APPLICATIONS

A. PREACHING

Even as Barth made it a main concern to work out the doctrine of biblical authority, he maintained a continuing interest in the practice of this authority in various fields. One such field was preaching, which he regarded as the supreme task of dogmatics to serve. Apart from examples in his own published sermons, Barth once gave a set of lectures on preaching, which finally made its way into print as *The Preaching of the Gospel*. Not unnaturally, the relationship of the sermon to Scripture claimed not a little of Barth's attention in this work.

The opening definition reminds us of the connection that Barth postulated between the word written and the word proclaimed: Preaching, as the word of God that He Himself has proclaimed, uses people speaking to other people, "in God's name, by means of a passage from Scripture." Preachers have the duty of proclaiming God's word by "explaining a passage of Scripture which concerns them (the hearers) personally."[90] They must speak what they have heard and received, in order that "when the Gospel is preached, God speaks."[91]

Along these lines, Barth resisted the notion that sermons should convey abstract truths or attempt rational proofs, which, he argued, cannot establish God's reality. He insisted that preaching is primarily explanation of Scripture. Predicated on God's willingness to reveal Himself, it draws from Scripture. Preachers must be ready to "follow the special trend of the text" no matter where it leads.[92] They must say nothing but what is found in the Bible. They must trust Scripture, respect it, and give it "close and detailed attention."[93]

In this connection Barth found a place for scientific exegetical methods and accurate linguistic and historical study. Since the original manuscripts were written in Hebrew and Greek, it is "necessary" to use those languages. Criticism has given "a better understanding of the Scriptures."[94] But Barth warned against the exaggerated importance that it has assumed. Above all, we must not let it sever the unity of the Old and New Testaments, which "are related to one another as prophecy to its fulfillment."[95] Historically, the Bible may be a monument to religious experience, but its real significance is as "the only record of Revelation" that gives witness to it in human terms.[96] Since the proper aim is to let Scripture speak for itself, preachers must ensure that their own ideas are "subject to correction by the text of Scripture" and yield themselves to "the movement of the Word of God."[97]

Preaching ought to respect the canon as the place "where the Word of God is to be heard." Accepting biblical rule safeguards against a sacerdotalist exalting of the ministry.[98] Although preaching must be

true to life as well as to the Bible—the great problem of the sermon—
expository preaching is better than topical preaching. One should "be
guided by the text, not by a topic."[99] So strongly did Barth underline
the need for biblical preaching that he thought a sermon needed only
a biblical introduction, and advised that it should end "when it
reaches the end of the text."[100]

He was confident that, as God's message for the world, the gospel
would have its own implications for political and social life. In
searching for God's answers to human questions, we should be
content with those that Scripture itself provides.[101] When giving these
a contemporary application, we need to be on constant guard against
"an arbitrary and too independent interpretation of Scripture."[102] The
best safeguards are an ongoing consultation of the Bible, regard for
the church's dogmatic teaching, and avoidance of the idea that one
can "approach Scripture with full freedom to exercise one's own
unfettered powers."[103]

The commitment to biblical authority comes out in the practical
aids that Barth offered for sermon preparation. He thought it unwise
to choose too short a text. He cautioned against easy and well-known
verses. He forbade the indulgence in allegory or the intrusion of too
much personal experience. He rejected utilitarian goals for preaching.
He advised planning that would prevent too strong a focus on favorite
passages or books. He insisted first on a word-for-word reading and
pondering of the text, for "here lies the content of the sermon." He
asked for thorough preparation; this is a prime duty "for those who
possess this treasure—the Word."[104]

B. DOGMATICS

As regards the practical application of scriptural authority to
dogmatics, Barth offered a mature discussion in his final course on
Evangelical Theology and ongoing examples in the volumes of his
Church Dogmatics.

In *Evangelical Theology* Barth repeated many of his main themes.
The prophets and apostles, he affirmed, were divinely appointed and
elected witnesses who spoke and wrote what they heard and saw.
Their words are thus "authentic, trustworthy, and authoritative
testimonies to the Word of God." Failure to recognize the unity of the
Old and New Testaments means that "theology is threatened by a
cancer in its very bones." Christ's own unity is also a basic premise; a
twofold Jesus "can be deduced from the New Testament texts only
after he has been arbitrarily read into them."[105]

On this basis Barth considered the special relation of theology to
Scripture. Theology knows God's Word "only at second hand, only in
the mirror and echo of the biblical witnesses." Theologians have no
right "to look over their shoulder benevolently or crossly, to correct
their notebooks, or to give them good, average, or bad marks." "Even

the smallest, strangest, simplest, or obscurest" of them "has an incomparable advantage over even the most pious, scholarly, or sagacious latter-day theologian." Heeding the "polyphonic" testimony of Scripture, theology must avoid being "monolithic, monomanic, monotonous," or "boring." Its task is not to put the Bible into "transitory jargon" but "to draw nearer to what stands *there*."[106]

Defining theology, Barth called it "a science learning in the school of Holy Scripture."[107] It should serve as simply "an introduction to the source and norm of all theology," that is, the Bible. The first discipline, then, is that of "biblical exegesis." Theology is "originally and especially the science of the Old and New Testaments." It seeks "to clarify what is actually written in the Scriptures and what is meant by all that is written." It must respect their own presupposition that they are "to be read and explained as attestation and proclamation of a divine act and speech" and that "testimony to the God who calls for faith will confront it in these texts." A truly biblical dogmatics will avoid systematization in the sense of construction upon or around a single doctrine, for "what should rule in the community is not a concept or principle, but solely the Word of God attested to in the Scripture and vivified by the Holy Spirit."[108]

How far Barth himself tried to base his dogmatics on the Bible is suggested at once by the 60 pages of Old Testament references and the 110 pages of New Testament references listed in the General Index to the *Church Dogmatics*. The quotations come in varying proportions from every biblical book and include not a few that are given intensive exposition. Barth used the Bible in many different ways. At times he heaped up verses (as in giving biblical backing for the divine perfections—II, 1). At times he offered extended exegesis of individual statements (e.g., Jn 1:14 in I, 2, or Jn 3:16 and 2Co 5:18ff. in IV, 1). At times he worked expository sections into the main discussion (e.g., Ro 9–11 in II, 2). At times he expounded whole books (e.g., Galatians in IV, 1 and Amos in IV, 2). At times he used Old Testament incidents as illustrations (as in the account of sin—IV, 1 and 2). At times he engaged in typology (as in II, 2). At times he even made a biblical commentary his main presentation (e.g., Ge 1 and 2 in III, 1).

Always he tried to take Scripture as it stood, paying scant attention to source analysis or alleged discrepancies. Always, too, he tried to give due weight to all relevant material, the only exceptions of a glaring nature being the references to the human spirit in 1 Thessalonians 5 and to the angelic fall in Jude, which did not harmonize with his own thinking or, he believed, with the main thrust of the biblical teaching. Whether or not his expositions are correct may obviously be debated. His understanding perhaps owed more than he realized to extraneous factors, although he was not unaware of the pressure they exerted. What is hardly contestable is that he did make a sincere and consistent effort to practice what he preached, namely, to give his own theology a solid grounding in Scripture and to test his dogmatic judgment by the biblical norm.

C. COUNSELING

Barth's letters shed interesting light on another aspect of his practical submission to biblical authority. Various pastoral and theological matters came up in his extensive correspondence, and in his initiatives and responses alike he often referred to Scripture and its authoritative role.

Thus, answering a person in prison who found no help in prayer or deep biblical study, he advised a reading of the Christmas story in Luke, "not deeply but very simply, with the thought that every word there, and every word in the Twenty-Third Psalm too, is meant for you too, and expressly for you."[109] To a railroad official wrestling with grace and freedom, he suggested: "Do not stop testing and correcting your insights by Holy Scripture."[110] When a pastor who was trying to interest him in the No Other Gospel movement mentioned that he suffered from profound depression, he sent him back to a quiet reading of the Bible and the hymnbook.[111]

Some remarks about Scripture in the letters have to do with aspects of liberal teaching. Barth told one professor he had become too American in treating the Bible as a kind of dish "from which all can serve themselves as they think good or as they desire."[112] When a Basel theological student was enthused about building up the kingdom, Barth said it was nonsense and that he did "not contradict merely one 'insight' but the whole message of the whole Bible." He also advised him that, unless he changed his mind, he should "take up any other career than that of a pastor."[113] In reply to the news from his daughter-in-law that her agnostic father was reading the Gospels and that she was trying to interest him in Teilhard de Chardin, he compared movements like Teilhard's to "giant snakes by which the poor gospel of the Old and New Testaments must let itself be gulped down," declared his "allergic reaction" to them, and asked why she could not quietly leave her father in the school of the Gospels "when you will probably annoy him again with T. de C. and at worst might even lead him to error."[114] To another pastor he expressed confidence that even in the age of Bultmann and Robinson the church need not be "too quickly flabbergasted by a handful of pompous professors and a few hundred excited students and candidates" when the Bible (and God) had already withstood many similar assaults "and will withstand this one too."[115]

Finally, in relation to Roman Catholicism, Barth welcomed the new weight that Vatican II gave to the Bible but still thought it necessary to stress the Scripture principle over against Roman Catholic teaching. Asked to distinguish between Evangelical and Roman Catholic confessions, he pointed out that in the former "the

Bible has strictly the first word over against church tradition," but the latter tends "to understand the Bible in the light of tradition."[116]

Again, when he took issue with the pope over the appeal to natural law in human life, he allowed some agreement that revelation "is to be found in the strict sense only in Holy Scripture" but complained that the encyclical "sets nature and conscience alongside revelation as equally divine," and asked: "Where does this equation occur in Holy Scripture? Where is it prescribed or even permitted . . . in Holy Scripture?" Whereas Cardinal Cicognani was claiming that revelation "does not suppress natural law, which is equally divine," Barth thought it better to uphold strictly "the irremovable distinction between the unequivocal word of God on the one side and the ambivalent voices of nature and conscience on the other" and in this way to give the encyclical "the character of a proclamation of the gospel," not a law.[117] He could have no real confidence that Vatican II had brought the Roman Catholic world to a full acceptance of the uniquely direct, absolute, and material authority of Scripture that he himself espoused and tried to practice.

V. EVALUATION

A. PROBLEMS

The many quotations from so many works of Barth, which could well be multiplied, demonstrate beyond cavil his resolute commitment to biblical authority and his sincere intention to observe it in his own Christian service. Nevertheless, certain problems arise regarding aspects of his understanding of this authority that might seem to weaken or compromise the very position that he ardently seeks to maintain.

First, his stress and insistence on the witnessing role of Scripture leave at times an impression of devaluation of Scripture as God's word. Barth's aim, of course, is the laudable one of differentiating Scripture from the incarnate Word (i.e., from God Himself). He also offers the safeguards that the Bible, although not revelation, is God's written word, that it was raised up within the event of revelation and as part of it, and that there is a perichoresis of the three forms of the word. Yet the accent falls so heavily on the function of witness as to suggest, even if unintentionally, that Scripture has an inferior role except in so far as the Holy Spirit empowers it in sovereign freedom. Indeed, some scholars have found in *Church Dogmatics* IV, 3 a tendency to retreat from the identification of Scripture as word, though this is saying too much in view of Barth's reference to his fuller discussion in I, 1. The true problem is that—perhaps even in I, 1 and I, 2—Scripture is to some extent undermined by the hierarchy of the threefold word rather than established by it (as Barth intended).

Second, Barth's muted championship of the past inspiration of Scripture as compared with its present inspiring produces further uncertainty about its objective authority. Is it authoritative because God inspired it once and for all, or is it authoritative only ad hoc as God inspires it when heard or read? Here again, of course, Barth made efforts to reduce the difficulty. He did not dispute the past act whereby God raised up prophets and apostles to speak and write the primary words of testimony. He insisted that the Holy Spirit speaks uniquely in Scripture. He did not view its present authority as a matter of human subjectivity. He contended that we may and should approach Scripture with the full expectation that God will impart His word in and through it. Yet the emphasis of his presentation leaves serious questions as to the scope, meaning, and solid objectivity of the authority that he proclaimed.

Third, Barth's dismissal of biblical inerrancy and his assigning of a special historical character to events like the Resurrection pose the question whether the biblical books can really enjoy the status of direct, absolute, material authority, except by a sacrifice of the intellect, if they do in fact contain demonstrably incorrect statements or tell of events that do not meet the test of normal historical verifiability. Barth himself apparently did not feel the difficulty. He accepted the general facticity of God's saving work and the veracity of the records. He never specified actual errors in the Bible. He saw no place from which to decide that the Bible is mistaken. He disputed the possibility of describing the Resurrection in ordinary historical categories, not that it really happened. He rejected the idea that the authority of Scripture should be suspended on inerrancy or its demonstration. For many people, however, doubt seems unavoidably to arise about the great reality to which the Bible bears witness if it might be in error, or even under suspicion of being in error, about plain facts.

Barth compounds his problem by speaking of a capacity for error but not giving examples of the types of error he has in mind. His supporting arguments are also weak. Undoubtedly, to err is human, but this does not entail a flat equation of humanity and error, as human experience amply demonstrates and the Incarnation itself should remind us. Again, God may speak through our own fallible human materials, so far as they are faithful to Scripture, but Barth himself sees a qualitative distinction between these materials and Scripture's normative testimony. Of no more value is the idea that God's speaking through what is erroneous at the human level is a greater miracle than His speaking through what He Himself has freed from error by His own prior action. Barth himself may ride roughshod over the problems that his teaching raises in this regard, but when essential facts or doctrines are at issue, as distinct perhaps from formal points of style or syntax, he seems to be unfortunately undercutting the very position on authority that he is passionately seeking to establish.

Finally, Barth's handling of biblical commands creates difficulties in the practical application of Scripture's authority in the ethical field. As Barth saw it, the commands were given to specific people in specific situations. Hence, we are not to make a simple transfer to different people in different situations. The commands are God's only as the Spirit so speaks through them that they go forth again as the direct voice of God. In this way, of course, Barth hoped to avoid legalism and casuistry, yet without falling into relativism or situationism. The Spirit speaks through the same commands without relinquishing personal control, whether to Scripture or to its hearers.

The problems arise, however, whether the commands have any real authority unless God speaks through them, and how one is to know that He really does speak, either enforcing the commands or making permissible exceptions. Barth himself in his conservatively biblical outworking of ethics could proceed only by finding criteria by which to assess the proper course in given circumstances. In so doing, he relieved the difficulty in practice. In principle, however, the problem still obtrudes that at any given time there may be no coincidence of the living voice of the Spirit and the permanent record of the commands. If not, Scripture may still have indirect, relative, formal authority, as church law also does, but its readers or hearers are deprived of the decisive divine authority that it ought to enjoy.

B. MERITS

Barth himself seemed not to feel the force of the problems that have arisen for others. He thought that he had provided sufficient safeguards against them. Even if not, he believed that the merits of his doctrine of authority outweighed possible disadvantages. There are indeed some real merits, which are for the most part the reverse side of the problems.

Thus, the emphasis on the witnessing aspect of Scripture has a twofold value. First, it clarifies the fact that God Himself is the true source of authority in the things of God; Scripture is authoritative because it is divinely authorized by Him who is always both subject and object. Second, it also points to God's authority as it is incarnate in the Son—who is Himself the truth of God in person, who as such is the origin and theme of Scripture, and who grants Scripture its authority as the written word by association with Himself as the revealed word. Scripture, then, is not left on its own in the conflict of competing human authorities. As itself God's word of witness to the incarnate Word, it stands against all comers as divine authority.

Second, the orientation to the present act of inspiring serves as a valuable reminder that God is no deistic or absentee God who has simply placed His authority elsewhere by a past act. The divine author of the Bible is the living God, who as Spirit still speaks and rules in and through the written word. Barth certainly uses the very text of Scripture; he insists on verbal inspiration in this sense, and so he demands careful exegesis. But God does not allow the recipients of Scripture to become its lords, nor does He allow Scripture to become a mere textbook of religion—as though its truths could be taught and learned like the truths of an academic discipline. Scripture has unique authority precisely because its divine author Himself speaks through it to call, claim, judge, enlighten, regenerate, and save. Barth saw in this emphasis no surrender to human subjectivity such as many fear. Instead, he found the very opposite, namely, an orientation to the objective reality of God, who as supreme object and subject speaks His own word in human words and thus gives the human words an authority that no human court can ever achieve.

Third, Barth was convinced that authority rather than inerrancy is the critical point in the doctrine of Scripture. In his view, it is a crippling mistake to suspend authority on the human ability to establish inerrancy. Liberation from the related defensive apologetics brings authority into proper focus, makes possible a fruitful use of the critical method in the exegetical task, dispels the insecurity that results when it is feared that possible errors will overturn the Bible's authority, and makes unnecessary the expenditure of time and labor on a buttressing of inerrancy that will not necessarily go hand in hand with a better hearing of God's message or a more faithful keeping of His commands.

Of course, Barth agreed that scientific criticism is a poor master in biblical studies. He saw no reason to make common cause with those who ignored the Bible's true status and function and focused on its humanity alone. He had no interest in publishing a message of biblical errancy. His primary concern was that God's authoritative word should come through the human authors and a proper exposition of their teaching. Concentration on the inerrancy of Scripture might seem to serve biblical authority by meeting critical objections on their own plane. In Barth's view, however, it involved a fatal shift of concern which could only weaken the true authority and use of Scripture that it desired to establish. Whether or not he judged rightly in this regard, his main point that authority on the basis of divine authorship and authorization is the real issue, so that inerrancy will be primarily an implication rather than a demonstrated presupposition, certainly deserves serious consideration.

Barth himself, of course, does not view inerrancy as an implication, and for this reason one may question whether he succeeds, or can succeed, in his desired aim of shifting the focus to authority. Thus, if Scripture is God's direct, material, and absolute Word, and if it also testifies to its own total reliability and truthfulness, then Barth's failure to accept the implication involves an inconsistency that already throws doubt on his assertion of biblical authority. Again, the supposed fallible humanity of Scripture stands in contradictory antithesis to the irrefutable infallibility of Scripture as God's Word. Thus, even though Barth may well be right that the ultimate issue in the church is the authority of Scripture, his denial of inerrancy as an implication means that he himself can make the shift only by the *tour de force* of self-contradictory disjunctions, which are unlikely to command substantial or lasting assent.

Fourth, Barth's insistence on God's direct commanding preserves a place for living divine authority, blocks the legalistic view of the Bible as merely a code of divine law, and resists the erosion of biblical commands on the plea of dispensational or cultural change. A problem of human caprice remains, for readers may always reject the divine direction, or pretend not to have heard it, or to have heard something else. But this is a problem in all ethics; even those who see in Scripture a set of given commands disagree widely on what the commands are or how to fulfill them. If, however, readers approach the Bible with the prayerful expectation that God will command, they need not suppose that He will withhold His voice, for He has specifically raised up Scripture in order to speak through it. It is through these texts that God does in fact issue His commands. Hence the subjective caprice of deafness, resistance, or evasion does not negate the objectivity of the authority in either the biblical embodiment or the free and living action of the Spirit.

A final merit of Barth's presentation demands brief notice. Making biblical authority dependent on God and not on human effort, Barth had full confidence that Scripture will never be reduced to a paper tiger any more than it should be exalted as a paper pope. It will always do its work, which is God's work, as God Himself decides. No fear need arise that unless it be supported by arguments, supplemented by reasoning, ornamented by rhetoric, or empowered by technique, it will be powerless to speak its message, exercise its rule, and make its impact. In every age, culture, and situation, God may be trusted to speak through the Word that He caused to be written as a normative word of witness. No doubt some aspects of Barth's presentation give rise to problems. No doubt faults may be perceived in both his understanding and practice of authority.[118] Nevertheless, the strength of his doctrine of scriptural authority comes to clear expression in the confidence in Scripture that it confers and in the attempted obedience that it consequently evokes.

CHAPTER NINE
THE BIBLICAL CANON
David G. Dunbar

David G. Dunbar

David G. Dunbar is President of Biblical Theological Seminary in Hatfield, Pennsylvania. He is a graduate of Pennsylvania State University (B.S.), Biblical Theological Seminary (M.Div.), Westminster Theological Seminary (Th.M.), and Drew University (Ph.D.). Prior to his present position he was Associate Professor of Biblical and Systematic Theology at Trinity Evangelical Divinity School, Deerfield, Illinois. He has published articles in *Vigiliae Christianae* and *The Westminster Theological Journal*.

CHAPTER NINE

THE BIBLICAL CANON

I. INTRODUCTION

A. THE RECENT PROMINENCE OF CANONICITY

> There are signs all about that major new developments with regard to the
> Christian Bible are just around the corner. I see six areas of intense activity
> which will sooner or later precipitate a massive series of changes regarding
> the shape and content of the Bible which should rival for creativity the
> Reformation period, if not the second through the fifth centuries.[1]

In the decade since David Dungan published these words, the
"massive series of changes" has not taken place and, in my judgment,
is not likely to occur. Though bold in his claims, the author
simultaneously underestimates the stability of the canon as it has
been held by the church during the last fifteen centuries and
overestimates the "creativity of the Reformation period," which was
marked indeed by a Protestant rejection of the Old Testament
apocrypha but no change at all in the New Testament canon.

It is nevertheless true that canon studies find a prominent place
on the contemporary theological agenda. This prominence reflects a
number of issues. First, there is the ongoing attempt of liberal
theology, perhaps best illustrated in the collection of essays edited by
Ernst Käsemann under the title *Das Neue Testament als Kanon* (1970),
to salvage some notion of biblical authority from the wreckage of three
centuries of historical-critical attacks on Scripture. The development
of the school of canon criticism, associated especially with the names
of Brevard Childs and James Sanders, forms only the most recent
attempt of critical scholars to find some abiding importance in the
traditional canon.[2]

Second, there continues to be a strong interest in the history of
the formation of the canons of both the Old and the New Testament.
This has certainly been stimulated by the mid-century discoveries
of the Dead Sea Scrolls and the Coptic Gnostic documents from
Nag Hammadi. Important monographs by Albert C. Sundberg, Jr., and
Sid Z. Leiman on the Old Testament and Hans von Campenhausen
and Isidore Frank[3] on the New Testament, along with a spate of
journal articles, have continued to focus attention on the historical
aspects of canonization.

A third issue contributing to interest in the canon is the growth of ecumenism and pluralism. Concern among the various separated communions for the reunification of Christendom has led to a search for a common Bible. Publishers like Doubleday (*Anchor Bible Commentary*) and Fortress (*Hermeneia*) are committed to publishing complete commentaries on the Apocrypha.[4] In this connection it is also significant to find Protestant scholars challenging the Reformers' rejection of the canonicity of the Apocrypha.[5]

However, many ecumenically minded theologians, particularly those of Protestant stripe, desire a unification that allows the fullest possible measure of doctrinal diversity. Theological pluralism is advocated not only as a fact of the modern ecclesiastical scene but as an inherent element of genuine and, therefore, original Christianity. This partially explains the great interest generated by the publication of the English translation of Walter Bauer's *Orthodoxy and Heresy in Earliest Christianity* (1971). Bauer saw the early church as marked by widespread pluralism that was eventually suppressed by the rise of Catholic orthodoxy. Since the present canon reflects the ascendancy of the orthodox party, the question must be raised as to the legitimacy of the canon as a norm for original Christianity. More recently, Bauer's emphasis on early Christian pluralism has been applied to the canonical materials themselves. According to James Dunn, diversity is fundamental to the canon: "We cannot claim to accept the authority of the NT unless we are willing to accept as valid *whatever* forms of Christianity can justifiably claim to be rooted in one of the strands that make up the NT."[6]

By contrast with the broad-based interest in the canon, Evangelical theology has devoted little attention to the current discussion. Major studies of biblical authority continue to be produced by Evangelicals who seldom interact with problems of canon.[7] Since Laird Harris's 1957 monograph, *The Inspiration and Canonicity of the Bible*, no attempt has been made at a comprehensive treatment of the historical and theological issues surrounding the canon.[8] Perhaps no further apology is needed for an Evangelical reconsideration of the canonization process.

B. DEFINITIONS

Etymologically, *kanōn* is a Semitic loan word that originally had the meaning "reed." From this came the figurative sense of a "measuring rod" or "ruler" and from this the general idea of a "norm" or "standard." Finally, the term could adopt the purely formal sense of a "list" or a "table." In ecclesiastical usage during the first three centuries of the Christian era, *kanōn* refers to the normative ethical and doctrinal content of the Christian faith. The use of *kanōn* to designate the Old or New Testament Scriptures originates in the latter half of the fourth century.[9]

In the present study, "canon" will be used to refer to a closed collection of documents regarded as Holy Scripture. As far as delimitation and closure belong to the idea of the canon, it will be necessary to distinguish canon from the concept of "Scripture"—although the former presupposes the latter. Canon, I shall argue, is a historical-theological idea that views the process of divine revelation as complete or at least in abeyance for the present. Only when the age of revelation is regarded as part of the past does the idea of a definite canon become explicit for the people of God. In what follows we will examine the process by which the writings of the Old Testament (and subsequently the New Testament) were explicitly recognized as belonging to a period of God's unique revelatory activity.

II. OLD TESTAMENT CANON

In the aftermath of the Babylonian exile, Ezra grieved over the destruction of the biblical books. Directed by God to choose five men as secretaries, he dictated in the course of forty days a total of ninety-four books. The first twenty-four, apparently corresponding to the entire Old Testament, were to be circulated generally, but the remaining seventy—apocryphal or pseudepigraphical works of some sort[10]—were to be delivered only "to the wise among your people." This account in 2 Esdras (= 4 Ezra) 14:44ff. (c. A.D. 100) is probably the source of similar Ezra traditions that appear in patristic literature from Irenaeus onward.[11] Jewish and Christian accounts of the canon have traditionally focused on the significance of Ezra for the establishment of the Old Testament in its present form. While the miraculous circumstances of the recollection and recovery of Scripture are not present in later Jewish literature, the association of Ezra with the closing of the canon is common. Through the work of the sixteenth-century Jewish writer Elias Levita, the notion was popularized that Ezra and his associates, the men of the Great Synagogue, not only established the correct text of the Bible but also collected the various books and arranged them in the traditional threefold form.[12]

This traditional view of the canon assumes a direct link between the writing of the books and their canonization: once a book has been written, it is virtually immediately recognized as authoritative and then added to the collection. No time is needed for books to be acknowledged as authoritative; therefore, the cessation of prophetic activity in Israel is followed immediately by the formation of the canon under Ezra.[13] When prophecy ceases, the canon is complete.

A. HISTORICAL-CRITICAL RECONSTRUCTION

This perception of the formation of the canon was dominant in Jewish and Christian circles until the nineteenth century but then gave way before Wellhausen's interpretation of Israel's history and literature. His partitioning of the Pentateuch into J, E, D, and P traditions led to massive revisions in the dating of all the Old Testament literature. Since the established view of the canon was incompatible with these revisions, an alternative model was proposed that is widely represented even among current Old Testament handbooks. The newer construction sees the first evidence of canonical activity in the discovery of the "Book of the Law" during the reign of Josiah (621 B.C.)—identified as the Book of Deuteronomy or a substantial portion of it. The final stages of the formation of the Pentateuch (Torah) are thought to have taken place during the fifth century, with canonization following (about 400 B.C.). Subsequently, the Prophets (nebi'im) were canonized about 200 B.C., and the Writings (ketubim) achieved canonical status as a result of rabbinic discussion at Jamnia during the closing decade of the first Christian century.[14]

While this reconstruction continues to enjoy wide endorsement, many of the arguments used to support it have been weakened by recent scholarship. Four factors should be especially noted.

First, the prevailing view assumes that the Old Testament canon developed in three consecutive stages and that the present tripartite form of the Hebrew Bible reflects the canonical process directly. But while this view "seems *prima facie* the simplest explanation of the tripartite division of the *tanak*," Jack Lightstone observes that its support is often grounded in arguments that are "circular, deductive, and question begging."[15] Arguments for the antiquity of other non-Masoretic orders and for the concurrent rather than successive development of the divisions of the canon call for a reexamination of the data.[16]

Second, the Samaritan schism is often dated prior to the close of the fourth century B.C. It is argued that since the Samaritans accepted only the Pentateuch as canonical, the general Jewish perspective did not view the prophets as canonical prior to about 200 B.C. It is gratuitous to assume that Jewish and Samaritan views of the canon prior to the schism were identical, but apart from this the question of dating the separation between the two groups and the development of the Samaritan recension of the Pentateuch has been reconsidered. R. J. Coggins concludes that "the decisive formative period for Samaritanism was the epoch from the third century B.C. to the beginning of the Christian era."[17] He follows F. M. Cross in arguing that "the Samaritan Pentateuch cannot have undergone its final redaction earlier than the first century B.C., and may have been influenced by Jewish tradition at an even later date."[18] Clearly, such a reassessment eliminates the appeal to the development of Samaritanism as a valid support for the higher critical account of the canon.

Third, a foundational argument for dating the prophetic canon at about 200 B.C. has been the alleged Maccabean provenance of the book of Daniel and its placement among the *ketubim*. If the traditional sixth-century dating of Daniel is correct, it is argued, the failure of Daniel to be included in the second section of the Hebrew Bible is inexplicable.[19] The late dating of Daniel is one of the most entrenched higher-critical opinions; even among those who call for a revision of the standard histories of the canon, the second-century date of Daniel remains a fundamental assumption.[20] But in view of the ongoing challenge by conservative scholars to the theory of Maccabean origins,[21] a major revision of the higher-critical consensus on Daniel is in order.

Fourth, since the latter part of the nineteenth century the idea has been widely advanced that the closure of the Hebrew Bible was the work of rabbinic scholars meeting at Jamnia (Jabneh) about A.D. 90. The work of the Council in fixing the limits of the canon was conceived as part of a larger effort to shore up the foundation of Judaism in the aftermath of A.D. 70. But here again it is on minimal grounds that a position has come to enjoy wide and continuing acceptance. Sid Leiman presents evidence that the rabbis at Jamnia discussed only the inspired character of Song of Songs and Ecclesiastes and that even in these cases the decisions of the Council were not binding, for these same questions were being discussed a century later.[22] Lightstone questions even the reliability of the available evidence for the Council: "Recent research, moreover, further dissolves the scenario of the Council, showing that the institution of the Yavnean college of rabbis (as commonly pictured) probably stems from the imagination of third- or fourth-century tradents."[23] The Jamnia hypothesis, concludes Jack P. Lewis, "appears to be one of those things that has come to be true due to frequent repetition of the assertion rather than to its being actually supported by the evidence."[24]

In light of the increasing ferment and diversity of opinion in canon studies it is appropriate to examine the primary evidence once again.

B. JOSEPHUS

The Jewish historian Josephus (c. A.D. 37–c. A.D. 100) is the first to discuss explicitly the formation and limitation of the Old Testament canon. In his treatise *Against Apion*[25] he writes:

> It therefore naturally, or rather necessarily, follows (seeing that with us it is not open to everybody to write the records, and that there is no discrepancy in what is written; seeing that, on the contrary, the prophets alone had this privilege, obtaining their knowledge of the most remote and ancient history through the inspiration which they owed to God, and committing to writing a clear account of the events of their own time just as they occurred)—it follows, I say, that we do not possess myriads of inconsistent books, conflicting with each other. Our books, those which are justly accredited, are but two and twenty, and contain the record of all time.

Of these, five are the books of Moses, comprising the laws and the traditional history from the birth of a man down to the death of the lawgiver. This period falls only a little short of three thousand years. From the death of Moses until Artaxerxes, who succeeded Xerxes as king of Persia, the prophets subsequent to Moses wrote the history of the events of their own times in thirteen books. The remaining four books contain hymns to God and precepts for the conduct of human life.

From Artaxerxes to our own time the complete history has been written but has not been deemed worthy of equal credit with the earlier records, because of the failure of the exact succession of the prophets.

We have given practical proof of our reverence for our own Scriptures. For, although such long ages have now passed, no one has ventured either to add, or to remove, or to alter a syllable; and it is an instinct with every Jew, from the day of his birth, to regard them as the decrees of God, to abide by them, and, if need be, cheerfully to die for them.

It is evident that at least by the end of the first century A.D. the Jews understood that the biblical canon was closed. For Josephus, canonicity is based upon prophetic inspiration (*tēn epipnoian*), and he is conscious of "the failure of the exact succession of the prophets." The biblical books were all produced during the period from Moses to Artaxerxes (i.e., to the time of Ezra and Nehemiah). Although the four books of "hymns to God and precepts for the conduct of human life" are not given explicit chronological placement, we may assume that these, too, were understood to belong to the age of the prophets.

The canon is fixed at a total of twenty-two books, which almost certainly correspond to the Talmudic canon of twenty-four books.[26] The smaller figure results probably from counting Judges-Ruth and Jeremiah-Lamentations as single books. The canon is tripartite and consists of the following: (1) the five books of Moses, (2) thirteen books of the prophets (Joshua, Judges-Ruth, Samuel, Kings, Isaiah, Jeremiah-Lamentations, Ezekiel, the Twelve Minor Prophets, Job, Daniel, Ezra-Nehemiah, Chronicles, Esther), and (3) four books of hymns and precepts (Psalms, Proverbs, Ecclesiastes, Song of Songs).

Later Jewish sources commonly number twenty-four books in the biblical canon. The earliest attestation of this number is in 2 Esdras 14:44ff. A specific list and order of biblical books is given in the Talmudic passage Baba Bathra 14b–15a, where the (unstated) total is twenty-four books. Although the tripartite division of the canon is clear, apart from the Torah (whose order is assumed rather than stated) the ordering of the books in the Prophets and Writings differs substantially from that of Josephus. Thus, the Prophets number eight in the following order: Joshua, Judges, Samuel, Kings, Jeremiah, Ezekiel, Isaiah, and the Twelve Minor Prophets. The order of the eleven Hagiographa is Ruth, Psalms, Job, Proverbs, Ecclesiastes, Song of Songs, Lamentations, Daniel, Esther, Ezra, and Chronicles.[27]

Later Jewish manuscripts are consistent with Baba Bathra in the books assigned to the Prophets and Hagiographa, although they register variations in ordering the books within each category.[28]

C. PHILO

For the evidence prior to Josephus we may consider first the Jewish philosopher Philo of Alexandria (c. 25 B.C.–c. A.D. 50). Philo does not list the contents of the biblical canon, although his *De Vita Contemplativa* shows an awareness of the tripartite division.[29] His writings contain about two thousand quotations from the Pentateuch as against fifty from the remaining two sections of the Hebrew Bible.[30] This could reflect a less authoritative status for the second and third divisions, or it may simply be due to Philo's adherence "to an Alexandrian tradition of exegesis which was established when the Pentateuch alone had been translated into Greek."[31] But then again, the larger part of Philo's works are given over to an allegorical exposition of the patriarchal and Exodus narratives; having chosen such a subject, the higher proportion of Pentateuchal quotations would not be surprising, nor would it necessarily tell us anything of the relative authority of divisions of the canon. Philo cites all of the Old Testament writings except Ezekiel, Song of Songs, Ruth, Lamentations, Ecclesiastes, Esther, and Daniel.[32] Whether his silence on these books is significant for his conception of the canon is impossible to judge. It is not clear whether Philo shows any knowledge of the Apocrypha[33]—certainly he never quotes them as Scripture.[34]

D. NEW TESTAMENT

The New Testament likewise bears witness to a tripartite division of the Jewish Scriptures: "the Law of Moses, the Prophets and the Psalms" (Lk 24:44). However, the threefold division is not emphasized. More common is the dual reference "the Law and the Prophets" or "Moses and the Prophets."[35] Alternatively, the Old Testament can be described generally as "the Law" or again as "the Prophets."[36] Paul's reference to the *reading* of the old covenant *(tēn anagnōsei palaias diathēkēs,* 2Co 3:14) probably is a similar collective reference to the entire Hebrew Bible. So also the term "Scripture" *(graphē)* or its plural "the Scriptures" frequently refers not to a particular passage but to the various biblical books conceived as a whole.[37]

The high authority accorded to the Old Testament by New Testament writers is reflected in the fact that "the books of the NT contain about 250 quotations, some of them fairly extensive, and in individual expressions and turns of speech more than 900 allusions to the Old Testament."[38] While debate can be raised on specific references, we may safely make the following generalizations about the New Testament use of the Old.[39] (1) The five books of the Law are cited and recognized as authoritative. (2) As far as the Prophets are concerned, Joshua, Judges, (perhaps) Ezekiel, Obadiah, Nahum, and Zephaniah are not cited. But the last three would have been included with the rest of the twelve Minor Prophets, and therefore the lack of citation suggests nothing about their canonical status. Ezekiel may be referred to in 2 Corinthians 6:16–17, and there are clear allusions to it in the Apocalypse. Joshua 1:5 may be quoted in Hebrews 13:5, and a knowledge of Judges is presupposed in Hebrews 11:32. It is safe to conclude, therefore, that all of the Prophets as they were later transmitted in the second division of the Old Testament canon were recognized by the New Testament writers as canonical Scripture. The reading of the Prophets alongside the Law in the synagogue in New Testament times (Lk 4:16–17; Ac 13:15ff.,27) supports the conclusion that by now the Prophets formed a recognized and defined corpus. (3) The Writings constitute the greatest problem for analysis. Clearly, Psalms is given canonical status, being quoted more than any other Old Testament book. The five Megilloth, Ezra, Nehemiah, and Chronicles are not quoted directly, although Matthew 1:5 is likely dependent on Ruth 3:21 and Matthew 23:34–35 (Lk 11:51) on 2 Chronicles 24:20–22.[40]

The Matthew 23 text is particularly interesting because of its possible implications for the concept of canon. Jesus warns the scribes and Pharisees, "upon you will come all the righteous blood that has been shed on earth, from the blood of righteous Abel to the blood of Zechariah son of Berekiah, whom you murdered between the temple and the altar" (Mt 23:35). If Abel is chosen because he was the first righteous man in history to suffer persecution from the wicked, why the mention of Zechariah? Many scholars judge that the reference is to Zechariah son of Jehoiada (2Ch 24:20,22).[41] Since Zechariah is not chronologically the last martyr named in the Old Testament,[42] it is assumed that he is mentioned here because Chronicles was, by New Testament times, understood to be the last book in the Hebrew Bible.[43] Thus, Jesus' statement would mean "the blood of all the martyrs mentioned in the Old Testament."

If this is the proper interpretation of the text, then it suggests that Matthew and Luke—and, assuming the reliability of their witness, Jesus also—regarded the canon as a completed entity with an order similar to that of Baba Bathra. Otto Eissfeldt notes that this would still fall short of demonstrating that the New Testament knew all the books of the third division of the canon.[44] True. But it coheres nicely with the rabbinic view, and it seems probable that the New Testament writers at least conceived of a closed canon of Jewish Scripture—and perhaps one identical with that of later Judaism.[45]

However, if we affirm that the New Testament witnesses to a closed canon, the question must be raised as to what use the New Testament makes of extracanonical literature—Apocrypha, pseude-pigrapha, or various other forms. Scholars vary greatly in their estimates of the influence of extracanonical materials on the thought forms and expressions of the New Testament authors. Without attempting a detailed consideration of all the alleged parallels,[46] we should make several observations. First, many of the parallels suggested do not show close correspondence, and this raises the possibility that such correspondence as there is may be either simply fortuitous or due to a mutual dependence of both the New Testament literature and the extracanonical sources on the Old Testament[47] or even on oral tradition.[48]

On the other hand, it is quite likely that New Testament writers do allude to extracanonical materials.[49] It would not be surprising, for example, that if Paul knew and cited secular Greek authors,[50] he would also be free to use materials of Jewish provenance.

Moreover, it is obvious that if the appeal to secular Greek authors does not entail that they are regarded as canonical by the New Testament writers, then the presence of allusions to the Apocrypha or (in a much smaller number of cases) to the pseudepigrapha does not establish the canonical status of such documents. Even the Old Testament writers used source material that they evidently did not regard as canonical (e.g., the Book of the Wars of the Lord, Nu 21:14). The New Testament authors never designate extracanonical literature as Scripture. The closest approach to such a designation occurs in Jude 14–15. Here a quotation of *1 Enoch* 1:9 is introduced as a genuine prophecy—*Proephēteusen de kai toutois hebdomos apo Adam Henōch*. Obviously *1 Enoch* was highly regarded by Jude, but whether it had canonical status cannot be determined.[51] As will be seen below, the Enoch literature was also valued by the Qumran community, but here, too, the question of its canonicity cannot be definitely answered. There seems to be no compelling reason, therefore, to conclude that the Old Testament canon of Jesus and the Apostles was other than the twenty-two (twenty-four) book canon of Josephus and later Rabbinic Judaism.

E. AN ALEXANDRIAN CANON?

Some assert that the Greek translation of the Old Testament (called the Septuagint or LXX) offers evidence that the canon of diaspora Judaism, particularly as it was represented in Alexandria, was different from that of Palestinian Judaism. While initially the Septuagint translation involved only the Pentateuch, the whole of the Old Testament was eventually rendered into Greek, most of it before the beginning of the Christian era.[52] The LXX codices preserved from the fourth and fifth centuries show significant variations from both the ordering and the number of books in the Jewish sources cited above.

While the books of Moses are always first in Septuagint ordering, the Prophets and Hagiographa are broken up and rearranged according to their literary style or content or their presumed authorship.[53] Further, the LXX enlarges upon the Old Testament canon by including a number of documents originating in the period from 200 B.C. to A.D. 100. Codex Vaticanus (4th c.) includes all of the Apocrypha with the exception of 1 and 2 Maccabees, Codex Sinaiticus (4th c.) has Tobit, Judith, 1 and 2 Maccabees, Wisdom, and Ecclesiasticus, and Codex Alexandrinus (5th c.) adds all of the Apocrypha plus 3 and 4 Maccabees and the Psalms of Solomon.[54]

Eighteenth-century scholars,[55] in an effort to explain the difference between the Septuagint codices and the Jewish reckoning (of twenty-two or twenty-four books), developed the hypothesis of a distinctive canon among Alexandrian Jews. According to this hypothesis, the liberal attitudes of diaspora Judaism would have permitted in Alexandria and elsewhere a more expansive biblical canon than that recognized in Palestine. It was this canon that was appropriated by the Christian church. As Christianity grew and expanded beyond the borders of Palestine, Christians would naturally have adopted the canon of the Hellenistic Jews around them. Consequently, the larger Alexandrian collection became the fixed canon in Christian usage.

With good reason this hypothesis has now largely been abandoned. (1) It has long been recognized that the evidence of the LXX is late and derives from Christian sources. The Septuagint, thus, cannot simply be assumed to give directed evidence for the canonical views of Alexandrian Jewry, certainly not those of the first century A.D.[56] (2) Alexandria itself yields little evidence for a broader canon. Philo does not cite extracanonical literature as Scripture, although, as noted above, he makes very few references even to biblical materials outside of the Pentateuch. Further, two Alexandrian Fathers (Origen and Athanasius) both state that the Jewish canon was twenty-two books, and both give canonical listings that vary only slightly from the Jewish reckoning.[57] (3) There is no evidence for the kind of independence of diaspora Judaism from Palestinian Judaism that is assumed by this theory. A. C. Sundberg, Jr., correctly asks,

> Do not the proponents of the Alexandrian canon hypothesis really have to show how it was that Alexandria and Judaism of the dispersion deviated from the practice in Palestine with respect to canon while the Temple (to which pilgrims from all Judaism made pilgrimages for holy days) stood but quickly submitted to the decision of the schools at Jamnia after the disruption of Palestinian Judaism in A.D. 70? Such acquiescence to the Jamnia decisions is hardly understandable except on the assumption of the accustomed leadership of Palestine throughout Judaism generally.[58]

F. THE APOCRYPHA

Sundberg's monograph, *The Old Testament of the Early Church* (1964), which has been widely influential in bringing about the demise of the Alexandrian hypothesis, has also served to revive another ancient question, namely, the authority of the Old Testament Apocrypha. While we have argued for a closed canon in Palestinian and diaspora Judaism during the first Christian century, Sundberg adopts the thesis that in Judaism prior to A.D. 90 the third division of the canon was amorphous: "in addition to closed collections of Law and Prophets, a wide religious literature without definite bounds circulated throughout Judaism as holy scripture before Jamnia."[59] Evidence for the openness of the third division of the canon is found in (a) the usage of extracanonical literature by the Qumran community, New Testament authors, and early church fathers, (b) the divergence in LXX codices, and (c) the difference of opinions among the early Fathers on the extent of the Old Testament canon.[60] After A.D. 70, Judaism and Christianity went their separate ways and thus established the bounds of the canon relatively independently of one another. In any case, no appeal can be made either to later Jewish statements or to New Testament writers to justify the Christian canon of the Old Testament; there are no historical antecedents upon which to ground the church's decisions.

The implications of Sundberg's position for Protestants are serious. Since the early days of the Reformation, Protestant theologians have supported their more restrictive view of the Old Testament canon by appeal to the presumed canon of Jesus and the Apostles. But, says Sundberg,

> there is reason to ask . . . whether this position is any longer tenable. It now appears that the bases upon which Luther and subsequent Protestants separated the books of the Apocrypha from the Christian Old Testament are historically inaccurate or misleading. Not only was the so-called Palestinian or Hebrew canon not closed in Jesus' day, but a *de facto* Hebrew canon paralleling the later Jamnia canon did not exist either.[61]

The alternative for Protestantism, Sundberg says, is either to return to a pre-Reformation position (implying acceptance of the canonical status of the Apocrypha) or to develop a new (nonhistorical) apologetic for its Old Testament canon.[62]

Several criticisms may be offered to the theory of an undefined pre-Jamnian canon. (1) Sundberg relies heavily on the thesis that the delimitation of the Hagiographa is the product of the Jamnia Council. However, the constitutive nature of these rabbinic discussions for the closure of the canon has been too severely undermined to bear the weight of Sundberg's hypothesis. (2) The appeal to the variation of the earliest (4th and 5th c.) Septuagint manuscripts from one another and from the order and numbering of the rabbinic sources is not decisive. These LXX codices are Christian productions and questionable sources from which to derive the shape of the Hebrew canon in New Testament times. If, as previously noted, this criticism is valid for the "Alexandrian hypothesis," it must also tell against Sundberg's reconstruction. (3) Reference to the church fathers for support of an undefined canon of the first century is open to precisely the same objection as the appeal to the LXX. Nor does Sundberg give sufficient attention to assessing the relative value of the patristic sources.[63] (4) Even if it is the case that the Qumran sect recognized as Scripture a broader range of materials than did later Judaism (see discussion below), the views of this group cannot without explicit evidence be extrapolated to all of Judaism outside Qumran.

There is then no compelling reason to revise the historic Protestant evaluation of the Apocrypha. The New Testament writers did not acknowledge these books as Scripture, nor did a significant number of the Patristic writers who witness to the Hebrew tradition of twenty-two biblical books.[64] That a wider range of books than those of the Hebrew canon came to be included in the Septuagint was due in part to the increasing ignorance among Gentile Christians of Jewish views on the subject. In addition, the move from scrolls to codex form may well have added to the confusion of the early Christians. As Bruce Metzger observes,

> Books which heretofore had never been regarded by the Jews as having any more than a certain edifying significance were now placed by Christian scribes in one codex side by side with the acknowledged books of the Hebrew canon. Thus it would happen that what was first a matter of convenience in making such books of secondary status available among Christians became a factor in giving the impression that all of the books within such a codex were to be regarded as authoritative.[65]

The translation of the Septuagint (including the Apocrypha) into Latin in the latter part of the second century A.D.[66] strengthened the case for a broader Old Testament canon in the Western church; and, in the fifth century, Augustine's advocacy of the Apocrypha prevailed over Jerome's endorsement of the Jewish canon.[67] Perhaps describing the Protestant canon as "a failure on historical grounds"[68] reveals more about the historian than about the canon.

G. THE DEAD SEA SCROLLS

The discovery of the first of the Dead Sea Scrolls in 1947 in a cave near the Wadi Qumran opened a whole new field for discussion relative to the Old Testament canon. During the decade to follow, some forty thousand manuscript fragments were recovered. These were originally parts of about 380 separate books, 100 of which were biblical texts.[69] Of the later Jewish canon, only Esther is unrepresented, whereas Deuteronomy, Isaiah, the Minor Prophets, and Psalms are represented by ten or more copies. The other manuscripts include works of the Apocrypha, pseudepigrapha, and writings that reflect the specific concerns of the Qumran sect.[70] However, while there is potentially a vast resource here for study of the progress of the canon during the closing centuries of the Second Jewish Commonwealth, the evidence is only indirect—the Qumran materials preserve no explicit dogmatic statement on the nature or limits of the canon.[71] Moreover, the canonical views of the Qumran Covenanters are not necessarily those of their contemporaries.[72]

Scholars generally agree that at Qumran the Law and the Prophets were regarded as fully authoritative Scripture.[73] The second of these categories, "the Prophets," may well have been a general category comprising all works outside the Pentateuch that were regarded as Scripture.[74] Among the *Nebi'im*, the twelve Minor Prophets already were copied together on a single scroll, and there were commentaries on six of the twelve.[75] As far as the Hagiographa are concerned, Psalms, Proverbs, Daniel,[76] and probably Job and Lamentations were considered Scripture,[77] but the position of Ruth, Song of Songs, Ecclesiastes, Ezra-Nehemiah, Chronicles, and Esther is not clear.[78]

Quite a few scholars believe that the absence of any manuscript evidence for Esther among the Dead Sea materials reflects a negative attitude toward the book. This is the view of Patrick Skehan, who notes, however, that the attitude of the community probably reflects its distinctive theological bias:

> Esther alone, of the Hebrew canon of the Old Testament, has still not been found at Qumran. It is easy to discount an argument from silence, but when one considers the late origin of the Purim festival with which Esther is connected, its partial identification with the victories of Judas the Maccabee (whose Hasmonean kindred were abhorred at Qumran), and rigidity in matters of the liturgical calendar that characterized the Qumran group, it seems more likely that the book was avoided than that it was simply not known.[79]

Of the Apocrypha, only manuscripts of Tobit, Ecclesiasticus, and perhaps the Epistle of Jeremiah have been identified, nor are there any distinct quotations from the Apocrypha, although there may be allusions to Ben Sirach.[80] There is no reason to think, therefore, that the Qumran sect regarded any of the Apocrypha as Scripture. Several other documents—Ian H. Eybers notes particularly *Jubilees*, the "Book of Meditation," *Enoch*, and *The Testament of Levi*[81]—enjoyed high esteem in the community, but whether they were regarded as Scripture is uncertain. Patrick Skehan speaks for a broad group of scholars when he concludes, "All in all, the Qumran library gives the impression of a certain selectivity, but hardly any fine distinction between a closed canon and all other texts."[82]

The discovery at Qumran of over thirty distinct texts of the Psalms has had particular significance for the discussion of the canon. Not only do these manuscripts provide exemplars a thousand years older than any previously known; they also include psalms additional to the biblical Psalter and arrange certain of the canonical psalms differently from the Masoretic order.[83] Attention has focused on the Psalms Scroll from Cave 11 (11QPs[a]).[84] This scroll contains forty-one biblical psalms plus another eight noncanonical compositions. Of the latter, three are psalms known from ancient versions of the Old Testament (Syriac, Greek, Latin),[85] one is a canticle from Ecclesiasticus (51:13ff.), and four are previously unknown compositions. Most of the variations from the "standard" Masoretic ordering are in the last third of the Psalter.[86] J. A. Sanders has argued from this evidence that as late as A.D. 50, the Psalter at Qumran, although authoritative, was not fully defined, at least in books III–V.[87] On the other hand, some suggest that the Psalms Scroll represents a nonauthoritative liturgical variant of a previously fixed Psalter.[88]

Thus, the Qumran materials witness to the scriptural status of the Law and the Prophets. The full extent of the second division is not established; possibly it included most or all of the materials presently grouped among the Hagiographa. The questions about books of the third division arise in part from lack of evidence. Certain extracanonical compositions (*Jubilees* and *1 Enoch*) were highly esteemed, and it is conceivable that they were acknowledged as Scripture, although again there is no positive evidence for such a view. The Book of Psalms was clearly canonical, but the precise order and content of the Psalter were still in question.

H. THE CESSATION OF PROPHECY

The remaining evidence from the pre-Christian centuries may be treated briefly. As with the Qumran materials, so here as well, we meet with no dogmatic or definitional statements relative to the canon. According to 2 Maccabees 2:13, Nehemiah "founded a library, and collected the books about the kings and prophets [*ta peri basileōn kai prophētōn biblia*], and the writings of David [*ta tou Daveid*] and letters of kings about votive offerings [*epistolas basileōn peri anathēmatōn*]." The first grouping apparently corresponds to the Former and Latter Prophets, the writings of David point to the Psalms, and letters of kings could well refer to Ezra-Nehemiah. Whether any sort of "canonization" is implied is uncertain. In 15:9 the dual title "the Law and the Prophets" suggests a usage similar to the New Testament.

The prologue to Sirach (c. 125 B.C.) witnesses to a tripartite division of Scripture;[89] however, the contents of the divisions are not specified. Some contend that Sirach itself (c. 180 B.C.) reflects a tripartite scheme, but this is unlikely.[90] Reference to "the twelve prophets" (49:10) indicates that at least by the beginning of the second century B.C. the Minor Prophets formed a recognized corpus. The sequence of Isaiah, Jeremiah, Ezekiel, and the twelve prophets (48:22–49:10) could reflect an early canonical ordering, but the context suggests that the order may be merely chronological.

What is more important for the development of the canon is that already in the centuries before the Christian era, Judaism understood that a qualitative change had taken place in the manner in which God spoke to His people. David Aune has recently argued that various manifestations of prophecy continued among the Palestinian Jews throughout the Second Temple period.[91] Yet, the term "prophet" (nabi'; prophētēs) was customarily used only of the classical Israelite prophets or of the eschatological prophets who were expected to appear at the end of the age. Aune judges that "canonical and eschatological prophecy had a special status that distinguished them from prophetic activity in the intervening period."[92] We have seen that Josephus viewed prophecy and canon as correlative phenomena; the canon was closed because the line of the prophets failed. But there is little doubt that Josephus reflected a more ancient conception.[93]

According to 1 Maccabees (c. 100 B.C.), prophetic ministry had ceased: "After the death of Judas, . . . there was great distress in Israel, such as had not been since the time that prophets had ceased to appear among them" (1Macc 9:23–27). The implication of this text is that there has already been an extended lapse of time since the days when God spoke to Israel through the prophets. The author also looks forward to the day when a "trustworthy prophet should arise" (1Macc 14:41; cf. 4:46). The hope for a renewal of prophecy may reflect biblical promises concerning the Day of the Lord (Joel 2:28–29; Mal 4:5–6) and the coming of the prophet like Moses (Dt 18:15).[94] This general perspective is paralleled at a later date by the New Testament. Both John the Baptist and Jesus are variously identified as "Elijah" or "the prophet" (Jn 1:19ff.; 6:14; 7:40; Ac 3:22–23; 7:37), and Peter interprets the Holy Spirit's coming at Pentecost as fulfilling Joel's prediction of the eschatological renewal of prophecy (Ac 2:16–21).

The same outlook may have been present at Qumran. The fact that the sect wrote commentaries only on biblical books suggests that these books stood in a place of unique authority that set them apart from later works. It should be noted that Qumran looked for the appearance of a prophet in connection with the coming of the two Messiahs of Aaron and Israel (1QS 9:11), and this may indicate that the covenanters recognized that prophecy was in abeyance. At least the two ideas are compatible.

On the other hand, the question is complicated by the enigmatic figure of the "Teacher of Righteousness." The Teacher was the leader and perhaps founder of the Qumran sect. Undoubtedly he was highly revered, and his exposition of the prophets carried great authority; in the view of the community, "the revelation was not complete or intelligible until the time of its fulfillment was made known, as it was to the Teacher of Righteousness."[95] David Aune follows a number of other scholars who believe that the Teacher was regarded by his followers as a prophet, even though he is never explicitly called such.[96] But even if prophecy was seen as operative in some sense at Qumran, this would not be incompatible with the understanding previously discussed that prophecy in its classical and canonical form had ceased. The great authority of the Teacher of Righteousness, therefore, says nothing for or against a fixed canon at Qumran.

I. SUMMARY

In the light of the preceding survey, we may attempt some reconstruction of the development of the Old Testament canon. In accord with the definition of canon given in the introduction, our concern is not merely with the status of a writing as inspired Scripture but also with its distinctiveness from other writings and its place as part of a recognized corpus. With regard to scriptural status, there is no historical evidence for the biblical books "acquiring" such a position. The earliest references to biblical books (or to portions of them) treat them as authoritative. Questions over a few of the books are raised by the rabbis at Jamnia or later, but these presuppose that the books are already generally accepted. The Protestant Reformers spoke of Scripture as "self-authenticated" (*autopiston*). Hence, its authority does not depend on its recognition by the people of God; rather, it is constitutive of the very existence of the people of God.[97] While the historical evidence does not demonstrate such a claim, neither does it disprove it. We have suggested, however, that the recognition of the canon is a related but slightly different issue: how and when were the books gathered into closed collections?

A number of scholars have questioned whether the tripartite division of the canon reflects directly the history of canonization. For example, E. J. Young writes that "there certainly is no evidence to support the view that there were three canons, that the Pentateuch was first accepted as canonical, then, at a later time, the Prophets and, finally, the Writings."[98] Yet, it is reasonable to assume that the canonical recognition of the Pentateuch took precedence chronologically over the rest of the Old Testament. According to R. T. Beckwith,

> The likelihood that this was so arises from the fact that it was basically the work of a single prophet of very early date, which was edited after his death but was not open to continual addition, whereas the other sections of the Old Testament were produced by authors of later date, whose number was not complete until after the return from exile.[99]

The formation of the remaining books of the Old Testament as a delimited corpus must obviously postdate the exile. A certain amount of time would have been necessary in order to confirm the cessation of classical prophecy. Only when the Jews became conscious of this qualitative change in the divine revelation would the idea of a limited canon surface. The earliest evidence, as we have seen, is Ecclesiasticus (c. 180 B.C.), yet the contents of the second and third divisions are not stated. That some collection of the prophetic writings was started much earlier is witnessed by Daniel 9:2, where the prophecy of Jeremiah is reckoned a part of the Scriptures.

It does not appear that the Prophets and the Writings formed two rigidly distinct categories prior to the second century A.D. Initially they may have formed one general collection that was only later divided into two sections. However, the division had been made at least by the end of the second century B.C., when it appears in the prologue of Ben Sirach.[100]

Placing a *terminus ad quem* on the completion of the Old Testament canon is difficult, partly due to an almost total lack of evidence. Ancient Jewish and Christian tradition connect the closing of the canon with the ministry of Ezra. But if the idea of the canon is a historical one that included the belief that the line of the ancient prophets had ceased, then a date subsequent to Ezra is more likely. R. K. Harrison suggests a date about 300 B.C. for the fixation of the essential parts of the Old Testament, even though discussion of certain books continued into the Christian era.[101] Beckwith contends, however, that the closing of the second and third divisions was the work of Judas Maccabaeus about 165 B.C.[102] Yet, the tradition concerning Judas (2Macc 2:14) says only that he collected books that were lost because of the war. This could have involved final collections of the canonical books, but this is not demanded by the text.

What can be said with confidence is that *at least* a century before the Christian era, the Jews were conscious that prophecy in its classical form belonged to the past. If the failure of prophecy and the closure of the canon were understood as correlative ideas in intertestamental Judaism (as they were later with Josephus), then a date of about 100 B.C. would seem to be the latest that could be entertained on the basis of our evidence. On the other hand, if Sirach 48:22–49:10 does reflect a canonical ordering, a substantially earlier date for closure would be likely.

III. NEW TESTAMENT CANON

New Testament canon study confronts us with the same problem as for the Old Testament, namely, that the New Testament nowhere includes a canonical list or table of contents. Rather, the collection and definition of a body of writings parallel in authority to the Old Testament was a process that spanned several centuries. The closing of the New Testament canon belongs to the fourth and fifth centuries, and here we shall begin our considerations. From this point of a formulated canonical consciousness we will turn to the earlier centuries to trace the lines of canonical development from the first through the third centuries.

A. THE CLOSING OF THE NEW TESTAMENT CANON

A principal source for establishing the canonical view of the early church is the *Ecclesiastical History* of Eusebius of Caesarea (c. 260– c. 340), whose own position is deeply indebted to two Alexandrian Fathers (Clement and Origen). Eusebius describes the canon using a threefold classification: the recognized books *(homologoumenoi)*, the disputed books *(antilegomenoi)*, and the writings advanced by heretics in the name of the apostles *(hai onomati tōn apostolōn pros tōn hairetikōn prophēromenai)*.[103] In the first category, Eusebius places the four Gospels, Acts, the Pauline Epistles, 1 Peter, 1 John, and (with some reservation) the Apocalypse of John. The fourteen letters of Paul include the Epistle to the Hebrews, although Eusebius is aware that the Roman church rejected the letter as not being from Paul.[104] The classification of disputed books is subdivided into those books that are generally accepted—James, Jude, 2 Peter, 2 and 3 John—and those that are not genuine *(nothoi)*—*The Acts of Paul*, *The Shepherd of Hermas*, *The Apocalypse of Peter*, *The Epistle of Barnabas*, *The Teachings of the Apostles*, and (perhaps) the Apocalypse of John. The third category of heretical writings comprises "gospels such as those of Peter and Thomas, and Matthias, and some others besides, or Acts such as those of Andrew and John and the other apostles."[105]

The main lines of the New Testament are evident. The Gospels, Acts, and the Pauline correspondence are universally recognized. Eusebius' statement about the remaining books reflects the discussions of the preceding centuries. Uncertainty about the Epistle to the Hebrews turned in part on the problem of authorship. Canonical recognition for the epistle had come earlier in the East because its Pauline authorship was maintained at least from the time of Pantaenus (teacher of Clement and the first known head of the catechetical school at Alexandria). In the West, recognition of Hebrews came only in the later part of the fourth century,[106] but eventually its association with Paul and its inclusion in Jerome's Vulgate were to secure its position. Eusebius knows that opinions on the seven Catholic Epistles varied. For his part, he accepts 1 Peter and 1 John. The two shorter letters of John, he suggests, may be the work of the Evangelist or of another with the same name.[107] However, he denies the authenticity of James, 2 Peter, and Jude, though he admits that they have been widely read and studied in the churches.[108] The Johannine Apocalypse, though recognized by most in the second century, had fallen under suspicion in the East.[109] Eusebius himself waffles on the status of Revelation, ranging from initial acceptance of the book as a genuine work of the apostle to its complete rejection as a forgery of the heretic Cerinthus. In the end, he seems to accept the canonical status of the book while denying its apostolic authorship.[110]

Questions regarding Eusebius' statements on the canon continued through the fourth century, although the various catalogues of the New Testament show an increasing agreement within the church. The Cheltenham manuscript discovered by Theodor Mommsen in 1885 is thought to represent the usage of North Africa about A.D. 360. It lists our present New Testament books with the exception of Hebrews, James, and Jude.[111] The first witness to the current twenty-seven books of the New Testament as alone canonical is Athanasius' Easter letter of A.D. 367. Even if his letter is only *prescriptive* rather than *descriptive* of the view of the Alexandrian church,[112] it remains as a straw in the wind. By the close of the fourth century a number of councils addressed themselves to the extent of the canon. The sixtieth canon of the Synod of Laodicea (A.D. 367) is a catalogue of all our present twenty-seven books except the Apocalypse. Although the manuscript evidence "is decidedly against the authenticity of the Catalogue as an integral part of the text," it may well represent a fourth-century addition to the Laodicean Canons.[113] Again, the Third Council of Carthage (A.D. 397) prescribed as canonical the current New Testament corpus, and the same list was confirmed at Carthage in 419. Augustine was present at both councils, and his views were probably decisive for the definition of the canon.

In the East a more restrictive outlook on the canon was represented among many Fathers. In Syria the usage of the churches at the end of the fourth and beginning of the fifth centuries is indicated by the Peshitta version, which includes twenty-two New Testament books (omitting 2 Peter, 2 and 3 John, Jude, and the Apocalypse). This conservatism marked various representatives of the school of Antioch and may be seen in John Chrysostom (c. A.D. 347–407), whose New Testament probably coincided with that of the Peshitta.[114] Outside the sphere of Syrian influence there was growing acceptance for all seven of the Catholic Epistles, while doubts still remained with many on the authenticity of the Apocalypse. Yet even in regard to the latter book there were voices of acceptance in different quarters.[115]

It is appropriate then to speak of the canon as having achieved its present form throughout most of the church during the fifth century. The consensus, to be sure, was not perfect. The native (as distinct from the Greek-speaking) Syrian church recognizes only the more limited canon of the Peshitta to the present day. The Ethiopian church, on the other hand, acknowledges the canonical books of the larger Christian church plus eight additional works dealing primarily with church order.[116] Yet it is fair to say that wherever Christians in particular localities have been concerned to know the extent of the

New Testament and have searched for this knowledge in a spirit of
open communication with the larger church, unanimity of opinion
has generally been the result. So it is significant that the reopening of
the questions of canon by the leaders of the Protestant Reformation
led to a narrowing of the Old Testament canon over against Roman
Catholic usage but effected no similar change in the extent of the New
Testament canon.[117]

B. THE FORMATION OF THE NEW TESTAMENT CANON

The present New Testament canon is the product of the fourth
and fifth centuries. But this raises two important questions. Is it
merely an offspring of the church's later history, thereby testifying
only to the wisdom (or foolishness!) of the early Christians in selecting
and authorizing particular writings from its past? Alternatively, is the
closed canon—even though not explicitly delineated in the apostolic
period or in the New Testament—yet properly seen as the logical and
organic development of certain principles resident in the New
Testament documents and in redemptive-historical events that
brought the church into existence? The New Testament itself suggests
four crucial factors that support the second possibility.[118]

1. The Authority of the Old Testament

From the beginning the church acknowledged the authority of
the Old Testament. The "Law," the "Law and the Prophets," or the
"Scriptures" were regarded as inspired *(theopneustos)* and, therefore,
"profitable" *(ōphelimos)* for believers (2Ti 3:16). Paul knew that
"everything that was written in the past was written to teach us, so
that through endurance and the encouragement of the Scriptures we
might have hope" (Ro 15:4; cf. 4:23–24; 1Co 9:10; 10:11).

This approach to the Old Testament is based on a view of history
framed in terms of prophecy and fulfillment. What the prophets had
foretold has been fulfilled in the death and resurrection of Jesus
Christ (1Pe 1:10–12); therefore, the words of the prophet had to be
attended to "as to a light shining in a dark place" (2Pe 1:19). With the
same understanding, Paul sought to evangelize his own people "and
tried to convince them about Jesus from the Law of Moses and from
the Prophets" (Ac 28:23).

Such a perspective on the Old Testament originated from Jesus
Himself. For our Lord, all of the Hebrew Scriptures could generally be
classified under the category of "Law" and thus could "not be broken"
(Jn 10:34–35). The divine pleasure in Jesus as the Servant of Yahweh
(Mt 3:17; cf. Isa 42:1) has its ground in His humble submission to
Scripture—"it is written" (Mt 4:4,7,10). Jesus' mission was not to
abolish the Law or the Prophets but to fulfill them (Mt 5:17). The
Christological interpretation of the Old Testament is thus seen to
have been rooted in Jesus' teachings; had His opponents believed the

words of Moses they would have believed His words, for Moses wrote of Him (Jn 5:46). Indeed, the whole Old Testament ("the Law of Moses, the Prophets, and the Psalms") prophesied of Jesus' death and resurrection (Lk 24:25–27,44–47; cf. 1Co 15:3–4).

The prominent place that Jesus and the early church gave to the Old Testament indicates that Christianity, from its inception, was a religion whose existence and self-identity were structured (in part) by a canon, a closed collection of uniquely authoritative writings. There was, thus, a canonical consciousness in the church from its very beginning. If this would not have led the church necessarily to *expect* an expansion of the canonical literature, it would surely have meant that such an expansion could not have seemed foreign or inappropriate.

2. The Authority of Jesus

"The earliest motive force, one that had been at work from the beginning of the Apostolic Age, was the supreme reverence in which the words and teachings of Christ Jesus were held."[119] We may go further to state that the words of Jesus and the revelatory events of His life, death, and resurrection formed the very heart and center of the canon that was to develop. In the freedom and confidence with which He opposed His own words to traditional teachings—"you have heard . . . but I say" (Mt 5:21–48)—His hearers recognized an authority above that of the custodians of the Law (Mt 7:28–29; cf. Mk 1:22; Lk 4:32). Jesus taught and acted as one conscious of His messianic dignity and divine prerogatives. If the claim to messiahship was nowhere overt, it was nevertheless sufficiently clear as to result in His crucifixion by the Jewish and Roman authorities.[120] In His bestowal of forgiveness (Mk 2:7; Lk 5:21), working of miracles (Jn 2:11), unique filial consciousness ("even calling God his own Father, making himself equal with God," Jn 5:18), and, above all, the Johannine "I am" statements, there was an implicit claim that the apostles made explicit in the light of the Resurrection.

The early church saw in the Resurrection the vindication (*edikaiōthē en pneumati*, 1Ti 3:16) of the person and ministry of Jesus. He had now been declared the Son of God with power (Ro 1:4), and His words were the rule of the church. Jesus was the Christ appointed for Israel, but He was also the prophet like Moses whose words could be ignored only with perilous consequence (Ac 3:19–23). But for the apostles, Jesus was not only the prophet *like* Moses; He was the eschatological prophet who brought God's word in its fullness and was therefore *superior* to Moses. The law came through Moses, but the revelation of God's truth and grace came through Jesus Christ (Jn 1:17). God had previously spoken by the prophets "at many times and in various ways," but He had now at the end of days spoken in one who was a son and whose intrinsic dignity was far above angels or prophets (Heb 1:1–3:6). If the word spoken by angels and mediated through the prophets was binding, how much more the word of the exalted Son (Heb 2:1–4; cf. 10:28–29)!

Here, then, lay the seed that would ultimately come to fruition in the church's recognition of the New Testament canon. From their conviction of the sovereign lordship of the resurrected Jesus and His presence with them in the ministry of the Holy Spirit grew the confidence with which they asserted their christological interpretation of the Old Testament. This conviction also ensured that the words of and about Jesus would be given the highest esteem, whether in oral or written form.

3. The authority of the apostles

The authority of Jesus for the early church was inseparable from the authority of the apostles. The word and work of Christ formed the "canon" of the first believers, but as part of that work "Jesus himself established the means, the formal authority, by which what was seen and heard in the fulness of time was to be *transmitted* and *communicated.*"[121]

The apostles were the official channels of revelation appointed by Christ Himself (Mk 3:14) as His plenipotentiary witnesses (Ac 10:39–42; 1Co 9:1; 15:5–7).[122] They were to speak for Him, and those who heard them heard Christ—"he who listens to you listens to me" (Lk 10:16). The apostles were pillars and foundation stones of the church (Mt 16:18; Gal 2:9; Eph 2:20; Rev 21:14), and therefore their function was unique and restricted to the first apostolic generation.[123]

The uniqueness of the apostolic ministry ensured that the words of the apostles would be regarded as a precious deposit entrusted to the church and in need of careful preservation (Jude 3; 1Ti 6:20; 2Ti 1:14; 2:2). New Testament references to "tradition" (*paradosis*) indicate the importance of the apostolic testimony. Tradition referred to the authoritative content of religious beliefs and practices that were to be "handed on" (*paradidōmi*) faithfully and "received" (*paralambanō*) in trust by the next generation.[124] While Jesus spoke critically of Jewish traditions that nullified the Word of God (Mt 15:6; Mk 7:13), Paul could use this terminology quite positively to designate various aspects of the apostolic message, whether doctrinal instruction (1Co 15:3ff.), ethical admonition (2Th 3:6; Ro 6:17; Php 4:9), or ecclesiastical practice (1Co 11:2,23).[125]

The authority of the tradition lay in its source; that is, it was "from the Lord" (*apo tou kyriou*, 1Co 11:23) in the sense that the historical Jesus stood at the chronological beginning of the chain of witnesses and, perhaps also, as Oscar Cullmann has argued, "that the exalted Lord acts through the apostles to authenticate and confirm the tradition."[126] The apostolic tradition could be oral or written, and both carried the same authority: "So then, brothers, stand firm and hold to the teachings we passed on to you, whether by word of mouth or by letter" (2Th 2:15). The oral proclamation claimed a chronological or historical priority; it was here that the message of redemption was first formed, and the New Testament documents took rise out of that proclamation. Subsequently, however, written deposit became the definitive form of the apostolic tradition. As Herman Ridderbos notes,

> That such would be the case is evident from the very nature of the matter; it is simply a natural development. With the passing of time and the church spreading over the whole world, the apostles could only keep written contact with the churches. And with the death of the apostles, oral tradition diminished in certainty and became less trustworthy, so that the written fixation of the apostolic tradition naturally acquired more significance.[127]

Although New Testament authors made no explicit claims to be writing Scripture, they did expect at least some of their writings to be circulated among the churches and read in the presence of the congregation (1Th 5:27; Col 4:16; 1Co 14:37; Rev 1:3,11), a practice paralleling the reading of the Old Testament in the synagogue. The Pauline correspondence was so highly esteemed it was placed on an equal footing with the Old Testament—"the other Scriptures" (2Pe 3:16).[128]

How early the New Testament literature was collected and circulated is impossible to establish. Jean Carmignac has argued that the contrast drawn by Paul between the New Testament and the Old (2Co 3:6,14) presupposes that if the latter could be read (v 14), so could the former. He does not suggest, of course, that the New Testament collection was complete but only that it was a "collection important enough and typical enough in order to have provoked the creation of a suitable comprehensive title: 'New Testament,' and to have imposed on the works of the Old Covenant the correlative term: 'Old Testament.'"[129] If Carmignac's position is valid, it confirms in a striking way that the notion of an authoritative body of literature parallel to the Old Testament was organically related to the church's beginning.

4. The rise of false teaching

The New Testament evidences the concern of the first-century church to preserve the apostolic tradition from distortion by false teachers. Both Matthew and Mark recall Jesus' warning of the coming of the false prophets (Mt 7:15; 24:11,24; Mk 13:22), a warning that His followers would repeat to their own congregations (1Jn 4:1; cf. 2Pe 2:1). Moreover, the New Testament writers considered false teaching of various types not only a threat but a common evil in first-century Christianity.[130]

This concern with false teaching also strengthens the connection between the apostolic church and the very idea of a New Testament canon. Since 1934, when Walter Bauer's *Rechtgläubigkeit und Ketzerei im ältesten Christentum* appeared,[131] the traditional use of "heresy" to designate movements that were theologically deviant and chronologically secondary has been strongly contested. "Orthodoxy" for Bauer was merely a tag for the winners of the political and theological battles in the early church. In many areas, in fact, the original manifestation of Christianity was one that would later be judged heretical by the orthodox. Bauer's thesis has had a profound influence on the understanding of the nature and formation of the New Testament canon.[132] Because the New Testament is understood as the documentary deposit of the process of self-definition by the "orthodox" party, it follows that the very notion of a canon—or at least *this particular canon*—must equally be as secondary as "orthodoxy" itself. The door is then open to discover some approach to Christian origins (other than a canonical one) as more in keeping with the original spirit of Christianity.

In this connection Bauer has found an articulate spokesman in Helmut Koester,[133] a former student of Rudolf Bultmann. Koester sees the first century as a period of doctrinal flux and change for which "the criteria for determining 'right' and 'wrong' belief which were worked out toward the end of the second century by anti-gnostic fathers have no validity."[134] Since these later criteria include the New Testament documents themselves, the modern theologian can no longer compellingly appeal to the New Testament for a standard of legitimatization. "For historical inquiry, the NT itself has no special claim to have made the correct and orthodox use of the criterion of faith. The canonical writings must be part and parcel of the historical questioning."[135] In the best existentialist fashion, Koester argues that no tradition—including the tradition incorporated into the canon—can function as a norm for what orthodox theology must say. *True* orthodoxy must sit loose to its past, and, paradoxically, *true* heresy is "the uncritical continued use of traditional language, whether the latter be of 'Christian' or of 'secular' origin."[136]

The New Testament concern to refute false teaching is instructive. There is no support here for Koester's laissez-faire interpretation of primitive Christianity, if such an understanding conceives of an ideal state in which the church existed free from the notion of authoritative traditions (the Old Testament, the teaching of Jesus, and the witness of the apostles). Such a reconstruction accords better with the disposition of twentieth-century existentialist philosophy than with the religious outlook of the first Christians.

An important article by I. Howard Marshall surveys the New Testament attitude toward false teaching in the light of Bauer's thesis on orthodoxy and heresy. Marshall grants that there was diversity and development in the theologies of the New Testament writings, but this is not to be equated, he argues, with a lack of distinction between orthodoxy and heresy.[137]

That the early Christians recognized a difference between true and false teaching is patent in the pages of the New Testament. In the Pastoral Epistles, "sound teaching" (1Ti 1:10; 6:3; 2Ti 1:13; 4:3; Tit 1:9; 2:1) rooted in "faithful words" (1Ti 1:15; 3:1; 4:9; 2Ti 2:11; Tit 1:9; 3:8) stands in contrast to "strange teaching" (1Ti 1:3; 6:3) or "the opposing ideas of what is falsely called knowledge" (1Ti 6:20) propagated by "mere talkers and deceivers" (Tit 1:10). Warnings elsewhere to guard against false teachers, false prophets, or false apostles (Mt 7:15; 24:11,24 [par. Mk 13:22]; 2Co 11:13; 2Pe 2:1; 1Jn 2:26–27; 4:1–6; 2Jn 7; Rev 2:2,20) who corrupt the gospel of Christ (2Co 11:4; Gal 1:6–9; Php 3:17–19; Jude 4) present a similar pattern. We may conclude with Marshall that the theory of Bauer (and Koester) does not fit the evidence of the New Testament:

> The New Testament writers one and all regard themselves as upholders of the truth of the gospel, and they often see quite clearly where the lines of what is compatible with the gospel and what is not compatible are to be drawn. And while it is possible that in some places the beginnings of Christianity came from people later regarded as heretical, it is not the case that orthodoxy was a later development.[138]

C. THE APOSTOLIC FATHERS

The writings of the Apostolic Fathers comprise a variety of materials that reflect the progress of Christianity from the closing decades of the first century to about the middle of the second century. Their concerns run more to practical and moral issues of the expanding church than to theological reflection. These works contain no formulated doctrine of Scripture or canon, and yet there is much that is suggestive of later development.

Though actually anonymous, *1 Clement* has from ancient times been associated with the presbyter-bishop of Rome who was active in that city during the closing decades of the first century A.D. The letter itself is most frequently dated c. A.D. 96.[139] Clement writes in behalf of the Roman church to the Corinthian church, encouraging peace, unity, and submission to their leaders.

Clement makes wide reference to the Old Testament, citing it with a variety of introductory formulas: "it is written," "Scripture says," "he/it says."[140] His approach is similar to what has already been observed in the New Testament. Clement can appeal to the Old Testament for prophecies regarding the coming of Christ or for direct moral teachings for the Christian church. Yet his method is thoroughly Christocentric: Christ Himself calls us through the words of the Old Testament,[141] the reality of salvation in Christ forms "the glorious and venerable canon of our tradition" (*kanōn tēs paradoseōs hēmōn*).[142] Thus, Jesus' words are quoted in parallel with those of the Old Testament and accorded equal authority.[143] It is evident that Clement is familiar with the traditions of the Synoptics (the Gospel of

John is less likely), but whether he knows these as embodied in our present Gospels or from extracanonical sources, either oral or written, is debated. Donald Hagner argues that Clement "probably knew at least one, if not more than one, of the Synoptics,"[144] although his two citations of the words of Jesus (13.1–2; 46.7–8) show no definite literary dependence on the Synoptics.

For Clement, the apostles also possess authority because they stand in a direct line of succession: "The Apostles received the Gospel for us from the Lord Jesus Christ, Jesus the Christ was sent from God. The Christ therefore is from God and the Apostles from the Christ."[145] So the apostles had received perfect foreknowledge (*prognōsis*) from the Lord on the basis of which they appointed successors to their own ministry. Clearly, Clement views the generation of the apostles as gone.[146] The obvious appeal, therefore, must be to the writings of the apostles: "Take up the epistle of the blessed Paul the Apostle. What did he first write to you at the beginning of his preaching?"[147]

Clement's reference to 1 Corinthians is the only time he explicitly identifies a New Testament writing; however, there is evidence of his familiarity with a wider range of the canonical materials. In addition to his probable knowledge of (at least one of) the Synoptics and the reference to 1 Corinthians, he demonstrates a knowledge of Hebrews and Romans. There are probable allusions to Acts, Galatians, Ephesians, Philippians, 1 Timothy, Titus, 1 Peter, and James, and possible references to Colossians and 2 Timothy. It is difficult, though, to identify any allusion to 1 and 2 Thessalonians, Philemon, 2 Peter, Jude, or the Johannine literature.[148]

But if Clement evidences the powerful influence of the writings later incorporated into the New Testament, he still has no formal theory of a New Testament Scripture or canon. While the tradition that derives from Jesus and His apostles is authoritative, it is not authoritative in a specific form; at this period, no distinction is made between oral or written tradition. Clement himself never cites the New Testament with the introductory formulas used for Old Testament citations.[149] Even the two quotations of Jesus mentioned above are introduced simply by the call to "remember" the words of the Lord Jesus. In a setting where the church may call on living memories, the form of the tradition as "written" is less likely to be emphasized.

Quite similar to the views of Clement are those of Ignatius of Antioch. Condemned to martyrdom in the arena during the reign of Trajan (A.D. 98–117), he wrote six letters to various churches and another to Polycarp, bishop of Smyrna. Ignatius discusses his coming martyrdom, warns the churches against heretics, and exhorts them to unity and submission to the bishop.

Although Ignatius uses the Old Testament less than does Clement,[150] he shares Clement's estimate of its authority and meaning. The prophets are heard because they "lived according to Jesus Christ" and were "inspired by his grace."[151] Christians ought to love not only the gospel and the apostles but also the prophets, because they announced the advent of Christ and became His disciples.[152] It is in this context that one should understand Ignatius' dialogue with his (Judaizing?) opponents:

> For I heard some men saying, "if I find it not in the charters I do not believe in the Gospel," and when I said to that that it is in the Scripture, they answered me, "that is exactly the question." But to me the charters are Jesus Christ, the inviolable charter is his cross, and death, and resurrection, and the faith which is through him.[153]

Against the objection that the gospel is not to be found in the Old Testament (the "charters"), Ignatius affirms a thoroughly Christocentric interpretation as the only appropriate understanding of the ancient revelation. The emphasis seems to be not "that what the prophets say is inferior to what Christ and the apostles say, but that it is essentially the same, though less complete."[154]

Therefore, for Ignatius, Jesus Christ is the full revelation of God. Jesus is "our only teacher,"[155] and Christians are to be "imitators" (*mimētai*) of Him[156] in accordance with His instruction.[157] But together with Jesus stand the apostles.[158] By contrast, Ignatius makes no such claims for his own writings. Even though his letters demand a high place for the office of the bishop, he does not give orders as did Peter and Paul: "They were apostles, I am a convict; they were free, I am even until now a slave."[159]

Ignatius, like Clement, shows acquaintance with a wide range of New Testament materials. He mentions sayings of Jesus based on the Synoptic tradition (Matthew in particular).[160] But, in contrast to Clement, there are also allusions to the Gospel of John. Ignatius seems to know most of the Pauline Epistles, especially Romans and 1 Corinthians. There is considerable evidence for his knowledge of Ephesians and Colossians and probably also 2 Corinthians, Galatians, Philippians, and the Pastorals. His statement that Paul makes reference to the Ephesians "in every epistle"[161] suggests that Ignatius may know a collection of the Pauline letters.[162] Additionally, he may allude to either James or 1 Peter.[163]

In summary, we may say that Ignatius stresses the authority of God's revelation in Jesus Christ. This revelation is proclaimed through the prophets and the apostles. The teachings of the former are known through the Old Testament; similarly, for Ignatius, the apostles' teachings are known through their writings. There is, however, no indication that Ignatius viewed the apostolic writings as Scripture parallel to the Old Testament. For him the issue is the authority of the revelation—not its form, whether oral or written.[164]

As Ignatius was on his way to martyrdom, the church of Philippi wrote to Polycarp to request copies of any letters of Ignatius in his possession. Polycarp's reply is given in his letter to the Philippians. It is thought that the last two chapters were written first (c. 110?) as a cover letter for the Ignatian correspondence and that chapters 1–12 were written later, perhaps about 135.[165]

Polycarp's letter is saturated with biblical language and imagery, so that "his letter is a veritable mosaic of quotation and allusion to [the New Testament writings]."[166] Like Clement and Ignatius, Polycarp sees an integral unity between the Old Testament prophets ("who foretold the coming of our Lord") and the apostles ("who brought us the gospel").[167] However, there is also a difference with Polycarp; for while the formal authority of the Old Testament is the same, the attention given it by comparison to the New is far less. Polycarp is acquainted with most of the present New Testament (including the Synoptics, Acts, the majority of the Pauline corpus, Hebrews, and most of the Catholic Epistles). There appear to be no allusions to the Fourth Gospel, Jude, or Revelation.[168]

Of particular interest is Polycarp's apparent designation of a Pauline text (Eph 4:26) as "Scripture":

> For I am confident that you are well versed in the Scripture [*sacris literis*], and from you nothing is hid; but to me this is not granted. Only, as it is said in these Scriptures [*his scripturis*], "Be ye angry and sin not," and "Let not the sun go down upon your wrath."[169]

It is generally accepted that Polycarp recognized the first part of Paul's exhortation as a quotation of Psalm 4:4 and that in the words *his scripturis* Polycarp points only to the Old Testament via Paul's quotation.[170] However, Charles Nielsen has championed the view that in the light of Polycarp's limited use of the Old Testament and his wide acquaintance with Paul, it is much more likely that Ephesians is here referred to as "Scripture."[171] His interpretation is persuasive.

So we see a movement in Polycarp beyond the position of Clement and Ignatius. The importance of the Old Testament has receded in favor of increased esteem given to the writings of the apostles, particularly Paul. Nielsen states:

> As we know, Polycarp hardly remembers the Old Testament at all, but he is very conscious of Paul. On this ground it would seem that the Pauline Epistles have more right to be called Scripture than the Old Testament, although let me say once again that I do not mean to imply that Polycarp had removed the Law, the Prophets and the Writings from the canon. What I am saying is that whereas the Old Testament was hardly a practical functioning authority for him, some Christian writings were. Surely this situation could have important consequences for one's view of the canon. Thus it is no accident that Polycarp calls Ephesians "sacred Scripture."[172]

The next work to be considered is the *Didache*. This composite
document in its present form probably dates from the first half of the
second century.[173] It introduces itself as "the Lord's teaching to the
heathen by the twelve apostles." The warning of Deuteronomy 4:2
neither to add to nor subtract from the word of the Lord is here
applied to the "apostolic" teaching.[174] The function of the apostles
blends together with that of the prophets. Any *apostle* who fails to
meet certain behavioral standards is a false *prophet*.[175]

There is a similarity between the need to distinguish true and
false prophets (or apostles) and the church's need to recognize the
canon. The issue is to identify that which is authentic and apostolic.
Denis Farkasfalvy notes that for the author of the *Didache*, this takes
place in part through a written standard:

> ... he produces this book of his as an instrument to be used by the
> Churches, and he gives his presentation under the title of "The Doctrine of
> the Twelve Apostles." *We see here the principle of apostolicity at work: it
> leads to the production of literary works enshrining old oral tradition and is
> used to give maximum authority to the resulting written work.*[176]

The Epistle of Barnabas (early 2nd c.?) is related to the *Didache* by
its use of the same "Two Ways" tradition of ethical paraenesis (*Barn.*
18–21; *Did.* 1–6).[177] Most of the Epistle (chs 2–17), however, is a
polemical foray into interpreting the Old Testament. Barnabas
wrestles with the problem of continuity/discontinuity between the
Old and New Covenants. How could Christianity maintain its
continuity with the Old Testament and recognize Abraham as the
father of all those who believe and at the same time proclaim that in
Christ God has established a New Covenant that made Judaism
obsolete? Barnabas resolves the problem by asserting that Israel,
because of its sin, had never actually received the covenant.

> Moses received it, but they were not worthy. But learn how we received it.
> Moses received it when he was a servant, but the Lord himself gave it to us,
> as the people of the inheritance, by suffering for our sakes.[178]

The way is hereby opened for Barnabas to appropriate almost
anything from the law, history, or prophetic literature of the Old
Testament, and, by means of allegorical or typological exegesis, apply
it to the church.

This "almost schizophrenic mentality with regard to Christianity's Jewish origins"[179] is important for reflecting the proportions of
the second-century doctrinal problem raised by the Old Testament.
The allegorical "gnosis" of the Old Testament provided by Barnabas[180] will become even more radical in the full bloom of Gnosticism,
and Marcion's complete rejection of the Old Testament will provide
the consistent, if unacceptable, resolution of the tension between Old
and New.

So it should not surprise us that as the problems of Old Testament interpretation grew, the church would become more conscious of its literature as forming a complementary Scripture, a *New* Testament. There is no need, therefore, to evade or minimize Barnabas' citation of Matthew 22:14—"many called but few chosen"—with the introductory formula "as it is written."[181] Apparently at least one of the Synoptics has, for Barnabas, a recognized status as *graphē* fully equivalent to the authority of the Old Testament.[182]

This interpretation is supported by the anonymous Christian sermon that goes under the misleading title *Clement's Second Letter to the Corinthians,* which probably originated before the middle of the second century.[183] The sermon distinguishes two coordinate authorities: "the books" (*ta biblia*), that is, the Old Testament, and "the apostles" (*hoi apostoloi*).[184] Both were probably read during public worship and were followed by the sermon.[185] We must give full weight therefore to the dominical quotation, "I have come not to call the righteous but sinners" (Mt 9:13; Mk 2:17; Lk 5:32), introduced by the phrase, "and another Scripture also says."[186]

In summary, the evidence from the Apostolic Fathers suggests that there was little conscious reflection on the authority of the apostolic witness in its written form during the later part of the first century and the opening of the second century. There is, however, a commonly shared assumption that the apostolic traditions stand alongside the Old Testament as a parallel authority. The hesitancy of some (e.g., Clement and Ignatius) to refer to the apostolic writings as *graphē* probably indicates only a deference to traditional modes of expression in which the Old Testament was Scripture par excellence. This does not entail a negative estimation of the authority of the New Testament. Moreover, at least by the middle of the century, church practice finds its echo in the formal citation of the apostolic documents as Scripture (Polycarp, Barnabas, and 2 *Clement*).

D. THE ROLE OF CONTROVERSY

The second century saw the rise of a number of groups outside the mainstream of Christianity whose challenges to church traditions and practices proved a stimulus to doctrinal development. Those controversies had their influence on the church's doctrine of Scripture and canon, although the nature of this influence is difficult to determine. Three movements will be examined: Gnosticism, Marcionism, and Montanism.

Gnosticism, which came to full bloom in the middle of the second century,[187] raised in more acute form the questions of tradition and authority that engaged the Apostolic Fathers. The study of Gnosticism was long hampered by the fact that little primary evidence survived from the Gnostic groups except such fragments as had been preserved in the anti-Gnostic church fathers like Irenaeus and Hippolytus. This situation changed radically after 1946 with the discovery and publication of thirteen Coptic Gnostic codices found at Nag Hammadi in Egypt. The codices were collected by a group of Gnostics or someone interested in the movement.[188] While they date from the fourth and fifth centuries, many of the works were written during the second century. The importance of this discovery for our knowledge of the second century ranks with that of the Dead Sea Scrolls for knowledge of Judaism during the Second Commonwealth.

The parallel between the Dead Sea finds and those of Nag Hammadi is germane to the present discussion because both have led to questions regarding the formation of the canon. The Coptic Gnostic materials have been proposed as a source for reliable traditions about the historical Jesus—a source independent of the Synoptics. The strongest claims for authenticity have been made on behalf of *The Gospel of Thomas*,[189] which, strictly speaking, is not a "gospel" at all[190] but a collection of 114 sayings of Jesus. Helmut Koester concludes that "the basis of the *Gospel of Thomas* is a sayings collection which is more primitive than the canonical gospel, even though its basic principle is not related to the creed of the passion and resurrection."[191] He infers from these sayings that "a direct and almost unbroken continuation of Jesus' own teaching takes place— unparalleled anywhere in the canonical tradition."[192]

Koester's positive valuation of *The Gospel of Thomas* is endorsed and even expanded in a recent work by Stevan Davies. He argues that Thomas is "in no meaningful sense" a Gnostic work and dates its composition extraordinarily early (c. A.D. 50–70). According to Davies, "If these conclusions are accepted, then the Gospel of Thomas can take a place in scholarship and in Christian self-understanding which it is now denied. . . . Only then will the question of the meaning of Thomas for Christian history be re-opened."[193]

Although the tradition represented by *The Gospel of Thomas* is not *necessarily* more authentic than the canonical Gospels, Davies believes that frequently it must be given preference by the historian.[194] Today the majority opinion appears to favor the idea that Thomas gives evidence for the existence of traditions independent of but parallel to the Synoptic materials,[195] though few are willing to say that these are more authentic than those preserved in the canonical Gospels.[196]

Do the independence and reliability of particular Gospel traditions in the apocryphal literature call into question the possibility of a canon? To quote Koester again, "It is difficult to understand why the apocryphal gospels and acts are separated from their canonical counterparts. Neither the external attestation nor the internal evidence permits such a separation."[197] Yet, only a position that holds that the apocryphal materials are *more historically* (or perhaps religiously?) *reliable* than the canonical traditions impinges on the church's understanding of the New Testament canon. Only then would there be a challenge to the authority of the canonical records. This position Koester and a few others are willing to take; but the evidence adduced is slender, and the judgments no more secure than the form- and redaction-critical criteria upon which they are based.[198] On the other hand, if some of the apocryphal literature— and *The Gospel of Thomas* seems the best candidate—does preserve authentic tradition independent of the canonical Gospels, this would not reopen the church's canon. To view *The Gospel of Thomas* as the foremost stimulus to "intense activity which will sooner or later precipitate a massive series of changes regarding the shape and content of the Bible"[199] exaggerates the significance of the Nag Hammadi finds.

The difference between the Gnostic groups and the mainline Christians over the issue of religious authority was a great stimulus to reflection on the canon. The Gnostics did not hesitate to make use of the documents of the New Testament. The first known biblical commentary was Heracleon's (fl. c. 145–80) interpretation of John's Gospel. W. C. Van Unnik states that the author of the Valentinian *Gospel of Truth* (140–50?) "used practically the same Books as constitute our present New Testament Canon" and that "the manner in which he treats these documents proves that they had authority for him."[200] Likewise, Wilson maintains "it is clear that for the author [of the Gospel] of Philip the greater part of our New Testament was recognized as authoritative, even if we can scarcely say that it was fully canonical."[201]

But while the Gnostics recognized the authority of the New Testament documents, it was fundamental to these groups that "the redeeming knowledge brought into this world by the Savior was a revelation and, as such, was not generally available to all men. It was not even available to all who styled themselves Christians."[202] This true gnosis was beyond Scripture. It had been delivered by Jesus Himself to a few disciples who in turn had written it down or passed it on orally. The attribution of many Gnostic writings to various of the apostles confirms that apostolicity was clearly recognized as a legitimizing principle by such groups. To be sure, some Gnostic writings defend their esoteric traditions by portraying the apostles themselves as deficient in knowledge. Nag Hammadi literature sets both Mary Magdalene and James, the brother of the Lord, in opposition to Peter and the rest of the apostles. The true tradition comes only through these "non-apostles."[203] But even the need to develop such an apologetic emphasizes the importance of the apostolic principle.

Gnosticism's effect on the church was to intensify its concern for faithful adherence to the teaching of the apostles. The necessity for a concrete standard by which to evaluate the church tradition pressed the orthodox Fathers from Irenaeus onward to focus more consciously on Scripture as the written fixation of the apostolic tradition.

E. MARCION

Marcion's role in canonical understanding was crucial, though there is much debate over the extent of his contribution. His teachings called forth a steady stream of orthodox polemic from Justin Martyr (c. 150) on into the fifth century. Under his influence, Marcionite churches were established that maintained their separate existence until late in the third century in the West and some two centuries longer in the East.[204] Yet, like so many figures in the early church, Marcion is surrounded by shadows. Information about his life and teaching comes almost entirely from the writings of his opponents,[205] and these are not always in agreement among themselves.[206] His excommunication by the church at Rome for false teaching is usually dated about A.D. 144, but it is safe to assume that Marcion engaged in an extensive teaching ministry in Asia Minor some decades earlier.[207]

Marcion's teaching was marked by a fundamental dualism that "looks like a combination of Christianity and Syrian gnosis."[208] He distinguished between the highest God (the merciful Father revealed in Jesus Christ) and the just but cruel God (the Creator and Lawgiver revealed in the Old Testament). He regarded matter as evil, denied the resurrection of the body, advocated a strict asceticism, and held to a docetic Christology. Correlative with his dualism of the two Gods, his complete disjunction between law and gospel entailed rejecting the Old Testament in its entirety and as well those New Testament writings he judged to be infected by the "Judaizing" error. In fact, Marcion believed that all of the original apostles had fallen away from the truth revealed in Jesus; only Paul represented Jesus' teaching in its pure form. Thus, the Marcionite canon consisted of the ten letters of the "Apostle"—the Pauline corpus minus the Pastoral Epistles— and the "Gospel"—an edited version of Luke.[209]

The influence of this Gospel-Apostle collection on the developing canon of the church "remains a subject for educated conjecture."[210] Although there is broad agreement that the crisis evoked by Marcion was not the only factor affecting the canon and that even apart from this crisis the church would certainly have arrived at the notion of a closed canon, Harnack, by contrast, argues that Marcion "is the creator of Christian Holy Scripture."[211] Similarly, Hans von Campenhausen says this:

> The idea of a normative Christian canon, of a new collection of writings, or "scripture", is as yet nowhere to be found [prior to Marcion]. . . . From every side we converge on the same result: the idea and the reality of a Christian Bible were the work of Marcion, and the Church which rejected his work, so

far from being ahead of him in this field, from a formal point of view simply followed his example.[212]

Now the truth of these assertions lies in the fact that Marcion seems to have been the first to advance the idea of a closed canon, but even here his originality must be stated cautiously. An edition of the Pauline letters may well have circulated prior to Marcion,[213] and it is possible that a four-Gospel collection did likewise, though there is no clear evidence for the idea of a fourfold Gospel prior to Tatian's *Diatessaron* (c. 150–60).[214] But if collections of New Testament writings were being formed prior to or concurrent with Marcion's efforts, then the question of closure was at least implicit in the church's action—even if largely unconscious.[215] Quite in accord with this are those few examples noted previously where Christian writers introduce New Testament quotations with formulas normally used for Old Testament citations.[216]

John Knox argues that Marcion's dual structural principle "Gospel and Apostle" became "the organizing idea of the catholic New Testament."[217] Other organizational principles would have been equally as possible, so it is argued, but because we are accustomed to the present canonical shape, we "easily overlook the fact that in itself there is nothing whatever obvious or inevitable about it."[218] Marcion, therefore, must be given his due as the prime shaper of the orthodox canon, for, according to Knox, the New Testament was a conscious creation of the church in reaction to Marcion.

But while the particular form was not *inevitable*, it is by no means surprising in the light of what we have discussed in regard to the authority of Jesus and the apostles; no categories would have been more appropriate than "Gospel" and "Apostle." Moreover, the concepts "Gospel" and "Apostle" had already been correlated by the church before Marcion.[219]

Finally, how did the church relate to Marcion's concept of the closure of the canon? Did the church appropriate this directly from him? In fact, Marcion's limitation of the canon was based squarely on his doctrine of true and false apostleship.[220] The canon was not formed to discriminate between that which was apostolic and that which was not but to distinguish the writings of the larger group of the apostles (who had "intermingled the things of the law with the words of the Savior")[221] from those of Paul (who had alone preserved the truth in its pristine purity). So the difference between the church and Marcion was not merely quantitative but qualitative: Marcion's principle of closure was theological in the strict sense. The church, on the other hand, was to conceive of the closure of the canon as a function of salvation history; all was canonical that derived from the ministry of the apostles.

Denis Farkasfalvy summarizes the distinction between Marcion and the orthodox church:

[Marcion's closure] was aimed at restricting the canon to the heritage of one apostle at the exclusion of the Twelve, rather than being the fruit of the realization that the formation period of the Church came to an end and thus the Church of the beginnings became the norm and guide for subsequent periods. When the anti-Gnostic Church settled for a closed canon because it acknowledged only apostolic books, the closure of the canon came about as a decision flowing from the principle of apostolicity against any other claim of later norms. Thus it seems that the closure of the canon as it happened after Marcion had a meaning different from what Marcion had in mind.[222]

F. JUSTIN MARTYR

The Marcionite challenge did not long go unanswered; and anti-Marcionite reaction was registered partly in the church's view of New Testament authority and tradition. Justin Martyr (c. 100–165) is the first writer known to us to respond to Marcion by name. Justin groups the Marcionites together with the Valentinians, Basilidians, Saturnalians, and others who, though they claim the name of Christ, are in reality "atheists, impious, unrighteous, and sinful, and confessors of Jesus in name only."[223] According to Irenaeus,[224] Justin wrote a treatise, now lost, against Marcion, but Justin's three extant works accepted as genuine—the two *Apologies* and the *Dialogue with Trypho the Jew*—do not deal specifically with Marcion or the Gnostics. For this reason, and also because his writings are addressed to—those outside the church, Justin's views on the extent and authority of the New Testament literature are unclear and are subject to varying interpretations.[225]

Like those before him, Justin stresses the importance of the apostolic witness. In his salvation-historical theology, the apostles speak in unity with the Old Testament prophets—the predictions of the prophets have been fulfilled in Christ, and to this the apostles bear witness.[226] It is only through the insight Jesus gave the apostles after the Resurrection that Christians are able (better than the Jews) to understand the meaning of the prophets.[227]

The witness of the apostles, however, is a written witness: "For the apostles, in the Memoirs composed by them, which are called Gospels, have thus delivered to us what was enjoined upon them."[228] Where Justin found the term "Memoirs" (*apomnemoneumata*) is not known—perhaps from Xenophon's "Memoirs of Socrates" (*apomnemoneumata Sokratous*)[229]—but evidently he preferred it to the term "Gospels"[230] because it better expressed the historical value of the documents, an important point for their apologetic use.[231] The contexts in which Justin discusses the Memoirs indicate that they "were in substance identical with our Synoptic Gospels, whatever else they contained."[232] Perhaps, as E. F. Osborn believes, Justin relied for his citations on a Synoptic harmony.[233] On the other hand, the references to the *Memoirs* never include any citations of the Gospel of

John, though there are a number of parallels between Justin and the Fourth Gospel. Probably the surest is the statement, "For Christ said, 'Unless you are born again [anagennēthete] you will not enter into the kingdom of heaven'" (1 Apol 61.4), which seems to conflate John 3:3,5.[234] Why Justin is reluctant to cite John's Gospel is not obvious, but it seems unlikely that it reflects a negative judgment on the apostolic character or scriptural status of the book.[235]

As concerns other New Testament writings, Justin mentions the Apocalypse by name and the apostle John as its author.[236] He evidences knowledge of Acts, a number of the Pauline letters, Hebrews, 1 John, and perhaps 1 Peter,[237] but again none is cited directly.

Therefore, an attempt to reconstruct Justin's views on the New Testament canon is beset with uncertainties. Willis A. Shotwell states that "whether or not Justin considered the writings that now constitute the New Testament to be inspired and canonical is a moot question. . . . From his extant writings no conclusions may be ascertained regarding the state of the New Testament canon."[238]

But this is too strong. Justin gives the fullest picture so far of the life of our Lord, and he does so by repeated appeal to documents written by the apostles. These apostolic *Memoirs* are regarded most probably as equal in authority to the Old Testament prophets. This is supported by Justin's report that both the prophets and the *Memoirs* were read in the weekly worship services of the church.[239] Thus, while our findings are somewhat tentative, it is reasonable to see Justin as part of the general movement in the church toward a fixed documentary authority. If he does not yet have a fourfold Gospel canon, he is not far from it, and his own student Tatian would shortly produce a harmony based on the four Gospels. Much of the rest of the New Testament is known to Justin, though the use he makes of it is limited, perhaps by virtue of his apologetic concerns. There is no reason to suspect that Justin is moving away from or in opposition to the general canonical developments in the church.[240]

G. IRENAEUS

A more thorough refutation of Marcion and the Gnostics appears with Irenaeus, bishop of Lyons (c. 178–200), in his work *Against All Heresies*. The *leitmotif* of Irenaeus' theology is unity. This theme is a conscious reaction to the pluralistic or dualistic tendencies characteristic of the Gnostic systems. The Gnostics distinguished a creator god from that god who was the savior and redeemer, they frequently differentiated the heavenly Christ from the earthly Jesus, and they maintained that beyond the publicly announced message of Christianity there were esoteric truths given only to the initiated. On the contrary, argues Irenaeus, there is but one God, one Christ, and one tradition passed on in the church.[241]

This unity also has implications for Irenaeus' theology of revelation. Commenting on John 5:39–40, Irenaeus says that all the Scriptures point to Christ because they all derive from one God: "How therefore did the Scriptures testify of Him, unless they were from one and the same Father, instructing men beforehand as to the advent of His Son, and foretelling the salvation brought in by Him?"[242] As Denis Farkasfalvy observes, "This uniqueness of the source of all revelations establishes the unity of the two Testaments and unites all scriptural records of revelation into one coherent collection of writings."[243] The unity of the Testaments means that citations from both are often quoted as parallel authorities whose difference is to be understood only by reference to salvation history: for Irenaeus, the truth is that "which the prophets proclaimed . . . but which Christ brought to perfection, and the apostles have handed down."[244]

His Christocentric interpretation of Old Testament revelation stands, as we have seen, in a line with the earlier picture of the church. But there is a change; in Irenaeus the accent falls decidedly upon the apostolic witness—and this in its specifically *written* form. After devoting the first two books of *Against All Heresies* to a description of the Gnostic systems, Irenaeus proposes in the introduction to book 3 to "adduce proofs from the Scriptures" in order to provide "the means of combatting and vanquishing those who, in whatever manner, are propagating falsehood."[245] But in the "proofs" that make up the bulk of books 3–5 a new prominence is given to the writings of the apostles.[246] Campenhausen observes that

> the appeals to the Old Testament and its prophecies have not disappeared; but they are far outnumbered by the innumerable quotations from the New Testament, and these too now serve to construct a formal "proof from scripture" such as had previously been drawn from the Old Testament. This is the really new thing which has to be explained.[247]

The explanation is partly to be found in the Gnostics' disparagement of the Old Testament, which made its witness apologetically less valuable. But even more significant for the shift toward the New Testament writings was the church's need to refute the Gnostic claims to a secret tradition that had preserved the true teaching of Christ and the apostles. Whereas the prophecy-fulfillment structure of Justin's apologetic focused attention more on the relation between Christ and the Old Testament, the Gnostic crisis raised the question of the relation between Christ and the church of the second century, i.e., the question of the nature and content of the apostolic tradition.[248] As a result, Irenaeus reflects with greater depth on the nature of the apostleship than any before him.

The church is founded upon the apostles.[249] They have received from the Lord the power to announce the gospel, and through them we know the truth. It was to the apostles that Jesus said, "He who hears you hears me, and he who despises you despises me and the one who sent me" (Lk 10:16).[250] The plan of salvation was first proclaimed publicly by the apostles and then later delivered to us in the Scriptures, to be "the future ground and pillar of our faith."[251] The two forms, oral and written, of the apostolic witness are a unity. Neither has preeminence over the other, and for Irenaeus there can be no thought of any contrast or conflict between them.[252] This is the error of the Gnostics, for they demean the Scriptures by appealing to esoteric traditions.[253] By contrast, Irenaeus argues that the testimony of the apostles is public, having been proclaimed in the most ancient (apostolically founded) churches and preserved by an unbroken succession of faithful bishops.[254] It is this same tradition, however, that is recorded in the (New Testament) Scriptures, "which are indeed perfect since they were spoken by the Word of God and his Spirit."[255] And it is this latter source, the corpus of the apostolic writings, that is given greatest emphasis: "for all practical purposes, when he wants to ascertain the apostolic teaching about any particular question, he turns to Scripture using practically those same books that figure in the canon of the Church in later centuries."[256]

Irenaeus sees the doctrine of the apostles in the gospel. Following the general custom of the early church, he often designates by this term simply the contents of the apostolic preaching.[257] "The Gospel(s)" can also refer, as in Justin Martyr, to written accounts of the preaching. But, moving beyond Justin, Irenaeus recognizes all four of the present canonical Gospels by name and argues that "it is not possible that the Gospels can be either more or fewer than they are."[258] Two of the Gospels were written by apostles (Matthew and John) and two by apostolic associates (Mark and Luke), yet they are "apostolic" and of equal authority, for Mark was the disciple and interpreter of Peter and Luke the companion of Paul.

To confirm the unique status of these particular writings, Irenaeus adduces the "proof" that there are four points of the compass and four principal winds. The church, which is spread throughout the world, appropriately rests on four pillars (the four Gospels). The four living creatures of the Apocalypse correspond to the four aspects of the person of Christ developed by the Evangelists. Moreover, the four Gospels correspond to the fourth and last of the covenants that God has made with the human race. This is an argument *a posteriori* given to defend the quadriform Gospel against the multiplication of Gospels by the Gnostics on the one hand and against the reductionism of groups like the Marcionites and the Alogi on the other.[259]

There is no need to be overly critical of the allegorical argument, for its purpose is only to defend the providential sufficiency of the church's gospel.[260] The allegorical justification does not in any case furnish a criterion of selection. The basis for all of Irenaeus' argumentation is the tradition of the church, which believes that these four Gospels alone had their origins in the ministry of the apostles.[261]

Irenaeus cites most of the other writings of the New Testament. With the exception of Philemon, he refers to all the Pauline Epistles, including the Pastorals.[262] In spite of some scholars' statements to the contrary, Irenaeus seems to regard Paul's writings as equal in authority to the Old Testament and the fourfold Gospel.[263] The Book of Acts is frequently quoted and fully authoritative. Irenaeus is perhaps the first of the Fathers to cite Acts explicitly, and it plays an important role in enabling him to affirm the unity of Paul with the rest of the apostles. Definitely cited are 1 Peter, 1 and 2 John, and the Apocalypse, and there are probably allusions to James and Hebrews.[264] It is evident, then, that Irenaeus used a body of authoritative literature whose lines conformed closely to our present canon.[265]

A number of advances are made for the church's canonical understanding. (1) More than ever before, the teaching of the apostles (particularly the written fixation of the teaching) is recognized as the norm of the church's existence. (2) Apostolicity is developed more extensively as a theological idea and as the criterion of canonicity. (3) The definiteness of the arguments for the fourfold Gospel shows that the process of closure was now consciously underway.

Whether Irenaeus had similar views on the definition and shape of the rest of the New Testament is debatable. For example, he gives no allegorical justification for a defined Pauline corpus parallel to the argument for the Gospels. Outside of the Gospels we should probably see a relatively well-defined body of literature that functions with full scriptural authority but whose canonical position is still more implicit and practical than explicit and theological.[266] In response (partly at least) to the Marcionite elevation of Paul to the detriment of the authority of the other apostles, Irenaeus upholds "the ascription of authority to the entire apostolic community and to the canon of the NT, and, consequently, the insistence that there was no conflict between the teaching of Paul and that of the other apostles."[267] In this sense Irenaeus may properly be spoken of as the first catholic theologian.

H. THE SPREAD OF THE CANONICAL IDEA

Irenaeus' contribution to the growth in canonical understanding was a straw in the wind. Very shortly the notion of a definite collection of Christian writings was widely accepted. We may assume that there was in the Christian community a readiness for the kind of formulations advanced by Irenaeus. This may well be suggested by the testimony of Melito of Sardis (c. 170), who states that he traveled to Palestine to ascertain "the books of the Old Covenant" (*ta tēs palaias diathēkēs biblia*).[268] While there is no explicit reference to books of the new covenant, the implications for a formulated "New Testament" are here.[269]

Closer to the end of the second century, the anti-Montanist writer quoted by Eusebius explains that his initial reluctance to write against the Montanists arises

> not from any lack of ability to refute the lie and testify to the truth, but from timidity and scruples lest I might seem to some to be adding to the writings or injunctions of the word of the new covenant of the gospel *[tō tēs-tou euangelious kainēs diathēkēs logō]*, to which no one who has chosen to live according to the gospel itself can add and from which he cannot take away.[270]

There is envisioned a definite collection of writings associated with the "New Testament." The collection is regarded as fixed, at least to the degree that writings of recent vintage could not qualify for inclusion. On the other hand, the term "New Testament" has still its broad sense as referring to the final period of salvation history. As Campenhausen notes, "We have not yet arrived at the purely literary meaning of the word."[271]

The polemics of the anti-Montanist raise the question of what impact Montanism or the "New Prophecy" had on the New Testament canon. The Montanist movement, which arose in Asia Minor not later than A.D. 170,[272] was an attempt to repristinate the church by stressing a fervent eschatological hope, a vigorous asceticism, and a renewal of the prophetic gift. "Montanus himself seems to have made the claim that the promise of Jesus concerning the Paraclete had been uniquely fulfilled in him."[273] It was this claim to the inspiration of the Holy Spirit, made not only by Montanus but also by some of his disciples, that challenged the church's understanding of authority.

The result of the Montanist challenge on the question of canon has long been debated.[274] Such influence as the New Prophecy had on the emergent canon was certainly indirect. Montanist polemic comprised no attack upon the authority or validity of the biblical writings, whether Old Testament or New Testament,[275] nor were Montanist oracles, collected in written form, seen as equivalent to Scripture. According to Andrew F. Walls, "It seems in fact, that while the Montanists always held the unique inspiration of Montanus and his colleagues as an article of faith, we have little evidence that in practice they attached overmuch weight to the writings of the New Prophecy."[276]

In fact, the real attacks upon the emergent canon came not from the Montanists but from some of their more radical opponents. The Roman presbyter Gaius rejected the authenticity of the Johannine Gospel and the Apocalypse presumably because both were important to Montanist teaching and apologetics. Against Gaius, Hippolytus of

Rome argued for the authenticity of the Johannine writings, while against Montanism he taught that the era of prophecy had ceased with the apostles. The task of the church was not to receive fresh revelation but to interpret the revelation already given through the apostles and recorded in the Scriptures.[277] So a collection of Scriptures rooted in the distinctive age of the apostles was by implication a *closed* collection.

The first extant canonical listing of the New Testament books is the Muratorian Canon, which probably originated in Rome about A.D. 200 or earlier.[278] The manuscript is fragmentary, but although it lacks reference to Matthew or Mark, these apparently headed the list, for Luke is mentioned as the third Gospel and John as the fourth. Luke is also recognized as the author of "the acts of all the apostles." Thirteen letters are acknowledged as authentically Pauline, while an *Epistle to the Laodiceans* and another to the Alexandrians (perhaps Hebrews?) are rejected as Marcionite forgeries. Two Johannine Epistles and Jude are also accepted. The Apocalypses ascribed to John and to Peter are received, but the Muratorianum affirms that there was some opposition to the public reading of the latter work. *The Shepherd of Hermas* is accepted for private but not public reading because it was written too recently. A strange reference to the Wisdom of Solomon finds it canonical.[279] All Gnostic, Marcionite, and Montanist writings are rejected.

Efforts to find a consistent rationale for the formation of Muratorianum have proved difficult. This gives some justification to the oft-repeated comment of Adolf Jülicher that, according to the Muratorian canon, "the principle of the Church in the origination of the canon was a lack of principle."[280] Certainly authorship by an apostle or an apostolic associate is stressed, yet this appears more as a justification *a posteriori* than as an actual criterion of selection. The specific shape of the canon undoubtedly reflects the church's controversy with heretical groups,[281] and yet this can only help in a subsidiary way to explain particular emphases or the exclusion of certain works like the Marcionite epistles. Isidore Frank has suggested that the Johannine logos theology forms a material principle for the selection or exclusion of works in the Muratorianum,[282] but this kind of theological sophistication can only be read into the relatively simple statements of the canon.

In the end we must conclude that the author of the Muratorian canon relies primarily on tradition. "In practice," says Campenhausen, "the crucial factor is clearly the usage and judgment of the one true Church, spread throughout the world."[283] The place of theological or historical criteria is more to defend the practice of the "catholic" church than to establish the practice. This is similar to what we encountered with Irenaeus, except that the definiteness of Irenaeus in regard to the fourfold Gospel has now expanded to a much larger body of literature.

Two writers of the early third century—the Roman presbyter Hippolytus (c. 170–236) and the North African apologist Tertullian (c. 160–225)—though providing no canonical list, use the New Testament in such a way as to suggest that their view of it was close to that of Canon Muratori. Hippolytus cites or alludes to all of the books of the present canon with the exception of Jude, Philemon, and 2 and 3 John.[284] He does not regard Hebrews as Pauline, but neither does he neglect to use it in his writings.[285]

Tertullian proposes apostolicity as the criterion of canonicity. Against the Marcionites he writes:

> I lay it down to begin with that the documents of the gospel have the apostles for their authors, and that this task of promulgating the gospel was imposed upon them by our Lord himself. If they also have for their authors apostolic men, yet these stand not alone, but as companions of apostles or followers of apostles.[286]

On this basis, Tertullian recognizes the canonicity of Mark, Luke, and Acts along with most of the other New Testament writings. Only James, 2 Peter, and 2 and 3 John find no definite citation in his works.[287] The Epistle to the Hebrews is referred to by Tertullian as the work of Barnabas, Paul's associate. Though it could by way of this apostolic connection qualify as Scripture, Tertullian is quite tentative in ascribing to it the full authority of the apostolic writings.[288] Nevertheless, it stands apart from *The Shepherd of Hermas*, which Tertullian disparages as an "apocryphal" book.[289] *The Shepherd* is rejected on the ground that it was not recognized in the churches in earlier times. Tertullian appeals to traditional usage and to the apostolic churches to determine which writings are apostolic.[290] Flesseman-van Leer concludes, "Thus the authority of the Church is necessary to decide which books are canonical, though certainly it is not the church which makes them so. Only their apostolicity makes them canonical."[291]

I. THE ALEXANDRIANS

A somewhat different picture is offered by Tertullian's contemporary Clement of Alexandria (c. 150–215). Clement is the first to use the term "testament" (*diathēkē*), in a literary sense not only in reference to the Old "Testament" but also to the New "Testament" writings.[292] Moreover, the New Testament is decidedly more prominent in his citations from Scripture.[293] According to Eusebius, Clement wrote brief commentaries on all of the canonical books, including those that were (in Eusebius' classification) disputed: the Epistle of Jude, the remaining Catholic Epistles, *The Epistle of Barnabas*, and *The Apocalypse of Peter*. Hebrews was acknowledged by Clement as originally written by Paul, but translated into Greek by Luke.[294]

In spite of this, it is difficult to draw any conclusions on

Clement's view of the shape of the New Testament. He provides no list of authoritative books and, like the rest of his contemporaries, never uses the word "canon" in this sense. Clement's theological method and appeal to authorities is thoroughly eclectic. If he cites the New Testament more than the Old, he refers to non-Christian works more frequently than either Testament.[295] Again, while he appears to recognize a (limited) fourfold Gospel canon, Clement is not adverse to citing various apocryphal Gospels.[296] His understanding of the universal working of the Logos, borrowed in part from Justin, allows him to view a wide range of literature as a source of insight to elaborate the truths of Christian faith.[297] The spirit is quite different from what we found in the West; Clement is far from asking Tertullian's rhetorical question, "What has Jerusalem to do with Athens?" In accord with this, "he by no means treats his biblical quotations in a separate category of their own. At every step they are entwined with the words of classical philosophers and poets, with heathen oracles and wisdom sayings."[298] Clement's breadth of vision, for better or for worse, prohibits any sharp discrimination of canonical and noncanonical writings. If he worked with such categories, he has not made them plain.[299]

Clement's illustrious successor at the catechetical school of Alexandria was Origen (c. 185–254), the greatest biblical scholar of antiquity. There are obvious similarities between Origen and Clement. Origen is explicit that only four Gospels are to be received as authoritative for the church.[300] He recognizes as well Acts, the thirteen letters of Paul, Hebrews—Pauline in thought but not in literary style—one epistle of Peter and perhaps a second that is disputed, the Apocalypse of John together with an epistle by the same author and perhaps two more of his letters, although these two are contested.[301] Beyond these it seems probable that Origen accepted as inspired most, if not all, of the rest of the New Testament, along with a few works that were ultimately excluded (notably *The Shepherd of Hermas* and *The Epistle of Barnabas*).[302] The attempt of some conservative scholars to find in Origen a New Testament canon limited to just the present twenty-seven books seems doomed to failure.[303] R. P. C. Hanson contrasts Origen with his predecessor:

> We can say without qualification that he regards the Canon of the Gospels as closed in a more final sense than did Clement, and that he displays a greater desire for definiteness than he, and a more sensitive appreciation of the possibilities of documents being spurious. But fundamentally Origen's attitude to the Canon is the same as Clement's; he will accept as Christian evidence any material that he finds convincing or appealing. Neither of them shows any signs of being conscious of the existence of a *list* of canonical works, apart from the list of four Gospels recognized as more authoritative than any others. Clement's promiscuous acceptance of any work, no matter how doubtful its relevance to the Christian dispensation, which appealed to

his curious and comprehensive intellect is in Origen's case modified by the accuracy of a scholar and the experience of a traveller. But that is all.[304]

But if the canonical outlook at Alexandria was looser and broader than that which obtained in some other sectors of the church, it was nevertheless not wildly divergent. And while Origen's "canon" may well have been slightly larger than the presently acknowledged New Testament books, it was probably as close to the mark as the more restrictive "canons" of contemporaries like Tertullian or Hippolytus. In any case, the shape of the canon would not undergo any significant variations from this point onward, as is shown by a comparison of Origen's position with that of Eusebius in the next century.

IV. THEOLOGICAL REFLECTION

To this point we have proceeded largely along historical lines. The final section of this study will consider some of the major theological issues that surround the canon. It will center around the work of four recent interpreters of the problem of the canon. These will set the stage for my own presentation. However, in this area of theology, as in so many others, the modern agenda has been set by the discussions that arose in the Reformation and the Enlightenment. We will consider these briefly.

A. BACKGROUNDS TO CURRENT CANON DISCUSSION

1. The Reformation

The Protestant Reformers structured their attack upon medieval Christendom around an appeal to the final authority of Scripture, the so-called "formal principle" of the Reformation. For Luther, "those things which have been delivered to us by God in the Sacred Scripture must be sharply distinguished from those that have been invented by men in the Church, it matters not how eminent they be for saintliness and scholarship."[305] Luther's contemporary, the English Reformer William Tyndale, wrote, "that Word is the chiefest of the apostles, and pope, and Christ's vicar, and head of the Church, and head of the general council. And unto the authority of that ought the children of God to harken without respect of person."[306] If the church and the papacy were corrupt and unwilling to enact necessary reforms, Luther and his followers would appeal to the Bible against the church.

But could the authority of the Scriptures so easily be divorced from the authority of the church? Roman Catholic apologists argued that it could not. The correct interpretation of the Bible was ensured only by the infallibility of the church. Romanist theologians cited Augustine's contention against the Manicheans, "I should not believe the Gospel except as moved by the authority of the Catholic Church."[307] To this Luther replied,

> We must not understand St. Augustine to say that he would not believe the Gospel unless he were moved thereto by the authority of the whole Church. . . . Every man must believe only because it is God's Word, and because he is convinced in his heart that it is true, although one angel from heaven and all the world preached to the contrary. His meaning is rather, as he himself says, that he finds the Gospel nowhere except in the Church, and that this external proof can be given heretics that their doctrine is not right, but that that is right which all the world has with one accord accepted.[308]

Calvin also rejected the Romanist interpretation of Augustine's words. Augustine did not mean to teach that faith in the Scriptures was dependent on the judgment of the church. The words of Augustine, Calvin argues, have reference not to Christians, but to non-Christians: "He is simply teaching that there would be no certainty of the gospel for unbelievers to win them to Christ if the consensus of the church did not impel them."[309]

This debate had implications for both sides relative to an understanding of the canon. For Roman Catholic theologians, not only the correct interpretation of Scripture but the shape and content of the canon were guaranteed by the infallibility of the church. The Reformers sensed here a threat to the principle of *sola scriptura* and denied that the church had the power to determine canonicity. It was God who established the canon; the role of the church was merely to witness to what God had already established. Nor was the church infallible in its role as witness. Luther, as we saw earlier, felt free to question the canonical status of the antilegomena, and other Lutheran theologians followed his example. Martin Chemnitz, for example, held that though the antilegomena ought not to be rejected, "no dogma ought therefore to be drawn out of these books which does not have reliable and clear foundations in other canonical books."[310] Thus, for Chemnitz, the antilegomena are not canonical in the pure sense. Later Lutheran dogmaticians generally (but not universally)[311] accepted the traditional twenty-seven books of the New Testament, while Reformed theologians were from the beginning less questioning in regard to the shape of the received canon.

But upon what ground could the Protestants base their confidence? That the authority of Scripture was self-authenticating *(autopistos)* and sealed to the hearts of God's people by the witness of the Holy Spirit alone was the Reformers' general position. However, among Lutheran and Reformed theologians, this witness was generally appealed to more to affirm the overall authority of the Bible than to validate the specific contents of the canon.[312] For the latter point, appeal was made to God's overriding providence. Calvin, in treating the question of certain lost letters of Paul, affirmed that

those which the Lord judged to be necessary for his church have been
selected by his providence for everlasting remembrance. Let us rest assured,
that what is left is enough for us, and that the smallness of the remaining
number is not the result of accident; but that the body of Scripture, which is
in our possession, has been adjusted by the wonderful counsel of God.[313]

In a similar fashion the nineteenth-century Reformed theologian
Louis Gaussen could point to "the marvelous, universal, immovable
unanimity with which all the churches of the world for the last
fourteen or fifteen centuries continue to present to us one and the
same Greek Testament" as evidence "that a concealed but almighty
hand has been here interposed, and that the Head of the church
watches in silence over the new Oracles as he has watched over the
old, preserving them from age to age against the folly of men."[314] So
conservative Protestant theologians stressed that the canonicity of the
biblical writings derived not from any human decision but from the
fact that their authors were inspired. Only in the context of
inspiration were Protestants willing to examine the history of the
canon. Thus, Princeton theologian Archibald Alexander wrote, "The
appeal to testimony, therefore, is not to obtain the judgment of the
Church, that these books were canonical; but to ascertain the fact,
that they are indeed the productions of the apostles, to whom our
Lord promised plenary inspiration."[315]

2. The Enlightenment

The contemporary discussion of the canon is indebted at least as
much to the critical scholarship of the Enlightenment as to the
theological controversies of the Reformation. While the form of the
Enlightenment varied from one country to another and its immediate
impact on the church is still being assessed by historians,[316] there is
no question that the rationalistic criticism of the Scriptures that arose
during the seventeenth and eighteenth centuries was to set much of
the agenda for modern biblical scholarship.

Johann Salomo Semler (1725–91) has been called by some the
founder of the historical-critical study of the New Testament.[317]
Semler's four volume *Treatise on the Free Investigation of the Canon*
(1771–75) was a sharp attack upon the orthodox doctrine of Scripture,
which, while not the first, was one of the most important in its
influence upon subsequent understanding of the canon.[318] For
Semler, not all of the Bible is inspired or authoritative; indeed, the
fundamental evil in theology is the equation of "Scripture" and "Word
of God":

Holy Scripture and the Word of God are clearly to be distinguished, for we
know the difference. If one has not previously been aware of this, that is no
prohibition that keeps us from making the distinction. To Holy Scripture
(using the particular historical expression that originated among the Jews)

belong Ruth, Esther, the Song of Songs, etc., but not all the books that are called holy belong to the Word of God, which at all times makes all men wise unto salvation.[319]

The corollary of Semler's distinction between Scripture and Word of God is that the shape of the canon is to be explained on purely historical grounds. The canonical books are those that were chosen by the early church to be used for public lections and instructions. But since the canon has no divine sanction, it is appropriate for any Christian to undertake a "free investigation" of the historical credentials of the biblical books in order to determine their religious value.[320]

Thus, for Semler and the many who have followed the same path, the canon as a whole is rejected, and at best what remains is some part of the biblical message, some abiding core of truth among the accidental historical and cultural trappings. To detect this core, one must find a standard, or canon, for the existing canon. Semler wished to retain from Scripture whatever contributed to moral improvement. But the problem of this approach is the subjectivism both of the choice of this particular inner canon as well as its application to the biblical materials. Modern historical-critical scholarship, which by and large accepts Semler's presuppositions, has failed to reach any consensus on the shape or content of the "canon within the canon." Gerhard Maier has fairly observed that Semler's legacy has "culminated in a universal Christian sickness."[321]

B. FOUR APPROACHES TO CANON HISTORY

At this point we will examine the work of a number of recent authors who are representative of the major lines of approach to the history of the canon.

1. James Barr

Oxford professor James Barr is chosen as a major representative of the historical-critical tradition.[322] He is antagonistic to the doctrine of Scripture held by "Protestant orthodoxy" and "Fundamentalism" and recently has become quite critical of the "canon criticism" of Brevard Childs. He believes the work of Childs "can be understood as very much an attempt to dispose of the Enlightenment, to destroy its values and drive out its way of dealing with biblical materials."[323] Integral to the historical-critical outlook is freedom—freedom to follow critical methods wherever they may lead. Such freedom is grounded not only in the secular outlook of the Enlightenment but also in the religious notion of freedom deriving from the Lutheran Reformation. Thus, the Christian scholar is free to pursue the task of biblical criticism, and in this way the Protestant principle of "the plain sense of Scripture" leads directly to Wellhausen.[324]

Barr appeals to Scripture itself to deny Protestant orthodoxy's understanding of the canon. He contends first that earliest Christianity was not concerned to be a religion of a book:

> The idea of a near-absolute scriptural *control* of faith is a quite foreign conception, based on a quite different construct of problems, and read into the New Testament statements about Old Testament scripture by a later generation, especially Protestant Orthodoxy, for which the concept of scriptural *control* of religion and doctrine was of absolute importance.[325]

Moreover, the notions of "Scripture" and "canon" are not the same. The idea of Scripture is that ,of certain writings held to be sacred and authoritative. Canon, on the other hand, entails the idea that these writings should be defined and limited, something that took place long after the biblical period.[326] "These considerations," Barr concludes "are . . . fatal to the notion that the idea of the canon is of first-rate importance for biblical Christianity. Scripture is essential, but canon is not."[327]

The shape of the canon is entirely the result of human decision. Such decisions are undoubtedly fallible, for Barr will allow no "special intervention" by God in the scriptural or canonical process.[328] This stands in full agreement with his larger conception of the Bible:

> My account of the formation of the biblical tradition is an account of a *human* work. It is *man's* statement of his beliefs, the events he has experienced, the stories he has been told, and so on. It has long been customary to align the Bible with concepts like Word of God, or revelation, and one effect of this has been to align the Bible with a movement *from God to man*. It is man who developed the biblical tradition and man who decided when it might be suitably fixed and made canonical. If one wants to use the Word-of-God type of language, the proper term for the Bible would be Word of Israel, Word of some leading early Christians.[329]

Barr allows that the church is entitled to change the canon should it desire to do so. Yet, from a practical standpoint, he thinks it most unlikely that such changes would ever be made, because

> . . . formation of scripture, and canonization of scripture, are processes which were characteristic of a certain time, a certain stage in the life of the people of God. We are in fact no longer in that stage; it is a matter of history to us, and even historically we are not too well informed of the arguments and categories which were employed—especially so, I would say, in the Jewish (as distinct from the Christian) process of scripture formation.[330]

One may ask, finally, what is Barr's conception of the authority of the Bible? The answer is none too clear. He holds that "the status of the Bible is something implied in the structure of Christian (and of Jewish) faith. This seems to be the basis for all involvement with the Bible: it is a corollary of the faith, something implied by the basic constituents of faith."[331] The Bible is this corollary of the faith because it embodies "the classic model for the understanding of God,"[332] a model first articulated in the Old Testament and then reformulated and reaffirmed in connection with Jesus Christ. Being a Christian means believing in "the God who has manifested himself in a way that has some sort of unique and specific expression in the Bible."[333] One ought not to approach the Bible as "a true book which contains true information about God and about various other persons and past events."[334] The concern of the Bible is rather to mediate an encounter with Jesus Christ—in this sense it "is able to speak to us as a message that reaches us from God."[335] The basis of Scripture's authority "lies in its efficacy in the faith-relation between men and God."[336] But Barr remains vague on what this might mean. It does not mean that the Bible functions as a comprehensive ethical or doctrinal norm. Rather, Scripture functions as part of the larger Christian vision for the church and society. Here it serves a critical role:

> It questions what people think, it queries the basis of their judgments, it asks whether the tradition which modern men form is really in continuity with its biblical origins. It is through this critical checking and questioning role that the Bible exercises its authority: the Bible queries the tradition of its own interpretation.[337]

In summary, Barr's notion of the canon is thoroughly within the parameters of historical-critical orthodoxy. Scripture is understood in naturalistic terms as a purely human production; much more is this true of the canon. But in denying any special divine intervention in the giving of Scripture, Barr attacks the root of any substantial notion of revelation or authority. The problem is not merely that the Bible is not for him revelation or the Word of God. The problem is whether Barr can consistently go on to speak of God manifesting himself to human beings in *any* way, since presumably any revelation involves some sort of "special intervention"—unless God has become purely immanent in the world process.

But, in fact, Barr holds that the Bible "is able to speak to us a message that reaches us from God."[338] Yet, given his presuppositions, we are entitled to ask what this can mean. Moreover, if the Bible itself is not a divine revelation, it is hard to see how Barr can maintain any sense of biblical authority. Evidently he struggles with the problem, for this issue is the foggiest part of his discussion. When Barr says that Scripture serves a critical role, he means that it acts as a foil for our own or the church's interpretation. The Bible is not an absolute standard, nor does it provide a comprehensive norm. While he is not happy with the expression "a canon within the canon," the reason is more semantic than principial; for "if the term is to be used, reasonably good supports and precedents for such an interior canon can be found."[339] That he does not specify such a canon suggests either an unwillingness or an inability to address the question of authority precisely.

Barr's sharp distinction between Scripture and canon is also problematic. By drawing the distinction sharply he is able to conclude that canon is a late idea, not of primary importance to Christianity. While I have argued previously that Scripture and canon are not identical ideas, it seems that Barr unduly separates them. But if Scripture does communicate a divine word to mankind—which Barr does not allow—then it would be natural and even imperative for God's people to distinguish that word from all other merely human words. And if this is the case, then the idea of canon would take on much more importance for biblical Christianity.[340]

2. Brevard Childs

Representative of quite a different approach to the canon is Brevard Childs, the best-known advocate of the hermeneutics of "canon criticism." In a series of major publications, he has defended the thesis that "the canon of the church is the most appropriate context from which to do Biblical Theology."[341] Childs is sharply critical of many of the effects of historical criticism upon the study of the Old Testament. Historical-critical introduction since Eichorn has been more concerned to reconstruct a history of Israel's religious and literary development than to analyze the canonical text itself. Further, critical scholars have failed to understand the inner dynamics of the process of canon formation and the dialectical relationship between the developing canon and the religious consciousness of the Israelite community.[342] The authoritative Scripture gave a distinctive shape to the people of God; but, on the other hand, those Scriptures were themselves shaped by the process of ordering and selection within the congregation.[343] In his most recent work, Childs directs a similar critique against the practitioners of New Testament introduction:

> It is assumed by many that the formation of a canon is a late, ecclesiastical activity, external to the biblical literature itself, which was subsequently imposed on the writings. Many of the questions which pose a polarity between the New Testament's real historical development and its ecclesiastical function, or between its genuine meaning and the sense later ascribed to it by clerics, reflect this basic confusion. Rather, it is crucial to see that the issue of canon turns on the authoritative role played by particular traditions for a community of faith and practice. Canon consciousness thus arose at the inception of the Christian church and lies deep within the New Testament literature itself.[344]

Canon criticism focuses attention on the final form of the biblical text. This text describes and defines the history of the encounter between God and His people in a way "which became normative for all successive generations of this community of faith. . . . It is only in the final form of the biblical text in which the normative history has reached an end that the full effect of this revelatory history can be perceived."[345] Childs is, therefore, critical of those who, like James Barr, see the canon only as a late development without hermeneutical significance.[346] He is also opposed to approaches like that of James Dunn that identify various levels of canonical authority as a function of differing historical contexts: "The function of a normative canon is to encompass the significance of the [canonical] process within the contours of a normative text, and the multi-layered text thus becomes the vehicle for the theological witness to the gospel."[347] So also Childs rejects the idea of "a canon within the canon" on the ground that the Scriptures as a whole must be the starting point for any exegesis.[348]

The history of the formation of the canonical text is for Childs a thoroughly human one. The canon did not fall from heaven, and we must not suppose that the decisions of the church were infallible, though there is a stable core of writings that ought not to be changed.[349] Thus, there can be no return to a traditional, pre-Enlightenment understanding of the canon; one cannot bypass two hundred years of critical research.[350]

On the other hand Childs wishes to maintain a theological as well as historical understanding of the canon.

> There is an analogy between the human and divine side of the Bible and the historical and theological aspects of the canon. The fact that the church confessed its faith in the divine origin of its Scripture in a thoroughly time-conditioned fashion can be readily acknowledged. But the theological issue at stake is the rightness of the claim for divine authority to which the church responded in setting aside certain writings as Scripture.[351]

The canon is authoritative because through this human word the living Lord continues to address His people; this can be understood only in the context of faith.[352] Childs does not explain exactly how the divine and human elements are related. He will say only that the canonical method

> . . . does run counter to two extreme theological positions. It is incompatible with a position on the far right which would stress the divine initiative in such a way as to rule out any theological significance to the response to the divine Word by the people of God. It is equally incompatible with a position on the far theological left, which would understand the formation of the Bible in purely naturalistic terms, such as Israel's search for self-identity, or a process within nature under which God is subsumed.[353]

Childs presents a learned and stimulating treatment of the canon. He has an admirable ability to synthesize a wide range of material and present it with clarity. He has identified the weakness of the traditional historical-critical approach to Scripture. His rejection of a "canon within the canon" is sound, as is also his concern to draw a more integral connection between Scripture and canon than that found in James Barr. His focus on the final form of the text provides a helpful corrective to overly atomistic exegesis and to that form of interpretation scored by Karl Barth when he wrote that "recent commentators confine themselves to an interpretation of the text which seems to me to be no commentary at all, but merely the first step towards the commentary."[354]

The reference to Barth is not without significance to assessing the position of Childs, for the great neoorthodox theologian and Childs present virtually the same position on Scripture and canon. While both affirm the divine authority of Scripture, they repeatedly stress the human and time-conditioned character of Scripture. Theology cannot return to a pre-Enlightenment stance—which means, on the one hand, that deference must be given to the broad lines of historical-critical orthodoxy and, on the other hand, that one cannot straightforwardly simply identify Scripture with the divine word.

Thus, while there is much that is refreshing and useful in Childs, I suspect that his uneasy synthesis of historical criticism with affirmations of canonical authority will not command wide assent.

3. Nicolaus Appel

A major voice in the contemporary discussion of the canon is that of Roman Catholic theologian Nicolaus Appel. He articulates a conservative Catholic understanding of canon formation—primarily the New Testament—in dialogue with a cross section of Protestant scholarship.[355]

For Appel, the fundamental difference between Protestant and Roman Catholic theology is found in their respective formulations of the doctrine of the Incarnation. The Reformation position is that of "solus Christus," which means that "in Jesus Christ and in him alone the Divine has become man, in him alone the revelation of God appears to us, in him alone God speaks to us."[356] Everyone stands in a direct, personal relationship to Christ, unmediated by human beings or the church. The Reformation *sola Scriptura* corresponds precisely to this notion of faith, "for through the word of Scripture alone can man meet Jesus Christ directly."[357] The Bible, therefore, may also function independently of the church, for Protestants conceive of a direct witness of the Holy Spirit to the hearts of believers, a witness that attests to the word of Scripture and is in turn dependent on Scripture.

But Reformation individualism faces a problem relative to the canon. The rise of historical criticism in the Enlightenment has focused attention on the human dynamics that entered into the production of Scripture and canon. How is this human element to be reconciled with the doctrine of Scripture as the Word of *God* testified to by the Holy Spirit? Are the traditionally established limits of the canon still to be accepted, even if the criteria used by the early church seem now naive or unworkable? Or if the traditional canon is retained, must not Protestant principles be surrounded with uncertainty and a consciousness of the church's fallibility even in the recognition of the canon? Such questions have initiated a crisis in Protestantism that to the present day remains unsolved.[358]

By contrast to the Reformation view, the Roman Catholic Church recognizes the "Christus totus." Protestants limit the Incarnation strictly to the man Jesus Christ, but the Roman church confesses not only the mystery of the God-man but also "the mystery of the emanation of the divine in the whole of humanity, especially in the Church of Christ."[359] For this reason, Christ and the church stand in greater unity for Rome than for the Reformation. Likewise, Scripture and the primitive church form a unity. It is not to be denied that Christ speaks to individual believers by the Word and by the Spirit, but He does so in conjunction with the witness of His body, the church.[360]

Appel recognizes the historical process that marks the formation of the canon. While some older Catholic writers posit a direct revelation given through the apostles in reference to the limits of the canon,[361] Appel sees the canon as an ecclesiastical decision made in the postapostolic age. In this period the church came to a deeper consciousness of the importance of a canon and to a true insight into the shape and boundaries of this canon. This was a human and historical process that came about only gradually in the midst of struggle and uncertainty.[362]

On the other hand, the growing canonical consciousness of the church must not be viewed merely as a profane historical process, for the testimony of the Holy Spirit in the faith of the church means that there is a theological dimension to the history of the canon. "The Spirit guides the Church into all the truth, including the truth of the profession of the canon."[363] For Appel, it is appropriate to speak with the Reformers of the *autopistia* of the Scriptures and, thus, of the canon. The Bible attests to its own authority because the Spirit bears witness in and through the words of Scripture. The process by which the church in history became conscious of the canon may be described as a growth of Scripture's *autopistia* under the guidance of the Holy Spirit.[364] But the Spirit does not witness to the canonicity of particular books; so there is a genuine process of recognition. On the other hand, the Spirit does attest to the truth of the gospel and, thus, to the evangelical content of the writings.[365] The recognition of the canon is, therefore, an expression of faith.

> The Church, confidently surrendering to Jesus Christ, professed its faith in the mysterious character of these books exclusively. As people of God, the Church knew and experienced itself bound to the Lord and received this personal relationship in accordance with the structures of the apostolic Church as they were "written."[366]

The Spirit who leads the body of Christ to confess this particular canon works infallibly to guarantee the correct consensus of the church in the recognition process. This consensus bears more than "mere historical certainty," and as a result "the boundaries of the canon are no longer revisable. The Spirit's witness does not bear or need reform or revision."[367]

Thus, the crucial issue for Appel is the nature of the church. The church as the body of Christ, understood in a much more literal sense than by Protestants, is the vehicle of the Holy Spirit. What the Spirit does He does infallibly, and this includes leading the church to recognize the canon. Only on the ground of an infallibly guided church can there be a sure canon. Protestants are left with uncertainty regarding the canon, for they cannot draw infallible limits without being untrue to their fundamental theological principles.[368]

Much of Appel's discussion is excellent. Conservative Protestants will appreciate his forthright affirmation of the infallible authority of Scripture and his rejection of any "canon within the canon." So also they will agree that the growth of the canon was not merely a profane historical process but included a theological dimension as well.

The major point of criticism, however, arises precisely over the assessment of this theological dimension. Protestants, who reject the doctrine of ecclesiastical infallibility in other matters, will likely dissent from the opinion that the witness of the Spirit guarantees the infallibility of the church's recognition of the canon. And in fact, one might question whether Appel himself can consistently maintain such a position once he has so clearly affirmed that the canon is the result of a historical process marked by "doubt," "struggle," "uncertainty and hesitation," and regional differences within the church.[369] Specifically, we must ask, when did the witness of the Spirit *in* and *through* the church become infallible? Surely the uncertainty of parts of the church about particular books suggests that this infallibility was not always operative.

Appel himself seems to sense the problem, for he raises the question: "Does this human struggle for certitude also have a theological meaning? In other words, does this human struggle tell us something about the essence of the canon itself?"[370] In the end, Appel's answer is merely that "an accurate investigation of the reasons why certain writings labored under difficulties is of interest for the study of dogma and its development."[371] But has he then faced the full implications of the historical process?

4. Herman Ridderbos

The New Testament scholar Herman Ridderbos is representative of those theologians who discuss the canon—here specifically the New Testament canon—from the perspective of salvation history.[372] This perspective is thoroughly Christological, for it maintains that the canon is properly understood only when seen in its connectedness with God's once-for-all redemptive action in Jesus Christ. As Ridderbos explains,

> ... the authority of God is in no wise limited to his mighty works in Jesus Christ, but ... it also extends to their proclamation in the words and writings of those who have been especially appointed as the authorized bearers and instruments of divine revelation. The written tradition established by the apostles, in analogy with the writings of the Old Testament, thereby acquires the significance of being the foundation and standard of the future church.[373]

There are both positive and negative entailments to a redemptive-historical understanding of the canon. Positively, it should be recognized that (1) in adopting a precise collection as authoritative, the church acted in accord with the facts of salvation history, namely, that Christ gave His disciples authority to serve as the foundation and "canon" of the primitive church. The priority is to be given to the action of Christ, however, not to the decision of the church: "the canon in its redemptive historical sense is not the product of the church; rather the church itself is the product of the canon."[374] Moreover, given the foundational and unrepeatable character of the writing of the apostles, it is clear that (2) the canon is in principle closed. Finally, the redemptive historical position of the canon necessitates that (3) this canon should be preserved for the church in written form. The Roman Catholic attempt to retain an oral tradition alongside the written can only lead to a relativizing of the New Testament canon.[375]

Negatively, Ridderbos argues against Harnack that (1) the growth of the recognition of the canon is not foreign to the character of earliest Christianity. According to Harnack, the church's original authority was charismatic. Later, as that authority took on an apostolic-institutional character, the canon was formed; thus was the Spirit "driven into a book." Yet, in the light of salvation history, the church never knew any authority but that which was founded on apostolic traditions. (2) Salvation history also speaks to the question of a canon within the canon. Luther's principle of canonicity ("whether it preaches Christ") effectively points to the intention of Christ in establishing the canon but must not be employed as a criterion of canonicity. What it means "to preach Christ" can be answered only in terms of the canon itself. (3) The redemptive-historical understanding of the canon is also opposed to a merely actualistic notion of canonicity (whereby the New Testament's authority consists only in the fact that the church continues to hear in these writings the word of God). To focus on the subjective reception of Scripture in this exclusive way undermines the objective validity of the canon.[376]

That Christ Himself as witnessed to by the apostles forms the ground of the canon is an *a priori* that must be received by faith. But, viewed as the canon of Christ, the canon cannot automatically be equated with our concrete collection of twenty-seven writings. Doubts exist about the apostolicity of particular writings of the present canon, and there is no *a posteriori* justification, whether by scientific investigation or certification by another external authority (Rome), that can eliminate all uncertainties. Some Protestants have also come close to a doctrine of ecclesiastical infallibility regarding the recognition of the canon by positing a special enduement of the Holy Spirit, a special providence of God, or an extension of the concept of inspiration to guide the canonization process.[377] Ridderbos, however, rejects all of these approaches. There is no escaping the fallibility of the church, even in connection with the recognition of the canon. Faith and history must be held in tension:

> The absoluteness of the canon is not to be separated from the relativity of history. It is true, however, that we shall have to view the history of the canon in the light of this a priori of faith; and we shall view it as a history in which not only the power of human sin and error, but, above all, Christ's promise works itself out, in order to build and to establish His church upon the testimony of the apostles.[378]

Concerning the actual history of the canon, Ridderbos makes several observations. First, he notes that the church prior to the end of the fourth century made no formal decisions on the shape or content of the canon, nor did it devise specific criteria to establish canonicity. The canon functioned more as a presupposition—at first largely unconscious—for the life of the early church. In this light, Ridderbos rejects the idea that the canon is merely a reaction to Marcion or to the Montanists; rather, both of these challenges only served to awaken the church's self-consciousness of its true origins.[379]

Second, the apostolic authority of the majority of the twenty-seven books was never questioned, and the differences that arose over the antilegomena should be seen in proper perspective. Compared to the conflicts that arose with Marcion and the Montanists, the debates over the limits of the canon were secondary and caused little distress. It is true that a variety of factors influenced the reception or rejection of the antilegomena, but ultimately two were decisive for acceptance. The first was growing ecumenical unity that showed the local and provincial character of many of the objections to particular books. Second was the overriding influence of the larger core of received books; no book was accepted whose content was seen to contradict the witness of the larger collection.[380]

The history of the canon, therefore, testifies to the great assurance with which the church received the canon; this is true in some sense even with respect to the antilegomena. Such assurance is indicative of the very nature of the canonical process.

The Church has dealt in this situation as does one who knows and points to a certain person as father and mother. Such a knowledge rests not on demonstration but upon direct experience; it is most closely connected with one's own identity. In this and no other way must we picture the knowledge and the "decision" of the Church concerning the canon. They have a direct character and flow forth out of the very existence of the Church itself.[381]

In this way the history of the canon *a posteriori* supports the salvation-historical *a priori*. Yet it remains a confession of faith that the canon of the New Testament corresponds exactly to Christ's canon, for their identity cannot be absolutely established by historical study.[382]

To summarize, Ridderbos consistently rejects the possibility that the church could or did establish its own canon. Christ alone and His appointed witnesses constitute the canon. The church can only point to this canon as that which lies at the foundation of its existence. Moreover, the reception of the canon by the church is a fallible reception. However, in the end, Ridderbos acknowledges (in faith) that the empirical canon coincides with the canon of Christ.

Ridderbos provides one of the most important studies of the theology of the canon. His stress on the redemptive-historical rootedness of the New Testament canon is both theologically and historically sound. The main question that arises concerning Ridderbos is the sharpness with which he distinguishes the canon of Christ from the empirical canon recognized by the church and rejects "every attempt to find an a posteriori element to justify the canon."[383]

While one may agree that "no historical argument, no recognition of the authority of the church, no appeal to the consensus of history can replace even to a small extent, the element of faith necessary in the recognition of the canon,"[384] certain issues are confused here. First, Ridderbos too easily lumps Protestant appeals to divine providence in guiding the church's recognition of the canon together with Roman Catholic claims to ecclesiastical infallibility. To be sure, there is a formal similarity, but materially there is a great difference in the theological program here at work (as Appel clearly sees).

Second, Ridderbos's strongly presuppositional apologetic for the canon sets too rigid an antithesis between historical evidence and faith. The appeal by many conservative Protestants to the history of the canon is not a denial of faith but a recognition that faith is rooted in history and thus is not without evidence. Happily, Ridderbos himself makes some appeal to the confirmatory witness of history, and in that sense he seems to transcend the dichotomy that he has drawn.

V. CONCLUSION

The preceding pages have surveyed the contemporary historical and theological discussions relative to the canon. In what follows I shall summarize my own position, restricting my comments largely to the New Testament·canon, although a number of the conclusions will hold for the Old Testament as well.

The account of the canon given by liberal Protestantism is unacceptable. Where the canon is seen to be purely and simply a consequence of the church's decision, with no divine or apostolic sanction, the results are disastrous. While many nice things may still be affirmed about the Bible—its uniqueness, its traditional prominence and influence in the Christian tradition, its proximity to the original revelatory events, etc.—in the end it remains no more than the fallible witness of a fallible church. It is this that constitutes the ongoing crisis of modern Protestantism, rightly critiqued by Gerhard Maier and Nicolaus Appel.

Moreover, the view of critical orthodoxy lacks sufficient historical evidence. The early church fathers show no consciousness that they are acting to establish the canon. Indeed, the basic shape of the New Testament canon was securely fixed long before any fourth-century councils declared themselves on the matter. The obvious *a posteriori* character of the arguments used by Irenaeus and his successors to defend particular aspects of the New Testament canon calls into question what it means to say that the church "chose" or "established" the canon. The apparently spontaneous development of the (New Testament) canon suggests that it is more appropriate to speak of a *recognition* rather than a selection of the New Testament books, and the same interpretation can be extended to the recognition of the Old Testament.

There is a general consensus among recent interpreters that the idea of canon is a theological construct that must be distinguished from the idea of "Scripture." Canon suggests the ideas of delimitation and selection that are not necessarily included in the term "Scripture."[385] Modern canon studies are quite conscious of the human elements—the doubts, the debates, and the delays—of the canonical process. "Canon," according to recent scholarship, is an idea that has arisen subsequent to the idea of "Scripture." As a developed theological construct, therefore, canon belongs not to the apostolic period so much as to the postapostolic period. I have no quarrel with this basic interpretation; there seems to be no other way to deal with the patristic materials. So, too, our discussion of the Old Testament canon showed that the idea of a closed canon appears only when Judaism had recognized that the period of classical prophecy was over.

This position has important consequences for many conservative

Protestant and Evangelical treatments of the canon. Frequently the ideas of canon, Scripture, and apostolic authority have been lumped together in a rather undifferentiated mass in which it is assumed that if one of these is present the others must be also. Thus, if it can be shown that the early church acknowledged apostolic authority, it is assumed that this proves that it also possessed rather complete ideas of New Testament Scripture and of canon. Something of this approach lies behind B. B. Warfield's statement that "the canon of the New Testament was completed when the last authoritative book was given to any church by the apostles" and that "the principle of canonicity was not apostolic authorship, but *imposition by the apostles as 'law.'*"[386] Now if Warfield by this statement intends merely to point to the objective aspect of canonical authority—what Ridderbos calls the redemptive-historical ground of the canon—I am quite in agreement with the statement. However, if Warfield means (as I believe he does) that the early church received the New Testament writings from the apostles with a consciousness that these documents had an inspired status that was fully parallel to the *graphai* of the Old Testament, I dissent. As Ned B. Stonehouse recognizes, " . . . this view lacks specific confirmation from the available evidence and, moreover, cannot account for the diversity with respect to the limits of the New Testament which prevailed for decades and even for centuries."[387] The seeming reluctance at an early period to designate the apostolic writings as "Scripture," the undifferentiating appeal to oral or written tradition, and the uncertainty over the status of certain books demand some adjustments in the traditional Evangelical approach.

Increasingly, modern students of the canon recognize not only the fact of historical process in the formation of the canon but also the genuine connections between the developed canon and the origins of the biblical literature. Specifically, they realize that the words and deeds of Jesus interpreted to the community by the apostles form the ultimate standard or "canon" for the nascent church. In this sense the developed canon is not only apostolic but fundamentally Christological or salvation-historical, as Ridderbos has correctly emphasized. The oral and written apostolic witness to Christ was that from which the primitive church drew its life. The process by which the written form of that witness rose to increasing prominence and was gradually defined in the canonical understanding of the church was both natural and spontaneous. The process was, to a great extent, underway before the Christian community was aware of its implications. From this perspective the sharp reaction of the Fathers to Marcion and the Gnostics is to be seen, not as a *de novo* selection of an alternative canon, but rather as a making explicit of what had always been implicit in the life of the church. Here again Ridderbos's analogy is apt: "the Church has dealt in this situation as

one who knows and points to a certain person as father and mother."
Such knowledge rests not "on demonstration but upon direct
experience."[388]

What does this imply for criteria of canonicity? Broadly stated,
the church regarded apostolicity as the qualifying factor for canonical
recognition;[389] however, this apostolicity should be understood not
strictly in terms of authorship but in terms of content and chronology. That which was canon must embody the apostolic tradition, and
this tradition was to be discerned in the most primitive documents:
"the normative testimonies must derive from the period closest to
Christ, namely that of Christian origins, the age of the apostles and
their disciples."[390] The recognition of this apostolicity, moreover, was
based primarily on the tradition of the church. Those books that had
functioned authoritatively for earlier Christians were received as an
authentic apostolic tradition. In turn, those documents were used in
a negative way to exclude works of later vintage or varying doctrinal
content, as happened, for example, in case of *The Gospel of Peter*.[391]

The importance of traditional usage provides a partial explanation for the debate that surrounded the antilegomena. The tradition
could not be expected to give a uniformly full witness to all of the
biblical books. In this situation, certain books might be questioned on
their relative lack of explicit testimony, not on the grounds of their
doctrinal content. For example, some of the doubts over James and 2
and 3 John[392] can be understood in this light. Obviously, it is not a
sufficient answer for all questions surrounding the antilegomena;
theological factors also played a part, conspicuously in connection
with Revelation[393] and perhaps also with Hebrews. Logistical factors
also influenced canonical development; restricted geographical circu-
lation hindered the ecumenical recognition of some books more than
others.

To what extent are the decisions of the early church permanently
binding on subsequent generations? Should the canon be regarded as
closed or still open? For example, should the church seriously
consider a document like *The Gospel of Thomas* as a candidate for
admission to the New Testament?

To this I respond first that the canon is in principle closed. This
is affirmed (following Ridderbos) on the basis of the salvation-
historical context of the New Testament canon. Christ and the
apostolic tradition constitute the eschatological fullness of divine
revelation. The canon, therefore, is limited to those documents that
the church experienced as foundational to its own existence. This
foundation is temporally limited. Dating this limit is not so important
as the fact that the church recognized there was such a limit and
therefore made a qualitative distinction between the age of the
apostles and the age of the church.[394] This insight remains valid
today.

Moreover, the Christian community of the second century was in a better position than the church of the later centuries to acknowledge the documents that *de facto* constituted the ground of its existence. The fact that the arguments used to defend the canonicity of certain books appear inadequate to some streams of modern scholarship does not necessarily disqualify the particular books in view since, as already noted, these arguments were generally *a posteriori*. The determining factor was usage, that is, the church's recognition of its own origins. This provides also an answer to the question of a "lost" apostolic document. Should such a document be found, would it be appropriate to include it in the canon? On the basis of what we have just said about usage, the answer will be no. The question here is not one of authenticity (although one wonders how agreement could ever be reached on such a question). The issue is rather that such a document certainly has not functioned for the church as foundational; therefore, it would be inappropriate to move beyond that foundation.

However, the closed status and enduring validity of the present canon is affirmed not merely on the ground of the close proximity of the second-century church to the original revelatory events or upon that community's supposedly clearer historical memory. The binding nature of the canon—binding here in the theological sense of "divinely authoritative"—is based upon the conviction that the canon acknowledged by the church is nothing other than the redemptive-historical canon given by Jesus Christ through the apostles and those whom the church recognized as "apostolic men." The truth of this conviction cannot be demonstrated unambiguously from historical analysis of the canonical process but is founded upon the presupposition of divine sovereignty in human history and the life of the church. Stonehouse observes:

> Although it is highly important that this historical process be studied and analyzed as a part of our effort to comprehend the implications of the Church's doctrine of Scripture, we also insist that the comprehension of the whole development depends on a recognition of divine control of history and of the special guidance of the Spirit of God.[395]

Ridderbos objects to any such *a posteriori* justification of the canon, and yet his appeal to the *a priori* of faith in reference to the New Testament canon seems only to shift the emphasis from faith in the providence of God and the leading of the Spirit to faith in the salvation-historical roots of the canon. But need these elements be placed in antithesis? Is not the *a priori* of faith a conviction that the God who spoke decisively to His people "in a Son" (Heb 1:2) has acted to preserve the message once given?

The objection of Ridderbos seems to derive from a fear that any appeal to a special providence or to the Spirit's leading for the recognition of the canon will eventuate in affirming the infallibility of the church, as in Roman Catholicism. A similar concern has led many Protestants to affirm a theoretically open canon. Yet the problem may not be so great as it appears at first. The idea of canon in its fully developed sense of a limited collection of documents uniquely authoritative for the life of the church is a theological Gestalt, or model, that parallels other major doctrines of the Christian community. As John Montgomery notes, "*absolute* certainty, both in science and theology, rests only with the data (for the former, natural phenomena; for the latter, scriptural affirmations)."[396] But the shape and limits of the canon are not scriptural affirmations. Therefore, if Montgomery is correct—and I believe he is—we cannot claim *absolute* empirical certainty for our canonical model. On the other hand, Montgomery allows that there are varying levels of certainty within theological formulations and that "some formulations are so well attested by the data that they acquire a practically (though not a theoretically) 'certain' status."[397]

It seems to me that the church's formulation of the canon falls within Montgomery's "practically certain" category. There is no claim here to ecclesiastical infallibility in the strict sense, yet there is great assurance to be drawn from the widespread judgment of the early Christians that this group of writings comprises the authoritative teachings of the apostles. Oscar Cullmann speaks of "the astonishing historical and theological assurance with which the Church proceeded when it settled on the fourfold canon."[398] Perhaps. But if the church's decision grew out of its direct experience with the foundational, normative, and life-sustaining character of these writings, is it really so astonishing? The early Christians believed that they knew where to find the canon of Christ and the apostles. Today we still so believe.

Abbreviations for Works Cited

ANF	*The Ante-Nicene Fathers*, ed. Alexander Roberts and James Donaldson, 10 vols. (Buffalo: Christian Literature, 1885–96; reprint, Grand Rapids: Eerdmans, 1950)
AUSS	*Andrews University Seminary Studies*
BA	*The Biblical Archaeologist*
BAGD	Walter Bauer, William F. Arndt, F. Wilbur Gingrich, and Frederick W. Danker, *A Greek-English Lexicon of the New Testament* (Chicago and London: University of Chicago Press, 1979)
BETS	*Bulletin of the Evangelical Theological Society*
Bib	*Biblica*
BJRL	*Bulletin of the John Rylands Library*
BS	*Bibliotheca Sacra*
BT	*The Bible Translator*
BTB	*Biblical Theology Bulletin*
CBQ	*Catholic Biblical Quarterly*
CQ	*Classical Quarterly*
CTM	*Concordia Theological Monthly*
DBSup	*Dictionnaire de la Bible, Supplement*, (Paris: Letourney, 1957)
EBC	*The Expositor's Bible Commentary*, ed. Frank E. Gaebelein, 12 vols. (Grand Rapids: Zondervan, 1976–)
EQ	*The Evangelical Quarterly*
ExpT	*The Expository Times*
GOR	*Greek Orthodox Review*
GCS	*Die griechischen christlichen Schriftsteller de ersten drei Jahrhunderte*, 40 vols. (Berlin: Akademie-Verlag, 1897–)
GTJ	*Grace Theological Journal*
H&T	*History and Theology*
HE	Eusebius, *Historia Ecclesiastica*
HeyJ	*Heythrop Journal*
HTR	*The Harvard Theological Review*
Int	*Interpretation*
IRM	*International Review of Mission*
JAAR	*Journal of the American Academy of Religion*
JBL	*Journal of Biblical Literature*
JBR	*Journal of Bible and Religion*

JETS	*Journal of the Evangelical Theological Society*
JPH	*Journal of Presbyterian History*
JQR	*Jewish Quarterly Review*
JR	*Journal of Religion*
JRT	*Journal of Religious Thought*
JSNT	*Journal for the Study of the New Testament*
JSOT	*Journal for the Study of the Old Testament*
JTS	*Journal of Theological Studies*
McCQ	*McCormick Quarterly*
NovT	*Novum Testamentum*
NPNF1	*The Nicene and Post-Nicéne Fathers*, ed. Philip Schaff, 1st ser., 14 vols. (repr. ed., Grand Rapids: Eerdmans, 1979)
NPNF2	*The Nicene and Post-Nicene Fathers*, ed. Philip Schaff and Henry Wace, 2d ser., 14 vols. (repr. ed., Grand Rapids: Eerdmans, 1975)
NTS	*New Testament Studies*
PEQ	*Palestine Exploration Quarterly*
PG	*Patrologia graeca*, ed. J. P. Migne, 162 vols. (Paris: Lutetiae, 1857–66)
PMLA	*Publications of the Modern Language Association*
PRS	*Perspectives in Religious Studies*
RB	*Revue Biblique*
RBén	*Revue bénédictine*
RTR	*The Reformed Theological Review*
SC	*Sources chrétiennes* (Paris: Editions du Cerf, 1940–)
SE	*Studia Evangelica*
SJT	*The Scottish Journal of Theology*
SNT	*Studien zum Neuen Testament*
SWJT	*Southwestern Journal of Theology*
TB	*Tyndale Bulletin*
TDNT	*Theological Dictionary of the New Testament*, ed. Gerhard Kittel and Gerhard Friedrich, 10 vols. (Grand Rapids: Eerdmans, 1964–76)
TJ	*Trinity Journal*
TP	*Theologie and Philosophie*
TS	*Theological Studies*
TSFB	*Theological Students Fellowship Bulletin*
TU	*Texte und Untersuchungen*
USQR	*Union Seminary Quarterly Review*
VC	*Vigiliae Christianae*
WTJ	*The Westminster Theological Journal*

Notes

CHAPTER ONE
RECENT DEVELOPMENTS IN THE DOCTRINE OF SCRIPTURE
D. A. Carson
1–48

[1] *Contra* Jack B. Rogers and Donald K. McKim, *The Authority and Interpretation of the Bible: An Historical Approach* (San Francisco: Harper & Row, 1979), 89ff.

[2] See especially H. D. McDonald, *Theories of Revelation: An Historical Study 1700–1960* [original titles *Ideas of Revelation* and *Theories of Revelation*] (1959 and 1963; reprint, Grand Rapids: Baker, 1979); and S. L. Greenslade, ed., *The Cambridge History of the Bible: The West from the Reformation to the Present Day* (Cambridge: Cambridge University Press, 1963).

[3] Viz., D. A. Carson and John D. Woodbridge, eds., *Scripture and Truth* (Grand Rapids: Zondervan, 1983).

[4] The recent literature is legion. The most important books and articles include the following: Paul J. Achtemeier, *The Inspiration of Scripture: Problems and Proposals* (Philadelphia: Westminster, 1980); M. R. Austin, "How Biblical is 'The Inspiration of Scripture'?" *ExpT* 93 (1981–82), 75–79; James Barr, *The Scope and Authority of the Bible* (London: SCM, 1980; Philadelphia: Westminster, 1981); idem, *Holy Scripture: Canon, Authority, Criticism* (Oxford: Oxford University Press, 1983); David L. Bartlett, *The Shape of Scriptural Authority* (Philadelphia: Fortress, 1983); Robert Gnuse, "Authority of the Scriptures: Quest for a Norm," *BTB* 13 (1983), 59–66; Paul D. Hanson, *The Diversity of Scripture: A Theological Interpretation* (Philadelphia: Fortress, 1982); Krister Stendahl, "The Bible as a Classic and the Bible as Holy Scripture," *JBL* 103 (1984), 3–10; idem, *Meanings: The Bible as Document and as Guide* (Philadelphia: Fortress, 1984). Also, many works on the interpretation of Scripture have important things to say about the Bible's authority. The same point could be made for some works published in other languages: the debate between Gerhard Maier, *Das Ende der historisch-kritischen Methode*, 5th ed. (Wuppertal: Brockhaus, 1984), and Peter Stuhlmacher, *Schriftauslegung auf dem Wege zur biblischen Theologie* (Göttingen: Vandenhoeck und Ruprecht, 1975); or the essay by Pierre Gisel, "Pour une theologie de l'Ecriture: Réactions face à la 'Théologie du mouvement évangelique,' " *Etudes théologiques et religieuses* 59 (1984), 509–21. Cf. also Eckhard Schnabel, "Die neuere Diskussion um die Inspiration der Heiligen Schrift," *Bibel und Gemeinde* 84 (1984), 409–30.

[5] So, for instance, James D. G. Dunn, "The Authority of Scripture According to Scripture," *Churchman* 96 (1982), 105–6. When Dunn argues that at the turn of the century the range of opinion among Evangelicals ranged from Warfield to Orr, he is, of course, right; but what he fails to assess is the *distribution* of those opinions among the Evangelicals. This sort of historical question receives a little more attention below.

[6] There is an enormous range of positions within this "left wing" of Evangelicals, as well as an enormous range of competency—from the mature and articulate to the astonishingly ignorant. Representative recent works include: William J. Abraham, *The Divine Inspiration of Holy Scripture* (New York/Oxford: Oxford University Press, 1981); idem, *Divine Revelation and the Limits of Historical Criticism* (Oxford: Oxford University Press, 1983); G. C. Berkouwer, *Studies in Dogmatics: Holy Scripture* (Grand Rapids:

Eerdmans, 1975); Donald G. Bloesch, *The Ground of Certainty: Toward an Evangelical Theology of Revelation* (Grand Rapids: Eerdmans, 1971); idem, *Essentials of Evangelical Theology*, vol. 1, *God, Authority, and Salvation* (San Francisco: Harper & Row, 1978), 51–87; Dunn, "The Authority of Scripture According to Scripture," 104–22, 201–25; I. Howard Marshall, *Biblical Inspiration* (Grand Rapids: Eerdmans, 1982); Robert M. Price, "Inerrant the Wind: The Troubled House of North American Evangelicals," *EQ* 55 (1983), 129–44; Bernard Ramm, *After Fundamentalism* (San Francisco: Harper & Row, 1983); Jack B. Rogers, "Biblical Authority and Confessional Change," *JPH* 59 (1981), 131–58; Jack B. Rogers and Donald K. McKim, *The Authority and Interpretation of the Bible.*

[7] In addition to some purely popular publications, the principal ICBI-sponsored publications are as follows: Norman L. Geisler, ed., *Inerrancy* (Grand Rapids: Zondervan, 1979); idem, *Biblical Errancy: Its Philosophical Roots* (Grand Rapids: Zondervan, 1981); Earl D. Radmacher and Robert D. Preus, eds., *Hermeneutics, Inerrancy, and the Bible* (Grand Rapids: Zondervan, 1984); John D. Hannah, ed., *Inerrancy and the Church* (Chicago: Moody, 1984); Gordon Lewis and Bruce Demarest, eds., *Challenges to Inerrancy* (Chicago: Moody, 1984).

[8] Paul D. Feinberg, "The Meaning of Inerrancy," in *Inerrancy*, ed. Norman L. Geisler (Grand Rapids: Zondervan, 1979), 267–304.

[9] Most of the contributors to this present volume and *Scripture and Truth*, including the two editors, have written nothing for ICBI. In addition, many books and articles have been published recently whose authors or editors may hold some connection with ICBI, even though the publication itself has not been sponsored by that organization: e.g., Roger R. Nicole and J. Ramsay Michaels, eds., *Inerrancy and Common Sense* (Grand Rapids: Baker, 1980); J. I. Packer, *God Has Spoken* (Downers Grove: InterVarsity, 1979); Paul Ronald Wells, *James Barr and the Bible: A Critique of the New Liberalism* (Phillipsburg, N.J.: Presbyterian and Reformed, 1980); Leon Morris, *I Believe in Revelation* (Grand Rapids: Eerdmans, 1976).

[10] Carl F. H. Henry, *God, Revelation and Authority*, 6 vols. (Waco: Word, 1976–83).

[11] I have defined the term in D. A. Carson, "Historical Tradition and the Fourth Gospel: After Dodd, What?" in *Gospel Perspectives II*, ed. R. T. France and David Wenham (Sheffield: JSOT, 1981), 83–145.

[12] Walter M. Abbott, ed., *The Documents of Vatican II* (New York: Guild, 1966), 119. See discussion by someone sympathetic to the final draft in Bruce Vawter, *Biblical Inspiration* (Philadelphia: Westminster, 1972; London: Hutchinson, 1972), 144–50.

[13] I am referring to commentaries, journal articles, published dissertations, works of theology, and the like that approach the truthfulness of Scripture in ways that an earlier generation of Catholic scholars could scarcely imagine. These include not only the contributions of North Atlantic scholars (e.g., Eduard Schillebeeckx and Hans Küng) but many "third world" works as well (e.g., the left wing of the largely Roman Catholic theology of liberation movement).

[14] E.g., *inter alia* Raymond E. Brown, "Rome and the Freedom of Catholic Biblical Studies," in *Search the Scriptures* [Festschrift for R. T. Stamm], ed. J. M. Myers et al. (Leiden: Brill, 1969) 129–50; idem, *The Critical Meaning of the Bible* (New York: Paulist, 1981); Vawter, *Biblical Inspiration*; Avery Dulles, *Models of Revelation* (New York: Doubleday, 1983).

[15] I am thinking of the works of such scholars as Albert Vanhoye and Ignace de la Potterie.

[16] E.g., George A. Kelly, *The New Biblical Theorists: Raymond E. Brown and Beyond* (Ann Arbor: Servant, 1983). For recent Protestant assessments, see Robert L. Saucy, "Recent Roman Catholic Theology," in *Challenges to Inerrancy: A Theological Response*, ed. Gordon Lewis and Bruce Demarest (Chicago: Moody, 1984), 215–46.

[17] The cohesiveness of this tradition I shall briefly mention below; but one caveat must be entered immediately. Differences between Protestants and Roman Catholics in the wake of the Reformation do not focus on the truthfulness of Scripture—or on its

authority *per se*—but on the means of obtaining an authoritative interpretation of Scripture and on whether the Scripture alone is the sole locus of absolute authority in the church. Whenever the present study appeals to the cohesiveness of the tradition across the centuries regarding the Bible's authority, it allows for this sort of caveat, since the issues raised by it are of little consequence to the present discussion.

[18] Martin E. Marty, "Tensions Within Contemporary Evangelicalism: A Critical Appraisal," in *The Evangelicals*, ed. David F. Wells and John D. Woodbridge (Nashville: Abingdon, 1975), 170–88.

[19] Ibid., 173, 180.

[20] See especially his *Biblical Study: Its Principles, Methods and History* (New York: Scribner, 1883).

[21] See especially the essays by Geoffrey Bromiley and John Frame in this volume.

[22] Rogers and McKim, *The Authority and Interpretation of the Bible*.

[23] John D. Woodbridge, "Biblical Authority: Towards an Evaluation of the Rogers and McKim Proposal," *TJ* 1 (1980), 165–236; idem, *Biblical Authority: A Critique of the Rogers/McKim Proposal* (Grand Rapids: Zondervan, 1982). One reviewer of Woodbridge's book rather badly missed the point by suggesting that although Rogers and McKim had been answered at the historical level, Woodbridge had failed to tackle the important hermeneutical issues that Rogers and McKim had raised. But, in fact, theirs was not a hermeneutical but a historical thesis. Another (William J. Abraham, "Redeeming the Evangelical Experiment," *TSFB* 8:3 [January–February 1985]: 12n.5) obliquely refers to Woodbridge's work to excoriate conservative claims "about the Bible" because "they rest on arguments which are narrowly historical in nature." The lack of evenhanded rigor in such a charge is frankly astonishing; Rogers and McKim set forth a thesis based on their historical understanding, and they were refuted in the same arena. Why, then, is it the conservative arguments that are "narrowly historical in nature"?

[24] The word is chosen by Rodney L. Petersen in his review of Rogers and McKim in *The Princeton Seminary Bulletin* 4 (1983), 61–63.

[25] Ernest R. Sandeen, *Roots of Fundamentalism: British & American Millenarianism, 1800–1930* (Chicago: University of Chicago Press, 1970; reprint, Grand Rapids: Baker, 1978).

[26] See especially Randall H. Balmer, "The Old Princeton Doctrine of Inspiration in the Context of Nineteenth-Century Theology: A Reappraisal" (M.A. thesis, Trinity Evangelical Divinity School, 1981); idem, "The Princetonians and Scripture: A Reconsideration," *WTJ* 44 (1982), 352–65; John D. Woodbridge and Randall H. Balmer, "The Princetonians and Biblical Authority: An Assessment of the Ernest Sandeen Proposal," in *Scripture and Truth*, ed. Carson and Woodbridge, 245–79, 396–410.

[27] Numerous writers have recently taken up this point (though a substantial part of contemporary scholarship continues to take the opposite view): e.g., James I. Packer, "John Calvin and the Inerrancy of Holy Scripture," in *Inerrancy and the Church*, 143–88; W. Robert Godfrey, "Biblical Authority in the Sixteenth and Seventeenth Centuries: A Question of Transition," in *Scripture and Truth*, ed. Carson and Woodbridge, 225–43, 391–97; Roger R. Nicole, "John Calvin and Inerrancy," *JETS* 25:4 (December 1982): 425–42; Eugene F. Klug, "Word and Spirit in Luther Studies since World War II," *TJ* 5 (1984), 3–46.

[28] Richard B. Gaffin, Jr., "Old Amsterdam and Inerrancy?" *WTJ* 44 (1982), 250–89; 45 (1983), 219–72.

[29] Ian S. Rennie, "Mixed Metaphors, Misunderstood Models, and Puzzling Paradigms: A Contemporary Effort to Correct Some Misunderstandings Regarding the Authority and Interpretation of the Bible: An Historical Response," a mimeographed but unpublished paper delivered at the conference, "Interpreting an Authoritative Scripture," in Toronto, Ontario, Canada, on June 22–26, 1981.

[30] Ibid., 11.

[31] For this paragraph and the next, I am heavily indebted to Richard Riss in an unpublished paper, "A Critical Examination of Ian Rennie's Historiography of Biblical Inspiration." See also his forthcoming thesis, "Early Nineteenth Century Protestant Views of Biblical Inspiration in the English Speaking World" (M.A. thesis, Trinity Evangelical Divinity School, 1986).

[32] Riss points out that "plenary inspiration" is not distinguished from "verbal inspiration" in Ebenezer Henderson's *Divine Inspiration* (1836), in Daniel Wilson's *The Evidences of Christianity* (1852), or in such important discussions of the doctrine as John Dick's *Essay on the Inspiration of the Holy Scriptures of the Old and New Testaments* (1811) or T. F. Curtis's *The Human Element in the Inspiration of the Sacred Scriptures* (1867).

[33] Thus, William Cooke, who held to verbal inspiration, could write that his "immediate object" was "to maintain the *plenary inspiration* of the sacred writers, and to show that the books of the Old and New Testament are the authentic oracles of God" (*Christian Theology* [London: Hamilton, Adams, and Co., 1879], 55). Cooke is not exceptional: cf. Eleazar Lord, *The Plenary Inspiration of the Holy Scriptures* (New York: A. D. F. Randolph, 1858); John Farrar, *Biblical and Theological Dictionary*, ed. J. Robinson Gregory (London: Charles H. Kelly, 1889), 354.

[34] So, for instance, Henry Alford, in the sixth section of the first chapter of his preface to *The Greek Testament*. Similarly, Daniel Wilson, whom Rennie lists as a fine exponent of plenary inspiration, can emphasize that the Bible is "the unerring standard of truth" and was "universally considered as the infallible word of God" throughout the preceding sixteen or seventeen centuries (*The Evidences of Christianity*, 254–55).

[35] See the discussion by David F. Wright, "Soundings in the Doctrine of Scripture in British Evangelicalism in the First Half of the Twentieth Century," *TB* 31 (1980): 87–106, who fails to treat this point adequately. He goes on to suggest that "[one] reason why Britain did not experience a Fundamentalist controversy in the 1910's and 1920's akin to the bitter battle in America lay in the more widespread acceptance of biological evolution by thinking evangelicals before the beginning of the century" (p. 92). But not only does this overlook the fact that Warfield himself was an evolutionist; it stands as an unproved judgment in need of immediate qualification by other factors. For instance, most Christians in England belonged to the state church; and a state church makes the kind of cleavage found in North America structurally almost impossible. The vast majority of institutions for theological training were either university faculties or state church theological colleges. Even so, the Baptist Union (a powerful independent denomination of Evangelicals in Britain as late as 1885) shortly thereafter split over the doctrine of Scripture, largely owing to the influence of C. H. Spurgeon. Moreover, many today would argue that the relative strength of American Evangelicals' institutions at the end of the twentieth century—and the consequent growth of the church—largely validates the painful and often courageous decisions to withdraw in the 1920s and 1930s from the parent organizations increasingly character-ized at the time by straightforward unbelief.

[36] Thomas Ridgley, *A Body of Divinity*, vol. 1 (New York: Robert Carter and Brothers, 1855), 57. Rennie's view needs further qualification from the thesis of Henning Graf Reventlow, *Bibelautorität und Geist der Moderne: Die Bedeutung des Bibelver-ständnisses für die geistesgeschichtliche und politische Entwicklung in England von der Reformation bis zur Aufklärung* (Göttingen: Vandenhoeck und Ruprecht, 1980), who argues that the eighteenth-century German moves adopting increasingly skeptical biblical criticism were dependent on seventeenth-century *English* developments. Reventlow's seminal study rightly debunks the stereotypical presentation of the rise of biblical criticism by showing that its roots are much earlier than the eighteenth century and are not simply German; but I suspect his important thesis unwittingly introduces a new reductionism by failing to discuss continental (especially French and Dutch) seventeenth-century intellectual history as well as English seventeenth-century intel-lectual history.

[37] Cf. Edward Norris Kirk, *Speech of Rev. E. N. Kirk at the Second Anniversary of the American Anti-Slavery Society* (New York: Anti-Slavery Society, 1835).

[38] Idem, *A Plea for the Poor* (Boston: Tappan and Dennet, 1843).

[39] Vawter, *Biblical Inspiration*; idem, "Creationism: Creative Misuse of the Bible," in *Is God a Creationist? The Religious Case Against Creation-Science*, ed. Roland Mushat Frye (New York: Scribner, 1983), 71–82.

[40] The title of the series is "Recent Interpretations of Biblical Authority." The third lecture is subtitled, "Does the Bible Teach 'Science'?" All are currently being published *ad seriatim* in *Bibliotheca Sacra*. I am indebted to Professor Woodbridge for stimulating discussions and important documentation in this area. See also his essay in this volume, "Some Misconceptions of the Impact of the 'Enlightenment' on the Doctrine of Scripture."

[41] The paradigmatic approach to the history of science was put on a respectable and influential footing by Thomas S. Kuhn, *The Structure of Scientific Revolutions* (Chicago: University of Chicago Press, 1962, 1970); but the theory has suffered a rather devastating attack in Frederick Suppe, ed., *The Structure of Scientific Theories*, 2d ed. (Urbana: University of Illinois Press, 1977); Gary Gutting, ed., *Paradigms and Revolutions: Applications and Appraisals of Thomas Kuhn's Philosophy of Science* (Notre Dame: University of Notre Dame Press, 1980).

[42] John D. Woodbridge, "Does the Bible Teach 'Science'?" *BS* 142 (1985): 199, referring to Wolfgang Milde.

[43] See especially Edward Rosen, "Kepler and the Lutheran Attitude Towards Copernicanism in the Context of the Struggle Between Science and Religion," in *Kepler, Four Hundred Years: Proceedings of Conferences held in honour of Johannes Kepler*, ed. Arthur Beer and Peter Beer (Oxford: Pergamon, 1975) 332–33.

[44] Ibid., 328.

[45] John D. Woodbridge, "Does the Bible Teach 'Science'?" p. 202.

[46] Cf. *inter alia*, Sydney E. Ahlstrom, "The Scottish Philosophy and American Theology," *Church History* 24 (1955): 257–72; Theodore Dwight Bozemann, *Protestants in an Age of Science: The Baconian Ideal and Antebellum American Religious Thought* (Chapel Hill: University of North Carolina Press, 1977); George M. Marsden, *The Evangelical Mind and the New School Presbyterian Experience* (New Haven: Yale University Press, 1970), 47–52; idem, *Fundamentalism and American Culture: The Shaping of Twentieth-Century Evangelicalism, 1870–1925* (New York: Oxford University Press, 1980), 55–61, 212–20; idem, "Preachers of Paradox: The Religious New Right in Historical Perspective," in *Religion in America: Spirituality in a Secular Age* (Boston: Beacon, 1982, 1983), 150–68 (esp. 163–64); Henry F. May, *The Enlightenment in America* (New York: Oxford University Press, 1976), 307–62; E. Brooks Holifield, *The Gentlemen Theologians: American Theology in Southern Culture, 1795–1860* (Durham: Duke University Press, 1978), 72–154; John C. Vander Stelt, *Philosophy and Scripture: A Study in Old Princeton and Westminster Theology* (Marlton: Mack, 1978); Mark A. Noll, "Common Sense Traditions and American Evangelical Thought" (unpublished paper read at the 1984 Annual Meetings of the Evangelical Theological Society). These works are not all of a piece: the Ahlstrom essay is seminal and judicious, virtues not present in all of the others.

[47] This is, of course, a simplification. Some antecedents in Common Sense can be traced to Aquinas and Aristotle; and the title of "founder" of the movement is often assigned to Gershom Carmichael or James McCosh. But Reid is widely recognized as the "archetypical Scottish Philosopher" (the language is that of Sydney Ahlstrom, "The Scottish Philosophy," 260).

[48] See especially Rogers and McKim, *The Authority and Interpretation of the Bible*, 235–48.

[49] Marsden, "Preachers of Paradox," 163.

[50] See David Hackett Fischer, *Historians' Fallacies: Toward a Logic of Historical Thought* (New York: Harper Torchbooks, 1970), 164–86, and the piercing critique of the method in the review by Gordon S. Woods of Gary Wills, *Explaining America: The Federalist*, in *The New York Review of Books* 28 (April 2, 1981): 16–18.

[51] See Charles Hodge, *Systematic Theology*, 4 vols. (New York: Scribner, Armstrong, and Co., 1872–74), 1:340–65, 2:278–309.

[52] At a generalizing level, several scholars have pointed out that Common Sense traditions had great impact on the broad sweep of American intellectual life (e.g., Sydney Ahlstrom, "The Scottish Philosophy"); but insufficient attention has been paid to particulars. Arguably, for instance, the Yale systematician Nathaniel W. Taylor, in his *Lectures on the Moral Government of God*, 2 vols. (New York: Clark, Austin, and Smith, 1859), especially in his understanding of free agency (see vol. 2, esp. chs. VII and XII), displays greater dependence on Common Sense categories than does any of the Princetonians.

[53] See the penetrating review of Marsden's *Fundamentalism* by Steve Martin in *TJ* 2 (1981): 94–99.

[54] Interestingly, in his most recent essay, Marsden has begun to back away from making Common Sense the general whipping boy. Impressed by the miasma of subjectivity into which certain strands of modern historiography have sunk, he now suggests we can learn from Thomas Reid—but not so far as Reid's approach to science is concerned. See George M. Marsden, "Common Sense and the Spiritual Vision of History," in *History and Historical Understanding*, ed. C. T. McIntire and Ronald A. Wells (Grand Rapids: Eerdmans, 1984), 55–68.

[55] Darryl G. Hart, "The Princeton Mind in the Modern World and the Common Sense of J. Gresham Machen," *WTJ* 46 (1984): 1–25.

[56] Charles Hodge, *Systematic Theology*, 1:10.

[57] Some of the problems involved in defining how one may legitimately go about constructing a systematic theology are discussed in the essays by Carson and by Packer in *Scripture and Truth*, ed. Carson and Woodbridge.

[58] Even Vander Stelt, *Philosophy and Scripture*, 125, points out that in 1841, Hodge was proving the Bible's divine origin by appealing to *internal* evidences.

[59] This attempt at redefinition is currently appearing in articles, books, and conferences: e.g., Thomas Finger, "Evangelical Theology: Where Do We Begin?" *TSFB* 8 (November–December 1984): 10–14; Clark H. Pinnock, *The Scripture Principle* (San Francisco: Harper & Row, 1984); Donald G. Bloesch, *Essentials of Evangelical Theology*, 2 vols. (San Francisco: Harper & Row, 1978–79).

[60] That the historian often becomes the persuader can scarcely be doubted. See, for instance, at least some of the essays in George M. Marsden, ed., *Evangelicalism and Modern America* (Grand Rapids: Eerdmans, 1984), especially the essays by Joel Carpenter, Grant Wacker, Martin E. Marty, Nathan O. Hatch, and Richard V. Pierard. Or again, while many Fundamentalists are claiming much more vibrant Christianity in America's early roots than the evidence allows, the response can be equally biased in the opposite direction—e.g., Mark A. Noll, Nathan O. Hatch, and George M. Marsden, *The Search for Christian America* (Westchester, Ill.: Crossway, 1983), and the review in *Church History* 53 (1984): 539–40.

[61] Marsden, *Fundamentalism and American Culture*, 230.

[62] *Churchman* 98 (1984): 208–16.

[63] Ibid., 210.

[64] Ibid., 211.

[65] Achtemeier, *The Inspiration of Scripture*, 95.

[66] James Barr, "The Problem of Fundamentalism Today," in *The Scope and Authority of the Bible*, 79. I have discussed that book at some length in D. A. Carson, "Three Books on the Bible: A Critical Review," *JETS* 26 (1983): 337–67.

⁶⁷Harold Lindsell, *The Battle for the Bible* (Grand Rapids: Zondervan, 1976), 174–76.

⁶⁸My library has many scores of Evangelicals' commentaries and expositions on the Gospels, and not one adopts Lindsell's interpretation.

⁶⁹See Wayne A. Grudem, "Scripture's Self-Attestation and the Problem of Formulating a Doctrine of Scripture," *Scripture and Truth*, ed. Carson and Woodbridge, 19–59 (esp. 51–53).

⁷⁰Ibid.

⁷¹Rudolf Bultmann, *The History of the Synoptic Tradition* (Oxford: Basil Blackwell, 1963).

⁷²E.g., E. J. Young, *Thy Word Is Truth* (Grand Rapids: Eerdmans, 1957).

⁷³One thinks, for instance, of William Lane, *The Gospel According to Mark* (Grand Rapids: Eerdmans, 1974), and Peter T. O'Brien, *Colossians, Philemon* (Waco: Word, 1982).

⁷⁴Douglas J. Moo, "Tradition and Old Testament in Matt 27:3–10," in *Gospel Perspectives III: Studies in Midrash and Historiography*, ed. R. T. France and David Wenham (Sheffield: JSOT, 1983), 157–75.

⁷⁵Gary V. Smith, "Paul's Use of Psalm 68:18 in Ephesians 4:8," *JETS* 15 (1975): 181–89.

⁷⁶Dewey M. Beegle, *The Inspiration of Scripture* (Grand Rapids: Eerdmans, 1963 [*Scripture, Tradition and Infallibility*, rev. ed. (Grand Rapids: Eerdmans, 1973)]).

⁷⁷Roger R. Nicole, "The Inspiration of Scripture: B. B. Warfield and Dr. Dewey M. Beegle," *The Gordon Review* 8 (1964–65): 106.

⁷⁸This same argument is especially stressed by William J. Abraham, *The Divine Inspiration of Holy Scripture* (Oxford: Oxford University Press, 1981). I have discussed that book at some length in Carson, "Three Books on the Bible."

⁷⁹R. C. Sproul, "The Case for Inerrancy: A Methodological Analysis," in *God's Inerrant Word: An International Symposium on the Trustworthiness of Scripture*, ed. John Warwick Montgomery (Minneapolis: Bethany House, 1973), 242–61; see also Paul Helm, "Faith, Evidence, and the Scriptures," in *Scripture and Truth*, ed. Carson and Woodbridge, 303–20, 411.

⁸⁰See Arthur F. Holmes, "Ordinary Language Analysis and Theological Method," *BETS* 11 (1968): 131–38; John Warwick Montgomery, "The Theologian's Craft: A Discussion of Theory Formation and Theory Testing in Theology, in *The Suicide of Christian Theology* (Minneapolis: Bethany House, 1970), 267–313; James I. Packer, "Hermeneutics and Biblical Authority," *Themelios* 1 (Autumn 1975): 3–12; Feinberg, "The Meaning of Inerrancy," 265–304, 468–71; and the literature cited in these works.

⁸¹Packer, "Hermeneutics and Biblical Authority," 3.

⁸²Roger R. Nicole, "The Biblical Concept of Truth," *Scripture and Truth*, ed. Carson and Woodbridge, 283–98.

⁸³Karl Barth, *Church Dogmatics* I, part 2, *The Doctrine of the Word of God* (Edinburgh: T. & T. Clark, 1956), 531. Similarly, see Ramm, *After Fundamentalism*, 103.

⁸⁴Vawter, *Biblical Inspiration*, 169.

⁸⁵Clark H. Pinnock, *The Scripture Principle* (San Francisco: Harper & Row, 1984), 97, 100.

⁸⁶Ibid., 99–100.

⁸⁷Richard A. Muller, *Dictionary of Latin and Greek Theological Terms: Drawn Principally from Protestant Scholastic Theology* (Grand Rapids: Baker, 1985), s.v. *accommodatio*, p. 19. See also John D. Woodbridge, "Some Misconceptions of the Impact of the 'Enlightenment' on the Doctrine of Scripture" (in this volume).

⁸⁸Vawter, *Biblical Inspiration*, 152.

⁸⁹See especially Ford Lewis Battles, "God Was Accommodating Himself to Human Capacity," *Interpretation* 31 (1977): 19–38.

[90] William J. Abraham, *The Divine Inspiration of Holy Scripture* (Oxford: Oxford University Press, 1981).

[91] See the review by Tony Lane in *Themelios* 8 (1982): 32–33; Carson, "Three Books on the Bible" (esp. 337–47).

[92] Louis Gaussen, *Theopneusty; or, The Plenary Inspiration of the Holy Scriptures*, trans. Edward Kirk (New York: John S. Taylor & Co., 1845 [French original 1841]).

[93] Ibid., 128.

[94] Grudem, "Scripture's Self-Attestation."

[95] Benjamin B. Warfield, " 'God-Inspired Scripture'," *The Presbyterian and Reformed Review* 11 (1900): 89–130; reprinted in idem, *The Inspiration and Authority of the Bible*, ed. Samuel G. Craig (Philadelphia: Presbyterian and Reformed, 1948), 245–96.

[96] Marshall, *Biblical Inspiration* (esp. ch. 3).

[97] E.g., the so-called Ligonier Affirmation.

[98] Feinberg, "The Meaning of Inerrancy"; see also Carson, "Three Books on the Bible" (esp. 354–67).

[99] D. A. Carson, "Redaction Criticism: On the Legitimacy and Illegitimacy of a Literary Tool," *Scripture and Truth*, ed. Carson and Woodbridge, 115–42.

[100] See, *inter alios*, Eta Linnemann, *Parables of Jesus* (London: SPCK, 1966); D. O. Via, *The Parables* (Philadelphia: Fortress, 1967); J. D. Crossan, *In Parables* (New York: Harper & Row, 1973). For surveys of the extraordinarily complex questions related to the interpretation of parables, see J. G. Little, "Parable Research in the Twentieth Century," *ExpT* 87 (1975–76): 356–60; 88 (1976–77): 40–44, 71–75; W. S. Kissinger, *The Parables of Jesus: A History of Interpretation and Bibliography* (Metuchen: Scarecrow, 1979); Craig L. Blomberg, "New Horizons in Parable Research," *TJ* 3 (1982): 3–17.

[101] E.g., B. Olsson, *Structure and Meaning in the Fourth Gospel: A Text-Linguistic Analysis of John 2:1–11 and 4:1–42* (Lund: C. W. K. Gleerup, 1974).

[102] E.g., Daniel Patte, *Paul's Faith and the Power of the Gospel: A Structural Introduction to the Pauline Letters* (Philadelphia: Fortress, 1983), 31ff., where the dependency on discovering certain structural opposites frequently leads to a distortion of Galatians.

[103] R. Alan Culpepper, *Anatomy of the Fourth Gospel: A Study in Literary Design* (Philadelphia: Fortress, 1983).

[104] See the review in *TJ* 4 (1983): 122–26.

[105] These developments have come about in part because of the influential work of Hans W. Frei, *The Eclipse of Biblical Narrative: A Study in Eighteenth and Nineteenth Century Hermeneutics* (New Haven: Yale University Press, 1974).

[106] James S. Ackerman, "Joseph, Judah, and Jacob," in *Literary Interpretations of Biblical Narratives Volume 2*, ed. Kenneth R. Gros Louis and James S. Ackerman (Nashville: Abingdon, 1982), 85–113. Of course, this does not mean that rhetorical criticism justifies the *historicity* of the passage in question. In one of his essays in the same volume (viz., "The Jesus Birth Stories," 273–84), Gros Louis stresses that Matthew and Luke display such different literary approaches in their respective birth narratives that it is improper to attempt conflation. More broadly, many practitioners of the new literary criticism begin with models drawn from novels—a form devoted to fiction.

[107] E.g., Gerd Thiessen, *The First Followers of Jesus: A Sociological Analysis of Earliest Christianity* (London: SCM, 1978); idem, *The Miracle Stories of the Early Christian Tradition* (Philadelphia: Fortress, 1983), especially the third part of the book; David L. Mealand, *Poverty and Expectation in the Gospels* (London: SPCK, 1979); Robert P. Carroll, *When Prophecy Failed* (London: SCM, 1979); John H. Elliott, *A Home for the Homeless* (London: SCM, 1982); E. A. Judge, *The Social Pattern of the Christian Groups in the First Century* (London: Tyndale, 1960). Cf. R. Scroggs, "The Sociological Interpretation of the New Testament: The Present State of Research," *NTS* 26 (1979–80): 164–79;

and especially the perceptive review article by Edwin Yamauchi, "Sociology, Scripture and the Supernatural," *JETS* 27 (1984): 169–92.

[108]E.g., John G. Gager, *Kingdom and Community* (Englewood Cliffs, N.J.: Prentice-Hall, 1975).

[109]Cyril S. Rodd, "On Applying a Sociological Theory to Biblical Studies," *JSOT* 19 (1981): 95–106. See also Derek Tidball, *An Introduction to the Sociology of the New Testament* (Exeter: Paternoster, 1983).

[110]I. Howard Marshall, *Luke: Historian and Theologian* (Exeter: Paternoster, 1970), 28.

[111]Craig L. Blomberg, "The Legitimacy and Limits of Harmonization."

[112]Robert H. Gundry, *Matthew: A Commentary on His Literary and Theological Art* (Grand Rapids: Eerdmans, 1982).

[113]See especially the unfortunate exchange: Norman L. Geisler, "Methodological Unorthodoxy," *JETS* 26 (1983): 87–94; Robert H. Gundry, "A Response to 'Methodological Unorthodoxy,' " 95–100; Norman L. Geisler, "Is There Madness in the Method? A Rejoinder to Robert H. Gundry," 101–8; Robert H. Gundry, "A Surrejoinder to Norman L. Geisler," 109–15.

[114]See D. A. Carson, "Gundry on Matthew: A Critical Review," *TJ* 3 (1982): 71–91; and the exchange: Douglas J. Moo, "Matthew and Midrash: An Evaluation of Robert H. Gundry's Approach," *JETS* 26 (1983): 31–39; Robert H. Gundry, "A Response to 'Matthew and Midrash,' " 41–56; Douglas J. Moo, "Once Again, 'Matthew and Midrash': A Rejoinder to Robert H. Gundry," 57–70; Robert H. Gundry, "A Surrejoinder to Douglas J. Moo," 71–86.

[115]E.g., C. H. Talbert, *What Is a Gospel? The Genre of the Canonical Gospels* (Philadelphia: Fortress, 1977); Philip L. Shuler, *A Genre for the Gospels: The Biographical Character of Matthew* (Philadelphia: Fortress, 1982).

[116]E.g., Marshall, *Luke: Historian and Theologian.*

[117]D. E. Aune, "The Problem of the Genre of the Gospels: A Critique of C. H. Talbert's *What Is a Gospel?*" in *Gospel Perspectives II*, 9–60.

[118]Richard N. Longenecker, "On the Form, Function, and Authority of the New Testament Letters," *Scripture and Truth*, ed. Carson and Woodbridge, 97–114.

[119]The literature on this subject is voluminous and generally well known; but often overlooked is the work of Loveday C. A. Alexander, "Luke-Acts in Its Contemporary Setting with Special Reference to the Prefaces (Luke 1:1-4 and Acts 1:1)" (D.Phil. diss., Oxford University, 1977). She argues that there is a distinct break from about the third century B.C. on in the formal characteristics of the prefaces to Greek books; the "historical" tradition is increasingly differentiated from the "scientific" tradition. The former works are characterized by much greater freedom from the historical reality they describe and much more rhetorical embellishment for various dramatic purposes; the latter are characterized by much greater fidelity to the historical reality. Luke's prologues, she demonstrates, are formally and substantially in the tradition of the prefaces to the latter works.

[120]Donald G. Bloesch, "In Defense of Biblical Authority," *The Reformed Journal* 34 (September 1984): 28–29.

[121]Ibid., 29.

[122]John M. Frame, "The Spirit and the Scriptures" (in this volume).

[123]The failure to make this distinction between "ordinary" usage and a more "technical" usage of "word" stands behind a plethora of slightly skewed criticisms— e.g., "Since the autographs of the Scriptures are collections of symbolic markings on objects suitable for the purpose, it seems odd to think of them as revealed of or by God. Any educated person can make intelligible marks on smooth, flat surfaces" (Stanley Obitts, "A Philosophical Analysis of Certain Assumptions of the Doctrine of the Inerrancy of the Bible," *JETS* 26 (1983): 129–36.

[124] Cf. Anthony C. Thiselton, *The Two Horizons* (Grand Rapids: Eerdmans, 1980), especially 432–38; John M. Frame, "God and Biblical Language: Transcendence and Immanence," in *God's Inerrant Word*, ed. John Warwick Montgomery (Minneapolis: Bethany Fellowship, 1974) 159–77; Brenton L. Thorwall, "Prolegomena for a Theocentric Theory of Language," (M.A. thesis, Trinity Evangelical Divinity School, 1981).

[125] Kevin J. Vanhoozer, "The Semantics of Biblical Literature: Truth and Scripture's Diverse Literary Forms" (in this volume).

[126] The most important work is that of Thiselton, *The Two Horizons;* but cf. also Hendrik Krabbendam, "The New Hermeneutic," *Hermeneutics, Inerrancy, and the Bible,* ed. Earl D. Radmacher and Robert D. Preus (Grand Rapids: Zondervan, 1984), 533–58, and the equally important "Responses" by J. I. Packer and Royce Gruenler (pp. 559–89); J. I. Packer, "Infallible Scripture and the Role of Hermeneutics," *Scripture and Truth,* ed. Carson and Woodbridge, 321–56. Broader treatments that shed considerable light on the topic include Richard E. Palmer, *Hermeneutics* (Evanston: Northwestern University Press, 1969), and Roy J. Howard, *Three Faces of Hermeneutics: An Introduction to Current Theories of Understanding* (Berkeley: University of California Press, 1982).

[127] Paul J. Achtemeier, *The Inspiration of Scripture,* 96–97.

[128] We have thus returned to the theories of Thomas Kuhn, briefly discussed earlier in this study.

[129] P. Joseph Cahill, in *CBQ* 46 (1984): 368, reviewing Rudolf Schnackenburg, *The Gospel According to St. John,* vol. 3, *Commentary on Chapters 13–21* (New York: Crossroad, 1982).

[130] The literature on this subject is now immense. See the bibliography of the essay by Kevin J. Vanhoozer, "The Semantics of Biblical Literature," in this volume; and cf. J. G. Davies, "Subjectivity and Objectivity in Biblical Exegesis," *BJRL* 66 (1983): 44–53.

[131] J. A. Passmore, "The Objectivity of History," in *Philosophical Analysis and History*, ed. W. H. Dray (New York/London: Harper & Row, 1966), 75–84. On the related questions of the nature of proof and belief in such matters, cf. George I. Mavrodes, *Belief in God: A Study in the Epistemology of Religion* (New York: Random House, 1970).

[132] One of the better brief introductions to the subject is the article by D. J. Hesselgrave, "Contextualization of Theology," in *Evangelical Dictionary of Theology*, ed. Walter A. Elwell (Grand Rapids: Baker, 1984), 271–72.

[133] D. A. Carson, "Reflections on Contextualization and the Third Horizon," in *The Church in the Bible and the World: An International Study*, ed. D. A. Carson (Exeter: Paternoster, 1986).

[134] Bruce D. Chilton, *A Galilean Rabbi and His Bible: Jesus' Use of the Interpreted Scripture of His Time* (Wilmington: Michael Glazier, 1984), 150.

[135] Charles H. Kraft, *Christianity in Culture: A Study in Dynamic Biblical Theologizing in Cross-Cultural Perspective* (Maryknoll: Orbis, 1980), 296.

[136] Daniel von Allmen, "The Birth of Theology: Contextualization as the dynamic element in the formation of New Testament theology," *IRM* 64 (1975): 37–52 [reprinted in *Readings in Dynamic Indigeneity*, ed. Charles H. Kraft and Tom N. Wisbey (South Pasadena, Calif.: William Carey Library, 1979). This work is discussed at length in Carson, "Reflections on Contextualization and the Third Horizon."

[137] For examples of such an appeal, see Daniel von Allmen, Charles H. Kraft, and G. C. Berkouwer, *Studies in Dogmatics: Holy Scripture* (Grand Rapids: Eerdmans, 1975).

[138] A devout Buddhist would take this to mean, among other things, that Jesus is inferior to the Buddha, since something is here predicated of Him.

[139] I have discussed this at greater length in "Reflections on Contextualization and the Third Horizon."

[140] Harold O. J. Brown, *Heresies: The Image of Christ in the Mirror of Heresy and Orthodoxy from the Apostles to the Present* (New York: Doubleday, 1984), 26.

141 Moisés Silva, "The New Testament Use of the Old Testament: Text Form and Authority," in *Scripture and Truth*, ed. Carson and Woodbridge, 143–65.

142 Idem, "The Place of Historical Reconstruction in New Testament Criticism" (in this volume).

143 Douglas J. Moo, "*Sensus Plenior* and the New Testament Use of the Old" (in this volume).

144 D. A. Carson, "Unity and Diversity in the New Testament: The Possibility of Systematic Theology," in *Scripture and Truth*, ed. Carson and Woodbridge, 61–95.

145 E.g., Helmut Koester, *Introduction to the New Testament*, 2 vols. (Philadelphia: Fortress, 1980, 1982), especially 2:1ff.

146 Cf. James A. Sanders, *Torah and Canon* (Philadelphia: Fortress, 1972); idem, "Adaptable for Life: The Nature and Function of Canon," in *Magnalia Dei* [Festschrift for G. Ernest Wright], ed. F. M. Cross et al. (Garden City: Doubleday, 1976), 531–60; idem, "Hermeneutics," *Interpreter's Dictionary of the Bible, Supplementary Volume* (Nashville: Abingdon, 1976), 404–5; idem, "Biblical Criticism and the Bible as Canon," *USQR* 32 (1977): 157–65; idem, "Text and Canon: Concept and Method," *JBL* 98 (1979): 5–29; idem, *Canon and Community: A Guide to Canonical Criticism* (Philadelphia: Fortress, 1984).

147 Brevard S. Childs, *Biblical Theology in Crisis* (Philadelphia: Westminister, 1970); idem, "The Canonical Shape of the Book of Jonah," in *Biblical and Near Eastern Studies* [Festschrift for W. S. LaSor], ed. G. Tuttle (Grand Rapids: Eerdmans, 1978), 122–28; idem, "The Canonical Shape of the Prophetic Literature," *Int* 32 (1978): 46–55; idem, *Introduction to the Old Testament as Scripture* (Philadelphia: Fortress, 1979); idem, "Some Reflections on the Search for a Biblical Theology," *Horizons in Biblical Theology* 4 (1982): 1–12; and his methods are well exemplified in idem, *The Book of Exodus: A Critical, Theological Commentary* (Philadelphia: Westminister/London: SCM, 1974).

148 David G. Dunbar, "The Biblical Canon in Recent Study" (in this volume).

149 For a balanced treatment (though now somewhat dated) of Calvin's appeal to evidence, see Kenneth S. Kantzer, "John Calvin's Theory of the Knowledge of God and the Word of God" (Ph.D. diss., Harvard University, 1950).

150 Jay M. Van Hook, "Knowledge, Belief, and Reformed Epistemology," *The Reformed Journal* 31:7 (July, 1981): 12–17.

151 Most recently, see Alvin Plantinga and Nicholas Wolterstorff, ed., *Faith and Rationality: Reason and Belief in God* (Notre Dame: University of Notre Dame Press, 1983).

152 Knowledge, unlike belief, is commonly defined in such a way as to make it immune to falsity. Belief may be mistaken; knowledge cannot be, or by definition it is not knowledge.

153 Richard Rorty, *Philosophy and the Mirror of Nature* (Princeton: Princeton University Press, 1979).

154 For instance, Colin Brown, *Miracles and the Critical Mind* (Grand Rapids: Eerdmans, 1984), brilliantly surveys a vast amount of literature and concludes that miracles cannot reasonably have any evidential force. In a perceptive review article (*JETS* 27:4 [December 1984]: 473–85), William Craig persuasively demonstrates that Brown forces later categories onto many of his historical sources by requiring that miracles address the radical, post-Kantian skepticism with which we have become familiar. Historically, appeals to miracles were far more likely made in the face of competing *theistic* claims; and here they do enjoy certain evidential force.

155 Helm, "Faith, Evidence, and the Scriptures," 299–320.

156 John Frame, "The Spirit and the Scriptures," in this volume.

157 Randall Basinger and David Basinger, "Inerrancy, Dictation and the Free Will Defence," *EQ* 55 (1983): 177–80.

[158]Ibid., 176.

[159]Cf. C. Samuel Storms, "Jonathan Edwards on the Freedom of the Will," *TJ* 3 (1982): 131–69.

[160]John Feinberg, *Theologies and Evil* (Washington: University Press of America, 1979); idem, "And the Atheist Shall Lie Down with the Calvinist: Atheism, Calvinism, and the Free Will Defence," *TJ* 1 (1980): 142–52; D. A. Carson, *Divine Sovereignty and Human Responsibility* (Atlanta: John Knox, 1981), especially the last chapter.

[161]The article was first published posthumously in *The Alliance Witness* on 15 May 1963 and has been republished many times—most recently in *BT* 255 (December 1984): 1–4.

[162]Carl F. H. Henry, "The Bible and the Conscience of Our Age," in *Hermeneutics, Inerrancy, and the Bible*, ed. Radmacher and Preus, 917.

[163]See especially David F. Wright, "Homosexuals or Prostitutes? The Meaning of ΑΡΣΕΝΟΚΟΙΤΑΙ (1 Cor. 6:9; 1 Tim. 1:10)," *VigChrist* 38 (1984): 125–53.

[164]See especially Wayne Grudem, "Does *kephalē* ('head') Mean 'Source' or 'Authority Over' in Greek Literature? A Survey of 2,336 Examples," *TJ* 6 (1985): 38–59.

CHAPTER TWO

THE SEMANTICS OF BIBLICAL LITERATURE: TRUTH AND SCRIPTURE'S DIVERSE LITERARY FORMS

Kevin J. Vanhoozer

49–104

[1]James Barr, *The Semantics of Biblical Language* (London and New York: Oxford University Press, 1961).

[2]Moisés Silva, *Biblical Words & Their Meanings: An Introduction to Lexical Statements* (Grand Rapids: Zondervan, 1983), 18.

[3]This is not to say that lexical semantics is unimportant, but only that Evangelicals must also respond to challenges on the level of literary semantics. For a fine introduction to lexical semantics and its bearing on biblical scholarship, see Silva, *Biblical Words*. Silva himself recognizes the need for a complementary study: "Perhaps someone can be persuaded to write a sequel on 'Biblical Sentences & Their Meaning' " (p. 11).

[4]Paul Ricoeur distinguishes semiotics from semantics by the size of the linguistic unit each studies: semiotics is the science of signs, semantics the science of sentences. We are using "semantics" in a fairly loose sense, to cover the various aspects of linguistic meaning. See Ricoeur's *Interpretation Theory* (Fort Worth: Texas Christian University, 1976), 6–7.

[5]I have elsewhere referred to the New Biblical Theology as "Aesthetic" theology— theology which is primarily concerned with the *form* or *shape* of biblical literature, sometimes to the exclusion of historical and truth content. See my forthcoming "The Hermeneutics of 'Aesthetic' Theology," *TJ*.

[6]Barr, *Semantics*, 10ff.

[7]James Barr, *The Bible in the Modern World* (London: SCM, 1973), p. 55.

[8]Barr, *Semantics*, 246.

[9]John Lyons, *Structural Semantics: An Analysis of Part of the Vocabulary of Plato* (Oxford: Basil Blackwell, 1963), 82–83, cited in Silva, *Biblical Words*, 144. At the same time, one must acknowledge that a genre is what it is only by virtue of the propositions that constitute it.

[10]James Barr, *Biblical Words for Time* (London: SCM, 1962), 138.

[11] See, for instance, Paul Ricoeur, *Time and Narrative* (Chicago: University of Chicago Press, 1984); Stephen Crites, "The Narrative Quality of Experience," *JAAR* 39 (1971): 290–307.

[12] See the extended footnote in David Tracy, *The Analogical Imagination* (London: SCM, 1981), 296n.81.

[13] See Silva, *Biblical Words*, 23–24, for a discussion of Hermann Cremer's attempt at a "theological lexicography."

[14] Compared to linguistics, literary criticism is usually regarded as less "scientific"—at least until the advent of structuralism. There is considerable internicene warfare among contemporary critics. See the excellent study by Frank Lentricchia, *After the New Criticism* (Chicago: University of Chicago Press, 1980).

[15] This in no way implies that Evangelicals have been remiss in studying biblical words. However, this chapter contends that Evangelicals have not come to grips with certain problems pertaining to the diverse literary forms of Scripture.

[16] Barr, *Bible in the Modern World*, 125.

[17] Ibid. (emphasis mine).

[18] James Barr, *Fundamentalism* (London: SCM, 1977), 46.

[19] See the helpful article by Paul Helm, "Revealed Propositions and Timeless Truths," *Religious Studies* 8 (1972): 126–36.

[20] Ronald Nash, *The Word of God and the Mind of Man* (Grand Rapids: Zondervan, 1982), 45.

[21] John Hick, "Revelation" in *The Encyclopedia of Philosophy*, ed. Paul Edwards, 8 vols. (London and New York: Macmillan, 1967), 7:189.

[22] Nash, *Word of God*, 53. Emil Brunner used the term as one of derision.

[23] H. D. McDonald, *Theories of Revelation: An Historical Study 1860–1960* (London: George Allen & Unwin, 1963), 162.

[24] J. I. Packer, "Contemporary Views of Revelation," in *Revelation and the Bible: Contemporary Evangelical Thought*, ed. Carl F. H. Henry (London: Tyndale, 1958), 90.

[25] Nash, *Word of God*, 50.

[26] Ibid.

[27] Ibid., 54.

[28] Stanley Obitts, "A Philosophical Analysis of Certain Assumptions of the Doctrine of the Inerrancy of the Bible," *JETS* 26:2 (1983): 129.

[29] Gordon R. Lewis, "What Does Biblical Infallibility Mean?" *BETS* 6:1 (1963): 18.

[30] It should be noted that Obitts, while making this distinction for analytic purposes, holds that the proposition is in practice inseparable from the sentence(s) that convey(s) it. Even in analysis, however, the problem remains of determining *which* proposition a given sentence conveys.

[31] Lewis, "What does Biblical Infallibility Mean?" 26.

[32] See Henry's thesis number ten in *God, Revelation & Authority*, 6 vols. (Waco: Word, 1976–83), vol. 3; and Clark Pinnock, *Biblical Revelation* (Chicago: Moody, 1971).

[33] Henry, *God, Revelation & Authority*, 3:456.

[34] Ibid., 4:205 (emphasis mine).

[35] Ibid., vol. 4, ch. 10 ("The Meaning of Infallibility").

[36] Pinnock, *Biblical Revelation*, 110n.6.

[37] Gordon Clark, *Karl Barth's Theological Method* (Nutley, N.J.: Presbyterian and Reformed, 1963), 150.

[38] See the six senses of "proposition" listed in the *Oxford English Dictionary*, 12 vols. (1933; reprint, Oxford: Clarendon, 1961), 8:1481–82.

[39] Aristotle, "On Interpretation," in *Aristotle*, The Loeb Classical Library, 23 vols. (Cambridge: Harvard University Press, 1973): 1:121.

[40] Richard Gale, "Propositions, Judgments, Sentences & Statements," *The Encyclopedia of Philosophy*, 6:494.

[41] Bernard Ramm, *Special Revelation and the Word of God* (Grand Rapids: Eerdmans, 1961), 154–55.

[42] So Gilbert Ryle in his "Are there Propositions?" *Proceedings of the Aristotelian Society* 30 (1929–30): 91–126.

[43] The example comes from Irving M. Copi, *Introduction to Logic*, 3d ed. (London: Macmillan, 1968), 6.

[44] W. V. Quine, *Philosophy of Logic*, Foundations of Philosophy Series (Englewood Cliffs, N.J.: Prentice-Hall, 1964), 1, 10.

[45] Ibid., 2.

[46] Ibid., 3.

[47] Karl R. Popper, *Objective Knowledge: An Evolutionary Approach*, rev. ed. (Oxford: Clarendon, 1979), 157.

[48] E. J. Lemmon, "Sentences, Statements and Propositions," in *British Analytical Philosophy*, ed. Bernard Williams and Alan Montefiore (London: Routledge & Kegan Paul, 1966), 87–107.

[49] Alan R. White, *Truth* (London: Macmillan, 1970), 11.

[50] Lemmon, "Sentences, Statements and Propositions," 96.

[51] White, *Truth*, 14.

[52] R. Cartwright distinguishes propositions from eight other related notions but still concludes that "it remains to be said *what* it is that is susceptible to truth or falsity." See his "Propositions," in *Analytical Philosophy*, ed. R. J. Butler (Oxford: Basil Blackwell, 1966), 103.

[53] Even White does not specify, however, the exact nature of the connection between what is said and the sentences used to say it.

[54] Quine here utilizes the "semantic theory" of truth that was formulated by Alfred Tarski in "The Semantic Conception of Truth and the Foundation of Semantics," *Philosophical and Phenomenological Research* 4 (1944): 341–76.

[55] Quine, *Philosophy of Logic*, 11.

[56] Henry Drummond, *Natural Law in the Spiritual World* (London: Hodder & Stoughton, 1899), 360.

[57] "The Chicago Statement on Biblical Hermeneutics," *JETS* 25:4 (December 1982): 397–401.

[58] David Kelsey, *The Uses of Scripture in Recent Theology* (Philadelphia: Fortress, 1975), ch. 2 ("Doctrine and Concept").

[59] The allusion is to Ludwig Wittgenstein's *Tractatus Logico-Philosophicus* (London: Routledge & Kegan Paul, 1961).

[60] Suggested parallels between the early Wittgenstein and Evangelical proponents of propositional revelation are restricted to his theory of meaning and language, not metaphysics or ethics.

[61] Cited in Norman Malcolm, "Wittgenstein" in the *Encyclopedia of Philosophy*, 8:330.

[62] References to the *Tractatus* will follow Wittgenstein's decimal numbering of his propositions.

[63] See Anthony Kenny, *Wittgenstein* (London: Penguin, 1973), ch. 4 ("The Picture Theory of a Proposition").

[64] Malcolm, "Wittgenstein," 337.

[65] Wittgenstein was influenced by the attempts of Bertrand Russell and Gottlob Frege to construct a formalized language, wherein every proposition would have a definite sense and truth value. See Kenny, *Wittgenstein*, ch. 2 ("The Legacy of Frege and Russell").

[66] Nash, *Word of God*, 50.

[67] See note 57.

[68] John R. Searle, "The Logical Status of Fictional Discourse," *New Literary History* 6 (1975): 319–32.

[69] *JETS* 21:4 (December 1978): 295.

[70] Henry, *God, Revelation and Authority*, 3:463.

[71] Ibid., 453.

[72] Ibid., 4:109.

[73] Ibid., 120.

[74] Ibid., 109.

[75] Cleanth Brooks, *The Well Wrought Urn* (New York: Harcourt, Brace & World, 1947).

[76] *Defense of Poesy* (1595).

[77] Paraphrase has a long and distinguished history. It flourished in sixteenth-century England, and Renaissance dictionaries refer readers to the standard treatment by Quintilian in his *Institutio Oratoria*.

[78] Barr, *Bible in the Modern World*, 57.

[79] Gerald Graff, *Poetic Statement and Critical Dogma* (Evanston: Northwestern University Press, 1970), xi.

[80] Lentricchia, *After the New Criticism*, 6.

[81] Ibid., 16–17.

[82] See I. A. Richards, *Science and Poetry* (London: Kegan Paul, 1926).

[83] Lentricchia, *After the New Criticism*, 324.

[84] Brooks, *The Well Wrought Urn*, 205.

[85] Northrop Frye, *The Anatomy of Criticism* (New York: Atheneum, 1967), 74.

[86] Lentricchia, *After the New Criticism*, 18.

[87] Ibid., 20.

[88] Friedrich von Schiller, *On the Aesthetic Education of Man*, cited in Lentricchia, *After the New Criticism*, 20–21.

[89] See Northrop Frye, *The Great Code: The Bible and Literature* (London: Routledge & Kegan Paul, 1982).

[90] Ibid., 29.

[91] Ibid.

[92] Ibid., 61.

[93] Ibid., 62.

[94] Hans Frei, *The Eclipse of the Biblical Narrative* (New Haven: Yale University Press, 1974).

[95] John Barton, *Reading the Old Testament: Method in Biblical Study* (London: Darton Longman & Todd, 1984), 163.

[96] D. H. Mellor, "Literary Truth," *Ratio* 10 (1968): 157.

[97] Ibid., 160.

[98] See note 79.

[99] Graff, *Poetic Statement*, 145.

[100] Ibid., 148–9.

[101]Ibid., 167. The definition of "literature" is one of the most difficult problems faced by the literary critic. Various criteria have been proposed, but a consensus is still lacking. This makes a topic like "the Bible as literature" all the more problematic.

[102]*Time*, March 19, 1984, 41.

[103]William Wordsworth, "The Tables Turned," (1798).

[104]This is an oversimplification of Geisler's argumentation but, I believe, an essentially accurate one. See the revealing exchange between Geisler and R. H. Gundry in *JETS* 26:1 (1983): 87–115.

[105]Robert Preus, "Notes on the Inerrancy of Scripture," in *Crisis in Lutheran Theology*, ed. John Warwick Montgomery, 2d rev. ed., 2 vols. (Minneapolis: Bethany Fellowship, 1974): 2:42.

[106]Ramm, *Special Revelation*, 64.

[107]Bernard Ramm, *Protestant Biblical Interpretation: A Textbook of Hermeneutics*, 3d rev. ed. (Grand Rapids: Baker, 1973), 144.

[108]Ramm, *Special Revelation*, 68.

[109]Barton, *Reading the Old Testament*, 140.

[110]Michael J. Christensen suggests that Lewis holds to a "literary inspiration" of the Bible: "The Bible is to be approached as inspired literature. Its literary elements— images, symbols, myths and metaphors—are actual *embodiments* of scriptural reality, *vehicles* of divine revelation" (*C. S. Lewis on Scripture* [London: Hodder & Stoughton, 1979], 77).

[111]C. S. Lewis, *Reflections on the Psalms* (London: Geoffrey Bles, 1958), 2–3. Cf. Lewis's comment in his essay "The Literary Impact of the Authorised Version": "But I cannot help suspecting, if I may make an Irish bull, that those who read the Bible as literature do not read the Bible" (*Selected Literary Essays* [London and New York: Cambridge University Press, 1969), 142.

[112]See C. S. Lewis and E. M. W. Tillyard, *The Personal Heresy: A Controversy* (London: Oxford University Press, 1939) for Lewis's early thoughts on the "objective" approach to poetry.

[113]C. S. Lewis, *A Preface to Paradise Lost* (London: Oxford University Press, 1942), 1.

[114]Ibid., 2.

[115]C. S. Lewis, "Myth Became Fact," in *Undeceptions*, ed. Walter Hooper (London: Geoffrey Bles, 1970), 41 [American reprint: *God in the Dock* (Grand Rapids: Eerdmans, 1985)].

[116]Ibid.

[117]Ibid., 42.

[118]Paul Holmer, *C. S. Lewis: The Shape of His Faith and Thought* (New York: Harper & Row, 1976), 20.

[119]In an excellent treatment of the tension between reason and imagination in Lewis's thought, Peter Schakel documents the decisive change in Lewis's thinking about the imagination—a change occasioned not by his conversion but by later factors in the late forties and early fifties. Schakel distinguishes the earlier role allotted the imagination from the more mature view that characterized Lewis's later thought. The former held that imagination was a "seeing" of universal objects, the latter that imagination was a "tasting" of reality. See Schakel's *Reason and Imagination of C. S. Lewis: A Study of Till We Have Faces* (Grand Rapids: Eerdmans, 1984), especially 138.

[120]C. S. Lewis *They Stand Together: The Letters of C. S. Lewis to Arthur Greeves (1914–1963)*, ed. Walter Hooper (London: Collins, 1979), 426–28.

[121]C. S. Lewis, *Letters to Malcolm: Chiefly on Prayer* (London: Geoffrey Bles, 1964).

[122]Schakel, *Reason and Imagination in C. S. Lewis*, 176.

[123]See C. S. Lewis, "The Language of Religion," in *Christian Reflections* (London: Geoffrey Bles, 1967).

[124]C. S. Lewis *An Experiment in Criticism* (London: Cambridge University Press, 1961), 30.

[125]Lewis, *Reflections on the Psalms*, 45.

[126]See his "Bluspels and Flalansferes: A Semantic Nightmare," in *Selected Literary Essays*, 251–65.

[127]"Bluspels and Flalansferes," 258.

[128]Lewis, *Reflections on the Psalms*, 112.

[129]Ibid., 113.

[130]Ibid.

[131]Ibid., 119.

[132]This is a quotation from Bernard Ramm's *Special Revelation*, 63n.30. Ramm is commenting on Kuyper's notion of "forms of inspiration," which Kuyper discusses in his *Principles of Sacred Theology*.

[133]Lewis, *Experiment*, 11.

[134]Cf. Augustine's distinction between enjoying (*frui*) and using (*uti*), in his *On Christian Doctrine* 1.3.3.

[135]Schakel, *Reason and Imagination in C. S. Lewis*, 165.

[136]So says Christensen in his Appendix "Lewis the rational romantic" of *C. S. Lewis on Scripture*. See also Schakel's account of the final reconciliation of reason and imagination in Lewis.

[137]See the letter from C. S. Lewis to Corbin Carnell in Appendix A of Christensen, *C. S. Lewis on Scripture*, and Ramm, *Protestant Biblical Interpretation*, 144.

[138]Ramm, *Protestant Biblical Interpretation*, 145.

[139]See, for instance, J. I. Packer, "Infallible Scripture and the Role of Hermeneutics," in *Scripture and Truth*, ed. D. A. Carson and John D. Woodbridge (Grand Rapids: Zondervan, 1983). The grammatico-historical method, writes Packer, "has been the historic evangelical method of exegesis, followed with more or less consistency and success since the Reformers' time" (p. 345).

[140]Letter to Carnell, in Christensen, *C. S. Lewis on Scripture*, 98.

[141]Letter to Clyde S. Kilby, in Christensen, *C. S. Lewis on Scripture*, 99.

[142]See, for instance, his articles in the *Revue Biblique* 4 (1895): 563–71 and 5 (1896): 199–220, as well as his *Historical Criticism and the Old Testament* (London: Catholic Truth Society, 1905).

[143]See the thorough discussion in James Burtchaell, *Catholic Theories of Biblical Inspiration since 1810* (London: Cambridge University Press, 1969). Burtchaell observes that the underlying issue that often shaped the debates over inspiration was the relation of nature and grace: to what extent can we account both for divine authorship of Scripture *and* human literary freedom?

[144]Burtchaell, *Catholic Theories of Biblical Inspiration*, 133.

[145]Ibid.

[146]Ibid., 140.

[147]Lagrange, *Historical Criticism and the Old Testament*, 98.

[148]Grant R. Osborne, "Genre criticism—*sensus literalis,*" *TJ*, n.s., 4:2 (1983): 1–27.

[149]E. D. Hirsch, *Validity in Interpretation* (New Haven: Yale University Press, 1967), 79.

[150]Gordon D. Fee and Douglas Stuart, *How to Read the Bible for All Its Worth* (Grand Rapids: Zondervan, 1982), 76.

[151]Ibid., 19.

[152]Ibid., 78.

[153]Ibid., 89.

[154]Paul Ricoeur, "Toward a Hermeneutic of the Idea of Revelation," in *Essays on Biblical Interpretation*, ed. Lewis Mudge (Philadelphia: Fortress, 1980), 75.

[155]Ibid.

[156]Luke 1:1–4

[157]Ricoeur, "Toward a Hermeneutic," 91.

[158]Ibid., 83.

[159]David L. Bartlett, *The Shape of Scriptural Authority* (Philadelphia: Fortress, 1983), 32.

[160]Ibid., 74.

[161]See, for instance, his *Introduction to the Old Testament as Scripture* (Philadelphia: Fortress, 1979). There seems to be some confusion in Childs as to whether the all-important "canonical context" refers to the *literary* context of canon (i.e., the final form of the biblical texts) or the *historical* context of the canonizers. Our interpretation of Childs understands canon-criticism in the former sense.

[162]Hirsch, *Validity in Interpretation*, 70. But note his qualification: "A genre is less like a game than like a code of social behavior, which provides rules of thumb such as, do not drink a toast to your hostess at a Scandinavian dinner party" (p. 93). Compiling the various metaphors and images for "genre" would itself be an interesting study.

[163]*Confessions*, 1.8.

[164]Note the parallel between Augustine's account and Wittgenstein's own earlier views.

[165]Thiselton lists several traditional assumptions about language that have proven false, and several of these are also criticized by Wittgenstein. Among those Thiselton lists are (1) that grammatical and logical structures are isomorphic, (2) that meaning involves a relation between a word and the object it refers to, and (3) that the basic kind of language use is the declarative proposition. See his "Semantics and New Testament Interpretation," in *New Testament Interpretation*, ed. I. H. Marshall (Exeter: Paternoster, 1977), 75–104.

[166]Ludwig Wittgenstein, *Philosophical Investigations*, (Oxford: Basil Blackwell, 1958), I §304.

[167]Stanley Cavell, *Must We Mean What We Say?* (London: Cambridge University Press, 1976), 36.

[168]See, for instance, *Philosophical Investigations*, I §664.

[169]Ibid., I §115.

[170]Ibid., I §11.

[171]Anthony Thiselton, *The Two Horizons* (Grand Rapids: Eerdmans, 1980), 372.

[172]See, for instance, Thiselton's examination of the concept of justification by faith in *The Two Horizons*, 415–22. Thiselton claims that the mystery of how human beings can be regarded as *simul iustus et peccator* is solved when we realize that the New Testament includes both a historical language-game (man as sinner) and an eschatological language-game (man as justified). Faith is thus the acceptance of this future-oriented "onlook" as being relevant in the present.

[173]*Philosophical Investigations*, I §68.

[174]Thiselton, *The Two Horizons*, 411.

[175]Anthony Thiselton, "Truth *(Alētheia)*," in *The New International Dictionary of New Testament Theology*, ed. Colin Brown, 3 vols. (Exeter: Paternoster, 1978), 3:874–902.

[176]Thiselton, *The Two Horizons*, 414.

[177] In an appendix entitled "Wittgenstein and the Debate about Biblical Authority," *The Two Horizons*, 432–38, Thiselton argues that while biblical authority may be *experienced* within a given language-game, the authority *rests* upon the truth of certain states of affairs that is independent of particular language-games. Thiselton tries to voice the relativity and absoluteness of truth in his "Truth *(Alētheia)*," 894: "On the one hand, truth is multiform, and criteria for different kinds of truth may vary. On the other hand, the truth of God lays claim to a universality which somehow undergirds and holds together particular expressions of truth in thought and life."

[178] See, for instance, Nicholas Lash, "How Large is a 'Language Game'?" *Theology* 87 (1984): 19–28; Patrick Sherry, *Religion, Truth and Language-Games* (London: Macmillan, 1977).

[179] See Sherry, "Validating: Does Religion Have a Special Kind of Truth?" *(Religion, Truth and Language-Games*, ch. 8). Again the example of Childs is interesting. Is a biblical book's genre constituted by its inclusion in the canon? I suggest (but cannot pursue here) that it is a book's *significance* (and not meaning) that is affected by its place in a specific literary context. It remains to be seen, however, whether the primary effect of canonization pertains to a *semantics* of biblical literature or merely to the nature of its *authority*.

[180] We shall see below that theology is, among other things, an "ordinary literature analysis" of the Bible. At the same time, however, one of the tasks of systematic theology is to show how the truths expressed in the various genres of Scripture interrelate to form a consistent, coherent, and comprehensive whole.

[181] Aristotle, *Metaphysics*, 4.2 and *passim*. For a brief introduction to Aristotle's thought on metaphysics, see G. E. R. Lloyd, *Aristotle: The Growth and Structure of his Thought* (Cambridge University Press, 1968), ch. 6.

[182] See C. S. Lewis, "The Language of Religion."

[183] Two possible exceptions, however, must be mentioned: the canon and the Gospels. Literary critics also speak of a "canon" of literature, but this is never rigidly circumscribed, as is the biblical canon. As to the Gospels, there is strong evidence that they are *sui generis*. R. H. Gundry writes that "the gospels resist categorization in terms of prior and contemporary genres of literature" ("Recent Investigations into the Literary Genre, 'Gospel'," *New Dimensions in New Testament Study*, ed. Richard N. Longenecker and Merrill C. Tenney [Grand Rapids: Zondervan, 1974], 112).

[184] As far as Searle's work on the fate of the "author's intention" is concerned, I have treated its importance in contemporary hermeneutics in "The Hermeneutics of 'Aesthetic' Theology," *TJ* (forthcoming).

[185] J. L. Austin, *How to Do Things with Words*, 2d ed. (Cambridge: Harvard University Press, 1975), 12.

[186] Ibid., 109.

[187] Ibid. Cf. further John R. Searle and David Vanderveken, *Foundations of Illocutionary Logic* (Cambridge: Cambridge University Press, 1985).

[188] Anthony Manser, "Austin's 'Linguistic Phenomenology'," in *Phenomenology and Philosophical Understanding*, ed. Edo Pivcevic (Cambridge: Cambridge University Press, 1975), 109–24, compares Austin's discovery of speech acts with Husserl's discovery of mental acts and suggests that Austin's work is a sort of "linguistic phenomenology."

[189] Austin, *How to Do Things with Words*, 117.

[190] William P. Alston, *Philosophy of Language*, Foundations of Philosophy Series (Englewood Cliffs, N.J.: Prentice-Hall, 1964), 39.

[191] Austin, *How to Do Things with Words*, 142.

[192] J. L. Austin, "Truth," in *Truth*, ed. George Pitcher (Englewood Cliffs N.J.: Prentice-Hall, 1964), 28.

[193]This should be taken not as a rejection of the correspondence theory of truth but as a modification or more careful application of it. One popular construal views facts as what are stated by true statements. But other speech acts—for instance a warning—can also "be about" a fact. Note, however, that warnings contain an implicit assertorical element. "You had better not skate on the ice," for example, may contain the latent assertion, "skating on that ice today is dangerous." Indeed, the warning derives no little part of its power precisely from this implied assertion. If the assertion is deemed false, the warning will likely be disregarded. There are, then, assertorical elements in other types of speech acts. But even the relation between assertion and facts can be notoriously complex—and this for two reasons. First, the *nature* of the facts. There are facts about past events, about patterns of human behavior, about the boiling point of various liquids, about the nuptial rites of honeybees, etc. To these facts "correspond" historical texts/truth, poetic texts/truth, scientific texts/truth, and so on. Second, the *nature* of correspondence. "Truth as correspondence" specifies neither the relation between statement and fact nor the requisite degree of "fit" between the two for such a relation to qualify as a bona fide instance of correspondence. Consider Austin's example: is the assertion "France is hexagonal" true? Does it "correspond to" reality? Austin replies: "It is good enough for a top-ranking general, perhaps, but not for a geographer. . . . It is a rough description; it is not a true or false one" (*How to Do Things with Words*, 143).

[194]See J. O. Urmson, "J. L. Austin," in *The Encyclopedia of Philosophy*, 1:211–15.

[195]Austin, *How to Do Things with Words*, 146.

[196]John R. Searle, *Speech Acts: An Essay in the Philosophy of Language* (London and New York: Cambridge University Press, 1969), 12.

[197]Cf. P. F. Strawson, "Intention and Convention in Speech Acts," in *Logico-Linguistic Papers* (London: Methuen, 1971).

[198]Searle, *Speech Acts*, 18. The two approaches are complementary rather than competing.

[199]Searle employs his own terminology and differs from Austin in a number of respects. See Searle's "Austin on Locutionary and Illocutionary Acts," *Philosophical Review* 77 (1968): 405–24.

[200]Searle, *Speech Acts*, 29.

[201]P. T. Geach, "Assertion," *Philosophical Review* 74 (1965): 449.

[202]Helm, "Revealed Propositions and Timeless Truths," 131.

[203]Searle, *Speech Acts*, 25.

[204]Ibid., 29.

[205]Perhaps Jesus was thinking about illocutionary force when He said, "He that hath ears let him hear."

[206]See the chart with analyses of seven speech acts in Searle, *Speech Acts*, 66–67.

[207]John Searle, *Expression and Meaning: Studies in the Theory of Speech Acts* (London and New York: Cambridge University Press, 1979), 29.

[208]Ibid. Searle labels these five illocutionary points Assertives, Directives, Commissives, Expressives, and Declaratives.

[209]Ricoeur, *Interpretation Theory*, 27.

[210]Searle, "Logical Status of Fictional Discourse," 325.

[211]Ibid., 326.

[212]Ibid., 332.

[213]Expressions such as "A man . . ." do not serve to refer at all. See *Speech Acts*, 27. Jesus, by omitting the definite article, perhaps signals the fictional nature of His narrative. The point of the narrative does not depend on its having actually happened.

[214]Mary Louise Pratt, *Towards a Speech Act Theory of Literary Discourse* (Bloomington and London: Indiana University Press, 1977).

[215]Pratt, *Towards a Speech Act Theory of Literary Discourse,* 86.

[216]Susan Snaider Lanser, *The Narrative Act: Point of View in Prose Fiction* (Princeton: Princeton University Press, 1981), 7.

[217]Ibid., 65.

[218]That all texts are about something goes for modern literature as well, even if the statement made by the literature is that literature cannot make any statements! See the insightful discussion of the paradox of modern fiction in Lentricchia, *After the New Criticism,* 313–14.

[219]Cf. C. S. Lewis's comments (*A Preface to Paradise Lost,* 3) about Milton's choice concerning the kind of "thing" he wanted to make in writing *Paradise Lost.*

[220]Richard N. Longenecker comments that the letter form was popular in antiquity because of its stress on the writer's "presence" with his addressees. See his "On the Form, Function, and Authority of the New Testament Letters," in *Scripture and Truth,* ed. Carson and Woodbridge, esp. 102.

[221]John Frame, "The Doctrine of the Word," unpublished classroom notes.

[222]See the comprehensive essay by Wayne A. Grudem entitled "Scripture's Self-attestation and the Problem of Formulating a Doctrine of Scripture," *Scripture and Truth,* ed. Carson and Woodbridge, 19–59.

[223]Ramm, *Protestant Biblical Interpretation,* 145.

[224]Austin, *How to Do Things with Words,* 45.

[225]Searle, *Speech Acts,* 47.

[226]Clark H. Pinnock, "Limited Inerrancy: A Critical Appraisal and Constructive Alternative" in *God's Inerrant Word,* ed. John Warwick Montgomery (Minneapolis: Bethany Fellowship, 1974), 148.

[227]I. Howard Marshall, *Biblical Inspiration* (Grand Rapids: Eerdmans, 1983), 53.

[228]D. A. Carson, "Three Books on the Bible: A Critical Review," *JETS* 26:3 (1983): 355.

[229]Paul Feinberg, "The Meaning of Inerrancy," in *Inerrancy,* ed. Norman L. Geisler (Grand Rapids: Zondervan, 1979), 293.

[230]Carson, "Three Books on the Bible," 359.

[231]Feinberg, "The Meaning of Inerrancy," 294.

[232]Arthur Holmes, "Ordinary Language Analysis and Theological Method," *BETS* 11:3 (1968): 133.

[233]I wish here to thank all those who participated in a seminar at Tyndale House Cambridge, on October 1, 1984, devoted to a discussion of a rough draft of this paper. Thanks go also to Mr. Philip Clayton for his many helpful suggestions.

CHAPTER THREE

THE PLACE OF HISTORICAL RECONSTRUCTION IN NEW TESTAMENT CRITICISM

Moisés Silva

105–33

[1]Since Bob Jones University is one of the few institutions that virtually everyone regards as Fundamentalist, it may be helpful to point out that, as a student there in the 1960s, I heard this theological point emphatically stated in a required course on Bible doctrines.

[2]See such commentators as Bengel, Alford, and Broadus. F. Godet, *A Commentary on the Gospel of St. Luke,* 2 vols. (Edinburgh: T. & T. Clark, 1890), 1:220, prefers Luke's order.

[3] As usual, John Calvin formulates the question soberly: "There is nothing very remarkable in Luke putting in second place the temptation which Matthew places last, for the Evangelists had no intention of so putting their narrative together as always to keep an exact order of events, but to bring the whole pattern together to produce a kind of mirror or screen image of those features most useful for the understanding of Christ. It is quite enough to grasp that Christ was put to three temptations. Which test came second or third, is not a matter for anxious debate" (*A Harmony of the Gospels: Matthew, Mark and Luke*, trans. A. W. Morrison, 3 vols. [Grand Rapids: Eerdmans, 1975], 1:139).

[4] J. Ramsey Michaels, *Servant and Son: Jesus in Parable and Gospel* (Atlanta: John Knox, 1981), 64. Incidentally, Calvin (*A Harmony*, 139–40) inclines toward the possibility that the temptations were visions.

[5] Josephus, *Antiquities of the Jews* 19.330, 334 (Loeb Classical Library translation).

[6] *Eadie's Biblical Cyclopaedia*, rev. ed. (London: Charles Griffin, [1901]), 520.

[7] Merrill F. Unger, *Unger's Bible Dictionary* (Chicago: Moody, 1957), 885–86. Much more balanced treatments by conservatives include the discussion by J. Ramsey Michaels in *Wycliffe Bible Encyclopedia*, ed. C. F. Pfeiffer et al., 2 vols. (Chicago: Moody, 1975), 2:1326–28, and Donald A. Hagner's more extensive article in *The Zondervan Pictorial Encyclopedia of the Bible*, ed. Merrill C. Tenney, 5 vols. (Grand Rapids: Zondervan, 1975), 4:745–52.

[8] Rabbi Samuel S. Cohon in James Hastings, ed., *Dictionary of the Bible*, ed. F. C. Grant and H. H. Rowley, rev. ed. (New York: Scribner, 1963), 761.

[9] Helmut Koester, *Introduction to the New Testament*, 2 vols. (Philadelphia: Fortress, 1982), 1:239–43.

[10] *Antiquities* 18.15.

[11] Some may wish to argue that the fault belongs not to Jesus but to the Gospel writers, who are sometimes unreliable, but this is no help for anyone who places the locus of authority on the canonical Scripture rather than on the teachings of Jesus as reconstructed by modern criticism. Cf. Moisés Silva, "Ned B. Stonehouse and Redaction Criticism," *WTJ* 40 (1977–78): 77–88, 281–303, esp. 286–89.

[12] This material is most accessible in C. G. Montefiore and H. Loewe, *A Rabbinic Anthology* (New York: Meridian, n.d.; reprint, New York: Schocken, 1970), 487–89.

[13] Regarding the famous Hillel, for example, J. Neusner comments: "The only firm conclusion is that Hillel was likely to have lived sometime before the destruction of the Temple and to have played an important part in the politics of the Pharisaic party" (*From Politics to Piety: The Emergence of Pharisaic Judaism* [Englewood Cliffs, N.J.: Prentice-Hall, 1973], 43).

[14] Phillip Sigal, *The Emergence of Contemporary Judaism*, Pittsburgh Theological Monograph Series 29a (Pittsburgh: Pickwick, 1980), 1/2:1.

[15] Cf. Neusner, *From Politics to Piety*, 64–66, building on the work of Morton Smith.

[16] J. Neusner, *Invitation to the Talmud: A Teaching Book*, rev. ed. (San Francisco: Harper & Row, 1984), 38.

[17] The most reliable attempt is E. E. Urbach, *The Sages: Their Concepts and Beliefs*, 2d ed., 2 vols. (Jerusalem: Magnes, 1979), esp. ch. 15; but even his work has not escaped criticism.

[18] The weaknesses in modern representations of rabbinic thought have been most thoroughly exposed by E. P. Sanders, *Paul and Palestinian Judaism: A Comparison of Patterns of Religion* (Philadelphia: Fortress, 1977), though his own interpretation of the evidence is hardly persuasive.

[19] On the other hand, such a caricature may correspond quite clearly to popular thought. A modern Jewish scholar, Ellis Rivkin, describes the inner turmoil of his youth in these terms: "On the unerring scales of God's justice, would my righteousness offset

my sinfulness and tip the scales to eternal life, or would the heavy weight of this or that sin, alone or in combination, bring the scales down on the side of eternal punishment?" (*A Hidden Revolution: The Pharisees' Search for the Kingdom Within* [Nashville: Abingdon, 1978], 22; cf. my review of this book, "The Pharisees in Modern Jewish Scholarship," *WTJ* 42 [1979–80]: 395–405). Rivkin's comments belie the claims of Pinchas Lapide that Jews are advocates of pure grace (Pinchas Lapide and Peter Stuhlmacher, *Paul: Rabbi and Apostle* [Minneapolis: Augsburg, 1984], 37–38).

[20] Cf. the summary in Urbach, *The Sages*, 1:496ff. For a classic and sympathetic exposition, see A. Marmorstein, *The Doctrine of Merits in Old Rabbinic Literature* (1920; reprint, New York: Ktav, 1968).

[21] Urbach, *The Sages*, 434.

[22] Mishnah, *Shebiit* 10:3–7. Cf. the discussion in Alexander Guttmann, *Rabbinic Judaism in the Making: A Chapter in the History of the Halakhah from Ezra to Judah I* (Detroit: Wayne State University Press, 1970), 71–72.

[23] Urbach, *The Sages*, 373.

[24] Damascus Document xi.13–14.

[25] Guttmann, *Rabbinic Judaism*, xii.

[26] See J. Gresham Machen, *The Origin of Paul's Religion* (1923; reprint, Grand Rapids: Eerdmans, 1947), 179.

[27] F. C. Baur, "Die Christuspartei in der korintischen Gemeinde, der Gegensatz des petrinischen und paulinischen Christenthums in der ältesten Kirche, der Apostel Paulus in Rom," *Tübingen Zeitschrift für Theologie* (1831), pt. 4, 61–206 [reprinted in *Ausgewählte Werke in Einzelusgaben*, 5 vols. (Stuttgart: Bad Cannstatt, 1963–75), 1:1–146.

[28] F. C. Baur, *Paul, the Apostle of Jesus Christ: His Life and Work, His Epistles and His Doctrine*, trans. A. Menzies, 2 vols. (London: Williams and Norgate, 1876). This English translation has received some criticism; when appropriate, I refer to the second German edition, *Paulus, der Apostel Jesu Christi. Sein Leben und Wirken, seine Briefe und seine Lehre*, ed. E. Zeller, 2 vols. (Leipzig: Fues, 1866–67).

[29] Baur, *Paul*, 1:5.

[30] Ibid., 1:6, 8, 11, 12.

[31] Cf. Werner George Kümmel, *The New Testament: The History of the Investigation of Its Problems* (Nashville: Abingdon, 1972), pt. IV. For a broader discussion, see Horton Harris, *The Tübingen School* (Oxford: Clarendon, 1975).

[32] J. B. Lightfoot, "St Paul and the Three," in *The Epistle of St. Paul to the Galatians* (1865; reprint, Grand Rapids: Zondervan, 1962), pp. 292–374. Johannes Munck, *Paul and the Salvation of Mankind* (Atlanta: John Knox, 1977). Walther Schmithals, *Paul and the Gnostics* (Nashville: Abingdon, 1972).

[33] See Stephen Neill, *The Interpretation of the New Testament 1861–1961* (London: Oxford University Press, 1964), 21, 27–28.

[34] Kümmel, *The New Testament*, 427n.177.

[35] Harris, *The Tübingen School*, 251–55.

[36] Ibid., 260.

[37] Kümmel, *The New Testament*, 127.

[38] Harris, *The Tübingen School*, 256.

[39] Prior to the publication of *Paulus* he had briefly stated the grounds for viewing Acts as an apologetic work in "Über den Ursprung des Episcopats in der christlichen Kirche," *Tübingen Zeitschrift für Theologie* (1838), pt. 3, 1–185, esp. 142 [reprinted in *Ausgewählte Werke*, 1:321–505); he then found extensive support for that thesis in Matthias Schneckenburger, *Über den Zweck der Apostelgeschichte* (Bern: C. Fischer, 1941).

40 Baur, *Paul*, 1:13. See also p. 38: " . . . the martyrdom of Stephen and the persecution of the Christians which was connected with it, wears the indubitable stamp of historical reality." Harris thus misrepresents matters when he says that Baur thought Acts "was unhistorical through and through" (*The Tübingen School*, 239).

41 Harris, *The Tübingen School*, 262.

42 Ibid., 251–52.

43 In addition to his programmatic essays—esp. *Die Epochen der kirchlichen Geschichtsschreibung* (Tübingen: Fues, 1852), reprinted in vol. 2 of *Ausgewählte Werke* and translated by P. C. Hodgson in *Ferdinand Christian Baur on the Writing of Church History* (New York: Oxford University Press, 1968)—note his explicit discussions in *Paul*, 1:23ff., 96ff., etc.

44 Harris, *The Tübingen School*, 257–58 (italics mine).

45 Baur, *Paul*, 1:8 (cf. the original, *Paulus*, 1:11).

46 Before sneering at this approach, we should recall that this is precisely how B. B. Warfield dealt with objections to biblical inerrancy; see "The Real Problem of Inspiration" (1893), in *The Inspiration and Authority of the Bible* (Philadelphia: Presbyterian and Reformed, 1964), 169–226, esp. 174, and N. M. de S. Cameron, "The Logic of Infallibility: An Evangelical Doctrine at Issue," *Scottish Bulletin of Evangelical Theology* 1 (1983): 39–44.

47 Baur, *Paul*, 1:vii. This translation takes some liberties with the original, which reads: "Mag Über Einzelnes fort und fort gestritten werden, es liegt ja ganz in der Natur der Sache, dass die abstracte Möglichkeit des Einzelnen nie widerlegt werden kann; was Über eine in grösserem Zusammenhang durchgeführte Ansicht in letzter Beziehung allein entscheiden kann, ist doch nur das Allgemeine, von welchem auch das Einzelne immer wieder abhängt, die Consequenz des Ganzen, die überwiegende, dem denkenden Bewusstsein von selbst sich aufdringende innere Wahrscheinlichkeit und Nothwendigkeit der Sache, gegen welche die Partei-Interessen des Tags früher oder später verstummen müssen" (*Paulus*, 1:ix; it should be noted that some material from the preface was omitted in the English edition). Additional evidence of Baur's concern for coherence appears in his introduction to Paul's theology, where he emphasizes the need "to maintain order, connection, and unity in our view of the whole" (*Paul*, 2:118). One curious result of his method is the way he relegates Christology to the category of subordinate issues: Paul's "doctrine of Christ is not indeed a key to his system; that system can be quite well examined and described even before this question is discussed" (2:234; cf. the original, 2:256).

48 Cf. Thomas S. Kuhn, *The Structure of Scientific Revolutions*, 2d ed. (Chicago: University of Chicago Press, 1970), esp. ch. 6. Note in this connection David Hollinger, "T. S. Kuhn's Theory of Science and Its Implications for History," in *Paradigms and Revolutions: Appraisals and Applications of Thomas Kuhn's Philosophy of Science*, ed. Gary Gutting (Notre Dame: University of Notre Dame Press, 1980), 195–222.

49 Neill, *Interpretation*, 37.

50 Otto Pfleiderer, *The Development of Theology in Germany since Kant, and Its Progress in Great Britain since 1825* (London: Swan Sonnenschein, 1890), 397. After vice-presidential candidate Geraldine Ferraro was examined by the press regarding her finances, an aide commented that in spite of thousands of facts being available, "only one thing matters: Will the public think she's honest? If so, none of the facts will be remembered. But if they decide she's not honest, then all the facts will be perceived as a mosaic of conspiracy and deceit" (*Time*, September 3, 1984, 17).

51 See note 32.

52 I cannot, therefore, agree with C. K. Barrett when he plays down Lightfoot's contribution to New Testament history ("Quomodo historia conscribenda sit," *NTS* 28 [1982]: 303–20, esp. 316).

[53] Lightfoot, *Galatians*, xi. Note also Barrett, "Quomodo," 310, and Bruce N. Kaye, "Lightfoot and Baur on Early Christianity," *NovT* 26 (1984): 193–224, esp. 214.

[54] Lightfoot, *Galatians*, 105–6.

[55] Ibid., 311.

[56] Ibid., 374.

[57] Ibid., 346.

[58] Ibid., 349.

[59] "The two first chapters of the Epistle to the Galatians form a historical document of the greatest importance into the true standpoint of the Apostle and his relation to the elder Apostles. . . . It is self-evident that as the Apostle appears as an eye-witness and an actor in his own personal affairs, his statement alone ought to be held as authentic" (Baur, *Paul*, 1:104). "The Epistles of the Apostle are thus the only authentic documents for the history of his apostolic labours, and of the entire relation in which he stood to his age" (1:245). It is, I hope, not unfair to point out that the same assumption plays the key role in more recent treatments, such as the highly regarded work by Alfred Wikenhauser and Josef Schmid, *Einleitung in das Neue Testament*, 6th ed. (Frieburg: Herder, 1973), 363–69, where the reliability of Acts is assessed exclusively on the basis of whether or not it agrees with the Pauline letters.

[60] For example, he affirms that "the historical character of the author [of Acts] can only be maintained at the cost of the moral character of the Apostle" (*Paul*, 1:11). And again: "All attempts to reconcile" Acts 15 and Galatians 2 result in "imputing to the Apostle what can only redound to the disadvantage of his character" (1:105). An interesting, though only partial, analogy is provided by Ernst Haenchen. After concluding that Acts was written by "someone of a later generation trying in his own way to give an account of things that can no longer be viewed in their true perspective," he assures us as follows: "We have no qualms about letting this truth be the last word, for without detracting from Luke's real merit, it ensures that the gospel according to Paul will not be robbed of its due" (*The Acts of the Apostles: A Commentary* [Oxford: Basil Blackwell, 1971], 116).

[61] Karl Barth, *Protestant Theology in the Nineteenth Century: Its Background and History* (London: SCM, 1972), 515.

[62] For example, Jack W. Meiland, *Scepticism and Historical Knowledge* (New York: Random House, 1965); more recently, Leon J. Goldstein, *Historical Knowing* (Austin: University of Texas, 1976). For a fine discussion of this problem, see R. F. Atkinson, *Knowledge and Explanation in History: An Introduction to the Philosophy of History* (Ithaca, N.Y.: Cornell University Press, 1978), ch. 2.

[63] H. Butterfield, *The Origins of History*, ed. Adam Watson (New York: Basic Books, 1981), 8–9. Incidentally, he believed that such objectivity was made possible by his own basic, religious presupposition: "Hold to Christ, and for the rest be totally uncommitted" (p. 9).

[64] Ibid., 163 (italics mine). It is remarkable, and probably significant, that in this book he does not interact with R. G. Collingwood's ideas on the writing of history. This is true even of Butterfield's contribution on the subject of "historiography" for the *Dictionary of the History of Ideas*, ed. P. P. Wiener, 5 vols. (New York: Scribner, 1968–74), 2:464–98.

[65] Unrestrained disavowals of objectivity are not very helpful, primarily because they operate with an artificial definition of *objectivity*; see, for example, J. G. Davies, "Subjectivity and Objectivity in Biblical Exegesis," *BJRL* 66 (1983–84): 44–53. Atkinson (*Knowledge and Explanation*, ch. 3) gives a carefully nuanced exposition of this question.

[66] As suggested earlier, Walther Schmithals (cf. note 32) shares with Baur an antisupernaturalist bias as well as the assumption that Paul faced a uniform front of opposition, yet his own reconstruction differs totally from Baur's. Quite a different example is J. D. G. Dunn, who is committed to what he considers a viable Evangelical

position, yet whose work leads him to conclusions that would have shocked some moderate nineteenth-century liberals (*Unity and Diversity in the New Testament: An Inquiry into the Character of Earliest Christianity* [London: SCM, 1977], especially 226, where he states that what many regard "as orthodox christology may be represented . . . as a curious amalgam of different elements taken from different parts of first-century Christianity").

⁶⁷ Lightfoot, *Galatians*, 347. In his article on Acts for Smith's *Dictionary of the Bible*, 3 vols. (London: John Murray, 1893), 1:25–43, esp. 35–37, Lightfoot illustrated this point. It is, therefore, perplexing that Barrett ("Quomodo," 313) views Lightfoot as simply assuming the credibility of Acts and so failing to indicate the "criteria by which these qualities may be assessed." In a letter dated January 19, 1985, Professor Barrett points out that the qualities to which he refers "are not credibility but 'simplicity, straight-forwardness, and naturalness', on which Lightfoot's argument for credibility rests." My concern, however, is that Lightfoot did provide evidence of other sorts to support his confidence in Acts.

⁶⁸ William M. Ramsay, *The Bearing of Recent Discovery on the Trustworthiness of the New Testament* (1915; reprint, Grand Rapids: Baker, 1979), esp. 3–89. Cf. also the summary in W. Ward Gasque, *A History of the Criticism of the Acts of the Apostle* (Grand Rapids: Eerdmans, 1975), 136–38.

⁶⁹ "One of the most impressive examples of Luke's accuracy is in the titles of the various officials in the Empire mentioned throughout his pages. . . . This accuracy is the more striking because titles of provincial governors changed suddenly at times if the status of provinces was changed. Luke's accuracy betokens not only contemporary knowledge but a natural accuracy of mind, and if his trustworthiness is vindicated in points where he can be checked, we should not assume that he is less trustworthy where we cannot test his accuracy" (F. F. Bruce, *The Acts of the Apostles: The Greek Text with Introduction and Commentary* [London: Tyndale, 1965], 17).

⁷⁰ Haenchen, *The Acts of the Apostles*. He includes a thirty-six-page survey of research during the nineteenth and twentieth centuries; I could not find one reference to Ramsay, not even in the footnotes. Similarly, the standard work by Werner Georg Kümmel, *Introduction to the New Testament*, rev. ed. (London: SCM, 1975), includes four pages (151–54) of bibliography on Acts, but Ramsay's name is missing. To "professional students of the ancient world," remarked A. T. Olmstead over forty years ago, "it seems unbelievable that [Ramsay's books] met an almost universally hostile reception from contemporary [New Testament] critics" ("History, Ancient World, and the Bible," *Journal of Near Eastern Studies* 2 [1943]: 23).

⁷¹ Koester, *Introduction*, 2:51. He says that "Luke might have attempted to write a historical account that could also have aided in the presentation of his apologetic interests. This, however, would have involved another problem: Luke intended to describe the activities of the Holy Spirit, an enterprise that is hardly reconcilable with the requirement that the historian critically investigate the causes behind the events he reports" (p. 316).

⁷² Cf. James M. Robinson, *A New Quest of the Historical Jesus* (London: SCM, 1959), 44. This type of remark, of course, is a commonplace of modern theology.

CHAPTER FOUR

THE LEGITIMACY AND LIMITS OF HARMONIZATION

Craig L. Blomberg

135–74

¹ P. J. Achtemeier, *The Inspiration of Scripture* (Philadelphia: Westminster, 1980), 59.

² Ibid., 66–67. Achtemeier cites Harold Lindsell's now infamous example of the six denials of Jesus by Peter, on which see page 148 and note 54.

[3] For a similar equivocation, see James Barr, *The Scope and Authority of the Bible* (Philadelphia: Westminster, 1980), 78.

[4] On which see especially D. A. Carson, "Unity and Diversity in the New Testament: The Possibility of Systematic Theology," in *Scripture and Truth*, ed. D. A. Carson and John D. Woodbridge (Grand Rapids: Zondervan, 1983), 65–95.

[5] Contrast the approaches of James D. G. Dunn, *Unity and Diversity in the New Testament* (London: SCM, 1977) and Donald Guthrie, *New Testament Theology* (Leicester: InterVarsity, 1981).

[6] F. W. Beare, *The Gospel According to Matthew* (San Francisco: Harper & Row, 1981), 189.

[7] See, for example, the masterful discussion of the first of these tensions in D. A. Carson, *Divine Sovereignty and Human Responsibility* (Atlanta: John Knox, 1981); cf. the comments of Bruce K. Waltke, "Historical Grammatical Problems," in *Hermeneutics, Inerrancy, and the Bible*, ed. Earl D. Radmacher and Robert D. Preus (Grand Rapids: Zondervan, 1984), 117; and Robert D. Preus, " A Response to the Unity of the Bible," in ibid., 684, 686.

[8] Of course, there are more than just two uses of the term, but these are the most prevalent and are sufficient to clarify the thesis defended here. For additional definitions, see Robert L. Thomas and Stanley N. Gundry, *A Harmony of the Gospels* (Chicago: Moody, 1978), 265, but note also their essay on "Problems and Principles of Harmonization," 302–8, in which not one of their "harmonistic" solutions to classic problem passages seems the most plausible!

[9] Robert H. Gundry, *Matthew: A Commentary on His Literary and Theological Art* (Grand Rapids: Eerdmans, 1982), 626; cf. J. Ramsey Michaels, *Servant and Son: Jesus in Parable and Gospel* (Atlanta: John Knox, 1981), 36.

[10] For insightful critiques of Gundry's work on this and other issues, see D. A. Carson, "Gundry on Matthew: A Critical Review," *TJ*, n.s., 3 (1982): 71–91; and Philip B. Payne, "Midrash and History in the Gospels with Special Reference to Robert H. Gundry's *Matthew*," in *Gospel Perspectives*, ed. R. T. France and D. Wenham, 6 vols. (Sheffield: JSOT, 1980–86), 3:177–215.

[11] The debate is well-chronicled in David L. Turner, "Evangelicals, Redaction Criticism and the Current Inerrancy Crisis," *GTJ* 4 (1983): 263–88; and idem, "Evangelicals, Redaction Criticism and Inerrancy: The Debate Continues," *GTJ* 5 (1984): 37–45.

[12] Moisés Silva, "Ned. B. Stonehouse and Redaction Criticism Part Two: The Historicity of the Synoptic Tradition," *WTJ* 40 (1978): 290.

[13] D. A. Carson, "Redaction Criticism: On the Legitimacy and Illegitimacy of a Literary Tool," in *Scripture and Truth*, ed. Carson and Woodbridge, 139.

[14] E.g., Greg L. Bahnsen, "The Inerrancy of the Autographs," in *Inerrancy*, ed. Norman L. Geisler (Grand Rapids: Zondervan, 1979), 151–93.

[15] On how this problem affects even simple translation of Scripture, see Paul Ellingworth, "Translating Parallel Passages in the Gospels," *BT* 34 (1983): 401–7.

[16] Perhaps the best brief introduction to the correct use of form criticism is Stephen H. Travis, "Form Criticism," in *New Testament Interpretation*, ed. I. Howard Marshall (Grand Rapids: Eerdmans, 1977), 153–64.

[17] J. A. Baird, *Audience Criticism and the Historical Jesus* (Philadelphia: Westminster, 1969); cf. the corroborating findings of Philip B. Payne's intensive study of the parables of Jesus in "Metaphor as a Model for Interpretation of the Parables of Jesus with Special Reference to the Parable of the Sower" (Ph.D. diss., Cambridge University, 1975); *contra* Joachim Jeremias, *The Parables of Jesus* (London: SCM, 1972).

[18] See further Craig L. Blomberg, "When Is a Parallel Really a Parallel? A Test Case: The Lucan Parables," *WTJ* 46 (1984): 78–103.

19 C. M. Tuckett, *The Revival of the Griesbach Hypothesis* (Cambridge: Cambridge University Press, 1983); K. Uchida, "The Study of the Synoptic Problem in the Twentieth Century: A Critical Assessment" (Ph.D. diss., University of Aberdeen, 1981).

20 E.g., J. Breckenridge, "Evangelical Implications of Matthean Priority," *JETS* (1983): 117–21.

21 Witness the examples, *par excellence*, of D. A. Carson, "Matthew," in *EBC*, 8:3–599; and I. Howard Marshall, *The Gospel of Luke* (Exeter: Paternoster, 1978).

22 See especially the treatment of this classic "contradiction" by Peter H. Davids, *Commentary on James* (Grand Rapids: Eerdmans, 1982), 19–21.

23 Cited by C. B. Joynt and N. Rescher, "The Problem of Uniqueness in History," *H&T* 1 (1960): 161.

24 See especially Norman Perrin, *What is Redaction Criticism?* (Philadelphia: Fortress, 1969).

25 Werner Georg Kümmel, *Introduction to the New Testament* (Nashville: Abingdon, 1975), 52; *contra*, e.g., Harold Lindsell, *The Bible in the Balance* (Grand Rapids: Zondervan, 1979), 296–97.

26 The best example of proper statistical method with respect to Synoptic studies is L. Gaston, *Horae Synopticae Electronicae* (Missoula: Scholars, 1973); *contra* Gundry, *Matthew*, 4; see further Craig L. Blomberg, "Tradition History in the Parables Peculiar to Luke's Central Section," (Ph.D. diss., University of Aberdeen, 1982), 312–18.

27 S. C. Goetz and C. L. Blomberg, "The Burden of Proof," *JSNT* 11 (1981): 52–58.

28 On the former, see especially J. Topolski, *Methodology of History* (Warsaw: PWN-Polish Scientific Publishers, 1976), 471–73; on the latter, J. Vansina, *Oral Tradition* (Chicago: Aldine, 1961), 138–39.

29 G. J. Garraghan, *A Guide to Historical Method* (New York: Fordham, 1946), 314.

30 See Jacques Barzun and Henry F. Graff, *The Modern Researcher*, 3d ed. (New York: Harcourt, Brace, Jovanovich, 1977), 87–88; M. Bloch, *The Historian's Craft* (New York: Knopf, 1962), 121, 130.

31 Goetz and Blomberg, "Burden," 44–53.

32 Philip L. Shuler, *A Genre for the Gospels* (Philadelphia: Fortress, 1982).

33 The Gospels could not pass the restricted, modern test of Nevins, cited in L. D. Stephens, *Probing the Past* (Boston: Allyn & Bacon, 1974), 5: "an integrated narrative description or analysis of past events or facts written in a spirit of critical inquiry for the whole truth," but they would measure well up against the requirements of Henry S. Commager (*The Nature and Study of History* [Columbus: Merrill, 1965], 3) that a historical narrative be a collection of what seem to be relevant facts organized into coherent patterns with interpretations of both facts and patterns.

34 Objections to the possibility of recovering *any* accurate information about the past (historical relativism) are well-refuted by R. D. Baird, "Factual Statements and the Possibility of Objectivity in History," *JRT* 26 (1969): 5–22; while those which impugn narrative genres, per se, as ancient outgrowth of myth, are well-answered by H. White, "The Question of Narrative in Contemporary Historical Theory," *H&T* 23 (1984): 1–33. White's work does, however, warn against any simplistic equation of an apparently historical form and historical intent, *contra*, e.g., the Chicago Statement on Biblical Hermeneutics, article 13 (see *Hermeneutics, Inerrancy, and the Bible*, ed. Radmacher and Preus, 884).

35 W. H. Kelber, "Redaction Criticism: On the Nature and Exposition of the Gospels," *PRS* 6 (1979): 4–16, though he unjustifiably rules out harmonization on the former count as well, along with much nonharmonistic historical reconstruction, when he declares (p. 13), "the very project of redaction criticism methodologically precludes the quest for the historical Jesus."

[36] Cf. H.-W. Bartsch, "Ein neuer Textus Receptus für das griechische Neue Testament?" *NTS* 2 (1981): 585–92, with K. Aland, "Ein neuer Textus Receptus für das griechische Neue Testament?" *NTS* 28 (1982): 145–53.

[37] See especially John W. Wenham, "Why Do You Ask Me About the Good? A Study of the Relation Between Text and Source Criticism," *NTS* 28 (1982): 106–25, though a more plausible explanation of the problem of Matthew 19:17 will be discussed on page 159.

[38] J. M. Ross, "The Harder Reading in Textual Criticism," *BT* 33 (1982): 138–39.

[39] For both statistical and heuristic principles involved in this kind of judgment, see Blomberg, "Parallel," esp. 80–83.

[40] C. S. Rodd, "Spirit or Finger," *ExpT* 72 (1960–61): 157–58.

[41] W. Grundmann, *Das Evangelium nach Lukas* (Berlin: Evangelische Verlagsanstalt, 1966), 235.

[42] R. Pesch, *Das Markusevangelium*, 2 vols. (Freiburg: Herder, 1976–77), 1:359; J. Gnilka, *Das Evangelium nach Markus*, 2 vols. (Neukirchen Vluyn: Neukirchen; Zürich: Benziger, 1978–79), 1:265; L. Williamson, *Mark* (Atlanta: John Knox, 1983), 130.

[43] D. Edmond Hiebert, *Mark: A Portrait of the Servant* (Chicago: Moody, 1974), 164.

[44] Leon Morris, *The Gospel according to John* (Grand Rapids: Eerdmans, 1971), 163n.98.

[45] Carson, "Matthew," 343.

[46] William L. Lane, *The Gospel According to Mark* (Grand Rapids: Eerdmans, 1974), 233n.111; C. E. B. Cranfield, *The Gospel According to St. Mark* (Cambridge: Cambridge University Press, 1959), 225; Vincent Taylor, *The Gospel According to St. Mark* (London: Macmillan, 1966), 327.

[47] Cf. H. Schürmann, *Das Lukasevangelium* (Freiburg: Herder, 1969), 320.

[48] See also *BGD*, 638, where πεδινός is contrasted not only with "high" or "elevated" but also with "steep" or "uneven."

[49] So William Hendriksen, *The Gospel of Matthew* (Grand Rapids: Baker, 1973), 260; William F. Arndt, *The Gospel According to St. Luke* (St. Louis: Concordia, 1956), 183; *contra* John F. Walvoord, *Matthew: Thy Kingdom Come* (Chicago: Moody, 1974), 43; Gleason L. Archer, Jr., *Encyclopedia of Bible Difficulties* (Grand Rapids: Zondervan, 1982), 366.

[50] *Contra* Taylor, *Mark*, 217.

[51] Pesch, *Markusevangelium*, 1:182n.15; Williamson, *Mark*, 73.

[52] William Hendriksen, *The Gospel of Mark* (Grand Rapids: Baker, 1975), 106–8.

[53] John W. Wenham, "Mark 2, 26" *JTS* 1 (1950): 156.

[54] As in the solutions of Harold Lindsell (*Battle for the Bible* [Grand Rapids: Zondervan, 1976] and J. M. Cheney (*The Life of Christ in Stereo* [Portland: Western Baptist Seminary Press, 1969], 218–20).

[55] Cf. Pesch (*Markusevangelium*, 2:450) with Hendriksen (*Mark*, 619–20).

[56] Walter W. Wessel, "Mark," in *EBC*, 8:657.

[57] Douglas J. Moo, "Tradition and Old Testament in Matt 27:3-10," in *Gospel Perspectives*, ed. France and Wenham, 3:157–75.

[58] Carson, "Matthew," 528–32; Archer, *Encyclopedia*, 375–76.

[59] Eugene A. Nida, *Good News for Everyone* (Waco: Word, 1977).

[60] David J. Hesselgrave, "Contextualization and Revelation Epistemology," in *Hermeneutics, Inerrancy, and the Bible*, ed. Radmacher and Preus (esp. 717–23).

[61] Jeremias, *Parables*, 26–27.

[62] J. Alexander Findlay, *Jesus and His Parables* (London: Epworth, 1950), 95–96; J. A. Fitzmyer, *The Gospel According to Luke I-IX* (Garden City: Doubleday, 1981), 644.

[63] Grant R. Osborne, "Redaction Criticism and the Great Commission: A Case Study Toward a Biblical Understanding of Inerrancy," *JETS* 19 (1976): 73–85.

[64] Idem, "The Evangelical and Redaction Criticism," *JETS* 22 (1979): 311, where he substitutes a view that sees Matthew 28:18–20 as an abbreviation of a fuller commissioning by Jesus.

[65] See H. H. Rowdon, ed., *Christ the Lord* (Leicester: InterVarsity, 1982), especially the articles by I. Howard Marshall, R. T. France, D. A. Carson, and M. M. B. Turner.

[66] As, for example, in John Warwick Montgomery, "Why Has God Incarnate Suddenly Become Mythical?" in *Perspectives on Evangelical Theology*, ed. Kenneth S. Kantzer and Stanley N. Gundry (Grand Rapids: Baker, 1979), 57–65.

[67] See especially S. Brown, "The Matthean Community and the Gentile Mission," *NovT* 22 (1980): 193–221.

[68] Craig L. Blomberg, "The Law in Luke-Acts," *JSNT* 22 (1984): 53–80; cf. M. M. B. Turner, "The Sabbath, Sunday, and the Law in Luke/Acts," in *From Sabbath to Lord's Day*, ed. D. A. Carson (Grand Rapids: Zondervan, 1982), 99–157.

[69] Carson, "Matthew," 413–19.

[70] Charles C. Ryrie, "Biblical Teaching on Divorce and Remarriage," *GTJ* 3 (1982): 177–92; W. A. Heth, "Another Look at the Erasmian View of Divorce and Remarriage," *JETS* 25 (1982): 263–72.

[71] For good surveys of the problem, see R. E. Brown, *The Birth of the Messiah* (Garden City: Doubleday, 1977): 547–56; Fitzmyer, *Luke*, 393–404; Harold W. Hoehner, *Chronological Aspects of the Life of Christ* (Grand Rapids: Zondervan, 1977), 14–22; Marshall, *Luke*, 99–104. Brown and Fitzmyer conclude that Luke has erred, Hoehner says he has not, and Marshall leaves the question open.

[72] J. Thorley, "The Nativity Census: What Does Luke Actually Say?" *Greece & Rome* 26 (1979): 84.

[73] J. R. McRay, "Birth of Jesus Christ," in *Evangelical Dictionary of Theology*, ed. W. A. Elwell (Grand Rapids: Baker, 1984), 156. In a personal conversation, Dr. Vardaman expressed his views more tentatively than McRay and would prefer that conclusions be deferred until the publication of his findings.

[74] I. Howard Marshall, *Biblical Inspiration* (Grand Rapids: Eerdmans, 1983), 63.

[75] Edwin M. Yamauchi, "Josephus and the Scriptures," *Fides et Historia* 13 (1980): 53.

[76] R. B. Rackham, *The Acts of the Apostles* (London: Methuen, 1901), 74.

[77] Recall the comments under "harmonization" (pp. 144–45) and the works cited in notes 28–30.

[78] E. P. Sanders, *The Tendencies of the Synoptic Tradition* (London: Cambridge University Press, 1969); L. R. Keylock, "Bultmann's Law of Increasing Distinctness," in *Current Issues in Biblical and Patristic Interpretation*, ed. Gerald F. Hawthorne (Grand Rapids: Eerdmans, 1975), 193–210.

[79] Craig L. Blomberg, "Tradition and Redaction in the Parables of the Gospel of Thomas," in *Gospel Perspectives*, ed. D. Wenham, 5:177–205.

[80] See, for example, the techniques for "telling a similitude," in Rudolf Bultmann, *The History of the Synoptic Tradition* (Oxford: Basil Blackwell, 1972), 188–91 (but not all of those on 192–97). Cf. W. Kelber, *The Oral and the Written Gospel* (Philadelphia: Fortress, 1983), 44–89.

[81] For a more detailed analysis of Luke's redaction of this parable, see Blomberg, "Tradition History," 278–83.

[82] G. Bornkamm, G. Barth, and H.-J. Held, *Tradition and Interpretation in Matthew* (Philadelphia: Westminster, 1963), 233.

[83] *Contra* Carson ("Matthew," 200) and Fitzmyer (*Luke*, 650), whose redaction-critical explanations are not based on clear-cut tendencies of the two Evangelists.

[84] Often, but by no means always, only one; see Craig L. Blomberg, "New Horizons in Parable Research," *TJ*, n.s., 3 (1982): 10–11; idem, "Preaching the Parables: Preserving Three Main Points," *PRS* 11 (1984): 31–41.

[85] A. M. Ward, *The Gospel According to St. Matthew* (London: Epworth, 1961), 108–9; cf. H. van der Loos, *The Miracles of Jesus* (Leiden: Brill, 1965), 686–87.

[86] G. M. Lee, "Studies in Texts: Matthew 17, 24–27," *Theology* 68 (1965): 380. For the most famous of these fables, see Herodotus 3:42 on Polycrates.

[87] Richard Bauckham, "The Coin in the Fish's Mouth," in *Gospel Perspectives*, ed. D. Wenham and C. L. Blomberg, 6 (forthcoming).

[88] So also Lee, "Studies," 381. Cf. also J. P. Meier, *The Vision of Matthew* (New York: Paulist, 1979), 127.

[89] Blomberg, "Parallel," 91–100.

[90] For a thorough survey of the literature on these passages, see Robert M. Fowler, *Loaves and Fishes* (Chico, Calif.: Scholars, 1980), who concludes the reverse, that Mark 6:32–44 is a secondary expansion of 8:1–10.

[91] N. A. Beck, "Reclaiming a Biblical Text: The Mark 8:14–21 Discussion about Bread in the Boat," *CBQ* 43 (1981): 52n.15; S. Masuda, "The Good News of the Miracle of the Bread: The Tradition and Its Markan Redaction," *NTS* 28 (1982): 211–12.

[92] J. Knackstedt, "Die beiden Brotvermehrungen im Evangelium," *NTS* 10 (1963-64): 315-16.

[93] Carson, "Matthew," 358.

[94] J. Goldingay, "The Chronicler as Theologian," *BTB* 5 (1975): 110.

[95] C. L. Blomberg, "Midrash, Chiasmus, and the Outline of Luke's Central Section," in *Gospel Perspectives*, ed. France and Wenham, 3:233–48.

[96] See idem, "Tradition History," 318–41.

[97] For example, S. T. Davis (*The Debate about the Bible* [Philadelphia: Westminster, 1977], 106) lists this as one of only six errors he can find in Scripture and declares flatly, "I know of no way to reconcile this inconsistency."

[98] Most recently, J. D. M. Derrett, "Peace, Sandals and Shirts (Mark 6:6b–13par.)," *HeyJ* 24 (1983): 255–56.

[99] For example, Archer, *Encyclopedia*, 326; Hendriksen, *Matthew*, 458.

[100] For a survey of proponents of this and the above views, see B. Ahern, "Staff or No Staff?" *CBQ* 5 (1943): 323–37.

[101] Schürmann, *Lukasevangelium*, 501.

[102] Osborne, "Evangelical and Redaction Criticism," 314.

[103] Carson, "Matthew," 241.

[104] For a recent assessment of its use and abuse, see Carson, "Redaction Criticism."

[105] Bornkamm, Barth, & Held, *Matthew*, 52–57; cf. especially Gundry, *Matthew*, 625–26.

[106] See especially G. Theissen, *The Miracle Stories of the Early Christian Tradition* (Philadelphia: Fortress, 1983), 137–38; P. F. Feiler, "The Stilling of the Storm in Matthew: A Response to Günther Bornkamm," *JETS* 26 (1983): 399–406.

[107] So even Robert H. Gundry, *A Survey of the New Testament* (Grand Rapids: Zondervan, 1981), 168.

[108] Hiebert, *Mark*, 262.

[109] Complete statistics appear in Blomberg, "Tradition History," 25–27; Luke is shorter than Mark in 71 of 92 paralleled pericopae.

[110] So Carson, "Matthew," 435, who argues that Luke "gains nothing" by its retention.

[111] Blomberg, "Midrash," 244-47.

[112] For similar explanations, see Marshall, *Luke*, 692; Walter L. Liefeld, "Luke," in *EBC*, 8:1006.

[113] Cf. Carson ("Matthew," *passim*, esp. p. 221) on the major problem with Mark's and Matthew's sequence for the Galilean ministry and (p. 90) on the consistent nonchronological meanings even for potentially temporal connectives like τότε.

[114] See the "episodic" outline of C. W. Hedrick, "What is a Gospel? Geography, Time and Narrative Structure," *PRS* 10 (1983): 255-68.

[115] R. J. Dillon, "Previewing Luke's Project from His Prologue (Luke 1:1-4)," *CBQ* 43 (1981): 205-27; G. Schneider, "Zur Bedeutung von καθεξῆς im lukanischen Doppel-werk," *Zeitschrift für die neutestamentliche Wissenschaft* 68 (1977): 128-31.

[116] *Contra*, for example, Thomas and Gundry (*Harmony*), J. Dwight Pentecost (*A Harmony of the Words and Works of Jesus Christ* [Grand Rapids: Zondervan, 1981]), and Robert D. Culver (*The Life of Christ* [Grand Rapids: Baker, 1976]).

[117] On the temptation narratives, see Carson ("Matthew," 111) and Marshall (*Luke*, 167); on the overall outline, see K. R. Wolfe ("The Chiastic Structure of Luke-Acts and Some Implications for Worship," *SWJT* 22 [1980]: 60-71).

[118] For a more detailed analysis of this miracle, see Craig L. Blomberg, "The Miracles as Parables," in *Gospel Perspectives*, ed. D. Wenham and C. L. Blomberg, 6 (forthcoming). W. Telford, *The Barren Temple and the Withered Tree* (Sheffield: JSOT, 1980), provides a comprehensive *Forschungsbericht* and defends the view that the mountain of Jesus' faith-sayings is not the Mount of Olives but Mount Zion.

[119] As, for example, in Robert L. Thomas, "The Rich Young Man in Matthew," *GTJ* 3 (1982): 256. Mark, in fact, uses the imperfect of ἐρωτάω and its compound form much more often than the aorist, and few of these references suggest an iterative emphasis.

[120] For example, J. P. Meier, *Matthew* (Wilmington: Glazier, 1980), 215; Eduard Schweizer, *The Good News According to Matthew* (Atlanta: John Knox, 1975), 387.

[121] Gundry, *Matthew*, 385; Taylor, *Mark*, 426-27.

[122] For a slightly freer harmonization, see Carson, "Redaction Criticism," 136.

[123] See Alfred Plummer, *A Critical and Exegetical Commentary on the Gospel According to St. Luke* (Edinburgh: T & T Clark, 1896), 539, for essentially the same solution.

[124] George E. Ladd, *I Believe in the Resurrection of Jesus* (Grand Rapids: Eerdmans, 1975), 91-93. Cf. now John W. Wenham, *Easter Enigma* (Grand Rapids: Zondervan, 1984), though Wenham's deliberate eschewal of redaction-critical considerations causes him at times to employ too much harmonization.

[125] See I. Howard Marshall, *Last Supper—Lord's Supper* (Exeter: Paternoster, 1980), especially 36-38, 179.

[126] On the historical probability of Mark's account, see A. N. Sherwin-White, "The Trial of Christ," in *Historicity and Chronology in the New Testament* (London: SPCK, 1965), 97-116; and for Luke, D. R. Catchpole, *The Trial of Jesus* (Leiden: Brill, 1971), 153-220, though neither admits the accuracy of the other account!

[127] As even F. J. Matera, *The Kingship of Jesus* (Chico, Calif.: Scholars, 1982), 9, admits, despite otherwise disparaging those who bring "an agenda that endeavors to synchronize the Synoptics" (p. 8).

[128] Carson, "Matthew," 243.

[129] *Contra* W. R. G. Loader, "Son of David, Blindness, Possession and Duality in Matthew," *CBQ* 44 (1982): 570-85, who argues that the motivation is forensic ("two or three witnesses").

[130] Cf. Archer, *Encyclopedia*, 325; Carson, "Matthew," 217; V. S. Poythress, "Adequacy of Language and Accommodation," in *Hermeneutics, Inerrancy, and the Bible*, ed. Radmacher and Preus, 373.

[131]Carl F. H. Henry, *God, Revelation and Authority*, 6 vols. (Waco: Word, 1976–83), 4:364.

[132]See especially David N. Freedman, "The Chronicler's Purpose," *CBQ* 23 (1961): 436–42; R. North, "Theology of the Chronicler," *JBL* 82 (1963): 369–81; Goldingay, "Chronicler"; J. D. Newsome, Jr., "Toward a New Understanding of the Chronicler and His Purposes," *JBL* 94 (1975): 201–17; T. D. Hanks, "The Chronicler: Theologian of Grace," *EQ* 53 (1981): 16–28; D. J. McCarthy, "Covenant and Law in Chronicles-Nehemiah," *CBQ* 44 (1982): 25–44.

[133]See especially F. L. Moriarty, "The Chronicler's Account of Hezekiah's Reform," *CBQ* 27 (1965): 401: "It is no longer fashionable to write off the historical validity of the Chronicler's narrative even when one takes into account that it reflects his own special interest and purpose"—though dissenting views have perhaps moderated this trend slightly.

[134]John W. Wenham, "Large Numbers in the Old Testament," *TB* 18 (1967): 19.

[135]Ibid., 21–24, 24–34.

[136]J. Barton Payne, "The Validity of the Numbers in Chronicles," *BS* 136 (1979): 109–28, 206–20, with a chart summarizing his findings (p. 125).

[137]Archer, *Encyclopedia*, 179; H. G. M. Williamson, *1 and 2 Chronicles* (Grand Rapids: Eerdmans, 1982), 142; T. Willi, *Die Chronik als Auslegung* (Göttingen: Vandenhoeck & Ruprecht, 1972): 138–39; *contra* P. K. McCarter, Jr., *2 Samuel* (Garden City: Doubleday, 1984), 450, who argues that the original Elhanan story attached itself to the better known hero, David, in oral tradition.

[138]I. W. Slotki, *Chronicles* (London: Soncino, 1952), 165.

[139]Williamson, *Chronicles*, 272; R. Dillard, "The Reign of Asa (2 Chronicles 14–16)," *JETS* 23 (1980): 212n.24; *contra* E. L. Curtis and A. A. Madsen, *A Critical and Exegetical Commentary on the Books of Chronicles* (Edinburgh: T & T Clark, 1910), 387, who argue that the Chronicler simply altered the facts since they portrayed Asa in a bad light.

[140]Wenham, "Numbers," 23; Payne, "Numbers," 122; Curtis and Madsen, *Chronicles*, 331.

[141]A. Zuidhof, "King Solomon's Molten Sea and (π)," *BA* 45 (1982): 181; cf. Slotki, *Chronicles*, 172.

[142]C. F. Keil, *The Books of the Chronicles* (reprint, Grand Rapids: Eerdmans, 1968), 413.

[143]R. J. Coggins, *The First and Second Books of the Chronicles* (Cambridge: Cambridge University Press, 1976), 236.

[144]Goldingay, "Chronicler," 110.

[145]Thiele's latest revision of *The Mysterious Numbers of the Hebrew Kings* (Grand Rapids: Zondervan, 1983), contains a complete review of his earlier studies and the responses they have received.

[146]See especially J. D. Shenkel, *Chronology and Recensional Development in the Greek Text of Kings* (Cambridge: Harvard University Press, 1968).

[147]S. H. Horn, "From Bishop Ussher to Edwin R. Thiele," *AUSS* 18 (1980): 49.

[148]Williamson, *Chronicles*, 103; J. B. Myers, *1 Chronicles* (Garden City: Doubleday, 1965), 90; Curties and Madsen, *Chronicles*, 15; *contra* J. Mauchline, *1 and 2 Samuel* (London: Oliphants, 1971), 321.

[149]A. G. Auld, "Prophets through the Looking Glass: Between Writings and Moses," *JSOT* 27 (1983): 15–16.

[150]*Contra* especially W. F. Stinespring, "Eschatology in Chronicles," *JBL* 80 (1961): 213.

[151]R. Dillard, "The Chronicler's Solomon," *WTJ* 43 (1981): 298n.18; cf. R. Mosis, *Untersuchungen zur Theologie des chronistischen Geschichtswerkes* (Freiburg: Herder, 1973), 137.

[152] Williamson, *Chronicles*, 18, argues that these and other titles all refer to canonical Samuel-Kings; cf. W. Rudolph, "Problems of the Books of Chronicles," *Vetus Testamentum* 4 (1954): 402–3.

[153] For example, R. Bauckham, "The Liber Antiquitatum Biblicarum of Pseudo-Philo and The Gospels as 'Midrash'," in *Gospel Perspectives*, ed. France and Wenham, 3:33–76.

[154] For example, B. D. Chilton, "Targumic Transmission and Dominical Tradition," in *Gospel Perspectives*, ed. France and Wenham, 1:21–45; idem, "A Comparative Study of Synoptic Development: The Dispute between Cain and Abel in the Palestinian Targums and the Beelzebul Controversy in the Gospels," *JBL* 101 (1982): 553–62.

[155] R. M. Johnston, "Parabolic Interpretations Attributed to Tannaim" (Ph.D. diss., Hartford Seminary Foundation, 1978).

[156] Blomberg, "Tradition History," 396–460.

[157] See the synoptic studies of H. W. Attridge (*The Interpretation of Biblical History in the Antiquitates Judaicae of Flavius Josephus* [Missoula: Scholars, 1976]) and F. G. Downing ("Redaction Criticism: Josephus' *Antiquities* and the Synoptic Gospels," *JSNT* 8–9 [1980]: 46–65, 29–48). See also N. G. Cohen, "Josephus and Scripture," *JQR* 54 (1964): 311–32.

[158] See S. J. D. Cohen, *Josephus in Galilee and Rome* (Leiden: Brill, 1979), esp. 3–64.

[159] Cf. W. C. van Unnik, *Flavius Josephus als historischer Schriftsteller* (Heidelberg: Lambert Schneider, 1978), 60–61.

[160] S. Cohen, *Josephus*, 33–34.

[161] A. Byatt, "Josephus and Population Numbers in First Century Palestine," *PEQ* 105 (1973): 51–60.

[162] C. G. Tuland, "Josephus, *Antiquities*, Book XI," *AUSS* 4 (1966): 192.

[163] Waltke, "Grammatical Problems," 93–99.

[164] Downing, "Redaction Criticism," 60; R. J. H. Shutt, *Studies in Josephus* (London: SPCK, 1961); Cohen, *Josephus*, 47.

[165] H. G. M. Williamson, "The Historical Value of Josephus's Jewish *Antiquities*, xi.297–301," *JTS* 28 (1977): 49.

[166] The pioneering work was R. Laqueur, *Der jüdische Historiker Flavius Josephus* (reprint, Darmstadt: Wissenschaftliche Buchgesellschaft, 1970); the state of the art appears in T. Rajak, *Josephus: The Historian and His Society* (Philadelphia: Fortress, 1984).

[167] Attridge, *Interpretation*, 50–51; Shutt, *Josephus* 122–27; *contra* Douglas J. Moo, "Once Again, 'Matthew and Midrash': A Rejoinder to Robert H. Gundry," *JETS* 26 (1983): 69–70.

[168] Downing, "Redaction Criticism," 33.

[169] *Josephus*, trans. L. H. Feldman, 9 vols. (Cambridge: Harvard University Press, 1926–65), 9:301, adds the word "total," while H. St. J. Thackeray, ibid., 2:403, adds the definite article ("the three").

[170] Rajak, *Josephus*, 16, 127, 211.

[171] Ibid., 15, 71, 88, 106, 154–55.

[172] C. B. Welles, "There Have Been Many Alexanders," in *The Impact of Alexander the Great*, ed. E. N. Borza (Hinsdale, Ill.: Dryden, 1974), 10.

[173] E. N. Borza, "The Nature of the Evidence," in ibid., 21–41. On the accuracy of Arrian, cf. the introduction, notes, and appendices in *Arrian*, trans. P. A. Brunt, 2 vols. (Cambridge: Harvard University Press, 1976) with A. B. Bosworth, "Errors in Arrian," *CQ* 26 (1976): 117–39. On the problem of biography versus history in Plutarch, see C. J. Gianakaris, *Plutarch* (New York: Twayne, 1970); and A. E. Wardman, "Plutarch's Methods in the Lives," *CQ* 21 (1971): 254–61. For a lone defender of the reliability of the "Vulgate,"

see N. G. L. Hammond, *Three Historians of Alexander the Great* (Cambridge: Cambridge University Press, 1983).

[174] For a convenient introduction to this material, see R. L. Fox, *The Search for Alexander* (Boston: Little, 1980): 38–46.

[175] On the twenty-plus primary sources for Arrian and Plutarch no longer extant, see especially L. Pearson, *The Lost Histories of Alexander the Great* (Oxford: Basil Blackwell, 1960).

[176] A. Wardman, *Plutarch's Lives* (London: Paul Elek, 1974), 161.

[177] J. R. Hamilton, *Plutarch, Alexander: A Commentary* (Oxford: Clarendon, 1969), xliv.

[178] A. B. Bosworth, *A Historical Commentary on Arrian's History of Alexander* (Oxford: Clarendon, 1980), 1:98–99.

[179] *Arrian*, 1:35.

[180] Hamilton, *Plutarch*, 32.

[181] *Arrian*, trans. E. I. Robson, 2 vols. (Cambridge: Harvard University Press, 1929), 1:449-50.

[182] J. G. Lloyd, *Alexander the Great: Selections from Arrian* (Cambridge; Cambridge University Press, 1981), 58.

[183] Bosworth, *Arrian's History*, 18.

[184] Cf. M. Hengel, *Acts and the History of Earliest Christianity* (London: SCM, 1979), on the practices of ancient historians most relevant to the study of Acts and the Gospels.

[185] Hamilton, *Plutarch*, xl.

[186] Bosworth, *Arrian's History*, 256; Hamilton, *Plutarch*, 77.

[187] Ibid., 83.

[188] P. A. Stadter, *Arrian of Nicomedia* (Chapel Hill: University of North Carolina Press, 1980), 99–100.

[189] A. Momigliano, "Biblical Studies and Classical Studies: Simple Reflections about Historical Method," *BA* 45 (1982): 224.

[190] Ibid., 225. For a masterful critique of the revisionism rampant among contemporary historians, see O. Handlin, *Truth in History* (Cambridge: Harvard University Press, 1979).

CHAPTER FIVE
THE PROBLEM OF *SENSUS PLENIOR*
Douglas J. Moo
175–211

[1] Robert H. Gundry, *Matthew: A Commentary on His Literary and Theological Art* (Grand Rapids: Eerdmans, 1982), 623–40. For critical reviews of Gundry's book, see D. A. Carson, "Gundry on Matthew: A Critical Review," *TJ* 3 (1982): 71–91; Philip Barton Payne, "Midrash and History in the Gospels with Special Reference to R. H. Gundry's *Matthew*," *Gospel Perspectives: Studies of History and Tradition in the Four Gospels*, vol. 3, *Studies in Midrash and History*, ed. R. T. France and David Wenham (Sheffield: JSOT, 1983), 177–215; Douglas Moo, "Matthew and Midrash: An Evaluation of Robert H. Gundry's Approach," *JETS* 26 (1983): 31–39.

[2] William J. Abraham, *The Divine Inspiration of Holy Scripture* (Oxford: Oxford University Press, 1981), 29.

[3] B. B. Warfield, *The Inspiration and Authority of the Bible* (reprint, Philadelphia: Presbyterian and Reformed, 1948), 201–26.

⁴See the brief discussion in Paul D. Feinberg, "The Meaning of Inerrancy," *Inerrancy*, ed. Norman L. Geisler (Grand Rapids: Zondervan, 1979), 270–76.

⁵Though dated now, the article of Moody Smith is still a valuable survey of the field ("The Use of the Old Testament in the New," *The Use of the Old Testament and Other Essays: Studies in Honor of William Franklin Stinespring*, ed. James M. Efird [Durham, N.C.: Duke University Press, 1972]). The most important monographs are: Leonhard Goppelt, *Typos. Die typologische Deutung des Alten Testaments im Neuen* (Gütersloh: Bertelmann, 1939) [now available in English (Grand Rapids: Eerdmans, 1982)]; C. H. Dodd, *According to the Scriptures: The Substructure of New Testament Theology* (London: Collins, 1952); Krister Stendahl, *The School of St. Matthew and Its Use of the Old Testament* (Lund: Gleerup, 1954); Barnabas Lindars, *New Testament Apologetic: The Doctrinal Significance of the Old Testament Quotations* (London: SCM, 1961); E. Earle Ellis, *Paul's Use of the Old Testament* (Edinburgh: Oliver & Boyd, 1957); Robert H. Gundry, *The Use of the Old Testament in St. Matthew's Gospel* (Leiden: Brill, 1967); J. W. Doeve, *Jewish Hermeneutics in the Synoptic Gospels and Acts* (Assen: van Gorcum, 1954); Alfred Suhl, *Die Funktion der alttestamentlichen Zitate und Anspielungen im Markusevangelium* (Gütersloh: Mohn, 1965); Friedrich Schröger, *Der Verfässer des Hebräerbriefes als Schriftausleger* (Biblische Untersuchungen 4; Regensburg: Pustet, 1968); Martin Rese, *Alttestamentliche Motive in der Christologie des Lukas* (SNT 1; Gütersloh: Mohn, 1969); W. Rothfuchs, *Die Erfüllungszitate des Matthäus-Evangeliums: eine biblische-theologische Untersuchung* (BWANT 5:8; Stuttgart: Kohlhammer, 1969); R. T. France, *Jesus and the Old Testament* (London: Tyndale, 1971); Richard N. Longenecker, *Biblical Exegesis in the Apostolic Period* (Grand Rapids: Eerdmans, 1975).

⁶Paul J. Achtemeier, *The Inspiration of Scripture: Problems and Proposals* (Philadelphia: Westminster, 1980), 64–65, 86–95, 112–13, 130; cf. the more negative assessment of S. Vernon McCasland, "Matthew Twists the Scripture," *JBL* 80 (1961): 143–48.

⁷See especially Origen's discussion in *De Principiis* 4; and cf. Jean Daniélou, *Origen* (New York: Shedd & Warner, 1959), 139–73.

⁸Henri de Lubac, *The Sources of Revelation* (New York: Herder and Herder, 1968), 49. The name to be given to this "sense beyond the literal"—typology, allegory, spiritual sense, mystical sense—and the different nuances within the sense are debated. See the helpful discussion of Glenn W. Olsen, "Allegory, Typology, and the *sensus spiritalis*. Part I: Definition and Earliest History," *Communio* 4 (1977): 161–79.

⁹See the Prologue to the Psalms by Diodore of Tarsus (translation in Karlfried Froelich, *Biblical Interpretation in the Early Church* [Philadelphia: Fortress, 1984], 82–86). On the Antiochians' Old Testament interpretation, see also A. Viccari, "La θεωρία nella scoula esegetica di Antiochia," *Bib* 1 (1920): 3–36.

¹⁰Geoffrey W. Bromiley, "The Church Fathers and Holy Scripture," *Scripture and Truth* (Grand Rapids: Zondervan, 1983), 214.

¹¹John Cassian (d. 435) speaks of these four senses; Rabanus Maurus (d. 856) solidified the "fourfold sense" as authoritative. See Peter Stuhlmacher, *Vom Verstehen des Neuen Testaments. Eine Hemeneutik* (Göttingen: Vandenhoeck & Ruprecht, 1979), 83; and the massive study of Henri de Lubac, *Exégèse Mediévale. Les Quatre Sens de l'écriture*, 4 vols. (Paris: Aubier, 1959).

¹²See, for this motivation in Origen, Daniélou, *Origen*, 140–43.

¹³Beryl Smalley, *The Study of the Bible in the Middle Ages* (Notre Dame: University of Notre Dame Press, 1964), 364–65; see also James Samuel Preus (*From Shadow to Promise: Old Testament Interpretation from Augustine to the Young Luther* [Cambridge: Belknap, 1969], 49–107), who surveys some of the medieval controversies over the meaning of the "literal" sense and its difference from the "spiritual" sense.

¹⁴Aquinas specifically ascribes the literal sense to what the author intends; and since the author is God, the literal sense of the text may have many meanings. See *Summa Theologiae* Ia. I, 10; and Smalley, *Study of the Bible*, 300.

[15] Preus, *From Shadow to Promise*, 106–7.

[16] *From Shadow to Promise*.

[17] Heinrich Bornkamm, *Luther and the Old Testament* (Philadelphia: Fortress, 1969), 96; cf. 87–101.

[18] Goppelt, *Typos*, 6–7 (ET).

[19] See Richard M. Davidson, *Typology in Scripture: A Study of Hermeneutical Τύπος Structures* (Andrews University Doctoral Diss. Series 2; Berrien Springs, Mich.: Andrews University Press, 1981), 33–36.

[20] See the essay by John W. Woodbridge (pp. 237–70 in this volume) for the degree to which these kinds of problems were already being discussed before the popularity of the "grammatical-historical" method.

[21] Stuhlmacher, *Vom Verstehen des Neuen Testaments*, 124; G. W. H. Lampe and K. J. Woollcombe, *Essays on Typology* (London: SCM, 1957), 15.

[22] *Weissagung und Erfullung im Alten und Neuen Testamente* (Nordlingen: C. H. Beck, 1841–44). See the discussion in Goppelt, *Typos*, 11–13; D. L. Baker, *Two Testaments: One Bible* (Leicester: InterVarsity, 1976), 299–300.

[23] Ernst Wilhelm Henstenberg, *The Christology of the Old Testament*, 2d ed. (Edinburgh: T. & T. Clark, 1854–58).

[24] Patrick Fairbairn, *The Typology of Scripture*, 2 vols. (New York: Funk & Wagnalls, 1876). Roger R. Nicole has recently advocated Fairbairn's approach as a way out of the difficulties Evangelicals find themselves in with respect to the use of the Old Testament in the New ("Patrick Fairbairn and Biblical Hermeneutics as Related to the Quotation of the Old Testament in the New," *Hermeneutics, Inerrancy, and the Bible*, ed. Earl D. Radmacher and Robert D. Preus [Grand Rapids: Zondervan, 1984], 767–76).

[25] John H. Newman, *An Essay on the Development of Christian Doctrine* (Westminster, Md.: Christian Classics, 1983), 74; cf. Nicholas Lash, *Newman on Development: The Search for an Explanation in History* (Shepherdstown, W.Va.: Patmos, 1975), 90–94.

[26] Lubac, *Sources of Revelation*, 14–31; Jean Daniélou, *From Shadows to Reality: Studies in the Biblical Typology of the Fathers* (London: Burns & Oates, 1960).

[27] The approach of Wilhelm Vischer (*The Witness of the Old Testament to Christ*, 3d ed., 2 vols. [London: Lutterworth, 1949], 28-29) comes very close to this position. See also Anthony Tyrrell Hanson, *Studies in Paul's Technique and Theology* (London: SPCK, 1974), 226.

[28] Moisés Silva, "New Testament Use of the Old Testament," in *Scripture and Truth*, ed. Carson and Woodbridge (Grand Rapids: Zondervan, 1983), 163.

[29] J. A. Sanders, "Habakkuk in Qumran, Paul, and the Old Testament," *JR* 39 (1959): 235.

[30] A. T. Hanson, *The New Testament Interpretation of the Old Testament* (London: SPCK, 1979), 13.

[31] See, for instance, J. I. Packer, "Infallible Scripture and the Role of Hermeneutics," *Scripture and Truth*, ed. Carson and Woodbridge, 325–56.

[32] Silva, "New Testament Use of the Old Testament," 163–64.

[33] S. Lewis Johnson, *The Old Testament in the New: An Argument for Biblical Inspiration* (Grand Rapids: Zondervan, 1980), 66.

[34] Bruce Vawter, *Biblical Inspiration* (Philadelphia: Westminster, 1972), 16; see also Abraham, *Inspiration*, 105–7.

[35] See, for instance, the discussion in Archibald A. Hodge and Benjamin B. Warfield, *Inspiration* (1881; reprint, Grand Rapids: Baker, 1979), 62–64.

[36] For discussions of the function of quotations and allusions, see J. A. E. van Dodewaard, "La Force évocatrice de la citation," *Bib* 36 (1955): 482–91; Rese,

Alttestamentliche Motive, 208–9; Suhl, *Funktion der alttestamentlichen Zitate*, 38–42; James Barr, *Old and New in Interpretation: A Study of the Two Testaments* (New York: Harper & Row, 1966), 115. Silva, "New Testament Use of the Old," 156–59, mentions similar considerations.

[37] Douglas J. Moo, *The Old Testament in the Gospel Passion Narratives* (Sheffield: Almond, 1983), 240–42.

[38] Silva, "New Testament Use of the Old," 157–58.

[39] Eric D. Hirsch, Jr., *Validity in Interpretation* (New Haven: Yale University Press, 1967), 121–26.

[40] Longenecker, *Biblical Exegesis*, 126–27.

[41] Hans Conzelmann, *1 Corinthians* (Philadelphia: Fortress, 1975), 154–55.

[42] Walter C. Kaiser, Jr., "The Current Crisis in Exegesis and the Apostolic Use of Deuteronomy 25:4 in 1 Corinthians 9:8–10," *JETS* 21:1 (March 1978): 3–18.

[43] See Luke 4:23, Acts 18:21, 21:22, 28:4, and Archibald T. Robertson and Alfred Plummer, *A Critical and Exegetical Commentary on the First Epistle of Paul to the Corinthians*, 2d ed. (Edinburgh: T. & T. Clark, 1914), 184.

[44] Although some scholars claim that the addition genuinely reflects Old Testament teaching, such as is found in the "imprecatory psalms" (Gundry, *Matthew*, 96–97), this is almost certainly not the case. The most likely origin is the Qumran community, whose members were instructed to hate "the sons of darkness."

[45] Silva, "New Testament Use of the Old," 159.

[46] Achtemeier, *Inspiration*, 113; Vawter, *Inspiration*, 5.

[47] Dewey Beegle, *Scripture, Tradition and Infallibility* (Grand Rapids: Eerdmans, 1973), 237.

[48] See the studies of Stendahl (*School of St. Matthew*), Gundry (*Use of the Old Testament*), and Rothfuchs (*Erfüllungszitate*).

[49] This is emphasized (perhaps too one-sidedly) by C. F. D. Moule, "Fulfillment-Words in the New Testament: Use and Abuse," *NTS* 14 (1967–68): 293–320. See also Bruce M. Metzger, "The Formulas Introducing Quotations of Scripture in the NT and the Mishnah," *JBL* 70 (1951): 297–307; Rothfuchs, *Erfüllungszitate*, 48–49; George M. Soares Prabhu, *The Formula Quotations in the Infancy Narrative of Matthew: An Enquiry into the Tradition History of Mt. 1–2* (Rome: Biblical Institute, 1976), 46–47; Gottlob Schrenk, *TDNT*, 1:758–59.

[50] For this interpretation of these key Matthean texts, see especially Robert Banks, *Jesus and the Law in the Synoptic Tradition* (Cambridge: Cambridge University Press, 1975), esp. 207–12; John P. Meier, *Law and History in Matthew's Gospel: A Redactional Study of Mt. 5:17–48* (Rome: Biblical Institute, 1976), esp. 66–75.

[51] D. A. Carson, "Matthew," *EBC*, 8:92–93.

[52] Beegle, *Scripture*, 237–38.

[53] Longenecker, *Biblical Exegesis*, 70–73, 211–13.

[54] The bibliography on "pesher" and "midrash" in Jewish literature and the New Testament is enormous. Useful surveys and discussions can be found in Longenecker, *Biblical Exegesis*, 32–45; Merrill P. Miller, "Targum, Midrash and the Use of the Old Testament in the New Testament," *Journal for the Study of Judaism in the Persian, Hellenistic and Roman Periods* 2 (1971): 29–82; E. Earle Ellis, "Midrash, Targum and New Testament Quotations," *Neotestamentica et Semitica: Studies in Honour of Matthew Black*, ed. E. Earle Ellis and Max Wilcox (Edinburgh: T. & T. Clark, 1969); idem, "How the New Testament Uses the Old," *New Testament Interpretation; Essays on Principles and Methods*, ed. I. Howard Marshall (Grand Rapids: Eerdmans, 1977); Joseph A. Fitzmyer, "The Use of Explicit Old Testament Quotations in Qumran Literature and in the New Testament," *NTS* 7 (1960–61): 297–333; Roger Le Déaut, "Apropos d'une définition du Midrash," *Bib* 50 (1969): 395–413 [ET in *Int* 25 (1971): 259–82]; F. F. Bruce,

Biblical Exegesis in the Qumran Texts (Grand Rapids: Eerdmans, 1960); R. Bloch, "Midrasch," *DBSup,* 5:1263-81; Otto Betz, *Offenbarung und Schriftforschung in der Qumransekte* (Tübingen: Mohr, 1960); Joseph Bonsirven, *Exégèse rabbinique et Exégèse paulinienne* (Paris: Beauchesne and Sons, 1939); *Gospel Perspectives,* Vol. 3, *Studies in Midrash and History,* ed. France and Wenham. I attempt to describe and categorize some of these methods in my book, *Old Testament in the Gospel Passion Narratives,* 5–78.

[55] See Moo, *Old Testament,* 388–92.

[56] Ibid., 75–78.

[57] "Midrash Pesher in Pauline Hermeneutics," *Prophecy and Hermeneutic in Early Christianity* (Grand Rapids: Eerdmans, 1978), 180 [= *NTS* 2 (1955–56): 127–33]. See, for a similar approach, Longenecker, *Biblical Exegesis,* 212.

[58] See, above all, Goppelt, *Typos* ("Die Typologie ist die im Schriftgebrauch des NT vorherrschende und für ihn charakteristische Deutungsweise . . . " [p. 239]). See also Fairbairn (*Typology*), Nicole ("Patrick Fairbairn and Biblical Hermeneutics"), and S. Lewis Johnson ("A Response to Patrick Fairbairn and Biblical Hermeneutics as Related to the Quotations of the Old Testament in the New," *Hermeneutics, Inerrancy, and the Bible,* ed. Radmacher and Preus, 794).

[59] David Baker, "Typology and the Christian Use of the Old Testament," *SJT* 29 (1976): 153.

[60] In the modern resurgence of interest in typology, it is often claimed that a historical basis for the type is unnecessary; all that is required is a "*salvation*-historical" basis (for instance, Gerhard von Rad, "Typological Interpretation of the Old Testament," *Essays on Old Testament Interpretation,* ed. Claus Westermann [London: SCM, 1963], 20–38). However, Davidson argues convincingly that the New Testament use of typology depends for its validity on the historical reality of the type (*Typology in Scripture,* 398).

[61] "Typology means not that there is a relation between things visible and invisible, but that there is a correspondence between historical realities at different stages of redemptive history" (Jean Daniélou, "The Fathers and the Scriptures," *Theology* 57 [1954]: 85). As Oscar Cullmann correctly notes, then, typology is inextricably bound up with a salvation-historical scheme, while allegory is not (*Salvation in History* [London: SCM, 1967], 132–33). See also Francis Foulkes, *The Acts of God: A Study of the Basis of Typology in the Old Testament* (London: Tyndale, 1958), 35.

[62] "Bei aller typologischen Wiederholung steht das Kommende im Gegensatz zum Alten. Es ist nicht eine reichere, vollkommene Form des Alten, auch keine neue Entwicklungsstufe . . . sondern die eschatologische Erfüllung. Es besteht also weder das Verhältnis der Repetition noch das Komparitius, sondern das der einzigartigen endzeitlichen Vollendung" (Kurt Frör, *Biblische Hermeneutik. Zur Schriftauslegung in Predigt und Unterricht,* 3d ed. [Munich: Kaiser, 1967], 86–87). See also Fairbairn, *Typology,* 1:150; Goppelt, *Typos,* 18–19.

[63] Davidson (*Typology in Scripture,* 94) points out that typology has traditionally been viewed as having a predictive function, while many modern advocates of the method see it as entirely retrospective. Thus Fairbairn (*Typology,* 1:46) makes a requirement for genuine typology that the type be designed and ordained by God (see also Goppelt, *Typos,* 18–19; Johnson, *Old Testament in the New,* 56). On the other hand, Baker ("Typology," 149), Foulkes (*Acts of God,* 20–34), and France (*Jesus and the Old Testament,* 39–40), among others, carefully distinguish typology from exegesis and claim that types need have no intrinsic prospective function.

[64] Goppelt, *Typos,* 244.

[65] Cullmann's *Salvation in History* is one of the more important statements of the position, but it is a widely recognized scheme (see also Hermann Ridderbos, *Paul: An Outline of His Theology* [Grand Rapids: Eerdmans, 1975], 44–90).

[66] See especially the careful exegesis of Davidson, *Typology in Scripture,* 193–297.

[67] Albert Vis, *The Messianic Psalm Quotations in the New Testament. A Critical Study on the Christian 'Testimonies' in the Old Testament* (Amsterdam: von Soest, 1936), 38–40.

[68] See Bruce Waltke, "A Canonical Approach to the Psalms," *Tradition and Testament: Essays in Honor of Charles Lee Feinberg*, ed. John S. Feinberg and Paul D. Feinberg (Chicago: Moody, 1981), 11–14. This larger theological setting and significance is too often ignored in modern scholarship. The strictures of George Dahl are worth quoting in full: "There seems to be abroad a strangely perverted and sadistically exaggerated sense of honesty in estimating our sacred writings, according to which one ought always to choose the less worthy and less religious of two possible interpretations of any given passage. Whenever in the Psalms the word 'Messiah' appears, every nerve is strained, and every device of forced exegesis utilized, in order to make it refer merely to the secular king and his mundane affairs. Even where the whole context is saturated with the characteristic motifs of Israel's dynamic and intensely religious Messianic expectation, one must never admit that the Messiah is meant" ("The Messianic Expectation in the Psalter," *JBL* 57 [1938]: 2).

[69] L. Ruppert, *Jesus als der leidende Gerechte? Der Weg Jesu im Lichte eines alt- und zwischentestamentlichen Motivs* (Stuttgart: Katholisches Bibelwerk, 1972); Eduard Schweizer, *Erniedrigung und Erhöhung bei Jesus und seinen Nachfolgern* (Zürich: Zwingli, 1962), 22–24. On the background of the concept, see Hans-Werner Surkau, *Martyrien in jüdischer und frühchristlicher Zeit* (Göttingen: Vandenhoeck & Ruprecht, 1938), 7–29.

[70] P. Grelot, *Sens Chrétien de l'Ancien Testament*, [Bibliothèque de Théologie, 1: Théologie Dogmatique, 3], 2d ed. (Paris: Desclee, 1962), 463–64; Donald A. Hagner, "The Old Testament in the New Testament," *Interpreting the Word of God* [Festschrift in Honor of Steven Barnabas], ed. Samuel J. Schultz and Morris A. Inch (Chicago: Moody, 1976), 94–102.

[71] Goppelt, *Typos*, 124; Moo, *Old Testament*, 289–300. For the Davidic connection, see John R. Donahue, "Temple, Trial and Royal Christology (Mk. 14:53–65)" *The Passion in Mark: Studies in Mark 14–16*, ed. Werner H. Kelber (Philadelphia: Fortress, 1976), 75–77.

[72] On this point, see the arguments of Fairbairn, *Typology*, 1:21.

[73] Most of the relevant articles have now been gathered into a book, with some revisions and additions: Walter C. Kaiser, Jr., *The Uses of the Old Testament in the New Testament* (Chicago: Moody, 1985).

[74] Walter C. Kaiser, Jr., "Legitimate Hermeneutics," *Inerrancy*, ed. Geisler, 135.

[75] Here Kaiser leans heavily on Hirsch, *Validity in Interpretation*.

[76] Kaiser has been strongly influenced by Willis J. Beecher, *The Prophets and the Promise* (New York: Thomas Y. Crowell, 1905; reprint, Grand Rapids: Baker, 1963).

[77] See the criticism of Philip B. Payne, "The Fallacy of Equating Meaning with the Human Author's Intention," *JETS* 20 (1977): 243–52. The "intentional fallacy" describes the notion that one can appeal behind the text to the intention of the author. But Kaiser clearly insists that intention be tied to the evidence of the text. See, further, John W. Montgomery, "Biblical Inerrancy: What Is at Stake?" *God's Inerrant Word* (Minneapolis: Bethany, 1973), 31.

[78] *Uses of the Old Testament*, 47–53.

[79] Raymond E. Brown, *The 'Sensus Plenior' of Sacred Scripture* (Baltimore: St. Mary's University, 1955), 92. See also Brown's later article "The 'Sensus Plenior' in the Last Ten Years," *CBQ* 25 (1963): 262–85; Grelot, *Sens Chrétien*, 458–97; Pierre Benoit, "La plénitude de Sens de Livres Saints," *RB* 67 (1960): 161–96; Edward F. Sutcliffe, "The Plenary Sense as a Principle of Interpretation," *Bib* 34 (1953): 333–43; and the survey in Henning Graf Reventlow, *Hauptprobleme der Biblischen Theologie im 20. Jahrhundert* (Erträge der Forschung 203; Darmstadt: Wissenschaftliche Buchgesellschaft, 1983), 39–49. The phrase *sensus plenior* was apparently first used in this sense by Andrea Fernández in 1927 (Brown, *Sensus Plenior*, 88).

[80] Brown, *Sensus Plenior*, 113. Grelot (*Sens Chrétien*, 453–55) argues that the author of a given text would not have been aware of the *sensus plenior* in a "notional" way but may have been conscious of a fuller meaning in some other sense.

[81] Brown, "Sensus Plenior," 277; Benoit, "La Plénitude," 189.

[82] Brown, *Sensus Plenior*, 92. As we have seen, a distinction of this sort can be traced back at least as far as Aquinas.

[83] *Sensus Plenior*, 70.

[84] Although Benoit ("La Plénitude," 184–86) wants to confine the *sensus plenior* to relationships between the Testaments.

[85] John W. Wenham succinctly states a kind of *sensus plenior* approach: "The Holy Spirit knew beforehand the course of history with its consummation in Christ, and so in guiding the writers he intended a deeper meaning than they understood" (*Christ and the Bible*, 2d ed. [Grand Rapids: Baker, 1984], 103). Cf. also Hagner, "Old Testament in the New Testament," 91–92.

[86] John L. McKenzie, "Problems of Hermeneutics in Roman Catholic Exegesis," *JBL* 77 (1958): 202.

[87] Cf. Hagner, "Old Testament in the New," 103 (though he overstates the case).

[88] The text often cited with respect to this question is 1 Peter 1:10–12: "The prophets who prophesied of the grace that was to be yours searched and inquired . . . what person or time [*tina ē poion kairon*] was indicated by the Spirit of Christ within them when predicting the sufferings of Christ and the subsequent glory. It was revealed to them that they were serving not themselves but you, in the things which have now been announced to you by those who preached the good news to you through the Holy Spirit sent from heaven, things into which angels long to look" (RSV). Kaiser has argued that both indefinite pronouns in verse 10 refer to *kairon*, so that Peter is not saying that the prophets were uncertain about the person (see, e.g., "The Current Crisis in Exegesis," 8n). But the grammar is not clear and, in any case, the text does not say that the prophets knew all that the New Testament claims to find in their prophecies.

[89] Vawter, *Inspiration*, 115–16; Kaiser, "Current Crisis," 8–9; Rudolf Bierberg, "Does Sacred Scripture Have a 'Sensus Plenior'?" *CBQ* 10 (1948): 195; John J. O'Rourke, "Marginal Notes on the 'Sensus Plenior,' " *CBQ* 21 (1959): 65–66.

[90] Brown, *Sensus Plenior*, 133.

[91] Walter C. Kaiser, Jr., "Author's Intention: Response," *Hermeneutics, Inerrancy, and the Bible*, ed. Radmacher and Preus, 444.

[92] Brown, "Sensus Plenior," 277.

[93] Packer, "Infallible Scripture and the Role of Hermeneutics," 350.

[94] See, however, Kaiser's attempt to demonstrate the messianic focus of the psalm ("The Promise to David in Psalm 16 and Its Application in Acts 2:25–33 and 13:32–37," *JETS* 23 (1980): 219–30). While Kaiser succeeds in showing that the psalm does have a legitimate messianic application, he has not shown that the specific application made by Peter (Jesus' resurrection) can be established exegetically in the psalm (see the criticisms of Elliot Johnson, "Author's Intention and Biblical Interpretation," *Hermeneutics, Inerrancy, and the Bible*, ed. Radmacher and Preus, 417–25).

[95] Norbert Lohfink, "The Inerrancy of Scripture," *The Christian Meaning of the Old Testament* (Milwaukee: Bruce, 1968), 42–43.

[96] William Sanford LaSor, "Prophecy, Inspiration, and *Sensus Plenior*," *TB* 29 (1978): 54–56; idem, "The 'Sensus Plenior' and Biblical Interpretation," *Scripture, Tradition and Interpretation*, ed. W. Ward Gasque and William Sanford LaSor (Grand Rapids: Eerdmans, 1978), 273–75; Waltke, "Canonical Approach to the Psalms," 5–13; Carson, "Matthew," 92–93; Packer, "Role of Hermeneutics," 350; cf. Bruce, *Biblical Exegesis*, 77.

[97]This phenomenon has been particularly emphasized in the salvation-historical approach of von Rad (see his *Old Testament Theology*, 2 vols. [Edinburgh: Oliver and Boyd, 1965] and also Walter Zimmerli, "Promise and Fulfillment," *Essays on Old Testament Interpretation*, 112).

[98]See, for example, Carson, "Matthew," 94–95.

[99]See the discussion of this question in Longenecker (*Biblical Exegesis*, 214–20), Silva ("New Testament Use of the Old," 162–64), and Johnson (*Old Testament in the New*, 78–83, 93–94).

[100]J. Lambrecht, "Paul's Christological Use of Scripture in 1 Cor. 15:20–28," *NTS* 28 (1982): 510.

[101]Charles Hodge, *An Exposition of the First Epistle to the Corinthians* (Robert Carter & Brothers, 1857; reprint, Grand Rapids: Baker, 1980), 332; Sutcliffe, "The Plenary Sense," 333–34.

[102]Joachim Jeremias, *TDNT*, 1:143; Oscar Cullmann, *The Christology of the New Testament* (London: SCM, 1959), 188; P. Giles, "The Son of Man in the Epistle to the Hebrews," *ExpT* 86 (1975): 330–31; George Wesley Buchanan, *The Epistle to the Hebrews* (New York: Doubleday, 1972), 38–51. Francis J. Moloney has argued that the targum on the psalm may preserve an early semimessianic interpretation that could have prepared for Paul's use ("The Reinterpretation of Psalm VIII and the Son of Man Debate," *NTS* 27 [1980–81]: 656–72).

[103]See particularly the discussion in Ridderbos, *Paul*, 85.

[104]"As ever, the coming of Christ revealed a whole landscape on the horizon to which the Old Testament was pointing" (Derek Kidner, *Psalms 1–72: An Introduction and Commentary on Books I and II of the Psalms* [Grand Rapids: Eerdmans, 1973], 68). Cf. also Dodd, *According to the Scriptures*, 117–18, 131; F. F. Bruce, *The Epistle to the Hebrews* (Grand Rapids: Eerdmans, 1964), 36; Philip Edgcumbe Hughes, *A Commentary on the Epistle to the Hebrews* (Grand Rapids: Eerdmans, 1977), 83–87; Robertson and Plummer, *First Corinthians*, 357.

[105]Yet J. Gerald Janzen has argued that the antecedent is "vision" and that Habakkuk is stressing the reliability of that vision ("Habakkuk 2:2–4 in the Light of Recent Philological Advances," *HTR* 73 [1980]: 53–78).

[106]Manuscript A of the LXX has *ho de dikaios mou ek pisteōs zēsetai*, but this word order may have been influenced by Hebrews 10:38. Other Greek versions use the third person qualifier (8 Hev XII gr, col. 12; Aquila) or the even more clear reflexive (Symmachus). On the textual situation, see Joseph A. Fitzmyer, "Habakkuk 2:3–4 and the New Testament," *To Advance the Gospel* (New York: Crossroad, 1981), 240–42; Lindars, *New Testament Apologetic*, 231.

[107]See the exchange between Torrance and Moule in *ExpT* 68 (1956–57): 111–14, 157, 221–22; D. W. B. Robinson, " 'Faith of Jesus Christ'—A New Testament Debate," *RTR* 29 (1970): 71–81. Arland Hultgren ("The ΠΙΣΤΙΣ ΧΡΙΣΤΟΥ Formulation in Paul," *NovT* 22 [1980]: 248–63) provides a valuable survey, arguing for a blending of objective and subjective genitives in the phrase. Richard B. Hays has recently argued that the phrase in Galatians 3:11 is purposely ambiguous, denoting both the faith of the Messiah and the faith of the righteous person (*The Faith of Jesus Christ: An Investigation of the Narrative Substructure of Galatians 3:1–4:11* [Chico, Calif.: Scholars, 1983], 150–56). Much depends on one's overall reading of Galatians 3, but I think Longenecker (who argues for "faithfulness of Christ" as the rendering in other occurrences of the formula) is right: the context demands that *pistis* means "human trust and reliance" (*Paul: Apostle of Liberty* [New York: Doubleday, 1964], 150).

[108]Lindars, *New Testament Apologetic*, 231.

[109]For arguments in favor of this reading, see especially J. B. Lightfoot, *Notes on Epistles of St. Paul*, ed. J. R. Harmer (London: Macmillan, 1895; reprint, Grand Rapids: Baker, 1980), 250–51; H. C. C. Cavallin, " 'The Righteous Shall Live by Faith.' A Decisive Argument for the Traditional Interpretation," *Studia Theologica* 32 (1978): 33–43.

[110]See, especially, A. Feuillet, "La citation d'Habacuc II.4 et les Huit premiers chapître de L'Epitre aux Romains," *NTS* 6 (1958–59): 52–80; C. E. B. Cranfield, *A Critical and Exegetical Commentary on the Epistle to the Romans*, 2 vols. (Edinburgh: T. & T. Clark, 1975, 1979), 1:101–2.

[111]Thus, Ernst Käsemann concludes that Paul's interpretation "neither does justice to the OT text nor finds any support in Jewish exegesis" (*Commentary on Romans* [Grand Rapids: Eerdmans, 1980], 32).

[112]See especially the still valuable treatment by Herman Cremer, *Die paulinische Rechtfertigungslehre im Zusammenhange ihrer geschichtlichen Voraussetzungen*, 2d ed. (Gütersloh: Bertelsmann, 1900), esp. 348–49.

[113]This usage is rooted especially in the Deuteronomic tradition.

[114]Cremer, *Rechtfertigungslehre*, 60–65.

[115]Habakkuk 2:4 is quoted in IQpHab 7:17 and is applied to "all the doers of the law in the house of Judah" who will be delivered out of the house of judgment because of their sufferings and their faith in the teacher of righteousness (8:1–3a). Clearly, "faith in the teacher of righteousness," linked as it is to the doing of the law, carries a far different meaning than Paul's "faith in Jesus Christ." The rabbis set forth Habakkuk 2:4 as a key summary of the demand of God, but it was related to keeping the law and monotheism (cf. b. Makk. 23b; Cranfield, *Romans*, 1:101).

[116]"Die alttestamentliche und jüdische Denkform wird durch das Evangelium gesprengt" (Otto Michel, *Der Brief an die Römer*, 5th ed. [MeyerK: Göttingen: Vandenhoeck & Ruprecht, 1978], 90). Cf. also Ridderbos, *Paul*, 172; Cremer, *Rechtfertigungslehre*, 348–49. A. Strobel ties Paul's use of this verse to a Jewish eschatological scheme based on Habakkuk 2:3 (*Untersuchungen zum eschatologischen Verzögerungsproblem auf Grund der spätjüdisch-urchristlichen Geschichte von Habakuk 2,2 ff* [Leiden: Brill, 1961], 173–202), while Ellis suggests that Habakkuk 2:4 may function as part of a midrashic structure with Genesis 15:6 as its basis ("Midrash Pesher," 174–77). Neither suggestion has enough evidence to make it convincing.

[117]"Sensus Plenior," 279.

[118]For some examples, see the passages treated in my book *Use of the Old Testament in the Gospel Passion Narratives*.

CHAPTER SIX

THE SPIRIT AND THE SCRIPTURES

John M. Frame

213–35

[1]On the general subject of the Spirit's witness to Scripture, I should mention some valuable works (not elsewhere directly cited in the notes) that I have found helpful. One is Bernard Ramm, *The Witness of the Spirit* (Grand Rapids: Eerdmans, 1957); then, two by Arthur Pink: *The Holy Spirit* (Grand Rapids: Baker, 1970) and *The Doctrine of Revelation* (Grand Rapids: Baker, 1975). Although he is probably to be classed as a popular rather than a scholarly writer, Pink's works are often remarkably thorough and insightful.

[2]Some of the most useful works today are these: Wayne A. Grudem, "Scripture's Self-Attestation and the Problem of Formulating a Doctrine of Scripture," in *Scripture and Truth*, ed. D. A. Carson and John W. Woodbridge (Grand Rapids: Zondervan, 1983), 19–59; Meredith G. Kline, *The Structure of Biblical Authority* (Grand Rapids: Eerdmans, 1975); John Murray, "The Attestation of Scripture," in *The Infallible Word*, ed. Ned Stonehouse and Paul Woolley (Grand Rapids: Eerdmans, 1946); Cornelius Van Til, *A Christian Theory of Knowledge* (Nutley, N.J.: Presbyterian and Reformed, 1969); Benjamin B. Warfield, *The Inspiration and Authority of the Bible* (Philadelphia: Presbyterian and Reformed, 1948); Edward J. Young, *Thy Word is Truth* (Grand Rapids: Eerdmans, 1957).

[3] " . . . the keystone of his doctrine of the knowledge of God," Benjamin B. Warfield, "Calvin's Doctrine of the Knowledge of God," in *Calvin and Calvinism* (New York: Oxford University Press, 1931), 113.

[4] John Calvin, *Institutes of the Christian Religion*, 2 vols. (Philadelphia: Westminster, 1960), 1:75.

[5] Idem.

[6] Ibid., 81.

[7] Ibid., 78.

[8] Ibid., 93.

[9] Ibid., 94–95.

[10] Ibid., 541–42.

[11] Ibid., 582–83.

[12] Ibid., 581–82.

[13] Karl Barth, *Church Dogmatics*, 4 vols. (Edinburgh: T. & T. Clark, 1936–56), 1:1, 207ff; 1:2, 523ff.

[14] Gerrit C. Berkouwer, *Holy Scripture* (Grand Rapids: Eerdmans, 1975), 39–66.

[15] Idem.

[16] Jack B. Rogers and Donald K. McKim, *The Authority and Interpretation of the Bible: A Historical Approach* (New York: Harper & Row, 1979).

[17] Such historical work, defending the orthodox tradition, has been done well, for example, by John D. Woodbridge in his *Biblical Authority: A Critique of the Rogers/McKim Proposal* (Grand Rapids: Zondervan, 1983) and in "The Princetonians and Biblical Authority," written with R. H. Balmer, in *Scripture and Truth*, ed. Carson and Woodbridge (Grand Rapids: Zondervan, 1983), 251–79. See also W. Robert Godfrey, "Biblical Authority in the Sixteenth and Seventeenth Centuries," *Scripture and Truth*, 225–43; John H. Gerstner, "The View of the Bible Held by the Church: Calvin and the Westminster Divines," in *Inerrancy*, ed. Norman L. Geisler (Grand Rapids: Zondervan, 1979), 385–412; idem., "Warfield's Case for Biblical Inerrancy," in *God's Inerrant Word*, ed. John W. Montgomery (Minneapolis: Bethany House, 1974), 115–42. Richard B. Gaffin argues in "Old Amsterdam and Inerrancy," *WTJ* 45:1 (Fall 1983): 219–72, that Kuyper and Bavinck—often appealed to by Rogers, McKim, and Berkouwer as representing a tradition opposed to "old Princeton"—were firm believers in inerrancy.

[18] Calvin, *Institutes*, 1:78–79.

[19] Helmut Thielicke, *The Evangelical Faith*, 3 vols. (Grand Rapids: Eerdmans, 1974), 1:105. Cf. 3:23.

[20] See, for example, Carl F. H. Henry, *God, Revelation and Authority*, 6 vols. (Waco: Word, 1976–79), 2:13ff.

[21] See, for example, R. C. Johnson, *Authority in Protestant Theology* (Philadelphia: Westminster, 1959), 54: "Just as scripture could become an instrument of redemption only by the action of the Spirit, so it could become theologically authoritative only under a personal relationship to the sovereign God through the personal presence of the Holy Spirit."

[22] See Karl Barth, *The Holy Ghost and the Christian Life* (London: Muller, 1938), 23.

[23] For example, John Baillie, *The Idea of Revelation in Recent Thought* (New York: Columbia University Press, 1956), 64ff., 83ff.

[24] This emphasis on obeying God's written words pervades Deuteronomy and many other parts of Scripture. See also the texts listed earlier in this article. A valuable study of the centrality of written revelation within God's covenant kingdom is Meredith G. Kline, *The Structure of Biblical Authority* (Grand Rapids: Eerdmans, 1975).

[25] Thielicke, *The Evangelical Faith*, 1:129ff.

[26] For Calvin, one main function of the doctrine is precisely to exalt the authority of Scripture, over against church tradition on the one hand and alleged modern prophets on the other. The idea that the internal testimony somehow removes the need for a fully authoritative Scripture is directly contrary to the intention of Calvin and the other Reformers. See Calvin, *Institutes*, 1:74ff.

[27] Three addenda to this distinction: (1) There is some confusion among Calvin scholars—and possibly in Calvin himself—as to his views on this matter. Geoffrey Bromiley writes that Calvin "perhaps does not sufficiently differentiate" the self-authentication of scripture from the spirit's testimony (*Historical Theology: An Introduction* [Grand Rapids: Eerdmans, 1978], 225). Seeberg indicates vagueness in Calvin: "Thus Calvin establishes the authority of the scriptures partly upon their divine dictation, and partly upon the testimony of the Holy Spirit working through them" (Reinhold Seeberg, *Textbook of the History of Doctrines*, 2 vols. [Grand Rapids: Baker, 1964], 2:395). The "partly . . . partly" formulation is understandable as an interpretation of Calvin, but it suggests at the same time Calvin's own vagueness as to the relation between the two factors. W. Niesel finds Calvin contradictory or "dialectical" here (see *The Theology of Calvin* [Philadelphia: Westminster, 1956], 30ff.). A good analysis of this issue, particularly as it relates to Calvin's statements, can be found in John Murray, *Calvin on Scripture and Divine Sovereignty* (Grand Rapids: Baker, 1960), republished in Murray, *Collected Writings*, 4 vols. (Edinburgh: Banner of Truth, 1982); in this latter collection, see 4:183–90. See also E. Dowey, *The Knowledge of God in Calvin's Theology* (New York: Columbia University Press, 1952), 106ff., esp. 111. (2) A good recent example of confusion created by a "partly . . . partly" scheme is the argument in David H. Kelsey's *The Uses of Scripture in Recent Theology* (Philadelphia: Fortress, 1975) that the *"discrimen"* for evaluating theological proposals is "the conjunction of certain uses of Scripture and the presence of God" (160). The result is vagueness and subjectivism. See my review article on this book in *WTJ* 39:2 (Spring, 1977): 328–53. (3) The distinction we have made, between objective and subjective authority, is, of course, the proper response to the neoorthodox idea that there is no revelation apart from our response. In the objective sense, they are wrong; in the subjective sense, they are right. Of course, their view actually is that there is no biblical authority in the objective sense. Yet some writers are remarkably inconsistent here. In Baillie, *The Idea of Revelation*, 134–48, the closing epilogue ("The Challenge of Revelation") exhorts the reader along this line: Don't criticize God for failing to reveal Himself; criticize yourself for failing to hear. But what sense can we make of this exhortation if there is no objective revelation that exists apart from our response?

[28] Berkouwer, *Holy Scripture*, 42–43.

[29] Ibid., 43, quoting Bavinck.

[30] Ibid., 43.

[31] Ibid., 51–52.

[32] Ibid., 44.

[33] This subtlety, however, makes it difficult to evaluate Berkouwer's criticisms of others. Has anyone ever taught that the Spirit *does* witness to the text "in abstraction from its message?" Has anyone, for example, argued that the Spirit witnesses to the isolated proposition that Scripture is God's Word, without at the same time witnessing to the message taught by that Word? Some theologians have, perhaps, failed to emphasize these connections as strongly as Berkouwer would like, but no one, to my knowledge, has ever denied them. When Berkouwer charges (p. 164) Edmund P. Clowney with "formalism" because Clowney wants us to hear what Christ says about the Bible (and not only *vice versa*), we wonder what is going on! Is Berkouwer really urging a much more radical view than he generally presents, namely a denial that we should have *any* concern with the authority of the text? No one can rightly accuse Edmund Clowney of neglecting the Christological focus of Scripture—not unless he means by "focus" something radically different from what the rest of us mean.

[34] Ibid., 53.

[35] Ibid., 52–53.

[36] Ibid., 252.

[37] The phrase comes from Murray, *Collected Writings*, 4:175, but the point has been made by a great many authors. I still think one of the best treatments is Edward J. Young, *Thy Word Is Truth* (Grand Rapids: Eerdmans, 1957).

[38] Berkouwer, *Holy Scripture*, 131ff., 227–28, *passim*.

[39] This is one of the *leitmotifs* of the book: ibid., 22, 135, 145, 184, 248–49, 272. It is disturbing that a man with Berkouwer's reputation as a responsible scholar would spend such a large part of a book impugning (gratuitously, I think, for the most part) the motives of others. Is it really the case that those who differ with Berkouwer on these issues hold their positions out of fear? Is it not equally plausible (and perhaps equally irresponsible!) to suggest that Berkouwer's own formulations arise out of his fear of being rejected by the academic establishment? And, of course, we must also raise the question of whether certain types of fear are justified.

[40] This, too: ibid., 11, 16, 25–26, 30, 135, 145, 150–51, 178, 183, 185, 189, 193, 207, 248–49, 365. Again, I think this talk is gratuitous. Maybe some conservative thinkers have sought to avoid difficult questions, but I hardly think that charge can be brought against such people as Warfield, Wilson, Van Til, and Machen. With at least equal plausibility, we could ask why Berkouwer is so vague in his formulations; is it perhaps to avoid the difficult process of speaking clearly to issues that are troubling the church? Is *he* avoiding something?

[41] Ibid., 253ff.

[42] Robert Dick Wilson, one of the great orthodox scholars of "Old Princeton," took as his motto the sentence "I have not shirked the difficult questions." Whatever else we may say about the Old Princeton theologians, we certainly have no right to accuse them of fearfulness.

[43] This can be an important point. Does a cultist who claims to believe in biblical inerrancy but denies the gospel of Christ qualify as a Bible-believer? Not in the eyes of God.

[44] This is clearly the position of Calvin: "Faith is certain that God is true in all things whether he command or forbid, whether he promise or threaten; and it also obediently receives his commandments, observes his prohibitions, heeds his threats. Nevertheless, faith properly begins with the promise, rests in it, and ends in it," *Institutes*, 1:575. In the second sentence, Calvin expresses Berkouwer's concern for the material content of the gospel; but in the first sentence he expresses a "formal" concern (though "formal" hardly seems the appropriate word to describe the profound attitude of obedience expressed here): to urge obedience to what God says, *whatever* he says. Cf. A. Lane, "John Calvin: the Witness of the Holy Spirit," in *Faith and Ferment* [Papers read at the 1982 Westminster Conference], ed. Robert S. Bilheimer (Minneapolis: Augsburg, 1983). George Hendry, *The Holy Spirit in Christian Theology* (Philadelphia: Westminster, 1956), criticizes Calvin since (Hendry thinks in contrast with Luther) he made Scripture itself not only an instrument but also an object of the Spirit's witness.

[45] As we have seen, Berkouwer frequently charges his conservative brethren with fearfulness; but there is more than one kind of fear. It is well to remind ourselves of the biblical admonitions to fear God rather than human beings. And, as we have also seen, there are plenty of admonitions in Scripture to "beware" of false teaching. (Whether the word "fear" is appropriate to describe this watchfulness is unimportant; the issue, however, is important.)

[46] Some of the Reformed confessions suggest that the witness of the Spirit is the basis for our confession of the canon. See the important distinctions made by Auguste Lecerf in an interesting (and somewhat subtle) analysis of this question, *An Introduction to Reformed Dogmatics* (Grand Rapids: Baker, 1949), 318–63. See also Berkouwer, *Holy Scripture*, 67ff., and Herman Ridderbos, *The Authority of the New Testament Scriptures* (Philadelphia: Presbyterian and Reformed, 1963).

⁴⁷On the question of the relation of "central message" to "peripheral matters" in Scripture, see also John M. Frame, "Rationality and Scripture," in *Rationality in the Calvinian Tradition*, ed. H. Hart, J. Van der Hoeven, and N. Wolterstorff (Lanham, Md.: University Press of America, 1983), 295ff.

⁴⁸I have discussed these matters at greater length in ibid., 293–317, and in my class syllabus, *Doctrine of the Knowledge of God.*

⁴⁹Here, of course, I am not thinking of the norm as "law" in distinction from "gospel." Here the word is both norm and good news at the same time.

⁵⁰Note here in the term *theopneustos* the implicit reference to the Spirit (*pneuma*).

⁵¹For the distinction (with biblical justification) between "illumination" and "persuasion" in the Spirit's witness, see John Murray, "The Attestation of Scripture," in *The Infallible Word*, ed. Stonehouse and Woolley, 1–52.

⁵²This is not to deny that sometimes our problems are intellectual, at least in part. However, I do not believe that our problems are ever the result of a lack of revelation (see Ro 1:18–21; Lk 16:27–31; 2Ti 3:16–17; 2Pe 1:3.

⁵³I have treated this subject, too, at greater length in "Rationality and Scripture," in *Rationality in the Calvinian Tradition*, ed. Hart, Van der Hoeven, and Wolterstorff, 304ff.

⁵⁴What else could it be? There is nothing else but morality that compels us to acknowledge valid inferences. We are not physically forced to draw them, and we are not always motivated to draw them by self-interest. Why, then, should we accept such inferences, if not because we simply *ought* to?

⁵⁵As argued, in effect, by Benjamin B. Warfield, *Inspiration and Authority*, and more recently in R. C. Sproul, J. Gerstner, A. Lindsley, *Classical Apologetics* (Grand Rapids: Zondervan, 1984), 162ff., 296ff. I won't go into this in detail, but I should say that their critique of my position is largely a misunderstanding, in my opinion. Actually, my view (and Van Til's) of the Spirit's testimony is very close to theirs, far closer than they realize. See my forthcoming review of this book in *WTJ* 47 (Fall 1985): 279–99. This position, however, has been sharply attacked by Rogers and McKim (*Authority and Interpretation*), Berkouwer (*Holy Scripture*), and others.

⁵⁶Calvin, *Institutes*, 1:78–80.

⁵⁷Jay M. Van Hook, "Knowledge, Belief and Reformed Epistemology," *Reformed Journal* 31:7 (July 1981): 12–17.

⁵⁸See my *Doctrine of the Knowledge of God.*

⁵⁹See, again, my "Rationality and Scripture," in *Rationality in the Calvinian Tradition*, ed. Hart, Van der Hoeven, and Wolterstorff, 305ff.

⁶⁰See, for example, T. Kuhn, *The Structure of Scientific Revolutions* (Chicago: University of Chicago Press, 1962). A considerable body of literature has developed over the past thirty years emphasizing that science is not a purely "objective" or "neutral" discipline, as many people still think it to be. This point has been made by N. R. Hanson and M. Polanyi, as well as by Christian thinkers like Dooyeweerd and Van Til.

⁶¹See Jonathan Edwards, *A Treatise on the Religious Affections* in *The Works of Jonathan Edwards*, ed. E. Hickman (Edinburgh: Banner of Truth, 1974), 281ff. Edwards' argument here is fascinating and perceptive in many ways. He says that in the internal testimony the Spirit reveals no new propositions to us and thus must reveal something of a different character than propositional truth. He settles on the "loveliness" of God and His Word; for unbelievers can know of God's existence, but they fail to acknowledge His loveliness, His desirability. Edwards' argument is useful in showing one of the important and neglected dimensions of the Spirit's work. At the same time, I would like to make some additional distinctions. In my view, unbelievers, even Satan, are capable of recognizing that God is lovely (objectively), while they prefer ugliness to loveliness (thus showing the irrationality of their unbelief). What the Spirit does is to give us a new heart, a heart that leads us to accept God's Word obediently. But that new heart of

obedience is also a crucial epistemological capacity. It cures us of the irrationality of unbelief and frees us to acknowledge with word and life the reality of what is.

[62]Valentine Hepp argued that the Holy Spirit also bears witness to general revelation—that is, that His witness is involved in all human knowledge, *Het Testimonium Spiritus Sancti* (Kampen, 1914).

[63]Of course, such a project would be under considerable disadvantage, for several reasons: (1) I believe that any valid proof of Christianity would be circular in a sense and, thus, not impressive to many people. See Cornelius Van Til, *The Defense of the Faith* (Philadelphia: Presbyterian and Reformed, 1955), and my "The Problem of Theological Paradox," in *Foundations of Christian Scholarship*, ed. G. North (Vallecito, Calif.: Ross House, 1976). (2) It is very difficult to capture in a formal proof the logical force of all the elements that *really* persuade people of the truth of Christianity, such as the love demonstrated by a Christian neighbor, the joy on the face of a church soloist, or a sudden awareness of one's sinfulness. (3) Finally, even if such a proof were sound and persuasive to normal (believing) minds, unbelievers would still resist it, and believers would not really need it.

CHAPTER SEVEN

SOME MISCONCEPTIONS OF THE IMPACT OF THE "ENLIGHTENMENT" ON THE DOCTRINE OF SCRIPTURE

John D. Woodbridge

237–70

[1]Portions of the present study come from the Griffith Thomas Memorial Lectures (November 6–9, 1984), which the author delivered at Dallas Theological Seminary. The lectures were published in fascicles of *Bibliotheca Sacra* during the year 1985. Used with permission.

[2]Cited in Walter M. Abbott, ed., *The Documents of Vatican II* (New York: Guild, 1966), 119, esp. n. 31.

[3]Cited in James T. Burtchaell, *Catholic Theories of Inspiration Since 1810: A Review and Critique* (Cambridge: Cambridge University Press, 1969), 1–2.

[4]See Oswald Loretz, *The Truth of the Bible* (New York: Herder and Herder, 1968).

[5]Hans Küng, on the other hand, frankly acknowledged that Saint Augustine believed in biblical inerrancy and that this belief "prevailed throughout the Middle Ages and right into the modern age." Küng attributed this stance to the alleged influence of a mantic theory of inspiration upon the thinking of Saint Augustine (Hans Küng, *Infallible? An Enquiry* [London: Collins, 1972], 173–74). See also John D. Woodbridge, *Biblical Authority: A Critique of the Rogers/McKim Proposal* (Grand Rapids: Zondervan, 1982), 37–46, 148–50.

[6]Consult, for example, Ernst Bizer's analysis of the thought of Lambert Daneau, in "Frühorthodoxie und Rationalismus," in *Theologische Studien*, Heft 71 (Zurich: EVZ-Verlag, 1963).

[7]Jill Raitt, "Introduction," in *Shapers of Religious Traditions in Germany, Switzerland, and Poland, 1560–1600*, ed. Jill Raitt (New Haven: Yale University Press, 1981), xix; Olivier Fatio, "Lambert Daneau," in *Shapers of Religious Traditions*, ed. Raitt, 111; Richard A. Muller, *Christ and the Decree: Christology and Predestination in Reformed Theology from Calvin to Perkins* (Durham, N.C.: Labyrinth, 1985).

[8]Geoffrey Bromiley, *Historical Theology: An Introduction* (Grand Rapids: Eerdmans, 1978), 328. See the comments of Professor David Lotz ("*Sola Scriptura*: Luther on Biblical Authority," *Interpretation* 35:3 [July 1981]: 273) of Union Theological Seminary (New York City) about the "neoorthodox" misunderstanding of Luther's views concerning biblical authority. He argues that Luther believed in biblical inerrancy but that he did not base his view of the Bible's authority upon its infallibility.

[9] See John D. Woodbridge, "A Neoorthodox Historiography under Siege," *BS*, 142 (January-March 1985): 3–15.

[10] Jack B. Rogers and Donald K. McKim, *The Authority and Interpretation of the Bible: An Historical Approach* (New York: Harper & Row, 1979).

[11] Professor Rogers wrote his doctoral dissertation on the views of Scripture upheld at the Westminster Assembly. See his *Scripture in the Westminster Confession* (Grand Rapids: Eerdmans, 1967). In October, 1984, Scott Thomas Murphy presented a Ph.D. dissertation entitled "The Doctrine of Scripture in the Westminster Assembly" to the Graduate School of Drew University. Contra Rogers' interpretation, Murphy argues that the Divines believed that "every jot and tittle is from God, so that Scripture is infallible, true, perfect, pure, certain, and harmonious in all subjects, whether historical or religious, and in all matters, whether fundamental or trivial" (from the abstract). He also proposes that they were defenders of a "mechanical dictation theory of inspiration." The latter observation needs further elaboration.

[12] See Gerald T. Sheppard, *Theology Today* 38 (October 1981): 330–37; Roger Nicole, *Christian Scholars Review*, 10:2 (1981): 161–65; David Wells, *WTJ* 43 (Fall 1980): 152–55; John H. Leith, *Int* 35 (January 1981): 75–78; Richard B. Gaffin, Jr., "Old Amsterdam and Inerrancy?" *WTJ* 44 (Fall 1982): 250–89; 45 (Fall 1983): 219–72; John D. Hannah, ed., *Inerrancy and the Church* (Chicago: Moody, 1984); Woodbridge, *Biblical Authority*.

[13] Bruce Vawter, "Creationism: Creative Misuse of the Bible," in *Is God a Creationist? The Religious Case Against Creation-Science*, ed. Roland M. Frye (New York: Scribner, 1983), 76.

[14] Ibid. Vawter's claim is simply not well-founded. Augustine, for example, did not describe condescension or accommodation in this fashion.

[15] Ibid.

[16] That Professor Vawter's essay is housed in a volume that generally defends macroevolution gives an indication that his interpretation does not lack for an apologetic impulse—to make the claims of macroevolutionary theory more acceptable to Christians.

[17] George M. Marsden, "Preachers of Paradox: The Religious New Right in Historical Perspective," *Religion and America: Spirituality in a Secular Age*, ed. Mary Douglas and Steven M. Tipton (Boston: Beacon, 1983), 163.

[18] George M. Marsden, *Fundamentalism and American Culture: The Shaping of Twentieth-Century Evangelicalism, 1870–1925* (New York: Oxford University Press, 1980), 214–15.

[19] In his treatment of the Princetonians (whose view of Scripture contributed to the beliefs of Fundamentalists), Marsden makes a series of claims about the impact of Common Sense philosophy on their formulations of verbal inspiration and inerrancy (ibid., 110–16). These claims deserve a critical assessment that we cannot give them here.

[20] Ibid., 57. Marsden provides no evidence for his claim that dispensationalists used the word *inerrancy* for the reason he indicates. His interpretation is a supposition given as fact. Nor does he tell us the names of the alleged innovators who chose the expression *inerrancy* because it had scientific connotations.

[21] In 1982, Marsden ("Everyone One's Own Interpreter? The Bible, Science, and Authority in Mid-Nineteenth-Century America," *The Bible in America: Essays in Cultural History*, ed. Nathan Hatch and Mark Noll, [New York: Oxford University Press, 1982], 99n.36) wrote: "The current debates over the precedents in church history for the doctrine of inerrancy can be clarified by observing that defenders of inerrancy are correct in showing that throughout church history the accuracy of the Bible in historical and scientific detail was often assumed or stated. Opponents of inerrancy, however, are correct in showing that such statements were seldom emphasized in unambiguous ways prior to the nineteenth century and that there are precedents for

seeing this issue as secondary or unimportant." Marsden made the remarkable claim, without citing evidence, that the doctrine of the "inerrancy of scripture" has had a more "prominent role in modern America than it has had at almost any other time or place in church history" (ibid., 91). It is, in fact, very difficult to know how Professor Marsden can ever justify this claim, given the commitment of Christians across many centuries to the Bible's complete infallibility. The only way he can apparently defend it is by asserting once again that biblical inerrancy represented in the nineteenth century something different from what it represented in earlier centuries. The strenuous debates about the infallibility of Scripture that ensued between Goeze and Lessing are a sample of scores of illustrations that deflate Marsden's thesis (Henry Chadwick, ed., *Lessing's Theological Writings* [Stanford: Stanford University Press, 1967], 36–37).

²²George M. Marsden, ed., *Evangelicalism and Modern America* (Grand Rapids: Eerdmans, 1984), ix. Marsden's definition is a sharp departure from the definition that Professor Martin Marty gave for Evangelicals and Fundamentalists as recently as 1975: " . . . both evangelicals and fundamentalists insist on the 'inerrancy of scripture' as being the most basic of all their fundamentals" ("Tensions Within Contemporary Evangelicalism: A Critical Appraisal," in *The Evangelicals*, ed. David Wells and John Woodbridge [Nashville: Abingdon, 1975], 180). Professor Marsden is apparently attempting to lead Evangelicals to abandon their commitment to biblical inerrancy as a defining characteristic of their own self-identity.

²³Augustine, *Letters* 28:3. See also *Letters* 40:1,4. The Roman Catholic John Eck and the Reformed theologian William Whitaker, among others, cited Augustine's argumentation when they encountered anyone who contested the infallibility of Holy Writ.

²⁴Bernard L. Ramm, *After Fundamentalism: The Future of Evangelical Theology* (San Francisco: Harper & Row, 1983), 6.

²⁵Ibid., 14, 17.

²⁶Ibid., 27, 43.

²⁷See Michel Baridon, "Lumières et Enlightenment Faux parallèle ou vraie dynamique du mouvement philosophique?" *Dix-huitième siècle* 10 (1978): 45–69.

²⁸See the studies of Lawrence Stone, Henri-Jean Martin, Raymond Birn, Paul Korshin, and others regarding literacy rates.

²⁹For a review of literature on the German Aufklärung, see Peter Pütz, *Die Deutsche Aufklärung* (Darmstadt: Wissenschaftliche Buchgesellschaft, 1979). Consult also: Klaus Scholder, "Grundzüge der theologischen Aufklärung in Deutschland," *Aufklärung Absolutismus und Bürgertum in Deutschland*, ed. Franklin Kopitzch (München: Nymphenburger Verlagshandlung, 1976), 294–318.

³⁰The troubles that Johann Christian Edelmann encountered as a religious dissenter in eighteenth-century Germany give ample evidence of the strength of "orthodoxy" and Pietism. See Walter Grossmann, *Johann Christian Edelmann: From Orthodoxy to Enlightenment* (The Hague: Mouton, 1976).

³¹The interpretation of this book remains a point of debate among scholars. Was Locke mincing words as he spoke about the truthfulness of the Christian religion, or was he sincerely attempting to draw up a list of beliefs upon which Christians could agree? The present author leans toward the second interpretation.

³²George Peabody Gooch, *Louis XV: The Monarchy in Decline* (London: Greenwood, 1956), 268.

³³C. J. Betts, *Early Deism in France* . . . (The Hague: Martinus Nijhoff, 1984), 270.

³⁴This edition, "Qu'est-ce que les lumières?" *Dix-huitième siècle* 10 (1978), was published by Editions Garnier Frères, Paris.

³⁵Hans Bots and Jan de Vet, "Les Provinces-Unies et les Lumières," *Dix-huitième siècle* 10 (1978): 119–20.

[36] For example, it is now clear that many members of the Republic of Letters received their impression of books, not from the volumes themselves, but from reviews in the some one thousand journals that existed at one time or another. A large number of people simply could not afford books in folio. Scholars are now giving journals like the Jesuit *Journal de Trévoux* their concerted attention.

[37] Aram Vartanian, "The *Annales* School and the Enlightenment," *Studies in Eighteenth-Century Culture*, ed. O. M. Brack, Jr. (Madison: University of Wisconsin Press, 1984), 13:237. Vartanian reviews Michel Vovelle's *Piété baroque et déchristianisation en Provence au XVIIIe siècle* (Paris: Plon, 1973), Daniel Roche's *Le siècle des lumières en province: Académies et académiciens provinciaux*, 2 vols. (Paris: Mouton, 1978), and Robert Darnton's *The Business of Enlightenment: A Publishing History of the Encyclopédie, 1775–1800* (Cambridge: Harvard University Press, 1979).

[38] Vartanian, "The *Annales* School, 234–39.

[39] Professor Van Kley teaches history at Calvin College.

[40] Consult Dale K. Van Kley, *The Damiens Affair and the Unraveling of the Ancien Régime: Church, State, and Society in France, 1750–1770* (Princeton: Princeton University Press, 1984); idem, *The Jansenists and the Expulsion of the Jesuits from France, 1757–1765* (New Haven: Yale University Press, 1975).

[41] Peter Gay, *The Enlightenment: An Interpretation—The Rise of Modern Paganism* (New York: Vintage, 1966), 33.

[42] The context of this 1784 statement should be explicated with more care than it usually receives.

[43] Vartanian, "The *Annales* School," 237.

[44] See Alan Charles Kors, *D'Holbach's Coterie: An Enlightenment in Paris* (Princeton: Princeton University Press, 1976).

[45] On various motifs in the thought of eighteenth-century Europeans, see Norman Hampson, *The Enlightenment* (New York: Penguin, 1979).

[46] Vartanian, "The *Annales* School," 246.

[47] Consult Vovelle, *Piété baroque et déchristianisation*; Margaret Jacob, *The Radical Enlightenment: Pantheists, Freemasons and Republicans* (London: George Allen & Unwin, 1981); Betts, *Early Deism in France*; John Redwood, *Reason, Ridicule and Religion: The Age of Enlightenment in England* (Cambridge: Harvard University Press, 1976); Marie-Hélène Cotoni, *L'Exégèse du Nouveau Testament dans la philosophie française du dix-huitième siècle* (Oxford: Voltaire Foundation, 1984).

[48] See John D. Woodbridge, "L'influence des philosophes français sur les pasteurs réformés du Languedoc pendant la deuxième moitié du dix-huitième siècle" (Université de Toulouse: Thèse pour le doctorat de troisième cycle, 1969), 291–371.

[49] Richard Popkin, *The History of Scepticism: From Erasmus to Descartes* (New York: Harper & Row, 1968), 68–69; R. M. Burns, *The Great Debate on Miracles: From Joseph Glanvill to David Hume* (Lewisburg: Bucknell University Press, 1981), 27–30; Woodbridge, *Biblical Authority*, 70–72.

[50] Earlier, Luther had linked the teachers of the church with fallibility and the Bible with infallibility: "We may trust unconditionally only in the Word of God and not in the teachings of the fathers; for the teachers of the church can err and have erred. Scripture never errs. Therefore it alone has unconditional authority" (cited in Paul Althaus, *The Theology of Martin Luther* [Philadelphia: Fortress, 1966], 6n.12).

[51] Woodbridge, *Biblical Authority*, 72–76.

[52] See Paul Auvray, "Jean Morin, 1591–1659," *RB* 66 (1959): 397–414; Jean Morin, *Exercitationes biblicae de hebraei graecique testus sinceritate* (1633).

[53] Popkin, *The History of Scepticism*, 69.

[54] Louis Bredvold, *The Intellectual Milieu of John Dryden* (1934; reprint, Ann Arbor: University of Michigan Press, 1966), 80.

[55] For a discussion of Roman Catholic apologists' use of the Masoretic pointing question for polemical purposes, see Richard Muller, "The debate over the vowel points and the crisis in orthodox hermeneutics," *The Journal of Medieval and Renaissance Studies*, 10 (1980): 55–58. Professor Muller's valuable essay deserves a careful assessment, which we cannot give it here.

[56] Jansenists, who were Roman Catholic Augustinians, believed that many Jesuits had succumbed to Molinism, allegedly a form of Pelagianism.

[57] On the several views of "tradition" defended by Roman Catholic theologians in the seventeenth century, see Georges Tavard, *La Tradition au XVIIe siècle en France et en Angleterre* (Paris: Cerf, 1969).

[58] Regarding the various stages of the Eucharistic controversy in France, see Remi Snoeks, *L'argument de tradition dans la controverse eucharistique entre catholiques et réformés français au XVII siècle* (Louvain: Editions J. Duculot, 1951).

[59] Earlier in the seventeenth century, Christians had struggled with the relationship between reason and revelation. See Sarah Hutton, "Reason and Revelation in the Cambridge Platonists, and their Reception of Spinoza," *Spinoza in der Frühzeit seiner religiösen Wirkung*, ed. Karlfried Gründer and Wilhelm Schmidt-Biggemann (Heidelberg: Verlag Lambert Schneider, 1984), 181–200; John Tulloch, *Rational Theology and Christian Philosophy*, 2 vols. (1874; reprint, Hildesheim: Georg Olms Verlagsbuchhandlung, 1966); see, too, the July 1980 edition of the *Revue des sciences philsophiques et théologiques*, which is dedicated to the theme "Révélation et rationalité au XVIIe siècle."

[60] Thomas Morgan, *The Moral Philosopher Being a Farther Vindication of Moral Truth and Reason* (London: Booksellers of London and Westminster, 1739), 2:3. The "to err is human" motif appears quite early in deistic literature as a justification for the denial of biblical infallibility.

[61] Professor McDonald's evaluation does not overlook the deficiencies of viewpoints proffered by Christians in the eighteenth century regarding theories of revelation. His *Ideas of Revelation: An Historical Study, A.D. 1700–1860* (London: Macmillan, 1959) remains one of the best studies in the field because its analysis is so balanced. See, too, the astute comments of R. M. Burns (*The Great Debate on Miracles*, 96–114) about the various forms of "evidentialism" in the early eighteenth century.

[62] See the somewhat questionable discussion of the background of these issues in Barbara J. Shapiro, *Probability and Certainty in Seventeenth-Century England: A Study of the Relationships between Natural Science, Religion, History, Law, and Literature* (Princeton: Princeton University Press, 1983).

[63] Desiderius Erasmus, *Collected Works of Erasmus*, trans. R. A. B. Mynors and D. F. S. Thomson, vol. 5, *The Correspondence of Erasmus* (Toronto: University of Toronto Press, 1976), 289–90, cited in Bruce Benson, "Erasmus and the Correspondence with Johann Eck" (unpublished paper; Trinity Evangelical Divinity School, 1983–84), 4.

[64] Ibid.

[65] Jacques Le Brun, "L'Institution dans la théologie de Henry Holden (1596–1662)," *Recherches de science religieuse* 71:2 (avril-juin 1983): 199.

[66] Ibid., 194.

[67] Bruce Vawter, *Biblical Inspiration* (Philadelphia: Westminster, 1972), 134.

[68] In his correspondence, Henri Justel, one of Simon's few confidants, portrayed the *Histoire critique du Vieux Testament* as a volume that denied the Mosaic authorship of all the Pentateuch.

[69] For Richard Simon's interaction with Spinoza's *Tractatus*, consult John D. Woodbridge, "Richard Simon's Reaction to Spinoza's 'Tractatus Theologico-Politicus,'" *Spinoza in der Frühzeit seiner religiösen Wirkung*, ed. Karlfried Gründer and Wilhelm Schmidt-Biggemann (Heidelberg: Verlag Lambert Schneider, 1984), 201–26.

[70] Françoise Charles-Daubert and Pierre-François Moreau, eds., *Pierre Bayle Ecrits sur Spinoza* (Paris: Berg International Editeurs, 1984), 22 [article, "Spinoza" from Bayle's

Dictionnaire historique et critique]. Concerning Pierre Bayle, consult the works of Paul Dibon, Elisabeth Labrousse, Walter Rex, Jacques Solé and Pierre Rétat.

[71] Paul Auvray, *Richard Simon (1632–1712)* (Paris: Presses Universitaires de France, 1974), 46-47.

[72] Le Brun, "Henry Holden (1596–1662)," 199.

[73] Jacques Le Brun, *Annuaire Résumés des conférences et travaux* [Hautes Etudes], 89 (1980–81), 559.

[74] Simon's theological "flexibility" was so extensive that he even penned an apology for Protestantism; it appears that money prompted him to do so. See Jacques Le Brun and John Woodbridge, eds., *Richard Simon Additions aux Recherches curieuses sur la diversité des langues et religions d'Edward Brerewood* (Paris: Presses Universitaires de France, 1983), 20–29.

[75] Robert Sullivan, *John Toland and the Deist Controversy: A Study in Adaptations* (Cambridge: Harvard University Press, 1982), 47, 57, 133. See Toland's discussion of the relationship between biblical infallibility and reason in his *Christianity Not Mysterious*, ed. Günder Gawlick (Stuttgart-Bad Cannstatt: Friedrich Fromman Verlag, 1964), 30–38.

[76] Matthew Tindal, *Christianity as Old as the Creation of the Gospel: a Republication of the Religion of Nature* (London: n.p., 1731), 5.

[77] Anthony Collins, *Discours sur la liberté de penser et de raisonner*, 2d ed. (London: n.p., 1727), 85. In his *Catholick Letters* (1687–), John Sergeant, the English Roman Catholic, had raised the issue of the difficulty of using unsure biblical texts to establish the faith (Robert Carroll, *The Common-Sense Philosophy of Religion of Bishop Edward Stillingfleet* [The Hague: Martinus Nijhoff, 1974], 41). On the other hand, even so conservative and controversial a Roman Catholic as François Garasse had a fully developed program of attempting to recover the "originals" by emending extant texts. Garasse set forth his program much earlier in the century. See his *La doctrine curieuse des beaux de ce temps . . .* (Paris: Sebastien Chappelet, 1623), 572–96, 625. See discussions concerning the debate in the second half of the seventeenth century over the issue of infallibility (Carroll, *Common Sense Philosophy*, 57–62).

[78] William Bentley, *La Friponniere laique des prétendus esprits-forts d'Angleterre* (Amsterdam: n.p., 1738), 219–20.

[79] Collins, *Discours sur la liberté*, 131–32. Matthew Tindel drew up a similar argument and referred to Bentley as well.

[80] Bentley, *La Friponniere laique*, 180–81. On the textual work of the classical scholar Bentley, see sections of E. J. Kenney, *The Classical Text* (Berkeley: University of California Press, 1974).

[81] Richard Baxter, *The Saints' Everlasting Rest* (1652), in the *Practical Works of Richard Baxter* (London: George Virtue, 1838), 3:92–93.

[82] See Jacques Le Brun, "Sens et portée du retour aux origines dans l'oeuvre de Richard Simon," *XVIIe siècle 33* (avril-juin 1981): 185–98.

[83] See Jacques Basnage's responses to various aspects of Roman Catholic polemics in his *Histoire du vieux et du nouveau testament* (Amsterdam: Pierre Mortier, 1721).

[84] In the first page of *Histoire critique du Vieux Testament* (1678), Richard Simon points out Augustine's stance as a justification for "textual criticism."

[85] Consult Hillel Schwartz, *The French Prophets: The History of a Millenarian Group in Eighteenth-Century England* (Berkeley: University of California Press, 1980), 1–36; Michel Heyd, "La réaction à l'enthousiasme et la sécularisation des sensibilités religieuses au début du dix-huitième siècle," *Sécularisation* (Brussels: Editions de l'Université de Bruxelles, 1984), 5–38.

[86] John Redwood, *Reason, Ridicule and Religion: The Age of Enlightenment in England, 1660–1750* (Cambridge: Harvard University Press, 1976), 116.

[87] Hillel, *The French Prophets*, 38.

⁸⁸Don Allen, *The Legend of Noah: Renaissance Rationalism in Art, Science, and Letters* (Urbana: University of Illinois Press, 1949), 71–74.

⁸⁹W. P. Stephens, *The Holy Spirit in the Theology of Martin Bucer* (Cambridge: Cambridge University Press, 1970), 129–38. See also the preface (1555) to Hartman Beyer's *Biblische Historien* (Franckfort a. M.: n.p., 1595), in which the author accepts the accounts of creation and the narrative thereafter as accurate "history." It is interesting to compare this work with Theodore Barin's *Le monde naissant ou la création du monde. Demonstrée par les principes très simples & très conformes à l'histoire de Moyse . . .* (Utrecht: Compagnie des Libraires, 1686). On what "history" represented in the sixteenth century, see C. B. Dubois, *La conception de l'histoire en France au XVIe siècle (1560–1610)* (Paris: Nizet, 1977).

⁹⁰The best study of the career of Jean Le Clerc remains Annie Barnes, *Jean Le Clerc (1657–1736) et la république des lettres* (Paris: Droz, 1938).

⁹¹Robert Preus, *The Theology of Post Reformation Lutheranism: A Study of Theological Prolegomena* (St. Louis: Concordia, 1970), 190; idem, *The Inspiration of Scripture: A Study of the Theology of the Seventeenth Century Lutheran Dogmaticians* (Edinburgh: Oliver and Boyd, 1957), 80–84.

⁹²See Glenn Sunshine, "Accommodation in Calvin and Socinus: A Study in Contrasts (M.A. thesis, Trinity Evangelical Divinity School, 1985). Professor Richard Muller (*Dictionary of Latin and Greek Theological Terms: Drawn Principally from Protestant Scholastic Theology* [Grand Rapids: Baker, 1985], article on "accommodatio") notes distinctions between an orthodox conception of accommodation and a Socinian definition.

⁹³On this conflict, see Woodbridge, *Biblical Authority*, 96–98. Deep into the eighteenth century, commentators (including writers for Diderot's *Encyclopédie*) continued to reflect upon the controversy between Simon and Le Clerc.

⁹⁴Le Brun and Woodbridge, eds., *Richard Simon*, 36.

⁹⁵For a singular eulogy of Reason's rights to stand in judgment of revelation, see Andreas Wissowatius, *Religio Rationalis Editio trilinguis,* ed. Zbigniew Ogonowski (Wolfenbüttel: Herzog August Bibliothek, 1982). Spinoza also criticized those political figures who defended biblical infallibility as a means to keep themselves in power. They demanded submission because the Bible calls us to submit to authorities over us. On occasion, debates over biblical infallibility were linked to political struggles in the seventeenth century. For background on the theological and philosophical debates at the end of the seventeenth century, see the excellent study by Erich Haase, *Einführung in die Literatur des Refuge Der Beitrag der französischen Protestanten zur Entwicklung analytischer Denkformen am Ende des 17 Jahrhunderts* (Berlin: Duncker & Humblot, 1959). This volume is the one with which to begin any serious analysis of these questions.

⁹⁶For background on physico-theological tractates in Germany, consult Walter Schatzberg, *Scientific Themes in the Popular Literature and the Poetry of the German Enlightenment, 1720–1760* (Berne: Herbert Lang, 1973).

⁹⁷For Lambert Daneau's thought, see Olivier Fatio, *Méthode et theologie: Lambert Daneau et les débuts de la scolastique réformée* (Genève: Droz, 1976).

⁹⁸Lambert Daneau, *The Wonderfull Workmanship of the World . . .* (London: n.p., 1578), 6v.

⁹⁹Consult Bizer's analysis of Daneau's thought in "Frühorthodoxie und Rationalismus," in *Theologische Studien,* 71 (Zurich: EVZ-Verlag, 1963). Bizer's very influential "neoorthodox" interpretation of Daneau's theological beliefs and methods is now being seriously challenged by Jill Raitt, Olivier Fatio, and others (Raitt, ed., *Shapers of Religious Traditions,* xix).

¹⁰⁰Daneau, *The Wonderful Workmanship of the World,* 13v. In response to those critics who indicated that Moses wrote "not truely and exactly expressed according to the truth of thinges," Daneau (p. 9) declared: "But, as it is to bee graunted that hee

spake simply, so can it not bee proved that hee spake or wrote lyingly, falsely, and ignorantly of those thinges. It is one thing therfore, to acknowledg that Moses stile is bare and simple, which kinde of utterance is meet for the truth: and another thing to say that hee is a false man and a lyar: which no man can affirme, but whoso is of a corrupt conscience. Wherfore simply, but truely: barely, but rightly: commonly, but purely doth hee deliver unto us those things which hee writeth, concerning the world."

[101] Hermann Heinrich Frey, *Therobiblia Biblisch Thier-Vogel-und Fischbuch* (Leipzig, 1595), ed. Heimo Reinitzer (Graz, Austria: Akademische Druck -u. Verlagsanstalt, 1978). Frey realized that his particular proposal had novel features. See also n. 89.

[102] Cited in Edward Rosen, "Kepler and the Lutheran Attitude Towards Copernicanism in the Context of the Struggle Between Science and Religion," *Kepler, Four Hundred Years: Proceedings of Conferences held in honour of Johannes Kepler,* ed. Arthur Beer and Peter Beer (Oxford: Pergamon, 1975), 329.

[103] Jean Bodin, *Les six livres de la république* (Lyon: Gabriel Cartier, 1593), 561.

[104] Rosen, "Kepler and the Lutheran Attitude," 332–33.

[105] Ibid., 332.

[106] Ibid., 328.

[107] Richard Popkin ("Scepticism, Theology, and the Scientific Revolution in the Seventeenth Century," *Problems in the Philosophy of Science,* ed. I. Lakatos and Alan Musgrave [Amsterdam: North Holland, 1968], 3:18) writes: "The whole enterprise of reconciling Scripture and the new science was blown apart by a mad genius, Isaac La Peyrère (Pereira), who, I believe, really set off the warfare between theology and science." On the career of La Peyrère, see David R. McKee, "Isaac de la Peyrère, a Precursor of Eighteenth Century Deists," *PMLA* 59 (1944): 456–85.

[108] Konrad Kratzsch, ed., *Illuminierte Holzschnitte der Luther-Bibel von 1534* (Hanau: Verlag Werner Dausien, 1982).

[109] This drawing is found on the dust jacket for the volume cited in n. 108.

[110] Michel Heyd, *Between Orthodoxy and the Enlightenment: Jean-Robert Chouet and the Introduction of Cartesian Science in the Academy of Geneva* (The Hague: Martinus Nijhoff, 1982), 84n.107. Heyd cites the reference for this quotation as *Calvini Opera,* 49:677.

[111] Frye, ed., *Is God a Creationist?,* 16–17, 200–204.

[112] Ibid., 202.

[113] Henri Blocher, *In the Beginning: The Opening Chapters of Genesis,* trans. David G. Preston (Downers Grove: InterVarsity, 1984), 223. Professor Blocher does not dismiss evolutionary theories on biblical grounds per se.

[114] Warfield's misleading perception of Calvin's viewpoint is receiving considerable play in scholarly literature. Consult Mark A. Noll, ed., *The Princeton Theology, 1812–1921]* (Grand Rapids: Baker, 1983), 293–94.

[115] Edward Rosen, "Copernicus and Renaissance Astronomy," *Renaissance Men and Ideas,* ed. Robert Schwoebel (New York: St. Martin's, 1971), 100.

[116] Hugh Kearney, *Science and Change, 1500–1700* (New York: McGraw-Hill, 1974), 104.

[117] It is true that there were apparently "allegorists" and others in the sixteenth century who did not view the Bible as speaking about the natural world in an authoritative fashion. Lambert Daneau makes reference to them. However, the Reformers were not known for their commitment to allegorizations. Who the other parties were, we do not know.

[118] The dispute between John Wilkins (1614–72) and Alexander Ross (1590–1654) over the interpretation of biblical passages that speak of the natural world may have turned on this point among others (Woodbridge, *Biblical Authority,* 108–10). The earlier Galileo-Bellarmine controversy also had elements of the same issue surrounding it.

[119]The influence of La Peyrère was quite notable on the continent, especially upon Spinoza and Simon; Hobbes's fame and infamy were much discussed in the coffeehouses of England.

[120]Consult Popkin, "Scepticism, Theology," 21–28. One senses an emerging lack of concern for this alignment in the correspondence of Henry Oldenburg, the influential secretary of the Royal Society in England. See the massive edition of his correspondence published by the University of Wisconsin Press (1965–73) and edited by A. Rupert Hall and Marie Boas Hall. On the other hand, several of the Boyle Lectures of the 1690s in particular reflect just such a concern. Consult James Force, "Hume and the Relation of Science to Religion among Certain Members of the Royal Society," *Journal of the History of Ideas* 45:4 (October–December 1984): 517–26.

[121]Jean-Robert Chouet (who taught at the Academy of Geneva), for one, began to think along these lines (Heyd, *Between Orthodoxy and the Enlightenment*, 82–86). Heyd argues that the doctrine of accommodation that Chouet used went back to Calvin and had been "transformed and radicalized by seventeenth-century scientists" (p. 86). But it is possible that Chouet may have simply espoused a Socinian doctrine of accommodation. Further research is needed on this point.

[122]John Weemses, *Exercitations Divine: Containing diverse Questions and Solutions for the right understanding of the Scriptures* (London: John Bellamie, 1634), 11. See also pp. 2, 5.

[123]H. J. DeJonge, "The Study of the New Testament," *Leiden University in the Seventeenth Century: An Exchange of Learning*, ed. Th. H. Lunsingh Scheurleer and G. H. M. Posthumus Meyjes (Leiden: Brill, 1975), 65. De Jonge's account continues: "There could be no clearer expression of what was expected before all else from the theological faculty: the unfolding of the Holy Scripture." But it is even clearer that, at least in theory, Scripture represented the dominant authority for the founders of the university.

[124]Our point is not that these Lutheran divines should have rejected the heliocentric theory but that their commitment to the premise that the Bible speaks authoritatively about the natural world is evidenced in their strong reactions.

[125]This is the judgment of Dr. Wolgang Milde (the Head Archivist for the manuscript collection of the Herzog August Bibliothek, Wolfenbüttel, West Germany). Dr. Milde has written on this subject. He discussed it at length with the present author. For a later period, see Wilhelm Schmidt-Biggemann, *Topica Universalis Eine Modellgeschichte humanistischer und barocker Wissenschaft* (Hamburg: Felix Meiner Verlag, 1983).

[126]William Mallard, "John Wyclif and the Tradition of Biblical Authority," *Church History* 30 (March 1961): 52. J. A. Robson (*Wyclif and the Oxford Schools* [Cambridge: Cambridge University Press, 1966], 96) describes Wyclif's beliefs about the Bible's truthfulness in this fashion: "Every word of Scripture was, and always had been, eternally true, in that it was an extension of the divine ideas."

[127]N. Max Wildiers, *The Theologian and His Universe: Theology and Cosmology from the Middle Ages to the Present* (New York: Seabury, 1982), 27.

[128]Ibid., 16.

[129]Ibid., 37.

[130]In seeking to explain Fundamentalist controversies regarding evolution, Professor George Marsden gives this ill-advised representation of Newton's views: "In the Newtonian worldview it had been possible, as indeed it was for Newton himself, to regard the Bible as a repository of facts on a par with the book of nature" (Marsden, *Fundamentalism and American Culture*, 214). Marsden's unfortunate analysis of this matter does not strengthen his interpretation of Fundamentalists' interaction with Darwinism.

[131]Richard Stoddard Brooks, "The Relationships between Natural Philosophy, Natural Theology and Revealed Religion in the Thought of Newton and their Historiographic Relevance" (Ph.D. diss., Northwestern University, 1976; Ann Arbor: Xerox University Microfilms, 1981), 117.

[132] Ibid.

[133] Ibid., 117–18.

[134] Rogers and McKim, *Authority and Interpretation*, 235.

[135] In the *Harmony of the Gospels* (I, 7, 10), Augustine noted that the foes of the Christian faith tried to discredit the faith by alleging that "the evangelists are not in harmony with each other." For his part, he wanted to prove that the Evangelists' writings could be harmonized; he even concerned himself with "one word" discrepancies (see his treatment of Mt 27:9).

[136] For a searching criticism of Thomas Kuhn's "paradigmatic" approach to the history of science (which seems to underlie portions of the interpretative analysis of Professor Marsden), see Frederick Suppe, *The Structure of Scientific Theories* (Urbana: University of Illinois Press, 1977), 633–49. Marsden plays down his debt to Kuhn, but it appears to remain. Many European historians (such as Wilhelm Schmidt-Biggemann and Hans Blumenberg) have long since abandoned Kuhn's proposals regarding the history of science. See Hans Blumenberg, *Die Genesis der kopernikanischen Welt* (Frankfurt am Main: Suhrkamp Verlag, 1975).

[137] The faulty syllogism inherent in Professor Vawter's definition of accommodation is expounded in his influential work, *Biblical Inspiration* (p. 169): "To conceive of an absolute inerrancy as the effect of inspiration was not really to believe that God had condescended to the human sphere but rather that He had transmuted it into something else. A human literature containing no error would indeed be a contradiction in terms, since nothing is more human than to err. Put in more vital terms, if the Scripture is a record of revelation, the acts of a history of salvation in which God has disclosed Himself by entering into the ways of man, it must be a record of trial and error as well as achievement, for it is in this way that man learns and comes to the truth."

[138] Professor Vawter even claims that for "fundamentalist minds," inerrancy signifies that the Bible is "the one and only source of every human affirmation in every conceivable field" (Vawter, "Creationism," 76). This is a breathtaking caricature.

[139] J. I. Packer argues that Calvin upheld a doctrine of accommodation. See Packer's "John Calvin and the Inerrancy of Scripture," *Inerrancy and the Church*, ed. John D. Hannah (Chicago: Moody, 1984), 166–68.

[140] Ramm, *After Fundamentalism*, 6.

[141] See Karl Aner, *Die Theologie der Lessingzeit* (Halle-Saale: Verlag von Max Niemeyer, 1929).

[142] Consult Hans Frei, *The Eclipse of Biblical Narrative: A Study in Eighteenth and Nineteenth Century Hermeneutics* (New Haven: Yale University Press, 1974); Peter H. Reill, *The German Enlightenment and the Rise of Historicism* (Berkeley: University of California Press, 1975).

[143] "An Account of the Life and Writings of John David Michaelis from Eichorn's *Allgemeine Bibliothek*," *Biblical Repertory* (1826), 2:261.

[144] Peter Stuhlmacher, *Vom Verstehen des Neuen Testaments Eine Hermeneutik* (Göttingen: Vandenhoeck & Ruprecht, 1979), 125.

[145] On the other hand, some scholars like the Pietist J. A. Bengel were very knowledgeable regarding "lower criticism." Moreover, several "orthodox" Lutheran scholars practiced "Critica Sacra" (essentially a form of lower criticism). In Switzerland, actual armed conflict broke out on occasion concerning the Masoretic point issue. See Barthélemy Barnaud, *Mémoires pour servir à l'histoire de troubles arrivés en Suisse à l'occasion du Consensus* (Amsterdam: J. Frédéric Barnard, 1727).

[146] Packer, "John Calvin and Inerrancy," 156–62.

[147] See Stephens, *The Holy Spirit*, 130–33. Bucer (130) described the Scriptures by saying that "without any sprinkling of error or any illusion they discourse on the divine works."

[148]Consult Gottfried Hornig, *Die Anfänge der historisch-kritischen Theologie Johann Salomo Semlers Schriftverständnis und seine Stellung zu Luther* (Göttingen: Vandenhoeck & Ruprecht, 1961).

[149]Semler had several of Simon's works on biblical criticism translated into German. He appended copious notes to them.

[150]In his comments regarding 1 John 5:7, Semler commends the critical work of Simon very highly. See the comments of Michaelis in his *Einleitung in die gottlichen Schriften des Neuen Bundes* (Göttingen: Verlag der Witwe Vandenhoek, 1765), Erster Theil, 678. J. Herder also made the claim about Simon as the "Father of Criticism of the Old and New Testament." The present author is preparing an essay on the reception of Richard Simon's works in Germany in the eighteenth century.

[151]Hornig, *Die Anfänge der historisch-kritischen*, 211–36. Hornig does not call Semler's version of accommodation "Socinian," but he recognizes that Semler was aware of the doctrine of accommodation as proposed by orthodox Lutheran theologians as well as by Jean Le Clerc, Thomas Burnet, and William Whiston. Semler's mentor (S. J. Baumgarten) had written a small history of accommodation (ibid., 215). On the career of Baumgarten, see Martin Schloemann, *Siegmund Jacob Baumgarten System und Geschichte in der Theologie des Überganges zum Neuprotestantismus* (Göttingen: Vandenhoeck & Ruprecht, 1974).

[152]Hornig, *Die Anfänge der historisch-kritischen*, 234–36.

[153]Ibid., 211n.1.

[154]Charles Hodge, ed., *Biblical Repertory* (Princeton: Princeton, 1825), 1:125.

[155]Ibid., 127. Hodge referred his readers to the article "Outlines of Hermeneutics" by Beck, found in the same edition of the *Biblical Repertory*. Beck wrote: "On the doctrine of accommodation, there is great diversity of opinion; whether it be considered in reference to the exposition and illustration of certain doctrines, to the mode of argument or narration, or to the manner in which the O.T. is quoted and employed in the New. Some of the Greek Fathers appear to have favoured the idea that the Sacred Writers did accommodate themselves even in matters of doctrine to popular opinions and modes of expression" (ibid., 19–20). Beck observed that " . . . Socinians and Grotius are the advocates of such accommodation, most of those of our communion are opposed to the doctrine (ibid., 20)." Besides Semler's doctrine of accommodation, Hodge also criticized the work of Paulus van Hemert (*Ueber Accommodationen im Neuen Testament* [Dortmund and Leipzig: Henrich Blothe and Compagnie, 1797]).

[156]See Norbert Schmidt, "The Concept of Scripture in the Theology of G. Ebeling: An Introduction to Important Aspects of Neoorthodox Thought and Its Relations to Reformation Theology," (unpublished paper, Trinity Evangelical Divinity School, February 29, 1984).

[157]See Wayne Grudem, "Scripture's Self-Attestation and the Problem of Formulating a Doctrine of Scripture," in *Scripture and Truth*, ed. D. A. Carson and John D. Woodbridge (Grand Rapids: Zondervan, 1983), 19–59.

[158]Reill, *The German Enlightenment*, 83.

[159]See John Goeze's complaints about the attacks upon the Christian religion in his day (*Theologische Untersuchung der Sittlichkeit der heutigen deutschen Schaübuhme* . . . [Hamburg: Johan Christian Brandt, 1770], 2). On Gotthold Lessing's views of Christianity, see Georges Pons, *Gotthold Ephraim Lessing et le christianisme* (Paris: Marcel Didier, 1964); Leonard Wesel, Jr., "The Problem of Lessing's Theology: A Prolegomenon to a New Approach," *Lessing Yearbook* 5:4 (Munchen: Max Hueber, 1972), 94–121.

[160]Those who argue that the commitment of Evangelicals to verbal inspiration and inerrancy leads them ineluctably to espouse a mechanical dictation theory of inspiration misunderstand what Evangelicals are saying. Professor John McNeill's discussion of John Calvin's views of inspiration is an illustration of this point (Woodbridge, *Biblical Authority*, 58–59).

161 Along with Professors Henning G. Reventlow and Walter Sparn, the present author recently chaired a symposium on biblical criticism in Germany during the eighteenth century (December 1985). A volume should emerge from the conference. See Henning G. Reventlow, *The Authority of the Bible and the Rise of the Modern World*, trans. John Bowden (Philadelphia: Fortress, 1984). Regarding Voltaire's criticism of the Bible, see David Levy, *Voltaire et son exégèse du Pentateuque: critique et polémique*, in *Studies on Voltaire and the Eighteenth Century* (Oxfordshire: Voltaire Foundation, 1975). See, too, Marie-Hélène Cotoni, *L'Exégèse du Nouveau Testament dans la philosophie françoise du dix huitième siècle* (Oxford: Voltaire Foundation, 1984).

162 Jack Rogers, "Biblical Authority and Confessional Change," *Journal of Presbyterian History* 59:2 (Summer 1982): 133.

163 In the 1670s both Baruch Spinoza and Richard Simon became very suspect for their criticism of traditional views regarding the Mosaic authorship of the Pentateuch. But by the 1680s the attacks began to fall on New Testament "difficulties" as well.

164 See Le Clerc's *Sentimens de quelques théolgiens de Hollande* . . . (1685). In his *Tractatus theologico-politicus* (1670) Spinoza also acknowledged that a belief in biblical infallibility dominated the theological thinking of his day.

165 See note 21.

166 Alvin Plantinga's essay, "Reason and Belief in God," in *Faith and Rationality*, ed. Alvin Plantinga and Nicholas Wolterstorff (Notre Dame: University of Notre Dame Press, 1983), 16–93, is a significant attempt to justify the merits of the "Reformed Epistemology" in the face of the alleged collapse of "classical foundationalism." Plantinga's debt to Barth is made clear in this piece. Despite his earnest attempts to fend off charges of fideism, Plantinga's proposal undoubtedly should be characterized in that fashion. Moreover, his understanding of the history of the various forms of "fideism" and Reformed thought in general will make specialists quite uncomfortable. See D. A. Carson's discussion of the "Reformed Epistemology" in his chapter above ("Recent Developments in the Doctrine of Scripture"). For a helpful essay on the relationship between faith and evidence, see Paul Helm's "Faith, Evidence, and the Scriptures," in *Scripture and Truth*, ed. Carson and Woodbridge, 303–20.

167 Tom Bethell, "Agnostic Evolutionists: The taxonomic case against Darwin," *Harper's Magazine*, February 1985, 61.

168 "Science Contra Darwin," *Newsweek*, April 8, 1985, 80–81. At last, the sizeable difficulties that challenge the validity of various versions of Darwinism are being communicated to a wider popular audience. These difficulties are recognized by a growing number of scientists who cannot be suspected of sympathy for an Evangelical faith. It is unfortunate that Marsden does not give any space in his analysis of current opinion to those Evangelicals (and non-Christians, for that matter) who do not uphold macroevolution. His identification of anti-evolutionary convictions with Fundamentalism does not capture the diversity of belief throughout the United States. See George Marsden, "Understanding Fundamentalist Views of Science," *Science and Creationism*, ed. Ashley Montagu (Oxford: Oxford University Press, 1984), 111–12.

CHAPTER EIGHT

THE AUTHORITY OF SCRIPTURE IN KARL BARTH

Geoffrey W. Bromiley

271–94

1 Karl Barth, *Final Testimonies* (Grand Rapids: Eerdmans, 1977), 23.

2 Karl Barth, *Barth–Bultmann Letters* (Grand Rapids: Eerdmans, 1981), 154.

3 Ibid.

4 Karl Barth, *The Word of God and the Word of Man*, trans. Douglas Horton (New York: Harper & Row, 1957), 34.

[5] Ibid., 35.

[6] Ibid., 41.

[7] Ibid., 60ff.

[8] Ibid., 112.

[9] Ibid., 114.

[10] Ibid., 120ff.

[11] Ibid., 230.

[12] Ibid., 235.

[13] Ibid., 241.

[14] Ibid.

[15] Ibid., 243.

[16] Ibid., 244

[17] Ibid.

[18] Ibid., 246ff.

[19] Karl Barth and Eduard Thurneysen, *Come Holy Spirit* (Oxford: A. R. Mowbray, 1978), 57.

[20] Ibid., 220.

[21] Ibid., 228–29.

[22] Karl Barth, *Epistle to the Romans*, trans. Edwin C. Hoskyns (London: Oxford University Press, 1932), 1.

[23] Ibid., 11.

[24] Ibid., 17ff.

[25] Barth, *Barth–Bultmann Letters*, 41, 142.

[26] Ibid., 4–5.

[27] Ibid., 146.

[28] Karl Barth, *The Theology of Schleiermacher*, trans. Geoffrey W. Bromiley (Grand Rapids: Eerdmans, 1982), 16ff.

[29] Ibid., 38.

[30] Ibid., 45–46.

[31] Ibid., 63.

[32] Ibid., 87.

[33] Ibid., 154.

[34] Ibid., 174–75.

[35] Ibid., 175, 182–83.

[36] Ibid., 210.

[37] Karl Barth, *Theology and Church* (New York: Harper & Row, 1962), 112ff.

[38] Ibid., 116.

[39] Ibid., 209ff.

[40] Ibid., 269ff.

[41] Ibid., 296.

[42] Ibid., 303.

[43] Karl Barth, *Ethics* (New York: Seabury, 1981), 13.

[44] Ibid., 80–81.

[45] Ibid., 310.

[46] Ibid., 355.

[47] Ibid., 112.

48 Karl Barth, *The Knowledge of God and the Service of God According to the Teaching of the Reformation: Recalling the Scottish Confession of 1560* (London: Hodder & Stoughton, 1938), 9ff.

49 Ibid., 66–67.

50 Ibid., 177ff.

51 Ibid., 178ff.

52 Ibid., 216.

53 Ibid., 197.

54 Karl Barth, *Learning Jesus Christ through the Heidelberg Catechism* (Grand Rapids: Eerdmans, 1981), 123.

55 Ibid., 20.

56 Karl Barth and Emil Brunner, *Natural Theology* (London: Geoffrey Bles, 1946), 68.

57 Ibid., 84; see also 90.

58 Ibid., 125.

59 Karl Barth, *Church Dogmatics*, 4 vols. (Edinburgh: T. & T. Clark, 1975), 1:1:4.

60 Ibid., 89ff.

61 Ibid., 102ff.

62 Ibid., 113ff.

63 Ibid., 101.

64 Barth, *Church Dogmatics*, 1:2:457ff.

65 Ibid., 463.

66 Ibid., 464ff.

67 Ibid., 469–70.

68 Ibid., 473ff.

69 Ibid., 481ff.

70 Ibid., 485ff.

71 Ibid., 492ff.

72 Ibid., 494–95.

73 Ibid., 496ff.

74 Ibid., 502ff.

75 Ibid., 527ff.

76 Ibid., 540–41.

77 Ibid., 542ff.

78 Ibid., 544–72.

79 Ibid., 573ff.

80 Ibid., 586ff.

81 Ibid., 601ff.

82 Ibid., 657ff.

83 Ibid., 672.

84 Ibid., 673–74.

85 Ibid., 680ff.

86 Ibid., 699ff.

87 Ibid., 715ff.

88 Ibid., 738–39.

89 Ibid.

90 Karl Barth, *The Preaching of the Gospel* (Philadelphia: Westminster, 1963), 9.

[91] Ibid., 10, 12.

[92] Ibid., 12, 15.

[93] Ibid., 43ff.

[94] Ibid., 45ff.

[95] Ibid., 62, 48–49.

[96] Ibid., 64.

[97] Ibid., 47–48.

[98] Ibid., 47.

[99] Ibid., 81.

[100] Ibid., 78ff., 82.

[101] Ibid., 45.

[102] Ibid., 66.

[103] Ibid., 56.

[104] Ibid., 56ff.

[105] Karl Barth, *Evangelical Theology: An Introduction*, trans. Grover Foley (Grand Rapids: Eerdmans, 1963), 26ff.

[106] Ibid., 31ff.

[107] Ibid., 49.

[108] Ibid., 173ff.

[109] Karl Barth, *Karl Barth Letters: 1961–1968*, trans. Geoffrey W. Bromiley (Grand Rapids: Eerdmans, 1981), 28.

[110] Ibid., 108.

[111] Ibid., 230.

[112] Ibid., 111.

[113] Ibid., 283.

[114] Ibid., 116–17.

[115] Ibid., 169–70.

[116] Ibid., 137.

[117] Ibid., 334–35; cf. 357.

[118] Indeed, one might ask whether a faulty hermeneutic does not erode even a staunch and sincere commitment to biblical authority. Yet one must allow that the degree of error, the readiness to correct it, and the debatable nature of every hermeneutic enter into the equation. If the commitment is explicit, fallibility of practice need hardly impair the validity of the principle.

CHAPTER NINE

THE BIBLICAL CANON

David G. Dunbar

295–360

[1] David L. Dungan, "The New Testament Canon in Recent Study," *Int* 29 (1975): 339.

[2] Brevard S. Childs, *Introduction to the Old Testament as Scripture* (Philadelphia: Fortress, 1979); idem, *The New Testament as Canon: An Introduction* (Philadelphia: Fortress, 1984); James A. Sanders, "Adaptable for Life: The Nature and Function of Canon," in *Magnalia Dei. Essays on the Bible and Archeology in Memory of G. Ernest Wright*, ed. F. M. Cross, W. E. Lemke, and P. D. Miller, Jr. (Garden City: Doubleday, 1976), 531–60; idem, *Torah and Canon* (Philadelphia: Fortress, 1972). Childs and Sanders are concerned with the same problem, even though their approaches are different. Childs

emphasizes the final form of the text as the principal concern of the exegete; Sanders is more concerned for the process of tradition that has given the canonical books their present form. Joseph Blenkinsopp (*Prophecy and Canon: A Contribution to the Study of Jewish Origins* [Notre Dame: University of Notre Dame, 1977]) shares Sanders' concern for the process that shaped the canon. He identifies the institutionalization of prophecy as the main impetus to canon formation.

³Albert C. Sundberg, Jr., *The Old Testament of the Early Church* (Cambridge: Harvard University Press, 1964); Sid Z. Leiman, *The Canonization of the Hebrew Scriptures: The Talmudic and Midrashic Evidence* (Hamden, Conn.: Archon, 1976); Hans F. von Campenhausen, *Die Entstehung der Christlichen Bibel* (Tübingen: Mohr, 1968; Philadelphia: Fortress, 1973); Isidore Frank, *Der Sinn der Kanonbildung* (Freiburg: Herder, 1971).

⁴Dungan, "Recent Study," 341–42.

⁵See the literature cited in n. 61.

⁶James D. G. Dunn, *Unity and Diversity in the New Testament* (Philadelphia: Westminster, 1977), 377. The problems raised by Dunn's approach have been dealt with by my colleague D. A. Carson ("Unity and Diversity in the New Testament: The Possibility of Systematic Theology," in *Scripture and Truth*, ed. D. A. Carson and John D. Woodbridge [Grand Rapids: Zondervan, 1983], 65–95).

⁷For example, Donald G. Bloesch, *Essentials of Evangelical Theology*, vol. 1, *God, Authority, Salvation* (New York: Harper, 1978); Millard J. Erickson, *Christian Theology*, 3 vols. (Grand Rapids: Baker, 1983–85), vol. 1; Clark Pinnock, *The Scripture Principle* (San Francisco: Harper & Row, 1984).

⁸Among the more important recent discussions of the canon by Evangelical scholars, one may cite F. F. Bruce, *The Books and the Parchments*, 3rd rev. ed. (Westwood, N.J.: Revell, 1963), 95–113; idem, "New Light on the Origins of the New Testament Canon," in *New Dimensions in New Testament Study*, ed. Merrill Tenney and Richard N. Longenecker (Grand Rapids: Zondervan, 1974), 3–18; idem, "Some Thoughts on the Beginning of the New Testament Canon," *BJRL* 65 (1983): 37-60; Theo Donner, "Some Thoughts on the History of the New Testament Canon," *Themelios* 7 (1982): 23-27; Simon J. Kistemaker, "The Canon of the New Testament," *JETS* 20 (1977): 3–14; Bruce M. Metzger, "Canon of the New Testament" in *Dictionary of the Bible*, ed. James Hastings, rev. ed. (New York: Scribner, 1963), 123–26; Herman Ridderbos, *The Authority of the New Testament Scriptures*, trans. H. De Jongste (Grand Rapids: Baker, 1963).

⁹Hermann Wolfgang Beyer, TDNT, 3:596–602.

¹⁰David S. Russell, *The Method and Message of Jewish Apocalyptic* (Philadelphia: Westminster, 1964), 85–88.

¹¹Recently, however, Jean-Daniel Kaestli ("Le Recit de IV Esdras 14 et sa Valeur pour l'Histoire du Canon de l'Ancien Testament," in *Le Canon de l'Ancien Testament*, ed. Jean-Daniel Kaestli and Otto Wermelinger [Geneva: Labor et Fides, 1984], 71–97) has argued for the probability of an independent tradition alongside 2 Esdras that has influenced certain of the patristic views on the canon.

¹²See Excursus A in Herbert E. Ryle, *The Canon of the Old Testament*, 2d ed. (London: Macmillan, 1985), 250–83. For a survey of the continuing debate on the development of the Great Synagogue, see Hugo Mandel, "The Nature of the Great Synagogue," *HTR* 60 (1967): 69–91.

¹³There are minor variations to this view. The Talmudic passage Baba Bathra 14b–15a regards Nehemiah as the last of the biblical writers. According to 2 Maccabees 2:13, Nehemiah founded a library and collected "books about the kings and the prophets, and the writings of David, and letters of kings about votive offerings." (All English citations of the Apocrypha will be taken from *The Apocrypha of the Old Testament*, ed. Bruce M. Metzger [New York: Oxford, 1965].) The following verse describes a similar effort by Judas in the aftermath of the Maccabean revolt. Whether such collections had significance for the formation of the canon, however, is uncertain.

¹⁴For this basic pattern in older works see Ryle, *Canon*, 47–62, 93, 123, 182–83, and G. Wildeboer, *The Origin of the Canon of the Old Testament*, trans. B. W. Bacon, ed. G. F. Moore (London: Luzac & Co., 1895), 101, 116, 146. For more recent statements, see G. N. Anderson, "Canonical and Non-Canonical" in *The Cambridge History of the Bible*, vol. 1: *From the Beginnings to Jerome*, ed. Peter R. Ackroyd and C. F. Evans (Cambridge: Cambridge University Press, 1970), 120–35; Otto Eissfeldt, *The Old Testament: An Introduction*, trans. P. Ackroyd (New York: Harper, 1965), 231–32, 565–68; Robert H. Pfeiffer, *Introduction to the Old Testament* (New York: Harper, 1948), 51–65; J. Alberto Soggin, *Introduction to the Old Testament*, trans. J. Bowden (London: SCM, 1976), 14–18; Artur Weiser, *Introduction to the Old Testament*, trans. D. M. Barton (London: Darton, Longman & Todd, 1961), 335–45.

¹⁵Jack N. Lightstone, "The Formation of the Biblical Canon in Judaism of Late Antiquity: Prolegomenon to a General Reassessment," *SR* 8 (1979): 136–37.

¹⁶See Childs, *Old Testament*, 53, and the literature cited there.

¹⁷R. J. Coggins, *Samaritans and Jews: The Origins of Samaritanism Reconsidered* (Oxford: Blackwell, 1975), 164.

¹⁸Ibid., 152; F. M. Cross, Jr. "Aspects of Samaritan and Jewish History in Late Persian and Hellenistic Times," *HTR* 59 (1966): 201–11.

¹⁹Note that the same type of argument is used by Theodore N. Swanson (*The Closing of the Collection of Holy Scriptures: A Study in the History of the Canonization of the Old Testament* [Ann Arbor: University Microfilms, 1970], 136) to date the closing of the prophetic canon in the second century: "If we accept this dating of the Samaritan schism and of the Samaritan recension of the Pentateuch as being correct, what are the implications of the fact that at the beginning of the last quarter of the second century B.C. the Samaritan community accepted only the Pentateuch as their Scriptures? The simplest and most natural explanation for this phenomenon is to assume that the Samaritans accepted only the Pentateuch as Scripture, and not prophetic writings, because either only the Pentateuch was regarded as Scripture at this time by the Jews, or prophetic writings had only just attained the status of full scriptural authority among the Jews (and perhaps among only a portion of the Jews, at that), a development of such recent standing that it was not reflected among the Samaritans."

²⁰For example, Ian H. Eybers, *Historical Evidence on the Canon of the Old Testament with Special Reference to the Qumran Sect* (Ann Arbor: University Microfilms, 1966), 236n.3; Leiman, *Canonization*, 29–30.

²¹For example, Gleason L. Archer, Jr., "The Aramaic of the 'Genesis Apocryphon' Compared with the Aramaic of Daniel," in *New Perspectives on the Old Testament*, ed. J. Barton Payne (Waco: Word, 1970), 160–69; J. G. Baldwin, *Daniel: An Introduction and Commentary* (Carol Stream: InterVarsity, 1978), 19–53; Arthur J. Ferch, "The Book of Daniel and the 'Maccabean Thesis,' " *AUSS* 21 (1983): 129–41; G. F. Hasel, "The Book of Daniel: Evidences Relating to Persons and Chronology," *AUSS* 19 (1981): 37–49; idem, "The Book of Daniel and Matters of Language: Evidence Relating to Names, Words, and the Aramaic Language," *AUSS* 19 (1981): 211–25; Robert I. Vasholz, "Qumran and the Dating of Daniel," *JETS* 21 (1978): 315–21; D. J. Wiseman et al., *Notes on some problems in the Book of Daniel* (London: Tyndale, 1965); Edwin M. Yamauchi, "The Archeological Background of Daniel," *BS* 137 (1980): 3–16.

²²Leiman, *Canonization*, 121–24.

²³Lightstone, "Formation," 141–42.

²⁴Jack P. Lewis, "What Do We Mean by Jabneh?" *JBR* 32 (1964): 132; see also the conclusions of Robert C. Newman, "The Council of Jamnia and the Old Testament Canon," *WTJ* 38 (1976): 319–49, and Günter Stemberger, "Die sogenannte 'Synode von Jabne' und das frühe Christentum," *Kairos* 29 (1977): 14–21.

²⁵Josephus, *Against Apion* 1.37–42 (Loeb 1:177–81).

²⁶Skepticism on this point by several scholars seems unwarranted in the light of later Palestinian witnesses. See the comments by Leiman, *Canonization*, 152nn.154,155;

Charles Augustus Briggs, *General Introduction to the Study of Holy Scripture* (Edinburgh: T. & T. Clark, 1899), 128. Cf. Solomon Zeitlin, "An Historical Study of the Canonization of the Hebrew Scriptures," in *Solomon Zeitlin's Studies in the Early History of Judaism*, 3 vols. (New York: Ktav, 1974), 2:9–10.

[27] The Talmudic and Midrashic evidence is gathered by Leiman, *Canonization*, 51–56.

[28] See Excursus C in Ryle, *Canon*, 292–94.

[29] Philo, *De Vita Contemplativa* 3.25 (Loeb, 9:127). Philo states that the Theraputae bring into their cells only "laws and oracles (*nomous kai logia*) delivered through the mouth of prophets, and psalms and anything else (*hymnous kai ta alla*) which fosters and perfects knowledge and piety."

[30] W. L. Knox, "A Note on Philo's Use of the Old Testament," *JTS* 41 (1940): 31.

[31] Ibid., 34.

[32] Ryle, *Canon*, 159.

[33] The Apocrypha (so designated by the Protestant churches) are those books accepted as part of the Old Testament by the Roman Catholic Church at the Council of Trent in 1546. They include Tobit, Judith, Wisdom, Ecclesiasticus (Sirach), Baruch, 1 and 2 Maccabees, and certain additions to Esther and Daniel. Roman Catholic scholars prefer the designation "deuterocanonical" or "protocanonical" for these books.

[34] Ryle, *Canon*, 158–59.

[35] "The Law and the Prophets" (Mt 5:17; 7:12; 11:13 [Lk 16:16]; 22:40; Ac 13:15; 24:15; Ro 3:21), "Moses and the Prophets" (Lk 16:29,31; Jn 1:45; Ac 26:22), "Law of Moses and the Prophets" (Lk 24:44; Ac 28:23).

[36] "Law" (Mt 5:18; Jn 10:34; 12:34; 15:25; Ro 3:31[?]; 1Co 14:21,34[?]), "Prophets" (Mt 26:56[?]; Lk 18:31[?]; Ac 3:17,21; 10:43[?]; 26:27[?]; Ro 16:26 (*graphon prophētikon*, cf. 1Pe 1:19, *ton prophētikon logon*); 2Pe 3:2).

[37] Gottlob Schrenk, "*graphē*," *TDNT*, 1:752–55.

[38] Curt Kuhl, *The Old Testament: Its Origins and Composition*, trans. C. T. M. Herriott (Richmond: John Knox, 1961), 3.

[39] A list of New Testament citations of the Old Testament may be found in the "Index of Quotations" in *The Greek New Testament*, ed. Kurt Aland et al., 2d ed. (Stuttgart: United Bible Societies, 1968), 897–918. A similar list with detailed discussion is given by Eybers, *Historical Evidence*, 63–82. Eybers (p. 73) in the following statistical summary gives first the number of "undoubted" citations and then in brackets a figure that includes the "very probable cases": (a) Torah—63[78]: Ge 14[15]; Ex 15[20]; Lev 8[11]; Nu 1[2]; Dt 25[27]; (b) Nebi'im—64[73]: Jos 0[1]; Jdg 0; Sa 4[5]; Ki 1[1]; Isa 37[40]; Jer 5[7]; Eze 0[1]; The Twelve 17[18]; (c) Ketubim—49[54]: Ps 44[49]; Pr 3[3]; Job 1[1]; the five Megillot 0; Da 1[1]; Ezr-Ne-Ch 0.

[40] I am indebted to Eybers (*Historical Evidence*, 75–82) for this analysis.

[41] For example, F. F. Bruce, *The Books*, 97; Eybers, *Historical Evidence*, 93; Ryle, *Canon*, 15; Weiser, *Old Testament*, 251.

[42] The last is Uriah son of Shemaiah (Jer 26:20–23).

[43] Two objections have been raised to this identification. (1) The difference in patronymic between Chronicles and Matthew is taken as evidence that another Zechariah must be intended by the latter reference. Frequently Matthew 23:34–35 is understood of Zechariah, son of Baris (or Baruch or Bariscaeus), who, according to Josephus [*Wars* 4.5 (Loeb, 3:99)], was killed in the temple precincts by Zealots in A.D. 68. Apart from the fact that the patronymic is still different, this identification labors under an untenable anachronism. A possible reconciliation of Matthew and Chronicles suggests that Jehoiada may have been the grandfather of Zechariah (D. A. Carson, *Matthew*, in *EBC*, ed. Frank E. Gaebelein, 12 vols. [Grand Rapids: Zondervan, 1976–], 8:486). (2) It is objected that there was no fixed sequence of books at this early period.

To find in Jesus' words evidence for a canonical order is anachronistic. But, of course, it is possible that the order later given by the rabbis preserves a much more primitive arrangement that, while not the only one known in the first century (cf. Josephus), may have been widely recognized.

[44] Eissfeldt, *Introduction*, 568.

[45] Cf. Leiman, *Canonization*, 41: "In summary, it can safely be said that while the New Testament does not prove the existence of a closed 22 or 24 book canon in the early first century, it is entirely consistent with such a possibility."

[46] See, for example, the list of Sundberg (*Early Church*, 54–55), which is based on the marginal references in *Novum Testamentum Graece*, ed. E. Nestle, 22d ed. (Stuttgart: Württembergische Bibelanstalt, 1948). A somewhat fuller list is given by T. R. Ferro, "References to Apocrypha, Pseudepigrapha, and Extrabiblical Literature as Noted in the Outer Margins of the Nestle-Aland Greek New Testament," *CTM* 39 (1968): 328–32.

[47] William Henry Green, *General Introduction to the Old Testament* (New York: Scribner, 1898; reprint, Grand Rapids: Baker, 1980), 146.

[48] For example, Origen assumed that there was a book about Jannes and Jambres that was the source of Paul's reference in 2 Timothy 3:8, but this may well have been an oral tradition. Cf. Eybers, *Historical Evidence*, 86–87; Albrecht Oepke, "*Bibloi apokryphoi* in Christianity," TDNT, 3:990. Moreover, at least two of the parallels between later pseudepigrapha and the New Testament (Gal 6:15, Apocrypha of Moses; 1Co 2:9, Apocalypse of Elijah) probably show a dependence of the extrabiblical materials on the New Testament; cf. Oepke, "*Bibloi apokryphoi*," 988–90.

[49] See the parallels discussed by Bruce M. Metzger, *An Introduction to the Apocrypha* (New York: Oxford, 1957), 157–70.

[50] Menander, 1Co 15:33; Cleanthes, Ac 17:28; Epimenides, Tit 1:12.

[51] Richard J. Bauckham (*Word Biblical Commentary: Jude, 2 Peter* [Waco: Word, 1983], 96) suggests, "While this word ["prophesied"] indicates that Jude regarded the prophecies in 1 Enoch as inspired by God, it need not imply that he regarded the book as canonical Scripture." Most Evangelicals have followed Augustine's position (*Civ. Dei* 15.23.4): Jude simply affirms the truthfulness of the quotation but implies nothing thereby for the canonicity of 1 Enoch.

[52] Ecclesiastes may not have been rendered into Greek before the second century A.D. version of Aquila. See Sidney Jellicoe, *The Septuagint and Modern Study* (Oxford: Clarendon, 1968), 69, 82.

[53] Henry B. Swete, *An Introduction to the Old Testament in Greek*, rev. R. R. Ottley (Cambridge: Cambridge University Press, 1914), 216–19.

[54] Ibid., 201–2.

[55] This hypothesis was first proposed by J. E. Grabe (1666–1711). Later it was independently elaborated by Johann Salomo Semler (1725–91). See Sundberg (*Early Church*, 3–40) for the history of the Alexandrian hypothesis.

[56] Ryle, *Canon*, 169; Wildeboer, *Origin*, 35.

[57] Eusebius, *HE* 4.26 (Loeb, 1:393), for Origen; Athanasius, *Ep. List.* 39 (*NPNF*2, 4:552).

[58] Sundberg, *Early Church*, 52. The reasoning seems cogent even if, as I have argued, the Jewish canon was closed before Jamnia.

[59] Ibid., 103.

[60] Ibid., 81–103.

[61] A. C. Sundberg, Jr. "The Protestant Old Testament Canon: Should It Be Re-Examined?" in "A Symposium on the Canon of Scripture," *CBQ* 28 (1966): 199. Similar is the view of Marvin E. Tate ("Old Testament Apocalyptic and the Old Testament Canon," *Review and Expositor* 65 [1968]: 353): "It seems clear that the Protestant position must be judged a failure on historical grounds, insofar as it sought to return to the canon of

Jesus and the Apostles. The Apocrypha belongs to this historical heritage of the Church." See also Richard Lyon Morgan, "Let's Be Honest about the Canon: A Plea to Reconsider a Question the Reformers Failed to Answer," *Christian Century* 84 (1967): 717–19; A. C. Sundberg, Jr., "The 'Old Testament': A Christian Canon," *CBQ* 30 (1968): 143–55.

[62] Sundberg, "Protestant," 203.

[63] Sundberg's treatment (*Early Church*, 56–60) of the patristic witness should be compared with that of Leiman, *Canonization*, 41–50.

[64] These would include, with minor variations, (a) among the Greek fathers: Melito of Sardis (perhaps), Origen, Athanasius, Cyril of Jerusalem, Epiphanius (who gives both 22 and 27 as the total), Gregory of Nazianzus and Amphilochius; and (b) among the Latin fathers: Hilary of Poitiers, Jerome, and Rufinus. See the canonical lists that are given by Swete (*Introduction*, 203–10), as well as the citations and commentary of Leiman (*Canonization*, 41–50).

[65] Metzger, *Introduction*, 178.

[66] Jellicoe, *Septuagint*, 249.

[67] For the contrast between Augustine and Jerome, see Samuel J. Schultz, "Augustine and the Old Testament Canon," *BS* 112 (1955): 225–34.

[68] See above, n. 61.

[69] F. F. Bruce, *Second Thoughts on the Dead Sea Scrolls*, 2d ed. (Grand Rapids: Eerdmans, 1964), 28.

[70] For a survey of the types of literature, see Jozef T. Milik, *Ten Years of Discovery in the Wilderness of Judea*, trans. J. Strugnall (London: SCM, 1959), 20–43.

[71] Eybers, *Historical Evidence*, 124.

[72] Leiman, *Canonization*, 36.

[73] See the detailed treatment of the data by Eybers, *Historical Evidence*, 124–59.

[74] Swanson, *Closing*, 198.

[75] Ibid., 182–83.

[76] Qumran's position on Daniel's canonicity has been questioned by F. M. Cross and W. Brownlee following J. T. Milik (D. Barthélemy and J. T. Milik, *Qumran Cave I*, vol. 1 of *Discoveries in the Judean Desert* [Oxford: Clarendon, 1955], 150). Milik argued that the manuscript format—the relative height and width of columns—suggested that Daniel was not regarded as canonical. This was confirmed, he believed, by the fact that Daniel was written on papyrus rather than leather like other biblical scrolls. But with the publication of 4Q Florelegium it has become clear that at least by the first century A.D., the members of the community viewed Daniel as a prophet and his book as Scripture. See Swanson, *Closing*, 189–93.

[77] Swanson, *Closing*, 197.

[78] Cf. the slightly varying accounts of Eybers, *Historical Evidence*, 171–85; P. W. Skehan, "The Biblical Scrolls from Qumran and the Text of the Old Testament," *BA* 28 (1965): 89; Swanson, *Closing*, 185–98.

[79] Skehan, "Scrolls from Qumran," 89.

[80] Eybers, *Historical Evidence*, 186–89. Eybers disagrees sharply with Bleddyn J. Roberts ("The Dead Sea Scrolls and the Old Testament Scriptures," *BJRL* 36 [1953–54]: 84), who speaks of "abundant quotations in the scrolls . . . from the present books of the Apocrypha."

[81] Eybers, *Historical Evidence*, 190–203.

[82] Skehan, "Scrolls from Qumran," 90. An interesting question, however, is raised by the text of Jubilees itself. Jubilees 2:23 reads, "there (were) two and twenty heads of mankind from Adam to Jacob, and two and twenty kinds of work were made until the seventh day" (R. H. Charles, *The Apocrypha and Pseudepigrapha of the Old Testament*, 2

vols. [Oxford: Clarendon, 1913], 2:15). The translation of Charles is based on the Ethiopic version. However, a Greek fragment of Jubilees preserved by Epiphanius (*de means. et pond.* 22) reads: *homou eikosiduo geneai. Dio kai eikosiduo eisi ta para tois Hebraiois grammata, kai pros auta kai tas biblous autōn kb' erithmēsan eikosiepta ousas.* ("Together there are twenty-two generations. Therefore also among the Hebrews there are twenty-two letters, and in reference to these things they also count twenty-two of their books, although there are actually twenty-seven.") Epiphanius is supported by several other Greek writers (see the quotations given by A.-M. Denis, *Fragmenta pseudepigraphorum quae supersunt Graeca, una cum historicorum et auctorum Judaeorum Hellenistarum fragmentis* [Leiden: Brill, 1970], 74–75). Charles (*Pseudepigrapha*, 2:15n.23) concludes that the Ethiopic manuscripts must have originally included the reference to twenty-two sacred books. Whether the original Hebrew text of Jubilees contained this reference is even more problematic. Jozef T. Milik ("Recherches sur la Version Grecque du Livre des Jubilés," *RB* 78 [1971]: 549–50) is emphatic that the Greek readings are secondary and based on Origen (*Hom. in Nu* 4:1 [*GCS*, 30:20]; cf. *in Ps. I* [*PG*, 12:1084A]). But R. T. Beckwith ("Canon [OT]" in *The Illustrated Bible Dictionary*, ed. J. D. Douglas, 3 vols. [Leicester: InterVarsity, 1980], 1:238) suggests that the reference to twenty-two books may have appeared in a Greek version of Jubilees as early as the first century B.C.

[83] The most recent survey of the question is that by G. H. Wilson, "The Qumran Psalms Manuscripts and the Consecutive Arrangement of Psalms in the Hebrew Psalter," *CBQ* 45 (1983): 377–88.

[84] The official publication is by J. A. Sanders, ed., *The Psalms Scroll of Qumran Cave 11, Discoveries in the Judean Desert*, vol. 4 (Oxford: Clarendon, 1965). This was followed by idem, ed., *The Dead Sea Psalms Scroll* (Ithaca: Cornell University Press, 1967). The latter work includes fragment E of the scroll, which became available only after the original publication.

[85] Sanders, *Dead Sea Psalms*, 93.

[86] Ibid., 13, 157–58; cf. idem, "Cave 11 Surprises and the Question of Canon," *McCQ* 21 (1968): 292.

[87] Sanders, *Dead Sea Psalms*, 13–14, 156–58; idem, "Cave 11 Surprises," 294. Sanders' analysis has been accepted recently by Wilson, "Qumran Psalms," 388.

[88] For example, Anderson, "Canonical and Non-Canonical," 153; M. H. Goshen-Gottstein, "The Psalms Scroll (11 QPs^a): A Problem of Canon and Text," *Textus* 5 (1966): 22–33; Leiman, *Canonization*, 154–55n.183; Skehan, "Biblical Scrolls," 100; Swanson, *Closing*, 240; S. Talman, "Pisgah be'emsa passuq and 11 QPs^a," *Textus* 5 (1966): 11–21.

[89] The prologue uses three similar designations: (1) "the law and the prophets and the others who followed after them" (*tou nomou kai tōn prophētōn kai tōn allōn tōn kat' autous ekolouthēkotōn*); (2) "the reading of the law and the prophets and the other books of the fathers" (*tēn tou nomou kai tōn prophētōn kai tōn allōn patriōn bibliōn anagnōsin*); and (3) "the law and the prophecies and the rest of the books" (*ho nomos kai hai prophēteiai kai ta loipa tōn bibliōn*).

[90] Sirach 38:13 describes the proper work of the sage: "(1) On the other hand, he who devotes himself to the study of the law of the Most High will seek out the wisdom of all the ancients, and will be concerned with prophecies; (2) he will preserve the discourse of notable men and penetrate the subtleties of parables; (3) he will seek out the hidden meanings of proverbs and be at home with the obscurities of parables."
   That verse 1 speaks of Scripture under the tripartite divisions and verses 2 and 3 refer to oral tradition has been suggested by a number of scholars (e.g., see the notes by J. G. Snaith, *Ecclesiasticus* [Cambridge: Cambridge University Press, 1974], 191–92). Swanson (*Closing*, 99–104) correctly argues that such an interpretation is strained.

[91] David E. Aune, *Prophecy in Early Christianity and in the Ancient Mediterranean World* (Grand Rapids: Eerdmans, 1983), 103–52. Aune is indebted to the similar views of Rudolf Meyer, "Prophecy and Prophets in Judaism of the Hellenistic-Roman Period," *TDNT*, 6:812–28.

[92] Aune, *Prophecy*, 368n.2; cf. 81, 103, 153, 187.

[93] Aune (*Prophecy*, 106) contends that there was apparently no connection between the notion of the cessation of prophecy and the formation of the canon. But here he minimizes the witness of Josephus (*Contra Ap.*, 1.37–41). While it is true that in the earlier literature there is no explicit connection between these ideas, we should point out that there are no explicit statements *whatever* on the motivation or criterion of canon formation. In view of this lack of direct evidence, the correlation between canon and prophecy seems reasonable.

[94] This is the view of Meyer, "Prophecy," 815. On the other hand, Aune (*Prophecy*, 105) holds that the theocratic outlook of 1 Maccabees excludes the possibility of a reference to an eschatological prophet.

[95] F. F. Bruce, "Holy Spirit in the Qumran texts," in *The Annual of Leeds University Oriental Society* 6 (1966–68): 51.

[96] Aune, *Prophecy*, 132–35; but cf. the opposite view of William Sanford LaSor (*The Dead Sea Scrolls and the New Testament* [Grand Rapids: Eerdmans, 1972], 119–20).

[97] For example, John Calvin, *Institutes of the Christian Religion*, trans. Ford Lewis Battles, 2 vols. (Philadelphia: Westminster, 1960), 1:7:1–5, 74–81.

[98] Edward J. Young, "The Authority of the Old Testament," in *The Infallible Word*, ed. Paul Woolley, 3d rev. ed. (Philadelphia: Presbyterian and Reformed, 1967), 89; cf. the similar view of R. Laird Harris, *Inspiration and Canonicity of the Bible* (Grand Rapids: Zondervan, 1957), 143.

[99] Beckwith, "Canon (OT)," 1:236.

[100] Ibid., 237.

[101] Roland K. Harrison, *Introduction to the Old Testament* (Grand Rapids: Eerdmans, 1969), 287.

[102] Beckwith, "Canon (OT)," 1:237.

[103] Eusebius, *HE* 3.25.

[104] Ibid., 3.3.4–5.

[105] Ibid., 3.25.6 (Loeb, 1:259).

[106] Hebrews is cited by Irenaeus and Hippolytus but not as a Pauline letter. It is omitted by the Muratorian Canon (c. A.D. 200) and the Cheltenham list (c. A.D. 360) and is never referred to by Cyprian. Donald Guthrie, *New Testament Introduction* (Downers Grove: InterVarsity, 1970), 687.

[107] Eusebius, *HE* 3.25.3.

[108] Ibid., 2.23.24–25; 3.3.1. M.-J. Lagrange (*Histoire Ancienne du Canon du Nouveau Testament* [Paris: J. Gabalda, 1933], 124) suggests that Eusebius' doubts regarding the four shorter Catholic letters may have derived from Lucian of Antioch (d. 312).

[109] The rejection of chiliastic movements like Montanism no doubt played a part in the Eastern reserve toward the Apocalypse as did also the denial of its apostolic authorship by Dionysius of Alexandria, bishop of Alexandria from 247 to 265. See R. H. Charles, *A Critical and Exegetical Commentary on the Revelation of St. John*, 2 vols. (Edinburgh: T. & T. Clark, 1920), 1:c–cii; Ned B. Stonehouse, *The Apocalypse in the Ancient Church* (Goes: Oosterbaan & Le Cointre, 1929).

[110] See the careful treatment of Eusebius' shifting views by Robert M. Grant (*Eusebius as Church Historian* [Oxford: Clarendon, 1980], 126–37).

[111] The limitation of the canon to twenty-four books may indicate a desire to conform the number of books to that of the Old Testament. The words *una sola* after the mention of the three Johannine Epistles and again after the two Petrine Epistles are probably marginal notes later incorporated into the texts. See the discussion of Lagrange, *Histoire*, 86–88.

[112] Bart D. Ehrman ("The New Testament Canon of Didymus the Blind," *VC* 37 [1983]: 1–21) argues that Didymus the Blind, appointed by Athanasius to head the

catechetical school at Alexandria, accepted as canonical most of Athanasius' canon but included with it a number of the Apostolic Fathers. He concludes, "While the entire church there [in Alexandria] seems to have agreed upon the canonical status of many books, there were others, notably several works of the Apostolic Fathers, that were still disputed. This means that although Athanasius listed no *antilegomena* in his thirty-ninth Paschal letter, the category did exist in his church" (p. 19).

[113]B. F. Westcott, *A General Survey of the History of the Canon of the New Testament*, 6th ed. (New York: Macmillan, 1889; reprint, Grand Rapids: Baker, 1980), 437; cf. Edgar J. Goodspeed, *The Formation of the New Testament* (Chicago: University of Chicago, 1926), 126.

[114]Westcott, *Survey*, 441–42; Goodspeed, *Formation*, 128–30.

[115]These would include Amphilocius of Iconium (c. 340–95), whose canon was precisely our present twenty-seven books, Epiphanius of Salamis (c. 315–403), Basil the Great (c. 330–79) and his brother Gregory of Nyssa (c. 330–95), and perhaps Gregory Nazianzus (329–89). See Lagrange, *Histoire*, 115–20; cf. Westcott, *Survey*, 445–48.

[116]Sean Kealy, "The Canon: An African Contribution," *BTB* 9 (1979): 19–21; cf. R. W. Cowley, "The Biblical Canon of the Ethiopian Orthodox Church Today," *Östkirchliche Studien* 23 (1974): 318–23.

[117]This is true even with Martin Luther, who, of all the Reformers, offered the strongest statements against the canonicity of certain of the antilegomena. In the table of contents to his 1522 translation of the New Testament, Luther separated Hebrews, James, Jude, and Revelation from the rest of the books by a space and discontinued the numbering of the books. This arrangement was abandoned in subsequent editions, and Luther's negative judgments on the value of these books (expressed in the Prefaces) were moderated. However, his reserve toward James continued throughout his life. See Paul Althaus, *Theology of Martin Luther*, trans. R. C. Schultz (Philadelphia: Fortress, 1966), 83–85; Willem Jan Kooiman, *Luther and the Bible*, trans. John Schmidt (Philadelphia: Muhlenberg, 1961), 110–15.

[118]For the New Testament witness see Raymond F. Collins, "The Matrix of the NT Canon," *BTB* 7 (1977): 51–59; Denis M. Farkasfalvy, "The Early Development of the New Testament Canon," in *The Formation of the New Testament Canon: An Ecumenical Approach*, by William R. Farmer and Denis M. Farkasfalvy (New York: Paulist, 1983), 103–23; Ralph P. Martin, "Authority in the Light of the Apostolate, Tradition and the Canon," *EQ* 40 (1968):66-82; Sigfried Pedersen, "Die Kanonfrage als historisches und theolgisches Problem," *Studia Theologica* 31 (1977): 83–136; Ridderbos, *Authority*, 18–33.

[119]Adolf von Harnack, *The Origin of the New Testament*, trans. J. R. Wilkinson (London: Williams & Norgate, 1925), 7.

[120]George E. Ladd, *A Theology of the New Testament* (Grand Rapids: Eerdmans, 1974), 140–43.

[121]Ridderbos, *Authority*, 14.

[122]K. H. Rengstorf (*apostolos, TDNT*, 1:407–47) has argued that *apostolos* is a literal rendering of a Jewish legal term *shaliach*. The *shaliach* is a commissioned representative. His position carries with it the full authority of the one who commissioned him, in accordance with the Rabbinic maxim that "the one sent by a man is as the man himself." Rengstorf's view has not gone unchallenged; see J. Andrew Kirk, "Apostleship Since Rengstorf: Towards a Synthesis," *NTS* 21 (1975): 249–64; Robert W. Herron, "The Origin of the New Testament Apostolate," *WTJ* 45 (1983): 101–31. What I have suggested regarding the position of the apostles may be maintained even if one judges that there is no direct equation between *shaliach* and *apostolos*.

[123]Hans von Campenhausen, *Ecclesiastical Authority and Spiritual Power in the Church of the First Three Centuries*, trans. J. A. Baker (Stanford: Stanford University Press, 1969), 23; Ridderbos, *Authority*, 15–17; Oscar Cullmann, "The Tradition," in *The Early Church*, abr. ed. (Philadelphia: Westminster, 1966), 75–79.

[124]The idea of tradition had taken on a technical sense in the rabbinic schools; it referred there to the haggadic and halakic interpretations of the Bible. *Pardosis* occurs thirteen times in the New Testament, and nine of these occurrences refer to the Rabbinic elaboration of the Law, the "tradition of the elders" (Mt 15:2,3,6; Mk 7:3,5,8,9,13; Gal 1:14; the phrase *kata tēn pardosin tōn anthrōpōn* [Col 2:8] is not clear). The Rabbinic concept of tradition has been explored most extensively by B. Gerhardsson, *Memory and Manuscript: Oral Tradition and Written Transmission in Rabbinic Judaism and Early Christianity*, trans. Eric J. Sharpe (Lund: Gleerup, 1961).

[125]F. F. Bruce, *Tradition: Old and New* (Grand Rapids: Zondervan, 1970), 29–38.

[126]Cullmann, "Tradition," 62–68.

[127]Ridderbos, *Authority*, 24.

[128]Note should also be made of 1 Timothy 5:18, where the introduction of a dominical saying together with an Old Testament text is a single phrase, "For the Scripture says" (*legei gar hē graphē*). If this cites the words of Jesus only via oral tradition, it confirms what we have said in reference to the authority of Jesus' teaching. If this is a direct reference to Luke 10:7, it provides another example of the high authority of the New Testament documents at an early period. It is recognized, of course, that the bulk of historical-critical scholarship places both 2 Peter and the Pastoral Epistles in the second century.

[129]Jean Carmignac, "II Corinthiens III. 6,14 et le Début de la Formation du Nouveau Testament," *NTS* 24 (1977–78): 386.

[130]Consult the excellent article by I. Howard Marshall, "Orthodoxy and Heresy in Earlier Christianity," *Themelios* 2 (1976–77): 5–14.

[131]Published as volume 10 in the series *Beiträge zur historischen Theologie* (Tübingen: Mohr-Siebeck, 1934). A new edition was published in 1964 by Georg Strecker. The first English translation appeared under the title *Orthodoxy and Heresy in Earliest Christianity* (Philadelphia: Fortress, 1971).

[132]For the continuing influence of Bauer on various areas of patristic and New Testament studies, see the literature cited in Daniel J. Harrington, "The Reception of Walter Bauer's *Orthodoxy and Heresy in Earliest Christianity* During the Last Decade," *HTR* 77 (1980): 289–98.

[133]Helmut Koester, "*Gnomai Diaphorai*: The Origin and Nature of Diversification in the History of Early Christianity," in *Trajectories through Early Christianity*, ed. James M. Robinson and Helmut Koester (Philadelphia: Fortress, 1971), 114–57 [repr. from *HTR* 58 (1965): 279–318]; idem, "The Theological Aspects of Primitive Christian Heresy," in *The Future of our Religious Past*, ed. James M. Robinson (London: SCM, 1971), 65–83.

[134]Koester, "Theological Aspects," 67. Evidence for this is found in the fact that, judged by second-century standards, "Paul himself stands in the twilight zone of heresy" (p. 68).

[135]Idem, "*Gnomai Diaphorai*," 118.

[136]Idem, "Theological Aspects," 83.

[137]Marshall, "Orthodoxy," 7.

[138]Ibid., 13.

[139]Earlier dates have been proposed. For example, John A. T. Robinson (*Redating the New Testament* [Philadelphia: Westminster, 1976], 327–35) argues for a date of A.D. 70. The balance of the evidence probably weighs toward the customary date; cf. J. B. Lightfoot, *The Apostolic Fathers: Part 1. Clement of Rome*, 2 vols. (London: Macmillan, 1980), 1:346–58.

[140]"It is written," *gegraptai*: 1 Clem 4.1; 14.4; 17.3; 29.2; et passim; "Scripture (the Writing) says," *graphē (to grapheion) legei*: 28.3; 34.6; 35.7; 42.5; "he/it says," *legei*: 29.3; 30.2,3.

[141]1 Clem 22.1ff.

[142]*1 Clem* 7.2 (Loeb, 1:18). Clement uses *kanōn* also in 1.3 and 41.1. In none of the three cases does the term refer to a "canon" of Scripture. For a discussion of Clement's usage see Frank, *Der Sinn*, 21–28.

[143]*1 Clem* 13.1–4; 46.1–8.

[144]Donald A. Hagner, *The Use of the Old and New Testament in Clement of Rome* (Leiden: Brill, 1973), 178. Hagner's conclusion is not shared by Helmut Koester.

[145]*1 Clem* 42.1–2 (Loeb, 1:78–81).

[146]*1 Clem* 44.1–2.

[147]*1 Clem* 47.1–2 (Loeb, 1:88–91).

[148]I am indebted here to the detailed analysis given by Hagner, *Use*, 179–271.

[149]For the list of Clement's citations and introductory formulas, see Robert M. Grant and Holt H. Graham, eds. *The Apostolic Fathers*, vol. 2, *First and Second Clement* (New York: Thomas Nelson, 1965), 133–34.

[150]There are only three direct quotations. Two are introduced by *gegraptai (Eph.* 5.3; *Magn.* 12). *Trall.* 8.2 introduces Isaiah 52:5 merely with *gar*.

[151]*Magn.* 8.2 (Loeb, 1:204–5).

[152]*Phil.* 5.2; *Magn.* 9.2.

[153]*Phil.* 8.2 (Loeb, 1:246–47).

[154]Ellen Flesseman-van Leer, *Tradition and Scripture in the Early Church* (Assen, The Netherlands: Van Gorcum 1954), 34.

[155]*Magn.* 9.1 (Loeb, 1:204–5).

[156]*Phil.* 7.2 (Loeb, 1:246–47).

[157]*Phil.* 8.2.

[158]*Magn.* 13.1.

[159]*Rom.* 4.3 (Loeb, 1:230–31); cf. *Trall.* 3.3 (Loeb, 1:214–15).

[160]Robert M. Grant, *The Apostolic Fathers*, vol. 1, *Introduction* (New York: Thomas Nelson, 1964), 59–61; Frank, *Der Sinn*, 39; *contra* Koester, *Uberlieferungen*, 24–61.

[161]*Eph.* 12.2 (Loeb, 1:186–87).

[162]Grant, *Introduction*, 57. Jack Finegan ("The Original Form of the Pauline Letter Collection," *HTR* 49 [1956]: 85–88) argues that both Ignatius and Clement of Rome had access to a collection of Pauline letters published originally in codex form prior to A.D. 95.

[163]For allusions to John, see *Rom.* 7.2; *Phil.* 7.1. Another passage, *Eph.* 5.3, may refer to James 4:6, 1 Peter 5:5, or perhaps Proverbs 3:34 (which is quoted in the two New Testament texts). That Ignatius introduces the quotation by *gegraptai gar* ("for it is written") may indicate that he is referring to Proverbs 3:34.

[164]Flesseman-van Leer, *Tradition*, 32–33.

[165]This position is set forth in detail by Paul N. Harrison, *Polycarp's Two Epistles to the Philippians* (Cambridge: Cambridge University Press, 1936). His interpretation is accepted by Johannes Quasten, *Patrology*, 3 vols. (Westminster, Maryland: Newman, 1962), 1:79–80. Cyril C. Richardson (ed., *Early Christian Fathers*, vol. 1 of *The Library of Christian Classics* [Philadelphia: Westminster, 1953], 124–25), following J. B. Lightfoot, rejects Harrison's interpretation in favor of the unity of the epistle and a date around A.D. 110.

[166]Richardson, *Fathers*, 123.

[167]*Phil.* 6.3 (Loeb, 1:290–91).

[168]See the detailed discussion by Harrison, *Polycarp's Two Epistles*, 285–310.

[169]*Phil.* 12.1 (Loeb, 1:298–99). Chapters 10–12 and 14 are extant only in Latin.

[170]For example, Koester, *Überlieferungen*, 113.

[171] Charles M. Nielsen, "Polycarp, Paul and the Scriptures," *Anglican Theological Review* 47 (1965): 199–205. Frank *(Der Sinn,* 47,52) sees *both* Psalm 4:5 and Ephesians 4:26 cited as *graphē.*

[172] Nielsen, "Polycarp," 207. By contrast to Nielsen, Flesseman-van Leer *(Tradition,* 44) makes the extraordinary judgment that "notwithstanding the many quotations, there is really no clear proof that Polycarp accepts any New Testament scriptural authority." But short of a formal statement to that effect, I am not sure what more could be expected from Polycarp.

[173] Robert A. Kraft, ed., *Barnabas and the Didache,* vol. 3 of *The Apostolic Fathers* (New York: Thomas Nelson, 1965), 72–77, argues for a mid-second century date. Quasten, *Patrology,* 1:36–37, places the origin between A.D. 100 and A.D. 150. F. E. Volkes, "The Didache and the Canon of the New Testament," *Studia Evangelica,* ed. F. L. Cross (Berlin: Akademie-Verlag, 1964), 3:431–32, dates the final form after A.D. 150. On the other hand, Frank *(Der Sinn* 33) judges that the author of the Didache was probably a Christian rabbi who wrote at Pella about A.D. 66. The complexities of the date and provenance of the document make it unwise to place great weight on the evidence of the Didache.

[174] *Did.* 4.13.

[175] *Did.* 11.3–6. Cited in Farkasfalvy, "Early Development," 129.

[176] Farkasfalvy, "Early Development," 129.

[177] On the literary-critical relationship between Barnabas and the Didache and their probable use of a common source, see Kraft, *Barnabas and the Didache,* 4–16. On the problems of dating see idem, 42–43.

[178] *Barn.* 14.4 (Loeb, 1:390–91).

[179] Farkasfalvy, "Early Development," 131.

[180] Barnabas uses the term *gnōsis* ten times (1.5; 2.3; 5.4; 6.9; 9.8; 10.10; 13.7; 18.1; 19.1; 21.5). For a discussion of the significance of the term, see Flesseman van-Leer, *Tradition,* 51–55.

[181] *Barn.* 4.14 (Loeb, 1:352): *prosechōmen, mēpote, hōs gegraptai, polloi, klētoi, oligoi de eklektoi heurethōmen.*

[182] This is correctly seen by Frank *(Der Sinn,* 58–59) and Grant *(Introduction,* 78).

[183] Richardson *(Early Christian Fathers,* 189) places the origin of the sermon at Alexandria prior to A.D. 150. Grant *(Introduction,* 46) suggests a "wild hypothesis" that the author was Hyginus (bishop of Rome c. 138–42).

[184] *2 Clem* 14.2.

[185] *2 Clem* 19.1 (Loeb, 1:158–59): "Therefore, brothers and sisters, following the God of truth, I am reading you an exhortation to pay attention to that which is written, that you may both save yourselves and him who is the reader among you." Justin Martyr *(1 Apol* 67) testifies to the combined reading of the Old Testament and apostolic literature in the Christian worship of the second century.

[186] *2 Clem* 2.4 (Loeb, 1:130–31): *kai hetera de graphē legei.*

[187] The problem of the definition and origins of Gnosticism need not detain us. A useful introduction appears in Jaroslav Pelikan, *The Emergence of the Catholic Tradition (100–600),* vol. 1 of *The Christian Tradition* (Chicago: University of Chicago Press, 1971), 81–97. Extensive discussions may be found in Ugo Bianchi, ed., *The Origins of Gnosticism: Colloquium of Messina 13–18 April 1966* (Leiden: Brill, 1967). On the issue of pre-Christian Gnosticism, see Edwin M. Yamauchi, *Pre-Christian Gnosticism: A Survey of the Proposed Evidences* (Grand Rapids: Eerdmans, 1973); idem, "Pre-Christian Gnosticism in the Nag Hammadi Texts?" *CH* 48 (1979): 129–41.

[188] Whether the collection belonged to a Gnostic group or a Gnostic believer, or whether it was a collection by orthodox Christians (perhaps from the monastery of Pachomias in nearby Chenoboskion) for heresiological purposes, is problematic. For

the latter view, see the article (with responses) by Torgny Save-Soderbergh, "Gnostic and Canonical Gospel Traditions," in Bianchi, *Origins*, 552–62; cf. Save-Soderbergh, "Holy Scriptures or Apologetic Documentations? The 'Sitz im Leben' of the Nag Hammadi Library," in J.-E. Ménard, *Les Textes de Nag Hammadi* (Leiden: Brill, 1975), 3–14. English translations of the Nag Hammadi materials are available in James M. Robinson, *The Nag Hammadi Library in English* (New York: Harper & Row, 1977). For a competent introduction to the literature, see Kurt Rudolf, *Gnosis. The Nature and History of Gnosticism*, ed. Robert McL. Wilson (San Francisco: Harper & Row, 1983), 34–52; cf. Andrew K. Helmbold, *The Nag Hammadi Gnostic Texts and the Bible* (Grand Rapids: Baker, 1967).

[189]Less attention has been given so far to the relationship between the Synoptic traditions and the rest of the Nag Hammadi literature, but see Robert McL. Wilson, "The New Testament in the Nag Hammadi Gospel of Philip," *NTS* 9 (1963): 291–94; Christopher Tuckett, "Synoptic Tradition in Some Nag Hammadi and Related Texts," *VC* 36 (1982): 173–90; Idem, "Synoptic Tradition in the Gospel of Truth and the Testimony of Truth," *JTS*, n.s., 35 (1984): 131–45. On Johannine traditions and Nag Hammadi cf. H. Koester, "Apocryphal and Canonical Gospels," *HTR* 73 (1980): 123–26.

[190]F. F. Bruce, "When is a Gospel not a Gospel?" *BJRL* 45 (1962–63): 319–39.

[191]Helmut Koester, "One Jesus and Four Primitive Gospels," *HTR* 61 (1968): 229 [reprinted in Robinson and Koester, *Trajectories*, 158–204].

[192]Koester, *"Gnomai Diaphoroi,"* 139. In a similar fashion Koester ("Apocryphal," 119–23) holds that the early second century *Papyrus Egerton 2* preserves traditions that antedate the canonical Gospels.

[193]Stevan L. Davies, *The Gospel of Thomas and Christian Wisdom* (New York: Seabury, 1983), 3.

[194]Cf. idem, "Thomas the Fourth Synoptic Gospel," *BA* 46 (1983): 14.

[195]See, for example, Gilles Quispel, "Some Remarks on the Gospel of Thomas, *NTS* 5 (1958–59): 276–90; "L'Evangile selon Thomas et les Clémentines," *VC* 12 (1958): 181–96; "L'Evangile selon Thomas et le Diatessaron," *VC* 13 (1959): 87–117; "The Gospel of Thomas and the New Testament," *VC* 11 (1957): 189–207 [the last three essays are reprinted in Quispel, *Gnostic Studies II* (Leiden: Nederlands Institute voor het Nabije Oosten, 1975)]; Hugh Montefiore, "A Comparison of the Parables of the Gospel According to Thomas and of the Synoptic Gospels," *NTS* 7 (1960–61): 220–48 (reprinted in H. E. W. Turner and Hugh Montefiore, *Thomas and the Evangelists* [Naperville: Allenson, 1962], 40–78).

More cautious treatments, which, however, do not deny the possibility of an independent tradition, include Oscar Cullmann, "The Gospel of Thomas and the Problem of the Age of the Tradition Contained Therein," *Int* 16 (1962): 418–38; Robert M. Grant and David N. Freedman, *The Secret Sayings of Jesus* (Garden City: Doubleday, 1960), 102–16; Hanson, *Tradition*, 228–32; H. E. W. Turner, "The Gospel of Thomas: Its History, Transmission and Sources," in Turner and Montefiore, *Thomas*, 11–39; Robert McL. Wilson, *Studies in the Gospel of Thomas* (London: Mowbray, 1960).

[196]"This does not necessarily imply that the new Sayings always represent a better tradition. The author of the Gospel of Thomas has modified the text which he found in his source, as can be proved in various cases; moreover the text we have now has undergone a revision by a gnosticizing redactor, as is proved by the Logia from Oxyrhynchus; and we cannot tell how much may have been lost in the translation from Greek into Coptic. We must have very strong arguments before we decide that in some cases the text of the new documents is to be preferred" (Quispel, *Gnostic Studies II*, 16).

[197]Koester, "Apocryphal," 107.

[198]See the arguments of Koester in the articles previously mentioned.

[199]Dungan, "Recent Study," 339.

[200]W. C. Van Unnik, "The 'Gospel of Truth' and the New Testament," in F. L. Cross, ed., *The Jung Codex* (London: Mowbray, 1955), 122. Van Unnik's ascription of this

writing to the pen of Valentinus himself has not been widely accepted, though most scholars recognize the *Gospel of Truth* as a product of Valentinian Gnosticism. See the discussion of Robert McL. Wilson, *Gnosis and the New Testament* (Oxford: Blackwell, 1968), 89–92.

[201] Robert McL. Wilson, *The Gospel of Philip* (New York: Harper & Row, 1962), 4–5. I am not sure on what grounds Wilson wishes to add the closing qualification in this sentence.

[202] Pelikan, *Catholic Tradition*, 92.

[203] Pheme Perkins, *The Gnostic Dialogue: The Early Church and the Crisis of Gnosticism* (New York: Paulist, 1980), 131–56; see also Elaine H. Pagels, "Visions, Appearances, and Apostolic Authority: Gnostic and Orthodox Traditions" in B. Aland, *Gnosis: Festschrift für Hans Jonas* (Göttingen: Vandenhoeck & Ruprecht, 1978), 415–30.

[204] E. C. Blackman, *Marcion and His Influence* London: SPCK, 1948), 3–4.

[205] Even the so-called "Marcionite Prologues" to the Pauline Epistles provide no unambiguous data for the reconstruction of Marcion's teaching. The Marcionite provenance of the prologues is questionable as well. See the discussions of Jürgen Regul (*Die Antimarcionitischen Evangelienprologe* [Freiburg: Herder, 1969], 84–94) and Nils A. Dahl ("The Origin of the Earliest Prologues to the Pauline Letters," *Semeia* 12 (1978): 233–77). The Marcionite character of the prologues has recently been affirmed by F. F. Bruce ("Some Thoughts on the Beginning of the New Testament Canon," *BJRL* 65 (1983): 45–46), and it forms an important assumption for the monograph by B. Joseph Hoffman, *Marcion: On the Restitution of Christianity* (Chico, Calif.: Scholars, 1984).

[206] Hoffman, *Marcion*, 31–74.

[207] Ibid. Hoffmann questions whether Marcion even journeyed to Rome.

[208] Robert M. Grant, *Gnosticism and Early Christianity* (New York: Columbia University Press, 1959), 126. Many have followed Harnack (*Marcion: Das Evangelium vom fremden Gott* [Leipzig: Hinrichs, 1924], 196–97) in arguing that the essence of Marcion's teaching was not Gnostic at all. For more recent discussion, see B. Aland "Marcion— Versuch einer neuen Interpretation," *Zeitschrift für Theologie und Kirche* 70 (1973): 420–47; David L. Balas, "Marcion Revisited: A 'Post-Harnack' Perspective," in *Texts and Testaments: critical essays on the Bible and early church fathers*, ed. W. Eugene March (San Antonio: Trinity University Press, 1980), 95–108; Ugo Bianchi, "Marcion: Théologien biblique ou docteur gnostique?" *VC* 21 (1967): 141–49; U. Schule, "Der Ursprung des Bosen bei Marcion," *Zeitschrift für Religions- und Geistegeschichte* 16 (1964): 23–42.

[209] Paul-Louis Couchoud ("Is Marcion's Gospel One of the Synoptics?" *Hibbert Journal* 34 [1935–36]: 265–77) argued that Luke's is an expanded and corrected edition of Marcion's gospel and was written about 145. A similar view was proposed by John Knox (*Marcion and the New Testament* [Chicago: University of Chicago Press, 1942], 114–39) who argued that Marcion's gospel was based on a proto-Luke that may have circulated as early as A.D. 116. Knox held that canonical Luke-Acts was written about 150 in response to Marcion. This position has recently been endorsed by Hoffman, *Marcion*, 113–34.

[210] Hoffman, *Marcion*, 107.

[211] Harnack, *Marcion*, 151. Harnack's view is adopted by Knox (*Marcion*, 19–31).

[212] Campenhausen, *Formation*, 148.

[213] For the literature regarding early Pauline collections see Guthrie, *Introduction*, 643–57.

[214] Defenders of a fourfold Gospel "canon" before Marcion have included Theodor Zahn (*Geschichte des Neutestamentlichen Kanons*, 2 vols. [Erlangen: Deichert, 1888–92], 1:654–80) and Harnack (*Origin*, 68–83). The idea is rejected by Campenhausen (*Formation*, 156–59), Knox (*Marcion*, 140–57), and Kenneth L. Carroll ("The Creation of the Fourfold Gospel," *BJRL* 37 [1954–55]: 68–77).

[215]Westcott's evaluation still wears well (*General Survey*, 317): "There is indeed no evidence to shew that any definite Canon of the Apostolic writings was already published in Asia Minor when Marcion's appeared; but the minute and varied hints which have been already collected tend to prove that if it were not expressly fixed it was yet implicitly determined by the practice of the Church. And though undue weight must not be attached to the language of his adversaries, it is not to be forgotten that they always charge him with mutilating something which already existed, and not with endeavouring to impose a test which was not generally received."

[216]See above, pp. 323–28.

[217]Knox, *Marcion*, 31.

[218]Campenhausen, *Formation*, 153; cf. Harnack, *Origin*, 59–60.

[219]For example, in Ignatius and Polycarp. See Farkasfalvy, "Early Development," 137–38.

[220]See the discussion of Hoffman, *Marcion*, 101–13.

[221]Irenaeus, *Haer.* 3.2.2. (*ANF*, 1:415).

[222]Farkasfalvy, "Early Development," 140.

[223]*Dial.* 35.5–6; cf. *1 Apol.* 26.5; 58.1.

[224]Irenaeus, *Haer.* 4.6.

[225]The intended audience of the *Dialogue*—whether Jewish, Pagan, or Christian—is itself a bone of contention and the ground of some of the divergence over Justin's canonical understanding. For surveys of this literature, see Charles H. Cosgrove, "Justin Martyr and the Emerging Christian Canon. Observations on the Purpose and Destination of the Dialogue with Trypho," *VC* 36 (1982): 209–32; Jon Nilson, "To Whom is Justin's *Dialogue with Trypho* Addressed?" *TS* 38 (1977): 538–46; Theodore Stylianopoulos, *Justin Martyr and the Mosaic Law* (Missoula: Scholars, 1975), 12-44, 169–95. My own opinion is that the *Dialogue* was intended to address Jews and at the same time function as a kind of apologetic manual for Christians. Cosgrove holds that the *Dialogue* was composed primarily for a Christian readership and that, therefore, the lack of reference to the subject of canon is indicative of Justin's own position. Thus, according to Cosgrove ("Justin Martyr," 209): "not only are the apostolic writings not esteemed as Scripture by Justin, but . . . he is in fact moving in an opposite direction from regarding them as such. Indeed, Justin represents a reversal of the trend of the church in the second century toward regarding apostolic writings as canon." I remain unconvinced by Cosgrove's reconstruction for a number of reasons: (1) Stylianopoulos's case for a Jewish readership and Justin's genuine concern for Jewish-Christian apologetics is stronger than Cosgrove allows; (2) at too many crucial points Cosgrove's case depends on the argument from silence; and (3) Cosgrove has probably understated the authority that Justin ascribed to the apostolic documents, at least to the Gospels.

[226]*Dial.* 119.9.

[227]*1 Apol.* 50.12; cf. 49.9.

[228]*1 Apol.* 66.3 (Otto, 1:182) *hoi gar apostoloi en tois genomenois hyp' autōn apomnemoneumasin, ha kaleitai euangelia, houtōs paredōkan entetalthai autois.*

[229]Leslie W. Barnard, *Justin Martyr. His Life and Thought* (Cambridge: Cambridge University Press, 1967), 56–57. R. G. Heard ("The *Apomnemoneumata* in Papias, Justin, and Irenaeus," *NTS* 1 [1954–55]: 122–29) contends that Justin's use of the term is dependent on Papias.

[230]In his writings, Justin refers to the "Memoirs" fifteen times but to the "Gospel(s)" only three times.

[231]Otto A. Piper, "The Nature of the Gospel According to Justin Martyr," *JR* 41 (1961): 159.

[232]Barnard, *Justin Martyr*, 58–60. Justin includes a very few details not given in the Synoptics, e.g., that Jesus was born in a cave and that the Magi came from Arabia

(*Dial.* 75). Whether this is oral tradition or based on some other written source cannot be determined. In any case, as Barnard notes, "The soberness of Justin's narrative is in marked contrast to the accounts in the second-century Apocryphal Gospels which go in for many embellishments" (p. 59).

²³³Eric Francis Osborn, *Justin Martyr* (Tübingen: Mohr, 1973), 125–31.

²³⁴A discussion of the parallels is found in Joseph N. Sanders, *The Fourth Gospel in the Early Church* (Cambridge: Cambridge University Press, 1943), 27–32.

²³⁵*Contra* Sanders, *Fourth Gospel*, 31. John S. Romanides ("Justin Martyr and the Fourth Gospel," *GOR* 4 (1958–59): 115–34) suggests that Justin's hesitancy in regard to citations of the Gospel of John derives from the more mystical quality of this Gospel compared with the Synoptics. The nature of the teaching in John would have been deemed less appropriate for non-Christians. "From all indications Justin was a catechist and as such based his whole method of teaching on the Old Testament and the Synoptic Tradition. It was more than natural that his dealings *tois ekso* be dominated more by these works than by the Gospel of John and the epistles of Paul" (p. 128).

²³⁶*Dial.* 81.4.

²³⁷Barnard, *Justin Martyr*, 62–63; cf. Osborn, *Justin Martyr*, 135–38.

²³⁸Willis A. Shotwell, *The Biblical Exegesis of Justin Martyr* (London: SPCK, 1965), 28.

²³⁹*1 Apol.* 67.3. This is the conclusion of Flesseman-van Leer (*Tradition*, 76) and Frank (*Der Sinn*, 124); but cf. Shotwell, *Biblical Exegesis*, 28.

²⁴⁰That Justin is out of step with the general development of the second century is held by Cosgrove (see discussions above, n. 225) and by Piper ("The Gospel"). The latter holds that the very nature of the gospel precludes for Justin the possibility of a New Testament canon. "The perfect work of Jesus does not allow the placement of the Scriptures of the New Covenant on the same level with the Savior. For it is the Logos himself whom we encounter in the work of Jesus, and thus the *euangelion* is not a word of God once spoken (= *Deus dixit*) but rather the Logos as he proclaims himself to us in the ongoing work of Jesus, just as he had done in the proclamation of the prophets" (p. 162). This is good rhetoric, but only an enthusiastic Barthian could find such a view in Justin.

. ²⁴¹On the importance of unity as a fundamental theme of Irenaean theology see the references and discussion in André Benoit, *Saint Irénée. Introduction à L'Etude de sa Théologie* (Paris: Presses Universitaires de France, 1960), 203–19.

²⁴²Irenaeus, *Haer.* 4.10.1 (*ANF*, 1:473); cf. ibid., 4.11.1 (*ANF*, 1:474).

²⁴³Denis Farkasfalvy, "Theology of Scripture in Irenaeus," *RBén* 78 (1968): 321.

²⁴⁴Irenaeus, *Haer.* 5. praef (*SC*, 153:10–11). For the variety of ways in which Irenaeus coordinates Old and New Testament citations, see J. Hoh, *Die Lehre des Hl. Irenaeus über des Neue Testament* (Münster: Aschendorffschen Verlagsbuchhandlung, 1919), 75–78, 200–202.

²⁴⁵Irenaeus, *Haer.* 3. praef. (*ANF*, 1:414); cf. ibid., 3.2.1; 3.5.1.

²⁴⁶In the whole of *Against All Heresies*, New Testament quotations are nearly twice as frequent as Old Testament quotations. See Benoit, *Saint Irénée*, 105–6.

²⁴⁷Campenhausen, *Formation*, 185.

²⁴⁸Ibid., 185–86.

²⁴⁹Irenaeus, *Haer.* 3.12.7 (*SC*, 211:212): *Ecclesia uero per uniuersum mundum, ab apostolis firmum habens initium.*

²⁵⁰Ibid., 3. praef. (*SC*, 211:20): *Etenim Dominus omnium dedit apostolis suis potestatem Euanglii, per quos et ueritatem, hoc est Dei Filii doctrinam, coegnouimus; et quibus dixit Dominus: Qui uos audit me audit, et qui uos contemnit me contemnit et eum qui me misit.*

²⁵¹Ibid., 3.1.1 (*SC*, 211:20): *postea uero per Dei uoluntatem in Scripturis nobis tradiderunt, fundamentum et columnam fidei nostrae futurum.*

²⁵²Flesseman-van Leer, *Tradition*, 139–44; cf. D. E. Lanne, "Le ministère apostolique dans l'oeuvre de Saint Irénée,"*Irénikon* 25 (1952): 133: "Prédication et Ecritures sont deux aspects de la même tradition apostolique vivante dans l'Eglise; quand il le faut, saint Irénée les distingue, mais dans son esprit elles sont constamment sur le même plan et ne forment qu'une unique réalité."

²⁵³Irenaeus, *Haer.* 3.2.1–2.

²⁵⁴Ibid., 3.3.1–4.

²⁵⁵Ibid., 2.28.2 (*SC*, 294:270): *rectissime scientes quia Scripturae quidem perfectae sunt, quippe a Verbo Dei et Spiritu eius dictae.*

²⁵⁶Farkasfalvy, "Early Development," 145.

²⁵⁷Hoh, *Die Lehre*, 5; Benoit, *Saint Irénée*, 109.

²⁵⁸Irenaeus, *Haer.* 3.11.8 (*SC*, 211:161).

²⁵⁹Ibid. 3.11.9.

²⁶⁰Oscar Cullmann ("The Plurality of the Gospels as the Theological Problem in Antiquity," in *The Early Church*, 39–54) criticizes Irenaeus for falling into a type of Docetism: "Irenaeus, therefore, represents the fourfold Gospel as a miracle. He tries to show that this is not based on a purely human situation at all. But this line of argument leads him into dangerous waters. For it means that at bottom he admits that purely human circumstances were left out of account when the Gospels were formed into a group" (p. 52). But could not Cullmann's talk of "purely human circumstances" equally easily be tagged as Ebionism? The problem is Cullmann's disjunction between human and divine activity.

²⁶¹Benoit (*Saint Irénée*, 120): "L'Evangile écrit appartient donc bien à la tradition de l'Eglise. C'est pour cette raison, et il n'y en a pas d'autre, que seul les quatre évangiles peuvent être reconnus par l'Eglise."

²⁶²Hoh, *Die Lehre*, 41–45; Benoit, *Saint Irénée*, 127–29.

²⁶³That the Pauline letters were not fully canonical for Irenaeus was first proposed by Johannes Werner (*Der Paulinismus des Irenaeus* [Leipzig: Hinrichs'sche, 1889], 46): "Nach alledem hat Iren. als Zuege der im Vollzug begriffenen Canonisierung der paulinischen Briefe zu gelten, nicht aber des vollendeten Abschlusses dieses Prozesses." Benoit (*Saint Irénée*, 130–41) follows Werner with reservations. Werner's thesis is rejected by F. R. M. Hitchcock, *Irenaeus of Lugdunum. A Study of His Teaching* (Cambridge: Cambridge University Press, 1914), 226–29; Hoh, *Die Lehre*, 64–65, 90–91; John Lawson, *The Biblical Theology of Saint Irenaeus* (London: Epworth, 1946), 46–49; Pierre Nautin, "Irénée et la canonicité des Epîtres pauliniennes," *RHR* 182 (1972): 113–30.

²⁶⁴Benoit, *Saint Irénée*, 122–27, 141–46; Lawson, *Biblical Theology*, 49–50.

²⁶⁵Irenaeus also refers to *Hermas* and *1 Clement* as *graphē*; however, this is not decisive in favor of the scriptural status of these writings, for Irenaeus is not entirely consistent in his usage. See Werner, *Der Paulinismus*, 36–37.

²⁶⁶Hoh (*Die Lehre*, 78–86) believes that if the New Testament writings functioned in a material sense on the same plane as the Old Testament, they must also have formed a well-circumscribed complex. But the logic of a theological construct is not necessarily the same as its historical development. Hoh's position is possible but not convincing.

²⁶⁷Pelikan, *Catholic Tradition*, 113.

²⁶⁸Eusebius, *HE* 4.26.14 (Loeb, 1:392–93).

²⁶⁹But cf. W. C. van Unnik, "*H kainē diathēkē*—a Problem in the early history of the Canon," *Studia Patristica* 4 (1961): 219.

²⁷⁰Eusebius, *HE* 5.16 (Loeb, 1:472–73).

[271] Campenhausen, *Formation*, 266. W. C. van Unnik ("De la règle *Mēte protheinai mēte aphelein* dans l'histoire du canon," *VC* 3 [1949]: 36) earlier argued, "il me parait incontestable qu'il faut penser chez Anti-montaniste à une *diathēkē* écrite et fixe, à un recueil d'écrits." Later, however, he took *kainē diathēkē* as a reference to the Christian era ("H *kainē diathēkē*," 218).

[272] Timothy D. Barnes, "The Chronology of Montanism," *JTS* 21 (1970): 403–8.

[273] Pelikan, *Catholic Tradition*, 100.

[274] See the discussion and literature cited by H. Paulsen, "Die Bedeutung des Montanismus für die Herausbildung des Kanons," *VC* 32 (1978): 19–52.

[275] Ibid., 22–23: "Prüft man unvoreingenommen die relevanten Texte—sei es des Montanismus selber, sei es seiner Gegner—, so zeigt sich allerdings, dass die Frage nach der Normativität und der Gültigkeit neutestamentlicher Texte überhaupt nicht strittig ist, jedenfalls eine auffallend geringe Rolle spielt."

[276] Andrew F. Walls, "The Montanist 'Catholic Epistle' and its New Testament Prototype," *SE* III (Berlin: Akademie-Verlag, 1964), 443; likewise Campenhausen, *Formation*, 227; Paulsen, "Die Bedeutung," 28–29.

[277] Adolf Hamel, *Kirche bei Hippolyt von Rom* (Gutersloh: Bertelsmann, 1951), 122; Pelikan, *Catholic Tradition*, 106–8.

[278] A major challenge to the common dating of the Muratorianum was offered by Albert C. Sundberg ("Canon Muratori: A Fourth Century List," *HTR* 66 (1973): 1–41), who contended that "there are several salient features of Canon Muratori that have no place in the early western church but find their earliest parallels in the eastern church during the late third and fourth centuries" (p. 34). Sundberg has been effectively answered and the traditional view defended by Everett Ferguson ("Canon Muratori: Date and Provenance," in *Studia Patristica*, ed. E. A. Livingstone (Oxford: Pergamon, 1982), 17:677–83). The Latin texts of the Muratorianum may be found in Zahn, *Geschichte*, 2:1:1–143 (with commentary); F. W. Grosheide, ed., *Some Early Lists of the Books of the New Testament* (Leiden: Brill, 1948), 5–11; Lagrange, *Canon*, 68–74 (with French translation and commentary). An English translation is given in Edgar Hennecke and Wilhelm Schneemelcher, *New Testament Apocrypha*, trans. Robert McL. Wilson, 2 vols. (Philadelphia: Westminster, 1963), 1:42–44.

[279] A clever conjecture by S. P. Tregelles, based upon the hypothesis of a Greek original for the Muratorianum, resolves the problem. By this conjecture the canon would ascribe the Wisdom of Solomon to Philo and, therefore, exclude it from either the Old Testament or the New. See the discussion of Lagrange (*Canon*, 74–75), who accepts the conjecture. But on the problem of a Greek original for the Muratorianum, see Bruce ("Some Thoughts," 56).

[280] Adolf Jülicher, *Einleitung in das Neue Testament*, 7th ed. (Tübingen: Mohr, 1931), 495. He is followed by Hennecke and Schneemelcher, *Apocrypha*, 1:36.

[281] Johannes Beumer, "Das Fragmentum Muratori und seine Ratsel," *TP* 48 (1973): 548–49; Campenhausen, *Formation*, 259–60.

[282] Frank, *Der Sinn*, 183–84. "Das Johannesevangelium ist für den Canon Muratori offensichtlich nicht nur einfach das bedeutendste Evangelium, es ist für den Verfasser offenbar überhaupt die massgebende Schrift des Kanons: Das Johannesevangelium ist kraft der Autorität aller Apostel offenkundig der 'Kanon im Kanon' " (p. 184).

[283] Campenhausen, *Formation*, 261.

[284] Lagrange, *Canon*, 61–63; cf. the very similar accounts of G. N. Bonwetsch, *Studien zu den Kommentaren Hippolyts zum Buche Daniel und Hohen Liede*, TU, 1:2 (Leipzig: Hinrich'sche, 1897), 21–26; Adhemar D'Ales, *La Théolgie de Saint Hippolyte* (Paris: Beauchesne, 1906), 114–15.

[285] See the list of citations in Bonwetsch, *Studien*, 25.

[286] Tertullian, *Marc.* 4.2.1 (Evans, 2:261).

287John F. Janson, "Tertullian and the New Testament," *The Second Century* 2 (1982): 191; cf. Adhemar D'Ales, *La Théologie de Tertullian* (Paris: Beauchesne, 1905), 227-29.

288Tertullian, *Pudic.* 20. Jansen ("Tertullian," 193) believes that Tertullian did not view Hebrews as "canonical"; likewise Westcott, *General Survey*, 371. Campenhausen (*Formation*, 233) writes that Tertullian "makes an attempt to rescue the canonicity of the epistle." Flesseman-van Leer (*Tradition*, 174) holds that Tertullian accepted the canonicity of Hebrews on the same grounds that he accepted Mark and Luke.

289Tertullian *Pudic* 20; cf. ibid., 10.12

290Tertullian *Marc* 4.5; *Praescrip* 36.

291Flesseman-van Leer, *Tradition*, 174.

292Campenhausen, *Formation*, 266.

293Otto Stählin, *Clemens Alexandrinus. Register. GCS* 39 (Leipzig: Hinrichs, 1934), 1-26.

294Eusebius *HE* 6.14.1-3.

295See the citations in Stählin, *Register*, 30-59.

296The most extensive discussion of Clement's canonical understanding (Old and New Testament) is J. Ruwet, "Clement d'Alexandria, Canon des Ecritures et apocryphes," *Bib* 29 (1948): 77-99, 240-68, 391-408. For Clement's use of apocryphal gospels, see 396-401.

297See, for example, Henry Chadwick, *Early Christian Thought and the Classical Tradition* (New York: Oxford University Press, 1966), 40-48; Jean Daniélou, *Gospel Message and Hellenistic Culture*, trans. J. A. Baker (Philadelphia: Westminster, 1973), 48-68.

298Campenhausen, *Formation*, 296. The attempt to distinguish levels of authority by examining the manner of citation is also rejected by Lagrange (*Histoire*, 90): "Cette tentative nous parait désespérée et d'ailleurs inutile."

299Campenhausen, *Formation*, 295-96; cf. R. B. Tollington, *Clement of Alexandria: A Study of Christian Liberalism*, 2 vols. (London: Williams and Norgate, 1914), 2:175: "His rule or canon is something other than a list of authoritative writings, and to a very large extent his strong preferences and affinities determine his use of the Church's literature, rather than any decision of authority from without. Thus, while it is quite clear that Clement attached less weight to the Epistle of Barnabas than he did to the Epistles of St. Paul, it would be going beyond our evidence to declare that this was because the latter were canonical and the former not. The grounds for the different degrees of authority are not explicitly declared. What the Lord had said was of primary weight. What could claim to be "Apostolic" came next in order. These distinctions were unquestioned and sufficient. Beyond them, lay a domain where some questions were still undecided or unrecognised."

300Origen, *Hom. on Luke I* (PG, 13:1801). Cf. also the quotation from Origen's *Commentaries on Matthew* preserved in Eusebius *HE* 6.25.3-6.

301Eusebius, *HE* 6.25.7-14. On the possibility that Eusebius has misrepresented Origen's views by unduly restricting the number of acknowledged books in Origen's "canon," see Lagrange, *Histoire*, 95-100.

302Cf. the slightly different conclusions of Goodspeed, *Formation*, 92; Hanson, *Origen's Doctrine*, 138-42; Souter, *Canon*, 183. Goodspeed (*Formation*, 93) argues for a twenty-nine book canon for Origen (our New Testament plus Hermas and Barnabas) and suggests that Origen's views were determinative for the shape of codex Sinaiticus, produced in Alexandria nearly a century later and consisting of precisely the same twenty-nine books.

303In an effort to maintain a more restrictive canon for Origen, some Roman Catholic scholars have distinguished between those books that Origen held to be both inspired and canonical and those he took to be inspired but *not* canonical (e.g.,

Barnabas, Hermas, Didache); thus, J. Ruwet, "Les 'Antilegomena' dans les Oeuvres d'Origène," *Bib* 23 (1942): 18–42; cf. Lagrange, *Histoire*, 101–3. Westcott (*General Survey*, 358–65) largely bypasses the question of the use of extracanonical writings by either Clement or Origen.

[304]Hanson, *Origen's Doctrine*, 143. William R. Farmer ("A Study of the Development of the New Testament Canon," in William R. Farmer and Denis Farkasfalvy, *The Formation of the New Testament Canon: An Ecumenical Approach* [New York: Paulist, 1983], 14–26) explains the difference between the two Alexandrians as deriving in part from "the diverging perception of martyrdom held by Clement and Origen. For Clement, martyrdom was not as important as it was for Origen" (p. 14). The suggestion is intriguing, but, as Farmer's long discussion confirms, it is more easily asserted than demonstrated by the evidence.

[305]*Works of Martin Luther*, 6 vols. (Philadelphia: Muhlenberg, 1943), 2:261.

[306]William Tyndale, *Expositions and Notes on Sundry Portions of the Holy Scriptures, together with the Practice of Prelates*, ed. Henry Walker, The Parker Society Series, 55 vols. (Cambridge: Cambridge University Press, 1849), 43:333.

[307]Augustine, *Against the Epistle of Manichaeus* 5 (*NPNF1*, 4:131).

[308]*Works of Martin Luther*, 2:452–53.

[309]Calvin, *Institutes*, 1.7.3 (Battles' ed., 77).

[310]Martin Chemnitz, *Examination of the Council of Trent. Part 1*, trans. Fred Kramer (St. Louis: Concordia, 1971), 189; cf. Heinrich Schmid, *The Doctrinal Theology of the Evangelical Lutheran Church*, 3d ed., rev., trans. C. A. Hay and H. E. Jacobs (Minneapolis: Augsburg, 1899), 89–91.

[311]For the more recent discussion among conservative Lutherans, see Francis Pieper, *Christian Dogmatics*, 4 vols. (St. Louis: Concordia, 1950), 1:330–38.

[312]Calvin, *Institutes* 1.7.1–5; Gerrit C. Berkouwer, *Holy Scripture*, trans. Jack Rogers (Grand Rapids: Eerdmans, 1975), 75; Schmid, *Doctrinal Theology*, 87.

[313]John Calvin, *Commentaries on the Epistles of Paul to the Galatians and Ephesians*, trans. William Pringle (Grand Rapids: Eerdmans, 1948), 249.

[314]Louis Gaussen, *The Canon of the Holy Scriptures Examined in the Light of History*, trans. Edward N. Kirk (Boston: American Tract Society, 1862), 422, 424.

[315]Archibald Alexander, *Evidences of the Authenticity, Inspiration, and Canonical Authority of the Holy Scripture* (Philadelphia: Presbyterian Board of Publication, n.d.), 269.

[316]See the chapter in this volume by John D. Woodbridge (pp. 237–70).

[317]Werner Georg Kümmel, *The New Testament: the History of the Investigation of Its Problems*, trans. S. McLean Gilmour and Howard C. Kee (Nashville: Abingdon, 1972), 68.

[318]Hermann Strathmann, "Die Krisis des Kanons der Kirche," in *Das Neue Testament als Kanon*, ed. Ernst Käsemann (Göttingen: Vandenhoeck & Ruprecht, 1970), 45.

[319]Quoted in Kümmel, *Investigation*, 63.

[320]Ibid., 62–65.

[321]Gerhard Maier, *The End of the Historical Critical Method*, trans. Edwin W. Levereng and Rudolf F. Norden (St. Louis: Concordia, 1977), 11.

[322]James Barr has discussed the canon in a series of works: *The Bible in the Modern World* (New York: Harper & Row, 1973); *Holy Scripture: Canon, Authority, Criticism* (Philadelphia: Westminster, 1983); *The Scope and Authority of the Bible* (Philadelphia: Westminster, 1980).

[323]Idem, *Holy Scripture*, 123.

[324]Ibid., 33–37.

[325] Ibid., 14.

[326] Idem, *Scope*, 120; *Holy Scripture*, 41; *Bible*, 155.

[327] Idem, *Holy Scripture*, 63.

[328] Idem, *Bible*, 118–19.

[329] Ibid., 120.

[330] Ibid., 154–55; cf. *Holy Scripture*, 74.

[331] Idem, *Bible*, 115.

[332] Ibid., 118; cf. *Scope*, 52.

[333] Idem, *Scope*, 52.

[334] Ibid., 53.

[335] Ibid., 64; cf. 55.

[336] Ibid., 54.

[337] Ibid., 62–63.

[338] Idem, *Scope*, 64.

[339] Idem, *Holy Scriptures*, 73.

[340] Concerning Barr's notion that "the men of the Bible had no Bible: there was no Bible in the biblical period" (idem, *Scope*, 56), see the critique of D. A. Carson, "Three Books on the Bible: A Critical Review," *JETS* 26 (1983): 351.

[341] Brevard S. Childs, *Biblical Theology in Crisis* (Philadelphia: Westminster, 1970), 99.

[342] Idem, *Old Testament*, 40–41.

[343] Ibid., 58–59.

[344] Idem, *New*, 21.

[345] Idem, *Old*, 75; cf. *New*, 21–22.

[346] Idem, *New*, 22.

[347] Ibid., 24.

[348] Ibid., 42; *Old*, 44.

[349] Idem, *New*, 44; cf. *Biblical Theology*, 99: "The fundamental theological issue at stake is not the extent of the canon, which has remained in some flux within Christianity, but the claim for a normative body of tradition contained in a set of books."

[350] Idem, *New*, 35.

[351] Idem, *Biblical Theology*, 105.

[352] Ibid., 104; cf. *New*, 29, 44.

[353] Idem, *Old*, 81–82.

[354] Karl Barth, *The Epistle to the Romans*, 6th ed., trans. Edwyn C. Hoskyns (London: Oxford University Press, 1933), 6.

[355] Nicolaus Appel, *Kanon und Kirche. Die Kanonkrise im heutigen Protestantismus als kontroverstheologisches Problem* (Paderborn: Bonifacius-Druckerei, 1964); "The New Testament Canon: Historical Process and Spirit's Witness," *TS* 32 (1971): 627–46.

[356] Idem, *Kanon*, 354.

[357] Ibid.

[358] Ibid., 17–23.

[359] Ibid., 355.

[360] Ibid., 353–60. On the biblical use of metaphors to describe the church, see Edmund P. Clowney, "Interpreting the Biblical Models of the Church: A Hermeneutical Deepening of Ecclesiology," in *Biblical Interpretation and the Church: The Problem of Contextualization*, ed. D. A. Carson (Nashville: Thomas Nelson, 1984), 64–109.

[361] Karl Rahner, *Inspiration of the Bible*, trans. Charles H. Henkey, 2d ed., rev. Martin Palmer (New York: Herder and Herder, 1964), 27–28. For Rahner's modification of the older view, see pp. 67–72.

[362] Appel, "New Testament," 629, 638, 645.

[363] Ibid., 640.

[364] Idem, *Kanon*, 377.

[365] Idem, "New Testament," 645; cf. 639.

[366] Ibid., 639.

[367] Ibid., 645–46; cf. *Kanon*, 363–64. Some recent Catholic writers are not sure that the infallibility of the church implies a closed canon; cf. Thomas A. Hoffman, "Inspiration, Normativeness, Canonicity, and the Unique Sacred Character of the Bible" *CBQ* 44 (1982): 462–65.

[368] Appel, *Kanon*, 364; cf. "New Testament," 641. Appel objects to Barth's suggestion (*Church Dogmatics*, trans. G. T. Thompson and Harold Knight [Edinburgh: T. & T. Clark, 1956], 1:2:476) that Scripture gives to the question of canonicity its own divine, infallible, and definitive answer, which is nevertheless heard by the church in a human and fallible way. Appel (*Kanon*, 55) replies, "Eine Antwort 'an sich' ist aber u. E. keine Antwort, sondern ein Selbst-gesprach . . . Eine unfehlbare Antwort, die nicht als unfehlbare gehört wird, is keine unfehlbare *Antwort*."

[369] Appel, "New Testament," 629, 638.

[370] Ibid., 629.

[371] Ibid., 646.

[372] Ridderbos, *Authority*; idem, "The Canon of the New Testament" in *Revelation and the Bible*, ed. Carl F. H. Henry (Grand Rapids: Baker, 1958), 189–201. Berkouwer (*Holy Scripture*, 67–104) follows Ridderbos very closely. A similar approach is developed independently by Oscar Cullmann (*Salvation in History*, trans. Sidney G. Sowers [London: SCM, 1967], 293–304).

[373] Ridderbos, *Authority*, 27; cf. "Canon," 192–96.

[374] Idem, *Authority*, 27.

[375] Ibid., 27–28.

[376] Ibid., 29–30.

[377] Ibid., 33–37; "Canon," 196–97.

[378] Idem, *Authority*, 41.

[379] Ibid., 42–45; idem, "Canon," 198–99.

[380] Idem, *Authority*, 47–51; idem, "Canon," 199–200.

[381] Idem, "Canon," 200.

[382] Ibid., 201; idem, *Authority*, 39, 51,

[383] Idem, *Authority*, 39.

[384] Ibid.

[385] For example, Barr, *Holy Scripture*, 41.

[386] Benjamin B. Warfield, *The Inspiration and Authority of the Bible* (Philadelphia: Presbyterian and Reformed, 1948), 415. The tendency to assume that for the early church the concepts of tradition, Scripture, and canon were equivalent is also present in the works of Alexander (*Canonical Authority*) and Harris (*Inspiration and Canonicity*).

[387] Ned B. Stonehouse, "The Authority of the New Testament" in *The Infallible Word*, ed. Woolley, 97.

[388] Ridderbos, "Canon," 200.

[389] Ellen Flesseman-van Leer, "Prinzipien der Sammlung und Ausscheidung bei der Bildung des Kanons," *Zeitschrift für Theologie und Kirche* 61 (1964): 418.

[390] Campenhausen, *Formation*, 330.

[391] Eusebius, *HE* 6.12.2ff.

[392] Guthrie, *Introduction*, 736–39, 884–86.

[393] See above, n. 109.

[394] This explicit distinction between the apostolic age and the subsequent history of the church was first formulated by Hippolytus of Rome (c. 200). See Pelikan, *Catholic Tradition*, 106–7.

[395] Stonehouse, "Authority," 138–39; cf. Farkasfalvy, "Early Development," 159–60.

[396] John Warwick Montgomery, "The Theologian's Craft" *CTM* 37 (1966): 86n.72.

[397] Ibid.

[398] Cullmann, "Plurality," 52.

Index of Persons

Abbott, Walter M., 364, 410
Abraham, William J., 29–30, 39–40, 179, 363, 365, 369, 370, 397, 399
Achtemeier, Paul, 20, 139–40, 180, 190–91, 363, 368, 372, 388, 398, 400
Ackerman, James S., 33, 370
Ackroyd, Peter R., 426
Aeschbacher, 275
Ahern, Barnabas M., 393
Ahlstrom, Sydney E., 367, 368
Aland, Barbara, 437
Aland, Kurt, 145, 391, 427
Alexander, Archibald, 11, 344, 443, 445
Alexander, Loveday C. A., 371
Alexander the Great, 141, 152, 169–73, 396, 397
Alford, Henry, 366, 383
Alleman, Daniel von, 43, 372
Allen, Don, 416
Alsted, Johann Heinrich, 256
Alston, William P., 87, 381
Althaus, Paul, 413, 432
Amphilochius, 429, 432
Anderson, G. N., 426, 430
Andrew of St. Victor, 182
Aner, Karl, 264, 419
Appel, Nicolaus, 350–52, 355–56, 444, 445
Aquinas, Thomas, 182, 367, 398, 403
Archer, Gleason L., Jr., 391, 393, 394, 395, 426
Aristandrus, 171
Aristobulus, 169, 173
Aristotle, 60, 85, 87, 367, 376, 381
Arnauld, 251
Arndt, William F., 391
Arrian, 152, 169–73, 396, 397
Arsames, 171
Athanasius, 14, 308, 317, 428, 429, 431, 432
Atkinson, R. F., 387
Attridge, H. W., 396
Augustine, 17, 22, 82, 244, 246, 253, 255–56, 258–59, 263–64, 269, 310, 317, 342–43, 379, 380, 410, 411, 412, 415, 419, 428, 429, 443
Auld, A. G., 165, 395
Aune, David, 36, 313, 371, 430, 431

Austin, J. L., 53, 86–88, 94–95, 381, 382, 383
Autophradates, 171
Auvray, Paul, 413, 415
Bacon, B. W., 426
Bacon, Francis, 53, 261
Bahnsen, Greg L., 389
Baile, Guillaume, 251
Baillie, John, 406, 407
Baird, J. A., 142, 389
Baird, R. D., 390
Baker, David, 195, 399, 401
Baker, J. A., 432, 442
Balas, David L., 437
Baldwin, J. G., 426
Balmer, Randall H., 365, 406
Banks, Robert, 400
Baridon, Michel, 412
Barin, Theodore, 416
Barnabas, 316, 327–28, 340, 341, 435, 442, 443
Barnabas, Steven, 402
Barnard, Leslie W., 438, 439
Barnaud, Barthélemy, 419
Barnes, Annie, 416
Barnes, Timothy, 441
Barr, James, 20, 53–56, 64–65, 69, 71, 81, 91, 97, 104, 345–49, 363, 364, 368, 374, 375, 377, 389, 400, 443, 444, 445
Barrett, C. K., 386, 388
Barth, G., 392, 393
Barth, Karl, 10–11, 26, 57–58, 128, 220–22, 224, 233, 246, 275–94, 350, 369, 387, 406, 421, 422, 423, 424, 444, 445
Barthélemy, D., 429
Bartlett, David L., 81, 363, 380
Barton, D. M., 426
Barton, John, 72, 75, 79, 377, 378
Bartsch, H. W., 391
Barzanes, 171
Barzun, Jacques, 390
Basil the Great, 432
Basinger, David, 45, 373
Basinger, Randall, 45, 373
Basnage, Jacques, 255, 415
Battles, Ford Lewis, 369, 431, 443

Bauckham, Richard, 153, 393, 396, 428
Bauer, Walter, 300, 322–23, 433
Baumgarten, S. J., 420
Baur, F. C., 43, 122–130, 132, 385, 386, 387
Bavinck, Herman, 11, 226, 233, 406, 407
Baxter, Richard, 255, 415
Bayle, Pierre, 252, 254, 414, 415
Beare, F. W., 140, 389
Beck, 420
Beck, N. A., 393
Beckwith, R. T., 314, 430, 431
Beecher, Willis J., 402
Beegle, Dewey, 24, 191, 193, 369, 400
Beer, Arthur, 367, 417
Beer, Peter, 367, 417
Bellarmine, Robert, 251, 417
Bengel, J. A., 383, 419
Benoit, André, 439, 440
Benoit, Pierre, 402, 403
Benson, Bruce, 414,
Bentley, William, 254–55, 415
Berkeley, George, 229
Berkouwer, Gerrit C., 11, 221, 225–29, 233, 363, 372, 406, 407, 408, 409, 443, 445
Bessus, 171
Bethell, Tom, 269, 421
Betts, C. J., 250, 412, 413
Betz, Otto, 401
Beumer, Johannes, 441
Beyer, Hartman, 416
Beyer, Hermann Wolfgang, 425
Bianchi, Ugo, 435, 436, 437
Bierberg, Rudolf, 403
Bilheimer, Robert S., 408
Birn, Raymond, 412
Bizer, Ernst, 258, 410, 416
Black, Matthew, 400
Blackman, E. C. 437
Blenkinsopp, Joseph, 425
Bloch, M., 390
Bloch, R., 401
Blocher, Henri, 260, 417
Bloesch, Donald G., 364, 368, 371, 425
Blomberg, Craig L., 22, 34, 370, 371, 389, 390, 391, 392, 393, 394, 396
Blumenberg, Hans, 419
Bodin, Jean, 258, 417
Bonsirven, Joseph, 401
Bonwetsch, G. N., 441
Bornkamm, Günther, 156, 392, 393
Bornkamm, Heinrich, 183, 399
Borza, E. N., 396
Bossuet, Jacques Bénigne, 254
Bosworth, A. B., 170–72, 396, 397
Bots, Hans, 247, 412
Bowden, John 421, 426

Bozemann, Theodore Dwight, 367
Brack, O. M., Jr., 413
Brahms, Johannes, 73
Breckenridge J., 390
Bredvold, Louis, 413
Brerewood, Edward, 415
Briggs, Charles, 10, 242, 427
Broadus, John Albert, 383
Bromiley, Geoffrey W., 36–37, 243, 365, 398, 407, 410, 422, 424
Brooks, Cleanth, 69–71, 73, 377
Brooks, Richard Stoddard, 418
Brown, Colin, 373, 380
Brown, Harold O. J., 43, 372
Brown, Raymond, 201–4, 209, 364, 392, 402, 403
Brown, S., 392
Brownlee, William H., 429
Bruce, F. F., 388, 400, 403, 404, 425, 427, 429, 431, 433, 436, 437, 441
Brunner, Emil, 57, 282, 375, 423
Brunt, P. A., 170, 396
Bucer, Martin, 256, 265, 416, 419
Buchanan, George Wesley, 404
Bultmann, Rudolf, 23, 151, 227, 278, 289, 322, 369, 392, 422
Burnet, Thomas, 420
Burns, R. M., 413, 414
Burke, Edmund, 75
Burtchaell, James T., 242, 253, 379, 410
Butler, R. J., 376
Butterfield, Herbert, 128–29, 387
Byatt, A., 167, 396
Cahill, P. Joseph, 40, 372
Callisthenes, 171
Calvin, John, 11, 13, 17, 28, 44, 183, 189, 220–21, 224, 232–33, 243–44, 256, 259–60, 263–65, 269, 275, 281–82, 343, 373, 384, 406, 407, 408, 409, 410, 416, 417, 418, 419, 420, 431, 443
Cameron, N. M. de S., 386
Campenhausen, Hans von, 299, 331, 335, 338–39, 425, 432, 437, 438, 439, 441, 442, 445
Camus, Albert, 254
Carmichael, Gershom, 367
Carmignac, Jean, 321, 433
Carnell, Corbin, 379
Carpenter, Joel, 368
Carroll, Kenneth L., 437
Carroll, Robert P., 370, 415
Carson, Alexander, 12
Carson, D. A., 102–103, 140, 146, 154, 161, 363, 364, 368, 369, 370, 371, 372, 373, 374, 379, 383, 389, 390, 391, 392, 393, 394, 397, 399, 400, 403, 404, 405, 406, 420, 421, 425, 427, 444

Cartwright, R., 376
Catchpole, D. R., 394
Cavallin, H. C. C., 404
Cavell, Stanley, 82, 380
Cerinthus, 317
Chadwick, Henry, 412, 442
Charles, R. H., 429, 430, 431
Charles-Daubert, Francois, 414
Charron, 254
Chemnitz, Martin, 343, 443
Cheney, J. M., 391
Childs, Brevard S., 44, 82, 209, 299, 345, 348–50, 373, 380, 381, 424, 426, 444
Chilton, Bruce D., 372, 396
Chouet, Jean-Robert, 417, 418
Christensen, Michael J., 378, 379
Cicero, 144
Cicognani, 290
Clark, Gordon H., 59–60, 62, 71, 375
Claude, Jean, 251
Cleanthes, 428
Cleitus, 171, 172
Clement of Alexandria, 316, 323–24, 325, 326, 328, 340–41, 442, 443
Clement of Rome, 434
Clowney, Edmund P., 407, 444
Coggins, R. J., 164, 302, 395, 426
Cohen, N. G., 396
Cohen, S. J. D., 166, 396
Cohon, Samuel S., 384
Coleridge, Samuel Taylor, 70, 242
Collingwood, R. G., 387
Collins, Anthony, 254–55, 257, 415
Collins, Raymond F., 432
Commager, Henry S., 390
Conzelmann, Hans, 400
Cooke, William, 366
Copernicus, 15, 258–60, 417
Copi, Irving M., 376
Cosgrove, Charles H., 438, 439
Cotoni, Marie-Hélène, 250, 413, 421
Couchoud, Paul-Louis, 437
Cowley, R. W., 432
Craig, Samuel G., 370
Craig, William, 373
Cranach, Lucas, 259
Cranfield, C. E. B., 146, 391, 405
Cremer, Hermann, 375, 405
Crites, Stephen, 375
Cross, Frank L., 435, 436
Cross, Frank Moore, Jr., 302, 373, 424, 426,
Crossan, J. D., 370
Cullman, Oscar, 360, 401, 404, 432, 433, 436, 440, 445, 446
Culpepper, R. Alan, 32, 370
Culver, Robert D., 394

Curtis, E. L., 163, 395
Curtis, T. F., 366
Cyprian, 431
Cyril of Jerusalem, 429
Dahl, George, 402
Dahl, Nils A., 437
D'Alembert, 248
D'Ales, Adhemar, 441, 442
Daneau, Lambert, 243, 258, 410, 416, 417
Daniélou, Jean, 184, 398, 399, 401, 442
Darius, 171–72
Darnton, Robert, 248, 413
Darwin, Charles, 421
Davids, Peter H., 390
Davidson, Richard M., 399
Davies, J. G., 372, 387
Davies, Stevan, 329, 393, 436
DeJonge, H. J., 418
De Jongste, H., 425
Demarest, Bruce A., 364
Denis, A. M., 430
Denney, James, 13
Derrett, J. D. M., 393
de Sales, François, 251, 254
Descartes, René, 413
Dibon, Paul, 415
Dick, John, 366
Diderot, 248, 416
Didymus the Blind, 431
Dillard, R., 165, 395
Dillon, R. J., 394
Diodore of Tarsus, 398
Diodorus, 169
Dionysius of Alexandria, 431
Dodd, C. H., 364, 398, 404
Dodewaard, J. A. E. van, 399
Dods, Marcus, 13
Doeve, J. W., 398
Donahue, John R., 402
Donner, Theo, 425
Dooyeweerd, Herman, 233, 409
Douglas, J. D., 430
Douglas, Mary, 411
Dowey, E., 407
Downing, F. G., 168, 396
Dray, W. H., 372
Drummond, Henry, 63, 376
Dryden, John, 413
Dubois, C. B., 416
Dulles, Avery, 364
Dunbar, David G., 44, 373
Dungan, David, 299, 424, 425, 436
Dunn, James D. G., 20, 22, 300, 349, 363, 364, 387, 389, 425
Dyson, "Hugo", 77

Eadie, John, 384
Ebeling, Gerhard, 420
Eck, John, 253, 412, 414
Edelmann, Johann Christian, 412
Edwards, Jonathan, 374, 409
Edwards, Paul, 375
Efird, James M., 398
Ehrman, Bart D., 431
Eichorn, Johann Gottfried, 265, 348, 419
Eissfeldt, Otto, 306, 426, 428
Eliot, T. S., 71
Ellingworth, Paul, 389
Elliott, John H., 370
Ellis, E. Earle, 195, 398, 400
Elwell, Walter A., 372, 392
Epidemides, 428
Epiphanius, 429, 430, 432
Erasmus, Desiderius, 253–54, 266, 413, 414
Erickson, Millard J., 425
Eusebius of Caesarea, 316–17, 338, 340, 342, 428, 431, 440, 442, 446
Evans, C. F., 426
Eybers, Ian H., 311, 426, 427, 428, 429
Fairbairn, Patrick, 184, 399, 401, 402
Farkasfalvy, Denis, 327, 332, 335, 432, 435, 438, 439, 440, 443, 446
Farmer, William R., 432, 443
Farrar, John, 366
Fatio, Oliver, 243, 410, 416
Fee, Gordon D., 80–81, 379
Feiler, P. F., 393
Feinberg, Charles Lee, 402
Feinberg, John S., 374, 402
Feinberg, Paul D., 7, 31, 103, 364, 369, 370, 383, 398, 402
Feldman, L. H., 396
Ferch, Arthur, J., 426
Ferguson, Everett, 441
Fernández, Andrea, 402
Ferraro, Geraldine, 386
Ferro, T. R., 428
Feuillet, A., 405
Findlay, J. Alexander, 391
Finegan, Jack, 434
Finger, Thomas, 368
Fischer, David Hackett, 368
Fitzmyer, J. A., 391, 392, 400, 404
Flacius Illyricus, 183, 243
Flesseman-van Leer, Ellen, 340, 434, 435, 439, 440, 442, 445
Foley, Grover, 424
Force, James, 418
Foulkes, Francis, 401
Fowler, Robert M., 393
Fox, R. L., 397

Frame, John, 37, 44, 93, 365, 371, 372, 373, 383, 409
France, R. T., 364, 369, 392, 393, 396, 397, 398, 401
Frank, Isidore, 299, 339, 425, 434, 435, 439, 441
Freedman, David Noel, 395, 436
Frege, Gottlob, 61, 377
Frei, Hans, 72, 264, 370, 377, 419
Frey, Hermann Heinrich, 258, 417
Froelich, Karlfried, 398
Fror, Kurt 401
Frye, Northrop, 70–72, 377
Frye, Roland Mushat, 15, 260–61, 367, 411, 417
Fuller, Daniel P., 102
Gaebelein, Frank E., 427
Gaffin, Richard B., Jr., 365, 406, 411
Gager, John G., 371
Gaius, 167, 338
Gale, Richard M., 60, 376
Galileo, 261, 417
Garasse, François, 415
Garraghan, Gilbert, 144, 390
Gaston, L., 390
Gasque, W. Ward, 388, 403
Gaussen, Louis, 13, 29, 344, 370, 443
Gawlick, Gunder, 415
Gay, Peter, 413
Geach, P. T., 88, 92, 382
Geisler, Norman L., 74–75, 364, 378, 383, 389, 398, 406
Genebrard, Gilbert, 251
Gerhardsson, Birger, 433
Gerstner, John H., 406, 409
Gianakaris, C. J., 396
Giles, P., 404
Gill, John, 13
Gilmour, S. McClean, 443
Gisel, Pierre, 363
Glanvill, Joseph, 413
Gnilka, J., 391
Gnuse, Robert, 363
Godet, Frédéric Louis, 189, 383
Godfrey, W. Robert, 365, 406
Goetz, Stewart, 144, 390
Goeze, John, 412, 420
Goldingay, John E., 154, 164, 393, 395
Goldstein, Leon J., 387
Gooch, George Peabody, 412
Goodspeed, Edgar J., 432, 442
Goppelt, Leonhard, 196, 398, 399, 401, 402
Goshen-Gottstein, M. H., 430
Grabe, J. E., 428
Graff, Gerald, 70, 72–73, 80, 377, 390
Graham, Holt H., 434

Grant, F. C., 384
Grant, Robert M., 431, 434, 435, 436, 437
Green, William Henry, 428
Greenslade, S. L., 363
Gregory, J. Robinson, 366
Gregory of Nazianzus, 429, 432
Gregory of Nyssa, 432
Grelot, P., 402, 403
Grosheide, F. W., 441
Grossmann, Walter, 412
Grotius, 15, 256, 420
Grudem, Wayne A., 36–37, 369, 370, 374, 383, 405, 420
Gruenler, Royce, 372
Gründer, Karlfried, 414
Grundmann, Walter, 146, 491
Gundry, Robert H., 35–36, 140, 144, 147, 179, 371, 378, 381, 389, 390, 393, 394, 396, 397, 398, 400
Gundry, Stanley, N., 389, 392, 394
Guthrie, Donald, 389, 431, 437, 446
Gutting, Gary, 367, 386
Guttmann, Alexander, 120, 385
Haase, Erich, 416
Haenchen, Ernst, 387, 388
Hagner, Donald A., 324, 384, 402, 403, 434
Haldane, Robert, 12
Hall, A. Rupert, 418
Hall, Marie Boas, 418
Hamel, Adolf, 441
Hamilton, J. R., 170, 172, 397
Hamilton, William, 16
Hamlet, 53
Hammond, N. G. L., 397
Hampson, Norman, 413
Handlin, Oscar, 397
Hanks, T. D., 395
Hannah, John D., 364, 411, 419
Hanson, A. T., 186, 399
Hanson, N. R., 409
Hanson, R. P. C., 341, 442, 443
Harmer, J. R., 404
Harnack, Adolf von, 181, 275, 331, 353, 432, 437, 438
Harrington, Daniel J., 433
Harris, Horton, 123–24, 385, 386
Harris, R. Laird, 300, 431, 445
Harrison, Paul N., 434
Harrison, R. K., 315, 431
Hart, Darryl G., 368
Hart, H., 409
Hasel, G. F., 426
Hastings, James, 384, 425
Hatch, Nathan O., 368, 411
Hay, C. A., 443
Hays, Richard B., 404

Hazard, Paul, 248
Heard, R. G., 438
Hedrick, C. W., 394
Hegel, Georg Wilhelm Friedrich, 123, 229
Heidegger, Martin, 278
Held, H. J., 152, 392, 393
Helm, Paul, 44, 88, 369, 373, 375, 382, 421
Helmbold, Andrew K., 436
Hemert, Paulus van, 266, 420
Henderson, Ebenezer, 366
Hendricksen, William, 147, 391, 393
Hendry, George, 408
Hengel, Martin, 397
Hengstengberg, Ernest W., 184, 399
Henkey, Charles H., 445
Hennecke, Edgar, 441
Henry, Carl F. H., 7, 47, 59–60, 63, 69, 161, 364, 374, 375, 377, 395, 406, 445
Hepp, Valentine, 410
Heracleon, 330
Herder, Johann Gottfried, 420
Hermas, 316, 339, 340, 341
Herodotus, 393
Herriott, C. T. M., 427
Herrmann, Johannes, 275
Herron, Robert W., 432
Hesselgrave, David J., 372, 391
Heth, W. A., 392
Heyd, Michel, 260, 415, 417, 418
Hick, John, 57, 375
Hickman, E., 409
Hiebert, D. Edmond, 156, 391, 393
Hilary of Poitiers, 429
Hillel the Elder, 119
Hippolytus, 329, 338, 340, 342, 431, 441, 446
Hirsch, E. D., 80, 82, 189, 379, 380, 400, 402
Hitchcock, F. R. M., 440
Hobbes, Thomas, 253, 261, 418
Hodge, Archibald, A., 399
Hodge, Charles, 10–11, 16–18, 220, 266, 368, 404, 420
Hodgson, P. C., 386
Hoehner, Harold W., 392
Hoffman, Joseph, 437, 438
Hoffman, Thomas A., 445
Hofmann, J. C. K. von, 184
Hoh, J., 439, 440
Holbach, Baron d', 249
Holden, Henry, 253–54, 414, 415
Holifield, E. Brooks, 367
Holmer, Paul, 76, 84, 378
Holmes, Arthur F., 104, 369, 383
Home, D. D., 153
Hooper, Walter, 378
Horn, Siegfried, 164, 395
Hornig, Gottfried, 266, 420

Horton, Douglas, 421
Hoskyns, Edwin C., 422, 444
Howard, Roy J., 372
Hughes, Philip Edgcumbe, 404
Hultgren, Arland, 404
Hume, David, 229, 413, 418
Husserl, Edmund, 381
Hutton, Sarah, 414
Hyginus, 435
Hyrcanus, 168
Ignatius, 324–26, 328, 434, 438
Inch, Morris A., 402
Irenaeus, 22, 301, 328, 331, 333–37, 339, 356, 431, 438, 439, 440
Jacob, Margaret, 250, 413
Jacobs, H. E., 443
James Perez of Valencia, 182
Janson, John F., 442
Janzen, J. Gerald, 404
Jellicoe, Sidney, 428, 429
Jeremias, Joachim, 148, 389, 391, 404
Jerome, 310, 429
John Cassion, 398
John Chrysostom, 244, 258, 317
Johnson, Elliot, 403
Johnson, R. C., 406
Johnson, S. Lewis, 187, 399, 401, 404
Johnston, Robert, 166, 396
Jonas, Hans, 437
Jonge, H. J. De, 262
Joseph, 167
Josephus, Flavius, 111–12, 114–15, 117, 141, 151, 166–68, 171–73, 303–4, 307, 313, 315, 384, 392, 396, 426, 427, 428, 431
Joynt, C. B., 390
Judge, E. A., 370
Jülicher, Adolf, 339, 441
Justel, Henri, 414
Justin, 169, 331, 333–36, 341, 435, 438, 439
Kaestli, Jean-Daniel, 425
Kaiser, Walter C., 189, 198–201, 204, 400, 402, 403
Kant, Immanuel, 230, 249, 275, 386
Kantzer, Kenneth S., 373, 392
Käsemann, Ernst, 299, 404, 443
Kaye, Bruce N., 387
Kealy, Sean, 432
Kearney, Hugh, 417
Keats, John, 70
Kee, Howard C., 443
Keil, C. F., 395
Kelber, Werner, 145, 390, 392, 402
Kelly, George A., 364
Kelsey, David, 64–65, 81, 104, 376, 407
Kenney, E. J., 415
Kenny, Anthony, 376, 377

Kepler, Johannes, 15, 258–59, 367, 417
Keylock, Leslie, 151, 392
Kidner, Derek, 404
Kilby, Clyde S., 379
Kirk, Edward, 13, 367, 370, 443
Kirk, J. Andrew, 432
Kissinger, W. S., 370
Kistemaker, Simon J., 425
Kline, Meredith G., 405, 406
Klug, Eugene F., 365
Knackstedt, J., 154, 393
Knight, Harold, 445
Knox, John, 332, 437, 438
Knox, W. L., 427
Koester, Helmut, 322–23, 329–30, 373, 384, 388, 433, 434, 436
Kooiman, Willem Jan, 432
Kopitzch, Franklin, 412
Kors, Alan Charles, 413
Korshin, Paul, 412
Krabbendam, Hendrick, 372
Kraft, Charles H., 42–43, 372
Kraft, Robert A., 435
Kramer, Fred, 443
Kratzswch, Konrad, 417
Kuhl, Curt, 427
Kuhn, Thomas S., 367, 372, 386, 409, 419
Kümmel, W. G., 143, 385, 388, 390, 443
Küng, Hans, 364, 410
Kutter, 275
Kuyper, Abraham, 11, 78, 233, 379, 406
Labrousse, Elisabeth, 415
Ladd, George E., 160, 394, 432
Lagrange, Marie-Joseph, 79–81, 379, 431, 432, 441, 442, 443
Lakatos, I., 417
Lambrecht, J., 404
La Mettrie, 248
Lampe, G. W. H., 399
Lane, A., 408
Lane, Tony, 370
Lane, William L., 146, 369, 391
Lanne, D. E., 440
Lanser, Susan S., 91, 383
La Peyrère, Isaac, 253, 259, 261, 417, 418
Lapide, Pinchas, 385
Laqueur, R., 396
Lash, Nicholas, 381, 399
LaSor, William Sanford, 373, 403, 431
Lawson, John, 440
Le Brun, Jacques, 254, 414, 415, 416
Lecerf, Auguste, 408
Le Clerc, Jean, 256–57, 266, 268, 416, 420, 421
Le Déaut, Roger, 400
Lee, G. M., 153, 393

Leibniz, Gottfried, 253
Leiman, Sid Z., 299, 303, 425, 426, 427, 428, 429, 430
Leith, John H., 411
Leland, John, 252
Lemke, W. E., 424
Lemmon, E. J., 61, 376
Lentricchia, Frank, 70–71, 375, 377, 383
Lessing, Gotthold, 267, 412, 420
Levereng, Edwin W., 443
Levita, Elias, 301
Levy, David, 421
Lewis, C. S., 75–79, 84, 94, 378, 379, 381, 383
Lewis, Gordon R., 58–60, 364, 375
Lewis, Jack P., 303, 426
Liefeld, Walter L., 394
Lightfoot, J. B., 123, 125–28, 131–32, 385, 386, 387, 388, 404, 433, 434
Lightstone, Jack N., 302, 303, 426
Lindars, Barnabas, 398, 404
Lindsell, Harold, 369, 388, 390, 391
Lindsley, A., 409
Linnemann, Eta, 370
Little, J. G., 370
Livingstone, E. A., 441
Lloyd, G. E. R., 381
Lloyd, J. G., 170, 397
Loader, W. R. G., 394
Locke, John, 243, 247, 253, 412
Loewe, H., 384
Lohfink, Norbert, 205, 403
Longenecker, Richard N., 36, 189, 193, 371, 381, 383, 398, 400, 401, 404, 425
Loos, H. van der, 393
Lord, Eleazar, 366
Loretz, Oswald, 242, 410
Lotz, David, 410
Louis, Kenneth R. Gros, 370
Louis XV, 412
Lubac, Henri de, 182, 184, 398, 399
Lucian, 144, 431
Luther, Martin, 183, 220, 224, 241, 243–44, 259, 262, 265–67, 269, 281, 309, 342–43, 353, 399, 408, 410, 413, 420, 432, 443
Lyons, John, 55, 374
Macaulay, Lord, 143
McCarter, Jr., P. K., 395
McCarthy, D. J., 395
McCasland, S. Vernon, 398
McCosh, James, 367
McDonald, H. D., 57, 252, 363, 375, 414
Machen, J. Gresham, 368, 385, 408
McIntire, C. T., 368
McKee, David R., 417
McKenzie, John L., 403

McKim, Donald K., 10–11, 15, 24, 221, 243–44, 261, 263, 267, 363, 364, 365, 367, 406, 409, 410, 411, 419
McNeill, John, 420
McRay, J. R., 392
Madsen, A. A., 163, 395
Magni, Valeriano, 254
Maier, Gerhard, 345, 356, 363, 443
Malcolm, Norman, 66, 84, 376
Mallard, William, 418
Mallarmé, Stéphane, 70
Mandel, Hugo, 425
Manichaeus, 443
Manser, Anthony, 381
March, W. Eugene, 427
Marcion, 181, 327, 331–334, 354, 357, 437, 438
Mariamme, 167
Marmorstein, A., 385
Marsden, George M., 16, 244–46, 250, 257, 263, 267–69, 367, 368, 411, 412, 418, 419, 421
Marshall, I. Howard, 30–31, 34, 102, 151, 322, 364, 370, 371, 380, 383, 389, 390, 392, 394, 400, 433
Martin, Henri-Jean, 412
Martin, Ralph P., 432
Martin, Steve, 368
Marty, Martin E., 10, 365, 368, 412
Masuda, S., 393
Matera, F. J., 394
Mauchline, J., 395
Mavrodes, George I., 372
May, Henry F., 367
Mealand, David L., 370
Mede, Joseph, 256
Meier, J. P., 393, 394, 400
Meiland, Jack W., 387
Melanchthon, 258
Melito of Sardis, 337, 429
Mellor, D. H., 72, 377
Menander, 428
Ménard, J.-E., 436
Menzies, A., 385
Metzger, Bruce M., 310, 400, 425, 428, 429
Meyer, Rudolf, 430, 431
Meyjes, G. H. M. Posthumus, 418
Michaelis, John David, 265, 266, 419, 420
Michaels, J. Ramsey, 364, 384, 389
Michel, Otto, 405
Milde, Wolgang, 418
Milik, Jozef T., 429, 430
Mill, John Stuart, 229
Miller, Merrill P., 400
Miller, P. D., Jr., 424
Milton, John, 383

Moloney, Francis J., 404
Momigliano, A., 173, 397
Mommsen, Theodor, 317
Montagu, Ashley, 421
Montanus, 338
Montefiore, Alan, 376
Montefiore, C. G., 384
Montefiore, Hugh, 436
Montesquieu, 247
Montgomery, John W., 360, 369, 372, 378, 383, 392, 402, 406, 446
Moo, Douglas J., 43, 369, 371, 373, 391, 396, 397, 400, 401, 402
Moore, George E., 229
Moreau, Pierre-François, 414
Morgan, Richard Lyon, 429
Morgan, Thomas, 252, 256, 414
Moriarty, F. L., 395
Morian, Jean, 251, 413
Moore, G. F., 426
Morris, Leon, 364, 391
Morrison, A. W., 384
Mosis, R., 395
Moule, C. F. D., 400, 404
Mudge, Lewis, 380
Muller, Richard, 243, 369, 410, 414, 416
Munck, Johannes, 123, 385
Murphy, Scott Thomas, 411
Murray, John, 260, 405, 407, 408, 409
Musgrave, Alan, 417
Myers, J. B., 395
Myers, J. M., 364
Mynors, R. A. B., 414
Nash, Ronald H., 57–60, 67, 375, 377
Nautin, Pierre, 440
Nearchus, 152
Neill, Stephen, 125, 385, 386
Neusner, Jacob, 116, 384
Nevins, 390
Newman, John H., 184, 399
Newman, Robert C., 426
Newsome, J. D., Jr., 395
Newton, Sir Isaac, 243, 263, 418
Nicole, 251
Nicole, Roger R., 20, 24, 26, 364, 365, 369, 399, 401, 411
Nida, Eugene A., 391
Nielsen, Charles, 326, 435
Niesel, W., 407
Nilson, Jon, 438
Noll, Mark A., 367, 368, 411, 417
Norden, Rudolf F., 443
North, G., 410
North, R., 395
Obitts, Stanley, 58–60, 371, 375
O'Brien, Peter T., 369

Oepke, Albrecht, 428
Ogonowski, Zbigniew, 416
Oldenburg, Henry, 418
Olmstead, A. T., 388
Olsen, Glenn W., 398
Olsson, B., 370
Origen, 181, 308, 316, 341–42, 398, 428, 429, 430, 442, 443
O'Rourke, John J., 403
Orpheus, 171
Orr, James, 13, 363
Osborne, E. F., 333, 439
Osborne, Grant R., 80, 149, 155, 379, 392, 393
Ottley, R. R., 428
Packer, James I., 25, 57, 139, 204, 264, 365, 368, 369, 372, 375, 379, 399, 403, 419
Pagels, Elaine H., 437
Palmer, Martin, 445
Palmer, Richard E., 372
Pantaenus, 316
Papius, 438
Parmenio, 171–73
Passmore, J. A., 41, 372
Patte, Daniel, 370
Paulsen, H., 441
Payne, J. Barton, 163, 395, 426
Payne, Philip B., 389, 397, 402
Pearson, L., 397
Pedersen, Sigfried, 432
Pelikan, Jaroslav, 435, 437, 440, 441, 446
Pentecost, J. Dwight, 394
Perkins, 410
Perkins, Pheme, 437
Perrin, Norman, 390
Pesch, R., 391
Petersen, Rodney L., 365
Pfeiffer, C. F., 384
Pfeiffer, Robert H., 426
Pfleiderer, Otto, 126, 386
Phillipps, D. Z., 84
Philo, 189, 305, 308, 427
Phrataphernes, 171
Pieper, Francis, 443
Pierard, Richard V., 368
Pink, Arthur W., 405
Pinnock, Clark H., 26–27, 59–60, 102, 368, 369, 375, 383, 425
Piper, Otto A., 438, 439
Pitcher, George, 381
Pivcevic, Edo, 381
Plantinga, Alvin, 44, 233, 373, 421
Plato, 120, 229–30
Plummer, Alfred, 394, 400, 404
Plutarch, 144, 152, 169–73, 396, 397
Polanyi, M., 409

Polonius, 53
Polybius, 144
Polycarp, 324, 326, 328, 434, 435, 438
Polycrates, 393
Pons, Georges, 420
Pope John XXIII, 8
Popkin, Richard, 413, 417, 418
Popper, Karl, 61, 376
Potterie, Ignace de la, 364
Poythress, V. S., 394
Prabhu, George M. Soares, 400
Pratt, Mary Louise, 91, 383
Preston, David G., 417
Preus, James Samuel, 183, 398, 399
Preus, Robert D., 74–75, 364, 372, 374, 378, 389, 390, 391, 394, 399, 401, 403, 416
Price, Robert M., 364
Pringle, William, 443
Ptolemy, 169
Pütz, Peter, 412
Quasten, Johannes, 434, 435
Quine, W. V., 60–62, 376
Quintilian, 377
Quintus Curtius, 169
Quispel, Gilles, 436
Rabanus Maurus, 398
Rackham, R. B., 392
Rad, Gerhard von, 401, 404
Rade, Martin, 275
Radmacher, Earl D., 364, 372, 374, 389, 390, 391, 394, 399, 401, 403
Ragaz, 275
Rahner, Karl, 445
Raitt, Jill, 243 410, 416
Rajak, T., 168, 396
Rambach, Johann Jakob, 265
Ramm, Bernard, 60, 74–75, 78, 95, 246, 250, 264–68, 364, 369, 376, 378, 379, 383, 405, 412, 419
Ramsay, William M., 132, 151, 388
Ranke, Leopold von, 40
Redwood, John, 250, 256, 413, 415
Regul, Jürgen, 437
Reid, Thomas, 15–17, 367, 368
Reill, Peter, 264, 419, 420
Reinitzer, Heimo, 417
Rembrandt, 73
Rengstorf, K. H., 432
Rennie, Ian, 11–13, 365, 366
Rescher, N., 390
Rese, Martin, 398, 399
Rétat, Pierre, 415
Reventlow, Henning Graf, 366, 402, 421
Rex, Walter, 415
Richards, I. A., 70, 377
Ricoeur, Paul, 81, 90, 374, 375, 380, 382

Ridderbos, N. Herman, 321, 352–55, 357–59, 401, 404, 405, 408, 425, 432, 433, 445
Ridgley, Thomas, 13, 366
Riss, Richard, 366
Richardson, Cyril C., 434, 435
Rivkin, Ellis, 384, 385
Roberts, Bleddyn J., 429
Robertson, Archibald T., 400, 404
Robinson, D. W. B., 404
Robinson, James M., 388, 433, 436
Robinson, John A. T., 21, 289, 433
Robson, E. I., 397
Robson, J. A., 418
Roche, Daniel, 248, 413
Rodd, Cyril S., 34, 146, 371, 391
Rogers, Jack B., 10–11, 15, 24, 221, 243–44, 261, 263, 267, 363, 364, 365, 367, 406, 409, 410, 411, 419, 421, 443
Romanides, John S., 439
Rorty, Richard, 44, 373
Rosen, Edward, 259, 367, 417
Ross, Alexander, 417
Ross, J. M., 391
Rothfuchs, W., 398, 400
Rousseau, Jean-Jacque, 249
Rowdon, H. H., 392
Rowley, H. H., 384
Rudolf, Kurt, 436
Rudolph, W., 396
Rufinus, 429
Ruppert, L., 402
Russell, Bertrand, 229, 377
Russell, David S., 425
Ruwet, J., 442, 443
Ryle, Gilbert, 376
Ryle, Herbert E., 425, 426, 427, 428
Ryle, J. C., 12
Ryrie, Charles C., 150, 392
Sandeen, Ernest, 11, 365
Sanders, E. P., 151, 384, 392
Sanders, James, 44, 185, 299, 312, 373, 399, 424, 425, 430
Sanders, Joseph N., 439
Saucy, Robert L., 364
Save-Soderbergh, Torgny, 436
Schakel, Peter, 77–78, 378–79
Schatzberg, Walter, 416
Scheurleer, Th. H. Lunsingh, 418
Schillebeeckx, Eduard, 364
Schiller, Friedrich von, 377
Schleiermacher, Friedrich Daniel Ernst, 275, 278–79
Schloemann, Martin, 420
Schmid, Heinrich, 443
Schmid, Josef, 387

Schmidt, John, 432
Schmidt, Norbert, 420
Schmidt-Biggemann, Wilhelm, 414, 418, 419
Schmithals, Walther, 123, 385, 387
Schnabel, Eckhard, 363
Schnackenburg, Rudolf, 40, 372
Schneckenburger, Matthias, 385
Schneemelcher, Wilhelm, 441
Schneider, G., 394
Scholder, Klaus, 412
Schrenk, Gottlob, 400, 427
Schröger, Friedrich, 398
Schule, U., 437
Schultz, R. C., 432
Schultz, Samuel J., 402, 429
Schürmann, H., 391, 393
Schwartz, Hillel, 415
Schweizer, Eduard, 394, 402
Schwoebel, Robert, 417
Scroggs, R., 370
Searle, John, 68, 86–92, 94, 377, 381, 382, 383
Seeberg, Reinhold, 407
Semler, Johann Salomo, 242, 266, 344–45, 420, 428
Sergeant, John, 415
Shapiro, Barbara J., 414
Sharpe, Eric J., 433
Shenkel, J. D., 395
Sheppard, Gerald T., 411
Sherry, Patrick, 381
Sherwin-White, A. N., 394
Shotwell, Willis A., 334, 439
Shuler, Philip, 144, 371, 390
Shutt, R. J. H., 396
Sidney, Sir Philip, 69
Sigal, Phillip, 117, 384
Silva, Moisés, 22, 43, 140, 181, 185–86, 189–90, 373, 374, 375, 384, 389, 399, 400, 404
Simon, Richard, 253–55, 257, 266, 414, 415, 416, 418, 420, 421
Skehan, Patrick, 311, 429, 430
Slotki, I. W., 395
Smalley, Beryl, 398
Smith, Gary V., 369
Smith, Moody, 398
Snaith, J. G., 430
Snoeks, Remi, 414
Socinus, 416
Socrates, 333
Soemius, 167
Soggin, J. Albert, 426
Solé, Jacques, 415
Souter, Alexander, 442

Sowers, Sidney G., 445
Sparn, Walter, 421
Spengler, Oswald, 129
Spinoza, Baruch, 253–54, 257, 414, 416, 417, 421
Sproul, R. C., 25, 369, 409
Spurgeon, Charles H., 366
Stadter, Philip, 173, 397
Stählin, Otto, 442
Stamm, R. T., 364
Stasanor, 171
Stauffer, Richard, 260
Stein, Sir Aurel, 170
Stemberger, Günter, 426
Stendahl, Krister, 363, 398, 400
Stephens, L. D., 390
Stephens, W. P., 416, 419
Stewart, Dugald, 16
Stillingfleet, Edward, 415
Stillingfleet, William, 253
Stinespring, W. F., 395, 398
Stone, Lawerence, 412
Stonehouse, Ned B., 357, 359, 384, 389, 405, 409, 431, 445, 446
Storms, C. Samuel, 374
Strathmann, Hermann, 443
Strawson, P. F., 382
Strecker, Georg, 433
Strobel, A., 405
Strugnall, J., 429
Stuart, Douglas, 80–81, 379
Stuhlmacher, Peter, 363, 385, 398, 399, 419
Stylianopoulos, Theodore, 438
Suhl, Alfred, 398, 400
Sullivan, Robert, 415
Sundberg, Albert C., Jr., 299, 308–10, 425, 428, 429, 441
Sunshine, Glenn, 416
Suppe, Frederick, 367, 419
Surkau, Hans-Werner, 402
Sutcliffe, Edward F., 402, 404
Swanson, Theodore N., 426, 429, 430
Swete, Henry B., 428, 429
Tacitus, 169
Talbert, C. H., 371
Talman, S., 430
Tarski, Alfred, 376
Tate, Marvin E., 428
Tatian, 332, 334
Tavard, Georges, 414
Taylor, Nathaniel W., 368
Taylor, Vincent, 146, 391
Teilhard de Chardin, 262, 289
Telford, W., 394
Tenney, Merrill C., 381, 384, 425
Tertullian, 255, 340–42, 441, 442

Thackeray, H. St. J., 396
Theissen, Gerd, 370, 393
Theodore of Mopsuestia, 244
Thiele, Edwin R., 164, 395
Thielicke, Helmut, 222, 225, 406
Thiselton, Anthony, 82–84, 372, 380, 381
Thomas, the apostle, 316, 329, 330, 358
Thomas, Robert L., 389, 394
Thomas, Aquinas. *See* Aquinas, Thomas
Thompson, G. T., 445
Thomson, D. F. S., 414
Thorley, John, 151, 392
Thorwall, Brenton L., 372
Thucydides, 169
Thurneysen, Rudolf, 276–77, 422
Tidball, Derek J., 371
Tillyard, E. M. W., 378
Tindal, Matthew, 243, 415
Tipton, Steven M., 411
Toland, John, 254, 257, 415
Tolkien, J. R. R., 77
Tollington, R. B., 442
Topolski, J., 390
Torrance, Thomas F., 404
Toynbee, Arnold, 129
Tozer, A. W., 46
Tracey, David, 375
Trajan, 324
Travis, Stephen H., 389
Tregelles, S. P., 441
Tuckett, C. M., 142, 390, 436
Tuland, C. G., 396
Tulloch, John, 414
Turner, David L., 389
Turner, H. E. W., 436
Turner, M. M. B., 392
Turretin, Francis, 17, 220, 243
Tuttle, G., 373
Tuya, Manuel de, 203
Tyndale, William, 342, 443
Uchida, K., 142, 390
Unger, Merrill F., 384
Unnik, W. C. van, 330, 396, 436, 440, 441
Urbach, E. E., 384, 385
Urmson, J. O., 382
Ussher, James, 256, 395
Valentinus, 437
Van der Hoeven, J., 409
Vander Stelt, John C., 367, 368
Vanderveken, David, 381
Van Hook, Jay M., 44, 233, 373, 409
Vanhoozer, Kevin, 38, 372
Vanhoye, Albert, 364
Van Kley, Dale K., 248, 413
Vansina, J., 390
Van Til, Cornelius, 405, 408, 409, 410

Vardaman, E. Jerry, 151, 392
Vartanian, Aram, 248–49, 413
Vasholz, Robert I., 426
Vawter, Bruce, 14–15, 16–28, 187, 190–91,
    244–46, 249–50, 252, 259, 261, 263–64,
    267–68, 364, 367, 369, 399, 400, 403, 411,
    414, 419
Veron, François, 251
Vet, Jan de, 247, 412
Via, D. O., 370
Viccari, A., 398
Vis, Albert, 197, 402
Vischer, Wilhelm, 399
Voetius, Gisbert, 220
Volkes, F. E., 435
Voltaire, 247–50, 421
Vovelle, Michel, 248, 250, 413
Wacker, Grant, 368
Walker, Henry, 443
Walls, Andrew F., 338, 441
Waltke, Bruce K., 167, 389, 396, 402, 403
Walvoord, John F., 391
Ward, A. M., 393
Ward, Marcus, 152
Wardman, Alan, 169, 396, 397
Warfield, Benjamin B., 10–11, 17, 29–30,
    65, 179, 220, 260, 357, 363, 366, 370, 386,
    397, 399, 405, 406, 408, 409, 417, 445
Watson, Adam, 128, 387
Weemses, John, 261, 418
Weiser, Artur, 426, 427
Welles, C. B., 169, 396
Wellhausen, Julius, 302, 345
Wells, David F., 365, 411, 412
Wells, Paul Ronald, 364
Wells, Ronald A., 368
Wenham, David, 364, 369, 392, 393, 394,
    396, 397, 400
Wenham, John W., 147–48, 162–63, 391,
    394, 395, 403
Wermelinger, Otto, 425
Werner, Johannes, 440
Wesel, Jr., Leonard, 420
Wesley, John, 249
Wessel, Walter W., 391
Westcott, B. F., 432, 438, 442, 443
Westermann, Claus, 401
Wheelwright, Philip, 70
Whiston, William, 420
Whitaker, William, 412
White, Alan R., 61–62, 376
White, H., 390
Whitefield, George, 249
Wiener, P. P., 387
Wikenhauser, Alfred, 387
Wilcox, Max, 400

Wildeboer, G., 426, 428
Wildiers, N. Max, 262, 418
Wilkins, John, 417
Wilkinson, J. R., 432
Willi, T., 395
Williams, Bernard, 376
Williamson, H. G. M., 395, 396
Williamson, L., 391
Wills, Gary, 368
Wilson, Daniel, 366
Wilson, G. H., 430
Wilson, Robert Dick, 408
Wilson, Robert McL., 330, 436, 437, 441
Wisbey, Tom N., 372
Wiseman, D. J., 426
Wissowatius, Andreas, 416
Wittgenstein, Ludwig, 53, 65–67, 82–84, 86–88, 90, 376, 377, 380, 381
Wolfe, K. R., 394
Wolff, Christian, 247
Wolterstorff, Nicholas, 44, 373, 409, 421

Woodbridge, John D., 11, 14–15, 363, 365, 367, 368, 369, 370, 371, 372, 373, 379, 383, 389, 399, 405, 406, 410, 411, 412, 413, 414, 416, 417, 420, 421, 425, 443
Woods, Gordon S., 368
Woollcombe, K. J., 399
Woolley, Paul, 405, 409, 431, 445
Wordsworth, William, 74, 378
Wright, David F., 366, 374
Wright, George Ernest, 373, 424
Wycliffe, John, 262, 418
Xenophon, 333
Yamauchi, Edwin, 151, 371, 392, 426, 435
Yeats, William Butler, 70
Young, Edward J., 314–15, 369, 405, 408, 431
Zahn, Theodor, 437, 441
Zeitlin, Solomon, 427
Zeller, E., 385
Zimmerli, Walter, 404
Zuidhof, A., 395

Index of Subjects

Accommodation: as recently treated, 26–28; its relation to alleged error in Scripture, 27–28, 266, 419n.137, 420n.155

Adduction. *See* Logic

Aesthetic Theology, 374n.5

Allegorization. *See* New Testament Use of the Old Testament

Audience Criticism: New Testament examples, 153–54; Old Testament example, 164; relation to harmonization, 142

Authority: of the biblical text itself, 37–38; crisis of, 8; declining influence of biblical authority in the churches, 46–48; multifaceted nature of, 94; its relation to literary genre, 81–82; of Scripture in Barth's thought, 222–24, 275–94

Baconianism, 17

Biblical Atomism, 65

Biblical Positivism, 65

Biblical Theology: its aversion to propositions, 54–55; its linguistic abuses, 53–54; ruled out by "ordinary" language, 85. *See also* New Biblical Theology

Canon: Alexandrian, 307–8, 340–42; and Apocrypha, 308–10; in apostolic fathers, 323–28; approaches to, 345–55; and the cessation of prophecy, 312–14; closing of the New Testament canon, 315–18; controversy over, 328–31; critical synthesis concerning, 356–60; and the Dead Sea Scrolls, 310–12; definition of, 300–301; in the Enlightenment, 344–45; formation of New Testament canon, 318–23; and Irenaeus, 334–37; in Josephus and Philo, 303–5; and Justin Martyr, 333–34, 439n.240; and literary genre, 82; and Marcion, 331–33, 438n.215; and the new hermeneutic, 43–44; in the New Testament, 305–7; Old Testament canon, 301–15; in the Reformation, 342–44, 432n.117; spread of notion of, 337–40; treatments of, 299–300, 300–303. *See also* Canon Criticism

Canon Criticism: confusion of context, 380n.161; and discussions of canon, 44, 348–50, 381n.179; and *sensus plenior*, 204–9

Chicago Statement on Biblical Hermeneutics, 64, 68–69

Chicago Statement on Biblical Inerrancy, 68

Common Sense Realism. *See* Scottish Common Sense Realism

Concursive Theory: criticism of, 45; and *sensus plenior* 203–4; and theodicy, 45

Contextualization: its relation to the new hermeneutic, 41–42; its relation to confessional statements, 42–43

Copernican Theory and biblical authority, 14–15

Council of Trent, 250

Cultural Conventions: and informal generalizations, 115; and speech arts, 91–92

Deduction. *See* Logic

Discourse Acts, 90–92, 93

Distanciation, its importance to interpretation, 41

Enlightenment: its alleged influence in evoking "Fundamentalist" creation of the doctrine of inerrancy, 244–65; elusive definition of, 246–49; and English influence on the Continent, 366n.36; misconceptions of its impact on the doctrine of Scripture, 241–69; its treatment of canon, 344–45

Epistemology: and the correspondence theory of truth, 382n.193; and fideism, 44–45; and foundationalism, 44–45; and the Holy Spirit's internal witness, 229–35; and miracles, 373n.154; in the natural sciences, 41; and the new hermeneutic, 38–45; and propositions, 37–38

Evangelicals: their abandonment of biblical authority, 47–48; their approach to "propositions," 55–56, 56–59, 66–67; their exegetical distortions, 21–22; their fragmentation, 6–8; their growth, 6, 46;

459

and Scripture, 5–6; Scripture as viewed by British Evangelicals, 366nn.34,35

Faith and Practice: as the Reformation understood it, 5; as a restrictive criterion, 14–15, 102–3

Form Criticism: and harmonization, 142; New Testament examples, 151–53; Old Testament example, 164

Fundamentalism: its alleged creation of the doctrine of inerrancy, 244–46; its connection with Evangelicalism, 10, 412n.22, 421n.168

Genre. *See* Literary Genre

Gnosticism, 328–31, 335–37

Harmonization: of the "additive" type, 144–45, 160–61, 165–66; and apparently contradictory passages, 149–51; legitimacy and limits of, 139–74; and literary genre, 144–45; of parallel documents, 34; problems and diverse definitions of, 139–41; in the study of Arrian's and Plutarch's lives of Alexander, 169–73; in the study of Josephus, 166–69; and sub-categories, 141–45; wise use of, 34

Hegelian Dialectic at Tübingen, 123

Hermeneutical Circle, 38–39. *See also* New Hermeneutic

Historical Reconstruction: of biblically described events, 110–12; and the burden of proof, 132; of first-century Christianity, 121–31; of first-century Pharisaism, 112–21; and historical objectivity, 128–30; need for and dangers of, 109–32; and related misunderstandings between conservative and nonconservatives, 130–32; and the slant of an evangelist, 116; uncertainty of, 111

Historiography: its agenda, 19–20; and the burden of proof, 18–20; dependence on restricted "paradigms," 14–15; of the Enlightenment, 241–46; 267–72; and historical skepticism, 390n.34; revisionist, 10–20. 365n.23, 368n.60, 511–12nn.19–22. *See also* Historical Reconstruction

Holy Spirit: diversity in His involvement with the Scriptures, 217; inspiration and internal witness in contemporary theology, 222–23; His internal witness, 219–35, 409–10n.60; His internal witness and Scripture's self-attestation, 407n.27; objects of His internal witness, 225–29; the rationality of His internal witness, 229–35; and revelation and inspiration, 217–29; the sovereignty of,

223–24, 225; His witness as understood in Protestant orthodoxy, 220–21

Hyperbole and historical reconstruction, 115

Illocutionary Act. *See* Speech Act

Imagination: its role in reading Scripture, 75–78; in tension with reason, 378n.119

Induction. *See* Logic

Inerrancy: in Barth's view, 293–94; definition of, 30–31; and literary phenomena in the Bible, 30–31; and propositions, 58–59; in recent historiography, 241–46; as a subset of infallibility, 94

Infallibility: believed by most Christians up to the early part of the Enlightenment, 250–57; history of the term, 101–2; its meaning related to achievement of the purposes of illocutionary forces, 94–103; and "natural philosophy," 257–64; as related to biblical sentences but not propositions, 58–59

Inspiration: and the confusion with the internal witness of the Spirit in contemporary theology, 222–23; current definitions of: 29–30; not entailing dictation, 29–30, 187; distinction between its results and its mode, 29–30; work of the Holy Spirit in, 217–19

International Council on Biblical Inerrancy, 7, 364n.9

Jamnia hypothesis, 301–3

Justification by faith, 380n.172

Language: "ordinary," 85–92; its relation to life, 82–84

Language-games: diverse kinds of, 83–84; and speech act, 90. *See also* Speech Act

Legalism: difficult definition of, 117–20; and Pharisaism, 118–20

Literary Criticism: and the doctrine of Scripture, 31–35; rhetorical criticism, 32–33; and structuralism, 375n.14. *See also* Literary Genre

Literary Genre: of Acts, 371n.119; and alleged (im)morality of forms, 74; and authorial intent, 79–80; and authority, 81–82; diversity of in Scripture, 69, 78–79; of an epistle, 36; of a gospel, 35–36, 381n.183; and harmonization, 144–45; importance of identifying inductively, 93; and interpretation, 35–38, 78–85; and life, 82–84; nature of, 380n.162; purposes of, 80–81, 82–83; and revelation, 81; and speech acts, 90–92; and truth, 68–75, 80–85. *See also* New Biblical Theology

Literature: "ordinary," 85–92. *See also* Literary Genre

Locutionary Act. *See* Speech Act

Logic: deduction allegedly abused by inerrantists, 179–80; the importance of induction, 179–80; its role in formulating a doctrine of Scripture, 24–25

Metaphor, value of, 78–79

Midrash, 35–36, 74, 193, 400–401n.54. *See also* New Testament Use of the Old Testament

Mishnah: date of, 116; nature of the history in, 116–17

Myth: and literary genre, 76–77; as providing a taste of history, 77

Narrative. *See* Literary Genre

Neologians, 264–67

New Biblical Theology: its aversion to propositions, 54–55; its dependence on literary forms, 54, 69–70, 71–72. *See also* Biblical Theology

New Hermeneutic: its appeal to paradigmatic dependency, 39–40; its connection with contextualization, 41–42; and epistemology, 38–45; lateness of Evangelicals' contribution, 39; its rejection of positivism, 40–41; its relation to the New Testament use of the Old, 186–87

New Testament Use of the Old Testament: adopting Jewish exegetical methods, 192–95; and allegorical exegesis, 181–83; and alternative points of view, 190–91; in application to new situations, 189–90; and the distinction between appropriation techniques and hermeneutical axioms, 194; and the distinction between "meaning" and "significance," 199–201; fideistic approaches of, 184–85; and "fulfillment" language, 191–92; and inerrancy, 209–11; and promise-fulfillment, 196; in Reformation thought, 183; and rejection of the Old Testament, 181; and "scientific" exegesis, 183–84; and *sensus plenior*, 201–4; and subjectivity of meaning, 186–87; and theologically controlled exegesis, 198–201; and typology, 195–98; using Old Testament language as a vehicle of expression, 188–89

Nonconservatives, the increasing discussion of Scripture by, 6–7; *passim*

Paradigmatic Dependency: in the New Hermeneutic, 39–40. *See also* Historiography

Performatives. *See* Speech Act

Perlocutionary Act. *See* Speech Act

Pesher, 193, 400–401n.54. *See also* New Testament Use of the Old Testament

Pharisaism: historical reconstruction of, 112–21; and legalism, 117–20

Plenary Inspiration, 11–14

Poetry: its functions, 76–78; and paraphrase, 69–73; and the real world, 69–71

Positivism and epistemology, 40–42

Presuppositions: and historical reconstruction, 123–25; need for sharper awareness of, 131; and the Tübingen School, 123–55

Princetonians: their courage, 408n.41; and reliance on induction, 17–18, 24–25; and Scottish Common Sense Realism, 16–18, 411n.19

Prophecy: cessation of in relation to canon, 312–14; as one paradigm of revelation, 81

Propositional revelation: dangers of, 63–64; difficulties in the expression, 56–60

Propositions: aversion to, 54–55; and biblical sentences, 58–59, 60–62; differentiated from other notions, 376n.52; and epistemology, 38; and Evangelicals, 55–56, 56–58; ordinary and philosophical senses of, 60; and the "picture-theory," 66–67; and poetry, 69–70; and revelation, 36–37, 56; and statements, 61–62; and truth, 56, 57, 72; and verbal inspiration, 57–58

Prozbul, 119–20

Pseudonymity as a literary form, 74

Qumran: and the canon, 310–12; and canonicity of Daniel, 429n.76; exegesis of, 194, 308

Redaction Criticism: and harmonization, 143–44, 390n.35; New Testament examples of, 155–60; Old Testament examples of, 165; stylistic redaction, 156–58; theological redaction, 158–60

Reductionism in the definition of theological terms, 25–26

Reformation, the: and accommodation, 27; and canon, 342–44; and Scripture, 5

Retroduction. *See* Logic

Revelation: Barthian view of, 58–59; and discourse acts, 90–92, 93; and reason, 416n.95

Roman Catholicism: and apologetics regarding the Bible following the Council of Trent, 250–52, 254–55; and canon, 350–52; and Scripture, 8–9, 364nn.13, 16, 379n.143; and *sensus plenior*, 201–2. *See also* Vatican II

Science: and the Bible, 14–15; at its rise and in discussion over biblical authority, 257–64

Scottish Common Sense Realism: its antecedents, 367n.47; and fundamentalism, 15–16, 411n.19; its origins and influence, 15–18, 368n.52

Sensus Plenior: and canon criticism, 204–9; and concursive theory, 203–4; its meaning as understood in Roman Catholicism, 201–2; and Scripture's appeal to Scripture, 43, 179–211. *See also* New Testament Use of the Old Testament

Sentences: their referents, 65; and speech acts, 86–90; and Wittgenstein, 65–67. *See also* Propositions; Speech Act

Sociology and New Testament interpretation, 33–34

Son of Man, 207

Source Criticism: and harmonization, 142–43; New Testament examples of, 154–55; Old Testament examples of, 164–65

Speech Act: as a theory of language, 86–92; commissive, 94; expressive, 94; successful or not, 95–103

Spirit. *See* Holy Spirit

Statements. *See* Propositions

Textual Criticism: and harmonization, 141; New Testament examples of, 145–47; Old Testament example of, 162–63

Theology: as defined by Barth, 287–89; as "ordinary literature" analysis of the Bible, 104, 381n.180; not a substitute for Scripture, 104

Torah, written and oral, 120–21

Translation and the problems of harmonization, 147–49

Truth: conception of, 95–103; definition of, 35–36; and language-games, 381n.177; and literary forms, 69; pragmatic theory of, 97–98; and successful speech acts, 96–98. *See also* Literary Genre; Propositions; Sentences

Tübingen School, 122–25, 386n.47, 387nn.59, 60; and the response of J. B. Lightfoot, 125–28

Typology: dependent on canon, 402n.68; as an interpretative key, 183, 184, 195–98, 399n.24. *See also Sensus Plenior*

Vatican II and Scripture, 8–9, 242

Verbal Inspiration, 11–14

Westminster Assembly, 411n.11

Word Studies, abuses of, 53–54

Index of Scripture References

Genesis

Book of	417, 427
1, 2	288
1	230
1:2	217, 260
1:16	263
1:28	230
3:1	63
15:6	405

Exodus

Book of	305, 373, 427
15	94
24:16	160
38:22−23	165

Leviticus

Book of	427
11:45	121
18:5	190−91
19:15	190

Numbers

| Book of | 427 |
| 21:14 | 307 |

Deuteronomy

Book of	93, 302, 310, 427
4:2	327
6:1	224
6:4−9	223
8:3	223
15:1−3	119
15:9	119−20
18:15	313
19:15	189
24:1−4	150
25:4	189, 200, 400

Joshua

Book of	164, 304, 306, 427
1:5	306
9:1	147
10:40	147

Judges

| Book of | 164, 304, 306, 427 |

Ruth

| Book of | 304, 305, 311 |
| 3:21 | 306 |

1 Samuel

Book of	304, 395, 396, 427
17:4, 7, 50	163
21:1−6	147

2 Samuel

Book of	93, 304, 395, 427
7:14	200
21:19	163
23:24−39	164
24:1	165

1 Kings

Book of	304, 395, 396, 427
3:6−14	164
7:13−14	165
7:13	166
7:23−26	163
15:16	163
15:23	166

2 Kings

Book of	304, 395, 396, 427
11:4−12	163
12:4−16	163
16:7−9	163
21:10	152

1 Chronicles

Book of	304, 306, 395, 396, 427
11:41−47	164
20:5	163
21:1	165
23:1	164
29:22	164
29:29	164

2 Chronicles

Book of	304, 306, 395, 396, 427
1:9−12	164
2:11	165
2:13−14	165
4:2−5	163
9:29	164
12:15	164
14−16	395
15:10, 19	163
16:11	166
23:1−11	163
24:4−14	163
24:20−22	306
26:10	147
28:16, 21	163
33:10	152

Ezra

| Book of | 304, 306, 311, 312, 427 |

Nehemiah

| Book of | 304, 306, 311, 312, 395, 427 |
| 2−6 | 167 |

464

Esther

Book of   304, 305, 310, 311, 427

Job

Book of   304, 311, 427
42:3   36

Psalms

Book of   93, 94, 304, 306, 310, 311, 312, 402, 403, 404, 427, 430
1   223
2:7   200, 202
4:4   326
4:5   435
8   207, 404
8:4   207
8:6   207
16   204, 209-11, 403
16:8-11   192
18:30   87
19:1, 3-4   100
19:7-14   223
22   197
22:18   197
33:6   217, 230
42, 43   188-89
68:18   369
71:15   36-37
104:30   217
110:1   192
119   223
119:18, 19   36
119:18   37
119:105   148
139:6   36

Proverbs

Book of   304, 311, 427
3:34   434

Ecclesiastes

Book of   304, 305, 311

Song of Solomon

Book of   304, 305, 311, 441

Isaiah

Book of   93, 304, 310, 312, 427
6:9   219
13:2   147
40:8   223
42:1   318
52:5   434
55:8, 9   36-37
55:11   95, 223
61:1-4   217
66:2   46

Jeremiah

Book of   304, 312, 427
4:7   86
20:14-18   35
26:20-23   427
31:8   147
31:15   206

Lamentations

Book of   304, 305, 311

Ezekiel

Book of   304, 305, 306, 312, 427

Daniel

Book of   303, 304, 305, 311, 426, 427, 429, 441
9:2   315
12:8   36

Hosea

11:1   191, 193, 200

Joel

2:28-29   313
2:32   200

Amos

Book of   288

Obadiah

Book of   306

Jonah

Book of   373

Nahum

Book of   306

Habbakuk

2:2-4   404
2:3-4   404
2:3   405
2:4   208, 405

Zephaniah

Book of   306

Malachi

4:5-6   313

Matthew

Book of   35-36, 339, 371, 384, 389, 390, 391, 392, 393, 394, 396, 397, 398, 400, 403, 404, 427, 442
1-2   148, 400
1:5   306
2:6   253
2:15   191, 200, 205
2:17-18   206
3:7   112
3:17   318
4:1-11   110
4:4   318
4:5   110, 158
4:7   318
4:8   110
4:10   318
4:24   147
5:1   147
5:17-20   223
5:17-48   400
5:17   191, 205, 318, 427
5:18   427
5:20   121
5:21-48   319
5:43   190

5:48	120–21
7:7–8	146
7:11	145
7:12	427
7:15–20	228
7:15	321, 323
7:24–27	111, 148
7:28–29	319
8–9	157
8:23b	156
8:26	156
8:28	161
9:13	328
9:37–10:16	155
10:5–6	150
10:10	154
11:13	191, 205, 427
12:40	148
13:31–32	148
14:22	146
15:2	433
15:3	433
15:6	320, 433
15:33	154
16:18	320
17:24–27	393
17:25–26	153
17:27	152–53
18:12–14	153
19:3–12	150
19:9	150
19:17	159, 391
20:30	161
21:12–17	158
21:18–22	158
22:1–10	154
22:14	328
22:40	427
23	116
23:3	113, 115
23:5–7	112
23:5	115
23:13, 15	112
23:23–24	117
23:25	112
23:34–35	306, 427
24:11, 24	321, 323
25:14–30	153
26:38	188
26:56	427
27:3–10	23, 369, 391
27:9	148, 419

27:26	152
27:46	197
28:18–20	150, 392
28:19	149

Mark

Book of	35, 339, 340, 384, 391, 394, 398, 442
1:15	191
1:22	319
2:1–3:6	157
2:7	319
2:17	328
2:26	147–48, 391
3:6	112
3:14	320
4:35	146
4:39–40	156
5:1	146, 148
5:2	161
5:21	146
6:6–13	393
6:8–9	154
6:32–44	393
6:33–44	153
6:43	146
6:45	146
6:53	146
7:1–13	120
7:3	433
7:5	433
7:8	121, 433
7:9	433
7:13	121, 320, 433
7:24–37	153
8:1–10	153, 393
8:4	154
8:8	153
8:13	146
8:14–21	393
8:19–20	153
8:22	146
9:2	159
10:1	146
10:2–12	150
10:11	150
10:17	159
10:18	159
10:46	156–57, 161
11:12–14	158
11:15–19	158
11:20–25	158

11:51	306
12:1–9	151
12:6	159
12:26	147, 204
12:34	115
12:40	115
13:22	321, 323
13:32	28
13:34–37	154
14–16	402
14:22–25	160
14:34	188
14:53–65	402
14:55–65	160
14:66–72	148
14:69	148
15:1	160
15:34	197
15:39	159
16:5	161

Luke

Book of	36, 331, 339, 340, 371, 383, 384, 390, 391, 392, 393, 394, 398, 437, 442
1:1–4	219, 371
1:3	157
1:35	230
1:46–55	94
4:1–12	110
4:5	110
4:9	110, 158
4:16–17	306
4:23	400
4:32	319
5:21	319
5:32	328
6:12	147
6:17–18	147
6:17	147
6:47–49	148
9:1–6	155
9:3	154
9:51–18:34	156
9:51	157
9:57–62	155
10:1–12	155
10:1	155
10:7	433
10:16	320, 336

10:17, 23	155	3:16	288	11:1−18		122
11:9−10	146	4:1−42	370	12	111−12,	116
11:13	145	5:18	319	13:15	306,	427
12:35−38	154	5:39−40	335	13:27		306
13:6−9	158	5:46	319	13:32−37		403
13:18−19	148	6:14	313	15	35,	387
14:16−24	154	6:17	146	15:1−21,		122
15:3−7	153	6:26	154	15:5		115
16:14	115	7:23	192	15:16−18		192
16:16	427	7:40	313	15:36−40		122
16:19−31	152	7:50−51	115	17:28		428
16:27−31	409	10:9	71	18:21		400
16:29, 31	427	10:34−35	318	21:20−26		122
17:7−10	121	10:34	427	21:22		400
18:9−12	121	11:39	30	24:15		427
18:9−14	113	11:47−53	112	26:22		427
18:13	121	11:49−52	204	26:27		427
18:21	121	12:21	146	28:4		400
18:31	427	12:34	427	28:23	318,	427
18:35−43	157	14:26	225			
18:35	156−57	15:25	427	**Romans**		
19:1−10	157	15:26	225	Book of	324,	325,
19:1	157	16:7	225			405
19:11−27	153, 157	16:13	225	1	228, 230,	232
19:11	157	16:14	225	1:4		319
19:28, 29	157	18:3	112	1:17		208
20:9−16a	151	20:31	218	1:18−21		409
20:13	159			1:19−21a		100
22:15−19	160	**Acts**		1:21		232
22:58	148			1:32		230
22:66−71	160	Book of	36, 132,	3:21	209,	427
23:47	159		316, 324, 326,	3:31		427
24:4	162		334, 337, 340,	4:23−24		318
24:25−27	319		341, 385, 386,	5:12−21		207
24:44−47	319		388, 392, 394,	6:17		320
24:44	305, 427		397, 398, 437	8:14−17	217,	226
		1:1	371	8:28		45
John		2	210, 217	9−11		288
Book of	324, 325,	2:16−21	313	10:4		205
	326, 334, 338,	2:25−34	192	10:5		190
	339, 364, 370,	2:25−33	403	10:13		200
	372, 391, 434,	2:25−28	204	15:4		318
	439, 441	2:31	209	16:16		148
1	230	3:17	427	16:26		427
1:14	288	3:18	205			
1:17	319	3:19−23	319	**1 Corinthians**		
1:19	313	3:21	427	Book of	324,	325,
1:45	427	3:22−23	313			400, 404
2:1−11	370	4:27	45	1, 2	228,	232
2:11	319	4:28	45	2:8, 9		36−37
3:3, 5	334	5:36	151	2:9, 10		217
3:8	219, 234	7:37	313	2:9		428
3:10	204	10:39−42	320	2:10−16	217,	222
		10:43	427			

6:9		374
6:12		190
7:1		190
8:1		190
9:1		320
9:8–10		400
9:9	189, 198,	200
9:10		318
10		196
10:11	74,	318
10:22		260
10:23		190
10:31		228
11		227
11:2		320
11:23		320
13:12		222
14:21, 34		427
14:37	223, 225,	321
15		207
15:3–4	319,	320
15:5–7		320
15:17		132
15:20–28		404
15:26		207
15:27		207
15:33		428
15:45–47		207

2 Corinthians

Book of		325
1:20		223
3:6	321,	433
3:14	305, 321,	433
5:18		288
6:16–17		306
10:5		228
11:4		323
11:13		323
13:1		189

Galatians

Book of	288, 324,	
	325, 370, 385,	
	387, 388,	433
1		228
1:6–9		323
1:14		433
2		387
2:4		126
2:9		320
2:11–21		122
3:1–4:11		404

3:11	208,	404
3:12		190
3:21		190
6:15		428

Ephesians

Book of	324, 325,	
		443
1:3		217
2:20		320
4:7–9		23
4:8		369
4:26	326,	435

Philippians

Book of	324,	325
3:17–19		323
4:9		320

Colossians

Book of	324,	325
2:8		433
4:16		321

1 Thessalonians

Book of		324
1:5	217,	225
2:13	217,	225
5		288
5:27		321

2 Thessalonians

Book of		324
2		228
2:15	223,	321
3:6	223,	320

1 Timothy

Book of		324
1:3	228,	323
1:10	323,	374
1:15		323
3:1		323
3:16		319
4:1		228
4:9		323
5:17		118
5:18		433
6:3		323
6:20	320,	323

2 Timothy

Book of		324
1:13		323
1:14		320
2:2		320
2:11		323
2:13		223
3:1		228
3:8		428
3:15–17		223
3:16–17		409
3:16	12, 30, 109,	
	217,	318
3:17		218
4:3		323

Titus

Book of		324
1:2		223
1:9		323
1:10		323
1:12		428
2:1		323
3:8		323

Philemon

Book of	324, 337,	
		340

Hebrews

Book of	316, 317,	
	324, 326, 334,	
	337, 339, 340,	
	341, 358, 398,	
	404, 431,	
	432,	442
1:1–3:6		320
1–2		93
1:1		79
1:2		359
2		207
2:1–4		320
2:10–18		218
4:14–16		218
6:18		223
10:28–29		320
10:38		404
11:32		306
13:15		306

468

James

Book of   316, 317,
324, 325, 337,
340, 358, 390,
432
4:6   434

1 Peter

Book of   316, 324,
325, 334,
337, 341
1:10–12   318, 403
1:10, 11   37
1:19   427
5:5   434

2 Peter

Book of   316, 317,
324, 340, 341,
428, 433
1:3   409
1:19–21   223
1:19   318
1:21   217
2   228

2:1   321, 323
3:2   427
3:15–16   223
3:16   132, 321

1 John

Book of   316, 334,
337
2:26–27   323
2:27   217
4:1–6   323
4:1–3   225
4:1   321
5:7   420
5:9   217

2 John

Book of   316, 317,
337, 339,
340, 358
7   323

3 John

Book of   316, 317,
339, 340, 358

Jude

Book of   288, 316,
317, 324, 326,
339, 340, 428,
432
3   223, 320
4   323
14–15   307

Revelation

Book of   316, 317,
326, 334,
336, 337,
338, 339,
341, 358,
431, 432
1:3, 11   321
2, 3   219
2:2   323
2:7   235
2:20   323
21:14   320

Note II Peter's recognition of Paul (120 AD at latest)

Eusebius list 316

1st witness - Athanasus - 377

Early christians deforest heresy 322-23 (did not ignore it)

I Clement 96 AD - appeals to OT as scripture as to words of Jesus + apostles (possibly pre-70 ? doc into chapter) - list of sources 324

Ignatius (325) - knows Matt (+ possibly rest of synoptics) John